Śrī Caitanya-caritāmṛta

BOOKS by
His Divine Grace A.C. Bhaktivedanta Swami Prabhupāda

Bhagavad-gītā As It Is
Śrīmad-Bhāgavatam, Cantos 1-5 (15 Vols.)
Śrī Caitanya-caritāmṛta (17 Vols.)
Teachings of Lord Caitanya
The Nectar of Devotion
Śrī Īśopaniṣad
Easy Journey to Other Planets
Kṛṣṇa Consciousness: The Topmost Yoga System
Kṛṣṇa, The Supreme Personality of Godhead (3 Vols.)
Transcendental Teachings of Prahlād Mahārāja
Kṛṣṇa, the Reservoir of Pleasure
The Perfection of Yoga
Beyond Birth and Death
On the Way to Kṛṣṇa
Rāja-vidyā: The King of Knowledge
Elevation to Kṛṣṇa Consciousness
Kṛṣṇa Consciousness: The Matchless Gift
Back to Godhead Magazine (Founder)

A complete catalogue is available upon request

International Society for Krishna Consciousness
3764 Watseka Avenue
Los Angeles, California 90034

All Glory to Śrī Guru and Gaurāṅga

ŚRĪ CAITANYA-CARITĀMṚTA

of Kṛṣṇadāsa Kavirāja Gosvāmī

v. 12

Madhya-līlā
Volume Nine

"The Lord Concludes His Travels"

with the original Bengali text, Roman transliterations, synonyms, translation and elaborate purports

by

HIS DIVINE GRACE

A.C. Bhaktivedanta Swami Prabhupāda

Founder-Ācārya of the International Society for Krishna Consciousness

THE BHAKTIVEDANTA BOOK TRUST
New York · Los Angeles · London · Bombay

Readers interested in the subject matter of this book
are invited by the International Society for Krishna Consciousness
to correspond with its Secretary.

International Society for Krishna Consciousness
3764 Watseka Avenue
Los Angeles, California 90034

Library of Congress Catalogue Card Number: 73-93206
International Standard Book Number: 0-912776-71-4

First printing, 1975: 20,000 copies

Printed in the United States of America

Contents

Introduction		vi
Chapter 23	Life's Ultimate Goal—Love of Godhead	1
Chapter 24	The Sixty-one Explanations of the Ātmārāma Verse	81
Chapter 25	How All the Residents of Vārāṇasī Became Vaiṣṇavas	295
References		455
Glossary		457
Bengali Pronunciation Guide		463
Index of Bengali and Sanskrit Verses		465
General Index		483
The Author		513

Introduction

Śrī Caitanya-caritāmṛta is the principal work on the life and teachings of Śrī Kṛṣṇa Caitanya. Śrī Caitanya is the pioneer of a great social and religious movement which began in India a little less than five hundred years ago and which has directly and indirectly influenced the subsequent course of religious and philosophical thinking not only in India but in the recent West as well.

Caitanya Mahāprabhu is regarded as a figure of great historical significance. However, our conventional method of historical analysis—that of seeing a man as a product of his times—fails here. Śrī Caitanya is a personality who transcends the limited scope of historical settings.

At a time when, in the West, man was directing his explorative spirit toward studying the structure of the physical universe and circumnavigating the world in search of new oceans and continents, Śrī Kṛṣṇa Caitanya, in the East, was inaugurating and masterminding a revolution directed inward, toward a scientific understanding of the highest knowledge of man's spiritual nature.

The chief historical sources for the life of Śrī Kṛṣṇa Caitanya are the *kaḍacās* (diaries) kept by Murāri Gupta and Svarūpa Dāmodara Gosvāmī. Murāri Gupta, a physician and close associate of Śrī Caitanya's, recorded extensive notes on the first twenty-four years of Śrī Caitanya's life, culminating in his initiation into the renounced order, *sannyāsa*. The events of the rest of Caitanya Mahāprabhu's forty-eight years are recorded in the diary of Svarūpa Dāmodora Gosvāmī, another of Caitanya Mahāprabhu's intimate associates.

Śrī Caitanya-caritāmṛta is divided into three sections called *līlās,* which literally means "pastimes"—*Ādi-līlā* (the early period), *Madhya-līlā* (the middle period) and *Antya-līlā* (the final period). The notes of Murāri Gupta form the basis of the *Ādi-līlā,* and Svarūpa Dāmodara's diary provides the details for the *Madhya-* and *Antya-līlās.*

The first twelve of the seventeen chapters of *Ādi-līlā* constitute the preface for the entire work. By referring to Vedic scriptural evidence, this preface establishes Śrī Caitanya as the *avatāra* (incarnation) of Kṛṣṇa (God) for the age of Kali—the current epoch, beginning five thousand years ago and characterized by materialism, hypocrisy and dissension. In these descriptions, Caitanya Mahāprabhu, who is identical with Lord Kṛṣṇa, descends to liberally grant pure love of God to the fallen souls of this degraded age by propagating *saṅkīrtana*—literally, "congregational glorification of God"—especially by organizing massive public chanting of the *mahā-mantra* (Great Chant for Deliverance). The esoteric purpose of Lord Caitanya's appearance in the world is revealed, his co-*avatāras* and principal devotees are described and his teachings are summarized. The remaining portion of *Ādi-līlā,* chapters thirteen through seventeen, briefly recounts his divine birth and his life until he accepted the renounced order. This includes his childhood miracles, schooling, marriage and early philosophical confrontations, as well as his organization of a widespread *saṅkīrtana* movement and his civil disobedience against the repression of the Mohammedan government.

The subject of *Madhya-līlā*, the longest of the three divisions, is a detailed narration of Lord Caitanya's extensive and eventful travels throughout India as a renounced mendicant, teacher, philosopher, spiritual preceptor and mystic. During this period of six years, Śrī Caitanya transmits his teachings to his principal disciples. He debates and converts many of the most renowned philosophers and theologians of his time, including Śaṅkarites, Buddhists and Muslims, and incorporates their many thousands of followers and disciples into his own burgeoning numbers. A dramatic account of Caitanya Mahāprabhu's miraculous activities at the giant Jagannātha Cart Festival in Orissa is also included in this section.

Antya-līlā concerns the last eighteen years of Śrī Caitanya's manifest presence, spent in semiseclusion near the famous Jagannātha temple at Jagannātha Purī in Orissa. During these final years, Śrī Caitanya drifted deeper and deeper into trances of spiritual ecstasy unparalleled in all of religious and literary history, Eastern or Western. Śrī Caitanya's perpetual and ever-increasing religious beatitude, graphically described in the eyewitness accounts of Svarūpa Dāmodara Gosvāmī, his constant companion during this period, clearly defy the investigative and descriptive abilities of modern psychologists and phenomenologists of religious experience.

The author of this great classic, Kṛṣṇadāsa Kavirāja Gosvāmī, born in the year 1507, was a disciple of Raghunātha dāsa Gosvāmī, a confidential follower of Caitanya Mahāprabhu. Raghunātha dāsa, a renowned ascetic saint, heard and memorized all the activities of Caitanya Mahāprabhu told to him by Svarūpa Dāmodara. After the passing away of Śrī Caitanya and Svarūpa Dāmodara, Raghunātha dāsa, unable to bear the pain of separation from these objects of his complete devotion, traveled to Vṛndāvana, intending to commit suicide by jumping from Govardhana Hill. In Vṛndāvana, however, he encountered Rūpa Gosvāmī and Sanātana Gosvāmī, the most confidential disciples of Caitanya Mahāprabhu. They convinced him to give up his plan of suicide and impelled him to reveal to them the spiritually inspiring events of Lord Caitanya's later life. Kṛṣṇadāsa Kavirāja Gosvāmī was also residing in Vṛndāvana at this time, and Raghunātha dāsa Gosvāmī endowed him with a full comprehension of the transcendental life of Śrī Caitanya.

By this time, several biographical works had already been written on the life of Śrī Caitanya by contemporary and near-contemporary scholars and devotees. These included *Śrī Caitanya-carita* by Murāri Gupta, *Caitanya-maṅgala* by Locana dāsa Ṭhākura and *Caitanya-bhāgavata*. This latter text, a work by Vṛndāvana dāsa Ṭhākura, who was then considered the principal authority on Śrī Caitanya's life, was highly revered. While composing his important work, Vṛndāvana dāsa, fearing that it would become too voluminous, avoided elaborately describing many of the events of Śrī Caitanya's life, particulary the later ones. Anxious to hear of these later pastimes, the devotees of Vṛndāvana requested Kṛṣṇadāsa Kavirāja Gosvāmī, whom they respected as a great saint, to compose a book to narrate these episodes in detail. Upon this request, and with the permission and blessings of the Madana-mohana Deity of Vṛndāvana, he began compiling *Śrī Caitanya-caritāmṛta,* which, due to its biographical excellence and thorough exposition of Lord Caitanya's profound philosophy and teachings, is regarded as the most significant of biographical works on Śrī Caitanya.

He commenced work on the text while in his late nineties and in failing health, as he vividly describes in the text itself: "I have now become too old and disturbed in invalidity. While writing, my hands tremble. I cannot remember anything, nor can I see or hear properly. Still I write, and this is a great wonder." That he nevertheless completed, under such debilitating conditions, the greatest literary gem of medieval India is surely one of the wonders of literary history.

This English translation and commentary is the work of His Divine Grace A. C. Bhaktivedanta Swami Prabhupāda, the world's most distinguished teacher of Indian religious and philosophical thought. His commentary is based upon two Bengali commentaries, one by his teacher Śrīla Bhaktisiddhānta Sarasvatī Gosvāmī, the eminent Vedic scholar who predicted, "The time will come when the people of the world will learn Bengali to read *Śrī Caitanya-caritāmṛta,"* and the other by Śrīla Bhaktisiddhānta's father, Bhaktivinoda Ṭhākura.

His Divine Grace A. C. Bhaktivedanta Swami Prabhupāda is himself a disciplic descendant of Śrī Caitanya Mahāprabhu, and he is the first scholar to execute systematic English translations of the major works of Śrī Caitanya's followers. His consummate Bengali and Sanskrit scholarship and intimate familiarity with the precepts of Śrī Kṛṣṇa Caitanya are a fitting combination that eminently qualifies him to present this important classic to the English-speaking world. The ease and clarity with which he expounds upon difficult philosophical concepts lures even a reader totally unfamiliar with Indian religious tradition into a genuine understanding and appreciation of this profound and monumental work.

The entire text, with commentary, presented in seventeen lavishly illustrated volumes by the Bhaktivedanta Book Trust, represents a contribution of major importance to the intellectual, cultural and spiritual life of contemporary man.

—The Publishers

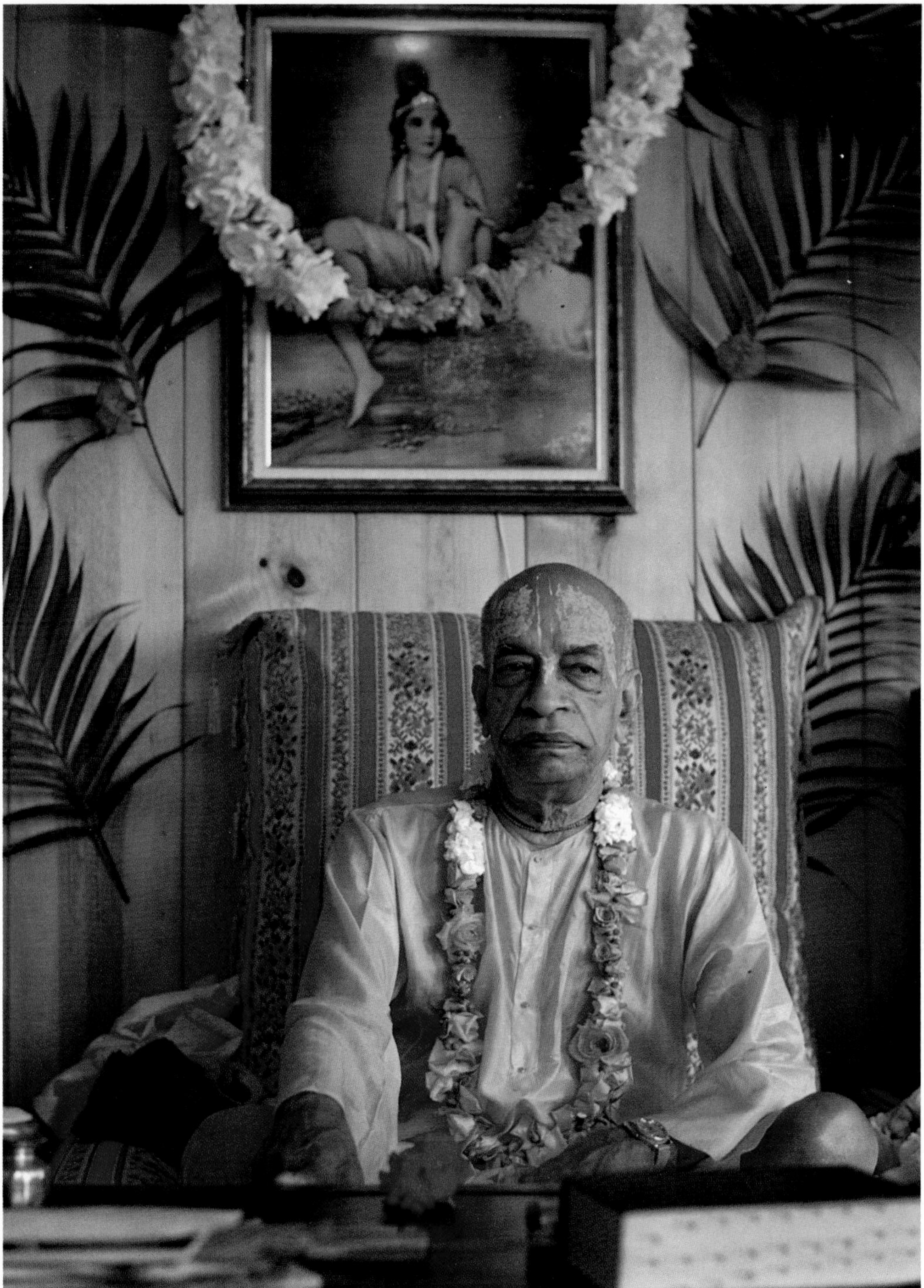

His Divine Grace
A. C. Bhaktivedanta Swami Prabhupāda
Founder-Ācārya of the International Society for Krishna Consciousness

Outside and inside views of the *samādhi* (tomb) of Śrīla Sanātana Gosvāmī at the Madana-mohana temple in Vṛndāvana. Sanātana Gosvāmī was instructed by the Lord Himself in the science of devotional service and thus empowered to establish the cult of Vaiṣṇavism.

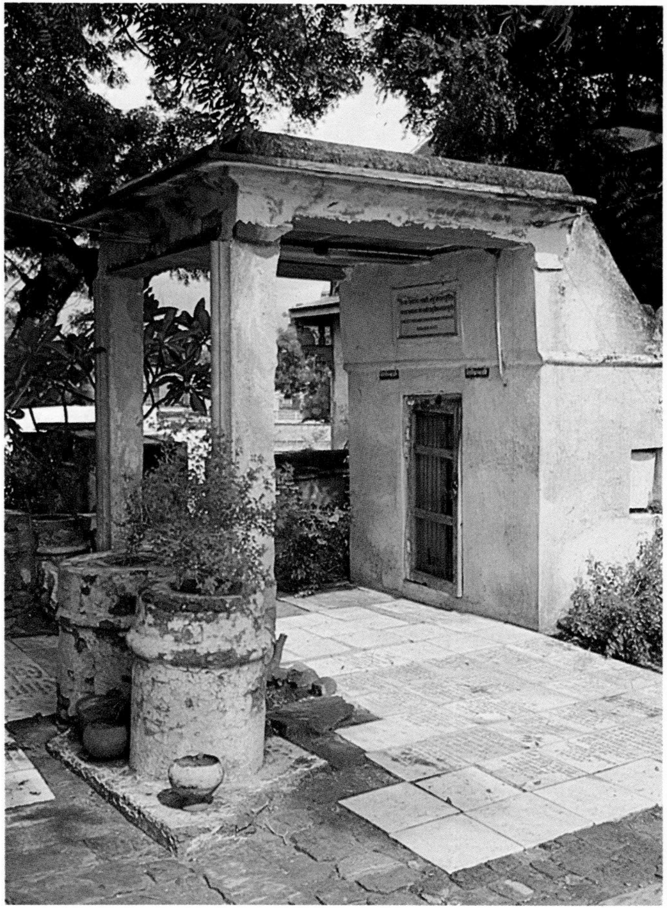

LEFT: The *bhajana-kuṭira* of Śrīla Sanātana Gosvāmī at Śrī Rādhā-kuṇḍa in the district of Mathurā.
RIGHT: The *samādhi* of Śrīla Gopāla Bhaṭṭa Gosvāmī, one of the great and exalted devotees of Śrī Caitanya Mahāprabhu, located at the Rādhā-ramaṇa temple in Vṛndāvana.

The temple and Deity of Śrī Rādhā-ramaṇa, established by Śrīla Gopāla Bhaṭṭa Gosvāmī under the direction of Śrīla Rūpa and Sanātana Gosvāmīs. Śrī Rādhā-ramaṇa manifested Himself from a *śālagrāma-silā* stone worshiped by Gopāla Bhaṭṭa Gosvāmī and is one of the seven principal Deities of Vṛndāvana.

The temple and Deities of Śrī Śrī Rādhā-Gopīnātha. Śrī Gopīnāthajī, one of the principal Deities of Vṛndāvana, was first acquired by Paramānanda Gosvāmī and worshiped by Madhu Paṇḍita, a disciple of Śrīla Gadādhara Paṇḍita.

The temple of Bindu Mādhava in Vārāṇasī (Benares), where Śrī Caitanya Mahāprabhu converted all the residents into Vaiṣṇavas by His ecstatic chanting and dancing in love of Godhead. (*p.331*)

The temple of Viśveśvara in Vārāṇasī, where countless thousands of people lined up to see Śrī Caitanya Mahāprabhu and received Him by chanting the Hare Kṛṣṇa *mahā-mantra*. (p.395)

PLATE ONE

"Lord Kṛṣṇa, the Supreme Personality of Godhead, who appeared as the son of Nanda Mahārāja, is the supreme hero in all dealings. Similarly, Śrīmatī Rādhārāṇī is the topmost heroine in all dealings. Kṛṣṇa is the Supreme Personality of Godhead Himself, and He is the crown jewel of all heroes. In Kṛṣṇa, all transcendental good qualities are permanently situated. The transcendental goddess Śrīmatī Rādhārāṇī is the direct counterpart of Lord Śrī Kṛṣṇa. She is the central figure for all the goddesses of fortune. She possesses all the attraction to attract the all-attractive Personality of Godhead. She is the primeval internal potency of the Lord." (*pp.43-44*)

PLATE TWO

"My dear Lord, I am a very lowborn person. Indeed, I am a servant to lowborn people; therefore I am very, very downtrodden. Nonetheless, You have taught me conclusions unknown even to Lord Brahmā. The conclusions that you have told me are the ocean of the ambrosia of truth. My mind is unable to approach even a drop of that ocean. If You want to make a lame man like me dance, kindly bestow Your transcendental blessings by keeping Your lotus feet on my head. Now, will You please tell me, 'Let whatever I have instructed all be fully manifest unto you.' By benedicting me in this way, You will give me strength to describe all this." Śrī Caitanya Mahāprabhu then placed His hand on Sanātana Gosvāmī's head and benedicted him, saying, "Let all these benedictions be manifest to you." (*pp.77-78*)

PLATE THREE

"O good fortune personified! O original Personality of Godhead, all these bees are chanting about Your transcendental fame, which will purify the entire universe. Indeed, they are following Your path in the forest and are worshiping You. Actually they are all saintly persons, but now they have taken the form of bees. Although You are playing like a human being, they could not forget that You are their worshipable Deity. This land Vṛndāvana (Vrajabhūmi) is glorified today. Your lotus feet have touched the earth and grass. Your fingers have touched the trees and creepers, and Your merciful eyes have glanced upon rivers, hills, birds and beasts. The gopīs have been embraced by Your arms, and even the goddess of fortune desires this. Now all of these are glorified." (*pp.179, 196*)

PLATE FOUR

"Nārada Muni saw that a deer was lying on the path through the forest and that it was pierced by an arrow. It had broken legs and was twisting due to much pain. Farther ahead, Nārada Muni saw a boar pierced by an arrow. Its legs were also broken, and it was twisting in pain. When he went farther, he saw a rabbit that was also suffering. Nārada Muni was greatly pained at heart to see living entities suffer so. When Nārada advanced farther, he saw a hunter behind a tree. This hunter was holding arrows, and he was ready to kill more animals. The hunter's body was blackish. He had reddish eyes, and he appeared fierce. It was as if the superintendent of death, Yamarāja, was standing there with bows and arrows in his hands. When Nārada left the forest path and went to the hunter, all the animals immediately saw him and fled. When all the animals fled, the hunter wanted to chastise Nārada with abusive language, but due to Nārada's presence, he could not utter anything abusive." (*pp.211-214*)

PLATE FIVE

"One day, while speaking to his friend Parvata Muni, Nārada Muni requested him to go with him to see his disciple the hunter. When the saintly sages came to the hunter's place, the hunter could see them coming from a distance. With great alacrity the hunter began to run toward his spiritual master, but he could not fall down and offer obeisances because ants were running hither and thither around his feet. Seeing the ants, the hunter whisked them away with a piece of cloth. After thus clearing the ants from the ground, he fell down flat to offer his obeisances. Nārada Muni said, 'My dear hunter, such behavior is not at all astonishing. A man in devotional service is automatically nonviolent. He is the best of gentlemen. O hunter, good qualities like nonviolence, which you have developed, are not very astonishing, for those engaged in the Lord's devotional service are never inclined to give pain to others because of envy.'" (*pp.234-236*)

PLATE SIX

"Upon reaching the temple of Bindu Mādhava, Śrī Caitanya Mahāprabhu, seeing the beauty of Lord Bindu Mādhava, became overwhelmed in ecstatic love. He then began to dance in the courtyard of the temple. There were four people accompanying Śrī Caitanya Mahāprabhu, and these were Candraśekhara, Paramānanda Purī, Tapana Miśra and Sanātana Gosvāmī. They were all chanting the Hare Kṛṣṇa *mahā-mantra* in the following way. In all directions, hundreds and thousands of people began to chant, 'Hari Hari.' Thus there arose a tumultuous and auspicious sound filling the entire universe. When Prakāśānanda Sarasvatī, who was staying nearby, heard this tumultuous chanting of the Hare Kṛṣṇa *mahā-mantra,* he and his disciples immediately came to see the Lord. When Prakāśānanda Sarasvatī saw the Lord, he and his disciples also joined the chanting with Śrī Caitanya Mahāprabhu. Prakāśānanda Sarasvatī was charmed by the Lord's dancing and ecstatic love, and by the transcendental beauty of His body." (*pp.331-333*)

PLATE SEVEN

"All the people were astonished to see the Lord's jubilation and humility and to hear Him talk in ecstasy. Indeed, all the residents of Benares (Kāśī) saw the bodily transformations and were astonished. When Śrī Caitanya Mahāprabhu regained His external consciousness, He saw that many Māyāvādī *sannyāsīs* and other people were gathering there. He therefore suspended His dancing for the time being. After stopping the *kīrtana,* Śrī Caitanya Mahāprabhu, who is a great example of humility, offered prayers unto the feet of Prakāśānanda Sarasvatī. At this, Prakāśānanda Sarasvatī immediately came forward and clasped the Lord's lotus feet. Prakāśānanda Sarasvatī said, 'Formerly I have committed many offenses against You by blaspheming You, but now the effects of my offenses are counteracted by touching Your lotus feet.' " (*pp.334-337*)

PLATE EIGHT

"The inhabitants of Vṛndāvana, under the leadership of Nanda Mahārāja, once wanted to go to the bank of the Sarasvatī on a pilgrimage. Nanda Mahārāja was fasting, and he lay down near the forest. At that time a serpent, who was formerly cursed by Āṅgirasa Ṛṣi, appeared. This serpent had formerly been named Sudarśana, and he had belonged to the Gandharvaloka planet. However, because he joked with the ṛṣi, he was condemned to take on the body of a big snake. When this serpent attacked Nanda Mahārāja, Nanda Mahārāja began to call, 'Kṛṣṇa! Help!' Kṛṣṇa immediately appeared and began to kick the serpent with His lotus feet. Due to being touched by the Lord's lotus feet, the serpent was immediately freed from the reactions of his sinful life. Being freed, he again assumed his original form of Sudarśana, the Gandharva." (*p.338*)

CHAPTER 23

Life's Ultimate Goal—Love of Godhead

The following summary study of the Twenty-third Chapter is given by Śrīla Bhaktivinoda Ṭhākura in his *Amṛta-pravāha-bhāṣya.* In this chapter Śrī Caitanya Mahāprabhu describes the symptoms of emotion and love and the awakening of one's original loving relationship with the Lord, as well as the characteristics of a devotee who has actually attained that stage. He then describes the gradual increase of love of God up to the point of *mahābhāva.* He then describes the five divisions of attraction and how they continue. He also describes the mellow derived from conjugal love, which is the supreme emotion. Conjugal love is divided into two categories—*svakīya* and *parakīya. Svakīya* refers to loving affairs between husband and wife, and *parakīya* refers to loving affairs between two lovers. There are a number of descriptions in this connection. There is also a description of the sixty-four transcendental qualities of Kṛṣṇa. Śrīmatī Rādhārāṇī has twenty-five transcendental qualities.

Śrī Caitanya Mahāprabhu then describes those candidates who are eligible to taste the mellows of devotional service. Their fundamental natures and their varieties are also described. The Lord also informs Sanātana Gosvāmī about all the confidential paraphernalia of devotional service. He gives a description of Goloka Vṛndāvana, where the Lord is engaged in His eternal pastimes described in the *Hari-vaṁśa.* There is also an opposing and favorable description of *keśa-avatāra.* All these instructions are mentioned herein.

In this way Śrī Caitanya Mahāprabhu blessed Sanātana Gosvāmī, placing His own hand on his head. Thus Sanātana received the power to describe these subjects in books like *Hari-bhakti-vilāsa.*

TEXT 1

চিরাদদত্তং নিজ-গুপ্তবিত্তং
স্বপ্রেম-নামামৃতমত্যুদারঃ ।
আপামরং যো বিততার গৌরঃ
কৃষ্ণো জনেভ্যস্তমহং প্রপদ্যে ॥ ১ ॥

cirād adattaṁ nija-gupta-vittaṁ
svaprema-nāmāmṛtam atyudāraḥ
āpāmaraṁ yo vitatāra gauraḥ
kṛṣṇo janebhyas tam ahaṁ prapadye

SYNONYMS

cirāt—for a long time; *adattam*—not given; *nija-gupta-vittam*—His own personal confidential property; *sva-prema*—of love for Him; *nāma*—of the holy name; *amṛtam*—the ambrosia; *ati-udāraḥ*—most munificent; *ā-pāmaram*—even down to the lowest of men; *yaḥ*—one who; *vitatāra*—distributed; *gauraḥ*—Śrī Gaurasundara; *kṛṣṇaḥ*—Lord Kṛṣṇa Himself; *janebhyaḥ*—to the people in general; *tam*—to Him; *aham*—I; *prapadye*—offer obeisances.

TRANSLATION

The most munificent Supreme Personality of Godhead, known as Gaurakṛṣṇa, distributed to everyone—even the lowest of men—His own confidential treasury in the form of the nectar of love of Himself and the holy name. This was never given to the people at any time before. I therefore offer my respectful obeisances unto Him.

TEXT 2

জয় জয় গৌরচন্দ্র জয় নিত্যানন্দ ।
জয়াদ্বৈতচন্দ্র জয় গৌরভক্তবৃন্দ ॥ ২ ॥

jaya jaya gauracandra jaya nityānanda
jayādvaita-candra jaya gaura-bhakta-vṛnda

SYNONYMS

jaya jaya—all glories; *gauracandra*—to Śrī Caitanya Mahāprabhu; *jaya*—all glories; *nityānanda*—to Nityānanda Prabhu; *jaya*—all glories; *advaita-candra*—to Advaita Ācārya; *jaya*—all glories; *gaura-bhakta-vṛnda*—to the devotees of Śrī Caitanya Mahāprabhu.

TRANSLATION

All glories to Śrī Caitanya Mahāprabhu! All glories to Lord Nityānanda! All glories to Advaita Ācārya! And all glories to all the devotees of Lord Caitanya Mahāprabhu!

TEXT 3

এবে শুন ভক্তিফল 'প্রেম'-প্রয়োজন ।
যাহার শ্রবণে হয় ভক্তিরস-জ্ঞান ॥ ৩ ॥

ebe śuna bhakti-phala 'prema'-prayojana
yāhāra śravaṇe haya bhakti-rasa-jñāna

SYNONYMS

ebe śuna—now hear; *bhakti-phala*—the result of the practice of devotional service; *prema*—love of Godhead; *prayojana*—the ultimate goal of life; *yāhāra śravaṇe*—by hearing of which; *haya*—there is; *bhakti-rasa-jñāna*—transcendental knowledge of the mellows of devotional service.

TRANSLATION

Śrī Caitanya Mahāprabhu continued, "Now hear, O Sanātana, about the result of devotional service, which is love of Godhead, life's ultimate goal. If one hears this description, he will be enlightened in the transcendental mellows of devotional service.

TEXT 4

কৃষ্ণে রতি গাঢ় হৈলে 'প্রেম'-অভিধান ।
কৃষ্ণভক্তি-রসের এই 'স্থায়িভাব'-নাম ॥ ৪ ॥

kṛṣṇe rati gāḍha haile 'prema'-abhidhāna
kṛṣṇa-bhakti-rasera ei 'sthāyi-bhāva'-nāma

SYNONYMS

kṛṣṇe—unto Lord Kṛṣṇa; *rati*—affection; *gāḍha*—deep; *haile*—when it becomes; *prema-abhidhāna*—called love of God; *kṛṣṇa-bhakti-rasera*—of the mellows of devotional service to Kṛṣṇa; *ei*—this; *sthāyi-bhāva-nāma*—called *sthāyi-bhāva.*

TRANSLATION

"When affection for Kṛṣṇa becomes deeper, one attains love of Godhead in devotional service. Such a position is called sthāyi-bhāva, permanent enjoyment of the mellows of devotional service to Kṛṣṇa.

TEXT 5

শুদ্ধসত্ত্ববিশেষাত্মা প্রেম-সূর্যাংশু-সাম্যভাক্ ।
রুচিভিশ্চিত্তম স্ণ্যকৃদসৌ ভাব উচ্যতে ॥ ৫ ॥

śuddha-sattva-viśeṣātmā
prema-sūryāṁśu-sāmya-bhāk
rucibhiś citta-masṛṇya-
kṛd asau bhāva ucyate

SYNONYMS

śuddha-sattva—by unadulterated goodness; *viśeṣa*—distinguished; *ātmā*—whose nature; *prema*—of love of God; *sūrya*—like the sun; *aṁśu*—a ray; *sāmya-bhāk*—which is similar to; *rucibhiḥ*—by different tastes; *citta*—of the heart; *masṛṇya*—softness; *kṛt*—which causes; *asau*—that softness; *bhāvaḥ*—emotion; *ucyate*—is called.

TRANSLATION

" 'When devotional service is situated on the transcendental platform of pure goodness, it is like a ray of the sunlight of love for Kṛṣṇa. At such a time, devotional service causes the heart to be softened by various tastes, and it is called bhāva [emotion].'

PURPORT

This verse is found in *Bhakti-rasāmṛta-sindhu* (1.3.1).

TEXT 6

এই দুই,—ভাবের 'স্বরূপ', 'তটস্থ' লক্ষণ ।
প্রেমের লক্ষণ এবে শুন, সনাতন ॥ ৬ ॥

e dui,——bhāvera 'svarūpa', 'taṭastha' lakṣaṇa
premera lakṣaṇa ebe śuna, sanātana

SYNONYMS

ei dui—these two; *bhāvera*—of emotion; *sva-rūpa*—constitutional; *taṭastha*—marginal; *lakṣaṇa*—symptoms; *premera*—of love; *lakṣaṇa*—the symptoms; *ebe*—now; *śuna*—hear; *sanātana*—O Sanātana.

TRANSLATION

"Bhāva [emotion] has two different symptoms—constitutional and marginal. Now, My dear Sanātana, listen to the symptoms of love.

PURPORT

The word *śuddha-sattva-viśeṣātmā* means "situated on the transcendental platform of pure goodness." In this way the soul is purified of all material contamination, and this position is called *svarūpa-lakṣaṇa,* the constitutional symptom of *bhāva,* emotion. By various tastes, one's heart is softened, and there is an awakening of one's loving propensity to render spontaneous service to the Lord. This is called *taṭastha-lakṣaṇa,* the marginal symptom of *bhāva.*

TEXT 7

সম্যঙ্‌মসৃণিতস্বান্তো মমত্বাতিশয়াঙ্কিতঃ ।
ভাবঃ স এব সান্দ্রাত্মা বুধৈঃ প্রেমা নিগদ্যতে ॥ ৭ ॥

samyaṅ masṛṇita-svānto
mamatvātiśayāṅkitaḥ
bhāvaḥ sa eva sāndrātmā
budhaiḥ premā nigadyate

SYNONYMS

samyak—completely; *masṛṇita-svāntaḥ*—which makes the heart soft; *mamatva*—of a sense of ownership; *atiśaya-aṅkitaḥ*—marked with an abundance; *bhāvaḥ*—emotion; *saḥ*—that; *eva*—certainly; *sāndra-ātmā*—whose nature is very condensed; *budhaiḥ*—by learned persons; *premā*—love of Godhead; *nigadyate*—is described.

TRANSLATION

" 'When that bhāva softens the heart completely, becomes endowed with a great feeling of possessiveness in relation to the Lord and becomes very much condensed and intensified, it is called prema [love of Godhead] by learned scholars.

PURPORT

This verse is found in *Bhakti-rasāmṛta-sindhu* (1.4.1).

TEXT 8

অনন্যমমতা বিষ্ণৌ মমতা প্রেমসঙ্গতা ।
ভক্তিরিত্যুচ্যতে ভীষ্মপ্রহ্লাদোদ্ধব-নারদৈঃ ॥ ৮ ॥

ananya-mamatā viṣṇau
mamatā prema-saṅgatā
bhaktir ity ucyate bhīṣma-
prahlādoddhava-nāradaiḥ

SYNONYMS

ananya-mamatā—having a sense of relationships with no others; *viṣṇau*—in Lord Viṣṇu, or Kṛṣṇa; *mamatā*—the sense of ownership; *prema-saṅgatā*—

endowed only with love; *bhaktiḥ*—devotional service; *iti*—thus; *ucyate*—is said; *bhīṣma*—by Bhīṣma; *prahlāda*—by Prahlāda Mahārāja; *uddhava*—by Uddhava; *nāradaiḥ*—and by Nārada.

TRANSLATION

" 'When one develops an unflinching sense of ownership or possessiveness in relation to Lord Viṣṇu, or, in other words, when one thinks Viṣṇu and no one else to be the only object of love, such an awakening is called bhakti [devotion] by exalted persons like Bhīṣma, Prahlāda, Uddhava and Nārada.'

PURPORT

This verse, quoted from the *Nārada-pañcarātra,* is found in *Bhakti-rasāmṛta-sindhu* (1.4.2).

TEXT 9

কোন ভাগ্যে কোন জীবের 'শ্রদ্ধা' যদি হয়।
তবে সেই জীব 'সাধুসঙ্গ' যে করয় ॥ ৯ ॥

kona bhāgye kona jīvera 'śraddhā' yadi haya
tabe sei jīva 'sādhu-saṅga' ye karaya

SYNONYMS

kona bhāgye—by some good fortune; *kona jīvera*—of some living entity; *śraddhā yadi haya*—if there is faith; *tabe*—then; *sei jīva*—that living entity; *sādhu-saṅga*—association with devotees; *ye*—certainly; *karaya*—makes.

TRANSLATION

"If, by good fortune, a living entity develops faith in Kṛṣṇa, he begins to associate with devotees.

TEXT 10

সাধুসঙ্গ হৈতে হয় 'শ্রবণ-কীর্তন'।
সাধনভক্ত্যে হয় 'সর্বানর্থনিবর্তন' ॥ ১০ ॥

sādhu-saṅga haite haya 'śravaṇa-kīrtana'
sādhana-bhaktye haya 'sarvānartha-nivartana'

SYNONYMS

sādhu-saṅga haite—from association with devotees; *haya*—there is; *śravaṇa-kīrtana*—hearing, chanting and so on; *sādhana-bhaktye*—by devotional service; *haya*—there is; *sarva*—all; *anartha-nivartana*—disappearance of unwanted things.

TRANSLATION

"When one is encouraged in devotional service by the association of devotees, one becomes free from all unwanted contamination by following the regulative principles and chanting and hearing.

TEXT 11

অনর্থনিবৃত্তি হৈলে ভক্ত্যে 'নিষ্ঠা' হয় ।
নিষ্ঠা হৈতে শ্রবণাদ্যে 'রুচি' উপজয় ॥ ১১ ॥

anartha-nivṛtti haile bhaktye 'niṣṭhā' haya
niṣṭhā haite śravaṇādye 'ruci' upajaya

SYNONYMS

anartha-nivṛtti—disappearance of all unwanted contamination; *haile*—when there is; *bhaktye*—in devotional service; *niṣṭhā*—firm faith; *haya*—there is; *niṣṭhā haite*—from such firm faith; *śravaṇa-ādye*—in hearing, chanting and so on; *ruci*—taste; *upajaya*—awakens.

TRANSLATION

"When one is freed from all unwanted contamination, he advances with firm faith. When firm faith in devotional service awakens, a taste for hearing and chanting also awakens.

TEXT 12

রুচি হৈতে ভক্ত্যে হয় 'আসক্তি' প্রচুর ।
আসক্তি হৈতে চিত্তে জন্মে কৃষ্ণে প্রীত্যঙ্কুর ॥ ১২ ॥

ruci haite bhaktye haya 'āsakti' pracura
āsakti haite citte janme kṛṣṇe prīty-aṅkura

SYNONYMS

ruci haite—from such a taste; *bhaktye*—in devotional service; *haya*—there is; *āsakti*—attachment; *pracura*—deep; *āsakti haite*—from attachment; *citte*—within the heart; *janme*—appears; *kṛṣṇe*—for Kṛṣṇa; *prīti-aṅkura*—the seed of affection.

TRANSLATION

"After taste is awakened, a deep attachment arises, and from that attachment the seed of love for Kṛṣṇa grows in the heart.

TEXT 13

সেই 'ভাব' গাঢ় হৈলে ধরে 'প্রেম'-নাম ।
সেই প্রেমা—'প্রয়োজন' সর্বানন্দ-ধাম ॥ ১৩ ॥

sei 'bhāva' gāḍha haile dhare 'prema'-nāma
sei premā——'prayojana' sarvānanda-dhāma

SYNONYMS

sei bhāva—that emotional condition; *gāḍha haile*—when it becomes intensified; *dhare*—takes; *prema-nāma*—the name love of Godhead; *sei premā*—that love of Godhead; *prayojana*—the ultimate goal of life; *sarva-ānanda-dhāma*—the reservoir of all pleasure.

TRANSLATION

"When that ecstatic emotional stage intensifies, it is called love of Godhead. Such love is life's ultimate goal and the reservoir of all pleasure.

PURPORT

Śrīla Bhaktivinoda Ṭhākura summarizes this growth of love of Godhead as a gradual process. A person becomes interested in devotional service by some good fortune. Eventually he becomes interested in pure devotional service without material contamination. At that point, a person wants to associate with devotees. As a result of this association, he becomes more and more interested in discharging devotional service and hearing and chanting. The more one is interested in hearing and chanting, the more he is purified of material contamination. Liberation from material contamination is called *anartha-nivṛtti,* indicating a diminishing of all unwanted things. This is the test of development in devotional service. If one actually develops the devotional attitude, he must be freed from the material contamination of illicit sex, intoxication, gambling and meat-eating. These are the preliminary symptoms. When one is freed from all material contamination, his firm faith awakens in devotional service. When firm faith develops, a taste arises, and by that taste, one becomes attached to devotional service. When this attachment intensifies, the seed of love of Kṛṣṇa fructifies. This position is called *prīti* or *rati* (affection) or *bhāva* (emotion). When *rati* intensifies, it is called love of Godhead. This love of Godhead is actually life's highest perfection and the reservoir of all pleasure.

Thus devotional life is divided into two stages—*sādhana-bhakti* and *bhāva-bhakti. Sādhana-bhakti* refers to the development of devotional service through the regulative principles. The basic principle for the execution of devotional service is faith. Above that, there is association with devotees, and after that there is initiation by a bona fide spiritual master. After initiation, when one follows the regulative principles of devotional service, one becomes freed from all unwanted things. In this way one becomes firmly fixed and gradually develops a taste for devotional service. The more the taste grows, the more one desires to render service to the Lord. In this way one becomes attached to a particular mellow in the Lord's service—*śānta, dāsya, sakhya, vātsalya* and *madhura*. As a result of such attachment, *bhāva* develops. *Bhāva-bhakti* is the platform of purified goodness. By such purified goodness, one's heart melts in devotional service. *Bhāva-bhakti* is the first seed of love of Godhead. This emotional stage is there before one attains pure love. When that emotional stage intensifies, it is called *prema-bhakti,* or transcendental love of Godhead. This gradual process is also described in the following two verses found in *Bhakti-rasāmṛta-sindhu* (1.4.15-16).

TEXTS 14-15

আদৌ শ্রদ্ধা ততঃ সাধুসঙ্গোঽথ ভজনক্রিয়া ।
ততোঽনর্থনিবৃত্তিঃ স্যাৎ ততো নিষ্ঠা রুচিস্ততঃ ॥ ১৪ ॥
অথাসক্তিস্ততো ভাবস্ততঃ প্রেমাভ্যুদঞ্চতি ।
সাধকানাময়ং প্রেম্ণঃ প্রাদুর্ভাবে ভবেৎ ক্রমঃ ॥ ১৫ ॥

ādau śraddhā tataḥ sādhu-
saṅgo 'tha bhajana-kriyā
tato 'nartha-nivṛttiḥ syāt
tato niṣṭhā rucis tataḥ

athāsaktis tato bhāvas
tataḥ premābhyudañcati
sādhakānām ayaṁ premṇaḥ
prādurbhāve bhavet kramaḥ

SYNONYMS

ādau—in the beginning; *śraddhā*—firm faith, or disinterest in material affairs and interest in spiritual advancement; *tataḥ*—thereafter; *sādhu-saṅgaḥ*—association with pure devotees; *atha*—then; *bhajana-kriyā*—performance of devotional service to Kṛṣṇa (surrendering to the spiritual master and being encouraged by the association of devotees, so that initiation takes place); *tataḥ*—thereafter; *anartha-nivṛttiḥ*—the diminishing of all unwanted habits; *syāt*—there should be; *tataḥ*—thereafter; *niṣṭhā*—firm faith; *ruciḥ*—taste; *tataḥ*—thereafter; *atha*—then; *āsaktiḥ*—attachment; *tataḥ*—then; *bhāvaḥ*—emotion or affection; *tataḥ*—thereafter; *prema*—love of God; *abhyudañcati*—arises; **sādhakānām**—of the devotees practicing Kṛṣṇa consciousness; *ayam*—this; *premṇaḥ*—of love of Godhead; *prādurbhāve*—in the appearance; *bhavet*—is; *kramaḥ*—the chronological order.

TRANSLATION

" 'In the beginning there must be faith. Then one becomes interested in associating with pure devotees. Thereafter one is initiated by the spiritual master and executes the regulative principles under his orders. Thus one is freed from all unwanted habits and becomes firmly fixed in devotional service. Thereafter, one develops taste and attachment. This is the way of sādhana-bhakti, the execution of devotional service according to the regulative principles. Gradually emotions intensify, and finally there is an awakening of love. This is the gradual development of love of Godhead for the devotee interested in Kṛṣṇa consciousness.'

TEXT 16

সতাং প্রসঙ্গান্মম বীর্যসংবিদো
ভবন্তি হৃৎকর্ণরসায়নাঃ কথাঃ ।
তজ্জোষণাদাশ্বপবর্গবর্ত্মনি
শ্রদ্ধা রতির্ভক্তিরনুক্রমিষ্যতি ॥ ১৬ ॥

satāṁ prasaṅgān mama vīrya-saṁvido
bhavanti hṛt-karṇa-rasāyanāḥ kathāḥ
taj-joṣaṇād āśv apavarga-vartmani
śraddhā ratir bhaktir anukramiṣyati

SYNONYMS

satām—of the devotees; *prasaṅgāt*—by the intimate association; *mama*—of Me; *vīrya-saṁvidaḥ*—talks full of spiritual potency; *bhavanti*—appear; *hṛt*—to the heart; *karṇa*—and to the ears; *rasa-āyanāḥ*—a source of sweetness; *kathāḥ*—talks; *tat*—of them; *joṣaṇāt*—from proper cultivation; *āśu*—quickly; *apavarga*—of liberation; *vartmani*—on the path; *śraddhā*—faith; *ratiḥ*—attraction; *bhaktiḥ*—love; *anukramiṣyati*—will follow one after another.

TRANSLATION

" 'The spiritually powerful message of Godhead can be properly discussed only in a society of devotees, and it is greatly pleasing to hear in that association. If one hears from devotees, the way of transcendental experience quickly opens to him, and gradually he attains firm faith that in due course develops into attraction and devotion.'

PURPORT

This is a quotation from *Śrīmad-Bhāgavatam* (3.25.25).

TEXT 17

যাঁহার হৃদয়ে এই ভাবাঙ্কুর হয়।
তাঁহাতে এতেক চিহ্ন সর্বশাস্ত্রে কয়॥ ১৭॥

yāṅhāra hṛdaye ei bhāvāṅkura haya
tāṅhāte eteka cihna sarva-śāstre kaya

SYNONYMS

yāṅhāra—of whom; *hṛdaye*—in the heart; *ei*—this; *bhāva-aṅkura*—seed of emotion; *haya*—there is; *tāṅhāte*—in him; *eteka*—these; *cihna*—symptoms; *sarva-śāstre*—all revealed scriptures; *kaya*—say.

TRANSLATION

"If one actually has the seed of transcendental emotion in his heart, the symptoms will be visible in his activities. That is the verdict of all revealed scriptures.

TEXTS 18-19

ক্ষান্তিরব্যর্থকালত্বং বিরক্তির্মানশূন্যতা।
আশাবন্ধঃ সমুৎকণ্ঠা নামগানে সদা রুচিঃ॥ ১৮॥
আসক্তিস্তদ্গুণাখ্যানে
প্রীতিস্তদ্বসতিস্থলে।
ইত্যাদয়োঽনুভাবাঃ স্যু
র্জাতভাবাঙ্কুরে জনে॥ ১৯॥

kṣāntir avyartha-kālatvaṁ
viraktir māna-śūnyatā
āśā-bandhaḥ samutkaṇṭhā
nāma-gāne sadā ruciḥ

āsaktis tad-guṇākhyāne
prītis tad-vasati-sthale
ity ādayo 'nubhāvāḥ syur
jāta-bhāvāṅkure jane

SYNONYMS

kṣāntiḥ—forgiveness; *avyartha-kālatvam*—being free from wasting time; *virak-tiḥ*—detachment; *māna-śūnyatā*—absence of false prestige; *āśā-bandhaḥ*—

hope; *samutkaṇṭhā*—eagerness; *nāma-gāne*—in chanting the holy names; *sadā*—always; *ruciḥ*—taste; *āsaktiḥ*—attachment; *tat*—of Lord Kṛṣṇa; *guṇa-ākhyāne*—in describing the transcendental qualities; *prītiḥ*—affection; *tat*—His; *vasati-sthale*—in places of residence (the temple or holy places); *iti*—thus; *ādayaḥ*—and so on; *anubhāvāḥ*—the signs; *syuḥ*—are; *jāta*—developed; *bhāva-aṅkure*—whose seed of ecstatic emotion; *jane*—in a person.

TRANSLATION

" 'When the seed of ecstatic emotion for Kṛṣṇa fructifies, the following nine symptoms manifest in one's behavior: forgiveness, concern that time should not be wasted, detachment, absence of false prestige, hope, eagerness, a taste for chanting the holy name of the Lord, attachment to descriptions of the transcendental qualities of the Lord, and affection for those places where the Lord resides—that is, a temple or a holy place like Vṛndāvana. These are all called anubhāva, subordinate signs of ecstatic emotion. They are visible in a person in whose heart the seed of love of God has begun to fructify.'

PURPORT

These two verses are found in *Bhakti-rasāmṛta-sindhu* (1.3.25-26).

TEXT 20

এই নব প্রীত্যঙ্কুর যাঁর চিত্তে হয়।
প্রাকৃত-ক্ষোভে তাঁর ক্ষোভ নাহি হয় ॥ ২০ ॥

ei nava prīty-aṅkura yāṅra citte haya
prākṛta-kṣobhe tāṅra kṣobha nāhi haya

SYNONYMS

ei—this; *nava*—nine; *prīti-aṅkura*—fructification of the seed of love; *yāṅra*—of whom; *citte*—in the mind; *haya*—there is; *prākṛta*—material; *kṣobhe*—in agitation; *tāṅra*—his; *kṣobha*—agitation; *nāhi haya*—there is not.

TRANSLATION

"If love for Kṛṣṇa in a seedling state has fructified in one's heart, one is not agitated by material things.

TEXT 21

তং মোপযাতং প্রতিযন্তু বিপ্রা
গঙ্গা চ দেবী ধৃতচিত্তমীশে ।

দ্বিজোপসৃষ্টঃ কুহকস্তক্ষকো বা
দশত্বলং গায়ত বিষ্ণুগাথাঃ ॥ ২১ ॥

taṁ mopayātaṁ pratiyantu viprā
gaṅgā ca devī dhṛta-cittam īśe
dvijopasṛṣṭaḥ kuhakas takṣako vā
daśatv alaṁ gāyata viṣṇu-gāthāḥ

SYNONYMS

tam—him; *mā*—me; *upayātam*—surrendered; *pratiyantu*—you may know; *viprāḥ*—O *brāhmaṇas; gaṅgā*—mother Ganges; *ca*—and; *devī*—the demigoddess; *dhṛta*—offered; *cittam*—whose mind; *īśe*—unto the Supreme Personality of Godhead; *dvija-upasṛṣṭaḥ*—created by the *brāhmaṇa; kuhakaḥ*—some trickery; *takṣakaḥ*—snake-bird; *vā*—or; *daśatu*—let it bite; *alam*—never mind; *gāyata*—chant; *viṣṇu-gāthāḥ*—the holy names of Lord Viṣṇu.

TRANSLATION

" 'O brāhmaṇas, just accept me as a completely surrendered soul, and let mother Ganges, the representative of the Lord, also accept me in that way, for I have already taken the lotus feet of the Lord into my heart. Let the snake-bird—or whatever magical thing the brāhmaṇa created—bite me at once. I only desire that you all continue singing the deeds of Lord Viṣṇu.'

PURPORT

This is a verse from *Śrīmad-Bhāgavatam* (1.19.15) spoken by Mahārāja Parīkṣit while he was sitting on the bank of the Ganges expecting to be bitten by a snake-bird summoned by the curse of a *brāhmaṇa* boy named Śṛṅgi, who was the son of a great sage named Śamīka. News of the curse was conveyed to the King, who prepared for his imminent death. Many great saintly persons, sages, *brāhmaṇas,* kings and demigods came to see him in his last days. Mahārāja Parīkṣit, however, was not at all afraid of being bitten by the snake-bird. Indeed, he requested all the great personalities assembled to continue chanting the holy name of Lord Viṣṇu.

TEXT 22

কৃষ্ণ-সম্বন্ধ বিনা কাল ব্যর্থ নাহি যায় ॥ ২২ ॥

kṛṣṇa-sambandha vinā kāla vyartha nāhi yāya

SYNONYMS

kṛṣṇa-sambandha vinā—without a connection with Kṛṣṇa; *kāla*—time; *vyartha*—useless; *nāhi yāya*—does not become.

TRANSLATION

"Not a moment should be lost. Every moment should be utilized for Kṛṣṇa or connected with Him.

PURPORT

Mahārāja Parīkṣit's expression of anxiety is explained in this verse. He says, "Let whatever is destined to happen take place. It doesn't matter. Just let me see that not a moment of my time is wasted without a relationship with Kṛṣṇa." One has to tolerate all obstacles on the path of Kṛṣṇa consciousness, and one has to see that not a moment of his life is wasted outside of Kṛṣṇa's service.

TEXT 23

বাগ্ভিঃ স্তুবন্তো মনসা স্মরন্তস্তন্বা নমন্তোঽপ্যনিশং ন তৃপ্তাঃ ।
ভক্তাঃ স্রবন্নেত্রজলাঃ সমগ্রমায়ুর্হরেরেব সমর্পয়ন্তি ॥ ২৩ ॥

vāgbhiḥ stuvanto manasā smarantas
tanvā namanto 'py aniśaṁ na tṛptāḥ
bhaktāḥ śravan-netra-jalāḥ samagram
āyūr harer eva samarpayanti

SYNONYMS

vāgbhiḥ—by words; *stuvantaḥ*—offering prayers to the Supreme Personality of Godhead; *manasā*—by the mind; *smarantaḥ*—remembering; *tanvā*—by the body; *namantaḥ*—offering obeisances; *api*—although; *aniśam*—all the time; *na tṛptāḥ*—not satisfied; *bhaktāḥ*—the devotees; *śravat*—shedding; *netra-jalāḥ*—tears from the eyes; *samagram*—the whole; *āyūḥ*—life; *hareḥ*—to Kṛṣṇa; *eva*—only; *samarpayanti*—dedicate.

TRANSLATION

" 'With their words, they offer prayers to the Lord. With their minds, they always remember the Lord. With their bodies, they offer obeisances to the Lord. Despite all these activities, they are still not satisfied. This is the nature of pure devotees. Shedding tears from their eyes, they dedicate their whole lives to the Lord's service.'

PURPORT

This verse from the *Hari-bhakti-sudhodaya* is found in *Bhakti-rasāmṛta-sindhu* (1.3.29).

TEXT 24

ভুক্তি, সিদ্ধি, ইন্দ্রিয়ার্থ তারে নাহি ভায় ॥ ২৪ ॥

bhukti, siddhi, indriyārtha tāre nāhi bhāya

SYNONYMS

bhukti—material enjoyment; *siddhi*—mystic power; *indriya-artha*—the objects of the senses; *tāre*—unto him; *nāhi bhāya*—do not appeal.

TRANSLATION

"In the material field, people are interested in material enjoyment, mystic power and sense gratification. However, these things do not appeal to the devotee at all.

TEXT 25

যো দুস্ত্যজান্ দারসুতান্ সুহৃদ্রাজ্যং হৃদিস্পৃশঃ ।
জহৌ যুবৈব মলবদুত্তমঃশ্লোকলালসঃ ॥ ২৫ ॥

yo dustyajān dāra-sutān
suhṛd-rājyaṁ hṛdi spṛśaḥ
jahau yuvaiva malavad
uttamaḥśloka-lālasaḥ

SYNONYMS

yaḥ—who (Bharata Mahārāja); *dustyajān*—difficult to give up; *dāra-sutān*—wife and children; *suhṛt*—friends; *rājyam*—kingdom; *hṛdi spṛśaḥ*—dear to the core of the heart; *jahau*—gave up; *yuvā*—youthful; *eva*—at that time; *mala-vat*—like stool; *uttamaḥ-śloka-lālasaḥ*—being captivated by the transcendental qualities, pastimes and association of the Supreme Personality of Godhead.

TRANSLATION

" 'King Bharata was very eager to attain the association of the Supreme Personality of Godhead, Kṛṣṇa, who is called uttama-śloka because poems and prayers are offered to Him for His favor. In his youth, King Bharata gave up his attractive wife and children, as well as his beloved friends and opulent kingdom, just as one gives up stool after passing it.'

PURPORT

These are the signs of *virakti* (detachment) found in a person who has developed *bhāva,* the preliminary stage of love of Godhead. This verse is quoted from *Śrīmad-Bhāgavatam* (5.14.43).

TEXT 26

'সর্বোত্তম' আপনাকে 'হীন' করি মানে ॥ ২৬ ॥

'sarvottama' āpanāke 'hīna' kari māne

SYNONYMS

sarva-uttama—although standing above all; *āpanāke*—himself; *hīna kari*—as the lowest; *māne*—considers.

TRANSLATION

"Although a pure devotee's standard is above all, he still considers himself to be in the lowest stage of life.

TEXT 27

হরৌ রতিং বহন্নেষ নরেন্দ্রাণাং শিখামণিঃ ।
ভিক্ষামটন্নরিপুরে শ্বপাকমপি বন্দতে ॥ ২৭ ॥

harau ratiṁ vahann eṣa
narendrāṇāṁ śikhāmaṇiḥ
bhikṣām aṭann ari-pure
śva-pākam api vandate

SYNONYMS

harau—toward the Supreme Personality of Godhead; *ratim*—affection; *vahan*—carrying; *eṣaḥ*—this one; *nara-indrāṇām*—of all the kings; *śikhā-maṇiḥ*—brilliant crown jewel; *bhikṣām*—begging alms; *aṭan*—wandering for; *ari-pure*—even in the city of enemies; *śva-pākam*—the fifth-grade *caṇḍālas; api*—even; *vandate*—worships.

TRANSLATION

" 'Bharata Mahārāja always carried affection for Kṛṣṇa within his heart. Although Bharata Mahārāja was the crown jewel of kings, he was still wandering about and begging alms in the city of his enemies. He was even offering respects to caṇḍālas, low-class men who eat dogs.'

PURPORT

This is a quotation from *Padma Purāṇa.*

TEXT 28

'কৃষ্ণ কৃপা করিবেন'— দৃঢ় করি' জানে ॥ ২৮ ॥

'kṛṣṇa kṛpā karibena'——dṛḍha kari' jāne

SYNONYMS

kṛṣṇa—Lord Kṛṣṇa; *kṛpā karibena*—will show His mercy; *dṛḍha kari'*—making firm; *jāne*—he believes.

TRANSLATION

"A fully surrendered devotee always hopes that Lord Kṛṣṇa will be kind to him. This hope is very firm in him.

TEXT 29

ন প্রেমা শ্রবণাদিভক্তিরপি বা যোগোঽথবা বৈষ্ণবো
জ্ঞানং বা শুভকর্ম বা কিয়দহো সজ্জাতিরপ্যস্তি বা ।
হীনার্থাধিকসাধকে ত্বয়ি তথাপ্যচ্ছেদ্যমূলা সতী
হে গোপীজনবল্লভ ব্যথয়তে হা হা মদাশৈব মাম্ ॥২৯॥

na premā śravaṇādi-bhaktir api vā yogo 'thavā vaiṣṇavo
jñānaṁ vā śubha-karma vā kiyad aho saj-jātir apy asti vā
hīnārthādhika-sādhake tvayi tathāpy acchedya-mūlā satī
he gopī-jana-vallabha vyathayate hā hā mad-āśaiva mām

SYNONYMS

na—not; *premā*—love of Godhead; *śravaṇa-ādi*—consisting of chanting, hearing and so on; *bhaktiḥ*—devotional service; *api*—also; *vā*—or; *yogaḥ*—the power of mystic *yoga; athavā*—or; *vaiṣṇavaḥ*—befitting a devotee; *jñānam*—knowledge; *vā*—or; *śubha-karma*—pious activities; *vā*—or; *kiyat*—a little; *aho*—O my Lord; *sat-jātiḥ*—birth in a good family; *api*—even; *asti*—there is; *vā*—or; *hīna-artha-adhika-sādhake*—who bestows greater benedictions upon one who is fallen and possesses no good qualities; *tvayi*—unto You; *tathāpi*—still; *acchedya-mūlā*—whose root is uncuttable; *satī*—being; *he*—O; *gopī-jana-vallabha*—most dear friend of the *gopīs; vyathayate*—gives pain; *hā hā*—alas; *mat*—my; *āśā*—hope; *eva*—certainly; *mām*—to me.

TRANSLATION

" 'O my Lord, I do not have any love for You, nor am I qualified for discharging devotional service by chanting and hearing. Nor do I possess the

mystic power of a Vaiṣṇava, knowledge or pious activities. Nor do I belong to a very high-caste family. On the whole, I do not possess anything. Still, O beloved of the gopīs, because You bestow Your mercy on the most fallen, I have an unbreakable hope that is constantly in my heart. That hope is always giving me pain.'

PURPORT

This verse is found in *Bhakti-rasāmṛta-sindhu* (1.3.35).

TEXT 30

সমুৎকণ্ঠা হয় সদা লালসা-প্রধান ॥ ৩০ ॥

samutkaṇṭhā haya sadā lālasā-pradhāna

SYNONYMS

samutkaṇṭhā—eagerness; *haya*—is; *sadā*—always; *lālasā*—ardent desire; *pradhāna*—chiefly characterized by.

TRANSLATION

"This eagerness is chiefly characterized by an ardent desire to associate with the Lord.

TEXT 31

ত্বচ্ছৈশবং ত্রিভুবনাদ্ভুতমিত্যবেহি
মচ্চাপলঞ্চ তব বা মম বাধিগম্যম্ ।
তৎ কিং করোমি বিরলং মুরলীবিলাসি
মুগ্ধং মুখাম্বুজমুদীক্ষিতুমীক্ষণাভ্যাম্ ॥ ৩১ ॥

tvac-chaiśavaṁ tri-bhuvanādbhutam ity avehi
mac-cāpalaṁ ca tava vā mama vādhigamyam
tat kiṁ karomi viralaṁ muralī-vilāsi
mugdhaṁ mukhāmbujam udīkṣitum īkṣaṇābhyām

SYNONYMS

tvat—Your; *śaiśavam*—early age; *tri-bhuvana*—within the three worlds; *adbhutam*—wonderful; *iti*—thus; *avehi*—know; *mat-cāpalam*—My unsteadiness; *ca*—and; *tava*—of You; *vā*—or; *mama*—of Me; *vā*—or; *adhigamyam*—to be understood; *tat*—that; *kim*—what; *karomi*—I do; *viralam*—in solitude; *muralī-vilāsi*—O player of the flute; *mugdham*—attractive; *mukha-ambujam*—lotuslike face; *udīkṣitum*—to see sufficiently; *īkṣaṇābhyām*—by the eyes.

TRANSLATION

" 'O Kṛṣṇa, O flute player, the sweetness of Your early age is wonderful within these three worlds. You know My unsteadiness, and I know Yours. No one else knows about this. I want to see Your beautiful, attractive face somewhere in a solitary place, but how can this be accomplished?'

PURPORT

This is a verse from *Kṛṣṇa-karṇāmṛta* (32).

TEXT 32

নাম-গানে সদা রুচি, লয় কৃষ্ণনাম ॥ ৩২ ॥

nāma-gāne sadā ruci, laya kṛṣṇa-nāma

SYNONYMS

nāma-gāne—in chanting the holy names; *sadā*—constantly; *ruci*—taste, relish; *laya*—takes; *kṛṣṇa-nāma*—the Hare Kṛṣṇa *mantra.*

TRANSLATION

"Due to having great relish for the holy name, one is inclined to chant the Hare Kṛṣṇa mahā-mantra constantly.

TEXT 33

রোদনবিন্দুমরন্দ-স্যন্দি-দৃগিন্দীবরাদ্য গোবিন্দ ।
তব মধুরস্বরকণ্ঠী গায়তি নামাবলীং বালা ॥ ৩৩ ॥

rodana-bindu-maranda-syandi-
dṛg-indīvarādya govinda
tava madhura-svara-kaṇṭhī
gāyati nāmāvalīṁ bālā

SYNONYMS

rodana-bindu—with teardrops; *maranda*—like the nectar or juice of flowers; *syandi*—pouring; *dṛk-indīvarā*—whose lotus eyes; *ādya*—today; *govinda*—O my Lord Govinda; *tava*—Your; *madhura-svara-kaṇṭhī*—who has a very sweet voice; *gāyati*—sings; *nāma-āvalīm*—holy names; *bālā*—this young girl (Rādhikā).

TRANSLATION

" 'O Govinda, this youthful girl named Rādhikā is today constantly pouring forth tears like nectar falling from flowers. She is also singing Your holy name in a sweet voice.'

PURPORT

This verse is found in *Bhakti-rasāmṛta-sindhu* (1.3.38).

TEXT 34

কৃষ্ণগুণাখ্যানে হয় সর্বদা আসক্তি ॥ ৩৪ ॥

kṛṣṇa-guṇākhyāne haya sarvadā āsakti

SYNONYMS

kṛṣṇa-guṇa-ākhyāne—in describing the transcendental qualities of Kṛṣṇa; *haya*—there is; *sarvadā*—always; *āsakti*—attachment.

TRANSLATION

"At this stage of bhāva, a devotee has awakened the tendency to chant and describe the transcendental qualities of the Lord. He has attachment for this process.

TEXT 35

মধুরং মধুরং বপুরস্য বিভোর্মধুরং মধুরং বদনং মধুরম্ ।
মধুগন্ধি মৃদুস্মিতমেতদহো মধুরং মধুরং মধুরং মধুরম্ ॥৩৫॥

madhuraṁ madhuraṁ vapur asya vibhor
madhuraṁ madhuraṁ vadanaṁ madhuram
madhu-gandhi mṛdu-smitam etad aho
madhuraṁ madhuraṁ madhuraṁ madhuram

SYNONYMS

madhuram—sweet; *madhuram*—sweet; *vapuḥ*—the transcendental form; *asya*—His; *vibhoḥ*—of the Lord; *madhuram*—sweet; *madhuram*—sweet; *vadanam*--face; *madhuram*—more sweet; *madhu-gandhi*—the fragrance of honey; *mṛdu-smitam*—soft smiling; *etat*—this; *aho*—oh; *madhuram*—sweet; *madhuram*—sweet; *madhuram*—sweet; *madhuram*—still more sweet.

TRANSLATION

" 'O my Lord, the transcendental body of Kṛṣṇa is very sweet, and His face is even sweeter than His body. The soft smile on His face, which is like the fragrance of honey, is sweeter still.'

PURPORT

This is a verse quoted from Bilvamaṅgala Ṭhākura's *Kṛṣṇa-karṇāmṛta* (92).

TEXT 36

কৃষ্ণলীলা-স্থানে করে সর্ব্বদা বসতি ॥ ৩৬ ॥

kṛṣṇa-līlā-sthāne kare sarvadā vasati

SYNONYMS

kṛṣṇa-līlā-sthāne—in the place where Kṛṣṇa has His pastimes; *kare*—makes; *sarvadā*—always; *vasati*—abode.

TRANSLATION

"A devotee absorbed in ecstatic emotion for Kṛṣṇa always resides in a place where Kṛṣṇa's pastimes were performed.

TEXT 37

কদাহং যমুনাতীরে নামানি তব কীর্ত্তয়ন্।
উদ্বাষ্পঃ পুণ্ডরীকাক্ষ রচয়িষ্যামি তাণ্ডবম্ ॥ ৩৭ ॥

kadāhaṁ yamunā-tīre
nāmāni tava kīrtayan
udbāṣpaḥ puṇḍarīkākṣa
racayiṣyāmi tāṇḍavam

SYNONYMS

kadā—when; *aham*—I; *yamunā-tīre*—on the bank of the Yamunā; *nāmāni*—holy names; *tava*—Your; *kīrtayan*—chanting; *udbāṣpaḥ*—full of tears; *puṇḍarīka-akṣa*—O lotus-eyed one; *racayiṣyāmi*—I shall create; *tāṇḍavam*—dancing like a madman.

TRANSLATION

" 'O Lord Puṇḍarīkākṣa, while chanting Your holy name with tears in my eyes, when shall I dance in ecstasy on the bank of the Yamunā?'

PURPORT

This verse is found in *Bhakti-rasāmṛta-sindhu* (1.2.156).

TEXT 38

কৃষ্ণে 'রতির' চিহ্ন এই কৈলুঁ বিবরণ ।
'কৃষ্ণপ্রেমের' চিহ্ন এবে শুন সনাতন ॥ ৩৮ ॥

kṛṣṇe 'ratira' cihna ei kailuṅ vivaraṇa
'kṛṣṇa-premera' cihna ebe śuna sanātana

SYNONYMS

kṛṣṇe—for Kṛṣṇa; *ratira*—of attraction; *cihna*—the symptoms; *ei*—all these; *kailuṅ vivaraṇa*—I have described; *kṛṣṇa-premera*—of love for Lord Kṛṣṇa; *cihna*—the symptoms; *ebe*—now; *śuna sanātana*—please hear, Sanātana.

TRANSLATION

"These are the symptoms of a person who has developed attraction [bhāva] for Kṛṣṇa. Now let me describe the symptoms of a person who is actually elevated to love of Kṛṣṇa. O Sanātana, please hear this from Me.

TEXT 39

যাঁর চিত্তে কৃষ্ণপ্রেমা করয়ে উদয় ।
তাঁর বাক্য, ক্রিয়া, মুদ্রা বিজ্ঞেহ না বুঝয় ॥ ৩৯ ॥

yāṅra citte kṛṣṇa-premā karaye udaya
tāṅra vākya, kriyā, mudrā vijñeha nā bujhaya

SYNONYMS

yāṅra citte—in whose heart; *kṛṣṇa-premā*—love of Kṛṣṇa; *karaye udaya*—awakens; *tāṅra*—his; *vākya*—words; *kriyā*—activities; *mudrā*—symptoms; *vijñeha*—even a learned scholar; *nā bujhaya*—does not understand.

TRANSLATION

"Even the most learned man cannot understand the words, activities and symptoms of a person situated in love of Godhead.

TEXT 40

ধন্যস্যায়ং নবপ্রেমা যস্যোন্মীলতি চেতসি ।
অন্তর্বাণিভিরপ্যস্য মুদ্রা সুষ্ঠু সুদুর্গমা ॥ ৪০ ॥

dhanyasyāyaṁ nava-premā
yasyonmīlati cetasi
antarvāṇibhir apy asya
mudrā suṣṭhu sudurgamā

SYNONYMS

dhanyasya—of a most fortunate person; *ayam*—this; *navaḥ*—new; *premā*—love of Godhead; *yasya*—of whom; *unmīlati*—manifests; *cetasi*—in the heart; *antarvāṇibhiḥ*—by persons well versed in *śāstras; api*—even; *asya*—of him; *mudrā*—symptoms; *suṣṭhu*—exceedingly; *sudurgamā*—difficult to understand.

TRANSLATION

" 'Even a most learned scholar cannot understand the activities and symptoms of an exalted personality in whose heart love of Godhead has awakened.'

PURPORT

This verse is also found in *Bhakti-rasāmṛta-sindhu* (1.4.17).

TEXT 41

এবংব্রতঃ স্বপ্রিয়নামকীর্ত্যা
জাতানুরাগো দ্রুতচিত্ত উচ্চৈঃ ।
হসত্যথো রোদিতি রৌতি গায়-
ত্যুন্মাদবন্নৃত্যতি লোকবাহ্যঃ ॥ ৪১ ॥

evaṁvrataḥ sva-priya-nāma-kīrtyā
jātānurāgo druta-citta uccaiḥ
hasaty atho roditi rauti gāyaty
unmādavan nṛtyati loka-bāhyaḥ

SYNONYMS

evam-vrataḥ—when one thus engages in a vow to chant and dance; *sva*—own; *priya*—very dear; *nāma*—the holy name; *kīrtyā*—by chanting; *jāta*—in this way develops; *anurāgaḥ*—attachment; *druta-cittaḥ*—very eagerly; *uccaiḥ*—loudly; *hasati*—laughs; *atho*—also; *roditi*—cries; *rauti*—becomes agitated; *gāyati*—chants; *unmāda-vat*—like a madman; *nṛtyati*—dances; *loka-bāhyaḥ*—not caring for outsiders.

TRANSLATION

" 'When a person is actually advanced and takes pleasure in chanting the holy name of the Lord, who is very dear to him, he is agitated and loudly chants the holy name. He also laughs, cries, becomes agitated and chants just like a madman, not caring for outsiders.'

PURPORT

This verse is quoted from *Śrīmad-Bhāgavatam* (11.2.40).

TEXT 42

প্রেমা ক্রমে বাড়ি' হয় – স্নেহ, মান, প্রণয় ।
রাগ, অনুরাগ, ভাব, মহাভাব হয় ॥ ৪২ ॥

premā krame bāḍi' haya——sneha, māna, praṇaya
rāga, anurāga, bhāva, mahābhāva haya

SYNONYMS

premā—love of God; *krame*—gradually; *bāḍi'*—increasing; *haya*—is; *sneha*—affection; *māna*—indignation due to affection; *praṇaya*—love; *rāga*—attachment; *anurāga*—subattachment; *bhāva*—ecstasy; *mahā-bhāva*—exalted ecstasy; *haya*—is.

TRANSLATION

"Love of Godhead increases and is manifest as affection, counter-love, love, attachment, subattachment, ecstasy and sublime ecstasy.

TEXT 43

বীজ, ইক্ষু, রস, গুড় তবে খণ্ডসার ।
শর্করা, সিতা-মিছরি, শুদ্ধমিছরি আর ॥ ৪৩ ॥

bīja, ikṣu, rasa, guḍa tabe khaṇḍa-sāra
śarkarā, sitā-michari, śuddha-michari āra

SYNONYMS

bīja—seeds; *ikṣu*—sugarcane plants; *rasa*—juice; *guḍa*—molasses; *tabe*—then; *khaṇḍa-sāra*—crude sugar; *śarkarā*—sugar; *sitā-michari*—sugar candy; *śuddha-michari*—rock candy; *āra*—also.

TRANSLATION

"This development is compared to sugarcane seeds, sugarcane plants, sugarcane juice, molasses, crude sugar, refined sugar, sugar candy and rock candy.

TEXT 44

ইহা যৈছে ক্রমে নির্মল, ক্রমে বাড়ে স্বাদ ।
রতি-প্রেমাদির তৈছে বাড়য়ে আস্বাদ ॥ ৪৪ ॥

ihā yaiche krame nirmala, krame bāḍe svāda
rati-premādira taiche bāḍaye āsvāda

SYNONYMS

ihā—this; *yaiche*—like; *krame*—by succession; *nirmala*—pure; *krame*—gradually; *bāḍe*—increases; *svāda*—taste; *rati*—from attachment; *prema-ādira*—of love of Godhead and so on; *taiche*—in that way; *bāḍaye*—increases; *āsvāda*—taste.

TRANSLATION

"Just as the taste of sugar increases as it is gradually purified, one should understand that when love of Godhead increases from rati, which is compared to the beginning seed, its taste increases.

TEXT 45

অধিকারি-ভেদে রতি—পঞ্চ পরকার ।
শান্ত, দাস্য, সখ্য, বাৎসল্য, মধুর আর ॥ ৪৫ ॥

adhikāri-bhede rati——pañca parakāra
śānta, dāsya, sakhya, vātsalya, madhura āra

SYNONYMS

adhikāri—of possessor; *bhede*—according to differences; *rati*—attachment; *pañca parakāra*—five varieties; *śānta*—neutral; *dāsya*—servitude; *sakhya*—friendship; *vātsalya*—paternal love; *madhura*—conjugal love; *āra*—also.

TRANSLATION

"According to the candidate possessing these transcendental qualities [sneha, māna and so on], there are five transcendental mellows—neutrality, servitorship, friendship, parental love and conjugal love.

PURPORT

In the *Bhakti-rasāmṛta-sindhu, rati* (attraction) is thus described:

vyaktaṁ masṛṇitevāntar-
lakṣyate rati-lakṣaṇam
mumukṣu-prabhṛtīnaṁ ced
bhaved eṣā ratir na hi

kintu bāla-camatkāra-
kārī tac-cihna-vīkṣayā
abhijñena subodho 'yaṁ
raty-ābhāsaḥ prakīrtitaḥ

The real symptoms of the fructification of the seed of love (*rati*) are manifest because the heart is melted. When such symptoms are found among speculators and fruitive actors, they cannot be accepted as real symptoms of attachment. Foolish people without knowledge of devotional service praise such symptoms of attachment even when they are based on something other than a desire to serve Kṛṣṇa. However, one who is expert in devotional service calls such symptoms *rati-ābhāsa,* a mere glimpse of attachment.

TEXT 46

এই পঞ্চ স্থায়ী ভাব হয় পঞ্চ 'রস' ।
যে-রসে ভক্ত 'সুখী', কৃষ্ণ হয় 'বশ' ॥ ৪৬ ॥

ei pañca sthāyī bhāva haya pañca 'rasa'
ye-rase bhakta 'sukhī', kṛṣṇa haya 'vaśa'

SYNONYMS

ei pañca—these five kinds of transcendental mellow; *sthāyī bhāva*—permanent ecstatic moods; *haya*—become; *pañca rasa*—five kinds of transcendental mellow; *ye-rase*—in a particular mellow; *bhakta sukhī*—a devotee becomes happy; *kṛṣṇa*—Lord Kṛṣṇa; *haya*—becomes; *vaśa*—under the control.

TRANSLATION

"These five transcendental mellows exist permanently. The devotee may be attracted to one of these mellows, and thus he becomes happy. Kṛṣṇa also becomes inclined toward such a devotee and comes under his control.

PURPORT

In *Bhakti-rasāmṛta-sindhu, sthāyi-bhāva,* permanent ecstasy, is thus described:

aviruddhān viruddhāṁś ca
bhāvān yo vaśatāṁ nayan
su-rājeva virājeta
sa sthāyī bhāva ucyate
sthāyī bhāvo 'tra sa proktaḥ
śrī-kṛṣṇa-viṣayā ratiḥ

These moods (*bhāvas*) bring under control the favorable ecstasies (such as laughing) and unfavorable ecstasies (such as anger). When these continue to remain as kings, they are called *sthāyi-bhāva,* or permanent ecstasies. Continuous ecstatic love for Kṛṣṇa is called permanent ecstasy.

TEXT 47

প্রেমাদিক স্থায়িভাব সামগ্রী-মিলনে ।
কৃষ্ণভক্তি রসরূপে পায় পরিণামে ॥ ৪৭ ॥

premādika sthāyi-bhāva sāmagrī-milane
kṛṣṇa-bhakti rasa-rūpe pāya pariṇāme

SYNONYMS

prema-ādika—love of Godhead, beginning with *śānta, dāsya* and so on; *sthāyi-bhāva*—the permanent ecstasies; *sāmagrī-milane*—by mixing with other ingredients; *kṛṣṇa-bhakti*—devotional service to Lord Kṛṣṇa; *rasa-rūpe*—composed of transcendental mellows; *pāya*—becomes; *pariṇāme*—by transformation.

TRANSLATION

"When the permanent ecstasies [neutrality, servitorship and so on] are mixed with other ingredients, devotional service in love of Godhead is transformed and becomes composed of transcendental mellows.

PURPORT

In *Bhakti-rasāmṛta-sindhu,* the following definition is given:

athāsyāḥ keśava-rater
lakṣitāyā nigadyate
sāmagrī-paripoṣeṇa
paramā rasa-rūpatā

vibhāvair anubhāvaiś ca
sāttvikair vyabhicāribhiḥ
svādyatvaṁ hṛdi bhaktānām
ānītā śravaṇādibhiḥ
eṣā kṛṣṇa-ratiḥ sthāyī
bhāvo bhakti-raso bhavet

Love for Kṛṣṇa, Keśava, as previously described, reaches the supreme state of being composed of mellows when its ingredients are fulfilled. By means of *vibhāva, anubhāva, sāttvika* and *vyabhicārī,* hearing and chanting are activated, and the devotee is able to taste love for Kṛṣṇa. Then attachment for Kṛṣṇa, or permanent ecstasy (*sthāyi-bhāva*), becomes the mellow of devotional service (*bhakti-rasa*).

TEXT 48

বিভাব, অনুভাব, সাত্ত্বিক, ব্যভিচারী ।
স্থায়িভাব 'রস' হয় এই চারি মিলি' ॥ ৪৮ ॥

vibhāva, anubhāva, sāttvika, vyabhicārī
sthāyi-bhāva 'rasa' haya ei cāri mili'

SYNONYMS

vibhāva—special ecstasy; *anubhāva*—subordinate ecstasy; *sāttvika*—natural ecstasy; *vyabhicārī*—transitory ecstasy; *sthāyi-bhāva*—permanent ecstasy; *rasa*—mellow; *haya*—becomes; *ei cāri*—these four; *mili'*—meeting.

TRANSLATION

"The permanent ecstasy becomes a more and more tasteful transcendental mellow through the mixture of special ecstasy, subordinate ecstasy, natural ecstasy and transitory ecstasy.

TEXT 49

দধি যেন খণ্ড-মরিচ-কর্পূর-মিলনে ।
'রসালাখ্য' রস হয় অপূর্বাস্বাদনে ॥ ৪৯ ॥

dadhi yena khaṇḍa-marica-karpūra-milane
'rasālākhya' rasa haya apūrvāsvādane

SYNONYMS

dadhi—yogurt; *yena*—as if; *khaṇḍa*—sugar candy; *marica*—black pepper; *karpūra*—camphor; *milane*—being mixed; *rasāla-ākhya*—known as delicious; *rasa*—mellow; *haya*—becomes; *apūrva-āsvādane*—by an unprecedented taste.

TRANSLATION

"Yogurt mixed with sugar candy, black pepper and camphor is very palatable and tasty. Similarly, when permanent ecstasy mixes with other ecstatic symptoms, it becomes unprecedentedly tasty.

TEXT 50

দ্বিবিধ 'বিভাব',—আলম্বন, উদ্দীপন ।
বংশীস্বরাদি—'উদ্দীপন', কৃষ্ণাদি—'আলম্বন' ॥৫০ ॥

dvividha 'vibhāva',——ālambana, uddīpana
vaṁśī-svarādi——'uddīpana', kṛṣṇādi——'ālambana'

SYNONYMS

dvi-vidha—two kinds; *vibhāva*—particular ecstasy; *ālambana*—the support; *uddīpana*—awakening; *vaṁśī-svara-ādi*—such as the vibration of the flute; *uddīpana*—exciting; *kṛṣṇa-ādi*—Kṛṣṇa and others; *ālambana*—the support.

TRANSLATION

"There are two kinds of particular ecstasies [vibhāva]. One is called the support, and the other is called the awakening. The vibration of Kṛṣṇa's flute is an example of the awakening, and Lord Kṛṣṇa Himself is an example of the support.

TEXT 51

'অনুভাব'—স্মিত, নৃত্য, গীতাদি উদ্ভাস্বর ।
স্তম্ভাদি—'সাত্ত্বিক' অনুভাবের ভিতর ॥ ৫১ ॥

'anubhāva'——smita, nṛtya, gītādi udbhāsvara
stambhādi——'sāttvika' anubhāvera bhitara

SYNONYMS

anubhāva—subordinate ecstasy; *smita*—smiling; *nṛtya*—dancing; *gīta-ādi*—songs and so on; *udbhāsvara*—symptoms of bodily manifestation; *stambha-ādi*—

being stunned and others; *sāttvika*—natural; *anubhāvera bhitara*—within the category of subordinate ecstasies.

TRANSLATION

"The subordinate ecstasies are smiling, dancing and singing, as well as different manifestations in the body. The natural ecstasies, such as being stunned, are considered among the subordinate ecstasies [anubhāva].

PURPORT

In the *Bhakti-rasāmṛta-sindhu, vibhāva* is described as follows:

tatra jñeyā vibhāvās tu
raty-āsvādana-hetavaḥ
te dvidhālambanā eke
tathaivoddīpanāḥ pare

"The cause bringing about the tasting of love for Kṛṣṇa is called *vibhāva. Vibhāva* is divided into two categories—*ālambana* (support) and *uddīpana* (awakening)."

In the *Agni Purāṇa* it is stated:

vibhāvyate hi raty-ādir
yatra yena vibhāvyate
vibhāvo nāma sa dvedhā-
lambanoddīpanātmakaḥ

"That which causes love for Kṛṣṇa to appear is called *vibhāva.* That has two divisions—*ālambana* [in which love appears] and *uddīpana* [by which love appears]."

In *Bhakti-rasāmṛta-sindhu,* the following is stated about *ālambana:*

kṛṣṇaś ca kṛṣṇa-bhaktāś ca
budhair ālambanā matāḥ
raty-āder viṣayatvena
tathādhāratayāpi ca

"The object of love is Kṛṣṇa, and the container of that love is the devotee of Kṛṣṇa. Both of them are called by the learned scholars *ālambana*—the foundations." Similarly, *uddīpana* is described:

uddīpanās tu te proktā
bhāvam uddīpayanti ye

"Those things which awaken ecstatic love are called *uddīpana.*"

te tu śrī-kṛṣṇa-candrasya
guṇāś ceṣṭāḥ prasādhanam

Mainly this awakening is made possible by the qualities and activities of Kṛṣṇa, as well as by His mode of decoration and the way His hair is arranged.

smitāṅga-saurabhe vaṁśa-
śṛṅga-nūpura-kambavaḥ
padāṅka-kṣetra-tulasī-
bhakta-tad-vāsarādayaḥ

"Kṛṣṇa's smile, the fragrance of His transcendental body, His flute, bugle, ankle bells, conchshell, the marks on His feet, His place of residence, His favorite plant [*tulasī*], His devotees, and the observance of fasts and vows connected to His devotion all awaken the symptoms of ecstatic love."

In *Bhakti-rasāmṛta-sindhu, anubhāva* is described as follows:

anubhāvās tu citta-stha-
bhāvānām avabodhakāḥ
te bahir vikriyā prāyāḥ
proktā udbhāsvarākhyayā

The many external ecstatic symptoms or bodily transformations which indicate ecstatic emotions in the mind, and which are also called *udbhāsvara,* are the *anubhāvas,* or subordinate ecstatic expressions of love. Some of these are dancing, falling down and rolling on the ground, singing and crying very loudly, bodily contortions, loud vibrations, yawning, deep breathing, disregard for others, the frothing of saliva, mad laughter, spitting, hiccups and other similar symptoms. All these symptoms are divided into two divisions—*śīta* and *kṣepaṇa.* Singing, yawning and so on are called *śīta.* Dancing and bodily contortions are called *kṣepaṇa.*

The *Bhakti-rasāmṛta-sindhu* describes *udbhāsvara* as follows:

udbhāsante svadhāmnīti
proktā udbhāsvarā budhaiḥ
nīvyuttarīya-dhammilla-
sraṁsanaṁ gātra-moṭanam
jṛmbhā ghrāṇasya phullatvaṁ
niśvāsādyāś ca te matāḥ

The ecstatic symptoms manifest in the external body of a person in ecstatic love are called by learned scholars *udbhāsvara*. Some of these are a slackening of the belt and a dropping of clothes and hair. Others are bodily contortions, yawning, a trembling of the front portion of the nostrils, heavy breathing, hiccupping and falling down and rolling on the ground. These are the external manifestations of emotional love. *Stambha* and other symptoms are described in *Madhya-līlā* (14.167).

TEXT 52

নির্বেদ-হর্ষাদি — তেত্রিশ 'ব্যভিচারী'।
সব মিলি' 'রস' হয় চমৎকারকারী ॥ ৫২ ॥

nirveda-harṣādi——tetriśa 'vyabhicārī'
saba mili' 'rasa' haya camatkārakārī

SYNONYMS

nirveda-harṣa-ādi—complete despondency, jubilation and so on; *tetriśa*—thirty-three; *vyabhicārī*—transitory elements; *saba mili'*—all meeting together; *rasa*—the mellow; *haya*—becomes; *camatkārakārī*—a causer of wonder.

TRANSLATION

"There are other ingredients beginning with complete despondency and jubilation. Altogether there are thirty-three varieties, and when these combine, the mellow becomes very wonderful.

PURPORT

Nirveda, harṣa, and other symptoms are explained in *Madhya-līlā* (14.167). The transitory elements (*vyabhicārī*) are described in *Bhakti-rasāmṛta-sindhu* as follows:

athocyante trayas triṁśad-
bhāvā ye vyabhicāriṇaḥ
viśeṣeṇābhimukhyena
caranti sthāyinaṁ prati
vāg-aṅga-sattva-sūcyā ye
jñeyās te vyabhicāriṇaḥ

sañcārayanti bhāvasya
gatiṁ sañcāriṇo 'pi te
unmajjanti nimajjanti
stāyiny-amṛta-vāridhau
ūrmivad vardhayanty enaṁ
yānti tad-rūpatāṁ ca te

There are thirty-three transitory elements known as *vyabhicārī*—ecstatic emotions. They especially wander about the permanent sentiments as assistants. They are to be known by words, by different symptoms seen in the limbs and in other parts of the body, and by the peculiar conditions of the heart. Because they set in motion the progress of the permanent sentiments, they are specifically called *sañcārī,* or impelling principles. These impelling principles rise up and fall back in the permanent sentiments of ecstatic love like waves in an ocean of ecstasy. Consequently they are called *vyabhicārī.*

TEXT 53

পঞ্চবিধ রস—শান্ত, দাস্য, সখ্য, বাৎসল্য ।
মধুর-নাম শৃঙ্গাররস—সবাতে প্রাবল্য ॥ ৫৩ ॥

pañca-vidha rasa——śānta, dāsya, sakhya, vātsalya
madhura-nāma śṛṅgāra-rasa——sabāte prābalya

SYNONYMS

pañca-vidha rasa—five kinds of mellows; *śānta*—neutrality; *dāsya*—servitorship; *sakhya*—friendship; *vātsalya*—paternal affection; *madhura*—sweet; *nāma*—named; *śṛṅgāra-rasa*—the conjugal mellow; *sabāte*—among all of them; *prābalya*—predominant.

TRANSLATION

"There are five transcendental mellows—neutrality, servitorship, friendship, paternal affection and conjugal love, which is also known as the mellow of sweetness. Conjugal love excels all others.

TEXT 54

শান্তরসে শান্তি-রতি 'প্রেম' পর্যন্ত হয় ।
দাস্য-রতি 'রাগ' পর্যন্ত ক্রমেত বাড়য় ॥ ৫৪ ॥

śānta-rase śānti-rati 'prema' paryanta haya
dāsya-rati 'rāga' paryanta krameta bāḍaya

SYNONYMS

śānta-rase—in the mellow of neutrality; *śānti-rati*—spiritual attachment in peacefulness; *prema paryanta*—up to love of Godhead; *haya*—is; *dāsya-rati*—attachment in servitude; *rāga*—spontaneous love; *paryanta*—up to; *krameta*—gradually; *bāḍaya*—increases.

TRANSLATION

"The position of neutrality increases up to the point where one can appreciate love of Godhead. The mellow of servitorship gradually increases to the point of spontaneous love of Godhead.

TEXT 55

সখ্য-বাৎসল্য-রতি পায় 'অনুরাগ'-সীমা ।
সুবলাদ্যের 'ভাব' পর্যন্ত প্রেমের মহিমা ॥ ৫৫ ॥

sakhya-vātsalya-rati pāya 'anurāga'-sīmā
subalādyera 'bhāva' paryanta premera mahimā

SYNONYMS

sakhya—in friendship; *vātsalya*—in paternal affection; *rati*—affection; *pāya*—obtains; *anurāga-sīmā*—up to the limit of subordinate spontaneous love; *subala-ādyera*—of friends like Subala and others; *bhāva*—ecstatic love; *paryanta*—up to; *premera mahimā*—the glory of the love of Godhead.

TRANSLATION

"After the mellow of servitorship, there are the mellows of friendship and paternal love, which increase to subordinate spontaneous love. The greatness of the love found in friends like Subala extends to the standard of ecstatic love of Godhead.

PURPORT

Śrīla Bhaktisiddhānta Sarasvatī Ṭhākura says that the mellow of neutrality increases to simple love of Godhead. In the mellow of servitorship, love of Godhead increases beyond that to affection, counter-love (anger based on love), love and attachment. Similarly, the mellow of friendship increases to affection, counter-love, love, attachment and subattachment. It is the same with the mellow of paternal affection. The special feature of the mellow of friendship exhibited by personalities like Subala is that it increases from fraternal affection to counter-love, to spontaneous attachment, to subordinate attachment, and finally to the ecstasy where all the ecstatic symptoms continuously exist.

TEXT 56

শান্তাদি রসের 'যোগ', 'বিয়োগ'—দুই ভেদ ।
সখ্য-বাৎসল্যে যোগাদির অনেক বিভেদ ॥ ৫৬ ॥

śānta-ādi rasera 'yoga', 'viyoga'——dui bheda
sakhya-vātsalye yogādira aneka vibheda

SYNONYMS

śānta-ādi rasera—of the mellows beginning from neutrality; *yoga*—connection; *viyoga*—separation; *dui bheda*—two divisions; *sakhya*—in the mellow of friendship; *vātsalye*—in paternal affection; *yoga-ādira*—of connection and separation; *aneka vibheda*—many varieties.

TRANSLATION

"There are two divisions of each of the five mellows—yoga [connection] and viyoga [separation]. Among the mellows of friendship and parental affection, there are many divisions of connection and separation.

PURPORT

In *Bhakti-rasāmṛta-sindhu,* these divisions are described:

ayoga-yogāvetasya
prabhedau kathitāv ubhau

In the mellows of *bhakti-yoga,* there are two stages—*ayoga* and *yoga. Ayoga* is described in *Bhakti-rasāmṛta-sindhu:*

saṅgābhāvo harer dhīrair
ayoga iti kathyate
ayoge tvan-manaskatvaṁ
tad-guṇādy-anusandhayaḥ
tat-prāpty-upāya-cintādyāḥ
sarveṣāṁ kathitāḥ kriyāḥ

Learned scholars in the science of *bhakti-yoga* say that when there is an absence of association with the Supreme Personality of Godhead, separation takes place. In the stage of *ayoga* (separation), the mind is filled with Kṛṣṇa consciousness and is fully absorbed in thoughts of Kṛṣṇa. In that stage, the devotee searches out the transcendental qualities of the Supreme Personality of Godhead. It is said that in that stage of separation, all the devotees in the different mellows are always active in thinking of ways to attain Kṛṣṇa's association.

The word *yoga* (connection) is thus described:

kṛṣṇena saṅgamo yas tu
sa yoga iti kīrtyate

"When one meets Kṛṣṇa directly, that is called *yoga.*"

In the transcendental mellows of neutrality and servitorship, there are similar divisions of *yoga* and *viyoga,* but they are not variegated. The divisions of *yoga* and *viyoga* are always existing in the five mellows. However, in the transcendental mellows of friendship and paternal affection, there are many varieties of *yoga* and *viyoga.* The varieties of *yoga* are thus described:

yogo 'pi kathitaḥ siddhis
tuṣṭiḥ sthitir iti tridhā

Yoga (connection) is of three types—success, satisfaction and permanence. The divisions of *ayoga* (separation) are thus described:

utkaṇṭhitaṁ viyogaś cety
ayogo 'pi dvidhocyate

Thus *ayoga* has two divisions—longing and separation.

TEXT 57

'রূঢ়', 'অধিরূঢ়' ভাব—কেবল 'মধুরে'।
মহিষীগণের 'রূঢ়', 'অধিরূঢ়' গোপিকা-নিকরে ॥৫৭॥

'rūḍha', 'adhirūḍha' bhāva——kevala 'madhure'
mahiṣī-gaṇera 'rūḍha', 'adhirūḍha' gopikā-nikare

SYNONYMS

rūḍha—advanced; *adhirūḍha*—highly advanced; *bhāva*—ecstasy; *kevala*—only; *madhure*—in the transcendental mellow of conjugal love; *mahiṣī-gaṇera*—of the queens of Dvārakā; *rūḍha*—advanced; *adhirūḍha*—highly advanced; *gopikā-nikare*—among the *gopīs.*

TRANSLATION

"Only in the conjugal mellow are there two ecstatic symptoms called rūḍha [advanced] and adhirūḍha [highly advanced]. The advanced ecstasy is found among the queens of Dvārakā, and the highly advanced ecstasies are found among the gopīs.

PURPORT

The *adhirūḍha* ecstasies are explained in the *Ujjvala-nīlamaṇi:*

rūḍhoktebhyo 'nubhāvebhyaḥ
kām apy āptā viśiṣṭatām
yatrānubhāvā dṛśyante
so 'dhirūḍho nigadyate

The very sweet attraction of conjugal love increases through affection, counter-love, love, attachment, subattachment, ecstasy and highly advanced ecstasy (*mahābhāva*). The platform of *mahābhāva* includes *rūḍha* and *adhirūḍha*. These platforms are possible only in conjugal love. Advanced ecstasy is found in Dvārakā, whereas highly advanced ecstasy is found among the *gopīs*.

TEXT 58

অধিরূঢ়-মহাভাব—দুই ত' প্রকার ।
সম্ভোগে 'মাদন', বিরহে 'মোহন' নাম তার ॥ ৫৮ ॥

adhirūḍha-mahābhāva——dui ta' prakāra
sambhoge 'mādana', virahe 'mohana' nāma tāra

SYNONYMS

adhirūḍha-mahābhāva—highly advanced ecstasy; *dui ta' prakāra*—two varieties; *sambhoge*—in actually meeting; *mādana—mādana; virahe*—in separation; *mohana—mohana; nāma*—the names; *tāra*—of them.

TRANSLATION

"Highly advanced ecstasy is divided into two categories—mādana and mohana. Meeting together is called mādana, and separation is called mohana.

TEXT 59

'মাদনে'—চুম্বনাদি হয় অনন্ত বিভেদ ।
'উদঘূর্ণা', 'চিত্রজল্প'—'মোহনে' দুই ভেদ ॥ ৫৯ ॥

'mādane'——cumbanādi haya ananta vibheda
'udghūrṇā', 'citra-jalpa'——'mohane' dui bheda

SYNONYMS

mādane—in the stage of *mādana; cumbana-ādi*—kissing and similar activities; *haya*—are; *ananta vibheda*—unlimited divisions; *udghūrṇā*—unsteadiness; *citra-jalpa*—various mad talks; *mohane*—the stage of *mohana; dui bheda*—two divisions.

TRANSLATION

"On the mādana platform there are kissing and many other symptoms, which are unlimited. In the mohana stage, there are two divisions—udghūrṇā [unsteadiness] and citra-jalpa [varieties of mad emotional talks].

PURPORT

For further information, see *Madhya-līlā* (1.87).

TEXT 60

চিত্রজল্পের দশ অঙ্গ—প্রজল্পাদি-নাম ।
'ভ্রমর-গীতা'র দশ শ্লোক তাহাতে প্রমাণ ॥ ৬০ ॥

citra-jalpera daśa aṅga——prajalpādi-nāma
'bhramara-gītā'ra daśa śloka tāhāte pramāṇa

SYNONYMS

citra-jalpera—of the mad talks; *daśa*—ten; *aṅga*—parts; *prajalpa-ādi-nāma*—named *prajalpa* and so on; *bhramara-gītāra*—of Rādhārāṇī's talks with the bumblebee (*Śrīmad-Bhāgavatam*, Canto Ten, Chapter Forty-seven); *daśa śloka*—ten verses; *tāhāte*—in that matter; *pramāṇa*—the evidence.

TRANSLATION

"Mad emotional talks include ten divisions, called prajalpa and other names. An example of this is the ten verses spoken by Śrīmatī Rādhārāṇī called 'song to the bumblebee.'

PURPORT

Imaginative mad talks known as *citra-jalpa* can be divided into ten categories—*prajalpa, parijalpa, vijalpa, ujjalpa, sañjalpa, avajalpa, abhijalpa, ājalpa, pratijalpa* and *sujalpa*. There are no English equivalents for these different features of *jalpa* (imaginative talk).

TEXT 61

উদ্ঘূর্ণা, বিবশ-চেষ্টা—দিব্যোন্মাদ-নাম ।
বিরহে কৃষ্ণস্ফূর্তি, আপনাকে 'কৃষ্ণ'-জ্ঞান ॥ ৬১ ॥

udghūrṇā, vivaśa-ceṣṭā——divyonmāda-nāma
virahe kṛṣṇa-sphūrti, āpanāke 'kṛṣṇa'-jñāna

SYNONYMS

udghūrṇā—unsteadiness; *vivaśa-ceṣṭā*—boastful activities; *divya-unmāda-nāma*—named transcendental madness; *virahe*—in separation; *kṛṣṇa-sphūrti*—manifestation of Kṛṣṇa; *āpanāke*—oneself; *kṛṣṇa-jñāna*—thinking as Kṛṣṇa.

TRANSLATION

"Udghūrṇā [unsteadiness] and vivaśa-ceṣṭā [boastful activities] are aspects of transcendental madness. In separation from Kṛṣṇa, one experiences the manifestation of Kṛṣṇa, and one thinks oneself to be Kṛṣṇa.

TEXT 62

'সম্ভোগ'-'বিপ্রলম্ভ'-ভেদে দ্বিবিধ শৃঙ্গার ।
সম্ভোগের অনন্ত অঙ্গ, নাহি অন্ত তার ॥ ৬২ ॥

'sambhoga'-'vipralambha'-bhede dvividha śṛṅgāra
sambhogera ananta aṅga, nāhi anta tāra

SYNONYMS

sambhoga—of meeting (enjoyment together); *vipralambha*—of separation; *bhede*—in two divisions; *dvi-vidha śṛṅgāra*—two kinds of conjugal love; *sambhogera*—of the stage of *sambhoga,* or meeting; *ananta aṅga*—unlimited parts; *nāhi*—not; *anta*—an end; *tāra*—of that.

TRANSLATION

"In conjugal love [śṛṅgāra] there are two departments—meeting and separation. On the platform of meeting, there are unlimited varieties that are beyond description.

PURPORT

Vipralambha is described in the *Ujjvala-nīlamaṇi:*

yūnor ayuktayor bhāvo
yuktayor vātha yo mithaḥ
abhīṣṭāliṅganādīnām
anavāptau prakṛṣyate
sa vipralambho vijñeyaḥ
sambhogonnatikārakaḥ

na vinā vipralambhena
sambhogaḥ puṣṭim aśnute

When the lover and the beloved meet, they are called *yukta* (connected). Previous to their meeting, they are called *ayukta* (not connected). Whether connected or not connected, the ecstatic emotion arising due to not being able to embrace and kiss each other as desired is called *vipralambha.* This *vipralambha* helps nourish emotions at the time of meeting. Similarly, *sambhoga* is thus described:

darśanāliṅganādīnām
ānukūlyān niṣevayā
yūnor ullāsam ārohan
bhāvaḥ sambhoga īryate

"Meeting each other and embracing each other are aimed at bringing about the happiness of both the lover and the beloved. When this stage becomes increasingly jubilant, the resultant ecstatic emotion is called *sambhoga.*" When awakened, *sambhoga* is divided into four categories:

(1) *pūrva-rāga-anantara*—after *pūrva-rāga* (attachment prior to meeting), *sambhoga* is called brief (*saṅkṣipta*);

(2) *māna-anantara*—after *māna* (anger based on love), *sambhoga* is called encroached (*saṅkīrṇa*);

(3) *kiñcid-dūra-pravāsa-anantara*—after being a little distance away for some time, *sambhoga* is called accomplished (*sampanna*);

(4) *sudūra-pravāsa-anantara*—after being far away, *sambhoga* is called perfection (*samṛddhimān*).

The meetings of the lovers that take place in dreams also have these four divisions.

TEXT 63

'বিপ্রলম্ভ' চতুর্বিধ —পূর্বরাগ, মান ।
প্রবাসাখ্য, আর প্রেমবৈচিত্ত্য-আখ্যান ॥ ৬৩ ॥

'vipralambha' catur-vidha——pūrva-rāga, māna
pravāsākhya, āra prema-vaicittya-ākhyāna

SYNONYMS

vipralambha—separation; *catuḥ-vidha*—four divisions; *pūrva-rāga*—*pūrva-rāga; māna*—*māna; pravāsākhya*—known as *pravāsa; āra*—and; *prema-vaicittya*—*prema-vaicittya; ākhyāna*—calling.

TRANSLATION

"Vipralambha has four divisions—pūrva-rāga, māna, pravāsa, and prema-vaicittya.

PURPORT

Pūrva-rāga is described in *Ujjvala-nīlamaṇi:*

ratir yā saṅgamāt pūrvaṁ
darśana-śravaṇādi-jā
tayor unmīlati prājñaiḥ
pūrva-rāgaḥ sa ucyate

When attachment produced in both the lover and beloved before their meeting by seeing, hearing and so on becomes very palatable by the mixture of four ingredients, such as *vibhāva* and *anubhāva,* this is called *pūrva-rāga.*

The word *māna* is also described:

dampatyor bhāva ekatra
sator apy anuraktayoḥ
svābhīṣṭāśleṣa-vīkṣādi-
nirodhī māna ucyate

Māna is a word used to indicate the mood of the lover and the beloved experienced whether they are in one place or in different places. This mood obstructs their looking at one another and embracing one another, despite the fact that they are attached to one another.

Pravāsa is also explained as follows:

pūrva-saṅga-tayor yūnor
bhaved deśāntarādibhiḥ
vyavadhānaṁ tu yat prājñaiḥ
sa pravāsa itīryate

Pravāsa is a word used to indicate the separation of lovers who were previously intimately associated. This separation is due to their being in different places.

Similarly, *prema-vaicittya* is explained:

priyasya sannikarṣe 'pi
premotkarṣa-svabhāvataḥ
yā viśeṣa-dhiyārtis tat
prema-vaicittyam ucyate

Prema-vaicittya is a word used to indicate an abundance of love that brings about grief from fear of separation, although the lover is present.

TEXT 64

রাধিকাদ্যে 'পূর্ব্বরাগ' প্রসিদ্ধ 'প্রবাস', 'মানে'।
'প্রেমবৈচিত্ত্য' শ্রীদশমে মহিষীগণে ॥ ৬৪ ॥

rādhikādye 'pūrva-rāga' prasiddha 'pravāsa', 'māne'
'prema-vaicittya' śrī-daśame mahiṣī-gaṇe

SYNONYMS

rādhikādye—in Śrīmatī Rādhārāṇī and the other *gopīs; pūrva-rāga*—feelings before union; *prasiddha*—celebrated; *pravāsa māne*—also *pravāsa* and *māna; prema-vaicittya*—feelings of fear of separation; *śrī-daśame*—in the Tenth Canto; *mahiṣī-gaṇe*—among the queens.

TRANSLATION

"Of the four kinds of separation, three [pūrva-rāga, pravāsa and māna] are celebrated in Śrīmatī Rādhārāṇī and the gopīs. In Dvārakā, among the queens, feelings of prema-vaicittya are very prominent.

TEXT 65

কুররি বিলপসি ত্বং বীতনিদ্রা ন শেষে
স্বপিতি জগতি রাত্র্যামীশ্বরো গুপ্তবোধঃ ।
বয়মিব সখি কচ্চিদ্গাঢ়নির্বিদ্ধচেতা
নলিন-নয়ন-হাসোদার-লীলেক্ষিতেন ॥ ৬৫ ॥

kurari vilapasi tvaṁ vīta-nidrā na śeṣe
svapiti jagati rātryām īśvaro gupta-bodhaḥ
vayam iva sakhi kaccid gāḍha-nirviddha-cetā
nalina-nayana-hāsodāra-līlekṣitena

SYNONYMS

kurari—O female osprey; *vilapasi*—are lamenting; *tvam*—you; *vīta-nidrā*—without sleep; *na*—not; *śeṣe*—rest; *svapiti*—sleeps; *jagati*—in the world; *rātryām*—at night; *īśvaraḥ*—Lord Kṛṣṇa; *gupta-bodhaḥ*—whose consciousness is hidden; *vayam*—we; *iva*—like; *sakhi*—O dear friend; *kaccid*—whether; *gāḍha*—deeply; *nirviddha-cetā*—pierced in the heart; *nalina-nayana*—of the lotus-eyed Lord; *hāsa*—smiling; *udāra*—liberal; *līlā-īkṣitena*—by the playful glancing.

TRANSLATION

" 'My dear friend kurarī, it is now night, and Lord Śrī Kṛṣṇa is sleeping. You yourself are not asleep or resting but are lamenting. Should I presume that you, like us, are affected by the smiling, liberal, playful glances of the lotus-eyed Kṛṣṇa? If so, your heart is deeply pierced. Is that why you are showing these signs of sleepless lamentation?'

PURPORT

This is a quotation from *Śrīmad-Bhāgavatam* (10.90.15). Although the queens were with Kṛṣṇa, they were still thinking of losing His company.

TEXT 66

ব্রজেন্দ্রনন্দন কৃষ্ণ—নায়ক-শিরোমণি ।
নায়িকার শিরোমণি - রাধা-ঠাকুরাণী ॥ ৬৬ ॥

vrajendra-nandana kṛṣṇa——nāyaka-śiromaṇi
nāyikāra śiromaṇi——rādhā-ṭhākurāṇī

SYNONYMS

vrajendra-nandana kṛṣṇa—Lord Kṛṣṇa, the son of Mahārāja Nanda; *nāyaka-śiromaṇi*—best of all heroes; *nāyikāra śiromaṇi*—the best of all heroines; rādhā-*ṭhākurāṇī*—Śrīmatī Rādhārāṇī.

TRANSLATION

"Lord Kṛṣṇa, the Supreme Personality of Godhead who appeared as the son of Nanda Mahārāja, is the supreme hero in all dealings. Similarly, Śrīmatī Rādhārāṇī is the topmost heroine in all dealings.

TEXT 67

নায়কানাং শিরোরত্নং কৃষ্ণস্তু ভগবান্ স্বয়ম্ ।
যত্র নিত্যতয়া সর্বে বিরাজন্তে মহাগুণাঃ ॥ ৬৭ ॥

nāyakānāṁ śiroratnaṁ
kṛṣṇas tu bhagavān svayam
yatra nityatayā sarve
virājante mahā-guṇāḥ

SYNONYMS

nāyakānām—of all heroes; *śiroratnam*—the crown jewel; *kṛṣṇaḥ*—Lord Kṛṣṇa; *tu*—but; *bhagavān svayam*—the Supreme Personality of Godhead Himself; *yatra*—in whom; *nityatayā*—with permanence; *sarve*—all; *virājante*—exist; *mahā-guṇāḥ*—transcendental qualities.

TRANSLATION

" 'Kṛṣṇa is the Supreme Personality of Godhead Himself, and He is the crown jewel of all heroes. In Kṛṣṇa, all transcendental good qualities are permanently situated.'

PURPORT

This verse is also found in *Bhakti-rasāmṛta-sindhu* (2.1.17).

TEXT 68

দেবী কৃষ্ণময়ী প্রোক্তা রাধিকা পরদেবতা ।
সর্বলক্ষ্মীময়ী সর্বকান্তিঃ সম্মোহিনী পরা ॥ ৬৮ ॥

devī kṛṣṇamayī proktā
rādhikā para-devatā
sarva-lakṣmīmayī sarva-
kāntiḥ sammohinī parā

SYNONYMS

devī—who shines brilliantly; *kṛṣṇa-mayī*—nondifferent from Lord Kṛṣṇa; *proktā*—called; *rādhikā*—Śrīmatī Rādhārāṇī; *para-devatā*—most worshipable; *sarva-lakṣmī-mayī*—presiding over all the goddesses of fortune; *sarva-kāntiḥ*—in whom all splendor exists; *sammohinī*—whose character completely bewilders Lord Kṛṣṇa; *parā*—the superior energy.

TRANSLATION

" 'The transcendental goddess Śrīmatī Rādhārāṇī is the direct counterpart of Lord Śrī Kṛṣṇa. She is the central figure for all the goddesses of fortune. She possesses all the attraction to attract the all-attractive Personality of Godhead. She is the primeval internal potency of the Lord.'

PURPORT

This text is found in the *Bṛhad-gautamīya-tantra*.

TEXT 69

অনন্ত কৃষ্ণের গুণ, চৌষট্টি—প্রধান ।
এক এক গুণ শুনি' জুড়ায় ভক্ত-কাণ ॥ ৬৯ ॥

ananta kṛṣṇera guṇa, causaṭṭi——pradhāna
eka eka guṇa śuni' juḍāya bhakta-kāṇa

SYNONYMS

ananta—unlimited; *kṛṣṇera*—of Lord Kṛṣṇa; *guṇa*—qualities; *causaṭṭi*—sixty-four; *pradhāna*—chief ones; *eka eka*—one by one; *guṇa*—qualities; *śuni'*—hearing; *juḍāya*—satisfies; *bhakta-kāṇa*—the ears of the devotees.

TRANSLATION

"The transcendental qualities of Lord Kṛṣṇa are unlimited. Out of these, sixty-four are considered prominent. The ears of the devotees are satisfied simply by hearing all these qualities one after the other.

TEXT 70

অয়ং নেতা সুরম্যাঙ্গঃ সর্বসল্লক্ষণান্বিতঃ ।
রুচিরস্তেজসা যুক্তো বলীয়ান্ বয়সান্বিতঃ ॥ ৭০ ॥

ayaṁ netā suramyāṅgaḥ
sarva-sal-lakṣaṇānvitaḥ
ruciras tejasā yukto
balīyān vayasānvitaḥ

SYNONYMS

ayam—this (Kṛṣṇa); *netā*—supreme hero; *suramya-aṅgaḥ*—having the most beautiful transcendental body; *sarva-sat-lakṣaṇa*—all-auspicious bodily marks; *anvitaḥ*—endowed with; *ruciraḥ*—possessing radiance very pleasing to the eyes; *tejasā*—with all power; *yuktaḥ*—bestowed; *balīyān*—very strong; *vayasa-anvitaḥ*—having a youthful age.

TRANSLATION

" 'Kṛṣṇa, the supreme hero, has the most beautiful transcendental body. This body possesses all good features. It is radiant and very pleasing to the eyes. His body is powerful, strong and youthful.

PURPORT

This verse and the following six verses are also found in *Bhakti-rasāmṛta-sindhu* (2.1.23-29).

TEXT 71

বিবিধাদ্ভুতভাষাবিৎ সত্যবাক্যঃ প্রিয়ংবদঃ ।
বাবদূকঃ সুপাণ্ডিত্যো বুদ্ধিমান্ প্রতিভান্বিতঃ ॥ ৭১ ॥

vividhādbhuta-bhāṣā-vit
satya-vākyaḥ priyaṁ vadaḥ
vāvadūkaḥ supāṇḍityo
buddhimān pratibhānvitaḥ

SYNONYMS

vividha—various; *adbhuta*—wonderful; *bhāṣā-vit*—knower of languages; *satya-vākyaḥ*—whose words are truthful; *priyam vadaḥ*—who speaks very pleasingly; *vāvadūkaḥ*—expert in speaking; *su-pāṇḍityaḥ*—very learned; *buddhimān*—very wise; *pratibhā-anvitaḥ*—genius.

TRANSLATION

" 'Kṛṣṇa is the linguist of all wonderful languages. He is a truthful and very pleasing speaker. He is expert in speaking, and He is a very wise, learned scholar and a genius.

TEXT 72

বিদগ্ধশ্চতুরো দক্ষঃ কৃতজ্ঞঃ সুদৃঢ়ব্রতঃ ।
দেশকালসুপাত্রজ্ঞঃ শাস্ত্রচক্ষুঃ শুচির্বশী ॥ ৭২ ॥

vidagdhaś caturo dakṣaḥ
kṛtajñaḥ sudṛḍha-vrataḥ
deśa-kāla-supātrajñaḥ
śāstra-cakṣuḥ śucir vaśī

SYNONYMS

vidagdhaḥ—expert in artistic enjoyment; *caturaḥ*—cunning; *dakṣaḥ*—expert; *kṛta-jñaḥ*—grateful; *sudṛḍha-vrataḥ*—firmly determined; *deśa*—of country; *kāla*—time; *supātra*—of fitness; *jñaḥ*—a knower; *śāstra-cakṣuḥ*—expert in the authoritative scriptures; *śuciḥ*—very clean and neat; *vaśī*—self-controlled.

TRANSLATION

" 'Kṛṣṇa is very expert in artistic enjoyment. He is highly cunning, expert, grateful and firmly determined in His vows. He knows how to deal according to time, person and country, and He sees through the scriptures and authoritative books. He is very clean and self-controlled.

TEXT 73

স্থিরো দান্তঃ ক্ষমাশীলো গম্ভীরো ধৃতিমান্ সমঃ ।
বদান্যো ধার্মিকঃ শূরঃ করুণো মান্যমানকৃৎ ॥ ৭৩ ॥

sthiro dāntaḥ kṣamā-śīlo
gambhīro dhṛtimān samaḥ
vadānyo dhārmikaḥ śūraḥ
karuṇo mānya-mānakṛt

SYNONYMS

sthiraḥ—steady; *dāntaḥ*—having controlled senses; *kṣamā-śīlaḥ*—forgiving; *gambhīraḥ*—grave; *dhṛtimān*—calm, never bereft of intelligence; *samaḥ*—equal; *vadānyaḥ*—magnanimous; *dhārmikaḥ*—religious; *śūraḥ*—chivalrous; *karuṇaḥ*—kind; *mānya-mānakṛt*—respectful to the respectable.

TRANSLATION

" 'Lord Kṛṣṇa is steady, His senses are controlled, and He is forgiving, grave and calm. He is also equal to all. Moreover, He is magnanimous, religious, chivalrous and kind. He is always respectful to respectable people.

TEXT 74

দক্ষিণো বিনয়ী হ্রীমান্ শরণাগতপালকঃ ।
সুখী ভক্তসুহৃৎ প্রেমবশ্যঃ সর্বশুভঙ্করঃ ॥ ৭৪ ॥

dakṣiṇo vinayī hrīmān
śaraṇāgata-pālakaḥ
sukhī bhakta-suhṛt prema-
vaśyaḥ sarva-śubhaṅkaraḥ

SYNONYMS

dakṣiṇaḥ—simple and liberal; *vinayī*—humble; *hrīmān*—bashful when glorified; *śaraṇāgata-pālakaḥ*—protector of the surrendered soul; *sukhī*—always happy; *bhakta-suhṛt*—well-wisher of the devotees; *prema-vaśyaḥ*—submissive to love; *sarva-śubhaṅkaraḥ*—all-auspicious.

TRANSLATION

" 'Kṛṣṇa is very simple and liberal, He is humble and bashful, and He is the protector of the surrendered soul. He is very happy, and He is always the well-wisher of His devotee. He is all-auspicious, and He is submissive to love.

TEXT 75

প্রতাপী কীর্তিমান্ রক্তলোকঃ সাধুসমাশ্রয়ঃ।
নারীগণ-মনোহারী সর্বারাধ্যঃ সমৃদ্ধিমান্ ॥ ৭৫ ॥

pratāpī kīrtimān rakta-
lokaḥ sādhu-samāśrayaḥ
nārīgaṇa-manohārī
sarvārādhyaḥ samṛddhimān

SYNONYMS

pratāpī—very influential; *kīrtimān*—famous for good works; *rakta-lokaḥ*—who is the object of the attachment of all people; *sādhu-sama-āśrayaḥ*—the shelter of the good and virtuous; *nārī-gaṇa*—to women; *manohārī*—attractive; *sarva-ārādhyaḥ*—worshipable by everyone; *samṛddhimān*—very rich.

TRANSLATION

" 'Kṛṣṇa is very influential and famous, and He is the object of attachment for everyone. He is the shelter of the good and the virtuous. He is attractive to the minds of women, and He is worshiped by everyone. He is very, very rich.

TEXT 76

বরীয়ানীশ্বরশ্চেতি গুণাস্তস্যানুকীর্তিতাঃ।
সমুদ্রা ইব পঞ্চাশদ্দুর্বিগাহা হরেরমী ॥ ৭৬ ॥

varīyān īśvaraś ceti
guṇās tasyānukīrtitāḥ
samudrā iva pañcāśad
durvigāhā harer amī

SYNONYMS

varīyān—the best; *īśvaraḥ*—the supreme controller; *ca*—and; *iti*—thus; *guṇāḥ*—the transcendental qualities; *tasya*—of Him; *anukīrtitāḥ*—described;

samudrāḥ—oceans; *iva*—like; *pañcāśat*—fifty; *durvigāhāḥ*—difficult to penetrate fully; *hareḥ*—of the Supreme Personality of Godhead; *amī*—all these.

TRANSLATION

" 'Kṛṣṇa is the Supreme, and He is always glorified as the Supreme Lord and controller. Thus all the previously mentioned transcendental qualities are in Him. The fifty qualities of the Supreme Personality of Godhead above mentioned are as deep as an ocean. In other words, they are difficult to fully comprehend.

TEXT 77

জীবেষ্বেতে বসন্তোঽপি বিন্দুবিন্দুতয়া ক্বচিৎ ।
পরিপূর্ণতয়া ভান্তি তত্রৈব পুরুষোত্তমে ॥ ৭৭ ॥

jīveṣv ete vasanto 'pi
bindu-bindutayā kvacit
paripūrṇatayā bhānti
tatraiva puruṣottame

SYNONYMS

jīveṣu—in the living entities; *ete*—these; *vasantaḥ*—are residing; *api*—though; *bindu-bindutayā*—with a very minute quantity; *kvacit*—sometimes; *paripūrṇatayā*—with fullness; *bhānti*—are manifest; *tatra*—in Him; *eva*—certainly; *puruṣa-uttame*—in the Supreme Personality of Godhead.

TRANSLATION

" 'These qualities are sometimes very minutely exhibited in living beings, but they are fully manifest in the Supreme Personality of Godhead.'

PURPORT

This verse is found in *Bhakti-rasāmṛta-sindhu* (2.1.30). Living entities are parts and parcels of the Supreme Personality of Godhead. As stated in *Bhagavad-gītā:*

mamaivāṁśo jīva-loke
jīva-bhūtaḥ sanātanaḥ
manaḥ ṣaṣṭhānīndriyāṇi
prakṛti-sthāni karṣati

"The living entities in this conditioned world are My eternal, fragmental parts. Due to conditioned life, they are struggling very hard with the six senses, which include the mind." (Bg. 15.7)

The qualities of Kṛṣṇa are present in the living entity in minute, atomic quantities. A small portion of gold is certainly gold, but it cannot be equal to a gold mine. Similarly, the living entities have all the characteristics of the Supreme Personality of Godhead in minute quantity, but the living entity is never equal to the Supreme Personality of Godhead. God is therefore described as the Supreme Being, and the living entity is described as a *jīva.* God is the Supreme Being, the chief of all living beings—*eko bahūnāṁ yo vidadhāti kāmān.* The Māyāvādīs maintain that everyone is God, but even if this philosophy is accepted, no one can maintain that everyone is equal to the Supreme Godhead. Only unintelligent men maintain that everyone is equal to God or that everyone is God.

TEXT 78

অথ পঞ্চগুণা যে স্যুরংশেন গিরিশাদিষু ॥ ৭৮ ॥

atha pañca-guṇā ye syur
aṁśena giriśādiṣu

SYNONYMS

atha—now (over and above these); *pañca-guṇāḥ*—five qualities; *ye*—which; *syuḥ*—may exist; *aṁśena*—by part; *giriśa-ādiṣu*—in demigods like Lord Śiva.

TRANSLATION

" 'Apart from these fifty qualities, there are five other qualities found in the Supreme Personality of Godhead that are partially present in demigods like Śiva.

PURPORT

This verse and the following seven verses are also found in *Bhakti-rasāmṛta-sindhu* (2.1.37-44).

TEXTS 79-81

সদা স্বরূপসংপ্রাপ্তঃ সর্বজ্ঞো নিত্যনূতনঃ ।
সচ্চিদানন্দসান্দ্রাঙ্গঃ সর্বসিদ্ধিনিষেবিতঃ ॥ ৭৯ ॥
অথোচ্যন্তে গুণাঃ পঞ্চ যে লক্ষ্মীশাদি-বর্তিনঃ ।
অবিচিন্ত্যমহাশক্তিঃ কোটিব্রহ্মাণ্ডবিগ্রহঃ ॥ ৮০ ॥
অবতারাবলীবীজং হতারিগতিদায়কঃ ।
আত্মারামগণাকর্ষীত্যমী কৃষ্ণে কিলাদ্ভুতাঃ ॥ ৮১ ॥

sadā svarūpa-samprāptaḥ
sarva-jño nity-nūtanaḥ
sac-cid-ānanda-sāndrāṅgaḥ
sarva-siddhi-niṣevitaḥ

athocyante guṇāḥ pañca
ye lakṣmīśādi-vartinaḥ
avicintya-mahā-śaktiḥ
koṭi-brahmāṇḍa-vigrahaḥ

avatārāvalī-bījaṁ
hatāri-gati-dāyakaḥ
ātmārāma-gaṇākarṣīty
amī kṛṣṇe kilādbhutāḥ

SYNONYMS

sadā—always; *svarūpa-samprāptaḥ*—situated in one's eternal nature; *sarva-jñaḥ*—omniscient; *nitya-nūtanaḥ*—ever-fresh; *sat-cit-ānanda-sāndra-aṅgaḥ*—the concentrated form of eternity, knowledge, bliss; *sarva-siddhi-niṣevitaḥ*—attended by all mystic perfections; *atha*—now; *ucyante*—are said; *guṇāḥ*—qualities; *pañca*—five; *ye*—which; *lakṣmī-īśa*—in the proprietor of the goddess of fortune; *ādi*—etc.; *vartinaḥ*—represented; *avicintya*—inconceivable; *mahā-śaktiḥ*—possessing supreme energy; *koṭi-brahmāṇḍa*—consisting of innumerable universes; *vigrahaḥ*—having a body; *avatāra*—of incarnations; *āvalī*—of groups; *bījam*—the source; *hata-ari*—to enemies killed by Him; *gati-dāyakaḥ*—giving liberation; *ātmārāma-gaṇa*—of those fully satisfied in themselves; *ākarṣī*—attracting; *iti*—thus; *amī*—these; *kṛṣṇe*—in Kṛṣṇa; *kila*—certainly; *adbhutāḥ*—very wonderful.

TRANSLATION

" 'These qualities are (1) the Lord is always situated in His original position, (2) He is omniscient, (3) He is always fresh and youthful, (4) He is the concentrated form of eternity, knowledge and bliss, and (5) He is the possessor of all mystic perfection. There are another five qualities, which exist in the Vaikuṇṭha planets in Nārāyaṇa, the Lord of Lakṣmī. These qualities are also present in Kṛṣṇa, but they are not present in demigods like Lord Śiva or in other living entities. These are (1) inconceivable supreme power, (2) generating innumerable universes from the body, (3) being the original source of all incarnations, (4) bestowing salvation upon enemies killed, and (5) the ability to attract exalted persons who are satisfied in themselves. Although these qualities are present in Nārāyaṇa, the dominating Deity of the Vaikuṇṭha planets, they are even more wonderfully present in Kṛṣṇa.

TEXTS 82-83

সর্বাদ্ভুতচমৎকার-লীলাকল্লোলবারিধিঃ ।
অতুল্যমধুরপ্রেম-মণ্ডিতপ্রিয়মণ্ডলঃ ॥ ৮২ ॥
ত্রিজগন্মানসাকর্ষি-মুরলীকলকূজিতঃ ।
অসমানোর্ধ্বরূপশ্রী-বিস্মাপিতচরাচরঃ ॥ ৮৩ ॥

sarvādbhuta-camatkāra-
līlā-kallola-vāridhiḥ
atulya-madhura-prema-
maṇḍita-priya-maṇḍalaḥ

trijagan-mānasākarṣi-
muralī-kala-kūjitaḥ
asamānordhva-rūpa-śrī-
vismāpita-carācaraḥ

SYNONYMS

sarva-adbhuta-camatkāra—bringing wonder to all; *līlā*—of pastimes; *kallola*—full of waves; *vāridhiḥ*—an ocean; *atulya-madhura-prema*—with incomparable conjugal love; *maṇḍita*—decorated; *priya-maṇḍalaḥ*—with a circle of favorite personalities; *tri-jagat*—of three worlds; *mānasa-ākarṣi*—attracting the minds; *muralī*—of the flute; *kala-kūjitaḥ*—the melodious vibration; *asamāna-ūrdhva*—unequaled and unsurpassed; *rūpa*—by beauty; *śrī*—and opulence; *vismāpita-cara-acaraḥ*—astonishing the moving and nonmoving living entities.

TRANSLATION

" 'Apart from these sixty transcendental qualities, Kṛṣṇa has an additional four transcendental qualities, which are not manifest even in the personality of Nārāyaṇa. These are: (1) Kṛṣṇa is like an ocean filled with waves of pastimes that evoke wonder within everyone in the three worlds. (2) In His activities of conjugal love, He is always surrounded by His dear devotees who possess unequaled love for Him. (3) He attracts the minds of all three worlds by the melodious vibration of His flute. (4) His personal beauty and opulence are beyond compare. No one is equal to Him, and no one is greater than Him. Thus the Personality of Godhead astonishes all living entities, both moving and nonmoving, within the three worlds. He is so beautiful that He is called Kṛṣṇa.

PURPORT

Māyāvādī philosophers, who have a poor fund of knowledge, simply dismiss the subject by explaining that Kṛṣṇa means black. Not understanding the qualities of Kṛṣṇa, these atheistic rascals do not accept Him as the Supreme Personality of Godhead. Although the Lord is described and accepted by great personalities, *ācāryas* and sages, the Māyāvādīs still do not appreciate Him. Unfortunately at the present moment human society is so degraded that people cannot even provide themselves with life's daily necessities, yet they are captivated by Māyāvādī philosophers and are being misled. According to *Bhagavad-gītā,* simply by understanding Kṛṣṇa one can get free from the cycle of birth and death. *Tyaktvā dehaṁ punar janma naiti mām eti so 'rjuna.* Unfortunately this great science of Kṛṣṇa consciousness has been impeded by Māyāvādī philosophers who are opposed to the personality of Kṛṣṇa. Those who are preaching this Kṛṣṇa consciousness movement must try to understand Kṛṣṇa from the statements given in *Bhakti-rasāmṛta-sindhu* (*The Nectar of Devotion*).

TEXT 84-85

লীলা প্রেম্ণা প্রিয়াধিক্যং মাধুর্যং বেণুরূপয়োঃ ।
ইত্যসাধারণং প্রোক্তং গোবিন্দস্য চতুষ্টয়ম্ ॥ ৮৪ ॥
এবং গুণাশ্চতুর্ভেদাশ্চতুঃষষ্টিরুদাহৃতাঃ ॥ ৮৫ ॥

līlā premṇā priyādhikyaṁ
mādhuryaṁ veṇu-rūpayoḥ
ity asādhāraṇaṁ proktaṁ
govindasya catuṣṭayam

evaṁ guṇāś catur-bhedāś
catuḥ-ṣaṣṭir udāhṛtāḥ

SYNONYMS

līlā—pastimes; *premṇā*—with transcendental love; *priya-ādhikyam*—an abundance of highly elevated devotees; *mādhuryam*—sweetness; *veṇu-rūpayoḥ*—of the flute and of the beauty of Kṛṣṇa; *iti*—thus; *asādhāraṇam*—uncommon; *proktam*—said; *govindasya*—of Lord Kṛṣṇa; *catuṣṭayam*—four special features; *evam*—thus; *guṇāḥ*—transcendental qualities; *catuḥ-bhedāḥ*—having four divisions; *catuḥ-ṣaṣṭiḥ*—sixty-four; *udāhṛtāḥ*—declared.

TRANSLATION

" 'Above Nārāyaṇa, Kṛṣṇa has four specific transcendental qualities—His wonderful pastimes, an abundance of wonderful associates who are very dear to Him [like the gopīs], His wonderful beauty and the wonderful vibration of His flute. Lord Kṛṣṇa is more exalted than ordinary living beings and demigods like Lord Śiva. He is even more exalted than His personal expansion Nārāyaṇa.

In all, the Supreme Personality of Godhead has sixty-four transcendental qualities in full.'

TEXT 86

অনন্ত গুণ শ্রীরাধিকার, পঁচিশ—প্রধান।
যেই গুণের 'বশ' হয় কৃষ্ণ ভগবান্ ॥ ৮৬ ॥

ananta guṇa śrī-rādhikāra, pañciśa——pradhāna
yei guṇera 'vaśa' haya kṛṣṇa bhagavān

SYNONYMS

ananta guṇa—unlimited qualities; *śrī-rādhikāra*—of Śrīmatī Rādhārāṇī; *pañciśa*—twenty-five; *pradhāna*—chief; *yei guṇera*—of those qualities; *vaśa*—under the control; *haya*—is; *kṛṣṇa*—Lord Kṛṣṇa; *bhagavān*—the Supreme Personality of Godhead.

TRANSLATION

"Similarly, Śrīmatī Rādhārāṇī has unlimited transcendental qualities, of which twenty-five qualities are principal. Śrī Kṛṣṇa is controlled by these transcendental qualities of Śrīmatī Rādhārāṇī.

TEXTS 87-91

অথ বৃন্দাবনেশ্বর্যাঃ কীর্ত্যন্তে প্রবরা গুণাঃ।
মধুরেয়ং নব-বয়াশ্চলাপাঙ্গোজ্জ্বলস্মিতা ॥ ৮৭ ॥
চারু-সৌভাগ্যরেখাঢ্যা গন্ধোন্মাদিতমাধবা।
সঙ্গীতপ্রসরাভিজ্ঞা রম্যবাঙ নর্মপণ্ডিতা ॥ ৮৮ ॥
বিনীতা করুণা-পূর্ণা বিদগ্ধা পাটবান্বিতা।
লজ্জাশীলা সুমর্যাদা ধৈর্য-গাম্ভীর্যশালিনী ॥ ৮৯ ॥
সুবিলাসা মহাভাবপরমোৎকর্ষতর্ষিণী।
গোকুল-প্রেমবসতির্জগচ্ছ্রেণীলসদ্‌যশাঃ ॥ ৯০ ॥
গুর্বর্পিতগুরুস্নেহা সখীপ্রণয়িতাবশা।
কৃষ্ণপ্রিয়াবলীমুখ্যা সন্ততাশ্রব-কেশবা।
বহুনা কিং গুণাস্তস্যাঃ সংখ্যাতীতা হরেরিব ॥ ৯১ ॥

atha vṛndāvaneśvaryāḥ
kīrtyante pravarā guṇāḥ
madhureyaṁ nava-vayāś
calāpāṅgojjvala-smitā

cāru-saubhāgya-rekhāḍhyā
gandhonmādita-mādhavā
saṅgīta-prasarābhijñā
ramya-vāṅ narma-paṇḍitā

vinītā karuṇā-pūrṇā
vidagdhā pāṭavānvitā
lajjā-śīlā sumaryādā
dhairya-gāmbhīrya-śālinī

suvilāsā mahābhāva-
paramotkarṣa-tarṣiṇī
gokula-prema-vasatir
jagac-chreṇī-lasad-yaśāḥ

gurv-arpita-guru-snehā
sakhī-praṇayitā-vaśā
kṛṣṇa-priyāvalī-mukhyā
santatāśrava-keśavā
bahunā kiṁ guṇās tasyāḥ
saṅkhyātītā harer iva

SYNONYMS

atha—now; *vṛndāvana-īśvaryāḥ*—of the Queen of Vṛndāvana (Śrī Rādhikā); *kīrtyante*—are glorified; *pravarāḥ*—chief; *guṇāḥ*—qualities; *madhurā*—sweet; *iyam*—this one (Rādhikā); *nava-vayāḥ*—youthful; *cala-apāṅga*—having restless eyes; *ujjvala-smitā*—having a bright smile; *cāru-saubhāgya-rekhāḍhyā*—possessing beautiful, auspicious lines on the body; *gandha*—by the wonderful fragrance of Her body; *unmādita-mādhavā*—exciting Kṛṣṇa; *saṅgīta*—of songs; *prasara-abhijñā*—knowledgeable in the expansion; *ramya-vāk*—having charming speech; *narma-paṇḍitā*—learned in joking; *vinītā*—humble; *karuṇā-pūrṇā*—full of mercy; *vidagdhā*—cunning; *pāṭava-anvitā*—expert in performing Her duties; *lajjā-śīlā*—shy; *su-maryādā*—respectful; *dhairya*—calm; *gāmbhīrya-śālinī*—and grave; *su-vilāsā*—playful; *mahā-bhāva*—of advanced ecstasy; *parama-utkarṣa*—in the highest excellence; *tarṣiṇī*—desirous; *gokula-prema*—the love of the residents of Gokula; *vasatiḥ*—the abode; *jagat-śreṇī*—among the surrendered devotees who are the abodes (*āśraya*) of love for Kṛṣṇa; *lasat*—shining; *yaśāḥ*—whose fame; *guru*—to the elders; *arpita*—offered; *guru-snehā*—whose great affection; *sakhī-praṇayitā-vaśā*—controlled by the love of Her *gopī* friends; *kṛṣṇa-priya-āvalī*—among those who are dear to Kṛṣṇa; *mukhyā*—the chief; *santata*—always; *āśrava-keśavāḥ*—to whom Lord Keśava is submissive; *bahunā kim*—in short; *guṇāḥ*—the qualities; *tasyāḥ*—of Her; *saṅkhyātītāḥ*—beyond count; *hareḥ*—of Lord Kṛṣṇa; *iva*—like.

TRANSLATION

" 'Śrīmatī Rādhārāṇī's twenty-five chief transcendental qualities are: (1) She is very sweet. (2) She is always freshly youthful. (3) Her eyes are restless. (4) She smiles brightly. (5) She has beautiful, auspicious lines. (6) She makes Kṛṣṇa happy with Her bodily aroma. (7) She is very expert in singing. (8) Her speech is charming. (9) She is very expert in joking and speaking pleasantly. (10) She is very humble and meek. (11) She is always full of mercy. (12) She is cunning. (13) She is expert in executing Her duties. (14) She is shy. (15) She is always respectful. (16) She is always calm. (17) She is always grave. (18) She is expert in enjoying life. (19) She is situated at the topmost level of ecstatic love. (20) She is the reservoir of loving affairs in Gokula. (21) She is the most famous of submissive devotees. (22) She is very affectionate to elderly people. (23) She is very submissive to the love of Her friends. (24) She is the chief gopī. (25) She always keeps Kṛṣṇa under Her control. In short, She possesses unlimited transcendental qualities, just as Lord Kṛṣṇa does.'

PURPORT

These verses are also found in *Ujjvala-nīlamaṇi, Śrī-rādhā-prakaraṇa* (11-15).

TEXT 92

নায়ক, নায়িকা,—দুই রসের 'আলম্বন'।
সেই দুই শ্রেষ্ঠ,—রাধা, ব্রজেন্দ্রনন্দন ॥ ৯২ ॥

nāyaka, nāyikā,——dui rasera 'ālambana'
sei dui śreṣṭha,——rādhā, vrajendra-nandana

SYNONYMS

nāyaka—hero; *nāyikā*—heroine; *dui*—two; *rasera*—of mellows; *ālambana*—the basis; *sei*—those; *dui*—two; *śreṣṭha*—chief; *rādhā*—Śrīmatī Rādhārāṇī; *vrajendra-nandana*—and Kṛṣṇa, the son of Mahārāja Nanda.

TRANSLATION

"The basis of all transcendental mellows is the hero and the heroine, and Śrīmatī Rādhārāṇī and Lord Kṛṣṇa, the son of Mahārāja Nanda, are the best.

TEXT 93

এইমত দাস্যে দাস, সখ্যে সখাগণ।
বাৎসল্যে মাতা পিতা আশ্রয়ালম্বন ॥ ৯৩ ॥

ei-mata dāsye dāsa, sakhye sakhā-gaṇa
vātsalye mātā pitā āśrayālambana

SYNONYMS

ei-mata—in this way; *dāsye*—in the transcendental mellow of servitude; *dāsa*—servants; *sakhye*—in the transcendental mellow of friendship; *sakhā-gaṇa*—the friends; *vātsalye*—in the transcendental mellow of paternal affection; *mātā pitā*—mother and father; *āśraya-ālambana*—the support or shelter of love as the abode or dwelling place of love.

TRANSLATION

"Just as Lord Kṛṣṇa and Śrīmatī Rādhārāṇī are the object and shelter of the mellow of conjugal love, so, in the mellow of servitorship, Kṛṣṇa, the son of Mahārāja Nanda, is the object, and servants like Citraka, Raktaka and Patraka are the shelter. Similarly, in the transcendental mellow of friendship, Lord Kṛṣṇa is the object, and friends like Śrīdāmā, Sudāmā and Subala are the shelter. In the transcendental mellow of paternal affection, Kṛṣṇa is the object, and mother Yaśodā and Mahārāja Nanda are the shelter.

TEXT 94

এই রস অনুভবে যৈছে ভক্তগণ ।
যৈছে রস হয়, শুন তাহার লক্ষণ ॥ ৯৪ ॥

ei rasa anubhave yaiche bhakta-gaṇa
yaiche rasa haya, śuna tāhāra lakṣaṇa

SYNONYMS

ei—this; *rasa*—mellow; *anubhave*—realize; *yaiche*—how; *bhakta-gaṇa*—the devotees; *yaiche*—how; *rasa*—the mellow; *haya*—appears; *śuna*—hear; *tāhāra*—of them; *lakṣaṇa*—the symptoms.

TRANSLATION

"Now hear how the mellows appear and how they are realized by the devotees on different transcendental platforms.

TEXTS 95-98

ভক্তিনির্ধূত-দোষাণাং প্রসন্নোজ্জ্বলচেতসাম্ ।
শ্রীভাগবতরক্তানাং রসিকাসঙ্গরঙ্গিণাম্ ॥ ৯৫ ॥

জীবনীভূত-গোবিন্দপাদভক্তিসুখশ্রিয়াম্ ।
প্রেমান্তরঙ্গভূতানি কৃত্যান্যেবানুতিষ্ঠতাম্ ॥ ২৬ ॥
ভক্তানাং হৃদি রাজন্তী সংস্কারযুগলোজ্জ্বলা ।
রতিরানন্দরূপৈব নীয়মানা তু রস্যতাম্ ॥ ২৭ ॥
কৃষ্ণাদিভির্বিভাবাদ্যৈর্গতৈরনুভবাধ্বনি ।
প্রৌঢ়ানন্দশ্চমৎকারকাষ্ঠামাপদ্যতে পরাম্ ॥ ২৮ ॥

bhakti-nirdhūta-doṣāṇāṁ
prasannojjvala-cetasām
śrī-bhāgavata-raktānāṁ
rasikāsaṅga-raṅgiṇām

jīvanī-bhūta-govinda-
pāda-bhakti-sukha-śriyām
premāntaraṅga-bhūtāni
kṛtyāny evānutiṣṭhatām

bhaktānāṁ hṛdi rājantī
saṁskāra-yugalojjvalā
ratir ānanda-rūpaiva
nīyamānā tu rasyatām

kṛṣṇādibhir vibhāvādyair
gatair anubhavādhvani
prauḍhānandaś camatkāra-
kāṣṭhām āpadyate parām

SYNONYMS

bhakti—by devotional service; *nirdhūta-doṣāṇām*—whose material contaminations are washed off; *prasanna-ujjvala-cetasām*—whose hearts are satisfied and clean; *śrī-bhāgavata-raktānām*—who are interested in understanding the transcendental meaning of *Śrīmad-Bhāgavatam; rasika-āsaṅga-raṅgiṇām*—who live with the devotees and enjoy their transcendental company; *jīvanī-bhūta*—has become the life; *govinda-pāda*—to the lotus feet of Govinda; *bhakti-sukha-śriyām*—those for whom the opulence of the happiness of devotional service; *prema-antaraṅga-bhūtāni*—which are of a confidential nature in the loving affairs of the devotees and Kṛṣṇa; *kṛtyāni*—activities; *eva*—certainly; *anutiṣṭhatām*—of those performing; *bhaktānām*—of the devotees; *hṛdi*—in the hearts; *rājantī*—existing; *saṁskāra-yugala*—by previous and current purificatory methods; *ujjvalā*—expanded; *ratiḥ*—love; *ānanda-rūpā*—whose form is transcendental bliss; *eva*—certainly; *nīyamānā*—being brought; *tu*—but; *rasyatām*—to tastefulness; *kṛṣṇa-ādibhiḥ*—by Kṛṣṇa and others; *vibhāva-ādyaiḥ*—by ingredients such as *vibhāva; gataiḥ*—gone; *anubhava-adhvani*—to the path of perception; *prauḍha-ānandaḥ*—mature bliss; *camatkāra-kāṣṭhām*—the platform of wonder; *āpadyate*—arrives at; *parām*—the supreme.

TRANSLATION

" 'Those who are completely washed of all material contamination by pure devotional service, who are always satisfied and brightly enlightened in the heart, who are always attached to understanding the transcendental meaning of Śrīmad-Bhāgavatam, who are always eager to associate with advanced devotees, whose happiness in the service of the lotus feet of Govinda is their very life, who always discharge the confidential activities of love—for such advanced devotees, who are by nature situated in bliss, the seed of love [rati] is expanded in the heart by previous and current reformatory processes. Thus the mixture of ecstatic ingredients becomes tasty and, being within the perception of the devotee, reaches the highest platform of wonder and deep bliss.'

PURPORT

These verses are also found in *Bhakti-rasāmṛta-sindhu* (2.1.7-10).

TEXT 99

এই রস-আস্বাদ নাহি অভক্তের গণে ।
কৃষ্ণভক্তগণ করে রস আস্বাদনে ॥ ৯৯ ॥

ei rasa-āsvāda nāhi abhaktera gaṇe
kṛṣṇa-bhakta-gaṇa kare rasa āsvādane

SYNONYMS

ei—this; *rasa-āsvāda*—tasting of transcendental mellows; *nāhi*—not; *abhaktera gaṇe*—among nondevotees; *kṛṣṇa-bhakta-gaṇe*—the pure devotees of Lord Kṛṣṇa; *kare*—do; *rasa*—these transcendental mellows; *āsvādane*—tasting.

TRANSLATION

"The exchange between Kṛṣṇa and different devotees situated in different transcendental mellows is not to be experienced by nondevotees. Advanced

devotees can understand and appreciate the different varieties of devotional service reciprocated with the Supreme Personality of Godhead.

TEXT 100

সর্বথৈব দুরূহোঽয়মভক্তৈর্ভগবদ্রসঃ ।
তৎপাদাম্বুজসর্বস্বৈর্ভক্তৈরেবানুরস্যতে ॥ ১০০ ॥

sarvathaiva durūho 'yam
abhaktair bhagavad-rasaḥ
tat pādāmbuja-sarvasvair
bhaktair evānurasyate

SYNONYMS

sarvathā—in all respects; *eva*—certainly; *durūhaḥ*—difficult to be understood; *ayam*—this; *abhaktaiḥ*—by nondevotees; *bhagavat-rasaḥ*—the transcendental mellow exchanged with the Supreme Personality of Godhead; *tat*—that; *pāda-ambuja-sarvasvaiḥ*—whose all in all is the lotus feet; *bhaktaiḥ*—by devotees; *eva*—certainly; *anurasyate*—are relished.

TRANSLATION

" 'Nondevotees cannot understand the transcendental mellows experienced between the devotee and the Lord. In all respects, this is very difficult, but one who has dedicated everything to the lotus feet of Kṛṣṇa can taste the transcendental mellows.'

PURPORT

This verse is also found in *Bhakti-rasāmṛta-sindhu* (2.5.131).

TEXT 101

সংক্ষেপে কহিলুঁ এই 'প্রয়োজন'-বিবরণ ।
পঞ্চম-পুরুষার্থ—এই 'কৃষ্ণপ্রেম'-ধন ॥ ১০১ ॥

saṅkṣepe kahiluṅ ei 'prayojana'-vivaraṇa
pañcama-puruṣārtha——ei 'kṛṣṇa-prema'-dhana

SYNONYMS

saṅkṣepe kahiluṅ—briefly I have spoken; *ei*—this; *prayojana-vivaraṇa*—description of the ultimate achievement; *pañcama-puruṣa-artha*—the fifth and ultimate goal of life; *ei*—this; *kṛṣṇa-prema-dhana*—the treasure of love of Kṛṣṇa.

TRANSLATION

"This brief description is an elaboration of the ultimate goal of life. Indeed, this is the fifth and ultimate goal, which is beyond the platform of liberation. It is called kṛṣṇa-prema-dhana, the treasure of love for Kṛṣṇa.

TEXT 102

পূর্বে প্রয়াগে আমি রসের বিচারে ।
তোমার ভাই রূপে কৈলুঁ শক্তি-সঞ্চারে ॥ ১০২ ॥

pūrve prayāge āmi rasera vicāre
tomāra bhāi rūpe kailuṅ śakti-sañcāre

SYNONYMS

pūrve—previously; *prayāge*—in Prayāga; *āmi*—I; *rasera vicāre*—in consideration of different mellows; *tomāra bhāi*—your brother; *rūpe*—unto Rūpa Gosvāmī; *kailuṅ*—I have done; *śakti-sañcāre*—endowment of all power.

TRANSLATION

"Previously I empowered your brother Rūpa Gosvāmī to understand these mellows. I did this while instructing him at the Daśāśvamedha-ghāṭa in Prayāga.

TEXT 103

তুমিহ করিহ ভক্তি-শাস্ত্রের প্রচার ।
মথুরায় লুপ্ততীর্থের করিহ উদ্ধার ॥ ১০৩ ॥

tumiha kariha bhakti-śāstrera pracāra
mathurāya lupta-tīrthera kariha uddhāra

SYNONYMS

tumiha—you also; *kariha*—should perform; *bhakti-śāstrera pracāra*—propagation of the revealed scriptures of devotional service; *mathurāya*—in Mathurā; *lupta-tīrthera*—of lost places of pilgrimage; *kariha*—should make; *uddhāra*—recovery.

TRANSLATION

"O Sanātana, you should broadcast the revealed scriptures on devotional service and excavate the lost places of pilgrimage in the district of Mathurā.

TEXT 104

বৃন্দাবনে কৃষ্ণসেবা, বৈষ্ণব-আচার ।
ভক্তিস্মৃতিশাস্ত্র করি' করিহ প্রচার ॥ ১০৪ ॥

vṛndāvane kṛṣṇa-sevā, vaiṣṇava-ācāra
bhakti-smṛti-śāstra kari' kariha pracāra

SYNONYMS

vṛndāvane—in Vṛndāvana; *kṛṣṇa-sevā*—the service of Lord Kṛṣṇa; *vaiṣṇava-ācāra*—behavior of Vaiṣṇavas; *bhakti-smṛti-śāstra*—the reference books of devotional service; *kari'*—compiling; *kariha*—do; *pracāra*—preaching.

TRANSLATION

"Establish devotional service to Lord Kṛṣṇa and Rādhārāṇī in Vṛndāvana. You should also compile bhakti scripture and preach the bhakti cult from Vṛndāvana."

PURPORT

Sanātana Gosvāmī was enjoined (1) to broadcast the revealed scriptures on devotional service and establish the conclusions of devotional service, (2) to re-establish lost places of pilgrimage like Vṛndāvana and Rādhā-kuṇḍa, (3) to establish the Vṛndāvana method of temple worship and install Deities in temples (Śrī Sanātana Gosvāmī established Madana-mohana temple, and Rūpa Gosvāmī established Govindajī temple.), and (4) to enunciate the behavior of a Vaiṣṇava (as Śrīla Sanātana Gosvāmī did in *Hari-bhakti-vilāsa*). In this way Sanātana Gosvāmī was empowered to establish the cult of Vaiṣṇavism. As stated by Śrīnivāsa Ācārya:

nānā-śāstra-vicāraṇaika-nipuṇau sad-dharma-saṁsthāpakau
lokānāṁ hita-kāriṇau tribhuvane mānyau śaraṇyākarau
rādhā-kṛṣṇa-padāravinda-bhajanānandena mattālikau
vande rūpa-sanātanau raghu-yugau śrī-jīva-gopālakau

"I offer my respectful obeisances unto the six Gosvāmīs, namely Śrī Sanātana Gosvāmī, Śrī Rūpa Gosvāmī, Śrī Raghunātha Bhaṭṭa Gosvāmī, Śrī Raghunātha dāsa Gosvāmī, Śrī Jīva Gosvāmī and Śrī Gopāla Bhaṭṭa Gosvāmī, who are very expert in scrutinizingly studying all the revealed scriptures with the aim of establishing eternal religious principles for the benefit of all human beings. Thus they are honored all over the three worlds, and they are worth taking shelter of because they are absorbed in the mood of the *gopīs* and are engaged in the transcendental loving service of Rādhā and Kṛṣṇa."

This Kṛṣṇa consciousness movement continues the tradition of the six Gosvāmīs, especially Śrīla Sanātana Gosvāmī and Śrīla Rūpa Gosvāmī. Serious students of this Kṛṣṇa consciousness movement must understand their great responsibility to preach the cult of Vṛndāvana (devotional service to the Lord) all over the world. We now have a nice temple in Vṛndāvana, and serious students should take advantage of it. I am very hopeful that some of our students can take up this responsibility and render the best service to humanity by educating people in Kṛṣṇa consciousness.

TEXT 105

যুক্তবৈরাগ্য-স্থিতি সব শিখাইল ।
শুষ্কবৈরাগ্য-জ্ঞান সব নিষেধিল ॥ ১০৫ ॥

yukta-vairāgya-sthiti saba śikhāila
śuṣka-vairāgya-jñāna saba niṣedhila

SYNONYMS

yukta-vairāgya—of proper renunciation; *sthiti*—the situation; *saba*—all; *śikhāila*—instructed; *śuṣka-vairāgya*—dry renunciation; *jñāna*—speculative knowledge; *saba*—all; *niṣedhila*—forbade.

TRANSLATION

Śrī Caitanya Mahāprabhu then told Sanātana Gosvāmī about proper renunciation according to a particular situation, and the Lord forbade dry renunciation and speculative knowledge in all respects.

PURPORT

This is the technique for understanding *śuṣka-vairāgya* and *yukta-vairāgya*. In *Bhagavad-gītā* (6.17) it is said:

yuktāhāra-vihārasya
yukta-ceṣṭasya karmasu
yukta-svapnāvabodhaśya
yogo bhavati duḥkha-hā

"He who is temperate in his habits of eating, sleeping, working and recreation can mitigate all material pains by practicing the *yoga* system." To broadcast the cult of Kṛṣṇa consciousness, one has to learn the possibility of renunciation in terms of country, time and candidate. A candidate for Kṛṣṇa consciousness in the Western countries should be taught about the renunciation of material existence, but one would teach candidates from a country like India in a different way. The teacher (*ācārya*) has to consider time, candidate and country. He must avoid the principle of *niyamāgraha*—that is, he should not try to perform the impossible. What is possible in one country may not be possible in another. The *ācārya's* duty is to accept the essence of devotional service. There may be a little change here and there as far as *yukta-vairāgya* (proper renunciation) is concerned. Dry renunciation is forbidden by Śrī Caitanya Mahāprabhu, and we have also learned this from our spiritual master, His Divine Grace Bhaktisiddhānta Sarasvatī Ṭhākura Gosvāmī Mahārāja. The essence of devotional service must be taken into consideration, and not the outward paraphernalia.

Sanātana Gosvāmī wrote his Vaiṣṇava *smṛti, Hari-bhakti-vilāsa,* which was specifically meant for India. In those days, India was more or less following the principle of *smārta-vidhi.* Śrīla Sanātana Gosvāmī had to keep pace with this, and his *Hari-bhakti-vilāsa* was compiled with this in mind. According to *smārta-brāhmaṇas,* a person not born in a *brāhmaṇa* family could not be elevated to the position of a *brāhmaṇa.* Sanātana Gosvāmī, however, says in *Hari-bhakti-vilāsa* (2.12) that anyone can be elevated to the position of a *brāhmaṇa* by the process of initiation.

yathā kāñcanatāṁ yāti
kāṁsyaṁ rasa-vidhānataḥ
tathā dīkṣā-vidhānena
dvijatvaṁ jāyate nṛṇām

There is a difference between the *smārta* process and the *gosvāmī* process. According to the *smārta* process, one cannot be accepted as a *brāhmaṇa* unless he is born in a *brāhmaṇa* family. According to the *gosvāmī* process, the *Hari-bhakti-vilāsa* and the *Nārada-pañcarātra,* anyone can be a *brāhmaṇa* if he is properly initiated by a bona fide spiritual master. This is also the verdict of Śukadeva Gosvāmī in *Śrīmad-Bhāgavatam* (2.4.18):

kirāta-hūṇāndhra-pulinda-pulkaśā
ābhīra-śumbhā yavanāḥ khasādayaḥ
ye 'nye ca pāpā yad-apāśrayāśrayāḥ
śudhyanti tasmai prabhaviṣṇave namaḥ

A Vaiṣṇava is immediately purified, provided he follows the rules and regulations of his bona fide spiritual master. It is not necessary that the rules and regulations followed in India be exactly the same as those in Europe, America and other Western countries. Simply imitating without effect is called *niyamāgraha.* Not following the regulative principles but instead living extravagantly is also called *niyamāgraha.* The word *niyama* means "regulative principles," and *āgraha* means "eagerness." The word *agraha* means "not to accept." We should not follow regulative principles without an effect, nor should we fail to accept the regulative principles. What is required is a special technique according to country, time and candidate. Without the sanction of the spiritual master, we should not try to imitate. This principle is recommended here: *śuṣka-vairāgya-jñāna saba niṣedhila.* This is Śrī Caitanya Mahāprabhu's liberal demonstration of the *bhakti* cult. We should not introduce anything whimsically, without the sanction of the bona fide spiritual master. In this connection, Śrīla Bhaktisiddhānta Sarasvatī Ṭhākura comments on these points by quoting two verses by Śrī Rūpa Gosvāmī (*Bhakti-rasāmṛta-sindhu* 1.2.255-256).

anāsaktasya viṣayān
yathārham upayuñjataḥ
nirbandhaḥ kṛṣṇa-sambandhe
yuktaṁ vairāgyam ucyate

prāpañcikatayā buddhyā
hari-sambandhi-vastunaḥ
mumukṣubhiḥ parityāgo
vairāgyaṁ phalgu kathyate

"When one is not attached to anything but at the same time accepts everything in relation to Kṛṣṇa, one is rightly situated above possessiveness. On the other hand, one who rejects everything without knowledge of its relationship to Kṛṣṇa is not as complete in his renunciation." To preach the *bhakti* cult, one should seriously consider these verses.

TEXTS 106-107

অদ্বেষ্টা সর্বভূতানাং মৈত্রঃ করুণ এব চ ।
নির্মমো নিরহঙ্কারঃ সমদুঃখসুখঃ ক্ষমী ॥ ১০৬ ॥
সন্তুষ্টঃ সততং যোগী যতাত্মা দৃঢ়নিশ্চয়ঃ ।
ময্যর্পিতমনোবুদ্ধির্যো মদ্ভক্তঃ স. মে প্রিয়ঃ ॥ ১০৭ ॥

adveṣṭā sarva-bhūtānāṁ
maitraḥ karuṇa eva ca
nirmamo nirahaṅkāraḥ
sama-duḥkha-sukhaḥ kṣamī

santuṣṭaḥ satataṁ yogī
yatātmā dṛḍha-niścayaḥ

mayy arpita-mano-buddhir
yo mad-bhaktaḥ sa me priyaḥ

SYNONYMS

adveṣṭā—not envious or jealous; *sarva-bhūtānām*—to all living entities in all parts of the world; *maitraḥ*—friendly; *karuṇaḥ*—compassionate; *eva*—certainly; *ca*—and; *nirmamaḥ*—with no sense of proprietorship; *nirahaṅkāraḥ*—without pride (without considering oneself a great preacher); *sama-duḥkha-sukhaḥ*—equal in distress and happiness (peaceful); *kṣamī*—tolerant of offenses created by others; *santuṣṭaḥ*—satisfied; *satatam*—continuously; *yogī*—engaged in *bhakti-yoga; yata-ātmā*—having controlled the senses and mind; *dṛḍha-niścayaḥ*—having firm confidence and determination; *mayi*—unto Me; *arpita*—dedicated; *manaḥ-buddhiḥ*—mind and intelligence; *yaḥ*—who; *mat-bhaktaḥ*—My devotee; *saḥ*—that person; *me*—My; *priyaḥ*—dear.

TRANSLATION

" 'One who is not envious but who is a kind friend to all living entities, who does not think himself a proprietor, who is free from false ego, equal in both happiness and distress, always satisfied, forgiving and self-controlled, who is engaged in devotional service with determination and whose mind and intelligence are dedicated to Me—he is very dear to Me.

PURPORT

One should not be jealous of members of other castes or nations. It is not that only Indians or *brāhmaṇas* can become Vaiṣṇavas. Anyone can become a Vaiṣṇava. Therefore one should recognize that the *bhakti* cult must be spread all over the world. That is real *adveṣṭā*. Moreover, the word *maitraḥ*, friendly, indicates that one who is able to preach the *bhakti* cult all over the world should be equally friendly to everyone. These two and the following six verses were spoken by Śrī Kṛṣṇa in *Bhagavad-gītā* (12.13-20).

TEXT 108

যস্মান্নোদ্বিজতে লোকো লোকান্নোদ্বিজতে তু যঃ ।
হর্ষামর্ষভয়োদ্বেগৈর্মুক্তো যঃ স চ মে প্রিয়ঃ ॥ ১০৮ ॥

yasmān nodvijate loko
lokān nodvijate tu yaḥ
harṣāmarṣa-bhayodvegair
mukto yaḥ sa ca me priyaḥ

SYNONYMS

yasmāt—from whom; *na*—not; *udvijate*—is agitated by fear or lamentation; *lokaḥ*—the people in general; *lokāt*—from the people; *na*—not; *udvijate*—is agitated; *tu*—but; *yaḥ*—who; *harṣa*—jubilation; *amarṣa*—anger; *bhaya*—fear; *udvegaiḥ*—and from anxiety; *muktaḥ*—liberated; *yaḥ*—anyone who; *saḥ*—he; *ca*—also; *me priyaḥ*—My very dear devotee.

TRANSLATION

" 'He for whom no one is put into difficulty and who is not disturbed by anxiety, who is liberated from jubilation, anger, fear and anxiety, is very dear to Me.

TEXT 109

অনপেক্ষঃ শুচির্দক্ষ উদাসীনো গতব্যথঃ ।
সর্বারম্ভপরিত্যাগী যো মে ভক্তঃ স মে প্রিয়ঃ ॥ ১০৯ ॥

anapekṣaḥ śucir dakṣa
udāsīno gata-vyathaḥ
sarvārambha-parityāgī
yo me bhaktaḥ sa me priyaḥ

SYNONYMS

anapekṣaḥ—indifferent; *śuciḥ*—clean; *dakṣaḥ*—expert in executing devotional service; *udāsīnaḥ*—without affection for anything material; *gata-vyathaḥ*—liberated from all material distress; *sarva-ārambha*—all kinds of endeavor; *parityāgī*—completely rejecting; *yaḥ*—anyone who; *me*—My; *bhaktaḥ*—devotee; *saḥ*—he; *me priyaḥ*—very dear to Me.

TRANSLATION

" 'A devotee who is not dependent on others but dependent solely on Me, who is clean inwardly and outwardly, who is expert, indifferent to material things, without cares, free from all pains, and who rejects all pious and impious activities, is very dear to Me.

PURPORT

The word *anapekṣaḥ* means that one should not be concerned with mundane people and should not depend upon them. One should depend solely on the Supreme Personality of Godhead and be free from material desires. One should also be clean, within and without. To be outwardly clean, one should regularly bathe with soap and oil, and to be inwardly clean one should always be absorbed in thoughts of Kṛṣṇa. The words *sarvārambha-parityāgī* indicate that one should not be interested in the so-called *smārta-vidhi* of pious and impious activities.

TEXT 110

যো ন হৃষ্যতি ন দ্বেষ্টি ন শোচতি ন কাঙ্ক্ষতি ।
শুভাশুভপরিত্যাগী ভক্তিমান্ যঃ স মে প্রিয়ঃ ॥ ১১০ ॥

yo na hṛṣyati na dveṣṭi
na śocati na kāṅkṣati
śubhāśubha-parityāgī
bhaktimān yaḥ sa me priyaḥ

SYNONYMS

yaḥ—he who; *na hṛṣyati*—is not jubilant (upon getting something favorable); *na dveṣṭi*—does not hate (being artificially influenced by something unfavorable); *na*—not; *śocati*—laments; *na*—not; *kāṅkṣati*—desires; *śubha-aśubha*—the materially auspicious and inauspicious; *parityāgī*—completely rejecting; *bhaktimān*—possessing devotion; *yaḥ*—anyone who; *saḥ*—that person; *me priyaḥ*—very dear to Me.

TRANSLATION

" 'One who neither rejoices nor hates, who neither laments nor desires, who renounces both auspicious and inauspicious things and who is devoted to Me is very dear to Me.

TEXTS 111-112

সমঃ শত্রৌ চ মিত্রে চ তথা মানাপমানয়োঃ ।
শীতোষ্ণসুখদুঃখেষু সমঃ সঙ্গবিবর্জিতঃ ॥ ১১১ ॥
তুল্যনিন্দাস্তুতির্মৌনী সন্তুষ্টো যেন কেনচিৎ ।
অনিকেতঃ স্থিরমতির্ভক্তিমান্ মে প্রিয়ো নরঃ ॥১১২॥

samaḥ śatrau ca mitre ca
tathā mānāpamānayoḥ
śītoṣṇa-sukha-duḥkheṣu
samaḥ saṅga-vivarjitaḥ

tulya-nindā-stutir maunī
santuṣṭo yena kenacit

aniketaḥ sthira-matir
bhaktimān me priyo naraḥ

SYNONYMS

samaḥ—equal; *śatrau*—to the enemy; *ca*—also; *mitre*—to the friend; *ca*—and; *tathā*—similarly; *māna-apamānayoḥ*—in honor and dishonor; *śīta*—in winter; *uṣṇa*—and in scorching heat; *sukha*—in happiness; *duḥkheṣu*—and in distress; *samaḥ*—equipoised; *saṅga-vivarjitaḥ*—without affection; *tulya*—equal; *nindā*—blasphemy; *stutiḥ*—and praise; *maunī*—grave; *santuṣṭaḥ*—always satisfied; *yena kenacit*—by whatever comes; *aniketaḥ*—without attachment for a residence; *sthira*—steady; *matiḥ*—minded; *bhaktimān*—devotee; *me*—My; *priyaḥ*—dear; *naraḥ*—a person.

TRANSLATION

" 'One who is equal to friends and enemies, who is equipoised in honor and dishonor, heat and cold, happiness and distress, fame and infamy, who is always free from contamination, always grave and satisfied with anything, who doesn't care for any residence, and who is fixed in devotional service, is very dear to Me.

TEXT 113

যে তু ধর্মামৃতমিদং যথোক্তং পর্যুপাসতে ।
শ্রদ্দধানা মৎপরমা ভক্তাস্তেঽতীব মে প্রিয়াঃ ॥ ১১৩ ॥

ye tu dharmāmṛtam idaṁ
yathoktaṁ paryupāsate
śraddadhānā mat-paramā
bhaktās te 'tīva me priyāḥ

SYNONYMS

ye—the devotees who; *tu*—but; *dharma-amṛtam*—eternal religious principle of Kṛṣṇa consciousness; *idam*—this; *yathā-uktam*—as mentioned above; *paryupāsate*—worship; *śraddadhānāḥ*—having faith and devotion; *mat-paramāḥ*—accepting Me as the Supreme or the ultimate goal of life; *bhaktāḥ*—such devotees; *te*—they; *atīva*—very much; *me*—My; *priyāḥ*—dear.

TRANSLATION

" 'He who thus follows this imperishable religious principle of Kṛṣṇa consciousness with great faith and devotion, fully accepting Me as the supreme goal, is very, very dear to Me.'

TEXT 114

চীরাণি কিং পথি ন সন্তি দিশন্তি ভিক্ষাং
নৈবাঙ্ঘ্রিপাঃ পরভৃতঃ সরিতোঽপ্যশুষ্যন্।
রুদ্ধা গুহাঃ কিমজিতোঽবতি নোপসন্নান্
কস্মাদ্ভজন্তি কবয়ো ধনদুর্মদান্ধান্ ॥ ১১৪ ॥

cīrāṇi kiṁ pathi na santi diśanti bhikṣāṁ
naivāṅghri-pāḥ parabhṛtaḥ sarito 'py aśuṣyan
ruddhā guhāḥ kim ajito 'vati nopasannān
kasmād bhajanti kavayo dhana-durmadāndhān

SYNONYMS

cīrāṇi—torn old clothes; *kim*—whether; *pathi*—on the path; *na*—not; *santi*—are; *diśanti*—give; *bhikṣām*—alms; *na*—not; *eva*—certainly; *aṅghri-pāḥ*—the trees; *parabhṛtaḥ*—maintainers of others; *saritaḥ*—rivers; *api*—also; *aśuṣyan*—have dried up; *ruddhāḥ*—closed; *guhāḥ*—caves; *kim*—whether; *ajitaḥ*—the Supreme Personality of Godhead, who is unconquerable; *avati*—protects; *na*—not; *upasannān*—the surrendered; *kasmāt*—for what reason, therefore; *bhajanti*—flatter; *kavayaḥ*—the devotees; *dhana-durmada-andhān*—persons who are puffed up with material possessions.

TRANSLATION

" 'Are there no torn clothes lying on the common road? Do the trees, which exist for maintaining others, no longer give alms in charity? Do the rivers, being dried up, no longer supply water to the thirsty? Are the caves of the mountains now closed, or, above all, does the unconquerable Supreme Personality of Godhead not protect the fully surrendered souls? Why then should learned persons like devotees go to flatter those who are intoxicated by hard-earned wealth?' "

PURPORT

This is a quotation from *Śrīmad-Bhāgavatam* (2.2.5). In this verse, Śukadeva Gosvāmī advises Mahārāja Parīkṣit that a devotee should be independent in all circumstances. The body can be maintained with no problem if one follows the instructions given in this verse. To maintain the body, we require shelter, food, water and clothing, and all these necessities can be obtained without approaching puffed-up rich men. One can collect old garments that have been thrown out, one can eat fruits offered by the trees, one can drink water from the rivers, and one can live within the caves of mountains. By nature's arrangements, shelter, clothing and food are supplied to the devotee who is completely surrendered to the Supreme Personality of Godhead. Such a devotee does not need a puffed-up materialistic person to maintain him. In other words, devotional service can be discharged in any condition. This is the version of *Śrīmad-Bhāgavatam* (1.2.6).

sa vai puṁsāṁ paro dharmo
yato bhaktir adhokṣaje
ahaituky apratihatā
yayātmā suprasīdati

"The supreme occupation [dharma] for all humanity is that by which men can attain to loving devotional service unto the transcendent Lord. Such devotional service must be unmotivated and uninterrupted in order to completely satisfy the self." This verse explains that devotional service cannot be checked by any material condition.

TEXT 115

তবে সনাতন সব সিদ্ধান্ত পুছিলা ।
ভাগবত-সিদ্ধান্ত গূঢ় সকলি কহিলা ॥ ১১৫ ॥

tabe sanātana saba siddhānta puchilā
bhāgavata-siddhānta gūḍha sakali kahilā

SYNONYMS

tabe—thereafter; *sanātana*—Sanātana Gosvāmī; *saba*—all; *siddhānta*—conclusive statements; *puchilā*—inquired about; *bhāgavata-siddhānta*—the conclusive statements about devotional service mentioned in *Śrīmad-Bhāgavatam; gūḍha*—very confidential; *sakali*—all; *kahilā*—Śrī Caitanya Mahāprabhu described.

TRANSLATION

Thus Sanātana Gosvāmī inquired from Śrī Caitanya Mahāprabhu about all the conclusive statements concerning devotional service, and the Lord very vividly explained all the confidential meanings of Śrīmad-Bhāgavatam.

TEXT 116

হরিবংশে কহিয়াছে গোলোকে নিত্যস্থিতি ।
ইন্দ্র আসি' করিল যবে শ্রীকৃষ্ণেরে স্তুতি ॥ ১১৬ ॥

hari-vaṁśe kahiyāche goloke nitya-sthiti
indra āsi' karila yabe śrī-kṛṣṇere stuti

SYNONYMS

hari-vaṁśe—the revealed scripture known as *Hari-vaṁśa; kahiyāche*—has told of; *goloke*—on the planet called Goloka; *nitya-sthiti*—the eternal situation; *indra*—King Indra of the heavenly planet; *āsi'*—coming; *karila*—offered; *yabe*—when; *śrī-kṛṣṇere stuti*—prayers to Lord Śrī Kṛṣṇa.

TRANSLATION

In the revealed scripture Hari-vaṁśa, there is a description of Goloka Vṛndāvana, the planet where Lord Śrī Kṛṣṇa eternally resides. This information was given by King Indra when he surrendered to Kṛṣṇa and offered prayers after Kṛṣṇa had raised Govardhana Hill.

PURPORT

In the Vedic scripture *Hari-vaṁśa* (*Viṣṇu-parva,* Chapter Nineteen), there is the following description of Goloka Vṛndāvana:

manuṣya-lokād ūrdhvaṁ tu
khagānāṁ gatir ucyate
ākāśasyopari rarir
dvāraṁ svargasya bhānumān
svargād ūrdhvaṁ brahma-loko
brahmarṣi-gaṇa-sevitaḥ

tatra soma-gatiś caiva
jyotiṣāṁ ca mahātmanām
tasyopari gavāṁ lokaḥ
sādhyās taṁ pālayanti hi
sa hi sarva-gataḥ kṛṣṇaḥ
mahā-kāśagato mahān

uparyupari tatrāpi
gatis tava tapomayī
yāṁ na vidmo vayaṁ sarve
pṛcchanto 'pi pitām aham

gatiḥ śama-damāṭyānāṁ
svargaḥ su-kṛta-karmaṇām
brāhmye tapasi yuktānāṁ
brahma-lokaḥ parā gatiḥ

gavām eva tu goloko
durārohā hi sā gatiḥ
sa tu lokas tvayā kṛṣṇa
sīdamānaḥ kṛtātmanā
dhṛto dhṛtimatā vīra
nighnatopadravān gavām

When the King of heaven, Indra, surrendered to Kṛṣṇa after Kṛṣṇa raised Govardhana Hill, Lord Indra stated that above the planetary systems wherein human beings reside is the sky, where birds fly. Above the sky is the sun and its orbit. This is the entrance to the heavenly planets. Above the heavenly planets are other planets, up to Brahmaloka, where those advancing in spiritual knowledge reside. The planets up to Brahmaloka are part of the material world (Devī-dhāma). Because the material world is under the control of Devī, Durgā, it is called Devī-dhāma. Above Devī-dhāma is a place where Lord Śiva and his wife Umā reside. Those brightened by spiritual knowledge and liberated from material contamination reside in that Śivaloka. Beyond that planetary system is the spiritual world, where there are planets called Vaikuṇṭha-lokas. Goloka Vṛndāvana is situated above all the Vaikuṇṭha-lokas. Goloka Vṛndāvana is the kingdom of Śrīmatī Rādhārāṇī and the parents of Kṛṣṇa, Mahārāja Nanda and mother Yaśodā. In this way there are various planetary systems, and they are all creations of the Supreme Lord. As stated in *Brahma-saṁhitā:*

goloka-nāmni nija-dhāmni tale ca tasya
devī-maheśa-hari-dhāmasu teṣu teṣu
te te prabhāva-nicayā vihitāś ca yena
govindam ādi-puruṣaṁ tam ahaṁ bhajāmi

Thus Goloka Vṛndāvana-dhāma is situated above the Vaikuṇṭha planets. The spiritual sky containing all the Vaikuṇṭha planets is very small compared to Goloka Vṛndāvana-dhāma. The space occupied by Goloka Vṛndāvana-dhāma is called *mahākāśa,* or "the greatest sky of all." Lord Indra said, "We asked Lord Brahmā about Your eternal planet, but we could not understand it. Those fruitive actors who have controlled their senses and mind with pious activities can be elevated to the heavenly planets. Pure devotees who are always engaged in Lord Nārāyaṇa's service are promoted to the Vaikuṇṭhalokas. However, my Lord Kṛṣṇa, Your Goloka Vṛndāvana-dhāma is very difficult to attain. Yet both You and that supreme planetary system have descended here upon this earth. Unfortunately, I have disturbed You by my misdeeds, and that was due to my foolishness. I am therefore trying to satisfy You by my prayers."

Śrī Nīlakaṇṭha confirms the existence of Goloka Vṛndāvana-dhāma by quoting the *Ṛg-saṁhitā* (*Ṛg Veda* 1.21.154.6):

tā vāṁ vāstūnyuśmasi gamadhyai
yatra gāvo bhūri-śṛṅgā ayāsaḥ
atrāha tad urugāyasya kṛṣṇaḥ
paramaṁ padam avabhāti bhūri

"We wish to go to Your [Rādhā's and Kṛṣṇa's] beautiful houses, about which cows with large, excellent horns are wandering. Yet distinctly shining on this earth is that supreme abode of Yours that showers joy on all, O Urugāya [Kṛṣṇa, who is much praised]."

TEXTS 117-118

মৌষল-লীলা, আর কৃষ্ণ-অন্তর্ধান ।
কেশাবতার, আর যত বিরুদ্ধ ব্যাখ্যান ॥ ১১৭ ॥
মহিষী-হরণ আদি, সব—মায়াময় ।
ব্যাখ্যা শিখাইল যৈছে সুসিদ্ধান্ত হয় ॥ ১১৮ ॥

mauṣala-līlā, āra kṛṣṇa-antardhāna
keśāvatāra, āra yata viruddha vyākhyāna

mahiṣī-haraṇa ādi, saba——māyāmaya
vyākhyā śikhāila yaiche susiddhānta haya

SYNONYMS

mauṣala-līlā—the pastimes of destroying the Yadu dynasty; *āra*—also; *kṛṣṇa-antardhāna*—the disappearance of Kṛṣṇa; *keśa-avatāra*—the incarnation of the hairs; *āra*—also; *yata*—all; *viruddha vyākhyāna*—statements against the Kṛṣṇa conscious conclusions; *mahiṣī-haraṇa*—kidnapping of the queens; *ādi*—and so on; *saba*—all; *māyā-maya*—made of the external energy; *vyākhyā*—explanations (countering the attack of the *asuras*); *śikhāila*—instructed; *yaiche*—which; *su-siddhānta*—proper conclusions; *haya*—are.

TRANSLATION

Illusory stories opposed to the conclusions of Kṛṣṇa consciousness concern the destruction of the Yadu dynasty, Kṛṣṇa's disappearance, the story that Kṛṣṇa and Balarāma arise from a black hair and a white hair of Kṣīrodakaśāyī Viṣṇu, and the story about the kidnapping of the queens. Śrī Caitanya Mahāprabhu explained to Sanātana Gosvāmī the proper conclusions of these stories.

PURPORT

Due to envy, many *asuras* describe Kṛṣṇa to be like a black crow or an incarnation of a hair. Śrī Caitanya Mahāprabhu told Sanātana Gosvāmī how to counteract all these asuric explanations of Kṛṣṇa. The word *kāka* means crow, and *keśa* means hair. The *asuras* describe Kṛṣṇa as an incarnation of a crow, an incarnation of a *śūdra* (a blackish tribe) and an incarnation of a hair, not knowing that the word *keśa* means *ka-īśa* and that *ka* means Lord Brahmā and *īśa* means Lord. Thus Kṛṣṇa is the Lord of Lord Brahmā.

Some of Lord Kṛṣṇa's pastimes are mentioned in the *Mahābhārata* as *mauṣala-līlā*. These include the stories of the destruction of the Yadu dynasty, Kṛṣṇa's disappearance, His being pierced by a hunter's arrow, the story of Kṛṣṇa's being an incarnation of a piece of hair (*keśa-avatāra*) as well as *mahiṣī-haraṇa,* the kidnapping of Kṛṣṇa's queens. Actually these are not factual but are related for the bewilderment of the *asuras* who want to prove that Kṛṣṇa is an ordinary human being. They are false in the sense that these pastimes are not eternal, nor are they transcendental or spiritual. There are many people who are by nature averse to the supremacy of the Supreme Personality of Godhead, Viṣṇu. Such people are called *asuras*. They have mistaken ideas about Kṛṣṇa. As stated in *Bhagavad-gītā,* the *asuras* are given a chance to forget Kṛṣṇa more and more, birth after birth. Thus they make their appearance in a family of *asuras* and continue this process, being kept in bewilderment about Kṛṣṇa. *Asuras* in the dress of *sannyāsīs* even explain *Bhagavad-gītā* and *Śrīmad-Bhāgavatam* in different ways according to their own imaginations. Thus they continue to remain *asuras* birth after birth.

As far as the *keśa-avatāra* (incarnation of hair) is concerned, it is mentioned in *Śrīmad-Bhāgavatam* (2.7.26). The *Viṣṇu Purāṇa* also states: *ujjahārātmanaḥ keśau sita-kṛṣṇau mahā-bala.*

Similarly, in the *Mahābhārata:*

sa cāpi keśau harir uccakarta
ekaṁ śuklam aparam cāpi kṛṣṇam
tau cāpi keśāvāv iśatāṁ yadūnāṁ
kule striyau rohiṇīṁ devakīṁ ca

tayor eko balabhadro babhūva
yo 'sau śvetas tasya devasya keśaḥ
kṛṣṇo dvitīyaḥ keśavaḥ saṁbabhūva
keśaḥ yo 'sau varṇataḥ kṛṣṇa uktaḥ

Thus in *Śrīmad-Bhāgavatam, Viṣṇu Purāṇa* and *Mahābhārata* there are references to Kṛṣṇa and Balarāma being incarnations of a black hair and a white hair. It is stated that Lord Viṣṇu snatched two hairs—one white and one black—from His head. These two hairs entered the wombs of Rohiṇī and Devakī, members of the Yadu dynasty. Balarāma was born from Rohiṇī, and Kṛṣṇa was born of Devakī. Thus Balarāma appeared from the first hair, and Kṛṣṇa appeared from the second hair. It was also foretold that all the *asuras,* who are enemies of the demigods, would be cut down by Lord Viṣṇu by His white and black plenary expansions and that the Supreme Personality of Godhead would appear and perform wonderful activities. In this connection, one should see *Laghu-bhāgavatāmṛta,* the chapter called *Kṛṣṇāmṛta,* verses 156-164. Śrīla Rūpa Gosvāmī has refuted this argument about the hair incarnation, and his refutation is supported by Śrī Baladeva Vidyābhūṣaṇa's commentaries. This matter is further discussed in the *Kṛṣṇa-sandarbha* (29) and in the commentary known as *Sarva-saṁvādinī,* by Śrīla Jīva Gosvāmī.

TEXT 119

তবে সনাতন প্রভুর চরণে ধরিয়া।
নিবেদন করে দন্তে তৃণ-গুচ্ছ লঞা॥ ১১৯॥

tabe sanātana prabhura caraṇe dhariyā
nivedana kare dante tṛṇa-guccha lañā

SYNONYMS

tabe—at that time; *sanātana*—Sanātana Gosvāmī; *prabhura*—of Śrī Caitanya Mahāprabhu; *caraṇe dhariyā*—catching the lotus feet; *nivedana kare*—submits a petition; *dante*—in the teeth; *tṛṇa-guccha*—a bunch of straw; *lañā*—taking.

TRANSLATION

Sanātana Gosvāmī then humbly accepted his position as lower than a piece of straw, and, symbolically holding some straw in his mouth, he fell down, clasped the lotus feet of Śrī Caitanya Mahāprabhu and submitted the following petition.

TEXT 120

"নীচজাতি, নীচসেবী, মুঞি – সুপামর।
সিদ্ধান্ত শিখাইলা,—যেই ব্রহ্মার অগোচর॥ ১২০॥

"nīca-jāti, nīca-sevī, muñi——supāmara
siddhānta śikhāilā,——yei brahmāra agocara

SYNONYMS

nīca-jāti—lower class; *nīca-sevī*—servant of lowborn people; *muñi*—I; *su-pāmara*—very, very fallen; *siddhānta śikhāilā*—You have taught the topmost conclusions in detail; *yei*—which; *brahmāra*—of Brahmā; *agocara*—beyond the reach.

TRANSLATION

Sanātana Gosvāmī said, "My dear Lord, I am a very lowborn person. Indeed, I am a servant to lowborn people; therefore I am very, very downtrodden. Nonetheless, You have taught me conclusions unknown even to Lord Brahmā.

TEXT 121

তুমি যে কহিলা, এই সিদ্ধান্তামৃত-সিন্ধু।
মোর মন ছুঁইতে নারে ইহার একবিন্দু॥ ১২১ ॥

tumi ye kahilā, ei siddhāntāmṛta-sindhu
mora mana chuṅite nāre ihāra eka-bindu

SYNONYMS

tumi ye—You; *kahilā*—have spoken; *ei*—this; *siddhānta-amṛta-sindhu*—the ocean of the ambrosia of conclusive truth; *mora mana*—my mind; *chuṅite*—to touch; *nāre*—is not able; *ihāra*—of it; *eka-bindu*—even a drop.

TRANSLATION

"The conclusions that You have told me are the ocean of the ambrosia of truth. My mind is unable to approach even a drop of that ocean.

TEXT 122

পঙ্গু নাচাইতে যদি হয় তোমার মন।
বর দেহ' মোর মাথে ধরিয়া চরণ॥ ১২২ ॥

paṅgu nācāite yadi haya tomāra mana
vara deha' mora māthe dhariyā caraṇa

SYNONYMS

paṅgu—lame man; *nācāite*—to make dance; *yadi*—if; *haya*—it is; *tomāra mana*—Your mind; *vara*—a benediction; *deha'*—kindly give; *mora māthe*—on my head; *dhariyā*—holding; *caraṇa*—Your lotus feet.

TRANSLATION

"If You want to make a lame man like me dance, kindly bestow Your transcendental blessings by keeping Your lotus feet on my head.

TEXT 123

'মুঞি যে শিখালুঁ তোরে স্ফুরুক সকল'।
এই তোমার বর হৈতে হবে মোর বল॥" ১২৩ ॥

'muñi ye śikhāluṅ tore sphuruka sakala'
ei tomāra vara haite habe mora bala"

SYNONYMS

muñi—I; *ye*—whatever; *śikhāluṅ*—have instructed; *tore*—unto you; *sphuruka sakala*—let it be manifested; *ei*—this; *tomāra vara*—Your benediction; *haite*—from; *habe*—there will be; *mora bala*—my strength.

TRANSLATION

"Now, will You please tell me, 'Let whatever I have instructed all be fully manifest unto you.' By benedicting me in this way, You will give me strength to describe all this."

TEXT 124

তবে মহাপ্রভু তাঁর শিরে ধরি' করে।
বর দিলা—'এই সব স্ফুরুক তোমারে'॥ ১২৪ ॥

tabe mahāprabhu tāṅra śire dhari' kare
vara dilā——'ei saba sphuruka tomāre'

SYNONYMS

tabe—after that; *mahāprabhu*—Śrī Caitanya Mahāprabhu; *tāṅra*—of Sanātana Gosvāmī; *śire*—on the head; *dhari'*—holding; *kare*—by the hand; *vara dilā*—gave the benediction; *ei saba*—all this; *sphuruka tomāre*—let it be manifested to you properly.

TRANSLATION

Śrī Caitanya Mahāprabhu then placed His hand on Sanātana Gosvāmī's head and benedicted him, saying, "Let all these instructions be manifest to you."

TEXT 125

সংক্ষেপে কহিলুঁ—'প্রেম'-প্রয়োজন-সংবাদ ।
বিস্তারি' কহন না যায় প্রভুর প্রসাদ ॥ ১২৫ ॥

saṅkṣepe kahiluṅ——'prema'-prayojana-saṁvāda
vistāri' kahana nā yāya prabhura prasāda

SYNONYMS

saṅkṣepe—briefly; *kahiluṅ*—I have described; *prema-prayojana-saṁvāda*—the discussion of the ultimate goal of life, love of Godhead; *vistāri'*—expansively; *kahana*—describing; *nā yāya*—not possible; *prabhura prasāda*—the benediction of Śrī Caitanya Mahāprabhu.

TRANSLATION

Thus I have briefly described a discussion of the ultimate goal of life, love of Godhead. The mercy of Śrī Caitanya Mahāprabhu cannot be described expansively.

TEXT 126

প্রভুর উপদেশামৃত শুনে যেই জন ।
অচিরাৎ মিলয়ে তাঁরে কৃষ্ণপ্রেমধন ॥ ১২৬ ॥

prabhura upadeśāmṛta śune yei jana
acirāt milaye tāṅre kṛṣṇa-prema-dhana

SYNONYMS

prabhura—of Śrī Caitanya Mahāprabhu; *upadeśa-amṛta*—the nectar of the instructions; *śune*—hears; *yei jana*—anyone who; *acirāt*—without delay; *milaye*—meets; *tāṅre*—him; *kṛṣṇa-prema-dhana*—the treasure of love of Kṛṣṇa.

TRANSLATION

Whoever hears these instructions given to Sanātana Gosvāmī by the Lord comes very soon to realize love of God, Kṛṣṇa.

TEXT 127

শ্রীরূপ-রঘুনাথ পদে যার আশ ।
চৈতন্যচরিতামৃত কহে কৃষ্ণদাস ॥ ১২৭ ॥

śrī-rūpa-raghunātha-pade yāra āśa
caitanya-caritāmṛta kahe kṛṣṇadāsa

SYNONYMS

śrī-rūpa—Śrīla Rūpa Gosvāmī; *raghunātha*—Śrīla Raghunātha dāsa Gosvāmī; *pade*—at the lotus feet; *yāra*—whose; *āśa*—expectation; *caitanya-caritāmṛta*—the book named *Caitanya-caritāmṛta; kahe*—describes; *kṛṣṇadāsa*—Śrīla Kṛṣṇadāsa Kavirāja Gosvāmī.

TRANSLATION

Praying at the lotus feet of Śrī Rūpa and Śrī Raghunātha, always desiring their mercy, I, Kṛṣṇadāsa, narrate Śrī Caitanya-caritāmṛta, following in their footsteps.

Thus end the Bhaktivedanta purports to the Śrī Caitanya-caritāmṛta, Madhya-līlā, *Twenty-third Chapter, describing love of Godhead.*

CHAPTER 24

The Sixty-One Explanations of the Ātmārāma Verse

The following summary of this chapter is given by Śrīla Bhaktivinoda Ṭhākura in his *Amṛta-pravāha-bhāṣya.* According to Śrī Sanātana Gosvāmī's request, Śrī Caitanya Mahāprabhu explained the well-known *Śrīmad-Bhāgavatam* verse beginning *ātmārāmāś ca munayo.* He explained this verse in sixty-one different ways. He analyzed all the words and described each word with its different connotations. Adding the words *ca* and *api,* He described all the different meanings of the verse. He then concluded that all classes of transcendentalists (*jñānīs, karmīs, yogīs*) utilize this verse according to their own interpretation, but if they gave up this process and surrendered to Kṛṣṇa, as indicated by the verse itself, they would be able to comprehend the real meaning of the verse. In this regard, Śrī Caitanya Mahāprabhu narrated a story about how the great sage Nārada converted a hunter into a great Vaiṣṇava, and how this was appreciated by Nārada's friend Parvata Muni. Sanātana Gosvāmī then offered a prayer to Śrī Caitanya Mahāprabhu, and Śrī Caitanya Mahāprabhu explained the glory of *Śrīmad-Bhāgavatam.* After this, the Lord gave Sanātana Gosvāmī a synopsis of *Hari-bhakti-vilāsa,* which Sanātana Gosvāmī later developed into the guiding principle of all Vaiṣṇavas.

TEXT 1

আত্মারামেতি পদ্যার্কস্যার্থাংশূন্ যঃ প্রকাশয়ন্ ।
জগত্তমো জহারাব্যাৎ স চৈতন্যোদয়াচলঃ ॥ ১ ॥

ātmārāmeti padyārkasy-
ārthāṁśūn yaḥ prakāśayan
jagat-tamo jahārāvyāt
sa caitanyodayācalaḥ

SYNONYMS

ātmārāma-iti—beginning with the word *ātmārāma; padya*—verse; *arkasya*—of the sunlike; *artha-aṁśūn*—the shining rays of different meanings; *yaḥ*—who; *prakāśayan*—manifesting; *jagat-tamaḥ*—the darkness of the material world; *jahāra*—

eradicated; *avyāt*—may protect; *saḥ*—He; *caitanya-udaya-acalaḥ*—Śrī Caitanya Mahāprabhu, who is like the eastern horizon, where the sun rises.

TRANSLATION

May Śrī Caitanya Mahāprabhu be glorified. It was He who acted as the eastern horizon where the sun of the ātmārāma verse rises and manifests its rays in the form of different meanings and thus eradicates the darkness of the material world. May He protect the universe.

TEXT 2

জয় জয় শ্রীচৈতন্য জয় নিত্যানন্দ।
জয়াদ্বৈতচন্দ্র জয় গৌরভক্তবৃন্দ ॥ ২ ॥

jaya jaya śrī-caitanya jaya nityānanda
jayādvaita-candra jaya gaura-bhakta-vṛnda

SYNONYMS

jaya jaya—all glories; *śrī-caitanya*—to Lord Caitanya Mahāprabhu; *jaya*—all glories; *nityānanda*—to Lord Nityānanda; *jaya*—all glories; *advaita-candra*—to Advaita Ācārya; *jaya*—all glories; *gaura-bhakta-vṛnda*—to all the devotees of Lord Caitanya Mahāprabhu.

TRANSLATION

All glories to Lord Caitanya! All glories to Lord Nityānanda! All glories to Advaitacandra! And all glories to all the devotees of Lord Caitanya!

TEXT 3

তবে সনাতন প্রভুর চরণে ধরিয়া।
পুনরপি কহে কিছু বিনয় করিয়া ॥ ৩ ॥

tabe sanātana prabhura caraṇe dhariyā
punarapi kahe kichu vinaya kariyā

SYNONYMS

tabe—thereafter; *sanātana*—Sanātana Gosvāmī; *prabhura caraṇe dhariyā*—catching the lotus feet of Śrī Caitanya Mahāprabhu; *punarapi*—again; *kahe*—says; *kichu*—something; *vinaya kariyā*—with great humility.

TRANSLATION

Thereafter, Sanātana Gosvāmī clasped the lotus feet of Śrī Caitanya Mahāprabhu and humbly submitted the following petition.

TEXT 4

'পূর্বে শুনিয়াছোঁ, তুমি সার্বভৌম-স্থানে ।
এক শ্লোকে আঠার অর্থ কৈরাছ ব্যাখ্যানে ॥ ৪ ॥

'pūrve śuniyāchoṅ, tumi sārvabhauma-sthāne
eka śloke āṭhāra artha kairācha vyākhyāne

SYNONYMS

pūrve—formerly; *śuniyāchoṅ*—I heard; *tumi*—You; *sārvabhauma-sthāne*—at the place of Sārvabhauma Bhaṭṭācārya; *eka śloke*—in one verse; *āṭhāra artha*—eighteen meanings; *kairācha vyākhyāne*—have explained.

TRANSLATION

Sanātana Gosvāmī said, "My Lord, I have heard that previously, at the home of Sārvabhauma Bhaṭṭācārya, You explained the ātmārāma verse in eighteen different ways.

TEXT 5

আত্মারামাশ্চ মুনয়ো নির্গ্রন্থা অপ্যুরুক্রমে ।
কুর্বন্ত্যহৈতুকীং ভক্তিমিত্থম্ভূতগুণো হরিঃ ॥ ৫ ॥

ātmārāmāś ca munayo
nirgranthā apy urukrame
kurvanty ahaitukīṁ bhaktim
ittham-bhūta-guṇo hariḥ

SYNONYMS

ātma-ārāmāḥ—persons who take pleasure in being transcendentally situated in the service of the Lord; *ca*—also; *munayaḥ*—great saintly persons who have completely rejected material aspirations, fruitive activities and so forth; *nirgranthāḥ*—without interest in any material desire; *api*—certainly; *urukrame*—unto the Supreme Personality of Godhead, Kṛṣṇa, whose activities are wonderful; *kurvanti*—do; *ahaitukīm*—causeless, or without material desires; *bhaktim*—devotional service; *ittham-bhūta*—so wonderful as to attract the attention of the self-satisfied; *guṇaḥ*—who has transcendental qualities; *hariḥ*—the Supreme Personality of Godhead.

TRANSLATION

" 'Those who are self-satisfied and unattracted by external material desires are also attracted to the loving service of Śrī Kṛṣṇa, whose qualities are

transcendental and whose activities are wonderful. Hari, the Personality of Godhead, is called Kṛṣṇa because He has such transcendentally attractive features.'

PURPORT

This is the famous *ātmārāma* verse from *Śrīmad-Bhāgavatam* (1.7.10).

TEXT 6

আশ্চর্য শুনিয়া মোর উৎকণ্ঠিত মন।
কৃপা করি' কহ যদি, জুড়ায় শ্রবণ ॥' ৬ ॥

āścarya śuniyā mora utkaṇṭhita mana
kṛpā kari' kaha yadi, juḍāya śravaṇa'

SYNONYMS

āścarya—wonderful; *śuniyā*—hearing; *mora*—my; *utkaṇṭhita*—desirous; *mana*—mind; *kṛpā kari'*—showing Your causeless mercy; *kaha yadi*—if You speak; *juḍāya*—pleases; *śravaṇa*—the ear.

TRANSLATION

"I have heard this wonderful story and am therefore very inquisitive to hear it again. If You would kindly repeat it, I would be very pleased to hear."

TEXT 7

প্রভু কহে,—"আমি বাতুল, আমার বচনে।
সার্বভৌম বাতুল তাহা সত্য করি' মানে ॥ ৭ ॥

prabhu kahe,—"āmi vātula, āmāra vacane
sārvabhauma vātula tāhā satya kari' māne

SYNONYMS

prabhu kahe—Śrī Caitanya Mahāprabhu said; *āmi*—I; *vātula*—a madman; *āmāra vacane*—in My words; *sārvabhauma*—Sārvabhauma Bhaṭṭācārya; *vātula*—another madman; *tāhā*—that (My explanation); *satya kari' māne*—took as truth.

TRANSLATION

Śrī Caitanya Mahāprabhu replied, "I am one madman, and Sārvabhauma Bhaṭṭācārya is another. Therefore he took My words to be the truth.

TEXT 8

কিবা প্রলাপিলাঙ, কিছু নাহিক স্মরণে ।
তোমার সঙ্গ-বলে যদি কিছু হয় মনে ॥ ৮ ॥

kibā pralāpilāṅa, kichu nāhika smaraṇe
tomāra saṅga-bale yadi kichu haya mane

SYNONYMS

kibā—what; *pralāpilāṅa*—I have said; *kichu*—anything; *nāhika*—there is not; *smaraṇe*—in memory; *tomāra*—of you; *saṅga-bale*—by the strength of association; *yadi*—if; *kichu*—something; *haya*—there is; *mane*—in My mind.

TRANSLATION

"I do not recall what I spoke in that connection, but if something comes to My mind due to association with you, I shall explain it.

TEXT 9

সহজে আমার কিছু অর্থ নাহি ভাসে ।
তোমা-সবার সঙ্গ-বলে যে কিছু প্রকাশে ॥ ৯ ॥

sahaje āmāra kichu artha nāhi bhāse
tomā-sabāra saṅga-bale ye kichu prakāśe

SYNONYMS

sahaje—generally; *āmāra*—My; *kichu*—any; *artha*—meaning; *nāhi bhāse*—does not manifest; *tomā-sabāra saṅga-bale*—by the strength of your association; *ye*—which; *kichu*—something; *prakāśe*—manifests.

TRANSLATION

"Generally by Myself I cannot give an explanation, but by the strength of your association something may manifest itself.

TEXT 10

একাদশ পদ এই শ্লোকে সুনির্মল ।
পৃথক্ নানা অর্থ পদে করে ঝলমল ॥ ১০ ॥

ekādaśa pada ei śloke sunirmala
pṛthak nānā artha pade kare jhalamala

SYNONYMS

ekādaśa pada—eleven words; *ei*—this; *śloke*—in the verse; *su-nirmala*—very clear; *pṛthak*—separately; *nānā*—various; *artha*—meanings; *pade*—in each word; *kare jhalamala*—are glittering.

TRANSLATION

"There are eleven clear words in this verse, but when they are studied separately, various meanings glitter from each word.

PURPORT

The eleven separate words are (1) *ātmārāmāḥ,* (2) *ca,* (3) *munayaḥ,* (4) *nirgranthāḥ,* (5) *api,* (6) *urukrame,* (7) *kurvanti,* (8) *ahaitukīm,* (9) *bhaktim,* (10) *ittham-bhūta-guṇaḥ,* and (11) *hariḥ*. Śrī Caitanya Mahāprabhu will explain the different connotations and imports of these words.

TEXT 11

'আত্মা'-শব্দে ব্রহ্ম, দেহ, মন, যত্ন, ধৃতি ।
বুদ্ধি, স্বভাব,—এই সাত অর্থ-প্রাপ্তি ॥ ১১ ॥

'ātmā'-śabde brahma, deha, mana, yatna, dhṛti
buddhi, svabhāva,——ei sāta artha-prāpti

SYNONYMS

ātmā-śabde—by the word *ātmā; brahma*—the Absolute Truth; *deha*—the body; *mana*—the mind; *yatna*—endeavor; *dhṛti*—firmness; *buddhi*—intelligence; *sva-bhāva*—nature; *ei sāta*—these seven; *artha-prāpti*—obtainment of meanings.

TRANSLATION

"The seven different meanings of the word ātmā are the Absolute Truth, the body, the mind, endeavor, firmness, intelligence and nature.

TEXT 12

"আত্মা দেহমনোব্রহ্মস্বভাবধৃতিবুদ্ধিষু । প্রযত্নে চ" ইতি ॥১২॥

"ātmā deha-mano-brahma-svabhāva-dhṛti-buddhiṣu
prayatne ca" iti

SYNONYMS

ātmā—the word *ātmā; deha*—the body; *manaḥ*—the mind; *brahma*—the Absolute Truth; *sva-bhāva*—nature; *dhṛti*—firmness; *buddhiṣu*—in the sense of intelligence; *prayatne*—in endeavor; *ca*—and; *iti*—thus.

TRANSLATION

" 'The following are synonyms of the word ātmā: the body, mind, Absolute Truth, natural characteristics, firmness, intelligence and endeavor.'

PURPORT

This is a quotation from the *Viśva-prakāśa* dictionary.

TEXT 13

এই সাতে রমে যেই, সেই আত্মারামগণ ।
আত্মারামগণের আগে করিব গণন ॥ ১৩ ॥

ei sāte rame yei, sei ātmārāma-gaṇa
ātmārāma-gaṇera āge kariba gaṇana

SYNONYMS

ei sāte—in these seven items; *rame*—enjoy; *yei*—those who; *sei*—they; *ātmārāma-gaṇa*—*ātmārāmas;* *ātmārāma-gaṇera*—of the *ātmārāmas;* *āge*—later; *kariba gaṇana*—shall make a count.

TRANSLATION

"The word ātmārāma refers to one who enjoys these seven items [the Absolute Truth, body, mind, and so on]. Later, I shall enumerate the ātmārāmas.

TEXT 14

'মুনি'-আদি শব্দের অর্থ শুন, সনাতন ।
পৃথক্ পৃথক্ অর্থ পাছে করিব মিলন ॥ ১৪ ॥

'muni'-ādi śabdera artha śuna, sanātana
pṛthak pṛthak artha pāche kariba milana

SYNONYMS

muni—the word *muni;* *ādi*—and the other; *śabdera*—of the words; *artha*—the meaning; *śuna*—hear; *sanātana*—My dear Sanātana; *pṛthak pṛthak*—separately; *artha*—meaning; *pāche*—after; *kariba milana*—I shall combine.

TRANSLATION

"My dear Sanātana, first hear the meanings of the other words, beginning with the word muni. I shall first explain their separate meanings, then combine them.

TEXT 15

'মুনি'-শব্দে মননশীল, আর কহে মৌনী ।
তপস্বী, ব্রতী, যতি, আর ঋষি, মুনি ॥ ১৫ ॥

'muni'-śabde manana-śīla, āra kahe maunī
tapasvī, vratī, yati, āra ṛṣi, muni

SYNONYMS

muni-śabde—by the word *muni; manana-śīla*—who is thoughtful; *āra*—also; *kahe*—it means; *maunī*—one who is silent; *tapasvī*—an ascetic; *vratī*—one who keeps great vows; *yati*—one in the renounced order of life; *āra*—and; *ṛṣi*—a saintly person; *muni*—they are called *muni.*

TRANSLATION

"The word muni refers to one who is thoughtful, one who is grave or silent, an ascetic, one who keeps great vows, one in the renounced order, a saint. These are the different meanings of the word muni.

TEXT 16

'নির্গ্রন্থ'-শব্দে কহে, অবিদ্যা-গ্রন্থি-হীন ।
বিধি-নিষেধ-বেদশাস্ত্র-জ্ঞানাদি-বিহীন ॥ ১৬ ॥

'nirgrantha'-śabde kahe, avidyā-granthi-hīna
vidhi-niṣedha-veda-śāstra-jñānādi-vihīna

SYNONYMS

nirgrantha—nirgrantha; śabde—by the word; *kahe*—one means; *avidyā*—of ignorance; *granthi-hīna*—without any knot; *vidhi-niṣedha*—regulative principles of rules and restrictions; *veda-śāstra*—the Vedic literature; *jñāna-ādi*—knowledge, and so on; *vihīna*—without.

TRANSLATION

"The word nirgrantha refers to one who is liberated from the material knots of ignorance. It also refers to one who is devoid of all regulative principles enjoined in the Vedic literature. It also refers to one who does not have knowledge.

TEXT 17

মূর্খ, নীচ, ম্লেচ্ছ আদি শাস্ত্ররিক্তগণ ।
ধনসঞ্চয়ী—নির্গ্রন্থ, আর যে নির্ধন ॥ ১৭ ॥

mūrkha, nīca, mleccha ādi śāstra-rikta-gaṇa
dhana-sañcayī——nirgrantha, āra ye nirdhana

SYNONYMS

mūrkha—foolish, illiterate persons; *nīca*—lowborn; *mleccha*—unclean persons with no principles; *ādi*—and others; *śāstra-rikta-gaṇa*—persons devoid of all regulative principles stated in *śāstra; dhana-sañcayī*—capitalist (one who gathers wealth); *nirgrantha*—called *nirgrantha; āra*—also; *ye*—anyone who; *nirdhana*—without riches.

TRANSLATION

"Nirgrantha also refers to one who is illiterate, lowborn, misbehaved, unregulated and devoid of respect for Vedic literature. The word also refers to one who is a capitalist and to one who has no riches.

TEXT 18

নির্নিশ্চয়ে নিষ্ক্রমার্থে নির্নির্মাণ-নিষেধয়োঃ ।
গ্রন্থো ধনেঽথ সন্দর্ভে বর্ণসংগ্রথনেঽপি চ ॥ ১৮ ॥

nir niścaye niṣ kramārthe
nir nirmāṇa-niṣedhayoḥ
grantho dhane 'tha sandarbhe
varṇa-saṅgrathane 'pi ca

SYNONYMS

niḥ—the prefix *niḥ; niścaye*—in the sense of ascertainment; *niḥ*—the prefix *niḥ; krama-arthe*—in the meaning of succession; *niḥ*—the prefix *niḥ; nirmāṇa*—in the sense of forming; *niṣedhayoḥ*—in the sense of forbidding; *granthaḥ*—the word *grantha; dhane*—in the sense of wealth; *atha*—also; *sandarbhe*—thesis; *varṇa-saṅgrathane*—in the sense of tying together words; *api*—also; *ca*—and.

TRANSLATION

" 'The prefix niḥ may be used for a sense of ascertainment, gradation, construction or forbidding. The word grantha means riches, thesis and composition.'

PURPORT

This is another quotation from the *Viśva-prakāśa* dictionary.

TEXT 19

'উরুক্রম'-শব্দে কহে, বড় যাঁর ক্রম ।
'ক্রম'-শব্দে কহে এই পাদবিক্ষেপণ ॥ ১৯ ॥

'urukrama'-śabde kahe, baḍa yāṅra krama
'krama'-śabde kahe ei pāda-vikṣepaṇa

SYNONYMS

urukrama—urukrama; *śabde*—by this word; *kahe*—one means; *baḍa*—great; *yāṅra*—whose; *krama*—step; *krama-śabde*—in this word *krama; kahe*—one means; *ei*—this; *pāda-vikṣepaṇa*—throwing forth of the foot.

TRANSLATION

"The word urukrama refers to one whose krama [step] is great. The word krama means 'throwing the foot forward,' that is, 'step.'

TEXT 20

শক্তি, কম্প, পরিপাটী, যুক্তি, শক্ত্যে আক্রমণ ।
চরণ-চালনে কাঁপাইল ত্রিভুবন ॥ ২০ ॥

śakti, kampa, paripāṭī, yukti, śaktye ākramaṇa
caraṇa-cālane kāṅpāila tribhuvana

SYNONYMS

śakti—power; *kampa*—trembling; *paripāṭī*—method; *yukti*—argument; *śaktye*—with great force; *ākramaṇa*—attacking; *caraṇa-cālane*—by moving the foot; *kāṅpāila*—caused to tremble; *tri-bhuvana*—the three worlds.

TRANSLATION

"Krama also means power, trembling, a systematic method, argument, and a forcible attack by stepping forward. Thus Vāmana caused the three worlds to tremble.

PURPORT

Uru means very great, and *krama* means step. When Lord Vāmanadeva was offered three steps of land, He expanded His three steps by covering the entire universe. In this way the three worlds trembled, and therefore Śrī Vāmanadeva, the incarnation of Lord Viṣṇu, is referred to as Urukrama.

TEXT 21

বিষ্ণোর্নু বীর্যগণনাং কতমোঽর্হতীহ
যঃ পার্থিবান্যপি কবির্বিমমে রজাংসি ।
চস্কম্ভ যঃ স্বরংহসাস্খলতা ত্রিপৃষ্ঠং
যস্মাত্রিসাম্যসদনাদুরুকম্পয়ানম্ ॥ ২১ ॥

viṣṇor nu vīrya-gaṇanāṁ katamo 'rhatīha
yaḥ pārthivāny api kavir vimame rajāṁsi
caskambha yaḥ sva-raṁhasāskhalatā tripṛṣṭhaṁ
yasmāt trisāmya-sadanād urukampayānam

SYNONYMS

viṣṇoḥ—of Lord Viṣṇu; *nu*—certainly; *vīrya-gaṇanām*—a counting of the different potencies; *katamaḥ*—who; *arhati*—is able to do; *iha*—in this world; *yaḥ*—who; *pārthivāni*—of the element earth; *api*—although; *kaviḥ*—a learned person; *vimame*—has counted; *rajāṁsi*—the atoms; *caskambha*—captured; *yaḥ*—who; *sva*—His own; *raṁhasā*—by potency; *askhalatā*—without hindrances; *tri-pṛṣṭham*—the topmost planet (Satyaloka); *yasmāt*—from some cause; *tri-sāmya*—where there is equilibrium of the three *guṇas; sadanāt*—from the place (from the root of the material world); *urukampayānam*—trembling greatly.

TRANSLATION

" 'Even if a learned man is able to count all the minute atoms in this material world, he still cannot count the potencies of Lord Viṣṇu. In the form of the Vāmana incarnation, Lord Viṣṇu, without hindrance, captured all the planets, beginning from the root of the material world up to Satyaloka. Indeed, He caused every planetary system to tremble by the force of His steps.'

PURPORT

This is a quotation from *Śrīmad-Bhāgavatam* (2.7.40). In the *Ṛg Veda mantra* (1.2.154.1), it is said:

oṁ viṣṇor nu vīryāṇi kaṁ prāvocaṁ
yaḥ pārthivāni vimame rajāṁsi
yo 'skambhayad uttaraṁ sadhasthaṁ
vicakramāṇas tredhorugāyaḥ

TEXT 22

বিভুরূপে ব্যাপে, শক্ত্যে ধারণ-পোষণ ।
মাধুর্যশক্ত্যে গোলোক, ঐশ্বর্যে পরব্যোম ॥ ২২ ॥

vibhu-rūpe vyāpe, śaktye dhāraṇa-poṣaṇa
mādhurya-śaktye goloka, aiśvarye paravyoma

SYNONYMS

vibhu-rūpe—in His all-pervasive feature; *vyāpe*—expands; *śaktye*—by His potency; *dhāraṇa-poṣaṇa*—maintaining and nourishing; *mādhurya-śaktye*—by

His potency of conjugal love; *goloka*—the planetary system Goloka Vṛndāvana; *aiśvarye*—and by opulence; *para-vyoma*—the spiritual world.

TRANSLATION

"Through His all-pervasive feature, the Supreme Personality of Godhead expanded the entire creation. He is holding and maintaining this creation by His extraordinary potency. By His conjugal potency, He maintains the planetary system known as Goloka Vṛndāvana. Through His six opulences, He maintains many Vaikuṇṭha planets.

PURPORT

In His gigantic form, Lord Kṛṣṇa has covered the creation. He holds all the planetary systems and maintains them by His inconceivable potencies. Similarly, He is maintaining His personal abode, Goloka Vṛndāvana, through His conjugal love, and He is maintaining the spiritual world containing the Vaikuṇṭha planets by His opulences.

TEXT 23

মায়া-শক্ত্যে ব্রহ্মাণ্ডাদি-পরিপাটী-সৃজন।
'উরুক্রম'-শব্দের এই অর্থ নিরূপণ॥ ২৩ ॥

māyā-śaktye brahmāṇḍādi-paripāṭī-sṛjana
'urukrama'-śabdera ei artha nirūpaṇa

SYNONYMS

māyā-śaktye—by His external potency; *brahmāṇḍa-ādi*—of material universes and so on; *paripāṭī*—an orderly arrangement; *sṛjana*—creating; *urukrama-śabdera*—of the word *urukrama; ei*—this; *artha*—of the meaning; *nirūpaṇa*—ascertainment.

TRANSLATION

"The word urukrama indicates the Supreme Personality of Godhead, who, by His external potency, has perfectly created innumerable universes.

TEXT 24

"ক্রমঃ শক্তৌ পরিপাট্যাং ক্রমশ্চালনকম্পয়োঃ ॥" ২৪ ॥

"kramaḥ śaktau paripāṭyāṁ kramaś cālana-kampayoḥ"

SYNONYMS

kramaḥ—the word *krama; śaktau*—in the meaning of potency; *paripāṭyām*—in the meaning of systematic arrangement; *kramaḥ*—the word *krama; cālana*—in moving; *kampayoḥ*—or in trembling.

TRANSLATION

" 'These are the different meanings of the word krama. It is used in the sense of potency, systematic arrangement, step, moving or trembling.'

PURPORT

This is a quotation from the *Viśva-prakāśa* dictionary. The Supreme Personality of Godhead is all-pervasive. Not only does He carry the three worlds by His inconceivable energy, but He maintains them also. He is also maintaining His spiritual planet, Goloka Vṛndāvana, by His conjugal love, and He is maintaining the Vaikuṇṭhalokas by His opulences. He maintains these material universes through the external energy. Material universes are perfectly situated because they are created by the Supreme Personality of Godhead.

TEXT 25

'কুর্বন্তি'-পদ এই পরস্মৈপদ হয়।
কৃষ্ণসুখনিমিত্ত ভজনে তাৎপর্য কহয়॥ ২৫॥

'kurvanti'-pada ei parasmaipada haya
kṛṣṇa-sukha-nimitta bhajane tātparya kahaya

SYNONYMS

kurvanti—they do (for others); *pada*—the word; *ei*—this; *parasmaipada*—a verb form indicating things done for others; *haya*—is; *kṛṣṇa-sukha-nimitta*—to satisfy Kṛṣṇa; *bhajane*—in devotional service; *tātparya*—the purport; *kahaya*—is said.

TRANSLATION

"The word kurvanti, which means 'they do something for others,' is a form of the verb 'things done for others.' It is used in connection with devotional service, which must be executed for the satisfaction of Kṛṣṇa. That is the purport of the word kurvanti.

PURPORT

In Sanskrit the verb "to do" has two forms, technically called *parasmaipada* and *ātmanepada*. When things are done for one's personal satisfaction, the form is called *ātmanepada*. In that case, the word "do" in English is *kurvante* in Sanskrit. When things are done for others, the verb form changes to *kurvanti*. Thus Śrī Caitanya Mahāprabhu informed Sanātana Gosvāmī that in the *ātmārāma* verse the verb *kurvanti* means that things should be done only for the satisfaction of Kṛṣṇa. This is supported by the grammarian Pāṇini. The verb is formed as *ātmanepada* when the work is to be done for one's own benefit, and when it is done for others, it is called *parasmaipada*. Thus the verb is formed according to whether something is done for one's self-satisfaction or for another's satisfaction.

TEXT 26

"স্বরিতঞিতঃ কর্ত্রভিপ্রায়ে ক্রিয়াফলে ॥" ২৬ ॥

"svaritañitaḥ kartrabhiprāye kriyā-phale"

SYNONYMS

svarita-ñitaḥ—of verbs having an indicatory *ñ* or a *svarita* accent; *kartṛ-abhiprāye*—is meant for the agent; *kriyā-phale*—when the fruit of the action.

TRANSLATION

" 'The terminations of the ātmanepada are employed when the fruit of the action accrues to the agent of verbs having an indicatory ñ or a svarita accent.'

PURPORT

This is a quotation from Pāṇini's *sūtras* (1.3.72).

TEXT 27

'হেতু'-শব্দে কহে—ভুক্তি-আদি বাঞ্ছান্তরে ।
ভুক্তি, সিদ্ধি, মুক্তি—মুখ্য এই তিন প্রকারে ॥ ২৭ ॥

'hetu'-śabde kahe——bhukti-ādi vāñchāntare
bhukti, siddhi, mukti——mukhya ei tina prakāre

SYNONYMS

hetu—cause; *śabde*—by the word; *kahe*—it is said; *bhukti*—enjoying the result by oneself; *ādi*—and so on; *vāñchā-antare*—because of a different ambition; *bhukti*—enjoying the result of action; *siddhi*—the perfection of doing something; *mukti*—liberation; *mukhya*—chief; *ei*—these; *tina prakāre*—in three ways.

TRANSLATION

"The word hetu [cause] means that a thing is done for some motive. There can be three motives. One may act to enjoy the result personally, to achieve some material perfection, or to act in such a way that one may be liberated.

TEXT 28

এক ভুক্তি কহে, ভোগ—অনন্ত-প্রকার ।
সিদ্ধি—অষ্টাদশ, মুক্তি—পঞ্চবিধাকার ॥ ২৮ ॥

eka bhukti kahe, bhoga——ananta-prakāra
siddhi——aṣṭādaśa, mukti——pañca-vidhākāra

SYNONYMS

eka—first; *bhukti*—material enjoyment by doing something; *kahe*—is known; *bhoga*—enjoyment; *ananta-prakāra*—unlimited varieties; *siddhi*—the yogic perfections; *aṣṭādaśa*—eighteen in number; *mukti*—liberation; *pañca-vidhā-ākāra*—five varieties.

TRANSLATION

"First we take the word bhukti [material enjoyment], which is of unlimited variety. We may also take the word siddhi [perfection], which has eighteen varieties. Similarly, the word mukti has five varieties.

TEXT 29

এই যাঁহা নাহি, তাহা ভক্তি—'অহৈতুকী' ।
যাহা হৈতে বশ হয় শ্রীকৃষ্ণ কৌতুকী ॥ ২৯ ॥

ei yāṅhā nāhi, tāhā bhakti——'ahaitukī'
yāhā haite vaśa haya śrī-kṛṣṇa kautukī

SYNONYMS

ei—these; *yāṅhā*—where; *nāhi*—not existing; *tāhā*—that; *bhakti*—the platform of devotional service; *ahaitukī*—unmotivated; *yāhā haite*—by which; *vaśa haya*—comes under control; *śrī-kṛṣṇa*—Lord Śrī Kṛṣṇa; *kautukī*—the most funny.

TRANSLATION

"Causeless devotional service is unmotivated by sense enjoyment, perfection or liberation. When one is freed from all these contaminations, he can bring Lord Kṛṣṇa, who is very funny, under control.

TEXT 30

'ভক্তি'-শব্দের অর্থ হয় দশবিধাকার ।
এক—'সাধন', 'প্রেমভক্তি'—নব প্রকার ॥ ৩০ ॥

'bhakti'-śabdera artha haya daśa-vidhākāra
eka——'sādhana', 'prema-bhakti'——nava prakāra

SYNONYMS

bhakti—bhakti; *śabdera*—of this word; *artha*—meanings; *haya*—are; *daśa-vidhā-ākāra*—ten varieties; *eka*—one; *sādhana*—the execution of regulative devotional service; *prema-bhakti*—ecstatic love; *nava prakāra*—nine kinds.

TRANSLATION

"There are ten meanings to the word bhakti, devotional service. One is execution of devotional service according to the regulative principles, and the other, called prema-bhakti [ecstatic love] has nine varieties.

PURPORT

The nine varieties are *rati, prema, sneha, māna, praṇaya, rāga, anurāga, bhāva* and *mahābhāva*—attraction, love, affection, adverse feelings, intimacy, attachment, subattachment, ecstatic love and sublime ecstatic love. For the execution of devotional service according to regulative principles, there is only one meaning.

TEXT 31

'রতি'-লক্ষণা, 'প্রেম'-লক্ষণা, ইত্যাদি প্রচার ।
ভাবরূপা, মহাভাব-লক্ষণরূপা আর ॥ ৩১ ॥

'rati'-lakṣaṇā, 'prema'-lakṣaṇā, ityādi pracāra
bhāva-rūpā, mahābhāva-lakṣaṇa-rūpā āra

SYNONYMS

rati—of attraction; *lakṣaṇā*—the symptoms; *prema*—of love; *lakṣaṇā*—the symptoms; *iti-ādi*—and so on; *pracāra*—are known; *bhāva-rūpā*—in the form of ecstatic love; *mahā-bhāva*—of higher ecstatic love; *lakṣaṇa-rūpā*—there are many symptoms; *āra*—other.

TRANSLATION

"Next are explained the symptoms of love of Godhead, which can be divided into nine varieties, beginning with attraction up to ecstatic love and finally up to the topmost ecstatic love [mahābhāva].

TEXT 32

শান্ত-ভক্তের রতি বাড়ে 'প্রেম'-পর্যন্ত ।
দাস্য-ভক্তের রতি হয় 'রাগ'-দশা-অন্ত ॥ ৩২ ॥

śānta-bhaktera rati bāḍe 'prema'-paryanta
dāsya-bhaktera rati haya 'rāga'-daśā-anta

SYNONYMS

śānta-bhaktera—of devotees on the platform of neutrality; *rati*—attraction; *bāḍe*—increases; *prema-paryanta*—up to love of Godhead; *dāsya-bhaktera*—of devotees on the platform of servitude; *rati*—attraction; *haya*—increases; *rāga-daśā-anta*—up to the point of spontaneous attachment.

TRANSLATION

"The attraction to Kṛṣṇa of devotees on the platform of neutrality increases up to love of Godhead [prema], and the attraction of devotees on the platform of servitorship increases to spontaneous attachment [rāga].

TEXT 33

সখাগণের রতি হয় 'অনুরাগ' পর্যন্ত ।
পিতৃ-মাতৃ-স্নেহ আদি 'অনুরাগ'-অন্ত ॥ ৩৩ ॥

sakhā-gaṇera rati haya 'anurāga' paryanta
pitṛ-mātṛ-sneha ādi 'anurāga'-anta

SYNONYMS

sakhā-gaṇera—of the friends; *rati*—the attraction; *haya*—becomes; *anurāga paryanta*—up to subecstatic love; *pitṛ-mātṛ-sneha*—paternal love; *ādi*—and so on; *anurāga-anta*—up to the end of subecstatic love.

TRANSLATION

"Devotees in Vṛndāvana who are friends of the Lord can increase their ecstatic love to the point of anurāga. Paternal affectionate lovers, Kṛṣṇa's father and mother, can increase their love of Godhead up to the anurāga point also.

TEXT 34

কান্তাগণের রতি পায় 'মহাভাব'-সীমা ।
'ভক্তি'-শব্দের এই সব অর্থের মহিমা ॥ ৩৪ ॥

kāntā-gaṇera rati pāya 'mahābhāva'-sīmā
'bhakti'-śabdera ei saba arthera mahimā

SYNONYMS

kāntā-gaṇera—of the devotees in conjugal love; *rati*—the attraction; *pāya*—attain; *mahā-bhāva-sīmā*—the limit of *mahābhāva; bhakti*—devotional service; *śabdera*—of the word; *ei saba*—all these; *arthera*—of the meanings; *mahimā*—of the glories.

TRANSLATION

"The gopīs of Vṛndāvana who are attached to Kṛṣṇa in conjugal love can increase their ecstatic love up to the point of mahābhāva [the greatest ecstatic love]. These are some of the glorious meanings of the word bhakti, devotional service.

TEXT 35

'ইত্থম্ভূতগুণঃ'-শব্দের শুনহ ব্যাখ্যান ।
'ইত্থং'-শব্দের ভিন্ন অর্থ, 'গুণ'-শব্দের আন ॥ ৩৫ ॥

'ittham-bhūta-guṇaḥ'-śabdera śunaha vyākhyāna
'itthaṁ'-śabdera bhinna artha, 'guṇa'-śabdera āna

SYNONYMS

ittham-bhūta-guṇaḥ—having qualities like this; *śabdera*—of the word; *śunaha*—please hear; *vyākhyāna*—the explanation; *ittham*—*ittham; śabdera*—of the word; *bhinna artha*—different meanings; *guṇa*—*guṇa; śabdera*—of the word; *āna*—other.

TRANSLATION

"Please hear the meaning of the word ittham-bhūta-guṇa, which is found in the ātmārāma verse. Ittham-bhūta has different meanings, and guṇa has other meanings.

TEXT 36

'ইত্থম্ভূত'-শব্দের অর্থ—পূর্ণানন্দময় ।
যাঁর আগে ব্রহ্মানন্দ তৃণপ্রায় হয় ॥ ৩৬ ॥

'ittham-bhūta'-śabdera artha—pūrṇānandamaya
yāṅra āge brahmānanda tṛṇa-prāya haya

SYNONYMS

ittham-bhūta-śabdera artha—the meaning or import of the word *ittham-bhūta; pūrṇa-ānanda-maya*—full of transcendental bliss; *yāṅra āge*—in front of which; *brahma-ānanda*—the transcendental bliss derived from impersonalism; *tṛṇa-prāya*—just like straw; *haya*—is.

TRANSLATION

"The word ittham-bhūta is transcendentally exalted because it means 'full of transcendental bliss.' Before this transcendental bliss, the bliss derived from merging into the existence of the Absolute [brahmānanda] becomes like a piece of straw in comparison.

TEXT 37

ত্বৎসাক্ষাৎকরণাহ্লাদবিশুদ্ধাব্ধিস্থিতস্য মে ।
সুখানি গোষ্পদায়ন্তে ব্রাহ্মাণ্যপি জগদ্‌গুরো ॥ ৩৭ ॥

tvat-sākṣāt-karaṇāhlāda-
viśuddhābdhi-sthitasya me
sukhāni goṣpadāyante
brāhmāṇy api jagad-guro

SYNONYMS

tvat—Your; *sākṣāt*—meeting; *karaṇa*—such action; *āhlāda*—pleasure; *vi-śuddha*—spiritually purified; *abdhi*—ocean; *sthitasya*—being situated; *me*—by me; *sukhāni*—happiness; *goṣpadāyante*—a small hole created by the hoof of a calf; *brāhmāṇi*—the pleasure derived from impersonal Brahman understanding; *api*—also; *jagat-guro*—O master of the universe.

TRANSLATION

" 'My dear Lord, O master of the universe, since I have directly seen You, my transcendental bliss has taken the shape of a great ocean. Being situated in that ocean, I now realize all other so-called happiness to be like the water contained in the hoofprint of a calf.'

PURPORT

This is a verse from the *Hari-bhakti-sudhodaya* (14.36).

TEXT 38

সর্বাকর্ষক, সর্বাহ্লাদক, মহারসায়ন ।
আপনার বলে করে সর্ব-বিস্মারণ ॥ ৩৮ ॥

sarvākarṣaka, sarvāhlādaka, mahā-rasāyana
āpanāra bale kare sarva-vismāraṇa

SYNONYMS

sarva-ākarṣaka—all-attractive; *sarva-āhlādaka*—all-pleasing; *mahā-rasa-ayana*—the complete abode of transcendental mellow; *āpanāra bale*—by His own strength; *kare*—causes; *sarva-vismāraṇa*—forgetfulness of all other bliss.

TRANSLATION

"Lord Kṛṣṇa is so exalted that He is more attractive than anything else and more pleasing than anything else. He is the most sublime abode of bliss. By His own strength, He causes one to forget all other ecstasies.

TEXT 39

ভুক্তি-মুক্তি-সিদ্ধি-সুখ ছাড়য় যার গন্ধে ।
অলৌকিক শক্তি-গুণে কৃষ্ণকৃপায় বান্ধে ॥ ৩৯ ॥

bhukti-mukti-siddhi-sukha chāḍaya yāra gandhe
alaukika śakti-guṇe kṛṣṇa-kṛpāya bāndhe

SYNONYMS

bhukti—material happiness; *mukti*—liberation from material suffering; *siddhi*—the perfection of mystic *yoga; sukha*—the happiness derived from these things; *chāḍaya*—one gives up; *yāra*—of which; *gandhe*—simply by the slight fragrance; *alaukika*—uncommon, transcendental; *śakti-guṇe*—by the power and quality; *kṛṣṇa-kṛpāya*—by the mercy of Lord Kṛṣṇa; *bāndhe*—one becomes bound.

TRANSLATION

"Pure devotional service is so sublime that one can very easily forget the happiness derived from material happiness, material liberation and mystic or yogic perfection. Thus the devotee is bound by Kṛṣṇa's mercy and His uncommon power and qualifications.

TEXT 40

শাস্ত্রযুক্তি নাহি ইহাঁ সিদ্ধান্ত-বিচার ।
এই স্বভাব-গুণে, যাতে মাধুর্যের সার ॥ ৪০ ॥

śāstra-yukti nāhi ihāṅ siddhānta-vicāra
ei svabhāva-guṇe, yāte mādhuryera sāra

SYNONYMS

śāstra-yukti—logic on the basis of revealed scripture; *nāhi*—there is not; *ihāṅ*—here; *siddhānta-vicāra*—consideration of logical conclusions; *ei*—this; *svabhāva-guṇe*—a natural quality; *yāte*—in which; *mādhuryera sāra*—the essence of all transcendental bliss.

TRANSLATION

"When one is attracted to Kṛṣṇa on the transcendental platform, there is no longer any logical argument on the basis of revealed scripture, nor are there considerations of such conclusions. This is His transcendental quality that is the essence of all transcendental sweetness.

TEXT 41

'গুণ' শব্দের অর্থ—কৃষ্ণের গুণ অনন্ত ।
সচ্চিদ্রূপ-গুণ সর্ব পূর্ণানন্দ ॥ ৪১ ॥

'guṇa' śabdera artha——kṛṣṇera guṇa ananta
sac-cid-rūpa-guṇa sarva pūrṇānanda

SYNONYMS

guṇa śabdera artha—the meaning of the word *guṇa; kṛṣṇera guṇa ananta*—Kṛṣṇa has unlimited qualities; *sat-cit-rūpa-guṇa*—such qualities are spiritual and eternal; *sarva pūrṇa-ānanda*—full of all transcendental bliss.

TRANSLATION

"The word guṇa means 'quality.' The qualities of Kṛṣṇa are transcendentally situated and are unlimited in quantity. All of the spiritual qualities are full of transcendental bliss.

TEXT 42

ঐশ্বর্য-মাধুর্য-কারুণ্যে স্বরূপ-পূর্ণতা ।
ভক্তবাৎসল্য, আত্মপর্যন্ত বদান্যতা ॥ ৪২ ॥

aiśvarya-mādhurya-kāruṇye svarūpa-pūrṇatā
bhakta-vātsalya, ātma-paryanta vadānyatā

SYNONYMS

aiśvarya—opulence; *mādhurya*—transcendental sweetness; *kāruṇye*—mercy; *svarūpa-pūrṇatā*—fullness of spiritual value; *bhakta-vātsalya*—affection for the devotee; *ātma-paryanta*—up to the point of His personal self; *vadānyatā*—magnanimity.

TRANSLATION

"Kṛṣṇa's transcendental qualities such as opulence, sweetness and mercy are perfect and full. As far as Kṛṣṇa's affectionate leaning toward His devotees is concerned, He is so magnanimous that He can give Himself to His devotees.

TEXT 43

অলৌকিক রূপ, রস, সৌরভাদি গুণ ।
কারো মন কোন গুণে করে আকর্ষণ ॥ ৪৩ ॥

alaukika rūpa, rasa, saurabhādi guṇa
kāro mana kona guṇe kare ākarṣaṇa

SYNONYMS

alaukika rūpa—uncommon beauty; *rasa*—mellows; *saurabha-ādi guṇa*—qualities like transcendental fragrance; *kāro mana*—the mind of a devotee; *kona guṇe*—by some particular quality; *kare*—does; *ākarṣaṇa*—attracting.

TRANSLATION

"Kṛṣṇa has unlimited qualities. The devotees are attracted by His uncommon beauty, mellows and fragrance. Thus they are differently situated in the different transcendental mellows. Therefore Kṛṣṇa is called all-attractive.

TEXT 44

সনকাদির মন হরিল সৌরভাদি গুণে ॥ ৪৪ ॥

sanakādira mana harila saurabhādi guṇe

SYNONYMS

sanaka-ādira mana—the minds of saintly sages like Sanaka and Sanātana; *harila*—attracted; *saurabha-ādi*—such as the transcendental aroma of His lotus feet; *guṇe*—by the quality.

TRANSLATION

"The minds of the four boy sages [Sanaka, Sanātana, Sanandana and Sanatkumāra] were attracted to the lotus feet of Kṛṣṇa by the aroma of the tulasī that had been offered to the Lord.

TEXT 45

তস্যারবিন্দনয়নস্য পদারবিন্দ-
কিঞ্জল্কমিশ্রতুলসীমকরন্দবায়ুঃ ।
অন্তর্গতঃ স্ববিবরেণ চকার তেষাং
সংক্ষোভমক্ষরজুষামপি চিত্ততন্বোঃ ॥ ৪৫ ॥

tasyāravinda-nayanasya padāravinda-
kiñjalka-miśra-tulasī-makaranda-vāyuḥ
antargataḥ svavivareṇa cakāra teṣāṁ
saṅkṣobham akṣara-juṣām api citta-tanvoḥ

SYNONYMS

tasya—of Him; *aravinda-nayanasya*—of the Supreme Personality of Godhead, whose eyes are like the petals of a lotus; *pada-aravinda*—of the lotus feet; *kiñjalka*—with saffron; *miśra*—mixed; *tulasī*—of *tulasī* leaves; *makaranda*—with the aroma; *vāyuḥ*—the air; *antargataḥ*—entered; *sva-vivareṇa*—through the nostrils; *cakāra*—created; *teṣām*—of them; *saṅkṣobham*—strong agitation; *akṣara-juṣām*—of the impersonally self-realized (Kumāras); *api*—also; *citta-tanvoḥ*—of the mind and body.

TRANSLATION

" 'When the breeze carrying the aroma of tulasī leaves and saffron from the lotus feet of the lotus-eyed Personality of Godhead entered through the nostrils into the hearts of those sages [the Kumāras], they experienced a change in both body and mind, even though they were attached to impersonal Brahman understanding.'

PURPORT

This is a verse from *Śrīmad-Bhāgavatam* (3.15.43). For an explanation, see *Madhya-līlā* (17.142).

TEXT 46

শুকদেবের মন হরিল লীলা-শ্রবণে ॥ ৪৬ ॥

śukadevera mana harila līlā-śravaṇe

SYNONYMS

śukadevera—of Śukadeva Gosvāmī; *mana*—the mind; *harila*—carried away; *līlā-śravaṇe*—by remembering the pastimes of the Lord.

TRANSLATION

"Śukadeva's mind was carried away by remembering the pastimes of the Lord.

TEXT 47

পরিনিষ্ঠিতোঽপি নৈর্গুণ্যে উত্তমঃশ্লোকলীলয়া।
গৃহীতচেতা রাজর্ষে আখ্যানং যদধীতবান্ ॥ ৪৭ ॥

pariniṣṭhito 'pi nairguṇye
uttamaḥśloka-līlayā
gṛhīta-cetā rājarṣe
ākhyānaṁ yad adhītavān

SYNONYMS

pariniṣṭhitaḥ—situated; *api*—although; *nairguṇye*—in the transcendental position, freed from the material modes of nature; *uttamaḥ-śloka-līlayā*—by the pastimes of the Supreme Personality of Godhead, Uttamaḥśloka; *gṛhīta-cetā*—the mind became fully taken over; *rājarṣe*—O great King; *ākhyānam*—the narration; *yat*—which; *adhītavān*—studied.

TRANSLATION

" 'Śukadeva Gosvāmī addressed Parīkṣit Mahārāja, "My dear King, although I was fully situated in the transcendental position, I was nonetheless attracted to the pastimes of Lord Kṛṣṇa. Therefore I studied Śrīmad-Bhāgavatam from my father." '

PURPORT

This is a quotation from *Śrīmad-Bhāgavatam* (2.1.9).

TEXT 48

স্বসুখনিভৃতচেতাস্তদ্‌ব্যুদস্তান্যভাবোঽ-
প্যজিতরুচিরলীলাকৃষ্টসারস্তদীয়ম্।
ব্যতনুত কৃপয়া যস্তত্ত্বদীপং পুরাণং
তমখিলবৃজিনঘ্নং ব্যাস-সূনুং নতোঽস্মি ॥ ৪৮ ॥

svasukha-nibhṛta-cetās tad-vyudastānya-bhāvo
'py ajita-rucira-līlākṛṣṭa-sāras tadīyam
vyatanuta kṛpayā yas tattva-dīpaṁ purāṇaṁ
tam akhila-vṛjina-ghnaṁ vyāsa-sūnuṁ nato 'smi

SYNONYMS

sva-sukha-nirbhṛta-cetāḥ—whose mind was always fully absorbed in the happiness of self-realization; *tat*—by that; *vyudasta-anya-bhāvaḥ*—being freed from all other attractions; *api*—although; *ajita-rucira-līlā*—by the most attractive pastimes of Ajita, the Supreme Personality of Godhead; *ākṛṣṭa*—attracted; *sāraḥ*—whose heart; *tadīyam*—in relation to the Lord; *vyatanuta*—described and spread; *kṛpayā*—out of mercy; *yaḥ*—he who; *tattva-dīpam*—which is the light of the Absolute Truth; *purāṇam*—the supplementary Vedic literature *Śrīmad-Bhāgavatam; tam*—to him; *akhila-vṛjina-ghnam*—who can destroy all kinds of material misery; *vyāsa-sūnum*—Śukadeva Gosvāmī, the son of Vyāsadeva; *nataḥ asmi*—I offer my respectful obeisances.

TRANSLATION

" 'I offer my respectful obeisances unto Śrīla Śukadeva Gosvāmī, the son of Vyāsadeva. He is the destroyer of all sinful reactions and is full in self-realization and bliss. Because of this, he has no other desire. Still, he was attracted by the transcendental pastimes of the Supreme Personality of Godhead, and out of compassion for the people, he described the transcendental historical literature called Śrīmad-Bhāgavatam. This is compared to the light of the Absolute Truth.'

PURPORT

This verse is from *Śrīmad-Bhāgavatam* (12.12.68).

TEXT 49

শ্রীঅঙ্গ-রূপে হরে গোপিকার মন ॥ ৪৯ ॥

śrī-aṅga-rūpe hare gopikāra mana

SYNONYMS

śrī-aṅga—of His transcendental body; *rūpe*—by the beauty; *hare*—attracts; *gopikāra mana*—the minds of the *gopīs.*

TRANSLATION

"Lord Śrī Kṛṣṇa attracts the minds of all the gopīs with His beautiful transcendental bodily features.

TEXT 50

বীক্ষ্যালকাবৃতমুখং তব কুণ্ডলশ্রি-
গণ্ডস্থলাধরসুধং হসিতাবলোকম্ ।

দত্তাভয়ঞ্চ ভুজদণ্ডযুগং বিলোক্য
বক্ষঃ শ্রিয়ৈকরমণঞ্চ ভবাম দাস্যঃ ॥ ৫০ ;

vīkṣyālakāvṛta-mukhaṁ tava kuṇḍala-śri-
gaṇḍa-sthalādhara-sudhaṁ hasitāvalokam
dattābhayaṁ ca bhuja-daṇḍa-yugaṁ vilokya
vakṣaḥ śriyaika-ramaṇaṁ ca bhavāma dāsyaḥ

SYNONYMS

vīkṣya—seeing; *alaka-āvṛta-mukham*—face decorated with curling tresses of hair; *tava*—Your; *kuṇḍala-śri*—beauty of earrings; *gaṇḍa-sthala*—falling on Your cheeks; *adhara-sudham*—and the nectar from Your lips; *hasita-avalokam*—Your smiling glance; *datta-abhayam*—which assure fearlessness; *ca*—and; *bhuja-daṇḍa-yugam*—the two arms; *vilokya*—by seeing; *vakṣaḥ*—chest; *śriyā*—by the beauty; *eka-ramaṇam*—chiefly producing conjugal attraction; *ca*—and; *bhavāma*—we have become; *dāsyaḥ*—Your maidservants.

TRANSLATION

" 'Dear Kṛṣṇa, we have simply surrendered ourselves as Your maidservants, for we have seen Your beautiful face decorated with tresses of hair, Your earrings falling upon Your cheeks and the nectar of Your lips. We have also seen the beauty of Your smile and have been embraced by Your arms, which give us courage. Because we have seen Your chest, which is beautiful and broad, we have surrendered ourselves.'

PURPORT

This verse from *Śrīmad-Bhāgavatam* (10.29.39) was spoken by the *gopīs* when they arrived near Kṛṣṇa for the *rāsa* dance on a full moonlit night. The attracted *gopīs* were awestruck, and they began to speak about how they came to Kṛṣṇa to enjoy the *rāsa* dance.

TEXT 51

রূপ-গুণ-শ্রবণে রুক্মিণ্যাদির আকর্ষণ ॥ ৫১ ॥

rūpa-guṇa-śravaṇe rukmiṇy-ādira ākarṣaṇa

SYNONYMS

rūpa—beauty; *guṇa*—qualities; *śravaṇe*—by hearing; *rukmiṇī-ādira*—of the queens, headed by Rukmiṇī; *ākarṣaṇa*—attracting.

TRANSLATION

"The queens in Dvārakā, who are headed by Rukmiṇī, are also attracted to Kṛṣṇa simply by hearing about His transcendental beauty and qualities.

TEXT 52

শ্রুত্বা গুণান্ ভুবনসুন্দর শৃণ্বতাং তে
নির্বিশ্য কর্ণবিবরৈর্হরতোঽঙ্গতাপম্ ।
রূপং দৃশাং দৃশিমতামখিলার্থলাভং
ত্বয্যচ্যুতাবিশতি চিত্তমপত্রপং মে ॥ ৫২ ॥

śrutvā guṇān bhuvana-sundara śṛṇvatāṁ te
nirviśya karṇa-vivarair harato 'ṅga-tāpam
rūpaṁ dṛśāṁ dṛśimatām akhilārtha-lābhaṁ
tvayy acyutāviśati cittam apatrapaṁ me

SYNONYMS

śrutvā—hearing; *guṇān*—the transcendental qualities; *bhuvana-sundara*—O most beautiful in the whole creation; *śṛṇvatām*—of those hearing; *te*—Your; *nirviśya*—entering; *karṇa-vivaraiḥ*—by the holes of the ears; *harataḥ aṅga-tāpam*—decreasing all the miserable conditions of the body; *rūpam*—the beauty; *dṛśām*—of the eyes; *dṛśimatām*—of those who can see; *akhila-artha-lābham*—the achievement of all kinds of gains; *tvayi*—unto You; *acyuta*—O infallible one; *āviśati*—enters; *cittam*—the consciousness; *apatrapam*—without shame; *me*—my.

TRANSLATION

" 'O most beautiful Kṛṣṇa, I have heard about Your transcendental qualities from others, and therefore all my bodily miseries are relieved. If one sees Your transcendental beauty, his eyes have attained everything profitable in life. O infallible one, I have become shameless after hearing of Your qualities, and I have become attracted to You.'

PURPORT

This verse (*Śrīmad-Bhāgavatam* 10.52.37) was written by Rukmiṇīdevī in a letter to Kṛṣṇa inviting Him to kidnap her. Śukadeva Gosvāmī described this to Mahārāja Parīkṣit when the King asked him how Rukmiṇī had been kidnapped. Rukmiṇī had heard about Kṛṣṇa's qualities from different people, and after she heard about them, she decided to accept Kṛṣṇa as her husband. Everything had been arranged for her marriage to Śiśupāla; therefore she wrote a letter to Kṛṣṇa, which she sent through a *brāhmaṇa,* and invited Him to kidnap her.

TEXT 53

বংশী-গীতে হরে কৃষ্ণ লক্ষ্ম্যাদির মন ॥ ৫৩ ॥

vaṁśī-gīte hare kṛṣṇa lakṣmy-ādira mana

SYNONYMS

vaṁśī-gīte—by the vibration of His flute; *hare*—attracts; *kṛṣṇa*—Lord Kṛṣṇa; *lakṣmī-ādira*—of the goddess of fortune and others; *mana*—the mind.

TRANSLATION

"Lord Kṛṣṇa even attracts the mind of the goddess of fortune simply by vibrating His transcendental flute.

TEXT 54

কস্যানুভাবোঽস্য ন দেব বিদ্মহে
তবাঙ্ঘ্রিরেণুস্পরশাধিকারঃ ।
যদ্বাঞ্ছয়া শ্রীর্ললনাচরত্তপো
বিহায় কামান্ সুচিরং ধৃতব্রতা ॥ ৫৪ ॥

kasyānubhāvo 'sya na deva vidmahe
tavāṅghri-reṇu-sparaśādhikāraḥ
yad-vāñchayā śrīr lalanācarat tapo
vihāya kāmān suciraṁ dhṛta-vratā

SYNONYMS

kasya—of what; *anubhāvaḥ*—a result; *asya*—of the serpent (Kāliya); *na*—not; *deva*—O Lord; *vidmahe*—we know; *tava-aṅghri*—of Your lotus feet; *reṇu*—of the dust; *sparaśa*—for touching; *adhikāraḥ*—qualification; *yat*—which; *vāñchayā*—by desiring; *śrīḥ*—the goddess of fortune; *lalanā*—the topmost woman; *acarat*—performed; *tapaḥ*—austerity; *vihāya*—giving up; *kāmān*—all desires; *suciram*—for a long time; *dhṛta*—a law upheld; *vratā*—as a vow.

TRANSLATION

" 'O Lord, we do not know how the serpent Kāliya attained such an opportunity to be touched by the dust of Your lotus feet. For this end, the goddess of

fortune performed austerities for centuries, giving up all other desires and taking austere vows. Indeed, we do not know how this serpent Kāliya got such an opportunity.'

PURPORT

This verse from *Śrīmad-Bhāgavatam* (10.16.36) was spoken by the wives of the Kāliya demon.

TEXT 55

যোগ্যভাবে জগতে যত যুবতীর গণ ॥ ৫৫ ॥

yogya-bhāve jagate yata yuvatīra gaṇa

SYNONYMS

yogya-bhāve—by proper behavior; *jagate*—within the three worlds; *yata*—all; *yuvatīra gaṇa*—the groups of young girls.

TRANSLATION

"Kṛṣṇa attracts not only the minds of the gopīs and the goddesses of fortune but the minds of all the young girls in the three worlds as well.

TEXT 56

কাস্ত্র্যঙ্গ তে কলপদামৃতবেণুগীত-
সম্মোহিতার্যচরিতান্ন চলেত্রিলোক্যাম্ ।
ত্রৈলোক্যসৌভগমিদঞ্চ নিরীক্ষ্য রূপং
যদ্গোদ্বিজদ্রুমমৃগাঃ পুলকান্যবিভ্রন্ ॥ ৫৬ ॥

kā stry aṅga te kala-padāmṛta-veṇu-gīta-
sammohitārya-caritān na calet trilokyām
trailokya-saubhagam idaṁ ca nirīkṣya rūpaṁ
yad go-dvija-druma-mṛgāḥ pulakāny abibhran

SYNONYMS

kā strī—who is that woman; *aṅga*—O Kṛṣṇa; *te*—of You; *kala-pada*—by the rhythms; *amṛta-veṇu-gīta*—and sweet songs of Your flute; *sammohitā*—being captivated; *ārya-caritāt*—from the path of chastity according to Vedic civilization; *na*—not; *calet*—would wander; *tri-lokyām*—within the three worlds; *trailokya-saubhagam*—which is the fortune of the three worlds; *idam*—this; *ca*—and;

nirīkṣya—by observing; *rūpam*—the beauty; *yat*—which; *go*—the cows; *dvija*—the birds; *druma*—the trees; *mṛgāḥ*—forest animals like the deer; *pulakāni*—transcendental jubilation; *abibhran*—manifested.

TRANSLATION

" 'My dear Lord Kṛṣṇa, where is that woman within the three worlds who cannot be captivated by the rhythms of the sweet songs coming from Your wonderful flute? Who cannot fall down from the path of chastity in this way? Your beauty is the most sublime within the three worlds. Upon seeing Your beauty, even cows, birds, animals and trees in the forest are stunned in jubilation.'

PURPORT

This verse is from *Śrīmad-Bhāgavatam* (10.29.40).

TEXT 57

গুরুতুল্য স্ত্রীগণের বাৎসল্যে আকর্ষণ ।
দাস্য-সখ্যাদি-ভাবে পুরুষাদি গণ ॥ ৫৭ ॥

guru-tulya strī-gaṇera vātsalye ākarṣaṇa
dāsya-sakhyādi-bhāve puruṣādi gaṇa

SYNONYMS

guru-tulya—on the level of a superior guardian; *strī-gaṇera*—of the ladies of Vṛndāvana; *vātsalye*—in parental affection; *ākarṣaṇa*—attracting; *dāsya-sakhya-ādi*—servants, friends, and others; *bhāve*—in the mode of; *puruṣa-ādi gaṇa*—all the males of Vṛndāvana.

TRANSLATION

"The women of Vṛndāvana, who are on the level of superior guardians, are attracted maternally. The men of Vṛndāvana are attracted as servants, friends and fathers to Lord Kṛṣṇa.

TEXT 58

পক্ষী, মৃগ, বৃক্ষ, লতা, চেতনাচেতন ।
প্রেমে মত্ত করি' আকর্ষয়ে কৃষ্ণগুণ ॥ ৫৮ ॥

pakṣī, mṛga, vṛkṣa, latā, cetanācetana
preme matta kari' ākarṣaye kṛṣṇa-guṇa

SYNONYMS

pakṣī—birds; *mṛga*—animals; *vṛkṣa*—trees; *latā*—creepers; *cetana-acetana*—living entities and even the stones and wood; *preme*—in ecstatic love; *matta*—captivated; *kari'*—making; *ākarṣaye*—attract; *kṛṣṇa-guṇa*—the qualities of Kṛṣṇa.

TRANSLATION

"The qualities of Kṛṣṇa captivate and attract everything, living and dead. Even birds, animals and trees are attracted to Kṛṣṇa's qualities.

TEXT 59

'হরিঃ'-শব্দে নানার্থ, দুই মুখ্যতম ।
সর্ব অমঙ্গল হরে, প্রেম দিয়া হরে মন ॥ ৫৯ ॥

'hariḥ'-śabde nānārtha, dui mukhyatama
sarva amaṅgala hare, prema diyā hare mana

SYNONYMS

hariḥ—*hari; śabde*—by this word; *nānā-artha*—different imports; *dui*—two; *mukhya-tama*—chief; *sarva*—all; *amaṅgala*—inauspiciousness; *hare*—takes away; *prema diyā*—by ecstatic love; *hare*—attracts; *mana*—the mind.

TRANSLATION

"Although the word hari has many different meanings, two of them are foremost. One meaning is that the Lord takes away all inauspicious things from His devotee, and the second meaning is that He attracts the mind by ecstatic love for God.

TEXT 60

যৈছে তৈছে যোহি কোহি করয়ে স্মরণ ।
চারিবিধ তাপ তার করে সংহরণ ॥ ৬০ ॥

yaiche taiche yohi kohi karaye smaraṇa
cāri-vidha tāpa tāra kare saṁharaṇa

SYNONYMS

yaiche taiche—somehow or other; *yohi kohi*—anywhere and everywhere; *karaye smaraṇa*—remembers; *cāri-vidha*—the four kinds; *tāpa*—miserable conditions of life; *tāra*—of the devotee; *kare saṁharaṇa*—He takes away.

TRANSLATION

"When the devotee somehow or other always remembers the Supreme Personality of Godhead anywhere and everywhere, Lord Hari takes away life's four miserable conditions.

PURPORT

The four miserable conditions are due to the four kinds of sinful activities, known as (1) *pātaka,* (2) *urupātaka,* (3) *mahā-pātaka* and (4) *atipātaka*—preliminary sin, very great sin, greater sin and topmost sin. However, Kṛṣṇa assures the devotee, *ahaṁ tvāṁ sarva-pāpebhyo mokṣayiṣyāmi mā śucaḥ:* "I will protect you from all sinful reactions. Do not fear." The word *sarva-pāpebhyaḥ* indicates four kinds of sinful activity. As soon as the devotee surrenders unto Kṛṣṇa's lotus feet, he is certainly relieved from all sinful activities and their results. The four basic sinful activities are summarized as illicit sex, intoxication, gambling and meat-eating.

TEXT 61

যথাগ্নিঃ সুসমৃদ্ধার্চিঃ করোত্যেধাংসি ভস্মসাৎ ।
তথা মদ্বিষয়া ভক্তিরুদ্ধবৈনাংসি কৃৎস্নশঃ ॥ ৬১ ॥

yathāgniḥ susamṛddhārciḥ
karoty edhāṁsi bhasmasāt
tathā mad-viṣayā bhaktir
uddhavaināṁsi kṛtsnaśaḥ

SYNONYMS

yathā—as; *agniḥ*—a fire; *su-samṛddha-arciḥ*—having a full flame; *karoti*—makes; *edhāṁsi*—fuel; *bhasmasāt*—into ashes; *tathā*—similarly; *mat-viṣayā bhaktiḥ*—devotional service in relation to Me; *uddhava*—O Uddhava; *enāṁsi*—all kinds of sinful activity; *kṛtsnaśaḥ*—totally.

TRANSLATION

" 'As all fuel is burned to ashes by a full-fledged fire, all sinful activities are totally erased when one engages in devotional service to Me.'

PURPORT

This verse is from *Śrīmad-Bhāgavatam* (11.14.19).

TEXT 62

তবে করে ভক্তিবাধক কর্ম, অবিদ্যা নাশ ।
শ্রবণাদ্যের ফল 'প্রেমা' করয়ে প্রকাশ ॥ ৬২ ॥

tabe kare bhakti-bādhaka karma, avidyā nāśa
śravaṇādyera phala 'premā' karaye prakāśa

SYNONYMS

tabe—thereafter; *kare*—does; *bhakti-bādhaka*—impediments on the path of devotional service; *karma*—activities; *avidyā*—ignorance; *nāśa*—vanquishing; *śravaṇa-ādyera*—of hearing, chanting and so forth; *phala*—the result; *premā*—love of Godhead; *karaye prakāśa*—causes a manifestation of.

TRANSLATION

"In this way, when all sinful activities are vanquished by the grace of the Supreme Personality of Godhead, one gradually vanquishes all kinds of impediments on the path of devotional service, as well as the ignorance resulting from these impediments. After this, one totally manifests his original love of Godhead through devotional service in nine different ways—hearing, chanting and so forth.

TEXT 63

নিজ-গুণে তবে হরে দেহেন্দ্রিয়মন ।
ঐছে কৃপালু কৃষ্ণ, ঐছে তাঁর গুণ ॥ ৬৩ ॥

nija-guṇe tabe hare dehendriya-mana
aiche kṛpālu kṛṣṇa, aiche tāṅra guṇa

SYNONYMS

nija-guṇe—by transcendental qualities; *tabe*—then; *hare*—attracts; *deha-indriya-mana*—the body, senses and mind; *aiche*—in that way; *kṛpālu kṛṣṇa*—merciful Kṛṣṇa; *aiche*—in that way; *tāṅra*—His; *guṇa*—transcendental qualities.

TRANSLATION

"When the devotee is freed from all sinful material activities, Kṛṣṇa attracts his body, mind and senses to His service. Thus Kṛṣṇa is very merciful, and His transcendental qualities are very attractive.

TEXT 64

চারি পুরুষার্থ ছাড়ায়, গুণে হরে সবার মন ।
'হরি'-শব্দের এই মুখ্য কহিলুঁ লক্ষণ ॥ ৬৪ ॥

cāri puruṣārtha chāḍāya, guṇe hare sabāra mana
'hari'-śabdera ei mukhya kahiluṅ lakṣaṇa

SYNONYMS

cāri puruṣa-artha—the four kinds of so-called goals of life; *chāḍāya*—causes to give up; *guṇe*—by the transcendental qualities; *hare*—attracts; *sabāra mana*—everyone's mind; *hari*—*hari; śabdera*—of the word; *ei*—this; *mukhya*—chief; *kahiluṅ*—I have explained; *lakṣaṇa*—the symptoms.

TRANSLATION

"When one's mind, senses and body are attracted to the transcendental qualities of Hari, one gives up the four principles of material success. Thus I have explained the chief meanings of the word hari.

PURPORT

The four principles of material success are (1) religious performance, (2) economic development, (3) sense gratification and (4) liberation, or merging in the impersonal effulgence of Brahman. These things do not interest the devotee.

TEXT 65

'চ' 'অপি', দুই শব্দ তাতে 'অব্যয়' হয় ।
যেই অর্থ লাগাইয়ে, সেই অর্থ হয় ॥ ৬৫ ॥

'ca' 'api', dui śabda tāte 'avyaya' haya
yei artha lāgāiye, sei artha haya

SYNONYMS

ca—*ca; api*—*api; dui*—two; *śabda*—words; *tāte*—in that way; *avyaya*—indeclinable words; *haya*—are; *yei*—whatever; *artha*—meaning; *lāgāiye*—they want to use; *sei*—that; *artha*—meaning; *haya*—can be used.

TRANSLATION

"When the conjunction ca [and] and the adverb api [although] are added to this verse, the verse can assume whatever meaning one wants to give it.

TEXT 66

তথাপি চ-কারের কহে মুখ্য অর্থ সাত ॥ ৬৬ ॥

tathāpi ca-kārera kahe mukhya artha sāta

SYNONYMS

tathāpi—still; *ca-kārera*—of the word *ca; kahe*—it is said; *mukhya*—chief; *artha*—meanings; *sāta*—seven.

TRANSLATION

"The word ca can be explained in seven ways.

TEXT 67

চান্বাচয়ে সমাহারেঽন্যোঽন্যার্থে চ সমুচ্চয়ে।
যত্নান্তরে তথা পাদপূরণেঽপ্যবধারণে ॥ ৬৭ ॥

cānvācaye samāhāre
'nyo 'nyārthe ca samuccaye
yatnāntare tathā pāda-
pūraṇe 'py avadhāraṇe

SYNONYMS

ca—this word *ca; anvācaye*—in connecting one with another; *samāhāre*—in the sense of aggregation; *anyo 'nya-arthe*—to help one another in the imports; *ca*—the word *ca; samuccaye*—in aggregate understanding; *yatna-antare*—in another effort; *tathā*—as well as; *pāda-pūraṇe*—in completing the verse; *api*—also; *avadhāraṇe*—in the sense of certainty.

TRANSLATION

" 'The word ca [and] is used to connect a word or sentence with a previous word or sentence, to give the sense of aggregation, to assist the meaning, to give a collective understanding, to suggest another effort or exertion, or to fulfill the meter of a verse. It is also used in the sense of certainty.'

PURPORT

This is a quotation from the *Viśva-prakāśa* dictionary.

TEXT 68

অপি-শব্দে মুখ্য অর্থ সাত বিখ্যাত ॥ ৬৮ ॥

api-śabde mukhya artha sāta vikhyāta

SYNONYMS

api-śabde—by the word *api; mukhya*—chief; *artha*—meanings; *sāta*—seven; *vikhyāta*—celebrated.

TRANSLATION

"There are seven chief meanings of the word api. They are as follows.

TEXT 69

অপি সম্ভাবনা-প্রশ্ন-শঙ্কা-গর্হা-সমুচ্চয়ে ।
তথা যুক্তপদার্থেষু কামচারক্রিয়াসু চ ॥ ৬৯ ॥

api sambhāvanā-praśna-
śaṅkā-garhā-samuccaye
tathā yukta-padārtheṣu
kāma-cāra-kriyāsu ca

SYNONYMS

api—the word *api; sambhāvanā*—possibility; *praśna*—question; *śaṅkā*—doubt; *garhā*—censure or abuse; *samuccaye*—aggregation; *tathā*—as well as; *yukta-pada-artheṣu*—the appropriate application of things; *kāma-cāra-kriyāsu*—of extravagance; *ca*—and.

TRANSLATION

" 'The word api is used in the sense of possibility, question, doubt, censure, aggregation, appropriate application of things, and extravagance.'

PURPORT

This is another quotation from the *Viśva-prakāśa.*

TEXT 70

এই ত' একাদশ পদের অর্থ-নির্ণয় ।
এবে শ্লোকার্থ করি, যথা যে লাগয় ॥ ৭০ ॥

ei ta' ekādaśa padera artha-nirṇaya
ebe ślokārtha kari, yathā ye lāgaya

SYNONYMS

ei ta'—this; *ekādaśa*—eleven; *padera*—of the words; *artha-nirṇaya*—demonstration of import; *ebe*—now; *śloka-artha*—the total meaning of the verse; *kari*—let Me do; *yathā*—as much as; *ye*—which; *lāgaya*—applicable.

TRANSLATION

"I have now described the different meanings of the eleven separate words. Now let Me give the complete meaning of the śloka, as it is applied in different places.

TEXT 71

'ব্রহ্ম' শব্দের অর্থ—তত্ত্ব সর্ব-বৃহত্তম ।
স্বরূপ ঐশ্বর্য করি' নাহি যাঁর সম ॥ ৭১ ॥

'brahma' śabdera artha——tattva sarva-bṛhattama
svarūpa aiśvarya kari' nāhi yāṅra sama

SYNONYMS

brahma—*brahma; śabdera artha*—the meaning of the word; *tattva*—the truth; *sarva-bṛhat-tama*—*summum bonum* among the relative truths; *sva-rūpa*—the original identity; *aiśvarya*—opulence; *kari'*—accepting; *nāhi*—not; *yāṅra*—whose; *sama*—equal.

TRANSLATION

"The word brahma indicates the summum bonum, the Absolute Truth, which is greater than all other truths. It is the original identity, and there can be no truth equal to that Absolute Truth.

TEXT 72

বৃহত্ত্বাদ্বৃংহণত্বাচ্চ তদ্ব্রহ্ম পরমং বিদুঃ ।
তস্মৈ নমস্তে সর্বাত্মন্ যোগিচিন্ত্যাবিকারবৎ ॥ ৭২ ॥

bṛhattvād bṛṁhaṇatvāc ca
tad brahma paramaṁ viduḥ
tasmai namas te sarvātman
yogi-cintyāvikāravat

SYNONYMS

bṛhattvāt—because of being all-pervasive; *bṛṁhaṇatvāt*—because of increasing unlimitedly; *ca*—and; *tat*—that; *brahma*—Absolute Truth; *paramam*—the ultimate; *viduḥ*—they know; *tasmai*—unto Him; *namaḥ*—obeisances; *te*—unto You; *sarva-ātman*—the Supreme Soul; *yogi-cintya*—appreciable by great *yogīs; avikāra-vat*—without change.

TRANSLATION

"'I offer my respectful obeisances to the Absolute Truth, the summum bonum. He is the all-pervasive, all-increasing subject matter for the great yogīs. He is changeless, and He is the soul of all.'

PURPORT

This is a quotation from the *Viṣṇu Purāṇa* (1.12.57).

TEXT 73

সেই ব্রহ্ম-শব্দে কহে স্বয়ং-ভগবান্ ।
অদ্বিতীয়-জ্ঞান, যাঁহা বিনা নাহি আন ॥ ৭৩ ॥

sei brahma-śabde kahe svayaṁ-bhagavān
advitīya-jñāna, yāṅhā vinā nāhi āna

SYNONYMS

sei—that; *brahma*—*brahma; śabde*—by the word; *kahe*—it is said; *svayam-bhagavān*—the Supreme Personality of Godhead; *advitīya-jñāna*—the supreme one, without duality; *yāṅhā*—which; *vinā*—without; *nāhi āna*—there is nothing else.

TRANSLATION

"The proper meaning of the word brahma is the Supreme Personality of Godhead, who is one without a second and without whom nothing exists.

TEXT 74

বদন্তি তত্তত্ত্ববিদস্তত্ত্বং যজ্‌জ্ঞানমদ্বয়ম্ ।
ব্রহ্মেতি পরমাত্মেতি ভগবানিতি শব্দ্যতে ॥ ৭৪ ॥

vadanti tat tattva-vidas
tattvaṁ yaj jñānam advayam
brahmeti paramātmeti
bhagavān iti śabdyate

SYNONYMS

vadanti—they say; *tat*—that; *tattva-vidaḥ*—learned souls; *tattvam*—the Absolute Truth; *yat*—which; *jñānam*—knowledge; *advayam*—nondual; *brahma*—Brahman; *iti*—thus; *paramātmā*—Paramātmā; *iti*—thus; *bhagavān*—Bhagavān; *iti*—thus; *śabdyate*—is known.

TRANSLATION

" 'Learned transcendentalists who know the Absolute Truth say that it is nondual knowledge and is called impersonal Brahman, localized Paramātmā and the Personality of Godhead.'

PURPORT

This is a quotation from *Śrīmad-Bhāgavatam* (1.2.11). For an explanation, see *Ādi-līlā* (2.11).

TEXT 75

সেই অদ্বয়-তত্ত্ব কৃষ্ণ—স্বয়ং-ভগবান্ ।
তিনকালে সত্য তিঁহো—শাস্ত্র-প্রমাণ ॥ ৭৫ ॥

sei advaya-tattva kṛṣṇa——svayaṁ-bhagavān
tina-kāle satya tiṅho——śāstra-pramāṇa

SYNONYMS

sei—that; *advaya-tattva*—Absolute Truth without a second; *kṛṣṇa*—Lord Kṛṣṇa; *svayam-bhagavān*—the Supreme Personality of Godhead; *tina-kāle*—in three phases of time (past, present and future); *satya*—truth; *tiṅho*—He; *śāstra-pramāṇa*—the verdict of all Vedic literature.

TRANSLATION

"That Absolute Truth without a second is Lord Kṛṣṇa, the Supreme Personality of Godhead. He is the supreme truth in the past, present and future. That is the evidence of all revealed scriptures.

TEXT 76

অহমেবাসমেবাগ্রে নান্যদ্‌যৎ সদসৎপরম্ ।
পশ্চাদহং যদেতচ্চ যোঽবশিষ্যেত সোঽস্ম্যহম্ ॥ ৭৬ ॥

aham evāsam evāgre
nānyad yat sad-asat-param

paścād ahaṁ yad etac ca
yo 'vaśiṣyeta so 'smy aham

SYNONYMS

aham—I, the Personality of Godhead; *eva*—certainly; *āsam*—existed; *eva*—only; *agre*—before the creation; *na*—never; *anyat*—anything else; *yat*—which; *sat*—the effect; *asat*—the cause; *param*—the supreme; *paścāt*—after; *aham*—I, the Personality of Godhead; *yat*—which; *etat*—this creation; *ca*—also; *yaḥ*—who; *avaśiṣyeta*—remains; *saḥ*—that; *asmi*—am; *aham*—I, the Personality of Godhead.

TRANSLATION

" 'Prior to the cosmic creation, only I exist, and no phenomena exist, either gross, subtle or primordial. After creation, only I exist in everything, and after annihilation only I remain eternally.'

PURPORT

This is a quotation from *Śrīmad-Bhāgavatam* (2.9.32). For an explanation see *Ādi-līlā* (1.53).

TEXT 77

'আত্ম'-শব্দে কহে কৃষ্ণ বৃহত্ত্বস্বরূপ ।
সর্বব্যাপক, সর্বসাক্ষী, পরমস্বরূপ ॥ ৭৭ ॥

'ātma'-śabde kahe kṛṣṇa bṛhattva-svarūpa
sarva-vyāpaka, sarva-sākṣī, parama-svarūpa

SYNONYMS

ātma—*ātmā; śabde*—by the word; *kahe*—it is said; *kṛṣṇa*—the Supreme Lord Kṛṣṇa; *bṛhattva*—the greatest of all; *sva-rūpa*—identity; *sarva-vyāpaka*—all-pervasive; *sarva-sākṣī*—the witness of all; *parama-svarūpa*—the supreme form.

TRANSLATION

"The word ātmā [self] indicates the highest truth, Kṛṣṇa. He is the all-pervasive witness of all, and He is the supreme form.

TEXT 78

আততত্বাচ্চ মাতৃত্বাদাত্মা হি পরমো হরিঃ ॥ ৭৮ ॥

ātatatvāc ca mātṛtvād
ātmā hi paramo hariḥ

SYNONYMS

ātatatvāt—due to being all-pervading; *ca*—and; *mātṛtvāt*—due to being the progenitor; *ātmā*—the soul; *hi*—certainly; *paramaḥ*—supreme; *hariḥ*—the Supreme Personality of Godhead.

TRANSLATION

" 'Hari, the Personality of Godhead, is the all-pervasive original source of everything; He is therefore the Supersoul of everything.'

PURPORT

This is a quotation from the *Bhāvārtha-dīpikā,* Śrīdhara Svāmī's commentary on *Śrīmad-Bhāgavatam.*

TEXT 79

সেই কৃষ্ণপ্রাপ্তি-হেতু ত্রিবিধ 'সাধন'।
জ্ঞান, যোগ, ভক্তি,—তিনের পৃথক্ লক্ষণ ॥ ৭৯ ॥

sei kṛṣṇa-prāpti-hetu trividha 'sādhana'
jñāna, yoga, bhakti,——tinera pṛthak lakṣaṇa

SYNONYMS

sei—those; *kṛṣṇa-prāpti*—of achieving the lotus feet of Kṛṣṇa; *hetu*—causes; *tri-vidha sādhana*—the three kinds of execution; *jñāna*—knowledge; *yoga*—mystic *yoga* practice; *bhakti*—and devotional service; *tinera*—of these three; *pṛthak lakṣaṇa*—the symptoms are different.

TRANSLATION

"There are three ways to attain the lotus feet of the Absolute Truth, Kṛṣṇa. There is the process of philosophical speculation, the practice of mystic yoga and the execution of devotional service. Each of these has its different characteristics.

TEXT 80

তিন সাধনে ভগবান্ তিন স্বরূপে ভাসে।
ব্রহ্ম, পরমাত্মা, ভগবত্তা,—ত্রিবিধ প্রকাশে ॥ ৮০ ॥

tina sādhane bhagavān tina svarūpe bhāse
brahma, paramātmā, bhagavattā,——trividha prakāśe

SYNONYMS

tina sādhane—by these three different processes; *bhagavān*—the Supreme Personality of Godhead; *tina*—three; *sva-rūpe*—in identities; *bhāse*—appears; *brahma*—the impersonal feature; *paramātmā*—the localized feature; *bhagavattā*—and the Supreme Personality of Godhead; *trividha prakāśe*—three manifestations.

TRANSLATION

"The Absolute Truth is the same, but according to the process by which one understands Him, He appears in three forms—as Brahman, Paramātmā, and Bhagavān, the Supreme Personality of Godhead.

TEXT 81

বদন্তি তত্ত্ববিদস্তত্ত্বং যজ্‌জ্ঞানমদ্বয়ম্‌ ।
ব্রহ্মেতি পরমাত্মেতি ভগবানিতি শব্দ্যতে ॥ ৮১ ॥

vadanti tat tattva-vidas
tattvaṁ yaj jñānam advayam
brahmeti paramātmeti
bhagavān iti śabdyate

SYNONYMS

vadanti—they say; *tat*—that; *tattva-vidaḥ*—learned souls; *tattvam*—the Absolute Truth; *yat*—which; *jñānam*—knowledge; *advayam*—nondual; *brahma*—Brahman; *iti*—thus; *paramātmā*—Paramātmā; *iti*—thus; *bhagavān*—Bhagavān; *iti*—thus; *śabdyate*—is known.

TRANSLATION

" 'Learned transcendentalists who know the Absolute Truth say that it is nondual knowledge and is called impersonal Brahman, localized Paramātmā and the Personality of Godhead.'

TEXT 82

'ব্রহ্ম-আত্মা'-শব্দে যদি কৃষ্ণেরে কহয় ।
'রূঢ়িবৃত্ত্যে' নির্বিশেষ অন্তর্যামী কয় ॥ ৮২ ॥

'brahma-ātmā'-śabde yadi kṛṣṇere kahaya
'rūḍhi-vṛttye' nirviśeṣa antaryāmī kaya

SYNONYMS

brahma-ātmā—*brahma* and *ātmā; śabde*—by these words; *yadi*—if; *kṛṣṇere kahaya*—Kṛṣṇa is indicated; *rūḍhi-vṛttye*—by the direct meaning; *nirviśeṣa*—impersonal; *antaryāmī*—the Supersoul; *kaya*—is said.

TRANSLATION

"Although the words brahma and ātmā indicate Kṛṣṇa, their direct meaning refers only to the impersonal Brahman and the Supersoul.

TEXT 83

জ্ঞানমার্গে—নির্বিশেষ-ব্রহ্ম প্রকাশে ।
যোগমার্গে—অন্তর্যামি-স্বরূপেতে ভাসে ॥ ৮৩ ॥

jñāna-mārge——nirviśeṣa-brahma prakāśe
yoga-mārge——antaryāmi-svarūpete bhāse

SYNONYMS

jñāna-mārge—the process of philosophical speculation; *nirviśeṣa-brahma*—the impersonal Brahman effulgence; *prakāśe*—becomes manifest; *yoga-mārge*—by practicing mystic *yoga; antaryāmi-svarūpete*—in the localized aspect, Supersoul; *bhāse*—appears.

TRANSLATION

"If one follows the path of philosophical speculation, the Absolute Truth manifests Himself as impersonal Brahman, and if one follows the path of mystic yoga, He manifests Himself as the Supersoul.

TEXT 84

রাগভক্তি-বিধিভক্তি হয় দুইরূপ ।
'স্বয়ং-ভগবত্ত্বে', ভগবত্ত্বে—প্রকাশ দ্বিরূপ ॥ ৮৪ ॥

rāga-bhakti-vidhi-bhakti haya dui-rūpa
'svayaṁ-bhagavattve', bhagavattve——prakāśa dvi-rūpa

SYNONYMS

rāga-bhakti—spontaneous devotional service; *vidhi-bhakti*—regulative devotional service; *haya*—are; *dui-rūpa*—the two kinds of devotional service; *svayam-*

bhagavattve—in the Supreme Personality of Godhead; *bhagavattve*—and in His personal expansion; *prakāśa dvi-rūpa*—the two kinds of manifestation.

TRANSLATION

"There are two kinds of devotional activity—spontaneous and regulative. By spontaneous devotional service, one attains the original Personality of Godhead, Kṛṣṇa, and by the regulative process one attains the expansion of the Supreme Personality of Godhead.

TEXT 85

রাগভক্ত্যে ব্রজে স্বয়ং-ভগবানে পায় ॥ ৮৫ ॥

rāga-bhaktye vraje svayaṁ-bhagavāne pāya

SYNONYMS

rāga-bhaktye—by the discharge of spontaneous devotional service; *vraje*—in Vṛndāvana; *svayam*—Himself; *bhagavāne*—the Supreme Personality of Godhead; *pāya*—one gets.

TRANSLATION

"By executing spontaneous devotional service in Vṛndāvana, one attains the original Supreme Personality of Godhead, Kṛṣṇa.

TEXT 86

নায়ং সুখাপো ভগবান্ দেহিনাং গোপিকাসুতঃ ।
জ্ঞানিনাঞ্চাত্মভূতানাং যথা ভক্তিমতামিহ ॥ ৮৬ ॥

nāyaṁ sukhāpo bhagavān
dehināṁ gopikā-sutaḥ
jñānināṁ cātma-bhūtānāṁ
yathā bhaktimatām iha

SYNONYMS

na—not; *ayam*—this Lord Śrī Kṛṣṇa; *sukha-āpaḥ*—easily available; *bhagavān*—the Supreme Personality of Godhead; *dehinām*—for materialistic persons who have accepted the body as the self; *gopikā-sutaḥ*—the son of mother Yaśodā; *jñāninām*—for persons addicted to mental speculation; *ca*—and; *ātma-bhūtānām*—for persons performing severe austerities and penances; *yathā*—as; *bhakti-matām*—for persons engaged in spontaneous devotional service; *iha*—in this world.

TRANSLATION

" 'The Supreme Personality of Godhead, Kṛṣṇa, the son of mother Yaśodā, is accessible to those devotees engaged in spontaneous loving service, but He is not as easily accessible to mental speculators, to those striving for self-realization by severe austerities and penances, or to those who consider the body the same as the self.'

PURPORT

This verse from *Śrīmad-Bhāgavatam* (10.9.21) is spoken by Śrīla Śukadeva Gosvāmī. It concerns the statement about Kṛṣṇa's being subjugated by the *gopīs* and thus glorifying them.

TEXT 87

বিধিভক্ত্যে পার্ষদদেহে বৈকুণ্ঠেতে যায় ॥ ৮৭ ॥

vidhi-bhaktye pārṣada-dehe vaikuṇṭhete yāya

SYNONYMS

vidhi-bhaktye—by executing regulative devotional service; *pārṣada-dehe*—in the form of an associate of the Lord; *vaikuṇṭhete yāya*—one achieves the Vaikuṇṭha planets.

TRANSLATION

"By executing regulative devotional service, one becomes an associate of Nārāyaṇa and attains the Vaikuṇṭhalokas, the spiritual planets in the spiritual sky.

TEXT 88

যচ্চ ব্রজন্ত্যনিমিষামৃষভানুবৃত্ত্যা
দূরে-যমা হ্যুপরি নঃ স্পৃহণীয়শীলাঃ ।
ভর্তুর্মিথঃ সুযশসঃ কথনানুরাগ-
বৈক্লব্যবাষ্পকলয়া পুলকীকৃতাঙ্গাঃ ॥ ৮৮ ॥

yac ca vrajanty animiṣām ṛṣabhānuvṛttyā
dūre-yamā hy upari naḥ spṛhaṇīya-śīlāḥ
bhartur mithaḥ suyaśasaḥ kathanānurāga-
vaiklavya-bāṣpa-kalayā pulakīkṛtāṅgāḥ

SYNONYMS

yat—which; *ca*—also; *vrajanti*—go; *animiṣām*—of the demigods; *ṛṣabha-anuvṛttyā*—by practicing the best means of spiritual life; *dūre*—keeping at a distance; *yamāḥ*—the regulative principles; *hi*—certainly; *upari*—above; *naḥ*—our;

spṛhaṇīya-śīlāḥ—decorated with desirable qualities; *bhartuḥ*—of the master; *mithaḥ*—mutually; *su-yaśasaḥ*—who has all transcendental qualities; *kathana-anurāga*—attracted to discussions; *vaiklavya*—transformation; *bāṣpa-kalayā*—with tears in the eyes; *pulakīkṛta*—jubilation; *aṅgāḥ*—bodily limbs.

TRANSLATION

" 'Those who discuss the activities of Lord Kṛṣṇa are on the highest platform of devotional life, and they evince the symptoms of tears in the eyes and bodily jubilation. Such persons discharge devotional service to Kṛṣṇa without practicing the rules and regulations of the mystic yoga system. They possess all spiritual qualities, and they are elevated to the Vaikuṇṭha planets, which exist above us.'

PURPORT

This is a quotation from *Śrīmad-Bhāgavatam* (3.15.25). In this verse Lord Brahmā is speaking to all the demigods, who feared the two *asuras* in Diti's womb. Lord Brahmā described the Kumāras' visit to Vaikuṇṭha, and this was again explained by Maitreya, the friend of Vyāsadeva, when he gave instructions to Vidura.

TEXT 89

সেই উপাসক হয় ত্রিবিধ প্রকার।
অকাম, মোক্ষকাম, সর্বকাম আর ॥ ৮৯ ॥

sei upāsaka haya trividha prakāra
akāma, mokṣa-kāma, sarva-kāma āra

SYNONYMS

sei upāsaka—those devotees; *haya*—are; *tri-vidha prakāra*—three varieties; *akāma*—without material desires; *mokṣa-kāma*—desiring to become liberated; *sarva-kāma*—filled with all material desires; *āra*—and.

TRANSLATION

"The devotees are divided into three categories—akāma [desireless], mokṣa-kāma [desiring liberation], and sarva-kāma [desiring material perfection].

TEXT 90

অকামঃ সর্বকামো বা মোক্ষকাম উদারধীঃ।
তীব্রেণ ভক্তিযোগেন যজেত পুরুষং পরম্ ॥ ৯০ ॥

akāmaḥ sarva-kāmo vā
mokṣa-kāma udāra-dhīḥ
tīvreṇa bhakti-yogena
yajeta puruṣaṁ param

SYNONYMS

akāmaḥ—without material desires; *sarva-kāmaḥ*—full of all material desires; *vā*—or; *mokṣa-kāmaḥ*—desiring liberation; *udāra-dhīḥ*—sincere and advanced in devotional service; *tīvreṇa*—firm; *bhakti-yogena*—by the practice of *bhakti-yoga; yajeta*—should worship; *puruṣam param*—the Supreme Personality of Godhead.

TRANSLATION

" 'One who is actually intelligent, although he may be a devotee free from material desires, a karmī desiring all kinds of material facilities, or a jñānī desiring liberation, should seriously engage in bhakti-yoga for the satisfaction of the Supreme Personality of Godhead.'

PURPORT

This is a quotation from *Śrīmad-Bhāgavatam* (2.3.10).

TEXT 91

বুদ্ধিমান্‌-অর্থে—যদি 'বিচারজ্ঞ' হয় ।
নিজ-কাম লাগিহ তবে কৃষ্ণেরে ভজয় ॥ ৯১ ॥

buddhimān-arthe——yadi 'vicāra-jña' haya
nija-kāma lāgiha tabe kṛṣṇere bhajaya

SYNONYMS

buddhimān-arthe—by the meaning of intelligent; *yadi*—if; *vicāra-jña*—expert in scrutinizing things; *haya*—is; *nija-kāma lāgiha*—even for sense gratification; *tabe*—then; *kṛṣṇere bhajana*—worships Lord Kṛṣṇa.

TRANSLATION

"The meaning of the word udāra-dhīḥ is buddhimān—intelligent or considerate. Because of this, even for one's own sense gratification one engages in the devotional service of Lord Kṛṣṇa.

TEXT 92

ভক্তি বিনু কোন সাধন দিতে নারে ফল ।
সব ফল দেয় ভক্তি স্বতন্ত্র প্রবল ॥ ৯২ ॥

bhakti vinu kona sādhana dite nāre phala
saba phala deya bhakti svatantra prabala

SYNONYMS

bhakti vinu—without devotional service; *kona*—some; *sādhana*—practice for perfection; *dite*—to give; *nāre*—not able; *phala*—any result; *saba phala*—all the results of different processes; *deya*—give; *bhakti*—devotional service; *svatantra*—independent; *prabala*—and powerful.

TRANSLATION

"The other processes cannot yield results unless they are associated with devotional service. Devotional service, however, is so strong and independent that it can give one all the desired results.

TEXT 93

অজাগলস্তন-ন্যায় অন্য সাধন ।
অতএব হরি ভজে বুদ্ধিমান্ জন ॥ ৯৩ ॥

ajā-gala-stana-nyāya anya sādhana
ataeva hari bhaje buddhimān jana

SYNONYMS

ajā-gala-stana-nyāya—like the nipples on the neck of a goat; *anya*—other; *sādhana*—execution of spiritual life; *ataeva*—therefore; *hari*—the Supreme Personality of Godhead; *bhaje*—one worships; *buddhimān jana*—the intelligent person.

TRANSLATION

"With the exception of devotional service, all the methods of self-realization are like nipples on the neck of a goat. An intelligent person adopts only devotional service, giving up all other processes of self-realization.

PURPORT

Without devotional service, other methods for self-realization and spiritual life are useless. Other methods cannot produce good results at any time, and therefore they are compared to the nipples on the neck of a goat. These nipples cannot produce milk, although it may appear that they can. An unintelligent person cannot understand that only devotional service can elevate one to the transcendental position.

TEXT 94

চতুর্বিধা ভজন্তে মাং জনাঃ সুকৃতিনোঽর্জুন ।
আর্তো জিজ্ঞাসুরর্থার্থী জ্ঞানী চ ভরতর্ষভ ॥ ৯৪ ॥

catur-vidhā bhajante māṁ
janāḥ sukṛtino 'rjuna
ārto jijñāsur arthārthī
jñānī ca bharatarṣabha

SYNONYMS

catuḥ-vidhāḥ—four kinds; *bhajante*—worship; *mām*—Me; *janāḥ*—persons; *sukṛtinaḥ*—who have obeyed the principles of human life or the regulative principles of *varṇa* and *āśrama; arjuna*—O Arjuna; *ārtaḥ*—the distressed; *jijñāsuḥ*—the inquisitive; *artha-arthī*—one in need of money; *jñānī*—one pursuing knowledge; *ca*—also; *bharata-ṛṣabha*—O best of the Bharata dynasty.

TRANSLATION

" 'O best among the Bharatas [Arjuna], four kinds of pious men render devotional service unto Me—the distressed, the desirer of wealth, the inquisitive, and he who is searching for knowledge of the Absolute.'

PURPORT

This is a quotation from *Bhagavad-gītā* (7.16). The word *sukṛtinaḥ* is very important in this verse. *Su* means "auspicious," and *kṛtī* means "meritorious" or "regulated." Unless one follows the regulative principles of religious life, human life is no different from animal life. Religious life means following the principles of *varṇa* and *āśrama*. In the *Viṣṇu Purāṇa* it is said:

varṇāśramācāravatā
pusuṣeṇa paraḥ pumān
viṣṇur ārādhyate panthā
nānyat tat-toṣa-kāraṇam

According to religious life, society is divided into four social divisions—*brāhmaṇa, kṣatriya, vaiśya* and *śūdra*—and four spiritual divisions—*brahmacarya, gṛhastha, vānaprastha* and *sannyāsa*. One needs to be trained to become a *brāhmaṇa, kṣatriya, vaiśya* or *śūdra*, just as one is trained to become an engineer, doctor or lawyer. Those who are properly trained can be considered human beings; if one is not trained socially and spiritually—that is, if one is uneducated and unregulated—his life is on the animal platform. Among animals there is no question of spiritual advancement. Spiritual life can be attained by proper training—either by following the principles of *varṇa* and *āśrama* or by being directly trained in the *bhakti* school by the methods of *śravaṇaṁ kīrtanaṁ viṣṇoḥ smaraṇaṁ pāda-sevanam/arcanaṁ vandanaṁ dāsyaṁ sakhyam ātma-nivedanam.* Without being trained, one cannot be *sukṛtī,* auspicious. In this verse Kṛṣṇa says that people approach Him when in distress, in need of money or when actually inquisitive to understand the Supreme Being or the original source of everything. Some people approach Him in the pursuit of knowledge of the Absolute Truth, and others approach Him when they are distressed, like the devotee Gajendra. Others are inquisitive, like the great sages headed by Sanaka, and others need money, like Dhruva Mahārāja. Śukadeva Gosvāmī approached the Lord when he pursued knowledge. All these great personalities thus took to the devotional service of the Supreme Personality of Godhead, Kṛṣṇa.

TEXT 95

আর্ত, অর্থার্থী,—দুই সকাম-ভিতরে গণি ।
জিজ্ঞাসু, জ্ঞানী,—দুই মোক্ষকাম মানি ॥ ৯৫ ॥

ārta, arthārthī,——dui sakāma-bhitare gaṇi
jijñāsu, jñānī,——dui mokṣa-kāma māni

SYNONYMS

ārta—distressed; *artha-arthī*—desirous of money; *dui*—two persons; *sakāma-bhitare*—in the division of material activities; *gaṇi*—we consider; *jijñāsu*—inquisitive; *jñānī*—pursuing knowledge; *dui*—two; *mokṣa-kāma*—transcendentalists pursuing spiritual knowledge for liberation; *māni*—I consider.

TRANSLATION

"Materialistic devotees take to devotional service and worship Kṛṣṇa when they are distressed or in need of money. Those who are actually inquisitive to understand the supreme source of everything and those who are in search of knowledge are called transcendentalists, for they desire liberation from all material contamination.

TEXT 96

এই চারি সুকৃতি হয় মহাভাগ্যবান্ ।
তত্তৎকামাদি ছাড়ি' হয় শুদ্ধভক্তিমান্ ॥ ৯৬ ॥

ei cāri sukṛti haya mahā-bhāgyavān
tat-tat-kāmādi chāḍi' haya śuddha-bhaktimān

SYNONYMS

ei cāri—these four persons; *sukṛti*—pious men; *haya*—are; *mahā-bhāgyavān*—highly fortunate; *tat-tat*—those respective; *kāma-ādi*—aspirations; *chāḍi'*—giving up; *haya*—become; *śuddha-bhaktimān*—pure devotees.

TRANSLATION

"Because they have a pious background, all four types of people are to be considered greatly fortunate. Such people gradually give up material desires and become pure devotees.

TEXT 97

সাধুসঙ্গ-কৃপা কিম্বা কৃষ্ণের কৃপায় ।
কামাদি 'দুঃসঙ্গ' ছাড়ি' শুদ্ধভক্তি পায় ॥ ৯৭ ॥

sādhu-saṅga-kṛpā kimvā kṛṣṇera kṛpāya
kāmādi 'duḥsaṅga' chāḍi' śuddha-bhakti pāya

SYNONYMS

sādhu-saṅga-kṛpā—by the mercy of association with devotees; *kimvā*—or; *kṛṣṇera kṛpāya*—by the mercy of Kṛṣṇa; *kāma-ādi*—material desires and so on; *duḥsaṅga*—unwanted association; *chāḍi'*—giving up; *śuddha-bhakti pāya*—one obtains the platform of pure devotional life.

TRANSLATION

"One is elevated to the platform of devotional life by the mercy of a Vaiṣṇava, the bona fide spiritual master, and by the special mercy of Kṛṣṇa. On that platform, one gives up all material desires and the association of unwanted people. Thus one is elevated to the platform of pure devotional service.

TEXT 98

সৎসঙ্গান্মুক্ত-দুঃসঙ্গো হাতুং নোৎসহতে বুধঃ ।
কীর্ত্যমানং যশো যস্য সকৃদাকর্ণ্য রোচনম্ ॥ ৯৮ ॥

sat-saṅgān mukta-duḥsaṅgo
hātuṁ notsahate budhaḥ

kīrtyamānaṁ yaśo yasya
sakṛd ākarṇya rocanam

SYNONYMS

sat-saṅgāt—by the association of pure devotees; *mukta*—freed; *duḥsaṅgaḥ*—the association of materialistic persons; *hātum*—to give up; *na*—not; *utsahate*—is able; *budhaḥ*—one who is actually learned; *kīrtyamānam*—being glorified; *yaśaḥ*—the glories; *yasya*—of whom (the Supreme Personality of Godhead); *sakṛt*—once; *ākarṇya*—hearing; *rocanam*—very pleasing.

TRANSLATION

" 'The intelligent, who have understood the Supreme Lord in the association of pure devotees and have become free from bad materialistic association, can never avoid hearing the glories of the Lord, even though they have heard them only once.'

PURPORT

This is a verse from *Śrīmad-Bhāgavatam* (1.10.11). All the members of the Kuru dynasty offered respects when Kṛṣṇa was leaving Hastināpura after the Battle of Kurukṣetra. Kṛṣṇa was going to His own kingdom, and all the members of the Kuru dynasty were overwhelmed by His departure. This verse was spoken in that connection by Śukadeva Gosvāmī. A pure devotee becomes attached to Kṛṣṇa by hearing the Lord's glories. The Lord's glories and the Lord Himself are identical. One has to be qualified to understand this Absolute Truth; therefore one should be given a chance to associate with a pure devotee. Our Kṛṣṇa consciousness movement is meant for this purpose. We want to create pure devotees so that other people will benefit by their association. In this way the number of pure devotees increases. Professional preachers cannot create pure devotees. There are many professional preachers of *Śrīmad-Bhāgavatam* who read this work to earn their livelihood. However, they cannot convert materialistic people to devotional service. Only a pure devotee can convert others to pure devotional service. It is therefore important for all the preachers in our Kṛṣṇa consciousness movement to first become pure devotees and follow the regulative principles, refraining from illicit sex, meat-eating, gambling and intoxication. They should regularly chant the Hare Kṛṣṇa *mahā-mantra* on their beads, follow the devotional process, rise early in the morning, attend *maṅgala-ārati* and recite *Śrīmad-Bhāgavatam* and *Bhagavad-gītā* regularly. In this way, one can become purified and free from all material contamination.

sarvopādhi-vinirmuktaṁ
tat-paratvena nirmalam

hṛṣīkeṇa hṛṣīkeśa-
sevanaṁ bhaktir ucyate
(*Nārada-pañcarātra*)

To make a show of devotional service will not help one. One must be a pure devotee following the devotional process; then one can convert others to devotional service. Śrī Caitanya Mahāprabhu practiced devotional service and preached (*āpani ācari' bhakti karila pracāra*). If a preacher behaves properly in devotional service, he will be able to convert others. Otherwise, his preaching will have no effect.

TEXT 99

'দুঃসঙ্গ' কহিয়ে—'কৈতব', 'আত্মবঞ্চনা' ।
কৃষ্ণ, কৃষ্ণভক্তি বিনু অন্য কামনা ॥ ৯৯ ॥

'duḥsaṅga' kahiye——'kaitava', 'ātma-vañcanā'
kṛṣṇa, kṛṣṇa-bhakti vinu anya kāmanā

SYNONYMS

duḥsaṅga—bad, unwanted association; *kahiye*—I say; *kaitava*—cheating; *ātma-vañcanā*—cheating oneself; *kṛṣṇa*—Lord Kṛṣṇa; *kṛṣṇa-bhakti*—devotional service to Kṛṣṇa; *vinu*—without; *anya*—other; *kāmanā*—desires.

TRANSLATION

"Cheating oneself and cheating others is called kaitava. Associating with cheaters is called duḥsaṅga, bad association. Those who desire things other than Kṛṣṇa's service are also called duḥsaṅga, bad association.

TEXT 100

ধর্মঃ প্রোজ্ঝিত-কৈতবোঽত্র পরমো নির্মৎসরাণাং সতাং
বেদ্যং বাস্তবমত্র বস্তু শিবদং তাপত্রয়োন্মূলনম্ ।
শ্রীমদ্ভাগবতে মহামুনিকৃতে কিংবা পরৈরীশ্বরঃ
সদ্যো হৃদ্যবরুধ্যতেঽত্র কৃতিভিঃ শুশ্রূষুভিস্তৎক্ষণাৎ ॥ ১০০ ॥

dharmaḥ projjhita-kaitavo 'tra paramo nirmatsarāṇāṁ satāṁ
vedyaṁ vāstavam atra vastu śivadaṁ tāpa-trayonmūlanam
śrīmad-bhāgavate mahāmuni-kṛte kiṁ vā parair īśvaraḥ
sadyo hṛdy avarudhyate 'tra kṛtibhiḥ śuśrūṣubhis tat-kṣaṇāt

SYNONYMS

dharmaḥ—religiosity; *projjhita*—completely rejected; *kaitavaḥ*—in which fruitive intention; *atra*—herein; *paramaḥ*—the highest; *nirmatsarāṇām*—of the fully pure in heart; *satām*—devotees; *vedyam*—to be understood; *vāstavam*—factual; *atra*—herein; *vastu*—substance; *śiva-dam*—giving well-being; *tāpa-traya*—of threefold miseries; *unmūlanam*—causing uprooting; *śrīmat*—beautiful; *bhāgavate*—in the *Bhāgavata Purāṇa; mahā-muni*—by the great sage (Vyāsadeva); *kṛte*—compiled; *kim*—what; *vā*—indeed; *paraiḥ*—with others; *īśvaraḥ*—the Supreme Lord; *sadyaḥ*—at once; *hṛdi*—within the heart; *avarudhyate*—becomes confined; *atra*—herein; *kṛtibhiḥ*—by pious men; *śuśrūṣubhiḥ*—desiring to hear; *tat-kṣaṇāt*—without delay.

TRANSLATION

" 'The great scripture Śrīmad-Bhāgavatam, compiled by Mahāmuni Vyāsadeva from four original verses, describes the most elevated and kindhearted devotees and completely rejects the cheating ways of materially motivated religiosity. It propounds the highest principle of eternal religion, which can factually mitigate the threefold miseries of a living being and award the highest benediction of full prosperity and knowledge. Those willing to hear the message of this scripture in a submissive attitude of service can at once capture the Supreme Lord in their hearts. Therefore there is no need for any scripture other than Śrīmad-Bhāgavatam.'

PURPORT

This is a quotation from *Śrīmad-Bhāgavatam* (1.1.2). For an explanation see also *Ādi-līlā* (1.91).

TEXT 101

'প্র'-শব্দে — মোক্ষবাঞ্ছা কৈতবপ্রধান ।
এই শ্লোকে শ্রীধরস্বামী করিয়াছেন ব্যাখ্যান ॥ ১০১ ॥

'pra'-śabde——mokṣa-vāñchā kaitava-pradhāna
ei śloke śrīdhara-svāmī kariyāchena vyākhyāna

SYNONYMS

pra-śabde—by the affix *pra; mokṣa-vāñchā*—the desire for being liberated; *kaitava-pradhāna*—first-class cheating; *ei śloke*—in this verse; *śrīdhara-svāmī*—the great commentator Śrīdhara Svāmī; *kariyāchena*—has made; *vyākhyāna*—explanation.

TRANSLATION

"The prefix pra in the word projjhita specifically refers to those desiring liberation or oneness with the Supreme. Such a desire should be understood to result from a cheating propensity. The great commentator Śrīdhara Svāmī has explained this verse in that way.

TEXT 102

সকাম-ভক্তে 'অজ্ঞ' জানি' দয়ালু ভগবান্ ।
স্ব-চরণ দিয়া করে ইচ্ছার পিধান ॥ ১০২ ॥

sakāma-bhakte 'ajña' jāni' dayālu bhagavān
sva-caraṇa diyā kare icchāra pidhāna

SYNONYMS

sakāma-bhakte—to devotees who still have material desires to fulfill; *ajña*—foolish; *jāni'*—knowing; *dayālu*—merciful; *bhagavān*—Śrī Kṛṣṇa; *sva-caraṇa*—His own lotus feet; *diyā*—giving; *kare*—does; *icchāra pidhāna*—the covering of other desires.

TRANSLATION

"When the merciful Lord Kṛṣṇa understands a devotee's foolish desire for material prosperity, He gratefully gives him the shelter of His lotus feet. In this way, the Lord covers his undesirable ambitions.

TEXT 103

সত্যং দিশত্যর্থিতমর্থিতো নৃণাং
নৈবার্থদো যৎ পুনরর্থিতা যতঃ ।
স্বয়ং বিধত্তে ভজতামনিচ্ছতা-
মিচ্ছাপিধানং নিজপাদপল্লবম্ ॥ ১০৩ ॥

satyaṁ diśaty arthitam arthito nṛṇāṁ
naivārthado yat punar arthitā yataḥ
svayaṁ vidhatte bhajatām anicchatām
icchā-pidhānaṁ nija-pāda-pallavam

SYNONYMS

satyam—it is true; *diśati*—He awards; *arthitam*—that which is desired; *arthitaḥ*—being requested; *nṛṇām*—by human beings; *na*—not; *eva*—certainly;

artha-daḥ—giving desired things; *yat*—which; *punaḥ*—again; *arthitā*—request; *yataḥ*—from which; *svayam*—Himself; *vidhatte*—He gives; *bhajatām*—of those engaged in devotional service; *anicchatām*—even though not desiring; *icchā-pidhānam*—covering all other desires; *nija-pāda-pallavam*—the shelter of His own lotus feet.

TRANSLATION

" 'Whenever Kṛṣṇa is requested to fulfill one's desire, He undoubtedly does so, but He does not award anything which, after being enjoyed, will cause someone to petition Him again and again to fulfill further desires. When one has other desires but engages in the Lord's service, Kṛṣṇa forcibly gives one shelter at His lotus feet, where one will forget all other desires.'

PURPORT

This is a quotation from *Śrīmad-Bhāgavatam* (5.19.26).

TEXT 104

সাধুসঙ্গ, কৃষ্ণকৃপা, ভক্তির স্বভাব ।
এ তিনে সব ছাড়ায়, করে কৃষ্ণে 'ভাব' ॥ ১০৪ ॥

sādhu-saṅga, kṛṣṇa-kṛpā, bhaktira svabhāva
e tine saba chāḍāya, kare kṛṣṇe 'bhāva'

SYNONYMS

sādhu-saṅga—the association of devotees; *kṛṣṇa-kṛpā*—the mercy of Lord Kṛṣṇa; *bhaktira*—of devotional service; *sva-bhāva*—nature; *e tine*—these three; *saba chāḍāya*—cause one to give up everything else; *kare*—do; *kṛṣṇe*—unto Lord Kṛṣṇa; *bhāva*—the loving affairs.

TRANSLATION

"Association with a devotee, the mercy of Kṛṣṇa, and the nature of devotional service help one to give up all undesirable association and gradually attain elevation to the platform of love of Godhead.

PURPORT

This verse refers to the association of pure devotees, the mercy of Kṛṣṇa and the rendering of devotional service. All these help one give up the association of nondevotees and the material opulence awarded by the external energy, *māyā*. A pure devotee is never attracted by material opulence, for he understands that wasting time to acquire material opulence is a misuse of the gift of human life. In

Śrīmad-Bhāgavatam it is said: *śrama eva hi kevalam.* In the eyes of a devotee, politicians, social workers, philanthropists, philosophers and humanitarians are simply wasting their time, for human society is not freed from the cycle of birth and death by their activity and propaganda. These so-called philanthropists, politicians and philosophers have no knowledge because they do not know that there is life after death. Understanding that there is life after death is the beginning of spiritual knowledge. A person can understand himself and what he is simply by understanding the first lessons of *Bhagavad-gītā.*

dehino 'smin yathā dehe
kaumāraṁ yauvanaṁ jarā
tathā dehāntara-prāptir
dhīras tatra na muhyati

"As the embodied soul continually passes, in this body, from boyhood to youth to old age, the soul similarly passes into another body at death. The self-realized soul is not bewildered by such a change." (Bg. 2.13)

Not knowing the real science of life one engages in the temporary activities of this life and thus becomes further entangled in the cycle of birth and death. Thus one always desires material opulence, which can be attained by *karma, jñāna* and *yoga.* However, when one is actually elevated to the devotional platform, he gives up all these desires. This is called *anyābhilāṣitā-śūnya.* Then one becomes a pure devotee.

TEXT 105

আগে যত যত অর্থ ব্যাখ্যান করিব ।
কৃষ্ণগুণাস্বাদের এই হেতু জানিব ॥ ১০৫ ॥

āge yata yata artha vyākhyāna kariba
kṛṣṇa-guṇāsvādera ei hetu jāniba

SYNONYMS

āge—ahead; *yata yata*—as many as; *artha*—meanings; *vyākhyāna kariba*—I shall explain; *kṛṣṇa-guṇa-āsvādera*—of tasting the transcendental qualities of Kṛṣṇa; *ei*—this; *hetu*—reason; *jāniba*—we shall understand.

TRANSLATION

"In this way I shall progressively explain all the words in the verse. It should be understood that all these words are meant to enable one to taste the transcendental quality of Kṛṣṇa.

TEXT 106

শ্লোকব্যাখ্যা লাগি' এই করিলুঁ আভাস ।
এবে করি শ্লোকের মূলার্থ প্রকাশ ॥ ১০৬ ॥

śloka-vyākhyā lāgi' ei kariluṅ ābhāsa
ebe kari ślokera mūlārtha prakāśa

SYNONYMS

śloka-vyākhyā—of the explanation of the verse; *lāgi'*—for the matter; *ei*—this; *kariluṅ*—I did; *ābhāsa*—indication; *ebe*—now; *kari*—let Me do; *ślokera*—of the verse; *mūla-artha*—the real meaning; *prakāśa*—the manifestation.

TRANSLATION

"I have given all these explanations just to indicate the purpose of the verse. Allow me to explain the real purpose of the verse.

TEXT 107

জ্ঞানমার্গে উপাসক—দুইত' প্রকার ।
কেবল ব্রহ্মোপাসক, মোক্ষাকাঙ্ক্ষী আর ॥ ১০৭ ॥

jñāna-mārge upāsaka——duita' prakāra
kevala brahmopāsaka, mokṣākāṅkṣī āra

SYNONYMS

jñāna-mārge—on the path of philosophical speculation; *upāsaka*—worshipers; *duita' prakāra*—two varieties; *kevala*—only; *brahma-upāsaka*—the worshiper of impersonal Brahman; *mokṣa-ākāṅkṣī*—desiring liberation; *āra*—and.

TRANSLATION

"There are two kinds of worshipers on the path of philosophical speculation—one is brahma-upāsaka, a worshiper of the impersonal Brahman, and the other is called mokṣākāṅkṣī, one who desires liberation.

TEXT 108

কেবল ব্রহ্মোপাসক তিন ভেদ হয় ।
সাধক, ব্রহ্মময়, আর প্রাপ্ত-ব্রহ্মলয় ॥ ১০৮ ॥

kevala brahmopāsaka tina bheda haya
sādhaka, brahmamaya, āra prāpta-brahma-laya

SYNONYMS

kevala brahma-upāsaka—the worshiper of only the impersonal Brahman; *tina bheda haya*—there are three different groups; *sādhaka*—the beginner; *brahma-maya*—absorbed in thought of Brahman; *āra*—and; *prāpta-brahma-laya*—actually merged into the Brahman effulgence.

TRANSLATION

"There are three types of people who worship the impersonal Brahman. The first is the beginner, the second is one whose thoughts are absorbed in Brahman, and the third is one who is actually merged in the impersonal Brahman.

TEXT 109

ভক্তি বিনা কেবল জ্ঞানে 'মুক্তি' নাহি হয়।
ভক্তি সাধন করে যেই 'প্রাপ্ত-ব্রহ্মলয়' ॥ ১০৯ ॥

bhakti vinā kevala jñāne 'mukti' nāhi haya
bhakti sādhana kare yei 'prāpta-brahma-laya'

SYNONYMS

bhakti—devotional service; *vinā*—without; *kevala*—only; *jñāne*—by philosophical speculation; *mukti*—liberation; *nāhi haya*—there is not; *bhakti*—devotional service; *sādhana*—practice; *kare*—does; *yei*—anyone who; *prāpta-brahma-laya*—as good as merging into the impersonal Brahman.

TRANSLATION

"One cannot attain liberation simply through philosophical speculation devoid of devotional service. However, if one renders devotional service, he is automatically on the Brahman platform.

TEXT 110

ভক্তির স্বভাব,—ব্রহ্ম হৈতে করে আকর্ষণ।
দিব্য দেহ দিয়া করায় কৃষ্ণের ভজন ॥ ১১০ ॥

bhaktira svabhāva,——brahma haite kare ākarṣaṇa
divya deha diyā karāya kṛṣṇera bhajana

SYNONYMS

bhaktira—of devotional service; *sva-bhāva*—nature; *brahma*—impersonal Brahman realization; *haite*—from; *kare*—does; *ākarṣaṇa*—attracting; *divya*—transcendental; *deha*—body; *diyā*—offering; *karāya*—causes to perform; *kṛṣṇera bhajana*—the service of Lord Kṛṣṇa.

TRANSLATION

"Characteristically, one in devotional service is attracted away from the impersonal Brahman platform. He is offered a transcendental body to engage in Lord Kṛṣṇa's service.

TEXT 111

ভক্তদেহ পাইলে হয় গুণের স্মরণ ।
গুণাকৃষ্ট হঞা করে নির্মল ভজন ॥ ১১১ ॥

bhakta-deha pāile haya guṇera smaraṇa
guṇākṛṣṭa hañā kare nirmala bhajana

SYNONYMS

bhakta-deha—the body of a devotee; *pāile*—when one gets; *haya*—there is; *guṇera smaraṇa*—remembrance of the transcendental qualities; *guṇa-ākṛṣṭa hañā*—being attracted by the transcendental qualities; *kare*—performs; *nirmala bhajana*—pure devotional service.

TRANSLATION

"When one gets a devotee's spiritual body, he can remember the transcendental qualities of Kṛṣṇa. Simply by being attracted to Kṛṣṇa's transcendental qualities, one becomes a pure devotee engaged in His service.

PURPORT

Śrīla Bhaktivinoda Ṭhākura has given the following summary of verses 107-111. Transcendentalists on the path of philosophical speculation can be divided into two categories—the pure worshiper of impersonal Brahman and he who wishes to merge into the existence of impersonal Brahman. When one is fully absorbed in the thought that one is not different from the Supreme Absolute Truth, one is said to be a worshiper of the impersonal Brahman. The impersonal worshipers of Brahman can again be divided into three categories—(1) *sādhaka,* those who are nearing perfect execution of the process of Brahman realization; (2) those who are fully absorbed in meditation on Brahman; and (3) those who are on the *brahma-bhūta* platform and have no relationship with material existence. Even though the worshiper of impersonal Brahman can be highly advanced, he cannot attain liberation without discharging devotional service. Anyone who has realized himself as spirit soul can engage in devotional service. This is the verdict of *Bhagavad-gītā:*

brahma-bhūtaḥ prasannātmā
na śocati na kāṅkṣati
samaḥ sarveṣu bhūteṣu
mad-bhaktiṁ labhate parām

"One who is thus transcendentally situated at once realizes the Supreme Brahman and is fully joyful. He never laments nor desires to have anything; he is equally disposed to every living entity. In that state he attains pure devotional service unto Me." (Bg. 18.54)

To attain the platform of pure devotional service, one has to become spiritually pure and attain the *brahma-bhūta* platform, which is beyond material anxiety and material discrimination. When one approaches pure devotional service after realizing Brahman, one becomes attracted by pure devotional service. At such a time, by rendering devotional service, one gets a spiritual body with purified senses.

sarvopādhi-vinirmuktaṁ
tatparatvena nirmalam
hṛṣīkeṇa hṛṣīkeśa-
sevanaṁ bhaktir ucyate

When one's senses are pure, one can render loving devotional service to Kṛṣṇa. A pure devotee can only remember Kṛṣṇa's transcendental qualities. Remembering them, he fully engages in the loving service of the Lord.

TEXT 112

"মুক্তা অপি লীলয়া বিগ্রহং কৃত্বা ভগবন্তং ভজন্তে ॥"১১২ ॥

"muktā api līlayā vigrahaṁ
kṛtvā bhagavantaṁ bhajante"

SYNONYMS

muktāḥ—liberated; *api*—although; *līlayā*—by pastimes; *vigraham*—the form of the Lord; *kṛtvā*—having installed; *bhagavantam*—the Supreme Personality of Godhead; *bhajante*—worship.

TRANSLATION

" 'Even a liberated soul merged in the impersonal Brahman effulgence is attracted to the pastimes of Kṛṣṇa. He thus installs a Deity and renders the Lord service.'

PURPORT

Highly elevated Māyāvādī *sannyāsīs* sometimes worship the Rādhā-Kṛṣṇa Deity and discuss the pastimes of the Lord, but their purpose is not elevation to Goloka Vṛndāvana. They want to merge into the Lord's effulgence. This statement is quoted from Śaṅkarācārya's commentary on the *Upaniṣad* known as *Nṛsiṁha-tāpanī.*

TEXT 113

জন্ম হৈতে শুক-সনকাদি 'ব্রহ্মময়' ।
কৃষ্ণগুণাকৃষ্ট হঞা কৃষ্ণেরে ভজয় ॥ ১১৩ ॥

janma haite śuka-sanakādi 'brahmamaya'
kṛṣṇa-guṇākṛṣṭa hañā kṛṣṇere bhajaya

SYNONYMS

janma haite—from birth; *śuka*—Śukadeva Gosvāmī; *sanaka-ādi*—the four Kumāras; *brahma-maya*—absorbed in the thought of impersonal Brahman; *kṛṣṇa-guṇa-ākṛṣṭa*—attracted by the transcendental pastimes of the Lord; *hañā*—becoming; *kṛṣṇere bhajaya*—worshiped Lord Kṛṣṇa.

TRANSLATION

"Although Śukadeva Gosvāmī and the four Kumāras were always absorbed in the thought of impersonal Brahman and were thus Brahmavādīs, they were nonetheless attracted by the transcendental pastimes and qualities of Kṛṣṇa. Therefore they later became devotees of Kṛṣṇa.

TEXT 114

সনকাদ্যের কৃষ্ণকৃপায় সৌরভে হরে মন ।
গুণাকৃষ্ট হঞা করে নির্মল ভজন ॥ ১১৪ ॥

sanakādyera kṛṣṇa-kṛpāya saurabhe hare mana
guṇākṛṣṭa hañā kare nirmala bhajana

SYNONYMS

sanaka-ādyera—of the four Kumāras, headed by Sanaka; *kṛṣṇa-kṛpāya*—by the mercy of the Lord; *saurabhe*—the fragrance; *hare*—took away; *mana*—the minds; *guṇa-ākṛṣṭa hañā*—thus being attracted by the qualities of Kṛṣṇa; *kare*—perform; *nirmala bhajana*—pure devotional service.

TRANSLATION

"The minds of the four Kumāras were attracted by the aroma of the flowers offered to Kṛṣṇa's lotus feet. Being thus attracted by the transcendental qualities of Kṛṣṇa, they engaged in pure devotional service.

TEXT 115

তস্যারবিন্দনয়নস্য পদারবিন্দ-
কিঞ্জল্কমিশ্রতুলসীমকরন্দবায়ুঃ।
অন্তর্গতঃ স্ববিবরেণ চকার তেষাং
সংক্ষোভমক্ষরজুষামপি চিত্ততন্বোঃ ॥ ১১৫ ॥

tasyāravinda-nayanasya padāravinda-
kiñjalka-miśra-tulasī-makaranda-vāyuḥ
antargataḥ svavivareṇa cakāra teṣāṁ
saṅkṣobham akṣara-juṣām api citta-tanvoḥ

SYNONYMS

tasya—of Him; *aravinda-nayanasya*—of the lotus-eyed Lord; *pada-aravinda*—of the lotus feet; *kiñjalka*—with the toes; *miśra*—mixed; *tulasī*—the *tulasī* leaves; *makaranda*—fragrance; *vāyuḥ*—breeze; *antargataḥ*—entered within; *sva-vivareṇa*—through their nostrils; *cakāra*—made; *teṣām*—of the Kumāras; *saṅkṣobham*—agitation for change; *akṣara-juṣām*—attached to impersonal Brahman realization; *api*—even though; *citta-tanvoḥ*—in both mind and body.

TRANSLATION

" 'When the breeze carrying the aroma of tulasī leaves and saffron from the lotus feet of the lotus-eyed Personality of Godhead entered through the nostrils into the hearts of those sages [the Kumāras], they experienced a change in both body and mind, even though they were attached to impersonal Brahman understanding.'

PURPORT

This is a verse from *Śrīmad-Bhāgavatam* (3.15.43).

TEXT 116

ব্যাসকৃপায় শুকদেবের লীলাদি-স্মরণ।
কৃষ্ণগুণাকৃষ্ট হঞা করেন ভজন ॥ ১১৬ ॥

vyāsa-kṛpāya śukadevera līlādi-smaraṇa
kṛṣṇa-guṇākṛṣṭa hañā karena bhajana

SYNONYMS

vyāsa-kṛpāya—by the mercy of Śrīla Vyāsadeva; *śukadevera*—of Śukadeva Gosvāmī; *līlā-ādi-smaraṇa*—remembrance of the transcendental pastimes of Kṛṣṇa; *kṛṣṇa guṇa-ākṛṣṭa*—attracted by the transcendental qualities of Kṛṣṇa; *hañā*—becoming; *karena*—performed; *bhajana*—loving service.

TRANSLATION

"By the mercy of Śrīla Vyāsadeva, Śukadeva Gosvāmī was attracted by the pastimes of Lord Kṛṣṇa. Being thus attracted by Kṛṣṇa's transcendental qualities, he also became a devotee and engaged in His service.

TEXT 117

হরের্গুণাক্ষিপ্তমতির্ভগবান্ বাদরায়ণিঃ ।
অধ্যগান্মহদাখ্যানং নিত্যং বিষ্ণুজনপ্রিয়ঃ ॥ ১১৭ ॥

harer guṇākṣipta-matir
bhagavān bādarāyaṇiḥ
adhyagān mahad-ākhyānaṁ
nityaṁ viṣṇu-jana-priyaḥ

SYNONYMS

hareḥ—of Lord Kṛṣṇa; *guṇa-ākṣipta-matiḥ*—whose mind was agitated by the qualities; *bhagavān*—the most powerful transcendentalist; *bādarāyaṇiḥ*—Śukadeva, son of Vyāsadeva; *adhyagāt*—studied; *mahat-ākhyānam*—the great epic description; *nityam*—eternally; *viṣṇu-jana-priyaḥ*—who is very dear to the Vaiṣṇavas, devotees of Lord Viṣṇu.

TRANSLATION

" 'Being very much attracted by the transcendental pastimes of the Lord, the mind of Śrīla Śukadeva Gosvāmī was agitated by Kṛṣṇa consciousness. He therefore began to study Śrīmad-Bhāgavatam by the grace of his father.'

PURPORT

This is a quotation from *Śrīmad-Bhāgavatam* (1.7.11).

TEXT 118

নব-যোগীশ্বর জন্ম হৈতে 'সাধক' জ্ঞানী ।
বিধি-শিব-নারদ-মুখে কৃষ্ণগুণ শুনি' ॥ ১১৮ ॥

nava-yogīśvara janma haite 'sādhaka' jñānī
vidhi-śiva-nārada-mukhe kṛṣṇa-guṇa śuni'

SYNONYMS

nava—nine; *yogi-īśvara*—great saintly *yogīs; janma haite*—from the very birth; *sādhaka*—practicers; *jñānī*—well versed in transcendental knowledge; *vidhi*—Lord Brahmā; *śiva*—Lord Śiva; *nārada*—the great sage Nārada; *mukhe*—in their mouths; *kṛṣṇa-guṇa śuni'*—hearing the transcendental qualities of Kṛṣṇa.

TRANSLATION

"From their very births, the nine great mystic yogīs [Yogendras] were impersonal philosophers of the Absolute Truth. However, because they heard about Lord Kṛṣṇa's qualities from Lord Brahmā, Lord Śiva and the great sage Nārada, they also became Kṛṣṇa's devotees.

TEXT 119

গুণাকৃষ্ট হঞা করে কৃষ্ণের ভজন ।
একাদশ-স্কন্ধে তাঁর ভক্তি-বিবরণ ॥ ১১৯ ॥

guṇākṛṣṭa hañā kare kṛṣṇera bhajana
ekādaśa-skandhe tāṅra bhakti-vivaraṇa

SYNONYMS

guṇa-ākṛṣṭa hañā—being attracted by the transcendental qualities; *kare*—engaged in; *kṛṣṇera bhajana*—the devotional service of the Lord; *ekādaśa-skandhe*—in the Eleventh Canto of *Śrīmad-Bhāgavatam; tāṅra*—of them; *bhakti-vivaraṇa*—description of the devotional service.

TRANSLATION

"In the Eleventh Canto of the Śrīmad-Bhāgavatam there is a full description of the devotional service of the nine Yogendras, who rendered devotional service because they were attracted by the Lord's transcendental qualities.

TEXT 120

অক্লেশাং কমলভুবঃ প্রবিশ্য গোষ্ঠীং
কুর্বন্তঃ শ্রুতিশিরসাং শ্রুতিং শ্রুতজ্ঞাঃ ।
উত্তুঙ্গং যদুপুরসঙ্গমায় রঙ্গং
যোগীন্দ্রাঃ পুলকভৃতো নবাপ্যবাপুঃ ॥ ১২০ ॥

akleśāṁ kamala-bhuvaḥ praviśya goṣṭhīṁ
kurvantaḥ śruti-śirasāṁ śrutiṁ śrutajñāḥ
uttuṅgaṁ yadu-pura-saṅgamāya raṅgaṁ
yogīndrāḥ pulaka-bhṛto navāpy avāpuḥ

SYNONYMS

akleśām—without material trouble; *kamala-bhuvaḥ*—of Lord Brahmā, who took his birth from the lotus flower; *praviśya*—entering; *goṣṭhīm*—the association; *kurvantaḥ*—continuously performing; *śruti-śirasām*—of the topmost Vedic knowledge; *śrutim*—hearing; *śruta-jñāḥ*—who are expert in Vedic knowledge; *uttuṅgam*—very high; *yadu-pura-saṅgamāya*—for going back home, back to Godhead, to Dvārakā; *raṅgam*—to Raṅga-kṣetra; *yogīndrāḥ*—great saintly persons; *pulaka-bhṛtaḥ*—being spiritually pleased; *nava*—nine; *api*—although; *avāpuḥ*—achieved.

TRANSLATION

" 'The nine Yogendras entered Lord Brahmā's association and heard from him the real meaning of the topmost Vedic literatures—the Upaniṣads. Although they were already conversant in Vedic knowledge, they became very jubilant in Kṛṣṇa consciousness just by listening to Brahmā. Thus they wanted to enter Dvārakā, the abode of Lord Kṛṣṇa. In this way they finally achieved the place known as Raṅga-kṣetra.'

PURPORT

This is a quotation from the *Mahā Upaniṣad.*

TEXT 121

মোক্ষাকাঙ্ক্ষী জ্ঞানী হয় তিনপ্রকার ।
মুমুক্ষু, জীবন্মুক্ত, প্রাপ্তস্বরূপ আর ॥ ১২১ ॥

mokṣākāṅkṣī jñānī haya tina-prakāra
mumukṣu, jīvan-mukta, prāpta-svarūpa āra

SYNONYMS

mokṣa-ākāṅkṣī—those who desire to merge into the impersonal Brahman; *jñānī*—advanced in knowledge; *haya*—are; *tina-prakāra*—three varieties; *mumukṣu*—desiring to be liberated; *jīvat-mukta*—already liberated, even in this life; *prāpta-svarūpa*—self-realized; *āra*—and.

TRANSLATION

"Those who wish to merge into the impersonal Brahman are also divided into three categories—those desiring to be liberated, those already liberated and those who have realized Brahman.

TEXT 122

'মুমুক্ষু' জগতে অনেক সংসারী জন ।
'মুক্তি' লাগি' ভক্ত্যে করে কৃষ্ণের ভজন ॥ ১২২ ॥

'mumukṣu' jagate aneka saṁsārī jana
'mukti' lāgi' bhaktye kare kṛṣṇera bhajana

SYNONYMS

mumukṣu—desiring to be liberated; *jagate*—in this world; *aneka*—many; *saṁsārī jana*—engaged in material activities; *mukti lāgi'*—for the sake of liberation; *bhaktye*—in devotional service; *kare*—perform; *kṛṣṇera bhajana*—the worship of Kṛṣṇa.

TRANSLATION

"There are many people within this material world who desire liberation, and for this purpose they render devotional service to Lord Kṛṣṇa.

TEXT 123

মুমুক্ষবো ঘোররূপান্ হিত্বা ভূতপতীনথ ।
নারায়ণ-কলাঃ শান্তা ভজন্তি হ্যনসূয়বঃ ॥ ১২৩ ॥

mumukṣavo ghora-rūpān
hitvā bhūta-patīn atha
nārāyaṇa-kalāḥ śāntā
bhajanti hy anasūyavaḥ

SYNONYMS

mumukṣavaḥ—those who are perfectly learned, who desire the highest perfection, and who, unlike demons and nondevotees, are never envious of anyone;

ghora-rūpān—demigods with fearful bodily features; *hitvā*—giving up; *bhūta-patīn*—the forefathers (*prajāpatis*); *atha*—therefore; *nārāyaṇa-kalāḥ*—the plenary expansions of Lord Nārāyaṇa; *śāntāḥ*—very peaceful; *bhajanti*—they worship; *hi*—certainly; *anasūyavaḥ*—nonenvious.

TRANSLATION

" 'Those who want to be relieved from the material clutches give up the worship of the various demigods, who have fearful bodily features. Such peaceful devotees, who are not envious of the demigods, worship the different forms of the Supreme Personality of Godhead, Nārāyaṇa.'

PURPORT

This is a quotation from the *Śrīmad-Bhāgavatam* (1.2.26). Those who actually want the highest perfection worship Lord Viṣṇu in His different incarnations. Those who are attracted to the materialistic way of life and who are always agitated and full of anxiety worship demigods who appear fierce, demigods like goddess Kālī and Kāla-bhairava (Rudra). The devotees of Kṛṣṇa, however, do not envy the demigods or their worshipers but peacefully render devotional service to the incarnations of Nārāyaṇa instead.

TEXT 124

সেই সবের সাধুসঙ্গে গুণ স্ফুরায় ।
কৃষ্ণভজন করায়, 'মুমুক্ষা' ছাড়ায় ॥ ১২৪ ॥

sei sabera sādhu-saṅge guṇa sphurāya
kṛṣṇa-bhajana karāya, 'mumukṣā' chāḍāya

SYNONYMS

sei sabera—of all those worshipers of different demigods; *sādhu-saṅge*—the contact of real devotees; *guṇa sphurāya*—awakens the appreciation of transcendental qualities; *kṛṣṇa-bhajana karāya*—engages in the devotional service of Lord Kṛṣṇa; *mumukṣā chāḍāya*—and causes to give up the desire to be liberated or merge into the impersonal feature of the Lord.

TRANSLATION

"If those who are attached to demigod worship fortunately associate with the devotees, their dormant devotional service and appreciation of the Lord's qualities gradually awaken. In this way they also engage in Kṛṣṇa's devotional service and give up the desire for liberation and the desire to merge into the existence of impersonal Brahman.

PURPORT

The four Kumāras (Catuḥsana), Śukadeva Gosvāmī and the nine Yogendras were absorbed in Brahman realization, and how they became devotees is described herein. There are three kinds of impersonalists—the *mumukṣu* (those desiring liberation), the *jīvan-muktas* (those liberated in this life) and the *prāpta-svarūpas* (those merged in Brahman realization). All three types of *jñānīs* are called *mokṣākāṅkṣīs,* those desiring liberation. By associating with devotees, such people give up the *mumukṣu* principle and render devotional service. The real cause for this change is the association of devotees. This Kṛṣṇa consciousness movement is meant to attract all types of men, even those who desire things other than the Lord's devotional service. Through the association of devotees, they gradually begin to render devotional service.

TEXT 125

অহো মহাত্মন্ বহুদোষদুষ্টোঽ-
পোকেন ভাত্যেষ ভবো গুণেন ।
সৎসঙ্গমাখ্যেন সুখাবহেন
কৃতাদ্য নো যেন কৃশা মুমুক্ষা ॥ ১২৫ ॥

aho mahātman bahu-doṣa-duṣṭo
'py ekena bhāty eṣa bhavo guṇena
sat-saṅgamākhyena sukhāvahena
kṛtādya no yena kṛśā mumukṣā

SYNONYMS

aho mahātman—O great devotee; *bahu-doṣa-duṣṭaḥ*—infected with varieties of material disease or attachment; *api*—although; *ekena*—with one; *bhāti*—shines; *eṣaḥ*—this; *bhavaḥ*—birth in this material world; *guṇena*—with a good quality; *sat-saṅgama-ākhyena*—known as association with devotees; *sukha-āvahena*—which brings about happiness; *kṛtā*—made; *adya*—now; *naḥ*—our; *yena*—by which; *kṛśā*—insignificant; *mumukṣā*—the desire for liberation.

TRANSLATION

" 'O great learned devotee, although there are many faults in this material world, there is one good opportunity—the association with devotees. Such association brings about great happiness. Due to this good quality, our strong desire to achieve liberation by merging into the Brahman effulgence has become weakened.'

PURPORT

This is a quotation from the *Hari-bhakti-sudhodaya.*

TEXT 126

নারদের সঙ্গে শৌনকাদি মুনিগণ ।
মুমুক্ষা ছাড়িয়া কৈলা কৃষ্ণের ভজন ॥ ১২৬ ॥

nāradera saṅge śaunakādi muni-gaṇa
mumukṣā chāḍiyā kailā kṛṣṇera bhajana

SYNONYMS

nāradera saṅge—by the association of the great saintly person Nārada; *śaunaka-ādi muni-gaṇa*—the great sages headed by Śaunaka Muni; *mumukṣā chāḍiyā*—giving up the desire for liberation; *kailā*—performed; *kṛṣṇera bhajana*—devotional service to Kṛṣṇa.

TRANSLATION

"By associating with the great saint Nārada, the great sages like Śaunaka and others gave up the desire for liberation and engaged in Kṛṣṇa's devotional service.

TEXT 127

কৃষ্ণের দর্শনে, কারো কৃষ্ণের কৃপায় ।
মুমুক্ষা ছাড়িয়া গুণে ভজে তাঁর পা'য় ॥ ১২৭ ॥

kṛṣṇera darśane, kāro kṛṣṇera kṛpāya
mumukṣā chāḍiyā guṇe bhaje tāṅra pā'ya

SYNONYMS

kṛṣṇera darśane—simply by meeting Kṛṣṇa; *kāro*—someone; *kṛṣṇera kṛpāya*—by the favor of Kṛṣṇa; *mumukṣā chāḍiyā*—giving up the desire for liberation; *guṇe*—being attracted by the transcendental qualities of Kṛṣṇa; *bhaje*—engages in service; *tāṅra pā'ya*—at the lotus feet of Kṛṣṇa.

TRANSLATION

"Simply by meeting Kṛṣṇa or receiving Kṛṣṇa's special favor, one can give up the desire for liberation. Being attracted by the transcendental qualities of Kṛṣṇa, one can engage in His service.

TEXT 128

অস্মিন্ সুখঘনমূর্ত্তৌ পরমাত্মনি বৃষ্ণিপত্তনে স্ফুরতি ।
আত্মারামতয়া মে বৃথা গতো বত চিরং কালঃ ॥ ১২৮ ॥

asmin sukha-ghana-mūrtau param-
ātmani vṛṣṇi-pattane sphurati
ātmārāmatayā me vṛthā
gato bata ciraṁ kālaḥ

SYNONYMS

asmin—when this; *sukha-ghana-mūrtau*—form of complete happiness; *parama-ātmani*—the Supreme Person; *vṛṣṇi-pattane*—in Dvārakā-dhāma; *sphurati*—exists; *ātmārāmatayā*—by the process of cultivating Brahman realization; *me*—my; *vṛthā*—uselessly; *gataḥ*—wasted; *bata*—alas, what can I say; *ciram*—for a long time; *kālaḥ*—time.

TRANSLATION

" 'In this Dvārakā-dhāma, I am being attracted by the Supreme Personality of Godhead, Kṛṣṇa, who is personified spiritual bliss. Simply by seeing Him, I am feeling great happiness. Oh, I have wasted so much time trying to become self-realized through impersonal cultivation. This is a cause for lamentation!'

PURPORT

This verse is also found in *Bhakti-rasāmṛta-sindhu* (3.1.34).

TEXT 129

'জীবন্মুক্ত' অনেক, সেই দুই ভেদ জানি ।
'ভক্ত্যে জীবন্মুক্ত', 'জ্ঞানে জীবন্মুক্ত' মানি ॥ ১২৯ ॥

'jīvan-mukta' aneka, sei dui bheda jāni
'bhaktye jīvan-mukta', 'jñāne jīvan-mukta' māni

SYNONYMS

jīvat-mukta—liberated in this life; *aneka*—there are many; *sei*—all of them; *dui bheda*—two divisions; *jāni*—we consider; *bhaktye jīvat-mukta*—one liberated in this life by pursuing the process of devotional service; *jñāne jīvat-mukta*—a person liberated in this life by following the process of philosophical speculation; *māni*—we can understand.

TRANSLATION

"There are many people who are liberated even in this lifetime. Some are liberated by discharging devotional service, and others are liberated through the philosophical speculative process.

TEXT 130

'ভক্ত্যে জীবন্মুক্ত' গুণাকৃষ্ট হঞা কৃষ্ণ ভজে।
শুষ্কজ্ঞানে জীবন্মুক্ত অপরাধে অধো মজে ॥ ১৩০ ॥

'bhaktye jīvan-mukta' guṇākṛṣṭa hañā kṛṣṇa bhaje
śuṣka-jñāne jīvan-mukta aparādhe adho maje

SYNONYMS

bhaktye jīvat-mukta—persons liberated in this life by discharging devotional service; *guṇa-ākṛṣṭa hañā*—being attracted by the transcendental qualities of Kṛṣṇa; *kṛṣṇa bhaje*—engage in the devotional service of the Lord; *śuṣka-jñāne jīvat-mukta*—so-called liberated in this life by dry, speculative knowledge; *aparādhe*—by offenses; *adho maje*—fall down.

TRANSLATION

"Those who are liberated by devotional service become more and more attracted by the transcendental qualities of Kṛṣṇa. Thus they engage in His service. Those who are liberated by the speculative process eventually fall down again due to offensive activity.

TEXT 131

যেঽন্যেঽরবিন্দাক্ষ বিমুক্তমানিন-
স্ত্বয্যস্তভাবাদবিশুদ্ধবুদ্ধয়ঃ।
আরুহ্য কৃচ্ছ্রেণ পরং পদং ততঃ
পতন্ত্যধোঽনাদৃতযুষ্মদঙ্ঘ্রয়ঃ ॥ ১৩১ ॥

ye 'nye 'ravindākṣa vimukta-māninas
tvayy asta-bhāvād aviśuddha-buddhayaḥ
āruhya kṛcchreṇa paraṁ padaṁ tataḥ
patanty adho 'nādṛta-yuṣmad-aṅghrayaḥ

SYNONYMS

ye—all those who; *anye*—others (nondevotees); *aravinda-akṣa*—O lotus-eyed one; *vimukta-māninaḥ*—who consider themselves liberated; *tvayi*—unto You;

asta-bhāvāt—without devotion; *aviśuddha-buddhayaḥ*—whose intelligence is not purified; *āruhya*—having ascended; *kṛcchreṇa*—by severe austerities and penances; *param padam*—to the supreme position; *tataḥ*—from there; *patanti*—fall; *adhaḥ*—down; *anādṛta*—without respecting; *yuṣmat*—Your; *aṅghrayaḥ*—lotus feet.

TRANSLATION

" 'O lotus-eyed one, those who think they are liberated in this life but are without devotional service to You are of impure intelligence. Although they accept severe austerities and penances and rise to the spiritual position, to impersonal Brahman realization, they fall down again because they neglect to worship Your lotus feet.'

PURPORT

This is a quotation from *Śrīmad-Bhāgavatam* (10.2.32).

TEXT 132

ব্রহ্মভূতঃ প্রসন্নাত্মা ন শোচতি ন কাঙ্ক্ষতি ।
সমঃ সর্বেষু ভূতেষু মদ্ভক্তিং লভতে পরাম্ ॥ ১৩২ ॥

brahma-bhūtaḥ prasannātmā
na śocati na kāṅkṣati
samaḥ sarveṣu bhūteṣu
mad-bhaktiṁ labhate parām

SYNONYMS

brahma-bhūtaḥ—being one with the Absolute; *prasanna-ātmā*—fully joyful; *na*—never; *śocati*—laments; *na*—never; *kāṅkṣati*—desires; *samaḥ*—equally disposed; *sarveṣu*—all; *bhūteṣu*—to living entities; *mat-bhaktim*—My devotional service; *labhate*—gains; *parām*—transcendental.

TRANSLATION

" 'One who is thus transcendentally situated at once realizes the Supreme Brahman and is fully joyful. He never laments nor desires to have anything; he is equally disposed to every living entity. In that state he attains pure devotional service unto Me.'

PURPORT

This is a quotation from *Bhagavad-gītā* (18.54).

TEXT 133

অদ্বৈতবীথীপথিকৈরুপাস্যাঃ
স্বানন্দসিংহাসনলব্ধদীক্ষাঃ।
শঠেন কেনাপি বয়ং হঠেন
দাসীকৃতা গোপবধূবিটেন ॥ ১৩৩ ॥

advaita-vīthī-pathikair upāsyāḥ
svānanda-siṁhāsana-labdha-dīkṣāḥ
śaṭhena kenāpi vayaṁ haṭhena
dāsī-kṛtā gopa-vadhū-viṭena

SYNONYMS

advaita-vīthī—of the path of monism; *pathikaiḥ*—by the wanderers; *upāsyāḥ*—worshipable; *svānanda*—of self-realization; *siṁhāsana*—on the throne; *labdha-dīkṣāḥ*—being initiated; *śaṭhena*—by a cheater; *kenāpi*—some; *vayam*—I; *haṭhena*—by force; *dāsī-kṛtā*—made into a maidservant; *gopa-vadhū-viṭena*—engaged in joking with the *gopīs.*

TRANSLATION

" 'Although I was worshiped by those on the path of monism and initiated into self-realization through the yoga system, I am nonetheless forcibly turned into a maidservant by some cunning boy who is always joking with the gopīs.'

PURPORT

This is a verse written by Bilvamaṅgala Ṭhākura.

TEXT 134

ভক্তিবলে 'প্রাপ্তস্বরূপ' দিব্যদেহ পায়।
কৃষ্ণগুণাকৃষ্ট হঞা ভজে কৃষ্ণ-পা'য় ॥ ১৩৪ ॥

bhakti-bale 'prāpta-svarūpa' divya-deha pāya
kṛṣṇa-guṇākṛṣṭa hañā bhaje kṛṣṇa-pā'ya

SYNONYMS

bhakti-bale—by the strength of devotional service; *prāpta-svarūpa*—attaining his original status; *divya-deha*—a transcendental body; *pāya*—one gets; *kṛṣṇa-guṇa-ākṛṣṭa*—attracted by the transcendental qualities of Kṛṣṇa; *hañā*—being; *bhaje*—takes to devotional service; *kṛṣṇa-pā'ya*—at Kṛṣṇa's lotus feet.

TRANSLATION

"One who has attained his constitutional position by the strength of devotional service attains a transcendental body even in this lifetime. Being attracted by Lord Kṛṣṇa's transcendental qualities, one fully engages in service at His lotus feet.

TEXT 135

নিরোধোঽস্যানুশয়নমাত্মনঃ সহ শক্তিভিঃ ।
মুক্তির্হিত্বান্যথারূপং স্বরূপেণ ব্যবস্থিতিঃ ॥ ১৩৫ ॥

nirodho 'syānu śayanam
ātmanaḥ saha śaktibhiḥ
muktir hitvānyathā-rūpaṁ
svarūpeṇa vyavasthitiḥ

SYNONYMS

nirodhaḥ—winding up; *asya*—of this; *anu*—after; *śayanam*—lying down; *ātmanaḥ*—of the Supreme Lord; *saha*—with; *śaktibhiḥ*—the energies (marginal and external); *muktiḥ*—liberation; *hitvā*—giving up; *anyathā*—other; *rūpam*—form; *svarūpeṇa*—with one's own eternal form; *vyavasthitiḥ*—staying.

TRANSLATION

" 'The living entities and other potencies merge in the Mahā-Viṣṇu as the Lord lies down and winds up [destroys] the cosmic manifestation. Liberation means being situated in one's eternal original form, which he attains after giving up the changeable gross and subtle bodies.'

PURPORT

This is a quotation from *Śrīmad-Bhāgavatam* (2.10.6).

TEXT 136

কৃষ্ণ-বহির্মুখ-দোষে মায়া হৈতে ভয় ।
কৃষ্ণোন্মুখ ভক্তি হৈতে মায়া-মুক্ত হয় ॥ ১৩৬ ॥

kṛṣṇa-bahirmukha-doṣe māyā haite bhaya
kṛṣṇonmukha bhakti haite māyā-mukta haya

SYNONYMS

kṛṣṇa-bahiḥ-mukha—of going against Kṛṣṇa consciousness; *doṣe*—by the fault; *māyā haite*—from the illusory energy; *bhaya*—fear; *kṛṣṇa-unmukha*—in favor of Kṛṣṇa consciousness; *bhakti*—devotional service; *haite*—from; *māyā-mukta*—liberated from *māyā; haya*—one becomes.

TRANSLATION

"By opposing Kṛṣṇa consciousness, one again becomes conditioned and fearful due to the influence of māyā. By executing devotional service faithfully, one is liberated from māyā.

TEXT 137

ভয়ং দ্বিতীয়াভিনিবেশতঃ স্যা-
দীশাদপেতস্য বিপর্যয়োঽস্মৃতিঃ ।
তন্মায়য়াতো বুধ আভজেত্তং
ভক্ত্যৈকয়েশং গুরুদেবতাত্মা ॥ ১৩৭ ॥

bhayaṁ dvitīyābhiniveśataḥ syād
īśād apetasya viparyayo 'smṛtiḥ
tan-māyayāto budha ābhajet taṁ
bhaktyaikayeśaṁ guru-devatātmā

SYNONYMS

bhayam—fear; *dvitīya-abhiniveśataḥ*—from the misconception of being a product of material energy; *syāt*—arises; *īśāt*—from the Supreme Personality of Godhead, Kṛṣṇa; *apetasya*—of one who has withdrawn (the conditioned soul); *viparyayaḥ*—reversal of position; *asmṛtiḥ*—no conception of his relationship with the Supreme Lord; *tat-māyayā*—because of the illusory energy of the Supreme Lord; *ataḥ*—therefore; *budhaḥ*—one who is wise; *ābhajet*—must worship; *tam*—Him; *bhaktyā*—by devotional service; *ekayā*—undiverted to *karma* and *jñāna; īśam*—the Supreme Personality of Godhead; *guru*—as the spiritual master; *devatā*—worshipable Lord; *ātmā*—Supersoul.

TRANSLATION

" 'When the living entity is attracted by the material energy that is separate from Kṛṣṇa, he is overpowered by fear. Because he is separated from the Supreme Personality of Godhead by the material energy, his conception of life is reversed. In other words, instead of being the eternal servant of Kṛṣṇa, he becomes Kṛṣṇa's competitor. This is called viparyayaḥ asmṛtiḥ. To nullify this mistake, one who is actually learned and advanced worships the Supreme Personality of Godhead as his spiritual master, worshipful Deity and source of life. He thus worships the Lord by the process of unalloyed devotional service.'

PURPORT

This verse is quoted from *Śrīmad-Bhāgavatam* (11.2.37).

TEXT 138

দৈবী হ্যেষা গুণময়ী মম মায়া দুরত্যয়া।
মামেব যে প্রপদ্যন্তে মায়ামেতাং তরন্তি তে ॥ ১৩৮ ॥

daivī hy eṣā guṇamayī
mama māyā duratyayā
mām eva ye prapadyante
māyām etāṁ taranti te

SYNONYMS

daivī—belonging to the Supreme Lord; *hi*—certainly; *eṣā*—this; *guṇa-mayī*—made of the three modes; *mama*—My; *māyā*—external energy; *duratyayā*—very difficult to surpass; *mām*—unto Me; *eva*—certainly; *ye*—those who; *prapadyante*—surrender fully; *māyām*—the illusory energy; *etām*—this; *taranti*—cross over; *te*—they.

TRANSLATION

" 'This divine energy of Mine, consisting of the three modes of material nature, is difficult to overcome. But those who have surrendered unto Me can easily cross beyond it.'

PURPORT

This is a quotation from *Bhagavad-gītā* (7.14).

TEXT 139

ভক্তি বিনু মুক্তি নাহি, ভক্ত্যে মুক্তি হয় ॥ ১৩৯ ॥

bhakti vinu mukti nāhi, bhaktye mukti haya

SYNONYMS

bhakti—devotional service; *vinu*—without; *mukti*—liberation; *nāhi*—there is not; *bhaktye*—actually by devotional service; *mukti haya*—liberation is attained.

TRANSLATION

"One does not attain liberation without rendering devotional service. Liberation is only attained by devotional service.

TEXT 140

শ্রেয়ঃস্হৃতিং ভক্তিমুদস্য তে বিভো
ক্লিশ্যন্তি যে কেবল-বোধলব্ধয়ে ।
তেষামসৌ ক্লেশল এব শিষ্যতে
নান্যদ্‌যথা স্থূলতুষাবঘাতিনাম্‌ ॥ ১৪০ ॥

śreyaḥ-sṛtiṁ bhaktim udasya te vibho
kliśyanti ye kevala-bodha-labdhaye
teṣām asau kleśala eva śiṣyate
nānyad yathā sthūla-tuṣāvaghātinām

SYNONYMS

śreyaḥ-sṛtim—the auspicious path of liberation; *bhaktim*—devotional service; *udasya*—giving up; *te*—of You; *vibho*—O my Lord; *kliśyanti*—accept increased difficulties; *ye*—all those persons who; *kevala*—only; *bodha-labdhaye*—for obtaining knowledge; *teṣām*—for them; *asau*—that; *kleśalaḥ*—trouble; *eva*—only; *śiṣyate*—remains; *na*—not; *anyat*—anything else; *yathā*—as much as; *sthūla*—bulky; *tuṣa*—husks of rice; *avaghātinām*—of those beating.

TRANSLATION

" 'My dear Lord, devotional service unto You is the only auspicious path. If one gives it up simply for speculative knowledge or the understanding that these living beings are spirit souls and the material world is false, he undergoes a great deal of trouble. He only gains troublesome and inauspicious activities. His actions are like beating a husk that is already devoid of rice. One's labor becomes fruitless.'

PURPORT

This is a quotation from *Śrīmad-Bhāgavatam* (10.14.4).

TEXT 141

যেঽন্যেঽরবিন্দাক্ষ বিমুক্তমানিন-
স্ত্বয্যস্তভাবাদবিশুদ্ধবুদ্ধয়ঃ ।
আরুহ্য কৃচ্ছ্রেণ পরং পদং ততঃ
পতন্ত্যধোঽনাদৃতযুষ্মদঙ্ঘ্রয়ঃ ॥ ১৪১ ॥

ye 'nye 'ravindākṣa vimukta-māninas
tvayy asta-bhāvād aviśuddha-buddhayaḥ

āruhya kṛcchreṇa paraṁ padaṁ tataḥ
patanty adho 'nādṛta-yuṣmad-aṅghrayaḥ

SYNONYMS

ye—all those who; *anye*—others (nondevotees); *aravinda-akṣa*—O lotus-eyed one; *vimukta-māninaḥ*—who consider themselves liberated; *tvayi*—unto You; *asta-bhāvāt*—without devotion; *aviśuddha-buddhayaḥ*—whose intelligence is not purified; *āruhya*—having ascended; *kṛcchreṇa*—by severe austerities and penances; *param padam*—to the supreme position; *tataḥ*—from there; *patanti*—fall; *adhaḥ*—down; *anādṛta*—without respecting; *yuṣmat*—Your; *aṅghrayaḥ*—lotus feet.

TRANSLATION

" 'O lotus-eyed one, those who think they are liberated in this life but are without devotional service to You are of impure intelligence. Although they accept severe austerities and penances and rise to the spiritual position, to impersonal Brahman realization, they fall down again because they neglect to worship Your lotus feet.'

PURPORT

This is a verse from *Śrīmad-Bhāgavatam* (10.2.32).

TEXT 142

য এষাং পুরুষং সাক্ষাদাত্মপ্রভবমীশ্বরম্ ।
ন ভজন্ত্যবজানন্তি স্থানাদ্ভ্রষ্টাঃ পতন্ত্যধঃ ॥ ১৪২ ॥

ya eṣāṁ puruṣaṁ sākṣād
ātma-prabhavam īśvaram
na bhajanty avajānanti
sthānād bhraṣṭāḥ patanty adhaḥ

SYNONYMS

ye—those who; *eṣām*—of those divisions of social and spiritual orders; *puruṣam*—the Supreme Personality of Godhead; *sākṣāt*—directly; *ātma-prabhavam*—the source of everyone; *īśvaram*—the supreme controller; *na*—do not; *bhajanti*—worship; *avajānanti*—or who neglect; *sthānāt*—from their proper place; *bhraṣṭāḥ*—being fallen; *patanti*—fall; *adhaḥ*—downward into hellish conditions.

TRANSLATION

" 'If one simply maintains an official position in the four varṇas and āśramas but does not worship the Supreme Lord Viṣṇu, he falls down from his puffed-up position into a hellish condition.'

PURPORT

This is also a quotation from *Śrīmad-Bhāgavatam* (11.5.3).

TEXT 143

ভক্ত্যে মুক্তি পাইলেহ অবশ্য কৃষ্ণেরে ভজয় ॥ ১৪৩ ॥

bhaktye mukti pāileha avaśya kṛṣṇere bhajaya

SYNONYMS

bhaktye—by devotional service; *mukti*—liberation; *pāileha*—if one gets; *avaśya*—certainly; *kṛṣṇere*—unto Lord Kṛṣṇa; *bhajaya*—renders service.

TRANSLATION

"When one is actually liberated by executing devotional service, he always engages in the transcendental loving service of the Lord.

TEXT 144

"মুক্তা অপি লীলয়া বিগ্রহং কৃত্বা ভগবন্তং ভজন্তে ॥" ১৪৪ ॥

"muktā api līlayā vigrahaṁ
kṛtvā bhagavantaṁ bhajante"

SYNONYMS

muktāḥ—liberated; *api*—although; *līlayā*—by the pastimes; *vigraham*—the form of the Lord; *kṛtvā*—having installed; *bhagavantam*—the Supreme Personality of Godhead; *bhajante*—worship.

TRANSLATION

" 'Even a liberated soul merged in the impersonal Brahman effulgence is attracted to the pastimes of Kṛṣṇa. He thus installs a Deity and renders the Lord service.'

PURPORT

This is a quotation from Śaṅkarācārya's commentary on the *Nṛsiṁha-tāpanī Upaniṣad.*

TEXT 145

এই ছয় আত্মারাম কৃষ্ণেরে ভজয় ।
পৃথক্ পৃথক্ চ-কারে ইহা 'অপি'র অর্থ কয় ॥ ১৪৫ ॥

ei chaya ātmārāma kṛṣṇere bhajaya
pṛthak pṛthak ca-kāre ihā 'api'ra artha kaya

SYNONYMS

ei chaya—all these six; *ātmārāma*—transcendentalists; *kṛṣṇere bhajaya*—render service to Kṛṣṇa; *pṛthak pṛthak*—separately; *ca-kāre*—in the use of the word *ca; ihā*—here; *'api'ra*—of the word *api; artha*—meaning; *kaya*—says.

TRANSLATION

"These six kinds of ātmārāmas engage in the loving service of Kṛṣṇa. The varieties of service are indicated by adding ca, and they also bear the meaning of api, 'indeed.'

PURPORT

There are six kinds of *ātmārāmas:* the neophyte (*sādhaka*) student who is absorbed in Brahman realization (*brahmamaya*), one who has already attained the Brahman position (*prāpta-brahma-laya*), one who desires to be liberated (*mumukṣu*), one who is liberated even in this life (*jīvan-mukta*), and one who is self-realized (*prāpta-svarūpa*).

TEXT 146

"আত্মারামাশ্চ অপি" করে কৃষ্ণে অহৈতুকী ভক্তি ।
"মুনয়ঃ সন্তঃ" ইতি কৃষ্ণমননে আসক্তি ॥ ১৪৬ ॥

"ātmārāmāś ca api" kare kṛṣṇe ahaitukī bhakti
"munayaḥ santaḥ" iti kṛṣṇa-manane āsakti

SYNONYMS

ātmārāmāḥ ca api—self-realized persons also; *kare*—do; *kṛṣṇe*—unto Kṛṣṇa; *ahaitukī bhakti*—unmotivated devotional service; *munayaḥ santaḥ*—great saintly persons and transcendentalists; *iti*—thus; *kṛṣṇa-manane*—in meditation on Kṛṣṇa; *āsakti*—attraction.

TRANSLATION

"The six kinds of ātmārāmas render devotional service to Kṛṣṇa without ulterior motives. The words munayaḥ and santaḥ indicate those who are very attached to meditating upon Kṛṣṇa.

TEXT 147

"নিগ্র'ন্থাঃ"—অবিদ্যাহীন, কেহ—বিধিহীন।
যাহাঁ যেই যুক্ত, সেই অর্থের অধীন ॥ ১৪৭ ॥

"nirgranthāḥ"——avidyā-hīna, keha——vidhi-hīna
yāhāṅ yei yukta, sei arthera adhīna

SYNONYMS

nirgranthāḥ—*nirgranthāḥ; avidyā-hīna*—without ignorance; *keha*—some of them; *vidhi-hīna*—without following any regulative principles; *yāhāṅ*—wherever; *yei*—which; *yukta*—appropriate; *sei arthera adhīna*—comes under that different import.

TRANSLATION

"The word nirgranthāḥ means 'without ignorance' and 'devoid of rules and regulations.' Whichever meaning fits may be applied.

TEXT 148

চ-শব্দে করি যদি 'ইতরেতর' অর্থ।
আর এক অর্থ কহে পরম সমর্থ ॥ ১৪৮ ॥

ca-śabde kari yadi 'itaretara' artha
āra eka artha kahe parama samartha

SYNONYMS

ca-śabde—by the word *ca; kari*—I do; *yadi*—if; *itaretara artha*—different and separate meanings; *āra*—another; *eka*—one; *artha*—meaning; *kahe*—is said; *parama samartha*—highly suitable.

TRANSLATION

"By using the word ca in different places, there are different meanings. Over and above them, there is another meaning that is very important.

TEXT 149

"আত্মারামাশ্চ আত্মারামাশ্চ" করি' বার ছয়।
পঞ্চ আত্মারাম ছয় চ-কারে লুপ্ত হয় ॥ ১৪৯ ॥

"ātmārāmāś ca ātmārāmāś ca" kari' bāra chaya
pañca ātmārāma chaya ca-kāre lupta haya

SYNONYMS

ātmārāmāḥ ca ātmārāmāḥ ca—repeating the words *ātmārāmāḥ* and *ca; kari'*—doing; *bāra chaya*—six times; *pañca ātmārāma*—five kinds of *ātmārāmas; chaya*—six; *ca-kāre*—by the word *ca; lupta haya*—become unpronounced.

TRANSLATION

"Although the words ātmārāmāś ca would be repeated six times, simply by adding the word ca, five ātmārāmas are deleted.

TEXT 150

এক 'আত্মারাম'-শব্দ অবশেষ রহে ।
এক 'আত্মারাম'-শব্দে ছয়জন কহে ॥ ১৫০ ॥

eka 'ātmārāma'-śabda avaśeṣa rahe
eka 'ātmārāma'-śabde chaya-jana kahe

SYNONYMS

eka—one; *ātmārāma*—*ātmārāma; śabda*—vibration; *avaśeṣa rahe*—remains at last; *eka ātmārāma*—one *ātmārāma; śabde*—by vibrating; *chaya-jana*—six persons; *kahe*—are indicated.

TRANSLATION

"Therefore there is no need to repeat the word ātmārāma. One is sufficient, and that one word indicates six persons.

TEXT 151

"সরূপাণামেকশেষ একবিভক্তৌ" ।
উক্তার্থানামপ্রয়োগঃ ।
রামশ্চ রামশ্চ রামশ্চ রামা ইতিবৎ ॥ ১৫১ ॥

"sarūpāṇām eka-śeṣa eka-vibhaktau"
uktārthānām aprayogaḥ
rāmaś ca rāmaś ca rāmaś ca rāmā itivat

SYNONYMS

sa-rūpāṇām—of words of the same form; *eka-śeṣaḥ*—only the last; *eka-vibhaktau*—in the same case; *ukta-arthānām*—of the previously spoken meanings; *aprayogaḥ*—nonapplication; *rāmaḥ ca*—and Rāma; *rāmaḥ ca*—and

Rāma; *rāmaḥ ca*—and Rāma; *rāmāḥ itivat*—in this way, by one *rāma,* many *rāmas* are indicated.

TRANSLATION

" 'Of words having the same form and case termination, the last one is the only one retained. For example, the word rāmaḥ is used to stand for rāmaś ca, rāmaś ca, rāmaś ca, etc.'

PURPORT

This is a quotation from Pāṇini's *sūtras* (1.2.64).

TEXT 152

তবে যে চ-কার, সেই 'সমুচ্চয়' কয় ।
"আত্মারামাশ্চ মুনয়শ্চ" কৃষ্ণেরে ভজয় ॥ ১৫২ ॥

tabe ye ca-kāra, sei 'samuccaya' kaya
"ātmārāmāś ca munayaś ca" kṛṣṇere bhajaya

SYNONYMS

tabe—then; *ye*—that; *ca-kāra*—syllable *ca; sei*—that; *samuccaya*—aggregation; *kaya*—is said; *ātmārāmāḥ ca*—all those who enjoy in the self; *munayaḥ ca*—all saintly persons; *kṛṣṇere bhajaya*—worship Kṛṣṇa.

TRANSLATION

"By the aggregate use of the word ca, it is indicated that all the ātmārāmas and saints serve and worship Kṛṣṇa.

TEXT 153

"নির্গ্রন্থা অপি"র এই 'অপি'—সম্ভাবনে ।
এই সাত অর্থ প্রথমে করিলুঁ ব্যাখ্যানে ॥ ১৫৩ ॥

"nirgranthā api"ra ei 'api'——sambhāvane
ei sāta artha prathame kariluṅ vyākhyāne

SYNONYMS

nirgranthāḥ apira—of the words *nirgranthāḥ api; ei*—this; *api*—*api; sambhāvane*—in the matter of exposition; *ei sāta artha*—these seven different meanings; *prathame*—in the beginning; *kariluṅ*—I have done; *vyākhyāne*—in explanation.

TRANSLATION

"Api added to the word nirgranthāḥ is used for exposition. Thus I have tried to clarify the seven types of meaning.

TEXT 154

অন্তর্যামি-উপাসক 'আত্মারাম' কয়।
সেই আত্মারাম যোগীর দুই ভেদ হয়॥ ১৫৪॥

antaryāmi-upāsaka 'ātmārāma' kaya
sei ātmārāma yogīra dui bheda haya

SYNONYMS

antaryāmi—of the Supersoul; *upāsaka*—worshiper; *ātmārāma kaya*—is also said to be an *ātmārāma; sei ātmārāma*—that *ātmārāma; yogīra*—of the mystic *yogī; dui bheda haya*—there are two kinds.

TRANSLATION

"The yogī who worships the Supersoul within himself is also called ātmārāma. There are two types of ātmārāma-yogīs.

TEXT 155

সগর্ভ, নিগর্ভ,—এই হয় দুই ভেদ।
এক এক তিন ভেদে ছয় বিভেদ॥ ১৫৫॥

sagarbha, nigarbha,——ei haya dui bheda
eka eka tina bhede chaya vibheda

SYNONYMS

sagarbha—*sagarbha; nigarbha*—*nigarbha; ei*—thus; *haya*—there are; *dui*—two; *bheda*—different varieties; *eka eka*—each one; *tina bhede*—in three varieties; *chaya vibheda*—therefore there are six varieties.

TRANSLATION

"The two ātmārāma-yogīs are called sagarbha and nigarbha. Each of these is divided into three; therefore there are six types of worshipers of the Supersoul.

PURPORT

The word *sagarbha-yogī* refers to a *yogī* who worships the Supersoul in the Viṣṇu form. The *nigarbha-yogī* worships the Supersoul without form. The *sagarbha* and *nigarbha yogīs* are further categorized: (1) *sagarbha-yogārurukṣu,* (2) *nigarbha-yogārurukṣu,* (3) *sagarbha-yogārūḍha,* (4) *nigarbha-yogārūḍha,* (5) *sagarbha-prāpta-siddhi* and (6) *nigarbha-prāpta-siddhi.*

TEXT 156

কেচিৎ স্বদেহান্তর্হৃদয়াবকাশে প্রাদেশমাত্রং পুরুষং বসন্তম্ ।
চতুর্ভুজং কঞ্জরথাঙ্গশঙ্খগদাধরং ধারণয়া স্মরন্তি ॥ ১৫৬ ॥

kecit svadehāntar hṛdayāvakāśe
prādeśa-mātraṁ puruṣaṁ vasantam
catur-bhujaṁ kañja-rathāṅga-śaṅkha-
gadā-dharaṁ dhāraṇayā smaranti

SYNONYMS

kecit—some of them; *sva-deha-antaḥ*—within one's own body; *hṛdaya-avakāśe*—in the cavity of the heart; *prādeśa-mātram*—with the measurement of six inches; *puruṣam*—the Supreme Personality of Godhead; *vasantam*—residing; *catuḥ-bhujam*—with four hands; *kañja*—a lotus flower; *ratha-aṅga*—a disc like the wheel of a chariot; *śaṅkha*—a conchshell; *gadā-dharam*—holding the club; *dhāraṇayā*—by such contemplation; *smaranti*—they remember.

TRANSLATION

" 'Some yogīs think of the Lord within their hearts as measuring about six inches. The Lord has four hands, in which He holds a conchshell, club, disc and lotus flower. Those who worship this form of Viṣṇu within the heart are called sagarbha-yogīs.'

PURPORT

This verse is from *Śrīmad-Bhāgavatam* (2.2.8).

TEXT 157

এবং হরৌ ভগবতি প্রতিলব্ধভাবো
ভক্ত্যা দ্রবদ্ধৃদয় উৎপুলকঃ প্রমোদাৎ ।
ঔৎকণ্ঠ্যবাষ্পকলয়া মুহুরর্দ্যমান-
স্তচ্চাপি চিত্তবড়িশং শনকৈর্বিযুঙ্ক্তে ॥ ১৫৭ ॥

evaṁ harau bhagavati pratilabdha-bhāvo
bhaktyā dravad-dhṛdaya utpulakaḥ pramodāt
autkaṇṭhya-bāṣpa-kalayā muhur ardyamānas
tac cāpi citta-baḍiśaṁ śanakair viyuṅkte

SYNONYMS

evam—thus; *harau*—unto the Supreme Personality of Godhead; *bhagavati*—the Lord; *pratilabdha-bhāvaḥ*—one who has awakened a sense of ecstatic love; *bhaktyā*—by devotional service; *dravat*—melting; *hṛdayaḥ*—the heart; *ut-pulakaḥ*—very pleased; *pramodāt*—because of happiness; *autkaṇṭhya*—with eagerness; *bāṣpa-kalayā*—with tears in the eyes; *muhuḥ*—always; *ardyamānaḥ*—merged in spiritual bliss; *tat ca api*—that also; *citta-baḍiśam*—with the heart like a fishing hook; *śanakaiḥ*—gradually; *viyuṅkte*—separates.

TRANSLATION

" 'When one is in ecstatic love with the Supreme Personality of Godhead, one's heart is melted by bhakti-yoga, and one feels transcendental bliss. There are bodily symptoms manifest, and, due to eagerness, there are tears in the eyes. Thus one is subjected to spiritual bliss. When the heart is overly afflicted, the meditative mind, like a fishing hook, is gradually separated from the object of meditation.'

PURPORT

This is also a quotation from *Śrīmad-Bhāgavatam* (3.28.34).

TEXT 158

'যোগারুরুক্ষু', 'যোগারূঢ়' 'প্রাপ্তসিদ্ধি' আর ।
এই তিন ভেদে হয় ছয় প্রকার ॥ ১৫৮ ॥

'yogārurukṣu', 'yogārūḍha' 'prāpta-siddhi' āra
ei tina bhede haya chaya prakāra

SYNONYMS

yoga-ārurukṣu—persons desiring elevation to the platform of yogic perfection; *yoga-ārūḍha*—persons already elevated to that position; *prāpta-siddhi*—persons who have achieved the success; *āra*—also; *ei tina*—these three; *bhede*—by varieties; *haya*—there are; *chaya prakāra*—six kinds.

TRANSLATION

"By these three divisions of advancement in yoga—yogārurukṣu, yogārūḍha and prāpta-siddhi—there are six kinds of mystic yogīs.

TEXT 159

আরুরুক্ষোর্মুনের্যোগং কর্ম কারণমুচ্যতে ।
যোগারূঢ়স্য তস্যৈব শমঃ কারণমুচ্যতে ॥ ১৫৯ ॥

ārurukṣor muner yogaṁ
karma kāraṇam ucyate
yogārūḍhasya tasyaiva
śamaḥ kāraṇam ucyate

SYNONYMS

ārurukṣoḥ—of a person desiring to rise to the platform of yogic perfection; *muneḥ*—of a saintly person; *yogam*—spiritual knowledge; *karma*—work; *kāraṇam*—the cause; *ucyate*—is said; *yoga-ārūḍhasya*—of one who has attained such perfect knowledge; *tasya*—for him; *eva*—certainly; *śamaḥ*—controlling the mind without being disturbed; *kāraṇam*—cause; *ucyate*—is said.

TRANSLATION

" 'Those who wish to rise to the platform of yogic perfection practice the yoga system and strictly follow its regulative principles. They practice the yoga postures, āsanas and breathing exercises. Those who are already elevated to this platform practice meditation and keep their minds on the Supreme Lord. They reject all material activity and keep their minds in an equipoised condition [śama].

PURPORT

Texts 159 and 160 are from *Bhagavad-gītā* (6.3-4).

TEXT 160

যদা হি নেন্দ্রিয়ার্থেষু ন কর্মস্বনুষজ্জতে ।
সর্বসংকল্পসন্ন্যাসী যোগারূঢ়স্তদোচ্যতে ॥ ১৬০ ॥

yadā hi nendriyārtheṣu
na karmasv anuṣajjate
sarva-saṅkalpa-sannyāsī
yogārūḍhas tadocyate

SYNONYMS

yadā—when; *hi*—certainly; *na*—not; *indriya-artheṣu*—sense gratification; *na*—not; *karmasu*—in activities; *anuṣajjate*—one becomes engaged; *sarva*—all kinds of; *saṅkalpa*—desires; *sannyāsī*—renouncing; *yoga-ārūḍhaḥ*—one who has actually attained perfection in the *yoga* system; *tadā*—at that time; *ucyate*—is said.

TRANSLATION

" 'When a person is no longer interested in acting for sense gratification and when he renounces all material desires, he is said to be situated in perfect yoga [yogārūḍha].'

TEXT 161

এই ছয় যোগী সাধুসঙ্গাদি-হেতু পাঞা ।
কৃষ্ণ ভজে কৃষ্ণগুণে আকৃষ্ট হঞা ॥ ১৬১ ॥

ei chaya yogī sādhu-saṅgādi-hetu pāñā
kṛṣṇa bhaje kṛṣṇa-guṇe ākṛṣṭa hañā

SYNONYMS

ei—this; *chaya*—six; *yogī*—mystics; *sādhu*—of devotees; *saṅga-ādi*—the association; *hetu*—because of; *pāñā*—getting; *kṛṣṇa bhaje*—render service to Kṛṣṇa; *kṛṣṇa-guṇe*—by the transcendental qualities of Kṛṣṇa; *ākṛṣṭa*—attracted; *hañā*—becoming.

TRANSLATION

"When a purified yogī associates with devotees, he engages in Lord Kṛṣṇa's devotional service, being attracted by the Lord's transcendental qualities.

TEXT 162

চ-শব্দে 'অপি'র অর্থ ইহাঁও কহয় ।
'মুনি', 'নিগ্রর্ন্থ'-শব্দের পূর্ব্ববৎ অর্থ হয় ॥ ১৬২ ॥

ca-śabde 'api'ra artha ihāṅo kahaya
'muni', 'nirgrantha'-śabdera pūrvavat artha haya

SYNONYMS

ca-śabde—by the word *ca; 'api'ra*—of the word *api; artha*—the meaning; *ihāṅo*—here also; *kahaya*—is applicable; *muni*—a saintly person; *nirgrantha*—fully liberated; *śabdera*—of the words; *pūrva-vat*—as mentioned above; *artha haya*—there are the meanings.

TRANSLATION

"The meanings of the words ca and api can be applied here. The meanings of the words muni and nirgrantha are the same as before.

TEXT 163

উরুক্রমে অহৈতুকী কাহাঁ কোন অর্থ।
এই তের অর্থ কহিলুঁ পরম সমর্থ॥ ১৬৩॥

urukrame ahaituki kāhān kona artha
ei tera artha kahiluṅ parama samartha

SYNONYMS

urukrame—unto the Supreme Personality of Godhead, who acts uncommonly; *ahaitukī*—without motives; *kāhāṅ*—wherever; *kona*—some; *artha*—import; *ei*—in this way; *tera artha*—thirteen imports; *kahiluṅ*—I have explained; *parama*—supremely; *samartha*—complete.

TRANSLATION

"The word ahaitukī is always applicable to the Supreme Personality of Godhead, Urukrama. In this way I have described the import of all these things in thirteen complete varieties.

PURPORT

The thirteen varieties mentioned are (1) *sādhaka,* the neophyte performer; (2) *brahmamaya,* one absorbed in the thought of impersonal Brahman; (3) *prāpta-brahma-laya,* one who has actually attained Brahman perfection; (4) *mumukṣu,* the desirer of liberation; (5) *jīvan-mukta,* one who is liberated in this life; (6) *prāpta-svarūpa,* one who has attained one's original consitutional position; (7) *nirgrantha-muni,* a completely liberated saint; (8) *sagarbha-yogārurukṣu,* a *yogī* meditating upon the four-handed Viṣṇu form or desiring yogic perfection; (9) *nigarbha-yogārurukṣu,* one who has attained perfection in impersonal meditation; (10) *sagarbha-yogārūḍha,* already elevated to the *yoga* perfection platform; (11) *nigarbha-yogārūḍha,* similarly impersonal *yogī;* (12) *sagarbha-prāpta-siddhi,* one who has already attained the perfectional stage; (13) *nigarbha-prāpta-siddhi,* one who has attained perfection by impersonal meditation.

TEXT 164

এই সব শান্ত যবে ভজে ভগবান্।
'শান্ত' ভক্ত করি' তবে কহি তাঁর নাম॥ ১৬৪॥

ei saba śānta yabe bhaje bhagavān
'śānta' bhakta kari' tabe kahi tāṅra nāma

SYNONYMS

ei saba—all these; *śānta*—neutral; *yabe*—when; *bhaje*—worship; *bhagavān*—the Supreme Personality of Godhead; *śānta bhakta*—devotees in the neutral stage of devotional service; *kari'*—describing as; *tabe*—that time; *kahi*—I speak; *tāṅra*—their; *nāma*—name.

TRANSLATION

"These thirteen types of yogīs and munis are called śānta-bhaktas, for they render transcendental loving service to the Supreme Personality of Godhead in the neutral stage.

TEXT 165

'আত্মা' শব্দে 'মন' কহ—মনে যেই রমে ।
সাধুসঙ্গে সেহ ভজে শ্রীকৃষ্ণচরণে ॥ ১৬৫ ॥

'ātmā' śabde 'mana' kaha——mane yei rame
sādhu-saṅge seha bhaje śrī-kṛṣṇa-caraṇe

SYNONYMS

ātmā—ātmā; śabde—by the word; *mana*—the mind; *kaha*—if you say; *mane*—within the mind; *yei rame*—one who is satisfied by speculation; *sādhu-saṅge*—by the association of devotees; *seha*—he also; *bhaje*—takes to devotional service; *śrī-kṛṣṇa-caraṇe*—at the lotus feet of Lord Kṛṣṇa.

TRANSLATION

"The word ātmā sometimes means 'the mind.' In this case, the word ātmārāma means 'a person who is satisfied by mental speculation.' When such a person associates with a pure devotee, he takes to devotional service at the lotus feet of Kṛṣṇa.

TEXT 166

উদরমুপাসতে য ঋষিবর্ত্মসু কূর্পদৃশঃ
পরিসরপদ্ধতিং হৃদয়মারুণয়ো দহরম্ ।
তত উদগাদনন্ত তব ধাম শিরঃ পরমং
পুনরিহ যৎ সমেত্য ন পতন্তি কৃতান্তমুখে ॥ ১৬৬ ॥

udaram upāsate ya ṛṣi-vartmasu kūrpa-dṛśaḥ
parisara-paddhatiṁ hṛdayam āruṇayo daharam
tata udagād ananta tava dhāma śiraḥ paramaṁ
punar iha yat sametya na patanti kṛtānta-mukhe

SYNONYMS

udaram—the abdomen*; *upāsate*—worship; *ye*—those who; *ṛṣi-vartmasu*—on the path marked out by the great saintly persons; *kūrpa-dṛśaḥ*—whose vision is grossly situated in the bodily conception of life; *parisara-paddhatim*—from which the system of the arteries comes; *hṛdayam*—the heart; *āruṇayaḥ*—saintly persons headed by Āruṇa Ṛṣi; *daharam*—the sky within the heart, the subtle conception of the Supersoul within the heart; *tataḥ*—from that; *udagāt*—went up; *ananta*—O unlimited one; *tava*—Your; *dhāma*—place; *śiraḥ*—the top of the head; *paramam*—supreme; *punaḥ*—again; *iha*—in this material world; *yat*—which; *sametya*—having achieved; *na*—not; *patanti*—fall down; *kṛta-anta-mukhe*—in the repetition of birth and death.

TRANSLATION

" 'Those who follow the path of great, saintly mystic yogīs take to the yogic gymnastic process and begin worshiping from the abdomen, where it is said that Brahman is located. Such people are called śārkarākṣa, which means that they are situated in the gross bodily conception. There are also followers of the ṛṣi known as Āruṇa. Following that path, they observe the activities of the arteries. Thus they gradually rise to the heart, where subtle Brahman, Paramātmā, is situated. They then worship Him. O unlimited Ananta! Better than these persons are the mystic yogīs who worship You from the top of their heads. Beginning with the abdomen and proceeding through the heart, they reach the top of the head and pass through the brahma-randhra, the hole at the top of the skull. Thus yogīs attain the perfectional platform and do not enter the cycle of birth and death again.'

PURPORT

This is a quotation from *Śrīmad-Bhāgavatam* (10.87.18).

TEXT 167

এহো কৃষ্ণগুণাকৃষ্ট মহামুনি হঞা ।
অহৈতুকী ভক্তি করে নির্গ্রন্থ হঞা ॥ ১৬৭ ॥

eho kṛṣṇa-guṇākṛṣṭa mahā-muni hañā
ahaitukī bhakti kare nirgrantha hañā

---

*For *yogīs,* the abdomen is technically understood to be *muni-purastha-brahman,* Brahman situated within the heart to digest food and keep the body fit.

SYNONYMS

eho—such *yogīs; kṛṣṇa guṇa-ākṛṣṭa*—attracted by the transcendental qualities of Kṛṣṇa; *mahā-muni hañā*—becoming great saintly persons; *ahaitukī bhakti kare*—they perform causeless devotional service; *nirgrantha hañā*—becoming indifferent to the mystic *yoga* process.

TRANSLATION

"Being attracted by the transcendental qualities of Kṛṣṇa, yogīs become great saints. At that time, not being hampered by the yogic process, they engage in unalloyed devotional service.

TEXT 168

'আত্মা'-শব্দে 'যত্ন' কহে—যত্ন করিয়া ।
"মুনয়োঽপি" কৃষ্ণ ভজে গুণাকৃষ্ট হঞা ॥ ১৬৮ ॥

'ātmā'-śabde 'yatna' kahe——yatna kariyā
"munayo 'pi" kṛṣṇa bhaje guṇākṛṣṭa hañā

SYNONYMS

ātmā-śabde—by the word *ātmā; yatna*—endeavor; *kahe*—one means; *yatna kariyā*—by great endeavor; *munayaḥ api*—even great saintly persons; *kṛṣṇa bhaje*—take to the devotional service of Kṛṣṇa; *guṇa-ākṛṣṭa hañā*—being attracted by His transcendental qualities.

TRANSLATION

"Ātmā also means 'endeavor.' Being attracted by Kṛṣṇa's transcendental qualities, some saints make a great endeavor to come to the point of rendering service to Him.

TEXT 169

তস্যৈব হেতোঃ প্রযতেত কোবিদো
ন লভ্যতে যদ্‌ভ্রমতামুপর্যধঃ ।
তল্লভ্যতে দুঃখবদন্যতঃ সুখং
কালেন সর্বত্র গভীর-রংহসা ॥ ১৬৯ ॥

tasyaiva hetoḥ prayateta kovido
na labhyate yad bhramatām upary adhaḥ

tal labhyate duḥkhavad anyataḥ sukhaṁ
kālena sarvatra gabhīra-raṁhasā

SYNONYMS

tasya eva—for that; *hetoḥ*—reason; *prayateta*—should endeavor; *kovidaḥ*—one who is learned and intelligent; *na*—not; *labhyate*—is achieved; *yat*—that which; *bhramatām*—of those wandering; *upari adhaḥ*—up and down; *tat*—that; *labhyate*—is achieved; *duḥkhavat*—exactly like unhappiness or distress; *anyataḥ*—from other reasons (one's past actions); *sukham*—happiness; *kālena*—by time; *sarvatra*—everywhere; *gabhīra*—insurmountable; *raṁhasā*—having force.

TRANSLATION

" 'The transcendental position cannot be attained by wandering up and down from Brahmaloka and Satyaloka to Pātālaloka. If one is actually intelligent and learned, he should endeavor for that rare transcendental position. Whatever material happiness is available within the fourteen worlds is attained by the force of time, just as one attains distress in due course of time. Since these are not attained by spiritual consciousness, one should not try for them.'

PURPORT

This verse was spoken by Nārada Muni in *Śrīmad-Bhāgavatam* (1.5.18). Nārada Muni was speaking to Vyāsadeva, who was morose even after he had compiled all Vedic literatures. In this connection, Nārada Muni advised Śrīla Vyāsadeva to attain devotional service.

TEXT 170

সদ্ধর্মস্যাববোধায় যেষাং নির্বন্ধিনী মতিঃ ।
অচিরাদেব সর্বার্থঃ সিধ্যত্যেষামভীপ্সিতঃ ॥ ১৭০ ॥

sad-dharmasyāvabodhāya
yeṣāṁ nirbandhinī matiḥ
acirād eva sarvārthaḥ
sidhyaty eṣām abhīpsitaḥ

SYNONYMS

sat-dharmasya—of the path of progressive devotional service; *avabodhāya*—for understanding; *yeṣām*—those whose; *nirbandhinī*—unflinching; *matiḥ*—intelligence; *acirāt*—very soon; *eva*—certainly; *sarva-arthaḥ*—the goal of life; *sidhyati*—becomes fulfilled; *eṣām*—of these persons; *abhīpsitaḥ*—desired.

TRANSLATION

" 'Those who are anxious to awaken their spiritual consciousness, who have unflinching intelligence and who are not deviated, certainly attain the desired goal of life.'

PURPORT

This is a quotation from the *Nāradīya Purāṇa.*

TEXT 171

চ-শব্দ অপি-অর্থে, 'অপি'—অবধারণে ।
যত্নাগ্রহ বিনা ভক্তি না জন্মায় প্রেমে ॥ ১৭১ ॥

ca-śabda api-arthe, 'api'——avadhāraṇe
yatnāgraha vinā bhakti nā janmāya preme

SYNONYMS

ca-śabda—the word *ca; api*—of the word *api; arthe*—in the meaning; *api avadhāraṇe*—this *api* is used in sense of emphasis; *yatna-āgraha vinā*—without sincere endeavor; *bhakti*—devotional service; *nā*—not; *janmāya*—begets; *preme*—love of Godhead.

TRANSLATION

"The word ca may be used in place of api, which gives emphasis to something. Thus it means that without sincere endeavor in devotional service, one cannot attain love of Godhead.

TEXT 172

সাধনৌঘৈরনাসঙ্গৈরলভ্যা স্থচিরাদপি ।
হরিণা চাশ্বদেয়েতি দ্বিধা সা স্যাৎ স্থদুর্লভা ॥ ১৭২ ॥

sādhanaughair anāsaṅgair
alabhyā sucirād api
hariṇā cāśv adeyeti
dvidhā sā syāt sudurlabhā

SYNONYMS

sādhana—activities of devotional service; *aughaiḥ*—by masses of; *anāsaṅgaiḥ*—without attachment; *alabhyā*—very difficult to achieve; *su-cirāt api*—even after a considerable duration of time; *hariṇā*—by the Supreme Lord;

ca—also; *āśu*—very soon; *adeyā*—not to be delivered; *iti*—thus; *dvidhā*—two ways; *sā*—that; *syāt*—is; *su-durlabhā*—very difficult to obtain.

TRANSLATION

" 'Devotional perfection is very difficult to attain for two reasons. First, unless one is attached to Kṛṣṇa, he cannot attain devotional perfection even if he renders devotional service for a long time. Second, Kṛṣṇa does not easily deliver perfection in devotional service.'

PURPORT

As stated in *Śrīmad-Bhāgavatam* (5.6.18): *muktiṁ dadāti karhicit.* Śrīla Śukadeva Gosvāmī told Mahārāja Parīkṣit that Kṛṣṇa readily grants liberation but does not very readily grant perfection in devotional service. This means that Kṛṣṇa wants to see that a devotee is actually sincere and serious and that he does not have ulterior motives. If this is the case, devotional service can very easily be successful; otherwise it is very difficult to obtain from the Supreme Personality of Godhead. This verse appears in the *Bhakti-rasāmṛta-sindhu* (1.1.35).

TEXT 173

তেষাং সততযুক্তানাং ভজতাং প্রীতিপূর্বকম্ ।
দদামি বুদ্ধিযোগং তং যেন মামুপযান্তি তে ॥ ১৭৩ ॥

teṣāṁ satata-yuktānāṁ
bhajatāṁ prīti-pūrvakam
dadāmi buddhi-yogaṁ taṁ
yena mām upayānti te

SYNONYMS

teṣām—to them; *satata-yuktānām*—always engaged; *bhajatām*—in devotional service; *prīti-pūrvakam*—in loving ecstasy; *dadāmi*—I give; *buddhi-yogam*—real intelligence; *tam*—that; *yena*—by which; *mām*—unto Me; *upayānti*—come; *te*—they.

TRANSLATION

" 'To those who are constantly devoted and worship Me with love, I give the understanding by which they can come to Me.'

PURPORT

This is a quotation from *Bhagavad-gītā* (10.10).

TEXT 174

'আত্মা'-শব্দে 'ধৃতি' কহে,—ধৈর্যে যেই রমে।
ধৈর্যবন্ত এব হঞা করয় ভজনে ॥ ১৭৪ ॥

'ātmā'-śabde 'dhṛti' kahe,——dhairye yei rame
dhairyavanta eva hañā karaya bhajane

SYNONYMS

ātmā-śabde—by the word *ātmā; dhṛti*—perseverance; *kahe*—it is said; *dhairye*—with perseverance; *yei rame*—anyone who endeavors; *dhairyavanta*—such persons with endurance; *eva*—certainly; *hañā*—becoming; *karaya*—perform; *bhajane*—devotional service.

TRANSLATION

"Another meaning of ātmā is dhṛti, or endurance. A person who endeavors with endurance is ātmārāma. With endurance, such a person engages in devotional service.

TEXT 175

'মুনি'-শব্দে—পক্ষী, ভৃঙ্গ ; 'নিগ্রর্ন্থে'—মূর্খজন।
কৃষ্ণকৃপায় সাধুকৃপায় দোঁহার ভজন ॥ ১৭৫ ॥

'muni'-śabde——pakṣī, bhṛṅga; 'nirgranthe'——mūrkha-jana
kṛṣṇa-kṛpāya sādhu-kṛpāya doṅhāra bhajana

SYNONYMS

muni-śabde—by the word *muni; pakṣī*—bird; *bhṛṅga*—bumblebee; *nirgranthe*—in the word *nirgrantha; mūrkha-jana*—foolish people; *kṛṣṇa-kṛpāya*—by the mercy of Lord Kṛṣṇa; *sādhu-kṛpāya*—by the mercy of a devotee; *doṅhāra bhajana*—engages in devotional service of both (Kṛṣṇa and his spiritual master or the *sādhu*).

TRANSLATION

"The word muni also means 'bird,' and 'bumblebee.' The word nirgrantha refers to foolish people. By the mercy of Kṛṣṇa, such creatures contact a sādhu [spiritual master] and thus engage in devotional service.

TEXT 176

প্রায়ো বতাম্ব মুনয়ো বিহগা বনেঽস্মিন্
কৃষ্ণেক্ষিতং তদুদিতং কলবেণুগীতম্ ।
আরুহ্য যে দ্রুমভুজান্ রুচিরপ্রবালান্
শৃণ্বন্তি মীলিতদৃশো বিগতান্যবাচঃ ॥ ১৭৬ ॥

prāyo batāmba munayo vihagā vane 'smin
kṛṣṇekṣitaṁ tad-uditaṁ kala-veṇu-gītam
āruhya ye druma-bhujān rucira-prabālān
śṛṇvanti mīlita-dṛśo vigatānya-vācaḥ

SYNONYMS

prāyaḥ—almost; *bata*—certainly; *amba*—O mother; *munayaḥ*—great sages; *vihagāḥ*—the birds; *vane*—in the forest; *asmin*—this; *kṛṣṇa-īkṣitam*—seeing the lotus feet of Kṛṣṇa; *tat-uditam*—created by Him; *kala-veṇu-gītam*—sweet vibrations made by playing the flute; *āruhya*—rising; *ye*—all of them; *druma-bhujān*—to the branches of the trees; *rucira-prabālān*—having beautiful creepers and twigs; *śṛṇvanti*—hear; *mīlita-dṛśaḥ*—closing their eyes; *vigata-anya-vācaḥ*—stopping all other sounds.

TRANSLATION

" 'My dear mother, in this forest, all the birds, after rising on the beautiful branches of the trees, are closing their eyes and, not being attracted by any other sound, are simply listening to the vibration of Kṛṣṇa's flute. Such birds and bees must be on the same level as great saints.'

PURPORT

This is a quotation from *Śrīmad-Bhāgavatam* (10.21.14). This statement was made by the *gopīs,* who were lamenting in separation from Kṛṣṇa and studying how the inhabitants of Vṛndāvana were enjoying life like saintly persons.

TEXT 177

এতেঽলিনস্তব যশোঽখিল-লোকতীর্থং
গায়ন্ত আদিপুরুষানুপথং ভজন্তে ।
প্রায়ো অমী মুনিগণা ভবদীয়মুখ্যা
গূঢ়ং বনেঽপি ন জহত্যনঘাত্মদৈবম্ ॥ ১৭৭ ॥

ete 'linas tava yaśo 'khila-loka-tīrthaṁ
gāyanta ādi-puruṣānupathaṁ bhajante
prāyo amī muni-gaṇā bhavadīya-mukhyā
gūḍhaṁ vane 'pi na jahaty anaghātma-daivam

SYNONYMS

ete—all these; *alinaḥ*—bees; *tava*—Your; *yaśaḥ*—reputation; *akhila*—all; *loka-tīrtham*—auspicious for the planets; *gāyante*—are singing; *ādi-puruṣa*—O original person; *anupatham*—along the path; *bhajante*—they are engaged in transcendental loving service; *prāyaḥ*—almost; *amī*—these; *muni-gaṇāḥ*—great saintly persons; *bhavadīya*—in relation with You; *mukhyāḥ*—very advanced devotees; *gūḍham*—unknown; *vane*—in the forest; *api*—although; *na*—not; *jahati*—give up; *anagha*—O personality of transcendental goodness; *ātma-daivam*—their worshipable Deity.

TRANSLATION

" 'O good fortune personified! O original Personality of Godhead, all these bees are chanting about Your transcendental fame, which will purify the entire universe. Indeed, they are following Your path in the forest and are worshiping You. Actually they are all saintly persons, but now they have taken the form of bees. Although You are playing like a human being, they could not forget that You are their worshipable Deity.'

PURPORT

This is a quotation from *Śrīmad-Bhāgavatam* (10.15.6). Kṛṣṇa and Balarāma were just on the verge of boyhood and were entering the forest of Vṛndāvana when Kṛṣṇa began to offer prayers to please Balarāma.

TEXT 178

সরসি সারসহংসবিহঙ্গাশ্চারুগীতহৃতচেতস এত্য ।
হরিমুপাসত তে যতচিত্তা হন্ত মীলিতদৃশো ধৃতমৌনাঃ ॥১৭৮॥

sarasi sārasa-haṁsa-vihaṅgāś
cāru-gīta-hṛta-cetasa etya
harim upāsata te yata-cittā
hanta mīlita-dṛśo dhṛta-maunāḥ

SYNONYMS

sarasi—in the water; *sārasa*—cranes; *haṁsa*—swans; *vihaṅgāḥ*—birds; *cāru-gīta*—by the melodious song of Kṛṣṇa's flute; *hṛta-cetasaḥ*—devoid of material consciousness; *etya*—coming near; *harim*—the Supreme Personality of Godhead; *upāsata*—worshiped; *te*—all of them; *yata-cittāḥ*—with full attention; *hanta*—alas; *mīlita-dṛśaḥ*—closing their eyes; *dhṛta-maunāḥ*—completely silent.

TRANSLATION

" 'All the cranes and swans in the water are being enchanted by the melodious song of Kṛṣṇa's flute. They have approached and are worshiping the Supreme Personality of Godhead with full attention. Alas, they are closing their eyes and are becoming completely silent.'

PURPORT

This is a quotation from *Śrīmad-Bhāgavatam* (10.35.11). In the day, Kṛṣṇa went to the forest of Vṛndāvana, and at that time, the *gopīs,* being morose due to separation from Him, were lamenting in this way.

TEXT 179

কিরাতহূনান্ধ্রপুলিন্দপুক্কশা
আভীরশুম্ভা যবনাঃ খশাদয়ঃ ।
যেঽন্যে চ পাপা যদুপাশ্রয়াশ্রয়াঃ
শুধ্যন্তি তস্মৈ প্রভবিষ্ণবে নমঃ ॥ ১৭৯ ॥

kirāta-hūnāndhra-pulinda-pukkaśā
ābhīra-śumbhā yavanāḥ khaśādayaḥ
ye 'nye ca pāpā yad-upāśrayāśrayāḥ
śudhyanti tasmai prabhaviṣṇave namaḥ

SYNONYMS

kirāta—the aborigines named Kirātas; *hūna*—the Hūnas; *āndhra*—Āndhras; *pulinda*—Pulindas; *pukkaśāḥ*—Pukkaśas; *ābhīra*—Ābhīras; *śumbhāḥ*—Śumbhas; *yavanāḥ*—persons who do not follow the Vedic injunctions and who eat cow's flesh; *khaśa-ādayaḥ*—Khaśas and others; *ye*—those who; *anye*—similar others; *ca*—also; *pāpāḥ*—sinful persons; *yat*—of the Supreme Personality of Godhead; *upāśraya*—of the devotees; *āśrayāḥ*—taking shelter; *śudhyanti*—become purified; *tasmai*—unto Him, Lord Viṣṇu, because of whom they become purified; *prabhaviṣṇave*—to Lord Viṣṇu, the most powerful; *namaḥ*—respectful obeisances.

TRANSLATION

" 'Kirāta, Hūna, Āndhra, Pulinda, Pukkaśa, Ābhīra, Śumbha, Yavana and the Khaśa races and even others who are addicted to sinful acts can be purified by

taking shelter of the devotees of the Lord due to His being the supreme power. I beg to offer my respectful obeisances unto Him.'

PURPORT

This is a quotation from *Śrīmad-Bhāgavatam* (2.4.18). This verse was spoken by Śukadeva Gosvāmī when Parīkṣit Mahārāja asked him for a description of the creation. While offering obeisances to the Supreme Personality of Godhead, Śukadeva Gosvāmī described the unlimited potencies of Lord Viṣṇu, who can purify the lowborn creatures mentioned herein.

TEXT 180

কিংবা 'ধৃতি'-শব্দে নিজপূর্ণতাদি-জ্ঞান কয়।
দুঃখাভাবে উত্তমপ্রাপ্ত্যে মহাপূর্ণ হয় ॥ ১৮০ ॥

kiṁvā 'dhṛti'-śabde nija-pūrṇatādi-jñāna kaya
duḥkhābhāve uttama-prāptye mahā-pūrṇa haya

SYNONYMS

kiṁvā—or; *dhṛti*—*dhṛti;* *śabde*—by this word; *nija*—own; *pūrṇatā-ādi*—perfection and so on; *jñāna*—knowledge; *kaya*—says; *duḥkha-abhāve*—in the absence of all material miseries; *uttama*—the best; *prāptye*—by obtaining; *mahā-pūrṇa haya*—becomes perfectly perfect.

TRANSLATION

"The word dhṛti is also used when one is fully perfect in knowledge. When due to having obtained the lotus feet of the Supreme Personality of Godhead, he has no material miseries, he attains mahā-pūrṇa, the highest level of perfection.

TEXT 181

ধৃতিঃ স্যাৎ পূর্ণতা জ্ঞান-দুঃখাভাবোত্তমাপ্তিভিঃ।
অপ্রাপ্তাতীত-নষ্টার্থানভিসংশোচনাদিকৃৎ ॥ ১৮১ ॥

dhṛtiḥ syāt pūrṇatā jñāna-
duḥkhābhāvottamāptibhiḥ
aprāptātīta-naṣṭārthā-
nabhisaṁśocanādikṛt

SYNONYMS

dhṛtiḥ—endurance; *syāt*—may become; *pūrṇatā*—fullness; *jñāna*—knowledge of the Supreme Personality of Godhead; *duḥkha-abhāva*—the absence of misery;

uttama-āptibhiḥ—by attainment of the highest platform of perfection; *aprāpta*—not obtained; *atīta*—gone; *naṣṭa*—destroyed; *artha*—object, goal; *anabhisaṁśocana*—absence of lamentation; *ādi*—and so on; *kṛt*—doing.

TRANSLATION

" 'Dhṛti is the fullness felt by the absence of misery and brought about by receiving knowledge of the Supreme Lord and by obtaining pure love for Him. The lamentation that accrues from not obtaining a goal or by loss of something already attained does not affect this completeness.'

PURPORT

This verse is found in *Bhakti-rasāmṛta-sindhu* (2.4.144).

TEXT 182

কৃষ্ণভক্ত— দুঃখহীন, বাঞ্ছান্তর-হীন ।
কৃষ্ণপ্রেম-সেবা-পূর্ণানন্দ-প্রবীণ ॥ ১৮২ ॥

kṛṣṇa-bhakta——duḥkha-hīna, vāñchāntara-hīna
kṛṣṇa-prema-sevā-pūrṇānanda-pravīṇa

SYNONYMS

kṛṣṇa-bhakta—a devotee of Lord Kṛṣṇa; *duḥkha-hīna*—not under miserable material conditions; *vāñchā-antara-hīna*—he has no other desire than to serve Kṛṣṇa; *kṛṣṇa-prema*—love of Kṛṣṇa; *sevā*—service; *pūrṇa-ānanda*—full in transcendental bliss; *pravīṇa*—and very expert or experienced in all subject matters.

TRANSLATION

"A devotee of Kṛṣṇa is never in a miserable condition, nor does he have any desire other than to serve Kṛṣṇa. He is experienced and advanced. He feels the transcendental bliss of love of Kṛṣṇa and always engages in His service fully protected.

TEXT 183

মৎসেবয়া প্রতীতং তে সালোক্যাদি-চতুষ্টয়ম্ ।
নেচ্ছন্তি সেবয়া পূর্ণাঃ কুতোঽন্যৎ কালবিপ্লুতম্ ॥ ১৮৩ ॥

mat-sevayā pratītaṁ te
sālokyādi-catuṣṭayam
necchanti sevayā pūrṇāḥ
kuto 'nyat kāla-viplutam

SYNONYMS

mat—of Me; *sevayā*—by service; *pratītam*—obtained; *te*—they; *sālokya-ādi*—liberation, beginning with *sālokya; catuṣṭayam*—the four kinds of; *na icchanti*—do not desire; *sevayā*—by service; *pūrṇāḥ*—complete; *kutaḥ*—where; *anyat*—other things; *kāla-viplutam*—which are lost in time.

TRANSLATION

" 'My devotees, having fulfilled their desires by serving Me, do not accept the four kinds of salvation that are easily earned by such service. Why then should they accept any pleasures that are lost in the course of time?'

PURPORT

This is a quotation from *Śrīmad-Bhāgavatam* (9.4.67).

TEXT 184

হৃষীকেশে হৃষীকাণি যস্য স্থৈর্যগতানি হি ।
স এব ধৈর্যমাপ্নোতি সংসারে জীবচঞ্চলে ॥ ১৮৪ ॥

hṛṣīkeśe hṛṣīkāṇi
yasya sthairya-gatāni hi
sa eva dhairyam āpnoti
saṁsāre jīva-cañcale

SYNONYMS

hṛṣīkeśe—to the master of the senses; *hṛṣīkāṇi*—all the senses; *yasya*—whose; *sthairya-gatāni*—fixed; *hi*—certainly; *saḥ*—that person; *eva*—of course; *dhairyam āpnoti*—attains the position of *dhairya,* endurance; *saṁsāre*—in the material world; *jīva-cañcale*—where everyone is disturbed.

TRANSLATION

"In this material world, all living entities are disturbed due to their flickering position. A devotee, however, is fixed in the service of the lotus feet of the Lord, the master of the senses. Such a person is to be considered situated in endurance and patience.

TEXT 185

'চ'—অবধারণে, ইহা 'অপি'—সমুচ্চয়ে ।
ধৃতিমন্ত হঞা ভজে পক্ষি-মূর্খ-চয়ে ॥ ১৮৫ ॥

'ca'——avadhāraṇe, ihā 'api'——samuccaye
dhṛtimanta hañā bhaje pakṣi-mūrkha-caye

SYNONYMS

ca—the word *ca; avadhāraṇe*—in emphasis; *ihā*—here; *api*—the word *api; samuccaye*—in the sense of an aggregate; *dhṛtimanta*—fully saturated; *hañā*—becoming; *bhaje*—worship; *pakṣi-mūrkha-caye*—dull creatures like the birds, the most foolish.

TRANSLATION

"The word ca is for emphasis, and the word api is used as an aggregate. It is to be understood that even dull creatures [birds and illiterates] can also be situated in endurance and engage in Kṛṣṇa's devotional service.

TEXT 186

'আত্মা'-শব্দে 'বুদ্ধি' কহে বুদ্ধিবিশেষ ।
সামান্যবুদ্ধিযুক্ত যত জীব অবশেষ ॥ ১৮৬ ॥

'ātmā'-śabde 'buddhi' kahe buddhi-viśeṣa
sāmānya-buddhi-yukta yata jīva avaśeṣa

SYNONYMS

ātmā-śabde—by the word *ātmā; buddhi*—intelligence; *kahe*—it is said; *buddhi-viśeṣa*—a particular type of intelligence; *sāmānya-buddhi-yukta*—endowed with common intelligence; *yata*—all; *jīva*—living entities; *avaśeṣa*—the rest.

TRANSLATION

"The word ātmā is also used for a particular type of intelligence. Since all living entities generally have some intelligence, more or less, they are included.

TEXT 187

বুদ্ধ্যে রমে আত্মারাম—দুই ত' প্রকার ।
'পণ্ডিত' মুনিগণ, নির্গ্রন্থ 'মূর্খ' আর ॥ ১৮৭ ॥

buddhye rame ātmārāma——dui ta' prakāra
'paṇḍita' muni-gaṇa, nirgrantha 'mūrkha' āra

SYNONYMS

buddhye—in intelligence; *rame*—who enjoys; *ātmārāma*—is *ātmārāma; dui ta' prakāra*—two varieties; *paṇḍita*—learned; *muni-gaṇa*—philosophers; *nir-grantha*—without education; *mūrkha*—foolish; *āra*—also.

TRANSLATION

"Everyone has some kind of intelligence, and one who utilizes his intelligence is called ātmārāma. There are two types of ātmārāma. One is a learned scholar and a philosopher, and the other is an uneducated, illiterate and foolish person.

TEXT 188

কৃষ্ণকৃপায় সাধুসঙ্গে রতি-বুদ্ধি পায় ।
সব ছাড়ি' শুদ্ধভক্তি করে কৃষ্ণপায় ॥ ১৮৮ ॥

kṛṣṇa-kṛpāya sādhu-saṅge rati-buddhi pāya
saba chāḍi' śuddha-bhakti kare kṛṣṇa-pāya

SYNONYMS

kṛṣṇa-kṛpāya—by the mercy of Kṛṣṇa; *sādhu-saṅge*—in the association of devotees; *rati-buddhi*—devotional attraction and intelligence; *pāya*—one obtains; *saba chāḍi'*—giving up everything; *śuddha-bhakti*—pure devotional service; *kare*—performs; *kṛṣṇa-pāya*—at the lotus feet of Kṛṣṇa.

TRANSLATION

"By the mercy of Kṛṣṇa and by the association of devotees, one increases his attraction to and intelligence for pure devotional service; therefore one gives up everything and engages himself at the lotus feet of Kṛṣṇa and His pure devotees.

TEXT 189

অহং সর্বস্য প্রভবো মত্তঃ সর্বং প্রবর্ততে ।
ইতি মত্বা ভজন্তে মাং বুধা ভাবসমন্বিতাঃ ॥ ১৮৯ ॥

ahaṁ sarvasya prabhavo
mattaḥ sarvaṁ pravartate
iti matvā bhajante māṁ
budhā bhāva-samanvitāḥ

SYNONYMS

aham—I, Lord Kṛṣṇa; *sarvasya*—of everyone; *prabhavaḥ*—the original source; *mattaḥ*—from Me; *sarvam*—everything; *pravartate*—emanates; *iti*—thus; *matvā*—understanding; *bhajante*—they engage in devotional service; *mām*—to Me; *budhāḥ*—those who are learned; *bhāva-samanvitāḥ*—with love and devotion.

TRANSLATION

" 'I [Kṛṣṇa] am the original source of everything. Everything emanates from Me. The wise who perfectly know this engage in My service with love and devotion.'

PURPORT

This is a quotation from *Bhagavad-gītā* (10.8).

TEXT 190

তে বৈ বিদন্ত্যতিতরন্তি চ দেবমায়াং
স্ত্রীশূদ্রহূনশবরা অপি পাপজীবাঃ।
যদ্যদ্ভুতক্রমপরায়ণ-শীল-শিক্ষা-
স্তির্যগ্‌জনা অপি কিমু শ্রুতধারণা যে ॥ ১৯০ ॥

te vai vidanty atitaranti ca deva-māyāṁ
strī-śūdra-hūna-śabarā api pāpa-jīvāḥ
yady adbhuta-krama-parāyaṇa-śīla-śikṣās
tiryag-janā api kimu śruta-dhāraṇā ye

SYNONYMS

te—all of them; *vai*—certainly; *vidanti*—understand; *atitaranti*—cross over; *ca*—also; *deva-māyām*—the influence of the external illusory energy; *strī*—women; *śūdra*—fourth-class men; *hūna*—uncivilized hill tribes; *śabarāḥ*—and hunters; *api*—even; *pāpa-jīvāḥ*—sinful creatures; *yadi*—if; *adbhuta-krama*—of the performer of wonderful activities; *parāyaṇa*—of the devotees; *śīla-śikṣāḥ*—characteristics and education; *tiryak-janāḥ*—birds and beasts; *api*—even; *kimu*—what to speak of; *śruta-dhāraṇāḥ ye*—persons advanced in the education of Vedic knowledge.

TRANSLATION

" 'Women, fourth-class men, uncivilized hill tribes, hunters and many others born of low families, as well as birds and beasts, can engage in the ser-

vice of the Supreme Personality of Godhead—who acts very wonderfully—and follow the path of the devotees and take lessons from them. Although the ocean of nescience is vast, they can still cross over it. What, then, is the difficulty for those who are advanced in Vedic knowledge?'

PURPORT

This is a quotation from *Śrīmad-Bhāgavatam* (2.7.46). Lord Brahmā said this when speaking to his disciple Nārada about the wonderful characteristics of Lord Viṣṇu. Simply by chanting the glories of Lord Viṣṇu, one can cross the ocean of nescience, even though one may be lowborn.

TEXT 191

বিচার করিয়া যবে ভজে কৃষ্ণ-পায় ।
সেই বুদ্ধি দেন তাঁরে, যাতে কৃষ্ণ পায় ॥ ১৯১ ॥

vicāra kariyā yabe bhaje kṛṣṇa-pāya
sei buddhi dena tāṅre, yāte kṛṣṇa pāya

SYNONYMS

vicāra—consideration; *kariyā*—doing; *yabe*—when; *bhaje*—one worships; *kṛṣṇa-pāya*—at the lotus feet of Kṛṣṇa; *sei buddhi*—that intelligence; *dena*—gives; *tāṅre*—to him; *yāte*—by which; *kṛṣṇa pāya*—one gets the shelter of the lotus feet of Kṛṣṇa.

TRANSLATION

"Considering all these points, when one engages in the service of Kṛṣṇa's lotus feet, Kṛṣṇa gives one the intelligence by which he can gradually progress toward perfection in service to the Lord.

TEXT 192

তেষাং সততযুক্তানাং ভজতাং প্রীতিপূর্বকম্ ।
দদামি বুদ্ধিযোগং তং যেন মামুপযান্তি তে ॥ ১৯২ ॥

teṣāṁ satata-yuktānāṁ
bhajatāṁ prīti-pūrvakam
dadāmi buddhi-yogaṁ taṁ
yena mām upayānti te

SYNONYMS

teṣām—to them; *satata-yuktānām*—always engaged; *bhajatām*—in devotional service; *prīti-pūrvakam*—in loving ecstasy; *dadāmi*—I give; *buddhi-yogam*—real intelligence; *tam*—that; *yena*—by which; *mām*—unto Me; *upayānti*—come; *te*—they.

TRANSLATION

" 'To those who are constantly devoted and worship Me with love, I give the understanding by which they can come to Me.'

PURPORT

This is a quotation from *Bhagavad-gītā* (10.10).

TEXT 193

সৎসঙ্গ, কৃষ্ণসেবা, ভাগবত, নাম ।
ব্রজে বাস,—এই পঞ্চ সাধন প্রধান ॥ ১৯৩ ॥

sat-saṅga, kṛṣṇa-sevā, bhāgavata, nāma
vraje vāsa,——ei pañca sādhana pradhāna

SYNONYMS

sat-saṅga—association with devotees; *kṛṣṇa-sevā*—engagement in the service of Kṛṣṇa; *bhāgavata*—devotees and the book known as *Śrīmad-Bhāgavatam; nāma*—the chanting of the holy name; *vraje vāsa*—residence in Vṛndāvana or Mathurā; *ei*—these; *pañca*—five; *sādhana pradhāna*—the chief processes of devotion.

TRANSLATION

"To be elevated to the platform of devotional service, the following five items should be observed: association with devotees, engagement in the service of Lord Kṛṣṇa, the reading of Śrīmad-Bhāgavatam, the chanting of the holy names and residence at Vṛndāvana or Mathurā.

TEXT 194

এই-পঞ্চ-মধ্যে এক 'স্বল্প' যদি হয় ।
সুবুদ্ধি জনের হয় কৃষ্ণপ্রেমোদয় ॥ ১৯৪ ॥

ei-pañca-madhye eka 'svalpa' yadi haya
subuddhi janera haya kṛṣṇa-premodaya

SYNONYMS

ei—these; *pañca-madhye*—out of the five; *eka*—of only one; *svalpa*—a small quantity; *yadi*—if; *haya*—there is; *su-buddhi*—intelligent; *janera*—of the person; *haya*—there is; *kṛṣṇa-prema-udaya*—awakening of dormant love for Kṛṣṇa.

TRANSLATION

"One's dormant love for Kṛṣṇa gradually awakens if one is a little advanced in one of these five items and is intelligent.

TEXT 195

দুরূহাদ্ভুতবীর্যেঽস্মিন্ শ্রদ্ধা দূরেঽস্তু পঞ্চকে ।
যত্র স্বল্পোঽপি সম্বন্ধঃ সদ্ধিয়াং ভাবজন্মনে ॥ ১৯৫ ॥

durūhādbhuta-vīrye 'smin
śraddhā dūre 'stu pañcake
yatra svalpo 'pi sambandhaḥ
saddhiyāṁ bhāva-janmane

SYNONYMS

durūha—difficult to be reconciled; *adbhuta*—wonderful; *vīrye*—in the power; *asmin*—in this; *śraddhā*—faith; *dūre*—far away; *astu*—let it be; *pañcake*—in the above-mentioned five principles; *yatra*—in which; *svalpaḥ*—a little; *api*—even; *sambandhaḥ*—connection; *sat-dhiyām*—of those who are intelligent and offenseless; *bhāva-janmane*—to awaken one's dormant love for Kṛṣṇa.

TRANSLATION

" 'The power of these five principles is very wonderful and difficult to reconcile. Even without faith in them, a person who is offenseless can experience dormant love of Kṛṣṇa simply by being a little connected with them.'

PURPORT

This verse is also found in *Bhakti-rasāmṛta-sindhu* (1.2.238).

TEXT 196

উদার মহতী যাঁর সর্বোত্তমা বুদ্ধি ।
নানা কামে ভজে, তবু পায় ভক্তিসিদ্ধি ॥ ১৯৬ ॥

udāra mahatī yāṅra sarvottamā buddhi
nānā kāme bhaje, tabu pāya bhakti-siddhi

SYNONYMS

udāra—liberal; *mahatī*—great; *yāṅra*—whose; *sarva-uttamā*—first-class; *buddhi*—intelligence; *nānā*—various; *kāme*—with desires; *bhaje*—engages in devotional service; *tabu*—still; *pāya*—gets; *bhakti-siddhi*—perfection in devotional service.

TRANSLATION

"If a person is actually liberal and intelligent, he can advance and become perfect in devotional service even if he has material desires and serves the Lord with some motive.

TEXT 197

অকামঃ সর্বকামো বা মোক্ষকাম উদারধীঃ।
তীব্রেণ ভক্তিযোগেন যজেত পুরুষং পরম্ ॥ ১৯৭ ॥

akāmaḥ sarva-kāmo vā
mokṣa-kāma udāra-dhīḥ
tīvreṇa bhakti-yogena
yajeta puruṣaṁ param

SYNONYMS

akāmaḥ—without material desires; *sarva-kāmaḥ*—full of all material desires; *vā*—or; *mokṣa-kāmaḥ*—desiring liberation; *udāra-dhīḥ*—sincere and advanced in devotional service; *tīvreṇa*—firm; *bhakti-yogena*—by the practice of *bhakti-yoga; yajeta*—should worship; *puruṣam param*—the Supreme Personality of Godhead.

TRANSLATION

" 'Whether one desires everything or nothing, or whether he desires to merge into the existence of the Lord, he is intelligent only if he worships Lord Kṛṣṇa, the Supreme Personality of Godhead, by rendering transcendental loving service.'

PURPORT

This is a quotation from *Śrīmad-Bhāgavatam* (2.3.10).

TEXT 198

ভক্তি-প্রভাব,—সেই কাম ছাড়াঞা।
কৃষ্ণপদে ভক্তি করায় গুণে আকর্ষিয়া ॥ ১৯৮ ॥

bhakti-prabhāva,——sei kāma chāḍāñā
kṛṣṇa-pade bhakti karāya guṇe ākarṣiyā

SYNONYMS

bhakti-prabhāva—the influence of devotional service; *sei*—that; *kāma*—material desire; *chāḍāñā*—causing to give up; *kṛṣṇa-pade*—unto the lotus feet of Kṛṣṇa; *bhakti karāya*—engages in devotional service; *guṇe*—by transcendental qualities; *ākarṣiyā*—attracting.

TRANSLATION

"Devotional service is so strong that when one engages in it, he gradually gives up all material desires and becomes fully attracted to the lotus feet of Kṛṣṇa. All this is brought about by attraction for the transcendental qualities of the Lord.

TEXT 199

সত্যং দিশত্যর্থিতমর্থিতো নৃণাং
নৈবার্থদো যৎ পুনরর্থিতা যতঃ ।
স্বয়ং বিধত্তে ভজতামনিচ্ছতা-
মিচ্ছা-পিধানং নিজপাদপল্লবম্ ॥ ১৯৯ ॥

satyaṁ diśaty arthitam arthito nṛṇāṁ
naivārthado yat punar arthitā yataḥ
svayaṁ vidhatte bhajatām anicchatām
icchā-pidhānaṁ nija-pāda-pallavam

SYNONYMS

satyam—it is true; *diśati*—He awards; *arthitam*—that which is desired; *arthitaḥ*—being requested; *nṛṇām*—by human beings; *na*—not; *eva*—certainly; *artha-daḥ*—giving desired things; *yat*—which; *punaḥ*—again; *arthitā*—request; *yataḥ*—from which; *svayam*—Himself; *vidhatte*—He gives; *bhajatām*—of those engaged in devotional service; *anicchatām*—even though not desiring; *icchā-pidhānam*—covering all other desires; *nija-pāda-pallavam*—the shelter of His own lotus feet.

TRANSLATION

" 'Whenever Kṛṣṇa is requested to fulfill one's desire, He undoubtedly does so, but He does not award anything which, after being enjoyed, will cause someone to petition Him again and again to fulfill further desires. When one has other desires but engages in the Lord's service, Kṛṣṇa forcibly gives one shelter at His lotus feet, where one will forget all other desires.'

PURPORT

This verse is from *Śrīmad-Bhāgavatam* (5.19.26).

TEXT 200

'আত্মা'-শব্দে 'স্বভাব' কহে, তাতে যেই রমে।
আত্মারাম জীব যত স্থাবর-জঙ্গমে ॥ ২০০ ॥

'ātmā'-śabde 'svabhāva' kahe, tāte yei rame
ātmārāma jīva yata sthāvara-jaṅgame

SYNONYMS

ātmā-śabde—by the word *ātmā; svabhāva*—nature; *kahe*—is sometimes said; *tāte*—in that; *yei rame*—one who takes pleasure; *ātmārāma*—called *ātmārāma; jīva*—the living entities; *yata*—all of them; *sthāvara-jaṅgame*—the moving and nonmoving.

TRANSLATION

"Another meaning of the word ātmā is 'one's characteristic nature.' Whoever enjoys his particular type of nature is called ātmārāma. Therefore, all living entities—be they moving or nonmoving—are also called ātmārāma.

TEXT 201

জীবের স্বভাব—কৃষ্ণ-'দাস'-অভিমান।
দেহে আত্ম-জ্ঞানে আচ্ছাদিত সেই 'জ্ঞান' ॥ ২০১ ॥

jīvera svabhāva——kṛṣṇa-'dāsa'-abhimāna
dehe ātma-jñāne ācchādita sei 'jñāna'

SYNONYMS

jīvera svabhāva—the original characteristic of all living entities; *kṛṣṇa-dāsa*—servant of Kṛṣṇa; *abhimāna*—the conception; *dehe*—in the material body; *ātma-jñāne*—by the conception of the self; *ācchādita*—covered; *sei jñāna*—that original consciousness.

TRANSLATION

"The original nature of every living entity is to consider himself the eternal servant of Kṛṣṇa. However, under the influence of māyā, he thinks himself to be the body, and thus his original consciousness is covered.

TEXT 202

চ-শব্দে 'এব', 'অপি'-শব্দ সমুচ্চয়ে।
'আত্মারামা এব' হঞা শ্রীকৃষ্ণ ভজয়ে ॥ ২০২ ॥

ca-śabde 'eva', 'api'-śabda samuccaye
'ātmārāmā eva' hañā śrī-kṛṣṇa bhajaye

SYNONYMS

ca-śabde—by the word *ca; eva*—the word *eva; api-śabda*—the word *api; samuccaye*—in the sense of aggregation; *ātmārāmāḥ eva*—all the *ātmārāmas* (all kinds of living entities); *hañā*—being; *śrī-kṛṣṇa bhajaye*—become engaged in the service of Lord Kṛṣṇa.

TRANSLATION

"In that case, by the word ca, the word eva is meant. The word api can be taken in the sense of aggregation. Thus the verse would read ātmārāmā eva; that is, 'even all kinds of living beings worship Kṛṣṇa.'

PURPORT

It is here mentioned that every living entity is *ātmārāma*. Temporarily covered by the influence of *māyā*, the living entity serves his senses, which are represented as *kāma-krodha-lobha-moha-mada-mātsarya*. In the material condition, all living entities are engaged in sense gratification, but when they associate with devotees who follow the regulative principles, they become purified and awakened to their original consciousness. They then attempt to satisfy the senses of Lord Kṛṣṇa and engage in His devotional service.

TEXT 203

এই জীব—সনকাদি সব মুনিজন।
'নিগ্রন্থ'—মূর্খ, নীচ, স্থাবর-পশুগণ ॥ ২০৩ ॥

ei jīva——sanakādi saba muni-jana
'nirgrantha'——mūrkha, nīca, sthāvara-paśu-gaṇa

SYNONYMS

ei jīva—these living entities; *sanaka-ādi saba muni-jana*—all the great personalities, such as Sanaka and Sanātana; *nirgrantha*—down to the illiterate; *mūrkha*—foolish person; *nīca*—lowborn; *sthāvara*—the trees and plants; *paśu-gaṇa*—the beasts and birds.

TRANSLATION

"Living entities include great personalities like the four Kumāras, low-class foolish people, trees, plants, birds and beasts.

TEXT 204

ব্যাস-শুক-সনকাদির প্রসিদ্ধ ভজন ।
'নির্গ্রন্থ' স্থাবরাদির শুন বিবরণ ॥ ২০৪ ॥

vyāsa-śuka-sanakādira prasiddha bhajana
'nirgrantha' sthāvarādira śuna vivaraṇa

SYNONYMS

vyāsa—of Vyāsadeva; *śuka*—of Śukadeva Gosvāmī; *sanaka-ādira*—of the four Kumāras; *prasiddha bhajana*—the devotional service is celebrated; *nirgrantha*—foolish, uneducated; *sthāvara-ādira*—of the immovable elements; *śuna vivaraṇa*—hear the description.

TRANSLATION

"The devotional service of Vyāsa, Śuka and the four Kumāras has already been well celebrated. Now let Me explain how immovable living entities like trees and plants engage in the Lord's devotional service.

TEXT 205

কৃষ্ণকৃপাদি-হেতু হৈতে সবার উদয় ।
কৃষ্ণগুণাকৃষ্ট হঞা তাঁহারে ভজয় ॥ ২০৫ ॥

kṛṣṇa-kṛpādi-hetu haite sabāra udaya
kṛṣṇa-guṇākṛṣṭa hañā tāṅhāre bhajaya

SYNONYMS

kṛṣṇa-kṛpā-ādi-hetu—the reason of Kṛṣṇa's mercy; *haite*—from; *sabāra udaya*—anyone becomes a devotee; *kṛṣṇa-guṇa-ākṛṣṭa hañā*—being attracted by the transcendental qualities of Kṛṣṇa; *tāṅhāre*—Him; *bhajaya*—worship.

TRANSLATION

"Everyone is eligible to receive Kṛṣṇa's mercy—including Vyāsadeva, the four Kumāras, Śukadeva Gosvāmī, lowborn creatures, trees, plants and beasts. By Kṛṣṇa's mercy they are elevated and engaged in His service.

PURPORT

This is also confirmed in *Bhagavad-gītā* wherein the Lord says:

māṁ hi pārtha vyapāśritya
ye 'pi syuḥ pāpa-yonayaḥ
striyo vaiśyās tathā śūdrās
te 'pi yānti parāṁ gatim

"O son of Pṛthā, those who take shelter in Me, though they be of lower birth—women, *vaiśyas* [merchants], as well as *śūdras* [workers]—can approach the supreme destination." (9.32)

Everyone is eligible to become Kṛṣṇa's devotee. One simply has to be trained according to the approved process. It is the work of Kṛṣṇa's confidential devotees to turn everyone into a Kṛṣṇa *bhakta*. If the confidential devotees do not take up the task of elevating everyone to Kṛṣṇa consciousness, then who will do it? Those who claim to be devotees but do not engage in Kṛṣṇa's service to elevate all living creatures to Kṛṣṇa consciousness are to be considered *kaniṣṭha-adhikārīs* (people in the lowest stage of devotional service). When one rises to the second platform of devotional service, his business is to propagate Kṛṣṇa consciousness all over the world. Those who are active in the Kṛṣṇa consciousness movement should not remain in the neophyte stage but should rise to the platform of preachers, the second platform of devotional service. Devotional service is so enchanting that even the first-class devotees (*uttama-adhikārīs*) also come down to the second platform to preach and render service to the Lord for the benefit of the whole world.

TEXT 206

ধন্যেয়মদ্য ধরণী তৃণ-বীরুধস্ত্বৎ-
পাদস্পৃশো দ্রুমলতাঃ করজাভিমৃষ্টাঃ ।
নদ্যোঽদ্রয়ঃ খগমৃগাঃ সদয়াবলোকৈ-
র্গোপ্যোঽন্তরেণ ভুজয়োরপি যৎস্পৃহা শ্রীঃ ॥ ২০৬ ॥

dhanyeyam adya dharaṇī tṛṇa-vīrudhas tvat-
pāda-spṛśo druma-latāḥ karajābhimṛṣṭāḥ
nadyo 'drayaḥ khaga-mṛgāḥ sadayāvalokair
gopyo 'ntareṇa bhujayor api yat-spṛhā śrīḥ

SYNONYMS

dhanyā—glorified; *iyam*—this; *adya*—today; *dharaṇī*—the surface of the globe; *tṛṇa-vīrudhaḥ*—the grass and herbs; *tvat*—Your; *pāda-spṛśaḥ*—from the touch of the lotus feet; *druma-latāḥ*—the creepers and trees; *karaja-abhimṛṣṭāḥ*—touched by Your nails; *nadyaḥ*—the rivers; *adrayaḥ*—the hills; *khaga-mṛgāḥ*—the birds and forest animals; *sadaya-avalokaiḥ*—because of Your merciful glances; *gopyaḥ*—the *gopīs,* the damsels of Vraja; *antareṇa*—by the region between; *bhujayoḥ*—Your two arms; *api*—also; *yat*—for which; *spṛhā*—desirous; *śrīḥ*—the goddess of fortune.

TRANSLATION

" 'This land Vṛndāvana [Vrajabhūmi] is glorified today. Your lotus feet have touched the earth and grass. Your fingers have touched the trees and creepers, and Your merciful eyes have glanced upon rivers, hills, birds and beasts. The gopīs have been embraced by Your arms, and even the goddess of fortune desires this. Now all of these are glorified.'

PURPORT

This verse from *Śrīmad-Bhāgavatam* (10.15.8) is spoken by Lord Kṛṣṇa to Śrī Balarāma.

TEXT 207

গা গোপকৈরনুবনং নয়তোরুদার-
বেণুস্বনৈঃ কলপদৈস্তনুভৃৎসু সখ্যঃ ।
অস্পন্দনং গতিমতাং পুলকস্তরূণাং
নির্যোগপাশকৃতলক্ষণয়োর্বিচিত্রম্ ॥ ২০৭ ॥

gā gopakair anuvanaṁ nayator udāra-
veṇu-svanaiḥ kala-padais tanu-bhṛtsu sakhyaḥ
aspandanaṁ gatimatāṁ pulakas tarūṇāṁ
niryoga-pāśa-kṛta-lakṣaṇayor vicitram

SYNONYMS

gāḥ—the cows; *gopakaiḥ*—with the cowherd boys; *anuvanam*—to each forest; *nayatoḥ*—leading; *udāra*—very liberal; *veṇu-svanaiḥ*—by the vibrations of the flutes; *kala-padaiḥ*—having sweet tones; *tanu-bhṛtsu*—among the living entities; *sakhyaḥ*—O friends; *aspandanam*—the lack of movement; *gatimatām*—of those living entities that can move; *pulakaḥ*—the ecstatic jubilation; *tarūṇām*—of the otherwise nonmoving trees; *niryoga-pāśa*—the ropes for binding the rear legs of the cows; *kṛta-lakṣaṇayoḥ*—of those two (Kṛṣṇa and Balarāma), who are characterized by; *vicitram*—wonderful.

TRANSLATION

" 'My dear friend, both Kṛṣṇa and Balarāma are passing through the forest leading Their cows with Their cowherd boy friends. They both carry ropes with which, at the time of milking, They bind the rear legs of the cows. When They play on Their flutes, all moving living entities are stunned, and non-moving living entities experience ecstatic jubilation by Their sweet music. All these things are certainly very wonderful.'

PURPORT

This is a quotation from *Śrīmad-Bhāgavatam* (10.21.19). All the *gopīs* were very attracted to Kṛṣṇa when they saw Him wandering in the forest with Baladeva. They thus praised the Lord's activities.

TEXT 208

বনলতাস্তরব আত্মনি বিষ্ণুং
ব্যঞ্জয়ন্ত্য ইব পুষ্পফলাঢ্যাঃ ।
প্রণতভারবিটপা মধুধারাঃ
প্রেমহৃষ্টতনবো ববৃষুঃ স্ম ॥ ২০৮ ॥

vana-latās tarava ātmani viṣṇuṁ
vyañjayantya iva puṣpa-phalāḍhyāḥ
praṇata-bhāra-viṭapā madhu-dhārāḥ
prema-hṛṣṭa-tanavo vavṛṣuḥ sma

SYNONYMS

vana-latāḥ—the herbs and plants; *taravaḥ*—the trees; *ātmani*—in the Supreme Soul; *viṣṇum*—the Supreme Personality of Godhead; *vyañjayantyaḥ*—manifesting; *iva*—like; *puṣpa-phala-āḍhyāḥ*—filled with luxuriant fruits and flowers; *praṇata-bhāra*—bowed down because of loads; *viṭapāḥ*—the trees; *madhu-dhārāḥ*—showers; *prema-hṛṣṭa*—inspired by love of Godhead; *tanavaḥ*—whose bodies; *vavṛṣuḥ*—constantly rained; *sma*—certainly.

TRANSLATION

" 'The plants, creepers and trees were full of fruits and flowers due to ecstatic love of Kṛṣṇa. Indeed, being so full, they were bowing down. They were inspired by such deep love for Kṛṣṇa that they were constantly pouring showers of honey. In this way the gopīs saw all the forest of Vṛndāvana.'

PURPORT

This verse is from *Śrīmad-Bhāgavatam* (10.35.9).

TEXT 209

কিরাতহূনান্ধ্র-পুলিন্দপুক্কশা
আভীরশুম্ভা যবনাঃ খসাদয়ঃ ।
যেঽন্যে চ পাপা যদুপাশ্রয়াশ্রয়াঃ
শুধ্যন্তি তস্মৈ প্রভবিষ্ণবে নমঃ ॥ ২০৯ ॥

kirāta-hūnāndhra-pulinda-pukkaśā
ābhīra-śumbhā yavanāḥ khaśādayaḥ
ye 'nye ca pāpā yad-upāśrayāśrayāḥ
śudhyanti tasmai prabhaviṣṇave namaḥ

SYNONYMS

kirāta—the aborigines named Kirātas; *hūna*—the Hūnas; *āndhra* —Āndhras; *pulinda*—Pulindas; *pukkaśāḥ*—Pukkaśas; *ābhīra*—Ābhīras; *śumbhāḥ*—Śumbhas; *yavanāḥ*—persons who do not follow the Vedic injunctions and who eat cow's flesh; *khaśa-ādayaḥ*—Khaśas and others; *ye*—those who; *anye*—similar others; *ca*—also; *pāpāḥ*—sinful persons; *yat*—of the Supreme Personality of Godhead; *upāśraya*—of the devotees; *āśrayāḥ*—taking shelter; *śudhyanti*—become purified; *tasmai*—unto Him, Lord Viṣṇu, because of whom they become purified; *prabhaviṣṇave*—to Lord Viṣṇu, the most powerful; *namaḥ*—respectful obeisances.

TRANSLATION

" 'Kirāta, Hūna, Āndhra, Pulinda, Pukkaśa, Ābhīra, Śumbha, Yavana and the Khaśa races and even others who are addicted to sinful acts can be purified by taking shelter of the devotees of the Lord due to His being the supreme power. I beg to offer my respectful obeisances unto Him.'

TEXT 210

আগে 'তের' অর্থ করিলুঁ, আর 'ছয়' এই ।
ঊনবিংশতি অর্থ হইল মিলি' এই দুই ॥ ২১০ ॥

āge 'tera' artha kariluṅ, āra 'chaya' ei
ūnaviṁśati artha ha-ila mili' ei dui

SYNONYMS

āge—previously; *tera*—thirteen; *artha*—meanings; *kariluṁ*—I have done; *āra*—another; *chaya*—six; *ei*—this; *ūnaviṁśati*—altogether nineteen; *artha*—meanings; *ha-ila*—there were; *mili'*—including; *ei dui*—these two.

TRANSLATION

"I have already spoken about the thirteen kinds of meaning. Now there are six more. Combined, these make nineteen.

PURPORT

The six different meanings are (1) mental speculators (vide verse 165), (2) those engaged in different types of endeavor (vide verse 168), (3) those who are patient and sober (vide verse 174), (4) those who are intelligent and learned scholars (vide verse 187), (5) those who are intelligent but illiterate and foolish (vide verse 187), and (6) those who are conscious of eternal servitorship to Kṛṣṇa (vide verse 201).

TEXT 211

এই ঊনিশ অর্থ করিলু, আগে শুন আর ।
'আত্ম'-শব্দে 'দেহ' কহে,—চারি অর্থ তার ॥ ২১১ ॥

ei ūniśa artha karilu, āge śuna āra
'ātma'-śabde 'deha' kahe,——cāri artha tāra

SYNONYMS

ei—these; *ūniśa*—nineteen; *artha*—meanings; *karilu*—I have done; *āge*—ahead; *śuna*—hear; *āra*—more; *ātma-śabde*—by the word *ātma; deha*—the body; *kahe*—is understood; *cāri artha*—four meanings; *tāra*—of that.

TRANSLATION

"I have already explained nineteen different meanings. Now please hear further meanings. The word ātma also refers to the body, and this can be taken in four ways.

PURPORT

The four divisions are (1) *aupādika-brahma-deha,* the material body considered as Brahman with designations (vide verse 212), (2) *karma-niṣtha yājñikera karma-deha,* the body engaged in ritualistic ceremonies of the Vedic injunctions (vide verse 214), (3) *tapo-deha,* the body engaged in austerities and penances (vide verse 216), and (4) *sarva-kāma-deha,* the body engaged for the satisfaction of all kinds of material desires (vide verse 218).

TEXT 212

দেহারামী দেহে ভজে 'দেহোপাধি ব্রহ্ম'।
সৎসঙ্গে সেহ করে কৃষ্ণের ভজন ॥ ২১২ ॥

dehārāmī dehe bhaje 'dehopādhi brahma'
sat-saṅge seha kare kṛṣṇera bhajana

SYNONYMS

dehārāmī—persons who have accepted this body as the self and are interested only in sense gratification; *dehe*—in the body; *bhaje*—worships; *deha-upādhi brahma*—Brahman having the body as a designation; *sat-saṅge*—in the association of devotees; *seha*—such a person; *kare*—does; *kṛṣṇera bhajana*—service to Lord Kṛṣṇa.

TRANSLATION

"One in the bodily conception worships his own body as Brahman, but when he comes in contact with the devotee, he gives up this mistaken idea and engages himself in the devotional service of Lord Kṛṣṇa.

TEXT 213

উদরমুপাসতে য ঋষিবর্ত্মসু কূর্পদৃশঃ
পরিসরপদ্ধতিং হৃদয়মারুণয়ো দহরম্ ।
তত উদগাদনন্ত তব ধাম শিরঃ পরমং
পুনরিহ যৎ সমেত্য ন পতন্তি কৃতান্তমুখে ॥ ২১৩ ॥

udaram upāsate ya ṛṣi-vartmasu kūrpa-dṛśaḥ
parisara-paddhatiṁ hṛdayam āruṇayo daharam
tata udagād ananta tava dhāma śiraḥ paramaṁ
punar iha yat sametya na patanti kṛtānta-mukhe

SYNONYMS

udaram—the abdomen; *upāsate*—worship; *ye*—those who; *ṛṣi-vartmasu*—on the path marked out by the great saintly persons; *kūrpa-dṛśaḥ*—whose vision is grossly situated in the bodily conception of life; *parisara-paddhatim*—from which the system of the arteries comes; *hṛdayam*—the heart; *āruṇayaḥ*—saintly persons headed by Āruṇa Ṛṣi; *daharam*—the sky within the heart, the subtle conception of the Supersoul within the heart; *tataḥ*—from that; *udagāt*—went up; *ananta*—O unlimited one; *tava*—Your; *dhāma*—place; *śiraḥ*—the top of the head; *paramam*—supreme; *punaḥ*—again; *iha*—in this material world; *yat*—which; *sametya*—having achieved; *na*—not; *patanti*—fall down; *kṛta-anta-mukhe*—in the repetition of birth and death.

TRANSLATION

" 'Those who follow the path of great, saintly mystic yogīs take to the yogic gymnastic process and begin worshiping from the abdomen, where it is said that Brahman is located. Such people are called śārk, which means that they are situated in the gross bodily conception. There are also followers of the ṛṣi known as Āruṇa. Following that path, they observe the activities of the arteries. Thus they gradually rise to the heart, where subtle Brahman, Paramātmā, is situated. They then worship Him. O, unlimited Ananta! Better than these persons are the mystic yogīs who worship You from the top of their heads. Beginning with the abdomen and proceeding through the heart, they reach the top of the head and pass through the brahma-randra, the hole at the top of the skull. Thus yogīs attain the perfectional platform and do not enter the cycle of birth and death again.'

PURPORT

This is a quotation from *Śrīmad-Bhāgavatam* (10.87.18).

TEXT 214

দেহারামী কর্মনিষ্ঠ—যাজ্ঞিকাদি জন ।
সৎসঙ্গে 'কর্ম' ত্যজি' করয় ভজন ॥ ২১৪ ॥

dehārāmī karma-niṣṭha——yājñikādi jana
sat-saṅge 'karma' tyaji' karaya bhajana

SYNONYMS

dehārāmī—those in the bodily concept of life; *karma-niṣṭha*—attracted to fruitive activities; *yājñika-ādi jana*—persons who perform ritualistic ceremonies for a better standard of life; *sat-saṅge*—in contact with devotees; *karma tyaji'*—giving up such fruitive activities; *karaya bhajana*—engages in the devotional service of the Lord.

TRANSLATION

"Those who are in the bodily conception mainly engage in fruitive activity. Those who perform yajñas and ritualistic ceremonies are also considered in the same category. However, when they are all in contact with the pure devotee, they give up their fruitive activity and fully engage in the service of the Lord.

TEXT 215

কর্মণ্যস্মিন্ননাশ্বাসে ধূমধূম্রাত্মনাং ভবান্ ।
আপায়য়তি গোবিন্দপাদপদ্মাসবং মধু ॥ ২১৫ ॥

karmaṇy asminn anāśvāse
dhūma-dhūmrātmanāṁ bhavān
āpāyayati govinda-
pāda-padmāsavaṁ madhu

SYNONYMS

karmaṇi—in fruitive activity; *asmin*—in this; *anāśvāse*—although not positive in result; *dhūma-dhūmra-ātmanām*—whose bodies are simply becoming blackish because of smoke; *bhavān*—you; *āpāyayati*—give a chance to drink; *govinda-pāda-padma-āsavam*—the nectarean beverage flowing from the lotus feet of Govinda; *madhu*—sweet.

TRANSLATION

" 'We have just begun performing this fruitive activity, a sacrificial fire, but due to the many imperfections in our action, we are not certain of its result. Our bodies have become black from the smoke, but we are factually pleased by the nectar of the lotus feet of the Personality of Godhead, Govinda, which you are distributing.'

PURPORT

This verse from *Śrīmad-Bhāgavatam* (1.18.12) was spoken to Sūta Gosvāmī at the meeting of great sages at Naimiṣāraṇya. The great sages were headed by Śaunaka, and Sūta Gosvāmī spoke of the glorious activities of the Supreme Personality of Godhead at that meeting. At that time, all the *ṛṣis* assembled there neglected to complete the ritualistic ceremonies because there was no positive assurance of the results. All the performers were coated with black ash due to the large amount of smoke coming from the fire.

TEXT 216

'তপস্বী' প্রভৃতি যত দেহারামী হয় ।
সাধুসঙ্গে তপ ছাড়ি' শ্রীকৃষ্ণ ভজয় ॥ ২১৬ ॥

'tapasvī' prabhṛti yata dehārāmī haya
sādhu-saṅge tapa chāḍi' śrī-kṛṣṇa bhajaya

SYNONYMS

tapasvī—persons who undergo severe penances; *prabhṛti*—and so on; *yata*—all; *dehārāmī haya*—are within the category of the bodily concept of life; *sādhu-saṅge*—in the association of devotees; *tapa chāḍi'*—giving up all such processes of penance and austerity; *śrī-kṛṣṇa bhajaya*—engage themselves in the service of Lord Kṛṣṇa.

TRANSLATION

"The tapasvīs, those who undergo severe austerities and penances to elevate themselves to the higher planetary systems, are also in the same category. When such persons come in contact with a devotee, they give up all those practices and engage in Lord Kṛṣṇa's service.

TEXT 217

যৎপাদসেবাভিরুচিস্তপস্বিনা-
মশেষজন্মোপচিতং মলং ধিয়ঃ।
সদ্যঃ ক্ষিণোত্যন্বহমেধতী সতী
যথা পদাঙ্গুষ্ঠবিনিঃসৃতা সরিৎ ॥ ২১৭ ॥

yat-pāda-sevābhirucis tapasvinām
aśeṣa-janmopacitaṁ malaṁ dhiyaḥ
sadyaḥ kṣiṇoty anvaham edhatī satī
yathā padāṅguṣṭha-viniḥsṛtā sarit

SYNONYMS

yat-pāda-sevā-abhiruciḥ—the taste for serving the lotus feet of Lord Kṛṣṇa; *tapasvinām*—of persons undergoing severe penances; *aśeṣa*—unlimited; *janma-upacitam*—contracted from life after life; *malam*—dirt; *dhiyaḥ*—of the intelligence; *sadyaḥ*—immediately; *kṣiṇoti*—vanquishes; *anvaham*—every day; *edhatī*—increasing; *satī*—being in the mode of goodness; *yathā*—as; *pada-aṅguṣṭha-viniḥsṛtā*—emanating from the toe of the Lord; *sarit*—the River Ganges.

TRANSLATION

" 'The taste for loving service is like the water of the River Ganges, which flows from the feet of Lord Kṛṣṇa. Every day that taste diminishes the results of sinful activities acquired over a period of many births by those who perform austerities.'

PURPORT

This is a quotation from *Śrīmad-Bhāgavatam* (4.21.31).

TEXT 218

দেহারামী, সর্বকাম—সব আত্মারাম ।
কৃষ্ণকৃপায় কৃষ্ণ ভজে ছাড়ি' সব কাম ॥ ২১৮ ॥

dehārāmī, sarva-kāma——saba ātmārāma
kṛṣṇa-kṛpāya kṛṣṇa bhaje chāḍi' saba kāma

SYNONYMS

dehārāmī—persons who are in the bodily concept of life; *sarva-kāma*—full of all material desires; *saba*—all; *ātmārāma*—enjoying self-satisfaction; *kṛṣṇa-kṛpāya*—by the mercy of Kṛṣṇa; *kṛṣṇa bhaje*—become engaged in the devotional service of Lord Kṛṣṇa; *chāḍi' saba kāma*—giving up all sorts of material desire.

TRANSLATION

"As long as one labors under the bodily conception, he must fulfill volumes and volumes of material desires. Thus a person is called ātmārāma. When such an ātmārāma is favored by the mercy of Kṛṣṇa, he gives up his so-called self-satisfaction and engages in the transcendental loving service of the Lord.

TEXT 219

স্থানাভিলাষী তপসি স্থিতোঽহং
ত্বাং প্রাপ্তবান্ দেবমুনীন্দ্রগুহ্যম্ ।
কাচং বিচিন্বন্নপি দিব্যরত্নং
স্বামিন্ কৃতার্থোঽস্মি বরং ন যাচে ॥ ২১৯ ॥

sthānābhilāṣī tapasi sthito 'haṁ
tvāṁ prāptavān deva-munīndra-guhyam
kācaṁ vicinvann api divya-ratnaṁ
svāmin kṛtārtho 'smi varaṁ na yāce

SYNONYMS

sthāna-abhilāṣī—desiring a very high position in the material world; *tapasi*—in severe austerities and penances; *sthitaḥ*—situated; *aham*—I; *tvām*—You; *prāptavān*—have obtained; *deva-muni-indra-guhyam*—difficult to achieve even for great demigods, saintly persons and kings; *kācam*—a piece of glass; *vicinvan*—

searching for; *api*—although; *divya-ratnam*—a transcendental gem; *svāmin*—O my Lord; *kṛta-arthaḥ asmi*—I am fully satisfied; *varam*—any benediction; *na yāce*—I do not ask.

TRANSLATION

[When he was being benedicted by the Supreme Personality of Godhead, Dhruva Mahārāja said], " 'O my Lord, because I was seeking an opulent material position, I was performing severe types of penance and austerity. Now I have gotten You, who are very difficult for the great demigods, saintly persons and kings to attain. I was searching after a piece of glass, but instead I have found a most valuable jewel. Therefore I am so satisfied that I do not wish to ask any benediction from You.'

PURPORT

This verse is from the *Hari-bhakti-sudhodaya* (7.28).

TEXT 220

এই চারি অর্থ সহ হইল 'তেইশ' অর্থ ।
আর তিন অর্থ শুন পরম সমর্থ ॥ ২২০ ॥

ei cāri artha saha ha-ila 'teiśa' artha
āra tina artha śuna parama samartha

SYNONYMS

ei—these; *cāri*—four; *artha*—meanings; *saha*—with; *ha-ila*—there were; *teiśa artha*—twenty-three different varieties of imports; *āra tina artha*—another three imports; *śuna*—hear; *parama samartha*—very strong.

TRANSLATION

"In addition to the nineteen other meanings, this ātmārāma meaning [including those laboring under the bodily conception] makes four meanings altogether and brings the total to twenty-three meanings. Now hear of another three meanings, which are very suitable.

PURPORT

The three different meanings are (1) the word *ca* meaning "in due course," (2) the words *ca* meaning *eva,* and *api* meaning "censure," and (3) *nirgrantha,* meaning "one who is very poor, without money."

TEXT 221

চ-শব্দে 'সমুচ্চয়ে', আর অর্থ কয় ।
'আত্মারামাশ্চ মুনয়শ্চ' **কৃষ্ণেরে ভজয় ॥ ২২১ ॥**

ca-śabde 'samuccaye', āra artha kaya
'ātmārāmāś ca munayaś ca' kṛṣṇere bhajaya

SYNONYMS

ca-śabde—by the word *ca; samuccaye*—in aggregation; *āra*—another; *artha*—import; *kaya*—is meant; *ātmārāmāḥ ca munayaḥ ca*—all the *ātmārāmas* and *munis; kṛṣṇere bhajaya*—worship Kṛṣṇa.

TRANSLATION

"As mentioned above, the word ca has been used to mean 'aggregate.' According to this meaning, all the ātmārāmas and the munis engage in Kṛṣṇa's service. Besides 'aggregate,' there is another meaning of the word ca.

TEXT 222

'নির্গ্রন্থাঃ' **হঞা ইহাঁ** 'অপি'—**নির্ধারণে ।**
'রামশ্চ কৃষ্ণশ্চ' **যথা বিহরয়ে বনে ॥ ২২২ ॥**

'nirgranthāḥ' hañā ihāṅ 'api'——nirdhāraṇe
'rāmaś ca kṛṣṇaś ca' yathā viharaye vane

SYNONYMS

nirgranthāḥ hañā—being liberated saintly persons; *ihāṅ*—here; *api*—the word *api; nirdhāraṇe*—in the sense of certainty; *rāmaḥ ca kṛṣṇaḥ ca*—both Rāma and Kṛṣṇa; *yathā*—as; *viharaye*—enjoy walking; *vane*—in the forest.

TRANSLATION

"The word nigranthāḥ is used as an adjective, and api is used in the sense of certainty. For instance, rāmaś ca kṛṣṇaś ca means that both Rāma and Kṛṣṇa enjoy walking in the forest.

PURPORT

Because it is said that both Rāma and Kṛṣṇa enjoy wandering in the forest, it is understood that both of Them are enjoying Their tour within the forest.

TEXT 223

চ-শব্দে 'অন্বাচয়ে' অর্থ কহে আর।
'বটো, ভিক্ষামট, গাঞ্চানয়' যৈছে প্রকার ॥ ২২৩ ॥

ca-śabde 'anvācaye' artha kahe āra
'baṭo, bhikṣām aṭa, gāṁ cānaya' yaiche prakāra

SYNONYMS

ca-śabde—by the word *ca; anvācaye*—in presenting an action of secondary importance; *artha*—meaning; *kahe*—says; *āra*—another; *baṭo*—O *brahmacārī; bhikṣām aṭa*—just bring some alms; *gām ca ānaya*—also, at the same time, bring the cows; *yaiche prakāra*—in this way.

TRANSLATION

"The word ca also means anvācaye, which means to present a secondary thing to be done at the same time. This is the way of understanding the word anvācaye. An example is: 'O brahmacārī, go out to collect alms and at the same time bring in the cows.'

TEXT 224

কৃষ্ণমননে মুনি কৃষ্ণে সর্বদা ভজয়।
'আত্মারামা অপি' ভজে,—গৌণ অর্থ কয় ॥ ২২৪ ॥

kṛṣṇa-manane muni kṛṣṇe sarvadā bhajaya
'ātmārāmā api' bhaje,——gauṇa artha kaya

SYNONYMS

kṛṣṇa-manane—in meditating on Kṛṣṇa; *muni*—saintly persons; *kṛṣṇe*—unto Lord Kṛṣṇa; *sarvadā*—always; *bhajaya*—perform devotional service; *ātmārāmāḥ api*—also those who are *ātmārāmas; bhaje*—engage themselves in devotional service; *gauṇa artha kaya*—this is also another secondary import.

TRANSLATION

"Saintly persons who are always meditating upon Kṛṣṇa are engaged in the devotional service of the Lord. The ātmārāmas are also engaged in the Lord's service. That is the indirect import.

PURPORT

The *anvācaye* meaning of the word *ca* indicates that between the two words compounded by the word *ca,* one is given more importance, and the other is considered subordinate. For example: "O *brahmacārī,* please go out and collect alms and at the same time bring in the cows." In this statement, the collection of alms is of first importance, and the second business of collecting the cows is subordinate. Similarly, one who always meditates upon Kṛṣṇa is mainly a devotee of Kṛṣṇa engaged in His devotional service. Other *ātmārāmas* are subordinate in devotional service.

TEXT 225

'চ' এবার্থে—'মুনয়ঃ এব' কৃষ্ণেরে ভজয় ।
"আত্মারামা অপি"—'অপি' 'গর্হা'-অর্থ কয় ॥ ২২৫ ॥

'ca' evārthe——'munayaḥ eva' kṛṣṇere bhajaya
"ātmārāmā api"——'api' 'garhā'-artha kaya

SYNONYMS

ca—the word *ca; eva-arthe*—in the sense of *eva; munayaḥ eva*—just the saintly persons; *kṛṣṇere bhajaya*—engage themselves in the devotional service of Lord Kṛṣṇa; *ātmārāmāḥ api*—also in this combination, *ātmārāmā api; api*—the word *api; garhā-artha kaya*—in the sense of censure.

TRANSLATION

"The word ca is also used to indicate the certainty that only saintly persons are engaged in rendering devotional service to Kṛṣṇa. In the combination ātmārāmā api, api is used in the sense of censure.

TEXT 226

'নিগ্রন্থ হঞা'—এই দুঁহার 'বিশেষণ' ।
আর অর্থ শুন, যৈছে সাধুর সঙ্গম ॥ ২২৬ ॥

'nirgrantha hañā'——ei duṅhāra 'viśeṣaṇa'
āra artha śuna, yaiche sādhura saṅgama

SYNONYMS

nirgrantha hañā—becoming *nirgrantha; ei*—this; *duṅhāra*—of both; *viśeṣaṇa*—the adjective; *āra artha*—another import; *śuna*—please hear; *yaiche*—in which; *sādhura saṅgama*—there is association with devotees.

TRANSLATION

"The word nirgrantha is taken as an adjective modifying muni and ātmārāma. There is another meaning, which you may hear from Me, indicating association with a devotee. Now I shall explain how it is that through the association of devotees, even a nirgrantha can become a devotee.

TEXT 227

নির্গ্রন্থ-শব্দে কহে তবে 'ব্যাধ', 'নির্ধন' ।
সাধুসঙ্গে সেহ করে শ্রীকৃষ্ণ-ভজন ॥ ২২৭ ॥

nirgrantha-śabde kahe tabe 'vyādha', 'nirdhana'
sādhu-saṅge seha kare śrī-kṛṣṇa-bhajana

SYNONYMS

nirgrantha-śabde—by the word *nirgrantha; kahe*—is said; *tabe*—therefore; *vyādha*—a hunter; *nirdhana*—without any riches; *sādhu-saṅge*—by the association of a saintly person; *seha*—he also; *kare*—engages himself; *śrī-kṛṣṇa-bhajana*—in the devotional service of Lord Kṛṣṇa.

TRANSLATION

"The word nirgrantha—when combined with api, used in the sense of certainty—indicates a person who is a hunter by profession or who is very poor. Nonetheless, when such a person associates with a great saint like Nārada, he engages in Lord Kṛṣṇa's devotional service.

TEXT 228

'কৃষ্ণারামাশ্চ' এব হয় কৃষ্ণ-মনন ।
ব্যাধ হঞা হয় পূজ্য ভাগবতোত্তম ॥ ২২৮ ॥

'kṛṣṇārāmāś ca' eva——haya kṛṣṇa-manana
vyādha hañā haya pūjya bhāgavatottama

SYNONYMS

kṛṣṇa-ārāmāḥ ca—one who takes pleasure in Kṛṣṇa; *eva*—certainly; *haya*—there is; *kṛṣṇa-manana*—meditation on Kṛṣṇa; *vyādha hañā*—being a hunter; *haya*—is; *pūjya*—worshipable; *bhāgavata-uttama*—the best of the devotees.

TRANSLATION

"The words kṛṣṇārāmaś ca refer to one who takes pleasure in thinking of Kṛṣṇa. Even though such a person may be a hunter, he is still worshipable and is the best of devotees.

TEXT 229

এক ভক্ত-ব্যাধের কথা শুন সাবধানে ।
যাহা হৈতে হয় সৎসঙ্গ-মহিমার জ্ঞানে ॥ ২২৯ ॥

eka bhakta-vyādhera kathā śuna sāvadhāne
yāhā haite haya sat-saṅga-mahimāra jñāne

SYNONYMS

eka bhakta-vyādhera—one devotee who was a hunter; *kathā*—narration; *śuna*—please hear; *sāvadhāne*—with attention; *yāhā haite*—from which; *haya*—there is; *sat-saṅga-mahimāra jñāne*—knowledge of the greatness of association with a great devotee.

TRANSLATION

"I shall now narrate the story of how the hunter became a great devotee by the association of such an exalted personality as Nārada Muni. From this story, one can understand the greatness of association with pure devotees.

TEXT 230

এক দিন শ্রীনারদ দেখি' নারায়ণ ।
ত্রিবেণী-স্নানে প্রয়াগ করিলা গমন ॥ ২৩০ ॥

eka dina śrī-nārada dekhi' nārāyaṇa
triveṇī-snāne prayāga karilā gamana

SYNONYMS

eka dina—one day; *śrī-nārada*—the great saintly person Nārada; *dekhi' nārāyaṇa*—after visiting Lord Nārāyaṇa; *tri-veṇī-snāne*—to bathe at the confluence of the Ganges, Yamunā and Sarasvatī rivers; *prayāga*—to Prayāga; *karilā gamana*—went.

TRANSLATION

"Once upon a time the great saint Nārada, after visiting Lord Nārāyaṇa in the Vaikuṇṭhas, went to Prayāga to bathe at the confluence of three rivers—the Ganges, Yamunā and Sarasvatī.

PURPORT

The great saint Nārada is so liberated that he can go to the Vaikuṇṭha planets to see Nārāyaṇa and then immediately come to this planet in the material world and go to Prayāga to bathe in the confluence of three rivers. The word *tri-veṇī* refers to a confluence of three rivers. This confluence is still visited by many hundreds of thousands of people who go there to bathe, especially during the month of January (Māgha-melā). A liberated person who has no material body can go anywhere and everywhere; therefore a living entity is called *sarva-ga,* which indicates that he can go anywhere and everywhere. Presently scientists are trying to go to other planets, but due to their material bodies, they are not free to move at will. However, when one is situated in his original spiritual body, he can move anywhere and everywhere without difficulty. Within this material world there is a planet called Siddhaloka, whose inhabitants can go from one planet to another without the aid of a machine or space rocket. In the material world every planet has a specific advantage (*vibhūti-bhinna*). In the spiritual world, however, all the planets and their inhabitants are composed of spiritual energy. Because there are no material impediments, it is said that everything in the spiritual world is one.

TEXT 231

বনপথে দেখে মৃগ আছে ভূমে পড়ি' ।
বাণ-বিদ্ধ ভগ্নপাদ করে ধড়্‌ফড়ি ॥ ২৩১ ॥

vana-pathe dekhe mṛga āche bhūme paḍi'
bāṇa-viddha bhagna-pāda kare dhaḍ-phaḍi

SYNONYMS

vana-pathe—on the forest path; *dekhe*—saw; *mṛga*—deer; *āche*—there was; *bhūme paḍi'*—lying on the ground; *bāṇa-viddha*—pierced by an arrow; *bhagna-pāda*—broken legs; *kare dhaḍ-phaḍi*—twisting with pain.

TRANSLATION

"Nārada Muni saw that a deer was lying on the path through the forest and that it was pierced by an arrow. It had broken legs and was twisting due to much pain.

TEXT 232

আর কতদূরে এক দেখেন শূকর ।
তৈছে বিদ্ধ ভগ্নপাদ করে ধড়্‌ফড় ॥ ২৩২ ॥

āra kata-dūre eka dekhena śūkara
taiche viddha bhagna-pāda kare dhaḍ-phaḍa

SYNONYMS

āra kata-dūre—still farther along; *eka*—one; *dekhena*—sees; *śūkara*—a boar; *taiche*—similarly; *viddha*—pierced; *bhagna-pāda*—broken legs; *kare dhaḍ-phaḍa*—twists in pain.

TRANSLATION

"Farther ahead, Nārada Muni saw a boar pierced by an arrow. Its legs were also broken, and it was twisting in pain.

TEXT 233

ঐছে এক শশক দেখে আর কতদূরে ।
জীবের দুঃখ দেখি' নারদ ব্যাকুল-অন্তরে ॥ ২৩৩ ॥

aiche eka śaśaka dekhe āra kata-dūre
jīvera duḥkha dekhi' nārada vyākula-antare

SYNONYMS

aiche—similarly; *eka śaśaka*—one rabbit; *dekhe*—he sees; *āra kata-dūre*—still farther ahead; *jīvera*—of the living entity; *duḥkha dekhi'*—seeing such horrible miseries; *nārada*—the great saintly person; *vyākula-antare*—very pained within himself.

TRANSLATION

"When he went farther, he saw a rabbit that was also suffering. Nārada Muni was greatly pained at heart to see living entities suffer so.

TEXT 234

কতদূরে দেখে ব্যাধ বৃক্ষে ওঁত হঞা ।
মৃগ মারিবারে আছে বাণ যুড়িয়া ॥ ২৩৪ ॥

kata-dūre dekhe vyādha vṛkṣe oṅta hañā
mṛga māribāre āche bāṇa yuḍiyā

SYNONYMS

kata-dūre—somewhat farther; *dekhe*—Nārada Muni saw; *vyādha*—the hunter; *vṛkṣe oṅta hañā*—hiding behind a tree; *mṛga māribāre*—to kill the animals; *āche*—was there; *bāṇa yuḍiyā*—with arrows in the hand.

TRANSLATION

"When Nārada Muni advanced farther, he saw a hunter behind a tree. This hunter was holding arrows, and he was ready to kill more animals.

TEXT 235

শ্যামবর্ণ রক্তনেত্র মহাভয়ঙ্কর ।
ধনুর্বাণ হস্তে,—যেন যম দণ্ডধর ॥ ২৩৫ ॥

śyāma-varṇa rakta-netra mahā-bhayaṅkara
dhanur-bāṇa haste,——yena yama daṇḍa-dhara

SYNONYMS

śyāma-varṇa—blackish color; *rakta-netra*—reddish eyes; *mahā-bhayaṅkara*—very fearful bodily features; *dhanuḥ-bāṇa haste*—with arrows and bow in hand; *yena yama daṇḍa-dhara*—exactly like the superintendent of death, Yamarāja.
ja.

TRANSLATION

"The hunter's body was blackish. He had reddish eyes, and he appeared fierce. It was as if the superintendent of death, Yamarāja, was standing there with bows and arrows in his hands.

TEXT 236

পথ ছাড়ি' নারদ তার নিকটে চলিল ।
নারদে দেখি' মৃগ সব পলাঞা গেল ॥ ২৩৬ ॥

patha chāḍi' nārada tāra nikaṭe calila
nārade dekhi' mṛga saba palāñā gela

SYNONYMS

patha chāḍi'—leaving aside the path; *nārada*—the saintly person Nārada; *tāra nikaṭe*—near him; *calila*—went; *nārade dekhi'*—seeing Nārada; *mṛga*—the animals; *saba*—all; *palāñā gela*—left, running away.

TRANSLATION

"When Nārada Muni left the forest path and went to the hunter, all the animals immediately saw him and fled.

TEXT 237

ক্রুদ্ধ হঞা ব্যাধ তাঁরে গালি দিতে চায় ।
নারদ-প্রভাবে মুখে গালি নাহি আয় ॥ ২৩৭ ॥

kruddha hañā vyādha tāṅre gāli dite cāya
nārada-prabhāve mukhe gāli nāhi āya

SYNONYMS

kruddha hañā—being very angry; *vyādha*—the hunter; *tāṅre*—him; *gāli dite cāya*—wanted to abuse; *nārada-prabhāve*—by the influence of Nārada; *mukhe*—in the mouth; *gāli*—abusive language; *nāhi āya*—did not come.

TRANSLATION

"When all the animals fled, the hunter wanted to chastise Nārada with abusive language, but due to Nārada's presence, he could not utter anything abusive.

TEXT 238

"গোসাঞি, প্রয়াণ-পথ ছাড়ি' কেনে আইলা ।
তোমা দেখি' মোর লক্ষ্য মৃগ পলাইলা ॥" ২৩৮ ॥

"gosāñi, prayāṇa-patha chāḍi' kene āilā
tomā dekhi' mora lakṣya mṛga palāilā"

SYNONYMS

gosāñi—O great saintly person; *prayāṇa-patha chāḍi'*—leaving aside the general path; *kene*—why; *āilā*—have you come; *tomā dekhi'*—seeing you; *mora lakṣya*—my targets; *mṛga*—the animals; *palāilā*—fled.

TRANSLATION

"The hunter addressed Nārada Muni: 'O gosvāmī! O great saintly person! Why have you left the general path through the forest to come to me? Simply by seeing you, all the animals I was hunting have now fled.'

TEXT 239

নারদ কহে,—"পথ ভুলি' আইলাঙ পুছিতে ।
মনে এক সংশয় হয়, তাহা খণ্ডাইতে ॥ ২৩৯ ॥

nārada kahe,—"patha bhuli' āilāṅa puchite
mane eka saṁśaya haya, tāhā khaṇḍāite

SYNONYMS

nārada kahe—Nārada Muni replied; *patha bhuli'*—leaving the general path; *āilāṅa*—I have come; *puchite*—to inquire from you; *mane*—in my mind; *eka*—one; *saṁśaya haya*—there is a doubt; *tāhā*—that; *khaṇḍāite*—to cause to break.

TRANSLATION

"Nārada Muni replied, 'Leaving the path, I have come to you to settle a doubt that is in my mind.

TEXT 240

পথে যে শূকর-মৃগ, জানি তোমার হয় ।"
ব্যাধ কহে,—"যেই কহ, সেই ত' নিশ্চয়" ॥ ২৪০ ॥

pathe ye śūkara-mṛga, jāni tomāra haya"
vyādha kahe,——"yei kaha, sei ta' niścaya"

SYNONYMS

pathe—on the path; *ye*—those; *śūkara-mṛga*—boars and other animals; *jāni*—I can understand; *tomāra haya*—all belong to you; *vyādha kahe*—the hunter replied; *yei kaha*—whatever you are saying; *sei ta' niścaya*—it is a fact.

TRANSLATION

" 'I was wondering whether all the boars and other animals that are half-killed belong to you.' The hunter replied, 'Yes, what you are saying is so.'

TEXT 241

নারদ কহে,—"যদি জীবে মার' তুমি বাণ ।
অর্ধ-মারা কর কেনে, না লও পরাণ ?" ২৪১ ॥

nārada kahe,——"yadi jīve māra' tumi bāṇa
ardha-mārā kara kene, nā lao parāṇa?"

SYNONYMS

nārada kahe—Nārada Muni said; *yadi*—if; *jīve*—in the animals; *māra'*—pierce; *tumi*—you; *bāṇa*—your arrows; *ardha-mārā kara*—you half-kill; *kene*—why; *nā lao parāṇa*—don't you take their lives completely.

TRANSLATION

"Nārada Muni then inquired, 'Why did you not kill the animals completely? Why did you half-kill them by piercing their bodies with arrows?'

TEXT 242

ব্যাধ কহে,—"শুন, গোসাঞি, 'মৃগারি' মোর নাম।
পিতার শিক্ষাতে আমি করি ঐছে কাম ॥ ২৪২ ॥

vyādha kahe,——"śuna, gosāñi, 'mṛgāri' mora nāma
pitāra śikṣāte āmi kari aiche kāma

SYNONYMS

vyādha kahe—the hunter replied; *śuna*—please hear; *gosāñi*—O great saintly person; *mṛga-ari*—the enemy of the animals; *mora nāma*—my name; *pitāra śikṣāte*—by the teaching of my father; *āmi*—I; *kari*—do; *aiche kāma*—such acts.

TRANSLATION

"The hunter replied, 'My dear saintly person, my name is Mṛgāri, enemy of animals. My father taught me to kill them in that way.

TEXT 243

অর্ধ-মারা জীব যদি ধড়্ফড় করে।
তবে ত' আনন্দ মোর বাড়য়ে অন্তরে ॥" ২৪৩ ॥

ardha-mārā jīva yadi dhaḍ-phaḍa kare
tabe ta' ānanda mora bāḍaye antare"

SYNONYMS

ardha-mārā jīva—half-killed living beings; *yadi*—if; *dhaḍ-phaḍa kare*—twist and turn because of suffering; *tabe*—then; *ta'*—certainly; *ānanda*—pleasure; *mora*—my; *bāḍaye antare*—increases within.

TRANSLATION

" 'When I see half-killed animals suffer, I feel great pleasure.'

TEXT 244

নারদ কহে,—'একবস্তু মাগি তোমার স্থানে'।
ব্যাধ কহে,—"মৃগাদি লহ, যেই তোমার মনে ॥২৪৪॥

nārada kahe,——'eka-vastu māgi tomāra sthāne'
vyādha kahe,——"mṛgādi laha, yei tomāra mane

SYNONYMS

nārada kahe—Nārada Muni said; *eka-vastu māgi*—I wish to beg one thing; *tomāra sthāne*—from you; *vyādha kahe*—the hunter replied; *mṛga-ādi laha*—take some of the hunted animals; *yei tomāra mane*—whatever you like.

TRANSLATION

"Nārada Muni then told the hunter, 'I have one thing to beg of you.' The hunter replied, 'You may take whatever animals or anything else you would like.

TEXT 245

মৃগছাল চাহ যদি, আইস মোর ঘরে ।
যেই চাহ তাহা দিব মৃগব্যাঘ্রাম্বরে ॥" ২৪৫ ॥

mṛga-chāla cāha yadi, āisa mora ghare
yei cāha tāhā diba mṛga-vyāghrāmbare"

SYNONYMS

mṛga-chāla—deerskin; *cāha yadi*—if you want; *āisa mora ghare*—come to my place; *yei cāha*—whatever you want; *tāhā*—that; *diba*—I shall give; *mṛga-vyāghra-ambare*—whether a deerskin or a tiger skin.

TRANSLATION

" 'I have many skins if you would like them. I shall give you either a deerskin or a tiger skin.'

TEXT 246

নারদ কহে,—"ইহা আমি কিছু নাহি চাহি ।
আর একদান আমি মাগি তোমা-ঠাঞি ॥ ২৪৬ ॥

nārada kahe,—"ihā āmi kichu nāhi cāhi
āra eka-dāna āmi māgi tomā-ṭhāñi

SYNONYMS

nārada kahe—Nārada Muni said; *ihā*—this; *āmi kichu nāhi cāhi*—I don't want any; *āra*—another; *eka-dāna*—one charity; *āmi*—I; *māgi*—beg; *tomā-ṭhāñi*—from you.

TRANSLATION

"Nārada Muni said, 'I do not want any of the skins. I am only asking one thing from you in charity.

TEXT 247

কালি হৈতে তুমি যেই মৃগাদি মারিবা।
প্রথমেই মারিবা, অর্ধ-মারা না করিবা॥" ২৪৭ ॥

kāli haite tumi yei mṛgādi māribā
prathamei māribā, ardha-mārā nā karibā"

SYNONYMS

kāli haite—from tomorrow; *tumi*—you; *yei*—whatever; *mṛga-ādi*—animals; *māribā*—you will kill; *prathamei māribā*—kill them in the beginning; *ardha-mārā*—half-killing; *nā karibā*—do not do.

TRANSLATION

" 'I beg you that from this day on you will kill animals completely and not leave them half-dead.'

TEXT 248

ব্যাধ কহে,—"কিবা দান মাগিলা আমারে।
অর্ধ মারিলে কিবা হয়, তাহা কহ মোরে॥" ২৪৮ ॥

vyādha kahe,—"kibā dāna māgilā āmāre
ardha mārile kibā haya, tāhā kaha more"

SYNONYMS

vyādha kahe—the hunter replied; *kibā dāna*—what kind of charity; *māgilā āmāre*—have you begged from me; *ardha mārile*—in half-killing; *kibā*—what; *haya*—there is; *tāhā*—that; *kaha more*—kindly explain to me.

TRANSLATION

"The hunter replied, 'My dear sir, what are you asking of me? What is wrong with the animals' lying there half-killed? Will you please explain this to me?'

TEXT 249

নারদ কহে,—"অর্ধ মারিলে জীব পায় ব্যথা।
জীবে দুঃখ দিতেছ, তোমার হইবে ঐছে অবস্থা ॥২৪৯॥

nārada kahe,—"ardha mārile jīva pāya vyathā
jīve duḥkha ditecha, tomāra ha-ibe aiche avasthā

SYNONYMS

nārada kahe—Nārada Muni replied; *ardha mārile*—by half-killing the animals; *jīva pāya vyathā*—the living beings suffer too much pain; *jīve duḥkha ditecha*—you are giving troubles to the living beings; *tomāra*—your; *ha-ibe*—there will be; *aiche avasthā*—the same suffering in retaliation.

TRANSLATION

"Nārada Muni replied, 'If you leave the animals half-dead, you are purposefully giving them pain. Therefore you will have to suffer in retaliation.'

PURPORT

This is an authoritative statement given by the greatest authority, Nārada Muni. If one gives another living entity unnecessary pain, one will certainly be punished by the laws of nature by a similar pain. Although the hunter Mṛgāri was uncivilized, he still had to suffer the results of his sinful activities. However, if a civilized man kills animals regularly in a slaughterhouse to maintain his so-called civilization, using scientific methods and machines to kill animals, one cannot even estimate the suffering awaiting him. So-called civilized people consider themselves very advanced in education, but they do not know about the stringent laws of nature. According to nature's law, it is a life for a life. We can hardly imagine the sufferings of one who maintains a slaughterhouse. He endures suffering not only in this life, but in his next life also. It is said that a hunter, murderer or killer is advised not to live and not to die. If he lives, he accumulates even more sins, which bring about more suffering in a future life. He is advised not to die because his dying means that he immediately begins to endure more suffering. Therefore he is advised not to live and not to die.

As followers of the Vedic principles, we accept the statements of Nārada Muni in this regard. It is our duty to see that no one suffers due to sinful activities. Foolish rascals are described in *Bhagavad-gītā* as *māyayāpahṛta-jñānāḥ,* which indicates that although they are superficially educated, *māyā* has taken their real knowledge away. Such people are presently leading human society. In *Śrīmad-Bhāgavatam* they are also described as *andhā yathāndhair upanīyamānāḥ*. These rascals are themselves blind, and yet they are leading others who are blind. When people follow such leaders, they suffer unlimited pains in the future. Despite so-called advancement, all this is happening. Who is safe? Who is happy? Who is without anxiety?

TEXT 250

ব্যাধ তুমি, জীব মার—'অল্প' অপরাধ তোমার ।
কদর্থনা দিয়া মার'—এ পাপ 'অপার' ॥ ২৫০ ॥

vyādha tumi, jīva māra——'alpa' aparādha tomāra
kadarthanā diyā māra'——e pāpa 'apāra'

SYNONYMS

vyādha tumi—you are a hunter; *jīva māra*—your occupation is to kill animals; *alpa*—slight; *aparādha*—offense; *tomāra*—your; *kadarthanā diyā*—unnecessarily giving them pain; *māra'*—when you kill; *e pāpa apāra*—this sinful activity is unlimited.

TRANSLATION

"Nārada Muni continued, 'My dear hunter, your business is killing animals. That is a slight offense on your part, but when you consciously give them unnecessary pain by leaving them half-dead, you incur very great sins.'

PURPORT

This is another good instruction to animal killers. There are always animal killers and animal eaters in human society because less civilized people are accustomed to eating meat. In Vedic civilization, meat-eaters are advised to kill an animal for the goddess Kālī or a similar demigod. This is in order not to give the animal unnecessary pain, as slaughterhouses do. In the *balidāna* sacrifice to a demigod, it is recommended to cut the throat of an animal with one slice. This should be done on a dark-moon night, and the painful noises expressed by the animal at the time of being slaughtered are not to be heard by anyone. There are also many other restrictions. Slaughter is only allowed once a month, and the killer of the animal has to suffer similar pains in his next life. At the present moment, so-called civilized men do not sacrifice animals to a deity in a religious or ritualistic way. They openly kill animals daily by the thousands for no purpose other than the satisfaction of the tongue. Because of this the entire world is suffering in so many ways. Politicians are unnecessarily declaring war, and, according to the stringent laws of material nature, massacres are taking place between nations.

prakṛteḥ kriyamāṇāni
guṇaiḥ karmāṇi sarvaśaḥ
ahaṅkāra-vimūḍhātmā
kartāham iti manyate

"The bewildered spirit soul, under the influence of the three modes of material nature, thinks himself to be the doer of activities, which are in actuality carried out by nature." (Bg. 3.27) The laws of *prakṛti* (nature) are very stringent. No one should think that he has the freedom to kill animals and not suffer the consequences. One cannot be safe by doing this. Nārada Muni herein says that animal killing is offensive, especially when animals are given unnecessary pain. Meat-eaters and animal killers are advised not to purchase meat from the slaughterhouse. They can worship Kālī once a month, kill some unimportant animal and eat it. Even by following this method, one is still an offender.

TEXT 251

কদর্থিয়া তুমি যত মারিলা জীবেরে ।
তারা তৈছে তোমা মারিবে জন্ম-জন্মান্তরে ॥" ২৫১ ॥

kadarthiyā tumi yata mārilā jīvere
tārā taiche tomā māribe janma-janmāntare"

SYNONYMS

kadarthiyā—giving unnecessary pangs; *tumi*—you; *yata*—all; *mārilā*—killed; *jīvere*—the living entities; *tārā*—all of them; *taiche*—similarly; *tomā*—you; *māribe*—will kill; *janma-janma-antare*—life after life.

TRANSLATION

"Nārada Muni continued, 'All the animals that you have killed and given unnecessary pain will kill you one after the other in your next life and in life after life.'

PURPORT

This is another authoritative statement made by the great sage Nārada. Those who kill animals and give them unnecessary pain—as people do in slaughterhouses—will be killed in a similar way in the next life and in many lives to come. One can never be excused from such an offense. If one kills many thousands of animals in a professional way so that other people can purchase the meat to eat, one must be ready to be killed in a similar way in his next life and in life after life. There are many rascals who violate their own religious principles. According to Judeo-Christian scriptures, it is clearly said, "Thou shalt not kill." Nonetheless, giving all kinds of excuses, even the heads of religions indulge in killing animals while trying to pass as saintly persons. This mockery and hypocrisy in human society bring about unlimited calamities; therefore occasionally there are great wars. Masses of such people go out onto battlefields and kill themselves. Presently they have discovered the atomic bomb, which is simply awaiting wholesale destruction. If people want to be saved from the killing business life after life, they must take to Kṛṣṇa consciousness and cease sinful activity. The International Society for Krishna Consciousness recommends that everyone abandon meat-eating, illicit sex, intoxication and gambling. When one gives up these sinful activities, he can understand Kṛṣṇa and take to this Kṛṣṇa consciousness movement. We therefore request everyone to abandon sinful activity and chant the Hare Kṛṣṇa *mantra.* In this way people can save themselves from repeated birth and death.

TEXT 252

নারদ-সঙ্গে ব্যাধের মন পরসন্ন হইল।
তাঁর বাক্য শুনি' মনে ভয় উপজিল ॥ ২৫২ ॥

nārada-saṅge vyādhera mana parasanna ha-ila
tāṅra vākya śuni' mane bhaya upajila

SYNONYMS

nārada-saṅge—in the association of the great sage Nārada Muni; *vyādhera*—of the hunter; *mana*—the mind; *parasanna ha-ila*—became cleansed and satisfied; *tāṅra*—his; *vākya*—words; *śuni'*—hearing; *mane*—in the mind; *bhaya upajila*—some fear arose.

TRANSLATION

"In this way, through the association of the great sage Nārada Muni, the hunter was a little convinced of his sinful activity. He therefore became somewhat afraid due to his offenses.

PURPORT

This is the effect of associating with a pure devotee. Our preachers who are preaching Kṛṣṇa consciousness all over the world should follow in the footsteps of Nārada Muni and become purified by following the four principles and chanting the Hare Kṛṣṇa *mahā-mantra.* This will make them fit to become Vaiṣṇavas. Then, when they speak to sinful people about the teachings of this Kṛṣṇa consciousness movement, people will be affected and take the instructions. We receive instructions in devotional service through the disciplic succession. Nārada Muni is our original *guru* because he is the spiritual master of Vyāsadeva. Vyāsadeva is the spiritual master of our disciplic succession; therefore we should follow in the footsteps of Nārada Muni and become pure Vaiṣṇavas. A pure Vaiṣṇava is one who has no ulterior motive. He has totally dedicated himself to the service of the Lord. He does not have material desires, and he is not interested in so-called learning and philanthropic work. The so-called learned scholars and philanthropists are actually *karmīs* and *jñānīs,* and some are actually misers engaged in sinful activity. All are condemned because they are not devotees of Lord Kṛṣṇa.

This is a chance to become purified by associating with this Kṛṣṇa consciousness movement and strictly following the rules and regulations. By chanting the Hare Kṛṣṇa *mahā-mantra,* one can become free from all contamination, especially contamination brought about by the killing of animals. Lord Kṛṣṇa Himself requested:

sarva-dharmān parityajya
māṁ ekaṁ śaraṇaṁ vraja
ahaṁ tvāṁ sarva-pāpebhyo
mokṣayiṣyāmi mā śucaḥ

"Abandon all varieties of religion and just surrender unto Me. I shall deliver you from all sinful reaction. Do not fear." (Bg. 18.66)

We should take this instruction from Kṛṣṇa and follow in the footsteps of Nārada Muni in the disciplic succession. If we simply surrender unto Kṛṣṇa's lotus feet and take this Kṛṣṇa consciousness movement seriously, we can be freed from the *karma* incurred by sin. If we are intelligent enough, we shall engage in the loving service of the Lord. Then our lives will be successful, and we shall not have to suffer like the hunter life after life. By killing animals, not only will we be bereft of the human form but we will have to take an animal form and somehow or other be killed by the same type of animal we have killed. This is the law of nature. The Sanskrit word *māṁsa* means "meat." It is said: *māṁ saḥ khadati iti māṁsaḥ*. That is, "I am now eating the flesh of an animal who will some day in the future be eating my flesh."

TEXT 253

ব্যাধ কহে,—"বাল্য হৈতে এই আমার কর্ম ।
কেমনে তরিমু মুঞি পামর অধম ? ২৫৩ ॥

vyādha kahe,——"bālya haite ei āmāra karma
kemane tarimu muñi pāmara adhama?

SYNONYMS

vyādha kahe—the hunter said; *bālya haite*—from the very beginning of my childhood; *ei āmāra karma*—I have been taught this business (half-killing animals); *kemane*—how; *tarimu*—shall become free from these sinful activities; *muñi*—I; *pāmara adhama*—sinful and misled.

TRANSLATION

"The hunter then admitted that he was convinced of his sinful activity, and he said, 'I have been taught this business from my very childhood. Now I am

wondering how I can become freed from these unlimited volumes of sinful activity.'

PURPORT

This kind of admission is very beneficial as long as one does not again commit sin. Cheating and hypocrisy are not tolerated by higher authorities. If one understands what sin is, he should give it up with sincerity and regret and surrender unto the lotus feet of the Supreme Personality of Godhead through His agent, the pure devotee. In this way, one can be freed from the reactions of sin and make progress in devotional service. However, if one continues committing sins after making some atonement, he will not be saved. In the *śāstras,* such atonement is compared to an elephant's bathing. An elephant takes a very good bath and cleanses its body very nicely, but as soon as it comes out of the water, it picks up some dust on the shore and throws it all over its body. Atonement may be carried out very nicely, but it will not help a person if he continues committing sins. Therefore the hunter first admitted his sinful activity before the saintly person Nārada and then asked how he could be saved.

TEXT 254

এই পাপ যায় মোর, কেমন উপায়ে ?
নিস্তার করহ মোরে, পড়োঁ তোমার পায়ে ॥" ২৫৪ ॥

ei pāpa yāya mora, kemana upāye?
nistāra karaha more, paḍoṅ tomāra pāye"

SYNONYMS

ei—this; *pāpa yāya mora*—sinful reaction of my life can be washed off; *kemana upāye*—by what means; *nistāra karaha more*—kindly deliver me; *paḍoṅ*—I fall down; *tomāra pāye*—at your lotus feet.

TRANSLATION

"The hunter continued, 'My dear sir, please tell me how I can be relieved from the reactions of my sinful life. Now I fully surrender unto you and fall down at your lotus feet. Please deliver me from sinful reactions.'

PURPORT

By the grace of Nārada Muni, the hunter came to his good senses and immediately surrendered unto the saint's lotus feet. This is the process. By associating with a saintly person, one is able to understand the reactions of his sinful life.

When one voluntarily surrenders to a saintly person who is a representative of Kṛṣṇa and follows his instructions, one can become freed from sinful reaction. Kṛṣṇa demands the surrender of a sinful man, and Kṛṣṇa's representative gives the same instructions. The representative of Kṛṣṇa never tells his disciple, "Surrender unto me." Rather he says, "Surrender unto Kṛṣṇa." If the disciple accepts this principle and surrenders himself through the representative of Kṛṣṇa, his life is saved.

TEXT 255

নারদ কহে,—'যদি ধর আমার বচন।
তবে সে করিতে পারি তোমার মোচন ॥' ২৫৫ ॥

nārada kahe,——'yadi dhara āmāra vacana
tabe se karite pāri tomāra mocana'

SYNONYMS

nārada kahe—Nārada Muni replied; *yadi dhara*—if you accept; *āmāra vacana*—my instruction; *tabe*—then; *se*—this; *karite pāri*—I can do; *tomāra*—your; *mocana*—liberation.

TRANSLATION

"Nārada Muni assured the hunter, 'If you listen to my instructions, I shall find the way you can be liberated.'

PURPORT

Gaurāṅgera bhakta-gaṇe jane jane śakti dhare. The purport of this song is that the devotees of Lord Śrī Caitanya Mahāprabhu are very powerful, and each and every one of them can deliver the whole world. What, then, to speak of Nārada Muni? If one follows the instructions of Nārada Muni, one can be delivered from any amount of sinful reactions. This is the process. One must follow the instructions of a spiritual master; then one will certainly be delivered from all sinful reaction. This is the secret of success. *Yasya deve parā bhaktir yathā deve tathā gurau.* If one has unflinching faith in Kṛṣṇa and the spiritual master, the result is *tasyaite kathitā hy arthāḥ prakāśante mahātmanaḥ:* all the conclusions of revealed scriptures will be open to such a person. A pure devotee of Kṛṣṇa can make the same demands that Nārada Muni is making. He says, "If you follow my instructions, I shall take responsibility for your liberation." A pure devotee like Nārada can give assurance to any sinful man because by the grace of the Lord such a devotee is empowered to deliver any sinful person if that person follows the principles set forth.

TEXT 256

ব্যাধ কহে,—'যেই কহ, সেই ত' করিব'।
নারদ কহে,—'ধনুক ভাঙ্গ, তবে সে কহিব' ॥ ২৫৬ ॥

vyādha kahe,——'yei kaha, sei ta' kariba'
nārada kahe,——'dhanuka bhāṅga, tabe se kahiba'

SYNONYMS

vyādha kahe—the hunter replied; *yei kaha*—whatever you say; *sei ta' kariba*—that I shall do; *nārada kahe*—Nārada Muni replied; *dhanuka bhāṅga*—break your bow; *tabe*—then; *se kahiba*—I shall speak to you.

TRANSLATION

"The hunter then said, 'My dear sir, whatever you say I shall do.' Nārada immediately ordered him, 'First of all, break your bow. Then I shall tell you what is to be done.'

PURPORT

This is the process of initiation. The disciple must admit that he will no longer commit sinful activity—namely illicit sex, meat-eating, gambling and intoxication. He promises to execute the order of the spiritual master. Then the spiritual master takes care of him and elevates him to spiritual emancipation.

TEXT 257

ব্যাধ কহে,—'ধনুক ভাঙ্গিলে বর্তিব কেমনে ?'
নারদ কহে,—'আমি অন্ন দিব প্রতিদিনে ॥' ২৫৭ ॥

vyādha kahe,——'dhanuka bhāṅgile vartiba kemane?'
nārada kahe,——'āmi anna diba prati-dine'

SYNONYMS

vyādha kahe—the hunter replied; *dhanuka bhāṅgile*—if I break my bow; *vartiba kemane*—what will be the source of my maintenance; *nārada kahe*—Nārada Muni replied; *āmi*—I; *anna*—food; *diba*—shall supply; *prati-dine*—every day.

TRANSLATION

"The hunter replied, 'If I break my bow, how shall I maintain myself?' Nārada Muni replied, 'Do not worry. I shall supply all your food every day.'

PURPORT

The source of our income is not actually the source of our maintenance. Every living being—from the great Brahmā down to an insignificant ant—is being maintained by the Supreme Personality of Godhead. *Eko bahūnāṁ yo vidadhāti kāmān.* The one Supreme Being, Kṛṣṇa, maintains everyone. Our so-called source of income is our own choice only. If I wish to be a hunter, it will appear that hunting is the source of my income. If I become a *brāhmaṇa* and completely depend on Kṛṣṇa, I do not conduct a business, but nonetheless my maintenance is supplied by Kṛṣṇa. The hunter was disturbed about breaking his bow because he was worried about his income. Nārada Muni assured the hunter because he knew that the hunter was not being maintained by the bow but by Kṛṣṇa. Being the agent of Kṛṣṇa, Nārada Muni knew very well that the hunter would not suffer by breaking the bow. There was no doubt that Kṛṣṇa would supply him food.

TEXT 258

ধনুক ভাঙ্গি' ব্যাধ তাঁর চরণে পড়িল ।
তারে উঠাঞা নারদ উপদেশ কৈল ॥ ২৫৮ ॥

dhanuka bhāṅgi' vyādha tāṅra caraṇe paḍila
tāre uṭhāñā nārada upadeśa kaila

SYNONYMS

dhanuka bhāṅgi'—breaking the bow; *vyādha*—the hunter; *tāṅra*—his (Nārada Muni's); *caraṇe*—at the lotus feet; *paḍila*—surrendered; *tāre*—him; *uṭhāñā*—raising; *nārada*—the great saint Nārada Muni; *upadeśa kaila*—gave instruction.

TRANSLATION

"Being thus assured by the great sage Nārada Muni, the hunter broke his bow, immediately fell down at the saint's lotus feet and fully surrendered. After this, Nārada Muni raised him with his hand and gave him instructions for spiritual advancement.

PURPORT

This is the process of initiation. The disciple must surrender to the spiritual master, the representative of Kṛṣṇa. The spiritual master, being in the disciplic succession stemming from Nārada Muni, is in the same category with Nārada Muni. A person can be relieved from his sinful activity if he surrenders to the lotus feet of a person who actually represents Nārada Muni. Nārada Muni gave instructions to the hunter after the hunter surrendered.

TEXT 259

"ঘরে গিয়া ব্রাহ্মণে দেহ' যত আছে ধন ।
এক এক বস্ত্র পরি' বাহির হও দুইজন ॥ ২৫৯ ॥

"ghare giyā brāhmaṇe deha' yata āche dhana
eka eka vastra pari' bāhira hao dui-jana

SYNONYMS

ghare giyā—returning home; *brāhmaṇe*—to the *brāhmaṇas,* the most intelligent men in spiritual understanding; *deha'*—give; *yata*—whatever; *āche*—you have; *dhana*—riches; *eka eka*—each of you; *vastra pari'*—just one cloth; *bāhira hao*—leave home; *dui-jana*—both of you.

TRANSLATION

"Nārada Muni then advised the hunter, 'Return home and distribute whatever riches you have to the pure brāhmaṇas who know the Absolute Truth. After distributing all your riches to the brāhmaṇas, both you and your wife should leave home, taking only one cloth to wear.'

PURPORT

This is the process of renunciation at the stage of *vānaprastha.* After enjoying householder life for some time, the husband and wife must leave home and distribute their riches to *brāhmaṇas* and Vaiṣṇavas. One can keep his wife as an assistant in the *vānaprastha* stage. The idea is that the wife will assist the husband in spiritual advancement. Therefore Nārada Muni advised the hunter to adopt the *vānaprastha* stage and leave home. It is not that a *gṛhastha* should live at home until he dies. *Vānaprastha* is preliminary to *sannyāsa.* In the Kṛṣṇa consciousness movement there are many young couples engaged in the Lord's service. Eventually they are supposed to take *vānaprastha,* and after the *vānaprastha* stage the husband may take *sannyāsa* in order to preach. The wife may then remain alone and serve the Deity or engage in other activities within the Kṛṣṇa consciousness movement.

TEXT 260

নদী-তীরে একখানি কুটীর করিয়া ।
তার আগে একপিণ্ডি তুলসী রোপিয়া ॥ ২৬০ ॥

nadī-tīre eka-khāni kuṭīra kariyā
tāra āge eka-piṇḍi tulasī ropiyā

SYNONYMS

nadī-tīre—on the bank of the river; *eka-khāni*—just one; *kuṭīra*—a cottage; *kariyā*—constructing; *tāra āge*—just in front of the cottage; *eka-piṇḍi*—one raised platform; *tulasī*—a *tulasī* plant; *ropiyā*—growing.

TRANSLATION

"Nārada Muni continued, 'Leave your home and go to the river. There you should construct a small cottage, and in front of the cottage you should grow a tulasī plant on a raised platform.

TEXT 261

তুলসী-পরিক্রমা কর, তুলসী-সেবন ।
নিরন্তর কৃষ্ণনাম করিহ কীর্তন ॥ ২৬১ ॥

tulasī-parikramā kara, tulasī-sevana
nirantara kṛṣṇa-nāma kariha kīrtana

SYNONYMS

tulasī-parikramā kara—circumambulate the *tulasī* plant; *tulasī-sevana*—just supply water to the root of *tulasī-devī; nirantara*—continuously; *kṛṣṇa-nāma*—the holy name of Kṛṣṇa; *kariha*—just perform; *kīrtana*—chanting.

TRANSLATION

" 'After planting the tulasī tree before your house, you should daily circumambulate that tulasī plant, serve her by giving her water and other things, and continuously chant the Hare Kṛṣṇa mahā-mantra.'

PURPORT

This is the beginning of spiritual life. After leaving householder life, one may go to a holy place, such as the bank of the Ganges or Yamunā, and erect a small cottage. A small cottage can be constructed without any expenditure. Four logs serving as pillars can be secured by any man from the forest. The roof can be covered with leaves, and one can cleanse the inside. Thus one can live very peacefully. In any condition, any man can live in a small cottage, plant a *tulasī* tree, water it in the morning, offer it prayers, and continuously chant the Hare Kṛṣṇa *mahā-mantra.* Thus one can make vigorous spiritual advancement. This is not at all difficult. One simply has to follow the instructions of the spiritual master strictly. Then everything will be successful in due course of time. As far as eating is concerned, there is no problem. If Kṛṣṇa, the Supreme Personality of Godhead, supplies everyone with eatables, why should He not supply His devotee? Sometimes a devotee will not even bother to construct a cottage. He will simply go to live in a mountain cave. One may live in a cave, in a cottage beside a river, in a palace or in a big city like New York or London. In any case, a devotee can follow the instructions of his spiritual master and engage in devotional service by watering the *tulasī* plant and chanting the Hare Kṛṣṇa *mantra.* Taking the advice of Śrī Caitanya Mahāprabhu and our spiritual master, Bhaktisiddhānta Sarasvatī Gosvāmī Mahārāja, one can go to any part of the world and instruct people to become devotees of the Lord by following the regulative principles, worshiping the *tulasī* plant and continuously chanting the Hare Kṛṣṇa *mahā-mantra.*

TEXT 262

আমি তোমায় বহু অন্ন পাঠাইমু দিনে ।
সেই অন্ন লবে, যত খাও দুইজনে ॥" ২৬২ ॥

āmi tomāya bahu anna pāṭhāimu dine
sei anna labe, yata khāo dui-jane"

SYNONYMS

āmi—I; *tomāya*—for you; *bahu*—much; *anna*—food; *pāṭhāimu*—shall send; *dine*—every day; *sei*—that; *anna*—food; *labe*—you shall take; *yata*—whatever; *khāo*—you can eat; *dui-jane*—both of you.

TRANSLATION

"Nārada Muni continued, 'I shall send sufficient food to you both every day. You can take as much food as you want.'

PURPORT

When a person takes to Kṛṣṇa consciousness, there is no need to care for material necessities. Kṛṣṇa says that He personally carries all the necessities to His devotees.

ananyāś cintayanto māṁ
ye janāḥ paryupāsate
teṣāṁ nityābhiyuktānāṁ
yoga-kṣemaṁ vahāmy aham

"Those who worship Me with love and devotion, meditating on My transcendental form—to them I carry what they lack and preserve what they have." (Bg. 9.22) Why should one be anxious about the necessities of life? The principle should be that one should not want more than what is absolutely necessary. Nārada Muni advises the hunter to accept only what is absolutely necessary for him and his wife. The devotee should always be alert to consume only those things that he absolutely requires and not create unnecessary needs.

TEXT 263

তবে সেই মৃগাদি তিনে নারদ সুস্থ কৈল ।
সুস্থ হঞা মৃগাদি তিনে ধাঞা পলাইল ॥ ২৬৩ ॥

tabe sei mṛgādi tine nārada sustha kaila
sustha hañā mṛgādi tine dhāñā palāila

SYNONYMS

tabe—thereafter; *sei*—those; *mṛga-ādi*—animals, beginning with the deer; *tine*—three; *nārada*—the sage Nārada; *sustha kaila*—brought to their senses; *sustha hañā*—coming to consciousness; *mṛga-ādi*—the pierced animals; *tine*—three; *dhāñā palāila*—very swiftly fled away from that place.

TRANSLATION

"The three animals that were half-killed were then brought to their consciousness by the sage Nārada. Indeed, the animals got up and swiftly fled.

TEXT 264

দেখিয়া ব্যাধের মনে হৈল চমৎকার ।
ঘরে গেল ব্যাধ, গুরুকে করি' নমস্কার ॥ ২৬৪ ॥

dekhiyā vyādhera mane haila camatkāra
ghare gela vyādha, guruke kari' namaskāra

SYNONYMS

dekhiyā—seeing; *vyādhera*—of the hunter; *mane*—in the mind; *haila*—there was; *camatkāra*—wonder; *ghare*—home; *gela*—went; *vyādha*—the hunter; *guruke*—to the spiritual master; *kari' namaskāra*—offering obeisances.

TRANSLATION

"When the hunter saw the half-killed animals flee, he was certainly struck with wonder. He then offered his respectful obeisances to the sage Nārada and returned home.

TEXT 265

যথা-স্থানে নারদ গেলা, ব্যাধ ঘরে আইল ।
নারদের উপদেশে সকল করিল ॥ ২৬৫ ॥

yathā-sthāne nārada gelā, vyādha ghare āila
nāradera upadeśe sakala karila

SYNONYMS

yathā-sthāne—to the proper destination; *nārada*—sage Nārada; *gelā*—went; *vyādha*—the hunter; *ghare āila*—came back to his house; *nāradera upadeśe*—under the instruction of the sage Nārada; *sakala karila*—he executed everything.

TRANSLATION

"After all this, Nārada Muni went to his destination. After the hunter returned home, he exactly followed the instructions of his spiritual master, Nārada.

PURPORT

For spiritual advancement one must have a bona fide spiritual master and follow his instructions in order to be assured of advancement.

TEXT 266

গ্রামে ধ্বনি হৈল, ব্যাধ 'বৈষ্ণব' হইল ।
গ্রামের লোক সব অন্ন আনিতে লাগিল ॥ ২৬৬ ॥

grāme dhvani haila,——vyādha 'vaiṣṇava' ha-ila
grāmera loka saba anna ānite lāgila

SYNONYMS

grāme—in the village; *dhvani haila*—there was news; *vyādha*—the hunter; *vaiṣṇava ha-ila*—has become a Vaiṣṇava, a lover and servitor of Lord Viṣṇu; *grāmera loka*—the villagers; *saba*—all kinds of; *anna*—food; *ānite lāgila*—began to bring.

TRANSLATION

"The news that the hunter had become a Vaiṣṇava spread all over the village. Indeed, all the villagers broughts alms and presented them to the Vaiṣṇava who was formerly a hunter.

PURPORT

It is the duty of the public to present a gift to a saintly person, Vaiṣṇava or *brāhmaṇa* when going to see him. Every Vaiṣṇava is dependent on Kṛṣṇa, and Kṛṣṇa is ready to supply all of life's necessities, provided a Vaiṣṇava follows the principles set forth by the spiritual master. There are certainly many householders in our Kṛṣṇa consciousness movement. They join the movement and live in the society's centers, but if they take advantage of this opportunity and do not work but live at the expense of the movement, eating *prasāda* and simply sleeping, they place themselves in a very dangerous position. It is therefore advised that *gṛhasthas* should not live in the temple. They must live outside the temple and maintain themselves. Of course, if the *gṛhasthas* are fully engaged in the Lord's service according to the directions of the authorities, there is no harm in their living in a temple. In any case, a temple should not be a place to eat and sleep. A temple manager should be very careful about these things.

TEXT 267

একদিন অন্ন আনে দশ-বিশ জনে ।
দিনে তত লয়, যত খায় দুই জনে ॥ ২৬৭ ॥

eka-dina anna āne daśa-biśa jane
dine tata laya, yata khāya dui jane

SYNONYMS

eka-dina—in one day; *anna*—food; *āne*—brought; *daśa-biśa jane*—enough for ten to twenty men; *dine*—in a day; *tata laya*—would accept only as much; *yata*—as; *khāya dui jane*—the two of them required to eat.

TRANSLATION

"In one day enough food was brought for ten or twenty people, but the hunter and his wife would accept only as much as they could eat.

TEXT 268

একদিন নারদ কহে,—"শুনহ, পর্বতে ।
আমার এক শিষ্য আছে, চলহ দেখিতে" ॥ ২৬৮ ॥

eka-dina nārada kahe,——"śunaha, parvate
āmāra eka śiṣya āche, calaha dekhite"

SYNONYMS

eka-dina—one day; *nārada kahe*—Nārada Muni said; *śunaha*—please hear; *parvate*—my dear Parvata; *āmāra*—my; *eka*—one; *śiṣya*—disciple; *āche*—there is; *calaha dekhite*—let us go see.

TRANSLATION

"One day, while speaking to his friend Parvata Muni, Nārada Muni requested him to go with him to see his disciple the hunter.

TEXT 269

তবে দুই ঋষি আইলা সেই ব্যাধ-স্থানে ।
দূর হৈতে ব্যাধ পাইল গুরুর দরশনে ॥ ২৬৯ ॥

tabe dui ṛṣi āilā sei vyādha-sthāne
dūra haite vyādha pāila gurura daraśane

SYNONYMS

tabe—thereafter; *dui ṛṣi*—two saintly persons; *āilā*—came; *sei vyādha-sthāne*—to the place of that hunter; *dūra haite*—from a distant place; *vyādha*—the hunter; *pāila*—got; *gurura daraśane*—vision of his spiritual master.

TRANSLATION

"When the saintly sages came to the hunter's place, the hunter could see them coming from a distance.

TEXT 270

আস্তে-ব্যস্তে ধাঞা আসে, পথ নাহি পায় ।
পথের পিপীলিকা ইতি-উতি ধরে পায় ॥ ২৭০ ॥

āste-vyaste dhāñā āse, patha nāhi pāya
pathera pipīlikā iti-uti dhare pāya

SYNONYMS

āste-vyaste—with great alacrity; *dhāñā*—running; *āse*—came; *patha nāhi pāya*—does not get the path; *pathera*—on the path; *pipīlikā*—ants; *iti-uti*—here and there; *dhare pāya*—touch the foot.

TRANSLATION

"With great alacrity the hunter began to run toward his spiritual master, but he could not fall down and offer obeisances because ants were running hither and thither around his feet.

TEXT 271

দণ্ডবৎ-স্থানে পিপীলিকারে দেখিয়া ।
বস্ত্রে স্থান ঝাড়ি' পড়ে দণ্ডবৎ হঞা ॥ ২৭১ ॥

daṇḍavat-sthāne pipīlikāre dekhiyā
vastre sthāna jhāḍi' paḍe daṇḍavat hañā

SYNONYMS

daṇḍavat-sthāne—in the place where he wanted to offer his obeisances; *pipīlikāre dekhiyā*—seeing the ants; *vastre*—by the cloth; *sthāna jhāḍi'*—cleansing the place; *paḍe daṇḍa-vat hañā*—falls down flat like a rod.

TRANSLATION

"Seeing the ants, the hunter whisked them away with a piece of cloth. After thus clearing the ants from the ground, he fell down flat to offer his obeisances.

PURPORT

The word *daṇḍa* means "rod," and *vat* means "like." To offer obeisances to the spiritual master, one must fall flat exactly as a rod falls on the ground. This is the meaning of the word *daṇḍavat.*

TEXT 272

নারদ কহে,—"ব্যাধ, এই না হয় আশ্চর্য ।
হরিভক্ত্যে হিংসা-শূন্য হয় সাধুবর্য ॥ ২৭২ ॥

nārada kahe,—"vyādha, ei nā haya āścarya
hari-bhaktye hiṁsā-śūnya haya sādhu-varya

SYNONYMS

nārada kahe—Nārada Muni said; *vyādha*—my dear hunter; *ei nā āścarya*—this is not wonderful for you; *hari-bhaktye*—by advancement in devotional service; *hiṁsā-śūnya haya*—one becomes nonviolent and nonenvious; *sādhu-varya*—thus one becomes the best of honest gentlemen.

TRANSLATION

"Nārada Muni said, 'My dear hunter, such behavior is not at all astonishing. A man in devotional service is automatically nonviolent. He is the best of gentlemen.

PURPORT

In this verse the word *sādhu-varya* means "the best of gentlemen." At the present moment there are many so-called gentlemen who are expert in killing animals and birds. Nonetheless, these so-called gentlemen profess a type of religion that strictly prohibits killing. According to Nārada Muni and Vedic culture, animal killers are not even gentlemen, to say nothing of being religious men. A religious person, a devotee of the Lord, must be nonviolent. Such is the nature of a religious person. It is contradictory to be violent and at the same time call oneself a religious person. Such hypocrisy is not approved by Nārada Muni and the disciplic succession.

TEXT 273

এতে ন হ্যদ্ভুতা ব্যাধ তবাহিংসাদয়ো গুণাঃ ।
হরিভক্তৌ প্রবৃত্তা যে ন তে স্যুঃ পরতাপিনঃ ॥ ২৭৩ ॥

ete na hy adbhutā vyādha
tavāhiṁsādayo guṇāḥ
hari-bhaktau pravṛttā ye
na te syuḥ paratāpinaḥ

SYNONYMS

ete—all these; *na*—not; *hi*—certainly; *adbhutāḥ*—wonderful; *vyādha*—O hunter; *tava*—your; *ahiṁsā-ādayaḥ*—nonviolence and others; *guṇāḥ*—qualities; *hari-bhaktau*—in devotional service; *pravṛttāḥ*—engaged; *ye*—those who; *na*—not; *te*—they; *syuḥ*—are; *paratāpinaḥ*—envious of other living entities.

TRANSLATION

" 'O hunter, good qualities like nonviolence, which you have developed, are not very astonishing, for those engaged in the Lord's devotional service are never inclined to give pain to others because of envy.'

PURPORT

This is a quotation from the *Skanda Purāṇa*.

TEXT 274

তবে সেই ব্যাধ দোঁহারে অঙ্গনে আনিল ।
কুশাসন আনি' দোঁহারে ভক্ত্যে বসাইল ॥ ২৭৪ ॥

tabe sei vyādha doṅhāre aṅgane ānila
kuśāsana āni' doṅhāre bhaktye vasāila

SYNONYMS

tabe—thereafter; *sei*—that; *vyādha*—hunter; *doṅhāre*—both Nārada Muni and Parvata; *aṅgane ānila*—brought in the courtyard of his house; *kuśa-āsana āni'*—bringing straw mats for sitting; *doṅhāre*—both of them; *bhaktye*—with great devotion; *vasāila*—made to sit down.

TRANSLATION

"The hunter then received both the great sages in the courtyard of his house. He spread out a straw mat for them to sit upon, and with great devotion he begged them to sit down.

TEXT 275

জল আনি' ভক্ত্যে দোঁহার পাদ প্রক্ষালিল ।
সেই জল স্ত্রী-পুরুষে পিয়া শিরে লইল ॥ ২৭৫ ॥

jala āni' bhaktye doṅhāra pāda prakṣālila
sei jala strī-puruṣe piyā śire la-ila

SYNONYMS

jala āni'—bringing water; *bhaktye*—with great devotion; *doṅhāra*—of both of them; *pāda prakṣālila*—washed the feet; *sei jala*—that water; *strī-puruṣe*—husband and wife; *piyā*—drinking; *śire la-ila*—put on their heads.

TRANSLATION

"He then fetched water and washed the sages' feet with great devotion. Then both husband and wife drank that water and sprinkled it on their heads.

PURPORT

This is the process one should follow when receiving the spiritual master or someone on the level of the spiritual master. When the spiritual master comes to the residence of his disciples, the disciples should follow in the footsteps of the former hunter. It doesn't matter what one was before initiation. After initiation, one must learn the etiquette mentioned herein.

TEXT 276

কম্প-পুলকাশ্রু হৈল কৃষ্ণনাম গাঞা।
ঊর্ধ্ব বাহু নৃত্য করে বস্ত্র উড়াঞা ॥ ২৭৬ ॥

kampa-pulakāśru haila kṛṣṇa-nāma gāñā
ūrdhva bāhu nṛtya kare vastra uḍāñā

SYNONYMS

kampa—trembling; *pulaka-aśru*—tears and jubilation; *haila*—there were; *kṛṣṇa-nāma gāñā*—chanting the Hare Kṛṣṇa *mantra; ūrdhva bāhu*—raising the arms; *nṛtya kare*—began to dance; *vastra uḍāñā*—waving his garments up and down.

TRANSLATION

"When the hunter chanted the Hare Kṛṣṇa mahā-mantra before his spiritual master, his body trembled, and tears welled in his eyes. Filled with ecstatic love, he raised his hands and began to dance, waving his garments up and down.

TEXT 277

দেখিয়া ব্যাধের প্রেম পর্বত-মহামুনি।
নারদেরে কহে,—তুমি হও স্পর্শমণি ॥ ২৭৭ ॥

dekhiyā vyādhera prema parvata-mahāmuni
nāradere kahe,——tumi hao sparśa-maṇi

SYNONYMS

dekhiyā—seeing; *vyādhera*—of the hunter; *prema*—the ecstatic love; *parvata-mahā-muni*—the great sage Parvata Muni; *nāradere kahe*—spoke to Nārada Muni; *tumi hao sparśa-maṇi*—you are certainly a touchstone.

TRANSLATION

"When Parvata Muni saw the ecstatic loving symptoms of the hunter, he told Nārada, 'Certainly you are a touchstone.'

PURPORT

When a touchstone touches iron, it turns the iron to gold. Parvata Muni called Nārada Muni a touchstone because by his touch the hunter, who was lowest among men, became an elevated and perfect Vaiṣṇava. Śrīla Bhaktivinoda Ṭhākura said that the position of a Vaiṣṇava can be tested by seeing how good a touchstone he is—that is, by seeing how many Vaiṣṇavas he has made during his life. A Vaiṣṇava should be a touchstone so that he can convert others to Vaiṣṇavism by his preaching, even though people may be fallen like the hunter. There are many so-called advanced devotees who sit in a secluded place for their personal benefit. They do not go out to preach and convert others into Vaiṣṇavas, and therefore they certainly cannot be called *sparśa-maṇi,* advanced devotees. *Kaniṣṭha-adhikārī* devotees cannot turn others into Vaiṣṇavas, but a *madhyama-adhikārī* Vaiṣṇava can do so by preaching. Śrī Caitanya Mahāprabhu advised His followers to increase the numbers of Vaiṣṇavas.

yāre dekha, tāre kaha 'kṛṣṇa'-upadeśa
āmāra ājñāya guru hañā tāra' ei deśa
(Cc. *Madhya* 7.128)

It is Śrī Caitanya Mahāprabhu's wish that everyone should become a Vaiṣṇava and *guru.* Following the instructions of Śrī Caitanya Mahāprabhu and His disciplic succession, one can become a spiritual master, for the process is very easy. One can go everywhere and anywhere to preach the instructions of Kṛṣṇa. *Bhagavad-gītā* is Kṛṣṇa's instructions; therefore the duty of every Vaiṣṇava is to travel and preach *Bhagavad-gītā,* either in his country or a foreign country. This is the test of *sparśa-maṇi,* following in the footsteps of Nārada Muni.

TEXT 278

"অহো ধন্যোঽসি দেবর্ষে কৃপয়া যস্য তৎক্ষণাৎ।
নীচোঽপ্যুৎপুলকো লেভে লুব্ধকো রতিমচ্যুতে ॥" ২৭৮ ॥

"aho dhanyo 'si devarṣe
kṛpayā yasya tat-kṣaṇāt
nīco 'py utpulako lebhe
lubdhako ratim acyute"

SYNONYMS

aho—oh; *dhanyaḥ*—glorified; *asi*—you are; *deva-ṛṣe*—O sage among the demigods; *kṛpayā*—by the mercy; *yasya*—of whom; *tat-kṣaṇāt*—immediately;

nīcaḥ api—even though one is the lowest of men; *utpulakaḥ*—becoming agitated in ecstatic love; *lebhe*—gets; *lubdhakaḥ*—a hunter; *ratim*—attraction; *acyute*—unto the Supreme Personality of Godhead.

TRANSLATION

"Parvata Muni continued, 'My dear friend Nārada Muni, you are glorified as the sage among the demigods. By your mercy, even a lowborn person like this hunter can immediately become attached to Lord Kṛṣṇa.'

PURPORT

A pure Vaiṣṇava believes in the statements of the *śāstras*. This verse is quoted from Vedic literature, the *Skanda Purāṇa*.

TEXT 279

নারদ কহে,—'বৈষ্ণব, তোমার অন্ন কিছু আয় ?'
ব্যাধ কহে, "যারে পাঠাও, সেই দিয়া যায় ॥ ২৭৯ ॥

nārada kahe,——'vaiṣṇava, tomāra anna kichu āya?'
vyādha kahe, "yāre pāṭhāo, sei diyā yāya

SYNONYMS

nārada kahe—Nārada Muni said; *vaiṣṇava*—O Vaiṣṇava; *tomāra*—your; *anna*—food; *kichu āya*—does any come; *vyādha kahe*—the hunter replied; *yāre pāṭhāo*—whoever you send; *sei*—that person; *diyā*—giving something; *yāya*—goes.

TRANSLATION

"Nārada Muni then asked the hunter, 'My dear Vaiṣṇava, do you have some income for your maintenance?' The hunter replied, 'My dear spiritual master, whoever you send gives me something when he comes to see me.'

PURPORT

This confirms the statement in *Bhagavad-gītā* (9.22) to the effect that the Lord carries all necessities to His Vaiṣṇava devotee. Nārada Muni asked the former hunter how he was being maintained, and he replied that everyone who came to see him brought him something for his maintenance. Kṛṣṇa, who is situated in everyone's heart, says, "I personally carry all necessities to a Vaiṣṇava." He can order anyone to execute this. Everyone is ready to give something to a Vaiṣṇava, and if a Vaiṣṇava is completely engaged in devotional service, he need not be anxious for his maintenance.

TEXT 280

এত অন্ন না পাঠাও, কিছু কার্য নাই ।
সবে দুইজনার যোগ্য ভক্ষ্যমাত্র চাই ॥" ২৮০ ॥

eta anna nā pāṭhāo, kichu kārya nāi
sabe dui-janāra yogya bhakṣya-mātra cāi"

SYNONYMS

eta anna—so much food; *nā pāṭhāo*—you do not need to send; *kichu kārya nāi*—there is no such need; *sabe*—only; *dui-janāra*—for two persons; *yogya*—requisite; *bhakṣya-mātra*—eatables; *cāi*—we want.

TRANSLATION

"The former hunter said, 'Please do not send so many grains. Only send what is sufficient for two people, no more.'

PURPORT

The former hunter only wanted enough for two people to eat, no more. It is not necessary for a Vaiṣṇava to keep a stock of food for the next day. He should receive only sufficient grains to last one day. The next day, he must again depend on the Lord's mercy. This is the instruction of Śrī Caitanya Mahāprabhu. When His personal servant Govinda sometimes kept a stock of *harītakī* (myrobalan), Śrī Caitanya Mahāprabhu chastised him, saying, "Why did you keep a stock for the next day?" Śrīla Rūpa Gosvāmī and others were begging daily from door to door for their sustenance, and they never attempted to stock their *āśrama* with food for the next day. We should not materially calculate, thinking, "It is better to stock food for a week. Why give the Lord trouble by having Him bring food daily?" One should be convinced that the Lord will provide daily. There is no need to stock food for the next day.

TEXT 281

নারদ কহে,—'ঐছে রহ, তুমি ভাগ্যবান্' ।
এত বলি' দুইজন হইলা অন্তর্ধান ॥ ২৮১ ॥

nārada kahe,——'aiche raha, tumi bhāgyavān'
eta bali' dui-jana ha-ilā antardhāna

SYNONYMS

nārada kahe—Nārada Muni said; *aiche raha*—live like that; *tumi bhāgyavān*—certainly you are very fortunate; *eta bali'*—saying this; *dui-jana*—both Nārada Muni and Parvata Muni; *ha-ilā antardhāna*—disappeared.

TRANSLATION

"Nārada Muni approved his not wanting more than a daily supply of food, and he blessed him, saying, 'You are fortunate.' Nārada Muni and Parvata Muni then disappeared from that place.

TEXT 282

এই ত' কহিলুঁ তোমায় ব্যাধের আখ্যান ।
যা শুনিলে হয় সাধুসঙ্গ-প্রভাব-জ্ঞান ॥ ২৮২ ॥

ei ta' kahiluṅ tomāya vyādhera ākhyāna
yā śunile haya sādhu-saṅga-prabhāva-jñāna

SYNONYMS

ei ta' kahiluṅ—thus I have narrated; *tomāya*—unto you; *vyādhera ākhyāna*—the story of the hunter; *yā śunile*—hearing which; *haya*—there is; *sādhu-saṅga*—of the association of devotees; *prabhāva*—of the influence; *jñāna*—knowledge.

TRANSLATION

"So far I have narrated the incident of the hunter. By hearing this narration, one can understand the influence derived by associating with devotees.

PURPORT

Śrī Caitanya Mahāprabhu wanted to stress that even a hunter, the lowest of men, could become a topmost Vaiṣṇava simply by associating with Nārada Muni or a devotee in his bona fide disciplic succession.

TEXT 283

এই আর তিন অর্থ গণনাতে পাইল ।
এই দুই অর্থ মিলি' 'ছাব্বিশ' অর্থ হৈল ॥ ২৮৩ ॥

ei āra tina artha gaṇanāte pāila
ei dui artha mili' 'chābbiśa' artha haila

SYNONYMS

ei—this example; *āra*—another; *tina artha*—three imports; *gaṇanāte*—in calculating; *pāila*—we have obtained; *ei dui artha mili'*—by adding these two imports; *chābbiśa*—twenty-six; *artha*—imports; *haila*—there have been.

TRANSLATION

"In this way we have found three more meanings. Combine these with the other meanings, and the total number of meanings add up to twenty-six in all.

TEXT 284

আর অর্থ শুন, যাহা —অর্থের ভাণ্ডার ।
স্থূলে 'দুই' অর্থ, সূক্ষ্মে 'বত্রিশ' প্রকার ॥ ২৮৪ ॥

āra artha śuna, yāhā——arthera bhāṇḍāra
sthūle 'dui' artha, sūkṣme 'batriśa' prakāra

SYNONYMS

āra—another; *artha*—import; *śuna*—hear; *yāhā*—which; *arthera bhāṇḍāra*—storehouse of knowledge; *sthūle*—grossly; *dui artha*—two meanings; *sūkṣme*—by a subtle import; *batriśa*—thirty-two; *prakāra*—varieties.

TRANSLATION

"There is yet another meaning, which is full of a variety of imports. Actually there are two gross meanings and thirty-two subtle meanings.

PURPORT

The two gross meanings refer to regulative devotional service and spontaneous devotional service. There are also thirty-two subtle meanings. Under the heading of regulative devotional service, there are sixteen meanings: (1) a servant of the Lord as His personal associate, (2) a personal friend, (3) personal parents or similar superiors, (4) a personal beloved, (5) a servant elevated by spiritual cultivation, (6) a friend by spiritual cultivation, (7) parents and superior devotees by cultivation of devotional service, (8) a beloved wife or female friend by cultivation of devotional service, (9) a mature devotee as a servant, (10) a mature devotee as a friend, (11) a mature devotee as a parent and superior, (12) a mature devotee as wife and beloved, (13) an immature devotee as servant, (14) an immature devotee as a friend, (15) an immature devotee as father and superior, and (16) an immature devotee as a beloved. Similarly, under the heading of spontaneous devotion there are also sixteen various associates. Therefore the total number of devotees under the headings of regular devotees and spontaneous devotees is thirty-two.

TEXT 285

'আত্মা'-শব্দে কহে —সর্ববিধ ভগবান্ ।
এক 'স্বয়ং ভগবান্', আর 'ভগবান্'-আখ্যান ॥২৮৫॥

'ātmā'-śabde kahe——sarva-vidha bhagavān
eka 'svayaṁ bhagavān', āra 'bhagavān'-ākhyāna

SYNONYMS

ātmā-śabde—by the word *ātmā; kahe*—it is said; *sarva-vidha bhagavān*—all types of Personalities of Godhead; *eka*—one; *svayam bhagavān*—the original Supreme Personality of Godhead, Kṛṣṇa; *āra*—another; *bhagavān-ākhyāna*—the Personality of Godhead by an expansive designation.

TRANSLATION

"The word ātmā refers to all the different expansions of the Supreme Personality of Godhead. One of them is the Supreme Personality of Godhead Himself, Kṛṣṇa, and the others are different incarnations or expansions of Kṛṣṇa.

PURPORT

The word *ātmā* also includes all kinds of Bhagavān, the Supreme Personality of Godhead. This means that Kṛṣṇa has unlimited expansions. This is described in *Brahmā-saṁhitā* (5.46):

dīpārcir eva hi daśāntaram abhyupetya
dīpāyate vivṛta-hetu-samāna-dharmā
yas tādṛg eva hi ca viṣṇutayā vibhāti
govindam ādi-puruṣaṁ tam ahaṁ bhajāmi

These expansions are thus compared to candles that have been lit from an original candle. All the secondary candles are equally powerful, but the original candle is that from which all the others have been lit. Kṛṣṇa is the original Supreme Personality of Godhead, and He is expanded as Balarāma, Saṅkarṣaṇa, Aniruddha, Pradyumna and Vāsudeva. In this way there are innumerable incarnations and expansions who are also called Bhagavān, the Supreme Personality of Godhead.

TEXT 286

তাঁতে রমে যেই, সেই সব—'আত্মারাম'।
'বিধিভক্ত', 'রাগভক্ত',—দুইবিধ নাম ॥ ২৮৬ ॥

tāṅte rame yei, sei saba——'ātmārāma'
'vidhi-bhakta', 'rāga-bhakta',——dui-vidha nāma

SYNONYMS

tāṅte—in all those Supreme Personalities of Godhead; *rame*—takes pleasure in devotional service; *yei*—those persons who; *sei saba*—all of them; *ātmārāma*—are also known as *ātmārāma; vidhi-bhakta*—devotees following the regulative principles; *rāga-bhakta*—devotees following spontaneous love; *dui-vidha nāma*—two different varieties.

TRANSLATION

"One who always engages in the service of the Supreme Personality of Godhead is called ātmārāma. There are two types of ātmārāma. One is an ātmārāma engaged in regulative devotional service, and the other is an ātmārāma engaged in spontaneous devotional service.

TEXT 287

দুইবিধ ভক্ত হয় চারি চারি প্রকার ।
পারিষদ, সাধনসিদ্ধ, সাধকগণ আর ॥ ২৮৭ ॥

dui-vidha bhakta haya cāri cāri prakāra
pāriṣada, sādhana-siddha, sādhaka-gaṇa āra

SYNONYMS

dui-vidha bhakta—these two varieties of *ātmārāma* devotees; *haya*—are; *cāri cāri prakāra*—each of four different categories; *pāriṣada*—personal associate; *sādhana-siddha*—liberated to the position of associates by perfection in devotional service; *sādhaka-gaṇa āra*—and devotees already engaged in the devotional service of the Lord.

TRANSLATION

"The ātmārāmas engaged in regulative and spontaneous devotional service are further categorized into four groups. There are the eternal associates, the associates who have become perfect by devotional service, and those who are engaged in devotional service and are called sādhaka.

TEXT 288

জাত-অজাত-রতিভেদে সাধক দুই ভেদ ।
বিধি-রাগ-মার্গে চারি চারি—অষ্ট ভেদ ॥ ২৮৮ ॥

jāta-ajāta-rati-bhede sādhaka dui bheda
vidhi-rāga-mārge cāri cāri——aṣṭa bheda

SYNONYMS

jāta-ajāta-rati-bhede—by distinction of mature love and immature love; *sādhaka dui bheda*—those practicing are of two varieties; *vidhi*—regulative devotion; *rāga*—spontaneous devotion; *mārge*—on both the paths; *cāri cāri*—there are four different varieties; *aṣṭa bheda*—a total of eight kinds.

TRANSLATION

"Those who are practicing devotional service are either mature or immature. Therefore the sādhakas are of two types. Since the devotees execute either regulative devotional service or spontaneous devotional service and there are four groups within these two divisions, altogether there are eight varieties.

PURPORT

Śrīla Bhaktisiddhānta Sarasvatī Ṭhākura says that the original Personality of Godhead, Kṛṣṇa, is the Supreme Personality of Godhead, and His expansions are also called the Personality of Godhead. However, Kṛṣṇa is the original Supreme Personality of Godhead. Speculative philosophers and mystic *yogīs* also meditate upon the form of Kṛṣṇa, but this form is not the form of the original Supreme Personality of Godhead. Such a Bhagavān is but a partial representation of the Lord's full potency. Nonetheless, He has to be understood to be the Supreme Personality of Godhead. To clarify this matter, one should simply understand that Kṛṣṇa, the son of Nanda Mahārāja in Vṛndāvana, the friend of the cowherd boys and lover of the *gopīs,* is actually the original Supreme Personality of Godhead. He is attained by spontaneous love. Although His expansions are also called the Supreme Personality of Godhead, They are attained only by the execution of regulative devotional service.

TEXT 289

বিধিভক্ত্যে নিত্যসিদ্ধ পারিষদ —'দাস'।
'সখা' 'গুরু', 'কান্তাগণ',—চারিবিধ প্রকাশ ॥ ২৮৯॥

vidhi-bhaktye nitya-siddha pāriṣada——'dāsa'
'sakhā' 'guru', 'kāntā-gaṇa',——cāri-vidha prakāśa

SYNONYMS

vidhi-bhaktye—by regulative devotional service; *nitya-siddha pāriṣada*—eternally perfect associate; *dāsa*—the servant; *sakhā guru kāntā-gaṇa*—friends, superiors and beloved damsels; *cāri-vidha prakāśa*—they are manifested in four varieties.

TRANSLATION

"By executing regulative devotional service, one is elevated to the platform of an eternally perfect associate—such as a servant, friend, superior or beloved woman. These are of four varieties.

TEXT 290

সাধনসিদ্ধ—দাস, সখা, গুরু, কান্তাগণ ।
জাতরতি সাধকভক্ত—চারিবিধ জন ॥ ২৯০ ॥

sādhana-siddha——dāsa, sakhā, guru, kāntā-gaṇa
jāta-rati sādhaka-bhakta——cāri-vidha jana

SYNONYMS

sādhana-siddha—those who have perfected themselves by devotional service; *dāsa*—servants; *sakhā*—friends; *guru*—superiors; *kāntā-gaṇa*—beloved damsels; *jāta-rati sādhaka-bhakta*—devotees who have become mature by devotional service; *cāri-vidha jana*—they are also of four varieties.

TRANSLATION

"Among those who have perfected themselves by devotional service, there are servants, friends, superiors and beloved damsels. Similarly, there are four types of mature devotees.

TEXT 291

অজাতরতি সাধকভক্ত,—এ চারি প্রকার ।
বিধিমার্গে ভক্তে ষোড়শ ভেদ প্রচার ॥ ২৯১ ॥

ajāta-rati sādhaka-bhakta,——e cāri prakāra
vidhi-mārge bhakte ṣoḍaśa bheda pracāra

SYNONYMS

ajāta-rati sādhaka-bhakta—immature devotees engaged in devotional service; e *cāri prakāra*—there are also the same four varieties; *vidhi-mārge*—on the path of regulative devotional service; *bhakte*—devotees; *ṣoḍaśa bheda pracāra*—there are sixteen varieties.

TRANSLATION

"Within the category of regulative devotional service, there are also immature devotees. These are also of four varieties. Thus in regulative devotional service there are altogether sixteen varieties.

TEXT 292

রাগমার্গে ঐছে ভক্তে ষোড়শ বিভেদ ।
দুই মার্গে আত্মারামের বত্রিশ বিভেদ ॥ ২৯২ ॥

rāga-mārge aiche bhakte ṣoḍaśa vibheda
dui mārge ātmārāmera batriśa vibheda

SYNONYMS

rāga-mārge—on the path of spontaneous loving service; *aiche*—in the same way; *bhakte*—all the devotees; *ṣoḍaśa vibheda*—divided into sixteen varieties; *dui mārge*—on the two paths, namely regulative devotional service and spontaneous devotional service; *ātmārāmera*—of persons enjoying with the Supreme Self; *batriśa vibheda*—there are thirty-two varieties of devotees.

TRANSLATION

"On the path of spontaneous devotional service, there are also sixteen categories of devotees. Thus there are thirty-two types of ātmārāmas enjoying the Supreme Lord on these two paths.

TEXT 293

'মুনি', 'নিগ্র্ন্থ', 'চ' 'অপি',—চারি শব্দের অর্থ ।
যাহাঁ যেই লাগে, তাহা করিয়ে সমর্থ ॥ ২৯৩ ॥

'muni', 'nirgrantha', 'ca' 'api',——cāri śabdera artha
yāhāṅ yei lāge, tāhā kariye samartha

SYNONYMS

muni—the sage; *nirgrantha*—either learned or foolish; *ca*—also; *api*—in spite of; *cāri śabdera artha*—the meanings of these four words; *yāhāṅ*—wherever; *yei lāge*—they apply; *tāhā kariye samartha*—make them sound.

TRANSLATION

"When these thirty-two types of devotees are qualified with the words muni nirgrantha ca api, they can be increased in different ways and very soundly elaborated upon.

TEXT 294

বত্রিশে ছাব্বিশে মিলি' অষ্টপঞ্চাশ ।
আর এক ভেদ শুন অর্থের প্রকাশ ॥ ২৯৪ ॥

batriśe chābbiśe mili' aṣṭa-pañcāśa
āra eka bheda śuna arthera prakāśa

SYNONYMS

batriśe—these thirty-two varieties; *chābbiśe*—the formerly described twenty-six varieties; *mili'*—added together; *aṣṭa-pañcāśa*—they become fifty-eight; *āra*—another; *eka*—one; *bheda*—different; *śuna*—please hear; *arthera prakāśa*—manifestation of import.

TRANSLATION

"When we add the twenty-six types of devotees to these thirty-two, they altogether number fifty-eight. You may now hear from Me of manifestations with different meanings.

TEXT 295

ইতরেতর 'চ' দিয়া সমাস করিয়ে।
'আটান্ন'বার আত্মারাম নাম লইয়ে ॥ ২৯৫ ॥

itaretara 'ca' diyā samāsa kariye
'āṭānna' bāra ātmārāma nāma la-iye

SYNONYMS

itaretara—in different varieties; *ca*—the word *ca; diyā*—adding; *samāsa kariye*—make a compound word; *āṭānna bāra*—fifty-eight times; *ātmārāma*—the *ātmārāma* devotees; *nāma la-iye*—I take their different names.

TRANSLATION

"In this way, as I add the word ca to one word after another, I make a compound. Thus the different names of ātmārāmas can be taken fifty-eight times.

TEXT 296

'আত্মারামাশ্চ আত্মারামাশ্চ' আটান্নবার।
শেষে সব লোপ করি' রাখি একবার ॥ ২৯৬ ॥

'ātmārāmāś ca ātmārāmāś ca' āṭānna-bāra
śeṣe saba lopa kari' rākhi eka-bāra

SYNONYMS

ātmārāmāḥ ca ātmārāmāḥ ca—repeating *ātmārāmāḥ; āṭānna-bāra*—fifty-eight times; *śeṣe*—at the end; *saba lopa kari'*—rejecting all; *rākhi*—we keep; *eka-bāra*—only one.

TRANSLATION

"In this way, one can repeat the word ātmārāmāḥ with ca for each of the fifty-eight meanings. By following the rule previously stated and rejecting all but the last, we retain that which represents all the meanings.

TEXT 297

সরূপাণামেকশেষ একবিভক্তৌ,
উক্তার্থানামপ্রয়োগ ইতি ॥ ২৯৭ ॥

sarūpāṇām eka-śeṣa eka-vibhaktau,
uktārthānām aprayoga iti

SYNONYMS

sa-rūpāṇām—of words of the same form; *eka-śeṣaḥ*—only the last; *eka-vibhaktau*—in the same case; *ukta-arthānām*—of the previously spoken meanings; *aprayogaḥ*—nonapplication; *iti*—thus.

TRANSLATION

" 'Of words having the same form and case termination, the last one is the only one retained.'

PURPORT

This is a quotation from Pāṇini's *sūtras* (1.2.64).

TEXT 298

আটান্ন চ-কারের সব লোপ হয়।
এক আত্মারাম-শব্দে আটান্ন অর্থ কয় ২৯৮ ॥

āṭānna ca-kārera saba lopa haya
eka ātmārāma-śabde āṭānna artha kaya

SYNONYMS

āṭānna—fifty-eight; *ca-kārera*—of the additions of the word *ca; saba lopa haya*—all of them are rejected; *eka*—one; *ātmārāma*—*ātmārāma; śabde*—by the word; *āṭānna artha kaya*—fifty-eight imports are automatically derived.

TRANSLATION

"When all the ca-kāra, or additions to the word ca, are taken away, fifty-eight different meanings can still be understood by the one word ātmārāma.

TEXT 299

অশ্বত্থবৃক্ষাশ্চ বটবৃক্ষাশ্চ কপিত্থবৃক্ষাশ্চ আম্রবৃক্ষাশ্চ বৃক্ষাঃ ॥ ২৯৯ ॥

aśvattha-vṛkṣāś ca baṭa-vṛkṣāś ca kapittha-vṛkṣāś ca āmra-vṛkṣāś ca vṛkṣāḥ

SYNONYMS

aśvattha-vṛkṣāḥ—banyan trees; *ca*—and; *baṭa-vṛkṣāḥ*—fig trees; *ca*—and; *kapittha-vṛkṣāḥ*—a type of tree named kapittha; *ca*—and; *āmra-vṛkṣāḥ*—mango trees; *ca*—and; *vṛkṣāḥ*—all indicated by the word "trees."

TRANSLATION

" 'By the plural word vṛkṣāḥ [trees], all trees, such as banyan trees, fig trees, kapittha trees and mango trees, are indicated.'

TEXT 300

"অস্মিন্ বনে বৃক্ষাঃ ফলন্তি" যৈছে হয়।
তৈছে সব আত্মারাম কৃষ্ণে ভক্তি করয় ॥ ৩০০ ॥

"asmin vane vṛkṣāḥ phalanti" yaiche haya
taiche saba ātmārāma kṛṣṇe bhakti karaya

SYNONYMS

asmin vane—in this forest; *vṛkṣāḥ phalanti*—different varieties of trees bear fruit; *yaiche haya*—just as in this sentence; *taiche*—similarly; *saba*—all; *ātmārāma*—self-realized souls; *kṛṣṇe bhakti karaya*—engage themselves in loving devotional service to Lord Kṛṣṇa.

TRANSLATION

"This ātmārāma verse is like the sentence, 'In this forest many different trees bear fruit.' All ātmārāmas render devotional service to Lord Kṛṣṇa.

TEXT 301

'আত্মারামাশ্চ' সমুচ্চয়ে কহিয়ে চ-কার।
'মুনয়শ্চ' ভক্তি করে,—এই অর্থ তার ॥ ৩০১ ॥

'ātmārāmāś ca' samuccaye kahiye ca-kāra
'munayaś ca' bhakti kare,——ei artha tāra

SYNONYMS

ātmārāmāḥ ca—similarly the word *ātmārāmāḥ* with the word *ca* added; *samuccaye*—in aggregation; *kahiye*—means; *ca-kāra*—the word *ca; munayaḥ ca*—the word *munayaḥ* with the word *ca* added; *bhakti kare*—all of them engage in devotional service; *ei artha tāra*—this is the perfect meaning of the verse.

TRANSLATION

"After fifty-eight times uttering the word ātmārāmāḥ and taking ca in a sense of aggregation, one may add the word munayaḥ. That will mean that they also render devotional service to Lord Kṛṣṇa. In this way there are fifty-nine meanings.

TEXT 302

'নির্গ্রন্থা এব' হঞা, 'অপি'—নির্ধারণে ।
এই 'ঊনষষ্টি' প্রকার অর্থ করিলুঁ ব্যাখ্যানে ॥ ৩০২ ॥

'nirgranthā eva' hañā, 'api'——nirdhāraṇe
ei 'ūnaṣaṣṭi' prakāra artha kariluṅ vyākhyāne

SYNONYMS

nirgranthā—the word *nirgranthā; eva*—also the word *eva; hañā*—becoming; *api*—the word *api; nirdhāraṇe*—in fixation; *ei ūnaṣaṣṭi prakāra artha*—in this way fifty-nine imports; *kariluṅ vyākhyāne*—I have described.

TRANSLATION

"Then taking the word nirgranthā and considering api in the sense of sustenance, I have tried to explain fifty-nine meanings of the word.

TEXT 303

সর্বসমুচ্চয়ে আর এক অর্থ হয় ।
'আত্মারামাশ্চ মুনয়শ্চ নির্গ্রন্থাশ্চ' ভজয় ॥ ৩০৩ ॥

sarva-samuccaye āra eka artha haya
'ātmārāmāś ca munayaś ca nirgranthāś ca' bhajaya

SYNONYMS

sarva-samuccaye—taking all of them together; *āra*—another; *eka*—one; *artha*—import; *haya*—there is; *ātmārāmāḥ ca munayaḥ ca nirgranthāḥ ca bha-*

jaya—the *ātmārāmas,* great sages and *nirgranthas* (the learned and the fools) are all eligible to engage in the transcendental loving service of the Lord.

TRANSLATION

"Taking all the words together, there is another meaning. Whether one is an ātmārāma, a great sage, or nirgrantha, everyone must engage in the service of the Lord.

PURPORT

The word *sarva-samuccaye* is significant here. It includes all classes of men—*ātmārāma, muni* and *nirgrantha.* Everyone engages in the service of the Lord. Taking the word *api* in the sense of ascertainment, there are, all together, sixty different meanings.

TEXT 304

'অপি'-শব্দ—অবধারণে, সেহ চারি বার ।
চারিশব্দ-সঙ্গে এবের করিবে উচ্চার ॥ ৩০৪ ॥

'api'-śabda——avadhāraṇe, seha cāri bāra
cāri-śabda-saṅge evera karibe uccāra

SYNONYMS

api-śabda—the word *api; avadhāraṇe*—in the matter of ascertaining; *seha cāri bāra*—those four times; *cāri-śabda*—four words; *saṅge*—with; *evera*—of the word *eva; karibe*—one can do; *uccāra*—pronouncing.

TRANSLATION

"The word api is then used in the sense of ascertainment, and then four times with four words the word eva can be uttered.

TEXT 305

"উরুক্রমে এব ভক্তিমেব অহৈতুকীমেব কুর্বন্ত্যেব" ॥ ৩০৫ ॥

"urukrame eva bhaktim eva ahaitukīm eva kurvanty eva"

SYNONYMS

urukrame—unto the most powerful; *eva*—only; *bhaktim*—devotional service; *eva*—only; *ahaitukīm*—without motives; *eva*—only; *kurvanti*—they perform; *eva*—only.

TRANSLATION

"The words urukrama, bhakti, ahaitukī and kurvanti are added to the word eva again and again. Thus another meaning is explained.

TEXT 306

এই ত' কহিলুঁ শ্লোকের 'ষষ্টি' সংখ্যক অর্থ।
আর এক অর্থ শুন প্রমাণে সমর্থ॥ ৩০৬॥

ei ta' kahiluṅ ślokera 'ṣaṣṭi' saṅkhyaka artha
āra eka artha śuna pramāṇe samartha

SYNONYMS

ei ta'—thus; *kahiluṅ*—I have explained; *ślokera*—of the verse; *ṣaṣṭi*—sixty; *saṅkhyaka*—numbering; *artha*—imports; *āra*—another; *eka*—one; *artha*—import; *śuna*—please hear; *pramāṇe samartha*—quite fit for giving evidence.

TRANSLATION

"Now I have given sixty different meanings to the verse, and yet there is another meaning which is also very strongly evident.

TEXT 307

'আত্মা'-শব্দে কহে 'ক্ষেত্রজ্ঞ জীব'-লক্ষণ।
ব্রহ্মাদি কীটপর্যন্ত- তাঁর শক্তিতে গণন॥ ৩০৭॥

'ātmā'-śabde kahe 'kṣetrajña jīva'-lakṣaṇa
brahmādi kīṭa-paryanta——tāṅra śaktite gaṇana

SYNONYMS

ātmā-śabde—by the word *ātmā; kahe*—it is said; *kṣetra-jña jīva*—the living entity who knows about his body; *lakṣaṇa*—symptom; *brahmā-ādi*—beginning from Lord Brahmā; *kīṭa-paryanta*—down to the insignificant ant; *tāṅra*—His; *śaktite*—as the marginal potency; *gaṇana*—counting.

TRANSLATION

"The word ātmā also refers to the living entity who knows about his body. That is another symptom. From Lord Brahmā down to the insignificant ant, everyone is counted as the marginal potency of the Lord.

TEXT 308

বিষ্ণুশক্তিঃ পরা প্রোক্তা ক্ষেত্রজ্ঞাখ্যা তথাপরা ।
অবিদ্যা-কর্ম-সংজ্ঞান্যা তৃতীয়া শক্তিরিষ্যতে ॥ ৩০৮ ॥

viṣṇu-śaktiḥ parā proktā
kṣetrajñākhyā tathā parā
avidyā-karma-saṁjñānyā
tṛtīyā śaktir iṣyate

SYNONYMS

viṣṇu-śaktiḥ—the potency of Lord Viṣṇu; *parā*—spiritual; *proktā*—it is said; *kṣetra-jña-ākhyā*—the potency known as *ksetrajña; tathā*—as well as; *parā*—spiritual; *avidyā*—ignorance; *karma*—fruitive activities; *saṁjñā*—known as; *anyā*—other; *tṛtīyā*—third; *śaktiḥ*—potency; *iṣyate*—known thus.

TRANSLATION

" 'The potency of Lord Viṣṇu is summarized in three categories—namely the spiritual potency, the living entities and ignorance. The spiritual potency is full of knowledge; the living entities, although belonging to the spiritual potency, are subject to bewilderment; and the third energy, which is full of ignorance, is always visible in fruitive activites.'

PURPORT

This is a quotation from *Viṣṇu Purāṇa*. For an explanation, see *Ādi-līlā* (7.119).

TEXT 309

"ক্ষেত্রজ্ঞ আত্মা পুরুষঃ প্রধানং প্রকৃতিঃ স্ত্রিয়াম্ ॥" ৩০৯ ॥

"kṣetrajña ātmā puruṣaḥ
pradhānaṁ prakṛtiḥ striyām"

SYNONYMS

kṣetra-jñaḥ—the word *kṣetrajña; ātmā*—the living entity; *puruṣaḥ*—the enjoyer; *pradhānam*—the chief; *prakṛtiḥ*—the material nature; *striyām*—in the feminine gender.

TRANSLATION

" 'The word kṣetrajña refers to the living entity, the enjoyer, the chief and material nature.'

PURPORT

This is a quotation from the *Svarga-varga* (7) of the *Amara-kośa* dictionary.

TEXT 310

ভ্রমিতে ভ্রমিতে যদি সাধুসঙ্গ পায় ।
সব ত্যজি' তবে তিঁহো কৃষ্ণেরে ভজয় ॥ ৩১০ ॥

bhramite bhramite yadi sādhu-saṅga pāya
saba tyaji' tabe tiṅho kṛṣṇere bhajaya

SYNONYMS

bhramite bhramite—wandering in different forms in different manners; *yadi*—if; *sādhu-saṅga pāya*—one obtains the association of devotees; *saba tyaji'*—giving up everything; *tabe*—then; *tiṅho*—he; *kṛṣṇere bhajaya*—engages himself in the service of Lord Kṛṣṇa.

TRANSLATION

"The living entities are wandering in different species of life on different planets, but if by chance they get the association of a pure devotee [sādhu] they give up all other engagements and engage in the service of Lord Kṛṣṇa.

TEXT 311

ষাটি অর্থ কহিলুঁ, সব—কৃষ্ণের ভজনে ।
সেই অর্থ হয় এই সব উদাহরণে ॥ ৩১১ ॥

ṣāṭi artha kahiluṅ, saba——kṛṣṇera bhajane
sei artha haya ei saba udāharaṇe

SYNONYMS

ṣāṭi—sixty; *artha*—imports; *kahiluṅ*—I explained; *saba*—all; *kṛṣṇera bhajane*—aiming at rendering transcendental loving service to Kṛṣṇa; *sei artha haya*—that is the only meaning; *ei saba*—all these; *udāharaṇe*—examples.

TRANSLATION

"I have thus explained sixty different meanings, and all of them aim at the service of Lord Kṛṣṇa. After giving so many examples, that is the only meaning.

TEXT 312

'একষষ্টি' অর্থ এবে স্ফুরিল তোমা-সঙ্গে ।
তোমার ভক্তিবশে উঠে অর্থের তরঙ্গে ॥ ৩১২ ॥

'eka-ṣaṣṭi' artha ebe sphurila tomā-saṅge
tomāra bhakti-vaśe uṭhe arthera taraṅge

SYNONYMS

eka-ṣaṣṭi—sixty-one; *artha*—imports; *ebe*—now; *sphurila*—has awakened; *tomā-saṅge*—because of your association; *tomāra*—your; *bhakti-vaśe*—by dint of devotional service; *uṭhe*—there arises; *arthera*—of imports; *taraṅge*—waves.

TRANSLATION

"Now, due to your association, another meaning has awakened. It is due to your devotional service that these waves of meaning are arising.

PURPORT

The word *ātmā* refers to the living entity. From Lord Brahmā down to an insignificant ant, everyone is considered a living entity. Living entities are considered part of the Lord's marginal potency. All of them are *kṣetrajña,* knowers of the body. When they become *nirgrantha,* or free, saintly persons, they engage in Lord Kṛṣṇa's service. That is the sixty-first meaning of the verse.

TEXT 313

অহং বেদ্মি শুকো বেত্তি ব্যাসো বেত্তি ন বেত্তি বা ।
ভক্ত্যা ভাগবতং গ্রাহ্যং ন বুদ্ধ্যা ন চ টীকয়া ॥ ৩১৩ ॥

ahaṁ vedmi śuko vetti
vyāso vetti na vetti vā
bhaktyā bhāgavataṁ grāhyaṁ
na buddhyā na ca ṭīkayā

SYNONYMS

aham—I (Lord Śiva); *vedmi*—know; *śukaḥ*—Śukadeva Gosvāmī; *vetti*—knows; *vyāsaḥ*—Vyāsadeva; *vetti*—knows; *na vetti vā*—or may not know; *bhaktyā*—by devotional service (executed in nine different processes); *bhāgavatam*—the *Bhāgavata Purāṇa* (called *Paramahaṁsa-saṁhitā,* the text or treatise readable by the topmost transcendentalists); *grāhyam*—to be accepted; *na*—not; *buddhyā*—

by so-called intelligence or experimental knowledge; *na*—nor; *ca*—also; *ṭīkayā*—by imaginary commentary.

TRANSLATION

"[Lord Śiva said,] 'I may know; Śukadeva Gosvāmī, the son of Vyāsadeva, may know; and Vyāsadeva may know or may not know the Śrīmad-Bhāgavatam. On the whole, the Śrīmad-Bhāgavatam, the spotless Purāṇa, can be learned only through devotional service, not by material intelligence, speculative methods or imaginary commentaries.' "

PURPORT

Devotional service includes nine processes, beginning with hearing, chanting and remembering the activities of Lord Viṣṇu. Only one who has taken to devotional service can understand *Śrīmad-Bhāgavatam,* which is the spotless *Purāṇa* for a transcendentalist (*paramahaṁsa*). So-called commentaries are useless for this purpose. According to the Vedic injunction: *yasya deve parā bhaktir yathā deve tathā gurau.* All Vedic literatures maintain that *Śrīmad-Bhāgavatam* has to be learned from the person *bhāgavata,* and to understand it one has to engage in pure devotional service. *Śrīmad-Bhāgavatam* cannot be understood by so-called erudite scholars or grammarians. One who has developed pure Kṛṣṇa consciousness and has served the pure devotee, the spiritual master, can understand *Śrīmad-Bhāgavatam.* Others cannot.

TEXT 314

অর্থ শুনি' সনাতন বিস্মিত হঞা।
স্তুতি করে মহাপ্রভুর চরণে ধরিয়া ॥ ৩১৪ ॥

artha śuni' sanātana vismita hañā
stuti kare mahāprabhura caraṇe dhariyā

SYNONYMS

artha śuni'—by hearing the meaning (of the *ātmārāma* verse); *sanātana*—Sanātana Gosvāmī; *vismita hañā*—becoming struck with wonder; *stuti kare*—offers prayers; *mahāprabhura*—of Śrī Caitanya Mahāprabhu; *caraṇe dhariyā*—touching the lotus feet.

TRANSLATION

After hearing all the explanations of all the different meanings of the ātmārāma verse, Sanātana Gosvāmī was struck with wonder. He fell down at the lotus feet of Śrī Caitanya Mahāprabhu and began to offer prayers.

TEXT 315

"সাক্ষাৎ ঈশ্বর তুমি ব্রজেন্দ্রনন্দন।
তোমার নিশ্বাসে সর্ববেদ-প্রবর্তন॥ ৩১৫॥

"sākṣāt īśvara tumi vrajendra-nandana
tomāra niśvāse sarva-veda-pravartana

SYNONYMS

sākṣāt īśvara tumi—You are the Supreme Personality of Godhead; *vrajendra-nandana*—the son of Mahārāja Nanda; *tomāra niśvāse*—by Your breathing; *sarva-veda*—all Vedic literatures; *pravartana*—are vibrated.

TRANSLATION

Sanātana Gosvāmī said, "My dear Lord, You are the Supreme Personality of Godhead, Kṛṣṇa, the son of Mahārāja Nanda. All the Vedic literatures are vibrated through Your breathing.

TEXT 316

তুমি—বক্তা ভাগবতের, তুমি জান অর্থ।
তোমা বিনা অন্য জানিতে নাহিক সমর্থ॥" ৩১৬॥

tumi——vaktā bhāgavatera, tumi jāna artha
tomā vinā anya jānite nāhika samartha"

SYNONYMS

tumi—Your Lordship; *vaktā*—the speaker; *bhāgavatera*—of *Śrīmad-Bhāgavatam; tumi*—You; *jāna*—know; *artha*—the import; *tomā vinā*—except for You; *anya*—anyone else; *jānite*—to know; *nāhika*—is not; *samartha*—able.

TRANSLATION

"My dear Lord, You are the original speaker of the Bhāgavatam. You therefore know its real import. But for You, no one can understand the confidential meaning of Śrīmad-Bhāgavatam."

PURPORT

Following this statement by Śrīla Sanātana Gosvāmī, we have written our introduction to *Śrīmad-Bhāgavatam* (First Canto, Part One, pages 7-41).

TEXT 317

প্রভু কহে,—"কেনে কর আমার স্তবন।
ভাগবতের স্বরূপ কেনে না কর বিচারণ ? ৩১৭ ॥

prabhu kahe,——"kene kara āmāra stavana
bhāgavatera svarūpa kene nā kara vicāraṇa?

SYNONYMS

prabhu kahe—Lord Śrī Caitanya Mahāprabhu said; *kene kara*—why do you do; *āmāra stavana*—My personal glorification; *bhāgavatera sva-rūpa*—the real form of *Śrīmad-Bhāgavatam; kene*—why; *nā kara*—you do not do; *vicāraṇa*—consideration.

TRANSLATION

Śrī Caitanya Mahāprabhu replied, "Why are you glorifying Me personally? You should understand the transcendental position of Śrīmad-Bhāgavatam. Why don't you consider this important point?

TEXT 318

কৃষ্ণ-তুল্য ভাগবত—বিভু, সর্বাশ্রয়।
প্রতি-শ্লোকে প্রতি-অক্ষরে নানা অর্থ কয় ॥ ৩১৮ ॥

kṛṣṇa-tulya bhāgavata——vibhu, sarvāśraya
prati-śloke prati-akṣare nānā artha kaya

SYNONYMS

kṛṣṇa-tulya bhāgavata—*Śrīmad-Bhāgavatam* is identical with Kṛṣṇa; *vibhu*—the supreme; *sarva-āśraya*—the origin of everything, or that which controls everything; *prati-śloke*—in every verse; *prati-akṣare*—in every syllable; *nānā artha kaya*—there are varieties of imports.

TRANSLATION

"Śrīmad-Bhāgavatam is as great as Kṛṣṇa, the Supreme Lord and shelter of everything. In each and every verse of Śrīmad-Bhāgavatam and in each and every syllable, there are various meanings.

TEXT 319

প্রশ্নোত্তরে ভাগবতে করিয়াছে নির্ধার।
যাঁহার শ্রবণে লোকে লাগে চমৎকার ॥ ৩১৯ ॥

praśnottare bhāgavate kariyāche nirdhāra
yāṅhāra śravaṇe loke lāge camatkāra

SYNONYMS

praśna-uttare—in the form of questions and answers; *bhāgavate*—in *Śrīmad-Bhāgavatam; kariyāche*—has made; *nirdhāra*—conclusion; *yāṅhāra śravaṇe*—hearing which; *loke*—in all people; *lāge*—there is; *camatkāra*—wonderful astonishment.

TRANSLATION

"The form of Śrīmad-Bhāgavatam is given in questions and answers. Thus the conclusion is established. By hearing these questions and answers, one is highly astonished.

TEXT 320

ব্রূহি যোগেশ্বরে কৃষ্ণে ব্রহ্মণ্যে ধর্মবর্মণি ।
স্বাং কাষ্ঠামধুনোপেতে ধর্মঃ কং শরণং গতঃ ॥ ৩২০ ॥

brūhi yogeśvare kṛṣṇe
brahmaṇye dharma-varmaṇi
svāṁ kāṣṭhām adhunopete
dharmaḥ kaṁ śaraṇaṁ gataḥ

SYNONYMS

brūhi—kindly explain; *yoga-īśvare*—the Supreme Personality of Godhead, the master of all mystic power; *kṛṣṇe*—Lord Kṛṣṇa; *brahmaṇye*—the protector of brahminical culture; *dharma-varmaṇi*—the strong arms of religious principles; *svām*—His own; *kāṣṭhām*—to the personal abode; *adhunā*—at present; *upete*—having returned; *dharmaḥ*—the religious principles; *kam*—unto what; *śaraṇam*—shelter; *gataḥ*—have gone.

TRANSLATION

" 'Now that Śrī Kṛṣṇa, the Absolute Truth, the master of all mystic powers, has departed for His own abode, please tell us by whom religious principles are presently protected.'

PURPORT

This verse from *Śrīmad-Bhāgavatam* (1.1.23) was a question raised by all the sages, who were headed by Śaunaka. This question put before the great devotee Sūta Gosvāmī is the foremost of the six questions raised. The answer to this important question is given in the next verse from *Śrīmad-Bhāgavatam* (1.3.43).

TEXT 321

কৃষ্ণে স্বধামোপগতে ধর্মজ্ঞানাদিভিঃ সহ ।
কলৌ নষ্টদৃশামেষ পুরাণার্কোঽধুনোদিতঃ ॥ ৩২১ ॥

kṛṣṇe svadhāmopagate
dharma-jñānādibhiḥ saha
kalau naṣṭa-dṛśām eṣa
purāṇārko 'dhunoditaḥ

SYNONYMS

kṛṣṇe—Lord Kṛṣṇa; *sva-dhāma*—to His personal abode; *upagate*—having returned; *dharma-jñāna-ādibhiḥ saha*—along with religious principles, transcendental knowledge, and so on; *kalau*—in this age of Kali; *naṣṭa-dṛśām*—of persons who have lost their spiritual vision; *eṣaḥ*—this; *purāṇa-arkaḥ*—*Purāṇa* or Vedic literature that shines like the sun; *adhunā*—at the present moment; *uditaḥ*—has arisen.

TRANSLATION

" 'After Lord Kṛṣṇa departed for His abode along with religious principles and transcendental knowledge, this Purāṇa, Śrīmad-Bhāgavatam, has arisen like the sun in this age of Kali to enlighten those who have no spiritual vision.'

TEXT 322

এই মত কহিলুঁ এক শ্লোকের ব্যাখ্যান ।
বাতুলের প্রলাপ করি' কে করে প্রমাণ ? ৩২২ ॥

ei mata kahiluṅ eka ślokera vyākhyāna
vātulera pralāpa kari' ke kare pramāṇa?

SYNONYMS

ei mata—in this way; *kahiluṅ*—I have spoken; *eka*—one; *ślokera*—of a verse; *vyākhyāna*—the explanation; *vātulera pralāpa*—the talking of a madman; *kari'*—doing; *ke kare pramāṇa*—who will accept this as evidential proof.

TRANSLATION

"In this way, like a madman, I have explained the meaning of just one verse. I do not know who will take this as evidence.

TEXT 323

আমা-হেন যেবা কেহ 'বাতুল' হয় ।
এইদৃষ্টে ভাগবতের অর্থ জানয় ॥" ৩২৩ ॥

āmā-hena yebā keha 'vātula' haya
ei-dṛṣṭe bhāgavatera artha jānaya"

SYNONYMS

āmā-hena—exactly like Me; *yebā*—anyone who; *keha*—a person; *vātula haya*—becomes a madman; *ei-dṛṣṭe*—according to this process; *bhāgavatera*—of *Śrīmad-Bhāgavatam; artha*—import; *jānaya*—he can understand.

TRANSLATION

"If one becomes a madman like Me, he may also understand the meaning of Śrīmad-Bhāgavatam by this process."

PURPORT

Śrī Caitanya Mahāprabhu plainly explains that *Śrīmad-Bhāgavatam* cannot be understood by those who are materially situated. In other words, one has to become a madman like Śrī Caitanya Mahāprabhu. Apart from being the Supreme Personality of Godhead, Śrī Caitanya Mahāprabhu is an *ācārya* who exhibited love of God like a madman. According to His own written verse: *yugāyitaṁ nimeṣeṇa.* He says that for Him, "a moment seems to last twelve years." *Cakṣuṣā prāvṛṣāyitam:* "My tears are flowing like torrents of rain." *Śūnyāyitaṁ jagat sarvam:* "I feel as if the entire universe were vacant." Why? *Govinda-viraheṇa me:* "Due to My being separated from Govinda, Kṛṣṇa."

One can understand *Śrīmad-Bhāgavatam* only by following in the footsteps of Śrī Caitanya Mahāprabhu, who was mad for Kṛṣṇa. We cannot, of course, imitate Śrī Caitanya Mahāprabhu. It is not possible. However, unless one is very serious about understanding Kṛṣṇa, he cannot understand *Śrīmad-Bhāgavatam. Śrīmad-Bhāgavatam* gives the full narration of Kṛṣṇa's transcendental activities. The first nine cantos explain who Kṛṣṇa is, and the Lord's birth and activities are narrated in the Tenth Canto. In *Bhagavad-gītā* it is stated: *janma karma ca me divyam.* Kṛṣṇa's appearance and disappearance are transcendental, not mundane. A person is eligible to return home, back to Godhead, if he perfectly understands Kṛṣṇa and His appearance and disappearance. This is verified by *Bhagavad-gītā: tyaktvā dehaṁ punar janma naiti mām eti so 'rjuna.*

It is therefore concluded that one has to learn about Kṛṣṇa from *Śrīmad-Bhāgavatam* and *Bhagavad-gītā,* and one has to follow in the footsteps of Śrī

Caitanya Mahāprabhu. Those who do not follow Śrī Caitanya Mahāprabhu cannot understand *Bhagavad-gītā* and *Śrīmad-Bhāgavatam.*

TEXT 324

পুনঃ সনাতন কহে যুড়ি' দুই করে।
"প্রভু আজ্ঞা দিলা 'বৈষ্ণবস্মৃতি' করিবারে ॥ ৩২৪ ॥

punaḥ sanātana kahe yuḍi' dui kare
"prabhu ājñā dilā 'vaiṣṇava-smṛti' karibāre

SYNONYMS

punaḥ—again; *sanātana*—Sanātana Gosvāmī; *kahe*—says; *yuḍi' dui kare*—folding his two hands; *prabhu ājñā dilā*—Your Lordship has ordered me; *vaiṣṇava-smṛti karibāre*—to write a dictionary of Vaiṣṇava activities.

TRANSLATION

Folding his hands, Sanātana Gosvāmī said, "My Lord, You ordered me to write a directory about the activities of Vaiṣṇavas.

TEXT 325

মুঞি—নীচ-জাতি, কিছু না জানোঁ আচার।
মো-হৈতে কৈছে হয় স্মৃতি-পরচার ॥ ৩২৫ ॥

muñi——nīca-jāti, kichu nā jānoṅ ācāra
mo-haite kaiche haya smṛti-paracāra

SYNONYMS

muñi—I; *nīca-jāti*—belong to a lower caste; *kichu*—anything; *nā*—not; *jānoṅ*—I know; *ācāra*—about proper behavior; *mo-haite*—from me; *kaiche*—how; *haya*—there is; *smṛti-paracāra*—propagation of the directions of Vaiṣṇava behavior.

TRANSLATION

"I am a most lowborn person. I have no knowledge of good behavior. How is it possible for me to write authorized directions about Vaiṣṇava activities?"

PURPORT

Actually Sanātana Gosvāmī belonged to a very respectable *brāhmaṇa* family. Nonetheless, he submitted himself as a fallen, lowborn person because he had served in the Mohammedan government. A *brāhmaṇa* is never supposed to be engaged for anyone's service. Accepting service for a livelihood (*paricaryātmakaṁ karma*) is the business of *śūdras*. The *brāhmaṇa* is always independent and busy studying *śāstra* and preaching *śāstra* to subordinate social members such as *kṣatriyas* and *vaiśyas*. Sanātana Gosvāmī felt unfit to write Vaiṣṇava *smṛti* about the behavior of Vaiṣṇavas because he had fallen from the brahminical position. Thus Sanātana Gosvāmī clearly admits that the brahminical culture should be standardized. Presently in India, so-called *brāhmaṇas* are almost all engaged in some mundane service, and they do not understand the import of the Vedic *śāstras*. Nonetheless, they are passing themselves off as *brāhmaṇas* on the basis of birth. In this connection, Sanātana Gosvāmī declares that a *brāhmaṇa* cannot be engaged in anyone's service if he wants to take a leading part in society. In *Śrīmad-Bhāgavatam* Nārada Muni states that even if a *brāhmaṇa* is in a difficult position, he should not accept the occupation of a *śūdra*. This means that he should not be engaged in service for another, for this is the business of dogs. Under the circumstances, Sanātana Gosvāmī felt very low because he had accepted the service of the Muslim government. The conclusion is that no one should claim to be a *brāhmaṇa* simply by birthright while engaging in someone else's service.

TEXT 326

সূত্র করি' দিশা যদি করহ উপদেশ ।
আপনে করহ যদি হৃদয়ে প্রবেশ ॥ ৩২৬ ॥

sūtra kari' diśā yadi karaha upadeśa
āpane karaha yadi hṛdaye praveśa

SYNONYMS

sūtra kari'—making a synopsis; *diśā*—direction; *yadi*—if; *karaha upadeśa*—You kindly instruct; *āpane*—personally; *karaha*—You do; *yadi*—if; *hṛdaye praveśa*—entering into me or manifesting in my heart.

TRANSLATION

Sanātana Gosvāmī then requested the Lord, "Please personally tell me how I can write this difficult book about Vaiṣṇava behavior. Please manifest Yourself in my heart.

PURPORT

The writing of Vaiṣṇava literatures is not a function for ordinary men. Vaiṣṇava literatures are not mental concoctions. They are all authorized literature meant to guide those who are going to be Vaiṣṇavas. Under these circumstances, an ordinary man cannot give his own opinion. His opinion must always correspond with the conclusion of the *Vedas*. Unless one is fully qualified in Vaiṣṇava behavior and authorized by superior authority (the Supreme Personality of Godhead), one cannot write Vaiṣṇava literatures or purports and commentaries on *Śrīmad-Bhāgavatam* and *Bhagavad-gītā*.

TEXT 327

তবে তার দিশা স্ফুরে মো-নীচের হৃদয়।
ঈশ্বর তুমি,— যে করাহ, সেই সিদ্ধ হয়॥" ৩২৭ ॥

tabe tāra diśā sphure mo-nīcera hṛdaya
īśvara tumi,——ye karāha, sei siddha haya"

SYNONYMS

tabe—if you do so; *tāra*—of that; *diśā*—the process of writing; *sphure*—manifests; *mo-nīcera*—of someone lowborn like me; *hṛdaya*—in the heart; *īśvara tumi*—You are the Supreme Personality of Godhead; *ye karāha*—whatever You cause to do; *sei siddha haya*—that is perfectly done.

TRANSLATION

"If You would please manifest Yourself within my heart and personally direct me in writing this book, then, although I am lowborn, I may hope to be able to write it. You can do this because You are the Supreme Personality of Godhead Yourself, and whatever You direct is perfect."

TEXT 328

প্রভু কহে,—"যে করিতে করিবা তুমি মন।
কৃষ্ণ সেই সেই তোমা করাবে স্ফুরণ॥ ৩২৮ ॥

prabhu kahe,——"ye karite karibā tumi mana
kṛṣṇa sei sei tomā karābe sphuraṇa

SYNONYMS

prabhu kahe—Śrī Caitanya Mahāprabhu said; *ye*—whatever; *karite*—to do; *karibā tumi mana*—you want; *kṛṣṇa*—Lord Kṛṣṇa; *sei sei*—that; *tomā*—to you; *karābe sphuraṇa*—will manifest.

TRANSLATION

Śrī Caitanya Mahāprabhu replied, "Whatever you want to do you will be able to do correctly by Lord Kṛṣṇa's favor. He will manifest the real purport.

PURPORT

Sanātana Gosvāmī was a pure devotee of Kṛṣṇa. A pure devotee has no business other than serving Kṛṣṇa; consequently Kṛṣṇa is always ready to help him. This benediction was given by Śrī Caitanya Mahāprabhu to Sanātana Gosvāmī, who was authorized to write Vaiṣṇava *smṛti*. Sanātana Gosvāmī was a pure devotee of the Lord, and through the blessings of Śrī Caitanya Mahāprabhu he was able to write the book perfectly.

TEXT 329

তথাপি এই সূত্রের শুন দিগ্‌দরশন ।
সকারণ লিখি আদৌ গুরু-আশ্রয়ণ ॥ ৩২৯ ॥

tathāpi ei sūtrera śuna dig-daraśana
sakāraṇa likhi ādau guru-āśrayaṇa

SYNONYMS

tathāpi—still; *ei sūtrera*—of the synopsis of this book; *śuna*—hear; *dik-daraśana*—an indication; *sakāraṇa*—the cause; *likhi*—we should write; *ādau*—in the beginning; *guru-āśrayaṇa*—accepting a bona fide spiritual master.

TRANSLATION

"Because you asked me for a synopsis, please hear these few indications. In the beginning one must take shelter of a bona fide spiritual master.

TEXT 330

গুরুলক্ষণ, শিষ্যলক্ষণ, দোঁহার পরীক্ষণ ।
সেব্য—ভগবান্, সর্বমন্ত্র-বিচারণ ॥ ৩৩০ ॥

guru-lakṣaṇa, śiṣya-lakṣaṇa, doṅhāra parīkṣaṇa
sevya——bhagavān, sarva-mantra-vicāraṇa

SYNONYMS

guru-lakṣaṇa—the symptoms of a bona fide spiritual master; *śiṣya-lakṣaṇa*—the symptoms of a bona fide disciple; *doṅhāra*—of both; *parīkṣaṇa*—the testing; *sevya-bhagavān*—the Supreme Personality of Godhead is worshipable; *sarva-mantra-vicāraṇa*—consideration of the different types of *mantras*.

TRANSLATION

"In your book there should be the characteristics of the bona fide guru and the bona fide disciple. Then, before accepting a spiritual master, one can be

assured of the spiritual master's position. Similarly, the spiritual master can also be assured of the disciple's position. The Supreme Personality of Godhead, Kṛṣṇa, should be described as the worshipable object, and you should consider the bīja-mantra for the worship of Kṛṣṇa, Rāma or any other expansion of the Supreme Personality of Godhead.

PURPORT

In the *Padma Purāṇa,* the characteristics of the *guru,* the bona fide spiritual master, have been described:

mahā-bhāgavata-śreṣṭho
brāhmaṇo vai gurur nṛṇām
sarveṣām eva lokānām
asau pūjyo yathā hariḥ

mahā-kula-prasūto 'pi
sarva-yajñeṣu dīkṣitaḥ
sahasra-śākhādhyāyī ca
na guruḥ syād avaiṣṇavaḥ

The *guru* must be situated on the topmost platform of devotional service. There are three classes of devotees, and the *guru* must be accepted from the topmost class. The first-class devotee is the spiritual master for all kinds of people. It is said: *gurur nṛṇām.* The word *nṛṇām* means "of all human beings." The *guru* is not limited to a particular group. It is stated in the *Upadeśāmṛta* of Rūpa Gosvāmī that a *guru* is a *gosvāmī,* a controller of the senses and the mind. Such a *guru* can accept disciples from all over the world. *Pṛthivīṁ sa śiṣyāt.* This is the test of the *guru.*

In India there are many so-called *gurus,* and they are limited to a certain district or a province. They do not even travel about India, yet they declare themselves to be *jagad-guru, gurus* of the whole world. Such cheating *gurus* should not be accepted. Anyone can see how the bona fide spiritual master accepts disciples from all over the world. The *guru* is a qualified *brāhmaṇa;* therefore he knows Brahman and Parabrahman. He thus devotes his life for the service of Parabrahman. The bona fide spiritual master who accepts disciples from all over the world is also worshiped all over the world because of his qualities. *Lokānām asau pūjyo yathā hariḥ:* the people of the world worship him just as they worship the Supreme Personality of Godhead. All these honors are offered to him because he strictly follows the brahminical principles and teaches these principles to his disciples. Such a person is called an *ācārya* because he knows the principles of devotional service, he behaves in that way himself, and he teaches his disciples to follow in his footsteps. Thus he is an *ācārya* or *jagad-guru.* Even though a person is born in a brahminical family and is very expert in performing sacrifices, he cannot be accepted as a *guru* if he is not a strict Vaiṣṇava. A *guru* is a *brāhmaṇa* by qualification, and he can turn others into *brāhmaṇas* according to the śāstric principles and brahminical qualifications. Brahmanism is not a question of heredity. In *Śrīmad-Bhāgavatam* (7.32.11) Śrī Nārada Muni tells Mahārāja Yudhiṣṭhira what a *brāhmaṇa* is. He states that if brahminical qualifications are observed in *kṣatriyas, vaiśyas* or even *śūdras,* one should accept them as *brāhmaṇas.* In this regard, Śrīla Śrīdhara Svāmī has commented: *śamādibhir eva brāhmaṇādi-vyavahāro mukhyaḥ, na jāti-mātrādīty āha—yasyeti. yad yadi anyatra varṇāntare 'pi dṛśyeta, tad-varṇāntaraṁ tenaiva lakṣaṇa-nimittenaiva varṇena vinirdiśet, na tu jāti-nimittenety arthaḥ.*

There is a similar statement made by Nīlakaṇṭha, the commentator on *Mahābhārata:*

śūdro 'pi śamādy-upeto brāhmaṇa eva
brāhmaṇo 'pi kāmādy-upetaḥ śūdra eva

"Although one may be born in a *śūdra* family, if he is endowed with the brahminical qualities beginning with *śama* [control of the mind], he is to be accepted as a *brāhmaṇa.* Although one may be born in a *brāhmaṇa* family, if he is endowed with the qualities beginning with *kāma* [lust], he is to be considered a *śūdra.*" No one should present himself as a *brāhmaṇa* simply on the basis of being born in a brahminical family. One must be qualified by the brahminical qualities mentioned in the *śāstras,* particularly *Bhagavad-gītā:*

śamo damas tapaḥ śaucaṁ
kṣāntir ārjavam eva ca
jñānaṁ vijñānam āstikyaṁ
brahma-karma svabhāva-jam

"Peacefulness, self-control, austerity, purity, tolerance, honesty, wisdom, knowledge and religiousness—these are the qualities by which the *brāhmaṇas* work." (Bg. 18.42)

Unless one is qualified with all these attributes, he cannot be accepted as a *brāhmaṇa.* It is not a question of simply taking birth in a *brāhmaṇa* family. In this regard, Śrīla Bhaktisiddhānta Sarasvatī Ṭhākura remarks that Narottama dāsa Ṭhākura and Śyāmānanda Gosvāmī, although not born in *brāhmaṇa* families, are accepted as bona fide spiritual masters because they were *brāhmaṇas* by qualification. Personalities like Śrī Gaṅgā-nārāyaṇa, Rāmakṛṣṇa and many others, who were actually born in *brāhmaṇa* families, accepted Narottama dāsa Ṭhākura and Śyāmānanda Gosvāmī as their spiritual masters.

The *mahā-bhāgavata* is one who decorates his body with *tilaka* and whose name indicates him to be a servant of Kṛṣṇa by the word *dāsa.* He is also initiated by a bona fide spiritual master and is expert in worshiping the Deity, chanting *mantras* correctly, performing sacrifices, offering prayers to the Lord, and performing *saṅkīrtana*. He knows how to serve the Supreme Personality of Godhead and how to respect a Vaiṣṇava. When one has attained the topmost position of *mahā-bhāgavata,* he is to be accepted as a *guru* and worshiped exactly like Hari, the Personality of Godhead. Only such a person is eligible to occupy the post of a *guru*. However, if one is highly qualified but is not a Vaiṣṇava, he cannot be accepted as a *guru*. One cannot be a *brāhmaṇa* unless one is a Vaiṣṇava. If one is a Vaiṣṇava, he is already a *brāhmaṇa*. If a *guru* is completely qualified as a Vaiṣṇava, he must be accepted as a *brāhmaṇa* even if he is not born in a *brāhmaṇa* family. The caste system method of distinguishing a *brāhmaṇa* by birth is not acceptable when applied to a bona fide spiritual master. A spiritual master is a qualified *brāhmaṇa* and *ācārya*. If one is not a qualified *brāhmaṇa,* he is not expert in studying Vedic literatures. *Nānā-śāstra-vicāraṇaika-nipuṇau*. Every Vaiṣṇava is a spiritual master, and a spiritual master is automatically expert in brahminical behavior. He also understands the Vedic *śāstras*.

Similarly, a disciple's qualifications must be observed by the spiritual master before he is accepted as a disciple. In our Kṛṣṇa consciousness movement, the requirement is that one must be prepared to give up the four pillars of sinful life—illicit sex, meat-eating, intoxication and gambling. In Western countries especially, we first observe whether a potential disciple is prepared to follow the regulative principles. Then he is given the name of a Vaiṣṇava servant and initiated to chant the Hare Kṛṣṇa *mahā-mantra,* at least sixteen rounds daily. In this way the disciple renders devotional service under the guidance of the spiritual master or his representative for at least six months to a year. He is then recommended for a second initiation, during which a sacred thread is offered and the disciple is accepted as a bona fide *brāhmaṇa*. Śrīla Bhaktisiddhānta Sarasvatī Ṭhākura introduced the system of giving the sacred thread to a bona fide Vaiṣṇava, and we are also following in his footsteps. The qualifications of a bona fide disciple are described in *Śrīmad-Bhāgavatam* (11.10.6) as follows:

amānya-matsaro dakṣo
nirmamo dṛḍha-sauhṛdaḥ
asatvaro 'rtha-jijñāsur
anasūyur amogha-vāk

The disciple must have the following qualifications. He must give up interest in the material bodily conception. He must give up material lust, anger, greed, illusion, madness and envy. He should be interested only in understanding the science of God, and he should be ready to consider all points in this matter. He should no longer think, "I am this body," or, "This thing belongs to me." One must love the spiritual master with unflinching faith, and one must be very steady and fixed. The bona fide disciple should be inquisitive to understand transcendental subject matter. He must not search out faults among good qualities, and he should no longer be interested in material topics. His only interest should be Kṛṣṇa, the Supreme Personality of Godhead.

As far as the mutual testing of the spiritual master and disciple is concerned, Śrīla Bhaktisiddhānta Sarasvatī Ṭhākura explains that a bona fide disciple must be very inquisitive to understand the transcendental subject matter. As stated in *Śrīmad-Bhāgavatam* (11.3.21):

tasmād guruṁ prapadyeta
jijñāsuḥ śreya uttamam

"One who is inquisitive to understand the highest goal and benefit of life must approach a bona fide spiritual master and surrender unto him." A serious disciple must be alert when selecting a bona fide spiritual master. He must be sure that the spiritual master can deliver all the transcendental necessities. The spiritual master must observe how inquisitive the disciple is and how eager he is to understand the transcendental subject matter. The spiritual master should study the disciple's inquisitiveness for no less than six months or a year. A spiritual master should not be very anxious to accept a disciple because of his material opulences. Sometimes a big businessman or landlord may approach a spiritual master for initiation. Those who are materially interested are called *viṣayīs* (*karmīs*), which indicates that they are very fond of sense gratification. Such *viṣayīs* sometimes approach a famous *guru* and ask to become a disciple just as a matter of fashion. Sometimes *viṣayīs* pose as disciples of a reputed spiritual master just to cover their activities and advertise themselves as advanced in spiritual knowledge. In other words, they want to attain material success. A spiritual master must be very careful in this regard. Such business is going on all over the world. The spiritual master does not accept a materially opulent disciple just to advertise the fact that he has such a big disciple. He knows that by associating with such *viṣayī* disciples, he may fall down. One who accepts a *viṣayī* disciple is not a bona fide spiritual master. Even if he is, his position may be damaged due to association with an unscrupulous *viṣayī*. If a so-called spiritual master accepts a disciple for his personal benefit or for material gain, the relationship between the spiritual master and the disciple turns into a material affair, and the spiritual master becomes like a *smārta-guru*. There are many caste *gosvāmīs* who professionally create some disciples who do not care for them or their instructions. Such spiritual masters are satisfied simply to get some material benefits from their disciples. Such a relationship is condemned by Śrīla Bhaktisiddhānta Sarasvatī Ṭhākura, who calls such spiritual masters and disciples a society of cheaters and cheated. They are also called *bāulas* or *prākṛta-sahajiyās*. Their aim is to make the connection between the spiritual master and the disciple into a very cheap thing. They are not serious in wanting to understand spiritual life.

The words *sevya bhagavān* in this verse are important. *Bhagavān* indicates the Supreme Personality of Godhead, Lord Viṣṇu. Lord Viṣṇu alone is worshipable. There is no need to worship demigods. This is confirmed in *Bhagavad-gītā:*

kāmais tais tair hṛta-jñānāḥ
prapadyante 'nya-devatāḥ
taṁ taṁ niyamam āsthāya
prakṛtyā niyatāḥ svayā

"Those whose minds are distorted by material desires surrender unto demigods and follow the particular rules and regulations of worship according to their own natures." (Bg. 7.20)

It is also stated in the *Skanda Purāṇa:*

vāsudevaṁ parityajya
yo 'anya-devam upāsate
svamātaraṁ parityajya
śva-pacīṁ vandate hi saḥ

"A person who worships the demigods and gives up Lord Vāsudeva is like a man who gives up the protection of his mother for the shelter of a witch."

It is also stated in *Bhagavad-gītā* (9.23):

ye 'py anya-devatā-bhaktā
yajante śraddhayānvitāḥ
te 'pi mām eva kaunteya
yajanty avidhi-pūrvakam

"Whatever a man may sacrifice to other gods, O son of Kuntī, is really meant for Me alone, but it is offered without true understanding."

Demigods are also living entities and parts and parcels of Kṛṣṇa. Therefore in one sense one worships Kṛṣṇa when one worships the demigods, but not in the proper way. There is a proper method to water a tree. One should water the roots, but if one waters the leaves and branches instead, he is simply wasting his time. If one worships the demigods to the exclusion of Lord Viṣṇu, his rewards will only be material. As confirmed in *Bhagavad-gītā:*

antavat tu phalaṁ teṣāṁ
tad bhavaty alpa-medhasām
devān deva-yajo yānti
mad-bhaktā yānti mām api

"Men of small intelligence worship the demigods, and their fruits are limited and temporary. Those who worship the demigods go to the planets of the demigods, but My devotees ultimately reach My supreme planet." (Bg. 7.23)

Demigod worship is meant for unintelligent men because the benefits derived from demigod worship are all material, temporary and retractable. It is also stated in the *Hari-bhakti-vilāsa:*

yas tu nārāyaṇaṁ devaṁ
brahma-rudrādi-devataiḥ
samatvenaiva vīkṣeta
sa pāṣaṇḍī bhaved dhruvam

"Whoever thinks Lord Viṣṇu and the demigods are on the same level is to be immediately considered a rogue as far as spiritual understanding is concerned."

There are three modes of nature in the material world, but when one is situated spiritually, he is above the material modes, even though he lives in this material world. Lord Kṛṣṇa states in *Bhagavad-gītā* (14.26):

māṁ ca yo 'vyabhicāreṇa
bhakti-yogena sevate
sa guṇān samatītyaitān
brahma bhūyāya kalpate

"One who engages in full devotional service, who does not fall down in any circumstances at once transcends the modes of material nature and thus comes to the level of Brahman." When one engages in the Supreme Lord's devotional service, he is in a transcendental position. Even though one may be situated in the mode of goodness in the material world, he is susceptible to pollution by the modes of passion and ignorance. When the mode of goodness is mixed with the mode of passion, one worships the sun-god, Vivasvān. When the mode of goodness is mixed with the mode of ignorance, he worships Gaṇapati, or Gaṇeśa. When the mode of passion is mixed with the mode of ignorance, one worships Durgā, or Kālī, the external potency. When one is simply in the mode of ignorance, he becomes a devotee of Lord Śiva because Lord Śiva is the predominating deity of the mode of ignorance within this material world. However, when one is completely free from the influence of all the modes of material nature, he becomes a pure Vaiṣṇava on the devotional platform. Śrīla Rūpa Gosvāmī states in *Bhakti-rasāmṛta-sindhu:*

anyābhilāṣitā-śūnyaṁ
jñāna-karmādy-anāvṛtam

ānukūlyena kṛṣṇānu-
śīlanaṁ bhaktir uttamā

The position of *viśuddha-sattva* is the position of uncontaminated goodness. On that platform, one can then understand, *ārādhyo bhagavān vrajeśa-tanayas tad-dhāma vṛndāvanam:* "The Supreme Personality of Godhead, the son of Nanda Mahārāja, is to be worshiped along with His transcendental abode, Vṛndāvana."

The word *sarva-mantra-vicāraṇa* means "considering all different types of *mantras.*" There are different kinds of *mantras* for different kinds of devotees. There are the *mantras* known as the *dvādaśākṣara,* and these are composed of twelve syllables. Similarly, there are *mantras* composed of eighteen syllables—the Nārasiṁha *mantra,* the Rāma *mantra,* Gopāla *mantra* and so on. Each and every *mantra* has its own spiritual significance. The spiritual master has to select a *mantra* for his disciple according to the disciple's ability to chant different *mantras.*

TEXT 331

মন্ত্র-অধিকারী, মন্ত্র-সিদ্ধ্যাদি-শোধন ।
দীক্ষা, প্রাতঃস্মৃতি-কৃত্য, শৌচ, আচমন ॥ ৩৩১ ॥

mantra-adhikārī, mantra-siddhy-ādi-śodhana
dīkṣā, prātaḥ-smṛti-kṛtya, śauca, ācamana

SYNONYMS

mantra-adhikārī—qualification for receiving *mantra* initiation; *mantra-siddhi-ādi*—the perfection of the *mantra* and so on; *śodhana*—purification; *dīkṣā*—initiation; *prātaḥ-smṛti-kṛtya*—morning duties and remembrance of the Supreme Lord; *śauca*—cleanliness; *ācamana*—washing the mouth and other parts of the body.

TRANSLATION

"You should discuss the qualifications necessary for receiving a mantra, the perfection of the mantra, the purification of the mantra, initiation, morning duties, remembrance of the Supreme Lord, cleanliness, and washing the mouth and other parts of the body.

PURPORT

The following injunction is given in the *Hari-bhakti-vilāsa* (1.194):

tāntrikeṣu ca mantreṣu
dīkṣāyāṁ yoṣitām api

sādhvīnām adhikāro 'sti
śūdrādīnāṁ ca sad-dhiyām

"*Śūdras* and women who are chaste and sincerely interested in understanding the Absolute Truth are qualified to be initiated with the *pāñcarātrika-mantras.*" This is also confirmed in *Bhagavad-gītā* (9.32):

māṁ hi pārtha vyapāśritya
ye 'pi syuḥ pāpa-yonayaḥ
striyo vaiśyās tathā śūdrās
te 'pi yānti parāṁ gatiṁ

"O son of Pṛthā, those who take shelter in Me, though they be of lower birth—women, *vaiśyas* [merchants], as well as *śūdras* [workers]—can approach the supreme destination."

If one actually wants to serve Kṛṣṇa, it doesn't matter whether one is a *śūdra, vaiśya,* or even a woman. If one is sincerely eager to chant the Hare Kṛṣṇa *mantra* or *dīkṣā-mantra,* he is qualified to be initiated according to the *pāñcarātrika* process. According to Vedic principles, only a *brāhmaṇa* who is fully engaged in his occupational duties can be initiated. *Śūdras* and women are not admitted to a *vaidika* initiation. Unless one is fit according to the estimation of the spiritual master, one cannot accept a *mantra* from the *pāñcarātrika-vidhi* or the *vaidika-vidhi.* When one is fit to accept the *mantra,* he is initiated by the *pāñcarātrika-vidhi* or the *vaidika-vidhi.* In any case, the result is the same.

Regarding *mantra-siddhi-ādi-śodhana,* the efficiency of the *mantra,* Śrīla Bhaktisiddhānta Sarasvatī Ṭhākura gives sixteen divisions, which are confirmed in the *Hari-bhakti-vilāsa* (beginning with 1.204):

siddha-sādhya-susiddhāri-
kramāj jñeyo vicakṣaṇaiḥ

These are (1) *siddha,* (2) *sādhya,* (3) *susiddha* and (4) *ari.* These four principles can be divided further: (1) *siddha-siddha,* (2) *siddha-sādhya,* (3) *siddha-susiddha,* (4) *siddha-ari,* (5) *sādhya-siddha,* (6) *sādhya-sādhya,* (7) *sādhya-susiddha,* (8) *sādhya-ari,* (9) *susiddha-siddha,* (10) *susiddha-sādhya,* (11) *susiddha-susiddha,* (12) *susiddha-ari,* (13) *ari-siddha,* (14) *ari-sādhya,* (15) *ari-susiddha,* and (16) *ari-ari.*

Those who are initiated with the eighteen-alphabet *mantra* do not need to consider the above-mentioned sixteen divisions. As enjoined in the *Hari-bhakti-vilāsa* (1.215, 219, 220):

na cātra śātravā doṣā
narṇasvādi-vicāraṇā

ṛkṣarāśi-vicāro vā
na kartavyo manau priye

nātra cintyo 'ri-śuddhyādir
nāri-mitrādi-lakṣaṇam

siddha-sādhya-susiddhāri-
rūpā nātra vicāraṇā

There is *śodhana,* or purification of the *mantra,* but there is no such consideration for the Kṛṣṇa *mantra. Balitvāt kṛṣṇa-mantrāṇāṁ saṁskārāpekṣaṇaṁ na hi.* "The Kṛṣṇa *mantra* is so strong that there is no question of *śodhana.* (1.235)

As far as *dīkṣā* is concerned, one should consult *Madhya-līlā,* Chapter Fifteen (108). On the whole, when a person is initiated according to the *pāñcarātrika-vidhi,* he has already attained the position of a *brāhmaṇa.* This is enjoined in the *Hari-bhakti-vilāsa* (2.12):

yathā kāñcanatāṁ yāti
kāṁsyaṁ rasa-vidhānataḥ
tathā dīkṣā-vidhānena
dvijatvaṁ jāyate nṛṇām

"As bell metal can be turned into gold when treated with mercury, a disciple initiated by a bona fide *guru* immediately attains the position of a *brāhmaṇa."*

As far as the time of *dīkṣā* (initiation) is concerned, everything depends on the position of the *guru.* As soon as a bona fide *guru* is received by chance or by a program, one should immediately take the opportunity to receive initiation. In the book called *Tattva-sāgara,* it is stated:

durlabhe sad-gurūṇāṁ ca
sakṛt-saṅga upasthite
tad-anujñā yadā labdhā
sa dīkṣāvasaro mahān

grāme vā yadi vāraṇye
kṣetre vā divase niśi
āgacchati gurur daivād
yathā dīkṣā tad-ājñayā

yadaivecchā tadā dīkṣā
guror ājñānurūpataḥ

na tīrthaṁ na vrataṁ hemo
na snānaṁ na japa-kriyā

dīkṣāyāḥ karaṇaṁ kintu
svecchā-prāpte tu sad-gurau

"If, by chance, one gets a *sad-guru,* it doesn't matter whether one is in the temple or the forest. If the *sad-guru,* the bona fide spiritual master, agrees, one can be initiated immediately, without waiting for a suitable time or place."

In the early morning hours (known as *brāhma-muhūrta*) one should get up and immediately chant the Hare Kṛṣṇa *mantra,* or, at least, "Kṛṣṇa, Kṛṣṇa, Kṛṣṇa." In this way, one should remember Kṛṣṇa. Some *ślokas* or prayers should also be chanted. By chanting, one immediately becomes auspicious and transcendental to the infection of material qualities. Actually one has to chant and remember Lord Kṛṣṇa twenty-four hours daily, or as much as possible.

smartavyaḥ satataṁ viṣṇur
vismartavyo na jātucit
sarve vidhi-niṣedhāḥ syur
etayor eva kiṅkarāḥ

"Kṛṣṇa is the origin of Lord Viṣṇu. He should always be remembered and never forgotten at any time. All the rules and prohibitions mentioned in the *śāstras* should be the servants of these two principles." This is a quotation from *Padma Purāṇa* in the portion called *Bṛhat-sahasra-nāma-stotra.*

Prātaḥ-kṛtya means that one should evacuate regularly and then cleanse himself by taking a bath. One has to gargle (*ācamana*) and brush his teeth (*danta-dhāvana*). He should do this either with twigs or a toothbrush—whatever is available. This will purify the mouth. Then one should take his bath. Actually householders and *vānaprasthas* should bathe two times a day (*prātar-madhyāhnayoḥ snānaṁ vānaprastha-gṛhasthayoḥ*). A *sannyāsī* should bathe three times daily, and a *brahmacārī* may take only one bath a day. Whenever one is not able to bathe in water, he can bathe by chanting the Hare Kṛṣṇa *mantra.* One also has to perform his *sandhyādi-vandana*—that is, one has to chant his Gāyatrī *mantra* three times daily—morning, noon and evening.

TEXT 332

দন্তধাবন, স্নান, সন্ধ্যাদি বন্দন।
গুরুসেবা, ঊর্ধ্ব পুণ্ড্র চক্রাদি-ধারণ ॥ ৩৩২ ॥

danta-dhāvana, snāna, sandhyādi vandana
guru-sevā, ūrdhva-puṇḍra-cakrādi-dhāraṇa

SYNONYMS

danta-dhāvana—washing the teeth; *snāna*—bath; *sandhyā-ādi vandana*—regular chanting of the *mantras; guru-sevā*—serving the spiritual master; *ūrdhva-puṇḍra*—wearing perpendicularly straight *tilaka; cakra-ādi-dhāraṇa*—stamping the body with different names and symbols of the Lord.

TRANSLATION

"In the morning, one should regularly brush his teeth, take his bath, offer prayers to the Lord and offer obeisances to the spiritual master. One should render service to the spiritual master and paint one's body in twelve places with ūrdhva-puṇḍra [tilaka]. One should stamp the holy names of the Lord on his body, or one should stamp the symbols of the Lord, such as the disc and club.

TEXT 333

গোপীচন্দন-মাল্য-ধৃতি, তুলসী-আহরণ ।
বস্ত্র-পীঠ-গৃহ-সংস্কার, কৃষ্ণ-প্রবোধন ॥ ৩৩৩ ॥

gopīcandana-mālya-dhṛti, tulasī-āharaṇa
vastra-pīṭha-gṛha-saṁskāra, kṛṣṇa-prabodhana

SYNONYMS

gopī-candana—*gopī-candana* (available in Vṛndāvana and Dvārakā); *mālya*—beads on the neck; *dhṛti*—wearing regularly; *tulasī-āharaṇa*—collecting *tulasī* leaves; *vastra*—cloth; *pīṭha*—temple; *gṛha*—the house; *saṁskāra*—cleansing; *kṛṣṇa-prabodhana*—awakening the Deity of Lord Kṛṣṇa.

TRANSLATION

"After this, you should describe how one should decorate his body with gopīcandana, wear neck beads, collect tulasī leaves from the tulasī tree, cleanse his cloth and the altar, cleanse one's own house or apartment and go to the temple and ring the bell just to draw the attention of Lord Kṛṣṇa.

TEXT 334

পঞ্চ, ষোড়শ, পঞ্চাশৎ উপচারে অর্চন ।
পঞ্চকাল পূজা আরতি, কৃষ্ণের ভোজন-শয়ন ॥৩৩৪॥

pañca, ṣoḍaśa, pañcāśat upacāre arcana
pañca-kāla pūjā ārati, kṛṣṇera bhojana-śayana

SYNONYMS

pañca—five; *ṣoḍaśa*—sixteen; *pañcāśat*—fifty; *upacāre*—with ingredients; *arcana*—offering worship; *pañca-kāla*—five times; *pūjā*—worshiping; *ārati*—offering *ārati; kṛṣṇera bhojana-śayana*—in this way offering eatables to Kṛṣṇa and laying Him down to rest.

TRANSLATION

"Also describe Deity worship, wherein one should offer food to Kṛṣṇa at least five times daily. One should in due time place Kṛṣṇa on a bed. You should also describe the process for offering ārati and the worship of the Lord according to the list of five, sixteen or fifty ingredients.

PURPORT

The five ingredients are (1) very good scents, (2) very good flowers, (3) incense, (4) a lamp and (5) something edible. As for *ṣoḍaśopacāra,* the sixteen ingredients, one should (1) provide a sitting place (*āsana*), (2) ask Kṛṣṇa to sit down, (3) offer *arghya,* (4) offer water to wash the legs, (5) wash the mouth, (6) offer *madhu-parka,* (7) offer water for washing the mouth, (8) bathe, (9) offer garments, (10) decorate the Lord's body with ornaments, (11) offer sweet scents, (12) offer flowers with good fragrance, like the rose or *campaka,* (13) offer incense, (14) offer a lamp, (15) give good food, and (16) offer prayers.

In the *Hari-bhakti-vilāsa* (Eleventh *Vilāsa,* verses 127-140) there is a vivid description of what is required in Deity worship. There are sixty-four items mentioned. In the temple, worship should be so gorgeous that all sixty-four items should be available for the satisfaction of the Personality of Godhead. Sometimes it is impossible to get all sixty-four items; therefore we recommend that at least on the first day of installation all sixty-four items should be available. When the Lord is established, worship with all sixty-four items should continue as far as possible. The sixty-four items are as follows: (1) There must be a big bell hanging in front of the temple room so that whoever comes in the room can ring the bell. This item is called *prabodhana,* or offering oneself submissively to the Lord. This is the first item. (2) The visitor must chant *jaya* Śrī Rādhā-Govinda, or *jaya* Śrī Rādhā-Mādhava when he rings the bell. In either case, the word *jaya* must be uttered. (3) One should immediately offer obeisances to the Lord, falling down like a stick. (4) There must be regular *maṅgala-ārati* in the temple during the early morning, an hour and a half before the sun rises. (5) There must be an *āsana,* a sitting place before the altar. This *āsana* is for the spiritual master. The disciple brings everything before the spiritual master, and the spiritual master offers everything to the Supreme Personality of Godhead. (6) After *maṅgala-ārati,* the Deity is supposed to wash His teeth by using a twig; therefore a twig must be offered. (7) Water must be offered for washing the Deity's feet. (8) *Arghya* should be offered. (9) Water for *ācamana* should be offered. (10) *Madhu-parka,* a small bowl containing *madhu* (honey, a little ghee, a little water, a little sugar, yogurt and milk) should be offered. This is called *madhu-parka-ācamana.* (11) One should place wooden slippers before the Lord. (12) One should massage the body of the Lord. (13) One should massage the body of the Lord with oil. (14) With a soft, wet sponge one should remove all the oil smeared over the Lord's body. (15) One should bathe the Lord with water in which nicely scented flowers have been soaking for some time. (16) After bathing the body of the Lord with water, one should bathe Him with milk. (17) Then with yogurt. (18) Then with ghee. (19) Then with honey. (20) Then with sugar. (21) Then one should wash the Deity with water and chant this *mantra:*

cintāmaṇi-prakara-sadmasu kalpa-vṛkṣa-
lakṣāvṛteṣu surabhīr abhipālayantam
lakṣmī-sahasra-śata-sambhrama-sevyamānaṁ
govindam ādi-puruṣaṁ tam ahaṁ bhajāmi

(22) One should dry the entire body with a towel. (23) A new dress should be put on the body. (24) A sacred thread should be given to the body. (25) Water should be offered for cleansing the mouth (*ācamana*). (26) Nicely scented oils like liquid sandalwood pulp should be smeared over the body. (27) All kinds of ornaments and crowns should be placed on the body. (28) Then one should offer flower garlands and decorative flowers. (29) One should burn incense. (30) Lamps should be offered. (31) Precautions should always be taken so that demons and atheists cannot harm the body of the Lord. (32) Food offerings should be placed before the Lord. (33) Spices for chewing should be offered. (34) Betel nuts should be offered. (35) At the proper time, there should be arrangements so that the Lord may take rest in bed. (36) The Lord's hair should be combed and decorated. (37) First-class garments should be offered. (38) A first-class helmet should be offered. (39) The garments should be scented. (40) There should be Kaustubha jewels and other ornaments offered. (41) A variety of flowers should be offered. (42) Another *maṅgala-ārati* should be offered. (43) A mirror should be offered. (44) The Lord should be carried on a nice palanquin to the altar. (45) The Lord should be seated on the throne. (46) Again water should be given for the washing of His feet. (47) Something again should be offered for eating. (48) Evening *ārati.* (49) The Lord should be fanned with a *cāmara* fan, and an umbrella should be placed over His head. (50) The Hare Kṛṣṇa *mantra* and approved songs should be sung. (51) Musical instruments should be played. (52) One should dance before the Deity. (53) One should circumambulate the Deity. (54) One should again offer obeisances. (55) One should offer different

types of prayers and hymns at the Lord's lotus feet. (56) One should touch the lotus feet of the Lord with one's head. This may not be possible for everyone, but at least the *pūjārī* should do this. (57) The flowers offered on the previous day should touch one's head. (58) One should take the remnants of the Lord's food. (59) One should sit before the Lord and think that he is massaging the Lord's legs. (60) One should decorate the Lord's bed with flowers before the Lord takes His rest. (61) One should offer one's hand to the Lord. (62) One should take the Deity to His bed. (63) One should wash the feet of the Lord and then sit Him on the bed. (64) One should place the Lord on the bed and then massage His feet.

Ārati should be offered to the Deities five times daily—early in the morning before sunrise, later in the morning, at noon, in the evening and at night. This means that there should be worship and a change of dress and flowers. As far as the eatables are concerned, all items should be first-class preparations. There should be first-class rice, dahl, fruit, sweet rice, vegetables and a variety of foods to be sucked, drunk and chewed. All the eatables offered to the Deities should be extraordinarily excellent. In Europe and America there is presently no monetary scarcity. People are not poor, and if they follow these principles of Deity worship, they will advance in spiritual life. As far as placing the Deity in the bed is concerned, if the Deity is large and heavy, it is not possible to move Him daily. It is better that a small Deity, which is also worshiped, be taken to the bed. This *mantra* should be chanted: *āgaccha śayana-sthānaṁ priyābhiḥ saha keśava.* "O Keśava, kindly come to Your bed along with Śrīmatī Rādhārāṇī." (*Hari-bhakti-vilāsa* 11.40)

The Deity should be placed in bed with Śrīmatī Rādhārāṇī, and this should be indicated by bringing the wooden slippers from the altar to the bedside. When the Deity is laid down, His legs should be massaged. Before laying the Deity down, a pot of milk and sugar should be offered to Him. After taking this thick milk, the Deity should lie down and should be offered betel nuts and spices to chew.

TEXT 335

শ্রীমূর্তিলক্ষণ, আর শালগ্রামলক্ষণ ।
কৃষ্ণক্ষেত্র-যাত্রা, কৃষ্ণমূর্তি-দরশন ॥ ৩৩৫ ॥

śrī-mūrti -lakṣaṇa, āra śālagrāma-lakṣaṇa
kṛṣṇa-kṣetra-yātrā, kṛṣṇa-mūrti-daraśana

SYNONYMS

śrī-mūrti-lakṣaṇa—characteristics of the Deity; *āra*—and; *śālagrāma-lakṣaṇa*—characteristics of the *śālagrāma-śilā; kṛṣṇa-kṣetra-yātrā*—visiting places like

Vṛndāvana, Dvārakā and Mathurā; *kṛṣṇa-mūrti-daraśana*—visiting the Deity in the temple.

TRANSLATION

"The characteristics of the Deities should be discussed as well as the characteristics of the śālagrāma-śilā. One should also discuss visiting the Deities in the temple and touring holy places like Vṛndāvana, Mathurā and Dvārakā.

TEXT 336

নামমহিমা, নামাপরাধ দূরে বর্জন ।
বৈষ্ণবলক্ষণ, সেবাপরাধ-খণ্ডন ॥ ৩৩৬ ॥

nāma-mahimā, nāmāparādha dūre varjana
vaiṣṇava-lakṣaṇa, sevāparādha-khaṇḍana

SYNONYMS

nāma-mahimā—the glories of the holy name; *nāma-aparādha*—offenses in chanting the holy name; *dūre varjana*—giving up very carefully; *vaiṣṇava-lakṣaṇa*—the symptoms of a Vaiṣṇava; *sevā-aparādha-khaṇḍana*—rejecting offenses in worshiping the Deity.

TRANSLATION

"You should glorify the holy name and carefully give up offenses when chanting the holy name. One should know the symptoms of a Vaiṣṇava. One must give up or nullify all kinds of sevā-aparādha, offenses in Deity worship.

PURPORT

The devotee should always be very careful not to commit the ten offenses when chanting the Hare Kṛṣṇa *mantra.* If a devotee very strictly follows the methods of Deity worship, he will naturally and quickly become a pure Vaiṣṇava. A pure Vaiṣṇava has unflinching faith in the Lord, and he does not deviate at all. He is always engaged in perfect Deity worship.

One should also notice the specific offenses against Deity worship. These are mentioned in the *Skanda Purāṇa* (*Avantī-khaṇḍa*), spoken by Vyāsadeva himself. One should liquidate all kinds of offenses.

The *śālagrāma-śilā* should be worshiped with *tulasī* where a sufficient quantity of *tulasī* leaves are available. Worship of *śālagrāma-śilā* should be introduced in all ISKCON temples. *Śālagrāma-śilā* is the form of the Lord's mercy. To worship the Deity with the sixty-four items mentioned may be a difficult job, but the Lord has become so small that anyone in any temple can carefully handle Deity worship simply by performing the same activities with *śālagrāma-śilā.*

There are thirty-two offenses that should be avoided. (1) One should not enter the temple in a vehicle. Shoes and slippers should be removed before entering the temple. (2) One should offer obeisances as soon as he sees the Deity. (3) One should enter the temple after taking a bath. In other words, one should be very clean. (4) One should not offer obeisances to the Lord with one hand. (5) One should not circumambulate demigods before the Deities. (6) One should not spread out his legs before the Deity. (7) One should not sit down before the Deity with his legs crossed, nor should one touch his legs with his hands. (8) One should not lie down before the Deity. (9) One should not eat before the Deity. (10) One should not speak lies before the Deity. (11) One should not speak very loudly before the Deity. (12) One should not talk nonsense before the Deity. (13) One should not cry before the Deity. (14) One should not deal with others before the Deity. (15) One should not utter harsh words before the Deity. (16) One should not cover himself with a blanket. (17) One should not talk enviously of others before the Deity. (18) One should not praise others before the Deity. (19) One should not use slang before the Deity. (20) One should not pass air before the Deity. (21) One should not neglect the sixty-four items of Deity worship. (22) One should not eat anything not offered to the Deity. (23) One should not neglect offering seasonal fruits as soon as they are available. (24) One should always offer fresh, untouched fruit to the Deity. (25) One should not sit with his back toward the Deity. (26) One should not offer obeisances to others before the Deity. (27) One should not sit near the Deity without taking the spiritual master's permission. (28) One should not be proud to hear himself praised before the Deity. (29) One should not blaspheme the demigods. (30) One should not be unkind to others before the Deities. (31) One should observe all festivals in the temple. (32) One should not fight or quarrel before the Deity.

TEXT 337

শঙ্খ-জল-গন্ধ-পুষ্প-ধূপাদি-লক্ষণ ।
জপ, স্তুতি, পরিক্রমা, দণ্ডবৎ বন্দন ॥ ৩৩৭ ॥

śaṅkha-jala-gandha-puṣpa-dhūpādi-lakṣaṇa
japa, stuti, parikramā, daṇḍavat vandana

SYNONYMS

śaṅkha—of a conchshell; *jala*—of water; *gandha*—of incense or scents; *puṣpa*—of flowers; *dhūpa-ādi*—of incense, and so on; *lakṣaṇa*—the characteristics; *japa*—murmuring; *stuti*—offering prayers; *parikramā*—circumambulation; *daṇḍavat*—offering obeisances; *vandana*—offering prayers.

TRANSLATION

"The items of worship, such as water, conchshell, flowers, incense and lamp, should be described. You should also mention chanting softly, offering prayers, circumambulating, and offering obeisances. All these should be carefully studied.

PURPORT

All these are mentioned in the *Hari-bhakti-vilāsa.* The *Aṣṭama Vilāsa* of that book should be consulted as far as possible.

TEXT 338

পুরশ্চরণ-বিধি, কৃষ্ণপ্রসাদ-ভোজন ।
অনিবেদিত-ত্যাগ, বৈষ্ণবনিন্দাদি-বর্জন ॥ ৩৩৮ ॥

puraścaraṇa-vidhi, kṛṣṇa-prasāda-bhojana
anivedita-tyāga, vaiṣṇava-nindādi-varjana

SYNONYMS

puraścaraṇa-vidhi—ritualistic ceremonies; *kṛṣṇa-prasāda-bhojana*—eating the remnants of food offered to the Lord; *anivedita-tyāga*—not touching anything not offered to the Lord; *vaiṣṇava-nindā-ādi-varjana*—completely avoiding blaspheming a Vaiṣṇava.

TRANSLATION

"Other items to be considered are the method of performing puraścaraṇa, taking kṛṣṇa-prasāda, giving up unoffered food and not blaspheming the Lord's devotees.

PURPORT

Regarding the *vaiṣṇava-nindā,* see *Madhya-līlā,* 15.260.

TEXT 339

সাধুলক্ষণ, সাধুসঙ্গ, সাধুসেবন ।
অসৎসঙ্গ-ত্যাগ, শ্রীভাগবত-শ্রবণ ॥ ৩৩৯ ॥

sādhu-lakṣaṇa, sādhu-saṅga, sādhu-sevana
asatsaṅga-tyāga, śrī-bhāgavata-śravaṇa

SYNONYMS

sādhu-lakṣaṇa—the symptoms of a devotee; *sādhu-saṅga*—association with devotees; *sādhu-sevana*—offering service to devotees; *asat-saṅga-tyāga*—giving up the company of nondevotees; *śrī-bhāgavata-śravaṇa*—regularly hearing the recitation of *Śrīmad-Bhāgavatam.*

TRANSLATION

"One should know the symptoms of a devotee and how to associate with devotees. One should know how to satisfy the devotee by rendering service, and one should know how to give up the association of nondevotees. One should also regularly hear the recitation of Śrīmad-Bhāgavatam.

TEXT 340

দিনকৃত্য, পক্ষকৃত্য, একাদশ্যাদি-বিবরণ।
মাসকৃত্য, জন্মাষ্টম্যাদি-বিধি-বিচারণ ॥ ৩৪০ ॥

dina-kṛtya, pakṣa-kṛtya, ekādaśy-ādi-vivaraṇa
māsa-kṛtya, janmāṣṭamyādi-vidhi-vicāraṇa

SYNONYMS

dina-kṛtya—daily duties; *pakṣa-kṛtya*—duties on the fortnights; *ekādaśī-ādi-vivaraṇa*—description of Ekādaśī and so on; *māsa-kṛtya*—duties every month; *janmāṣṭamī-ādi*—of performing Janmāṣṭamī and other ceremonies; *vidhi*—of the process; *vicāraṇa*—consideration.

TRANSLATION

"You should describe the ritualistic duties of every day, and you should describe the fortnightly duties—especially observing Ekādaśī fast, which comes every fortnight. You should also describe the duties of every month, especially the observance of ceremonies like Janmāṣṭamī, Rāma-navamī and Nṛsiṁha-caturdaśī.

TEXT 341

একাদশী, জন্মাষ্টমী, বামনদ্বাদশী।
শ্রীরামনবমী, আর নৃসিংহচতুর্দশী ॥ ৩৪১ ॥

ekādaśī, janmāṣṭamī, vāmana-dvādaśī
śrī-rāma-navamī, āra nṛsiṁha-caturdaśī

SYNONYMS

ekādaśī—the eleventh day of the fortnight; *janmāṣṭamī*—the birthday ceremony of Lord Kṛṣṇa; *vāmana-dvādaśī*—the birthday or appearance day of Lord Vāmana; *śrī-rāma-navamī*—the birthday ceremony of Lord Rāmacandra; *āra*—and; *nṛsiṁha-caturdaśī*—the appearance day of Lord Nṛsiṁha.

TRANSLATION

"Ekādaśī, Janmāṣṭamī, Vāmana-dvādaśī, Rāma-navamī and Nṛsiṁha-caturdaśī should all be observed.

TEXT 342

এই সবে বিদ্ধা-ত্যাগ, অবিদ্ধা-করণ ।
অকরণে দোষ, কৈলে ভক্তির লম্ভন ॥ ৩৪২ ॥

ei sabe viddhā-tyāga, aviddhā-karaṇa
akaraṇe doṣa, kaile bhaktira lambhana

SYNONYMS

ei sabe—all these things; *viddhā-tyāga*—to avoid *viddha-ekādaśī* or mixed Ekādaśī; *aviddhā-karaṇa*—performing the pure Ekādaśī; *akaraṇe doṣa*—the fault of not performing them; *kaile*—if done so; *bhaktira lambhana*—there will be discrepancies in devotional service.

TRANSLATION

"You should recommend the avoidance of mixed Ekādaśī and the performance of pure Ekādaśī. You should also describe the fault in not observing this. One should be very careful as far as these items are concerned. If one is not careful, one will be negligent in executing devotional service.

TEXT 343

সর্বত্র প্রমাণ দিবে পুরাণ-বচন ।
শ্রীমূর্তি-বিষ্ণুমন্দিরকরণ-লক্ষণ ॥ ৩৪৩ ॥

sarvatra pramāṇa dibe purāṇa-vacana
śrī-mūrti-viṣṇu-mandira karaṇa-lakṣaṇa

SYNONYMS

sarvatra—everywhere; *pramāṇa*—evidence; *dibe*—you should give; *purāṇa-vacana*—quoting from the *Purāṇas; śrī-mūrti*—the Deity; *viṣṇu-mandira*—of the Viṣṇu temple; *karaṇa-lakṣaṇa*—the characteristics of constructing.

TRANSLATION

"Whatever you say about Vaiṣṇava behavior, the establishment of Vaiṣṇava temples and Deities and everything else should be supported by evidence from the Purāṇas.

TEXT 344

'সামান্য' সদাচার, আর 'বৈষ্ণব'-আচার ।
কর্তব্যাকর্তব্য সব 'স্মার্ত' ব্যবহার ॥ ৩৪৪ ॥

'sāmānya' sad-ācāra, āra 'vaiṣṇava'-ācāra
kartavyākartavya saba 'smārta' vyavahāra

SYNONYMS

sāmānya—general; *sat-ācāra*—good behavior; *āra*—and; *vaiṣṇava*—of devotees of Lord Viṣṇu; *ācāra*—etiquette; *kartavya-akartavya*—things which are to be done and which are not to be done; *saba*—all; *smārta*—connected with regulative principles; *vyavahāra*—business.

TRANSLATION

"You should give general and specific descriptions of the behavior and activities of a Vaiṣṇava. You should outline things that are to be done and things that are not to be done. All this should be described as regulations and etiquette.

TEXT 345

এই সংক্ষেপে সূত্র কহিলুঁ দিগ্‌দরশন ।
যবে তুমি লিখিবা, কৃষ্ণ করাবে স্ফুরণ ॥ ৩৪৫ ॥

ei saṅkṣepe sūtra kahiluṅ dig-daraśana
yabe tumi likhibā, kṛṣṇa karābe sphuraṇa

SYNONYMS

ei—thus; *saṅkṣepe*—in brief; *sūtra*—codes; *kahiluṅ*—I have described; *dik-daraśana*—just a little direction; *yabe*—whenever; *tumi*—you; *likhibā*—will attempt to write; *kṛṣṇa*—Lord Kṛṣṇa; *karābe*—will do; *sphuraṇa*—manifesting.

TRANSLATION

"I have thus given a synopsis of the Vaiṣṇava regulative principles. I have given this in brief just to give you a little direction. When you write on this subject, Kṛṣṇa will help you by spiritually awakening you."

PURPORT

One cannot write on spiritual matters without being blessed by Kṛṣṇa and the disciplic succession of *gurus*. The blessings of the authorities are one's power of attorney. One should not try to write anything about Vaiṣṇava behavior and activities without being authorized by superior authorities. This is confirmed in *Bhagavad-gītā: evaṁ paramaparā-prāptam imaṁ rājarṣayo viduḥ.*

TEXT 346

এই ত' কহিলুঁ প্রভুর সনাতনে প্রসাদ ।
যাহার শ্রবণে চিত্তের খণ্ডে অবসাদ ॥ ৩৪৬ ॥

ei ta' kahilu prabhura sanātane prasāda
yāhāra śravaṇe cittera khaṇḍe avasāda

SYNONYMS

ei ta'—in this way; *kahilu*—I have described; *prabhura*—of Lord Śrī Caitanya Mahāprabhu; *sanātane*—unto Sanātana Gosvāmī; *prasāda*—mercy; *yāhāra śravaṇe*—hearing which; *cittera*—of the mind; *khaṇḍe*—disappears; *avasāda*—all moroseness.

TRANSLATION

Thus I have narrated Lord Caitanya's mercy upon Sanātana Gosvāmī. When one hears these topics, one's heart will be cleansed of all contamination.

TEXT 347

নিজ-গ্রন্থে কর্ণপূর বিস্তার করিয়া ।
সনাতনে প্রভুর প্রসাদ রাখিয়াছে লিখিয়া ॥ ৩৪৭ ॥

nija-granthe karṇapūra vistāra kariyā
sanātane prabhura prasāda rākhiyāche likhiyā

SYNONYMS

nija-granthe—in his own book; *karṇapūra*—Kavi-karṇapūra; *vistāra kariyā*—vividly describing; *sanātane*—unto Sanātana Gosvāmī; *prabhura*—of Lord Śrī Caitanya Mahāprabhu; *prasāda*—the mercy; *rākhiyāche*—has kept; *likhiyā*—writing.

TRANSLATION

The authorized poet Kavi-karṇapūra has written a book named Caitanya-candrodaya-nāṭaka. This book tells how Śrī Caitanya Mahāprabhu blessed Sanātana Gosvāmī with His specific mercy.

TEXT 348

গৌড়েন্দ্রস্য সভা-বিভূষণমণিস্ত্যক্ত্বা য ঋদ্ধাং শ্রিয়ং
রূপস্যাগ্রজ এষ এব তরুণীং বৈরাগ্যলক্ষ্মীং দধে।
অন্তর্ভক্তিরসেন পূর্ণহৃদয়ো বাহ্যেঽবধূতাকৃতিঃ
শৈবালৈঃ পিহিতং মহা-সর ইব প্রীতিপ্রদস্তদ্বিদাম্ ॥ ৩৪৮॥

gauḍendrasya sabhā-vibhūṣaṇa-maṇis tyaktvā ya ṛddhāṁ śriyaṁ
rūpasyāgraja eṣa eva taruṇīṁ vairāgya-lakṣmīṁ dadhe
antar-bhakti-rasena pūrṇa-hṛdayo bāhye 'vadhūtākṛtiḥ
śaivālaiḥ pihitaṁ mahā-sara iva prīti-pradas tad-vidām

SYNONYMS

gauḍa-indrasya—of the ruler of Gauḍa-deśa (Bengal); *sabhā*—of the parliament; *vibhūṣaṇa*—fundamental; *maṇiḥ*—the gem; *tyaktvā*—relinquishing; *yaḥ*—one who; *ṛddhām*—opulent; *śriyam*—kingly enjoyment; *rūpasya agrajaḥ*—the elder brother of Śrīla Rūpa Gosvāmī; *eṣaḥ*—this; *eva*—certainly; *taruṇīm*—youthful; *vairāgya-lakṣmīm*—the fortune of renunciation; *dadhe*—accepted; *antaḥ-bhakti-rasena*—by the mellows of inner love of Kṛṣṇa; *pūrṇa-hṛdayaḥ*—satisfied fully; *bāhye*—externally; *avadhūta-ākṛtiḥ*—the dress of a mendicant; *śaivālaiḥ*—by moss; *pihitam*—covered; *mahā-saraḥ*—a great lake or very deep lake; *iva*—like; *prīti-pradaḥ*—very pleasing; *tat-vidām*—to persons acquainted with the science of devotional service.

TRANSLATION

"Śrīla Sanātana Gosvāmī, the elder brother of Śrīla Rūpa Gosvāmī, was a most important minister in the government of Hussain Shah, the ruler of Bengal, and he was considered a most brilliant gem in that assembly. He possessed all the opulences of a royal position, but he gave up everything just to accept the youthful goddess of renunciation. Although he externally appeared to be a mendicant who had renounced everything, he was filled with the pleasure of devotional service within his heart. Thus he can be compared to a deep lake covered with moss. He was the object of pleasure for all the devotees who knew the science of devotional service.

PURPORT

This and the following two verses are from *Caitanya-candrodaya-nāṭaka* (9.34, 35, 38).

TEXT 349

তং সনাতনমুপাগতমক্ষ্ণো-
দৃষ্টমাত্রমতিমাত্রদয়ার্দ্রঃ ।
আলিলিঙ্গ পরিঘায়ত-দোর্ভ্যাং
সানুকম্পমথ চম্পক-গৌরঃ ॥ ৩৪৯ ॥

taṁ sanātanam upāgatam akṣṇor
dṛṣṭa-mātram atimātra-dayārdraḥ
āliliṅga parighāyata-dorbhyāṁ
sānukampam atha campaka-gauraḥ

SYNONYMS

tam—unto him; *sanātanam*—Sanātana Gosvāmī; *upāgatam*—having arrived; *akṣṇoḥ*—with the eyes; *dṛṣṭa-mātram*—being only seen; *ati-mātra*—greatly; *dayā-ārdraḥ*—merciful; *āliliṅga*—embraced; *parighāyata-dorbhyām*—with His two arms; *sa-anukampam*—with great affection; *atha*—thus; *campaka-gauraḥ*—Lord Śrī Caitanya Mahāprabhu, who has a complexion the color of a *campaka* flower (golden).

TRANSLATION

"As soon as Sanātana Gosvāmī arrived in front of Lord Caitanya, the Lord, seeing him, became merciful to him. The Lord, who has the complexion of a golden campaka flower, opened His arms and embraced him while expressing great affection."

TEXT 350

কালেন বৃন্দাবনকেলি-বার্তা
লুপ্তেতি তাং খ্যাপয়িতুং বিশিষ্য ।
কৃপামৃতেনাভিষিষেচ দেব-
স্তত্রৈব রূপঞ্চ সনাতনঞ্চ ॥ ৩৫০ ॥

kālena vṛndāvana-keli-vārtā
lupteti tāṁ khyāpayituṁ viśiṣya
kṛpāmṛtenābhiṣiṣeca devas
tatraiva rūpaṁ ca sanātanaṁ ca

SYNONYMS

kālena—in the course of time; *vṛndāvana-keli-vārtā*—topics concerning the transcendental mellows of the pastimes of Lord Kṛṣṇa in Vṛndāvana; *luptā*—

almost lost; *iti*—thus; *tām*—all those; *khyāpayitum*—to enunciate; *viśiṣya*—making specific; *kṛpā-amṛtena*—with the nectar of mercy; *abhiṣiṣeca*—sprinkled; *devaḥ*—the Lord; *tatra*—there; *eva*—indeed; *rūpam*—Śrīla Rūpa Gosvāmī; *ca*—and; *sanātanam*—Sanātana Gosvāmī; *ca*—as well as.

TRANSLATION

"In the course of time, the transcendental news of Kṛṣṇa's pastimes in Vṛndāvana was almost lost. To enunciate explicitly those transcendental pastimes, Śrī Caitanya Mahāprabhu, at Prayāga, empowered Śrīla Rūpa Gosvāmī and Sanātana Gosvāmī with the nectar of His mercy to carry out this work in Vṛndāvana."

TEXT 351

এই ত' কহিলুঁ সনাতনে প্রভুর প্রসাদ ।
যাহার শ্রবণে চিত্তের খণ্ডে অবসাদ ॥ ৩৫১ ॥

ei ta' kahiluṅ sanātane prabhura prasāda
yāhāra śravaṇe cittera khaṇḍe avasāda

SYNONYMS

ei ta'—thus; *kahiluṅ*—I have explained; *sanātane*—unto Sanātana Gosvāmī; *prabhura prasāda*—the mercy of Lord Śrī Caitanya Mahāprabhu; *yāhāra śravaṇe*—hearing which; *cittera*—of the heart; *khaṇḍe*—disappears; *avasāda*—moroseness.

TRANSLATION

I have thus explained the mercy bestowed on Sanātana Gosvāmī by Śrī Caitanya Mahāprabhu. If one hears this, all moroseness in the heart will diminish.

TEXT 352

কৃষ্ণের স্বরূপগণের সকল হয় 'জ্ঞান' ।
বিধি-রাগ-মার্গে 'সাধনভক্তি'র বিধান ॥ ৩৫২ ॥

kṛṣṇera svarūpa-gaṇera sakala haya 'jñāna'
vidhi-rāga-mārge 'sādhana bhakti'ra vidhāna

SYNONYMS

kṛṣṇera svarūpa-gaṇera—of Lord Kṛṣṇa in His various expansions; *sakala*—all; *haya*—there is; *jñāna*—knowledge; *vidhi-rāga-mārge*—in the process of devotional service under regulative principles or in spontaneous love; *sādhana bhaktira vidhāna*—the authorized means of executing devotional service.

TRANSLATION

By reading these instructions to Sanātana Gosvāmī, one will become fully aware of Lord Kṛṣṇa's various expansions and the process of devotional service according to the regulative principles and spontaneous love. Thus everything can be fully known.

TEXT 353

'কৃষ্ণপ্রেম', 'ভক্তিরস', 'ভক্তির সিদ্ধান্ত' ।
ইহার শ্রবণে ভক্ত জানেন সব অন্ত ॥ ৩৫৩ ॥

'kṛṣṇa-prema', 'bhakti-rasa', 'bhaktira siddhānta'
ihāra śravaṇe bhakta jānena saba anta

SYNONYMS

kṛṣṇa-prema—love of Godhead; *bhakti-rasa*—the mellows of devotional service; *bhaktira siddhānta*—the conclusions of devotional service; *ihāra śravaṇe*—by hearing this chapter; *bhakta*—a devotee; *jānena*—knows; *saba*—all; *anta*—limits.

TRANSLATION

By reading this chapter, a pure devotee can understand love of Kṛṣṇa, the mellows of devotional service and the conclusion of devotional service. Everyone can understand all these things to their ultimate end by studying this chapter.

TEXT 354

শ্রীচৈতন্য-নিত্যানন্দ-অদ্বৈত-চরণ ।
যাঁর প্রাণধন, সেই পায় এই ধন ॥ ৩৫৪ ॥

śrī-caitanya-nityānanda-advaita-caraṇa
yāṅra prāṇa-dhana, sei pāya ei dhana

SYNONYMS

śrī-caitanya-nityānanda-advaita-caraṇa—the lotus feet of Lord Śrī Caitanya Mahāprabhu, Lord Nityānanda and Advaita Prabhu; *yāṅra prāṇa-dhana*—whose life and soul; *sei*—such a person; *pāya*—gets; *ei dhana*—this treasure-house of devotional service.

TRANSLATION

The conclusion of this chapter can be known to one whose life and soul are the lotus feet of Śrī Caitanya Mahāprabhu, Nityānanda Prabhu and Advaita Prabhu.

TEXT 355

শ্রীরূপ-রঘুনাথ-পদে যার আশ।
চৈতন্যচরিতামৃত কহে কৃষ্ণদাস ॥ ৩৫৫ ॥

śrī-rūpa-raghunātha-pade yāra āśa
caitanya-caritāmṛta kahe kṛṣṇadāsa

SYNONYMS

śrī-rūpa—Śrīla Rūpa Gosvāmī; *raghunātha*—Śrīla Raghunātha dāsa Gosvāmī; *pade*—at the lotus feet; *yāra*—whose; *āśa*—expectation; *caitanya-caritāmṛta*—the book named *Caitanya-caritāmṛta; kahe*—describes; *kṛṣṇadāsa*—Śrīla Kṛṣṇadāsa Kavirāja Gosvāmī.

TRANSLATION

Praying at the lotus feet of Śrī Rūpa and Śrī Raghunātha, always desiring their mercy, I, Kṛṣṇadāsa, narrate Śrī Caitanya-caritāmṛta, following in their footsteps.

Thus end the Bhaktivedanta purports to the Śrī Caitanya-caritāmṛta, Madhya-līlā, *Chapter Twenty-four, describing the* ātmārāma *verse and the Lord's mercy upon Sanātana Gosvāmī.*

CHAPTER 25

How All the Residents of Vārāṇasī Became Vaiṣṇavas

The following is a summary of Chapter Twenty-five. A Mahārāṣṭrian *brāhmaṇa* who was living in Benares was a great devotee of Śrī Caitanya Mahāprabhu. He was always very happy to hear of the glories of the Lord, and it was by his arrangement that all the *sannyāsīs* of Vārāṇasī became devotees of Lord Caitanya Mahāprabhu. He invited all the *sannyāsīs* to his house to meet Śrī Caitanya Mahāprabhu, and this incident has been described in the Seventh Chapter of *Ādi-līlā.* From that day, Śrī Caitanya Mahāprabhu became famous in the city of Vārāṇasī, and many important men in that city became His followers. By and by, one of the disciples of the great *sannyāsī* Prakāśānanda Sarasvatī became devoted to Śrī Caitanya Mahāprabhu, and this devotee explained Śrī Caitanya Mahāprabhu to Prakāśānanda Sarasvatī and supported His views with various arguments.

One day Śrī Caitanya Mahāprabhu went to take a bath at Pañca-nada, and afterwards all His devotees began chanting the Hare Kṛṣṇa *mantra* in front of the temple of Bindu Mādhava. At this time Prakāśānanda Sarasvatī and all his devotees approached the Lord. Prakāśānanda Sarasvatī immediately fell down at the lotus feet of Śrī Caitanya Mahāprabhu and very much regretted his past behavior toward the Lord. He asked Śrī Caitanya Mahāprabhu about devotional service in terms of the *Vedānta-sūtra,* and the Lord told him about devotional service that is approved by great personalities who know the *Vedānta-sūtra.* Śrī Caitanya Mahāprabhu then pointed out that *Śrīmad-Bhāgavatam* is the proper commentary on the *Vedānta-sūtra.* He then explained the *catuḥ-ślokī* (four *ślokas*) of *Śrīmad-Bhāgavatam,* the essence of that great scripture.

From that day on, all the *sannyāsīs* of Vārāṇasī became devotees of Śrī Caitanya Mahāprabhu. Before returning to His headquarters at Jagannātha Purī, the Lord advised Sanātana Gosvāmī to go to Vṛndāvana. The Lord then departed for Jagannātha Purī. Kavirāja Gosvāmī then describes something about Śrīla Rūpa Gosvāmī, Sanātana Gosvāmī and Subuddhi Rāya. Śrī Caitanya Mahāprabhu returned to Jagannātha Purī through the great forest of Jhārikhaṇḍa in central India. At the end of this chapter, Kavirāja Gosvāmī sums up the incidents of *Madhya-līlā* and instructs every living being to read this sublime book of Śrī Caitanya Mahāprabhu's pastimes.

TEXT 1

বৈষ্ণবীকৃত্য সন্ন্যাসিমুখান্ কাশীনিবাসিনঃ।
সনাতনং সুসংস্কৃত্য প্রভুর্নীলাদ্রিমাগমৎ ॥ ১ ॥

vaiṣṇavī-kṛtya sannyāsi-
mukhān kāśī-nivāsinaḥ
sanātanaṁ susaṁskṛtya
prabhur nīlādrim āgamat

SYNONYMS

vaiṣṇavī-kṛtya—making into Vaiṣṇavas; *sannyāsi-mukhān*—headed by the *sannyāsīs; kāśī-nivāsinaḥ*—the residents of Vārāṇasī; *sanātanam*—Sanātana Gosvāmī; *su-saṁskṛtya*—completely purifying; *prabhuḥ*—Lord Śrī Caitanya Mahāprabhu; *nīlādrim*—to Jagannātha Purī; *āgamat*—returned.

TRANSLATION

After converting into Vaiṣṇavas all the residents of Vārāṇasī, who were headed by the sannyāsīs, and after completely educating and instructing Sanātana Gosvāmī at Vārāṇasī, Śrī Caitanya Mahāprabhu returned to Jagannātha Purī.

TEXT 2

জয় জয় শ্রীচৈতন্য জয় নিত্যানন্দ।
জয়াদ্বৈতচন্দ্র জয় গৌরভক্তবৃন্দ ॥ ২ ॥

jaya jaya śrī-caitanya jaya nityānanda
jayādvaita-candra jaya gaura-bhakta-vṛnda

SYNONYMS

jaya jaya—all glories; *śrī-caitanya*—to Śrī Caitanya Mahāprabhu; *jaya*—all glories; *nityānanda*—to Nityānanda Prabhu; *jaya*—all glories; *advaita-candra*—to Advaita Prabhu; *jaya*—all glories; *gaura-bhakta-vṛnda*—to the devotees of Lord Śrī Caitanya Mahāprabhu.

TRANSLATION

All glories to Lord Caitanya! All glories to Lord Nityānanda! All glories to Advaitacandra! And all glories to all the devotees of Lord Caitanya!

TEXT 3

এই মত মহাপ্রভু দুই মাস পর্যন্ত।
শিখাইলা তাঁরে ভক্তিসিদ্ধান্তের অন্ত ॥ ৩ ॥

ei mata mahāprabhu dui māsa paryanta
śikhāilā tāṅre bhakti-siddhāntera anta

SYNONYMS

ei mata—in this way; *mahāprabhu*—Śrī Caitanya Mahāprabhu; *dui māsa paryanta*—for two months; *śikhāilā*—instructed; *tāṅre*—him; *bhakti-siddhāntera anta*—all the conclusions of devotional service.

TRANSLATION

Lord Caitanya Mahāprabhu instructed Śrī Sanātana Gosvāmī in all the conclusions of devotional service for two consecutive months.

TEXT 4

'পরমানন্দ কীর্তনীয়া'—শেখরের সঙ্গী।
প্রভুরে কীর্তন শুনায়, অতি বড় রঙ্গী ॥ ৪ ॥

'paramānanda kīrtanīyā'——śekharera saṅgī
prabhure kīrtana śunāya, ati baḍa raṅgī

SYNONYMS

paramānanda kīrtanīyā—Paramānanda Kīrtanīyā; *śekharera saṅgī*—a friend of Candraśekhara's; *prabhure*—unto Śrī Caitanya Mahāprabhu; *kīrtana śunāya*—sings and chants; *ati baḍa raṅgī*—very humorous.

TRANSLATION

For as long as Śrī Caitanya Mahāprabhu was in Vārāṇasī, Paramānanda Kīrtanīyā, who was a friend of Candraśekhara's, chanted the Hare Kṛṣṇa mahā-mantra and other songs to Śrī Caitanya Mahāprabhu in a very humorous way.

TEXT 5

সন্ন্যাসীর গণ প্রভুরে যদি উপেক্ষিল।
ভক্ত-দুঃখ খণ্ডাইতে তারে কৃপা কৈল ॥ ৫ ॥

sannyāsīra gaṇa prabhure yadi upekṣila
bhakta-duḥkha khaṇḍāite tāre kṛpā kaila

SYNONYMS

sannyāsīra gaṇa—all the *sannyāsīs; prabhure*—Lord Śrī Caitanya Mahāprabhu; *yadi*—when; *upekṣila*—criticized; *bhakta-duḥkha*—the unhappiness of the devotees; *khaṇḍāite*—to drive away; *tāre*—to them; *kṛpā kaila*—showed His mercy.

TRANSLATION

When the Māyāvādī sannyāsīs at Vārāṇasī criticized Śrī Caitanya Mahāprabhu, the Lord's devotees became very depressed. To satisfy them, Śrī Caitanya Mahāprabhu showed His mercy to the sannyāsīs.

TEXT 6

সন্ন্যাসীরে কৃপা পূর্বে লিখিয়াছোঁ বিস্তারিয়া ।
উদ্দেশে কহিয়ে ইহাঁ সংক্ষেপ করিয়া ॥ ৬ ॥

sannyāsīre kṛpā pūrve likhiyāchoṅ vistāriyā
uddeśe kahiye ihāṅ saṅkṣepa kariyā

SYNONYMS

sannyāsīre kṛpā—mercy upon the *sannyāsīs; pūrve*—before this; *likhiyāchoṅ*—I have described; *vistāriyā*—elaborately; *uddeśe*—in reference to that; *kahiye*—let me speak; *ihāṅ*—here; *saṅkṣepa kariyā*—in brief.

TRANSLATION

In the Seventh Chapter of Ādi-līlā I have already elaborately described Śrī Caitanya Mahāprabhu's deliverance of the sannyāsīs at Vārāṇasī, but I shall briefly repeat it in this chapter.

TEXT 7

যাহাঁ তাহাঁ প্রভুর নিন্দা করে সন্ন্যাসীর গণ ।
শুনি' দুঃখে মহারাষ্ট্রীয় বিপ্র করয়ে চিন্তন ॥ ৭ ॥

yāhāṅ tāhāṅ prabhura nindā kare sannyāsīra gaṇa
śuni' duḥkhe mahārāṣṭrīya vipra karaye cintana

SYNONYMS

yāhāṅ tāhāṅ—anywhere and everywhere; *prabhura nindā*—criticism of Śrī Caitanya Mahāprabhu; *kare*—do; *sannyāsīra gaṇa*—the Māyāvādī *sannyāsīs;*

śuni'—hearing; *duḥkhe*—in great unhappiness; *mahārāṣṭrīya vipra*—the *brāhmaṇa* of Mahārāṣṭra province; *karaye cintana*—was contemplating.

TRANSLATION

When the Māyāvādī sannyāsīs were criticizing Śrī Caitanya Mahāprabhu anywhere and everywhere in Vārāṇasī, the Mahārāṣṭrian brāhmaṇa, hearing this blasphemy, began to think about this unhappily.

TEXT 8

"প্রভুর স্বভাব,—যেবা দেখে সন্নিধানে।
'স্বরূপ' অনুভবি' তাঁরে 'ঈশ্বর' করি' মানে ॥ ৮ ॥

"prabhura svabhāva,——yebā dekhe sannidhāne
'svarūpa' anubhavi' tāṅre 'īśvara' kari' māne

SYNONYMS

prabhura sva-bhāva—the characteristics of Śrī Caitanya Mahāprabhu; *yebā*—anyone who; *dekhe*—sees; *sannidhāne*—nearby; *sva-rūpa*—His personality; *anubhavi'*—realizing; *tāṅre*—Him; *īśvara kari'*—as the Supreme Lord; *māne*—accepts.

TRANSLATION

The Mahārāṣṭrian brāhmaṇa thought, "Whoever closely sees the characteristics of Śrī Caitanya Mahāprabhu immediately realizes His personality and accepts Him as the Supreme Lord.

TEXT 9

কোন প্রকারে পারোঁ যদি একত্র করিতে।
ইহা দেখি' সন্ন্যাসিগণ হবে ইহাঁর ভক্তে ॥ ৯ ॥

kona prakāre pāroṅ yadi ekatra karite
ihā dekhi' sannyāsi-gaṇa habe iṅhāra bhakte

SYNONYMS

kona prakāre—by some means; *pāroṅ*—I am able; *yadi*—if; *ekatra karite*—to assemble; *ihā dekhi'*—by seeing this (Śrī Caitanya Mahāprabhu's personal characteristics); *sannyāsi-gaṇa*—the Māyāvādī *sannyāsīs* of Vārāṇasī; *habe*—will become; *iṅhāra bhakte*—His devotees.

TRANSLATION

"If by some means I can assemble all the sannyāsīs together, they will certainly become His devotees after seeing His personal characteristics.

PURPORT

If one saw the personal characteristics and activities of Śrī Caitanya Mahāprabhu, one would certainly be convinced that He was the Supreme Personality of Godhead. One can ascertain this by following in the footsteps of the śāstric injunctions. This sincere study and appreciation of Śrī Caitanya Mahāprabhu is also applicable to His authorized devotees, and it is clearly stated in the *Caitanya-caritāmṛta* (*Antya-līlā,* 7.11):

kali-kālera dharma——kṛṣṇa-nāma-saṅkīrtana
kṛṣṇa-śakti vinā nāhe tāra pravartana

In this age of Kali, real religious propaganda should induce people to chant the Hare Kṛṣṇa *mahā-mantra.* This is possible for someone who is especially empowered by Kṛṣṇa. No one can do this without being especially favored by Kṛṣṇa. Śrīla Bhaktisiddhānta Sarasvatī Ṭhākura comments in this regard in his *Anubhāṣya,* wherein he quotes a verse from *Nārāyaṇa-saṁhitā:*

dvāparīyair janair viṣṇuḥ
pañcarātrais tu kevalaiḥ
kalau tu nāma-mātreṇa
pūjyate bhagavān hariḥ

"In Dvāpara-yuga, devotees of Lord Viṣṇu and Kṛṣṇa rendered devotional service according to the principles of *pāñcarātrika.* In this age of Kali, the Supreme Personality of Godhead is worshiped simply by the chanting of His holy names." Śrīla Bhaktisiddhānta Sarasvatī Ṭhākura then comments: "Without being empowered by the direct potency of Lord Kṛṣṇa to fulfill His desire and without being specifically favored by the Lord, no human being can become the spiritual master of the whole world. He certainly cannot succeed by mental concoction, which is not meant for devotees or religious people. Only an empowered personality can distribute the holy name of the Lord and enjoin all fallen souls to worship Kṛṣṇa. By distributing the holy name of the Lord, he cleanses the hearts of the most fallen people; therefore he extinguishes the blazing fire of the material world. Not only that, he broadcasts the shining brightness of Kṛṣṇa's effulgence throughout the world. Such an *ācārya,* or spiritual master, should be considered nondifferent from Kṛṣṇa—that is, he should be considered the incarnation of Lord Kṛṣṇa's potency. Such a personality is *kṛṣṇāliṅgita-vigraha*—that is, he is always embraced by the Supreme Personality of Godhead, Kṛṣṇa. Such a person is above the considerations of the *varṇāśrama* institution. He is the *guru* or spiritual master for the entire world, a devotee on the topmost platform, the *mahā-bhāgavata* stage, and a *paramahaṁsa-ṭhākura,* a spiritual form only fit to be addressed as *paramahaṁsa* or *ṭhākura.*"

Nonetheless, there are many people who are just like owls but never open their eyes to see the sunshine. These owlish personalities are inferior to the Māyāvādī *sannyāsīs* who cannot see the brilliance of Kṛṣṇa's favor. They are prepared to criticize the person engaged in distributing the holy name all over the world and following in the footsteps of Śrī Caitanya Mahāprabhu, who wanted Kṛṣṇa consciousness preached in every town and city.

TEXT 10

বারাণসী-বাস আমার হয় সর্বকালে।
সর্বকাল দুঃখ পাব, ইহা না করিলে॥" ১০ ॥

vārāṇasī-vāsa āmāra haya sarva-kāle
sarva-kāla duḥkha pāba, ihā nā karile"

SYNONYMS

vārāṇasī-vāsa—residence at Vārāṇasī; *āmāra*—my; *haya*—there is; *sarva-kāle*—always; *sarva-kāla*—always; *duḥkha pāba*—I will suffer unhappiness; *ihā*—this; *nā karile*—if I do not execute.

TRANSLATION

"I shall have to reside at Vārāṇasī the rest of my life. If I do not try to carry out this plan, I shall certainly continue to suffer mental depression."

TEXT 11

এত চিন্তি' নিমন্ত্রিল সন্ন্যাসীর গণে।
তবে সেই বিপ্র আইল মহাপ্রভুর স্থানে॥ ১১ ॥

eta cinti' nimantrila sannyāsīra gaṇe
tabe sei vipra āila mahāprabhura sthāne

SYNONYMS

eta cinti'—thinking this; *nimantrila*—he invited; *sannyāsīra gaṇe*—all the *sannyāsīs; tabe*—then; *sei vipra*—that *brāhmaṇa; āila*—approached; *mahāprabhura sthāne*—the lotus feet of Śrī Caitanya Mahāprabhu.

TRANSLATION

Thinking like this, the Mahārāṣṭrian brāhmaṇa extended an invitation to all the sannyāsīs of Vārāṇasī. After doing this, he finally approached Śrī Caitanya Mahāprabhu to extend Him an invitation.

TEXT 12

হেনকালে নিন্দা শুনি' শেখর, তপন ।
দুঃখ পাঞা প্রভু-পদে কৈলা নিবেদন ॥ ১২ ॥

hena-kāle nindā śuni' śekhara, tapana
duḥkha pāñā prabhu-pade kailā nivedana

SYNONYMS

hena-kāle—exactly at this time; *nindā śuni'*—by hearing the criticism (of Lord Caitanya by the Māyāvādī *sannyāsīs*); *śekhara tapana*—Candraśekhara and Tapana Miśra; *duḥkha pāñā*—feeling very unhappy; *prabhu-pade*—unto the lotus feet of Śrī Caitanya Mahāprabhu; *kailā nivedana*—submitted a request.

TRANSLATION

At this time, Candraśekhara and Tapana Miśra both heard blasphemous criticism against Śrī Caitanya Mahāprabhu and felt very unhappy. They came to Śrī Caitanya Mahāprabhu's lotus feet to submit a request.

TEXT 13

ভক্ত-দুঃখ দেখি' প্রভু মনেতে চিন্তিল ।
সন্ন্যাসীর মন ফিরাইতে মন হইল ॥ ১৩ ॥

bhakta-duḥkha dekhi' prabhu manete cintila
sannyāsīra mana phirāite mana ha-ila

SYNONYMS

bhakta-duḥkha dekhi'—seeing the unhappiness of the devotees; *prabhu*—Śrī Caitanya Mahāprabhu; *manete cintila*—considered within His mind; *sannyāsīra mana*—the minds of the Māyāvādī *sannyāsīs; phirāite*—to turn; *mana ha-ila*—Śrī Caitanya Mahāprabhu decided.

TRANSLATION

They submitted their request, and Śrī Caitanya Mahāprabhu, seeing His devotees' unhappiness, decided to turn the minds of the Māyāvādī sannyāsīs.

TEXT 14

হেনকালে বিপ্র আসি' করিল নিমন্ত্রণ ।
অনেক দৈন্যাদি করি' ধরিল চরণ ॥ ১৪ ॥

hena-kāle vipra āsi' karila nimantraṇa
aneka dainyādi kari' dharila caraṇa

SYNONYMS

hena-kāle—at this time; *vipra*—the Mahārāṣṭrian *brāhmaṇa; āsi'*—coming; *karila nimantraṇa*—invited Śrī Caitanya Mahāprabhu; *aneka*—various; *dainya-ādi*—submissions; *kari'*—doing; *dharila caraṇa*—touched His lotus feet.

TRANSLATION

While Śrī Caitanya Mahāprabhu was seriously considering meeting with the Māyāvādī sannyāsīs, the Mahārāṣṭrian brāhmaṇa approached Him and extended an invitation. The brāhmaṇa submitted his invitation with great humility, and he touched the lotus feet of Śrī Caitanya Mahāprabhu.

TEXT 15

তবে মহাপ্রভু তাঁর নিমন্ত্রণ মানিলা ।
আর দিন মধ্যাহ্ন করি' তাঁর ঘরে গেলা ॥ ১৫ ॥

tabe mahāprabhu tāṅra nimantraṇa mānilā
āra dina madhyāhna kari' tāṅra ghare gelā

SYNONYMS

tabe—after this; *mahāprabhu*—Śrī Caitanya Mahāprabhu; *tāṅra*—his; *nimantraṇa*—invitation; *mānilā*—accepted; *āra dina*—the next day; *madhyāhna kari'*—after finishing His *madhyāhna* activities (taking bath and murmuring *mantras*); *tāṅra ghare gelā*—He went to the house of the Mahārāṣṭrian *brāhmaṇa.*

TRANSLATION

Śrī Caitanya Mahāprabhu accepted his invitation, and the next day, after finishing His noontime activities, He went to the brāhmaṇa's house.

TEXT 16

তাহাঁ যৈছে কৈলা প্রভু সন্ন্যাসীর নিস্তার ।
পঞ্চতত্ত্বাখ্যানে তাহা করিয়াছি বিস্তার ॥ ১৬ ॥

tāhāṅ yaiche kailā prabhu sannyāsīra nistāra
pañca-tattvākhyāne tāhā kariyāchi vistāra

SYNONYMS

tāhāṅ—there; *yaiche*—how; *kailā*—performed; *prabhu*—Śrī Caitanya Mahāprabhu; *sannyāsīra*—of the Māyāvādī *sannyāsīs; nistāra*—deliverance; *pañca-tattva-ākhyāne*—in describing the glories of the Pañca-tattva (Śrī Kṛṣṇa Caitanya, Prabhu Nityānanda, Śrī Advaita, Gadādhara and Śrīvāsa); *tāhā*—that subject matter; *kariyāchi vistāra*—have described elaborately.

TRANSLATION

I have already described Śrī Caitanya Mahāprabhu's deliverance of the Māyāvādī sannyāsīs in the Seventh Chapter when I described the glories of the Pañca-tattva—Śrī Caitanya Mahāprabhu, Śrī Nityānanda Prabhu, Advaita Prabhu, Gadādhara Prabhu and Śrīvāsa.

TEXT 17

গ্রন্থ বাড়ে, পুনরুক্তি হয় ত' কথন।
তাহাঁ যে না লিখিলুঁ, তাহা করিয়ে লিখন ॥ ১৭ ॥

grantha bāḍe, punarukti haya ta' kathana
tāhāṅ ye nā likhiluṅ, tāhā kariye likhana

SYNONYMS

grantha—the size of the book; *bāḍe*—increases; *punaḥ-ukti*—repetition; *haya*—would be; *ta' kathana*—of subject matters once described; *tāhāṅ*—there (in the Seventh Chapter); *ye*—whatever; *nā likhiluṅ*—I have not described; *tāhā*—that; *kariye likhana*—I am writing.

TRANSLATION

Since I have already described this incident very elaborately in the Seventh Chapter of Ādi-līlā, I do not wish to increase the size of this book by giving another description. However, I shall try to include in this chapter whatever was not described there.

TEXT 18

যে দিবস প্রভু সন্ন্যাসীরে কৃপা কৈল।
সে দিবস হৈতে গ্রামে কোলাহল হৈল ॥ ১৮ ॥

ye divasa prabhu sannyāsīre kṛpā kaila
se divasa haite grāme kolāhala haila

SYNONYMS

ye divasa—the day when; *prabhu*—Śrī Caitanya Mahāprabhu; *sannyāsīre*—to the Māyāvādī *sannyāsīs; kṛpā kaila*—showed His mercy; *se divasa haite*—beginning from that day; *grāme*—in the locality; *kolāhala haila*—there were many talks about this incident.

TRANSLATION

Beginning from the day on which Śrī Caitanya Mahāprabhu showed His mercy to the Māyāvādī sannyāsīs, there were vivid discussions about this conversion among the inhabitants of Vārāṇasī.

TEXT 19

লোকের সংঘট্ট আইসে প্রভুরে দেখিতে ।
নানা শাস্ত্রে পণ্ডিত আইসে শাস্ত্র বিচারিতে ॥ ১৯ ॥

lokera saṅghaṭṭa āise prabhure dekhite
nānā śāstre paṇḍita āise śāstra vicārite

SYNONYMS

lokera saṅghaṭṭa—crowds of men; *āise*—come; *prabhure dekhite*—to see Lord Śrī Caitanya Mahāprabhu; *nānā śāstre paṇḍita*—scholars learned in various scriptures; *āise*—used to come; *śāstra vicārite*—to talk on various scriptures.

TRANSLATION

Crowds of people came to see Śrī Caitanya Mahāprabhu from that day on, and scholars of various scriptures discussed different subject matters with the Lord.

TEXT 20

সর্বশাস্ত্র খণ্ডি' প্রভু 'ভক্তি' করে সার ।
সযুক্তিক বাক্যে মন ফিরায় সবার ॥ ২০ ॥

sarva-śāstra khaṇḍi' prabhu 'bhakti' kare sāra
sayuktika vākye mana phirāya sabāra

SYNONYMS

sarva-śāstra khaṇḍi'—defeating all the false conclusions of different scriptures; *prabhu*—Śrī Caitanya Mahāprabhu; *bhakti kare sāra*—established the predominance of devotional service; *sa-yuktika vākye*—by talks full of pleasing logic and arguments; *mana phirāya*—turns the minds; *sabāra*—of everyone.

TRANSLATION

When people came to Śrī Caitanya Mahāprabhu to discuss the principles of various scriptures, the Lord defeated their false conclusions and established the predominance of devotional service to the Lord. With logic and argument He very politely changed their minds.

PURPORT

We have been spreading this *saṅkīrtana* movement in the Western countries, and in our recent tour of European cities like Rome, Geneva, Paris and Frankfurt, many learned Christian scholars, priests, philosophers and *yogīs* came to see us, and by the grace of Kṛṣṇa they agreed that this Kṛṣṇa consciousness movement, the *bhakti* cult, offers the topmost conclusion. Following in the footsteps of Śrī Caitanya Mahāprabhu, we are trying to convince everyone that the devotional service of the Lord is enjoined in every scripture. If a person is religious, he must accept the supreme authority of the Lord, become His devotee and try to love Him. This is the real principle of religion. It does not matter whether one is Christian, Mohammedan or whatever. He simply must accept the sublime position of the Supreme Personality of Godhead and render service unto Him. It is not a question of being Christian, Mohammedan or Hindu. One should be purely religious and freed from all these material designations. In this way one can learn the art of devotional service. This argument appeals to all intelligent men, and consequently this Kṛṣṇa consciousness movement is gaining ground throughout the world. Due to our solid logic and scientific presentation, Śrī Caitanya Mahāprabhu's prediction that Kṛṣṇa consciousness will spread in every town and village throughout the world is gradually being realized.

TEXT 21

উপদেশ লঞা করে কৃষ্ণ-সংকীর্তন।
সর্বলোক হাসে, গায়, করয়ে নর্তন ॥ ২১ ॥

upadeśa lañā kare kṛṣṇa-saṅkīrtana
sarva-loka hāse, gāya, karaye nartana

SYNONYMS

upadeśa lañā—getting instructions from Śrī Caitanya Mahāprabhu; *kare*—join; *kṛṣṇa-saṅkīrtana*—the *saṅkīrtana* movement; *sarva-loka hāse*—everyone began to laugh in pleasure; *gāya*—chant; *karaye nartana*—and dance.

TRANSLATION

As soon as people received instructions from Śrī Caitanya Mahāprabhu, they began to chant the Hare Kṛṣṇa mahā-mantra. Thus everyone laughed, chanted and danced with the Lord.

TEXT 22

প্রভুরে প্রণত হৈল সন্ন্যাসীর গণ ।
আত্মমধ্যে গোষ্ঠী করে ছাড়ি' অধ্যয়ন ॥ ২২ ॥

prabhure praṇata haila sannyāsīra gaṇa
ātma-madhye goṣṭhī kare chāḍi' adhyayana

SYNONYMS

prabhure—unto Lord Śrī Caitanya Mahāprabhu; *praṇata haila*—offered obeisances; *sannyāsīra gaṇa*—all the Māyāvādī *sannyāsīs; ātma-madhye*—among themselves; *goṣṭhī kare*—discussed; *chāḍi' adhyayana*—giving up so-called studies of Vedānta.

TRANSLATION

All the Māyāvādī sannyāsīs offered their obeisances unto Śrī Caitanya Mahāprabhu and then began to discuss His movement, giving up their studies of Vedānta and Māyāvāda philosophy.

TEXT 23

প্রকাশানন্দের শিষ্য এক তাঁহার সমান ।
সভামধ্যে কহে প্রভুর করিয়া সম্মান ॥ ২৩ ॥

prakāśānandera śiṣya eka tāṅhāra samāna
sabhā-madhye kahe prabhura kariyā sammāna

SYNONYMS

prakāśānandera śiṣya eka—one of the disciples of Prakāśānanda Sarasvatī; *tāṅhāra samāna*—equal in learning with Prakāśānanda Sarasvatī; *sabhā-madhye*—in the assembly of the *sannyāsīs; kahe*—explains; *prabhura kariyā sammāna*—respecting Śrī Caitanya Mahāprabhu seriously.

TRANSLATION

One of the disciples of Prakāśānanda Sarasvatī, who was as learned as his guru, began to speak in that assembly, offering all respects to Śrī Caitanya Mahāprabhu.

TEXT 24

শ্রীকৃষ্ণচৈতন্য হয় 'সাক্ষাৎ নারায়ণ' ।
'ব্যাসসূত্রের' অর্থ করেন অতি-মনোরম ॥ ২৪ ॥

śrī-kṛṣṇa-caitanya haya 'sākṣāt nārāyaṇa'
'vyāsa-sūtrera' artha karena ati-manorama

SYNONYMS

śrī-kṛṣṇa-caitanya—Lord Śrī Kṛṣṇa Caitanya Mahāprabhu; *haya*—is; *sākṣāt nārāyaṇa*—directly the Supreme Personality of Godhead, Nārāyaṇa; *vyāsa-sūtrera*—the codes of Vyāsadeva (*Vedānta-sūtra*); *artha karena*—He explains; *ati-manorama*—very nicely.

TRANSLATION

He said, "Śrī Caitanya Mahāprabhu is the Supreme Personality of Godhead, Nārāyaṇa Himself. When He explains the Vedānta-sūtra, He does so very nicely.

TEXT 25

উপনিষদের করেন মুখ্যার্থ ব্যাখ্যান ।
শুনিয়া পণ্ডিত-লোকের জুড়ায় মন-কাণ ॥ ২৫ ॥

upaniṣadera karena mukhyārtha vyākhyāna
śuniyā paṇḍita-lokera juḍāya mana-kāṇa

SYNONYMS

upaniṣadera—of the Vedic version known as the *Upaniṣads; karena*—He does; *mukhya-artha*—the original meaning; *vyākhyāna*—explanation; *śuniyā*—hearing; *paṇḍita-lokera*—of the learned scholars; *juḍāya*—satisfies; *mana-kāṇa*—the minds and ears.

TRANSLATION

"Śrī Caitanya Mahāprabhu explains the direct meaning of the Upaniṣads. When all learned scholars hear this, their minds and ears are satisfied.

TEXT 26

সূত্র-উপনিষদের মুখ্যার্থ ছাড়িয়া ।
আচার্য 'কল্পনা' করে আগ্রহ করিয়া ॥ ২৬ ॥

sūtra-upaniṣadera mukhyārtha chāḍiyā
ācārya 'kalpanā' kare āgraha kariyā

SYNONYMS

sūtra-upaniṣadera—of the *Vedānta-sūtra* and the *Upaniṣads; mukhya-artha*—the direct meaning; *chāḍiyā*—giving up; *ācārya*—Śaṅkarācārya; *kalpanā*—imagination; *kare*—does; *āgraha kariyā*—with great eagerness.

TRANSLATION

"Giving up the direct meaning of the Vedānta-sūtra and the Upaniṣads, Śaṅkarācārya imagines some other interpretation.

TEXT 27

আচার্য-কল্পিত অর্থ যে পণ্ডিত শুনে।
মুখে 'হয়' 'হয়' করে, হৃদয় না মানে ॥ ২৭ ॥

ācārya-kalpita artha ye paṇḍita śune
mukhe 'haya' 'haya' kare, hṛdaya nā māne

SYNONYMS

ācārya-kalpita—imagined by Śaṅkarācārya; *artha*—meaning; *ye paṇḍita śune*—any learned person who hears; *mukhe*—only in the mouth; *haya haya*—yes it is, yes it is; *kare*—does; *hṛdaya*—his heart; *nā māne*—does not accept.

TRANSLATION

"All the interpretations of Śaṅkarācārya are imaginary. Such imaginary interpretations are verbally accepted by learned scholars, but they do not appeal to the heart.

TEXT 28

শ্রীকৃষ্ণচৈতন্য-বাক্য দৃঢ় সত্য মানি।
কলিকালে সন্ন্যাসে 'সংসার' নাহি জিনি ॥ ২৮ ॥

śrī-kṛṣṇa-caitanya-vākya dṛḍha satya māni
kali-kāle sannyāse 'saṁsāra' nāhi jini

SYNONYMS

śrī-kṛṣṇa-caitanya-vākya—the words of Śrī Caitanya Mahāprabhu; *dṛḍha*—very firm and convincing; *satya māni*—I admit as truth; *kali-kāle*—in this age of Kali;

sannyāse—simply by accepting the renounced order of life; *saṁsāra nāhi jini*—one cannot escape the material clutches.

TRANSLATION

"The words of Śrī Kṛṣṇa Caitanya Mahāprabhu are firm and convincing, and I accept them as true. In this age of Kali, one cannot be delivered from material clutches simply by formally accepting the renounced order.

TEXT 29

হরের্নাম-শ্লোকের যেই করিলা ব্যাখ্যান ।
সেই সত্য সুখদার্থ পরম প্রমাণ ॥ ২৯ ॥

harer nāma-ślokera yei karilā vyākhyāna
sei satya sukhadārtha parama pramāṇa

SYNONYMS

harer nāma-ślokera—of the verse beginning *harer nāma harer nāma; yei*—whatever; *karilā*—made; *vyākhyāna*—the explanation; *sei*—that; *satya*—true; *sukha-da-artha*—a meaning that is pleasing to accept; *parama pramāṇa*—the supreme evidence.

TRANSLATION

"Śrī Caitanya Mahāprabhu's explanation of the verse beginning 'harer nāma harer nāma' is not only pleasing to the ear but is strong, factual evidence.

TEXT 30

ভক্তি বিনা মুক্তি নহে, ভাগবতে কয় ।
কলিকালে নামাভাসে সুখে মুক্তি হয় ॥ ৩০ ॥

bhakti vinā mukti nahe, bhāgavate kaya
kali-kāle nāmābhāse sukhe mukti haya

SYNONYMS

bhakti vinā—without devotional service; *mukti nahe*—there is no question of liberation; *bhāgavate kaya*—it is said in *Śrīmad-Bhāgavatam; kali-kāle*—in this age of Kali; *nāma-ābhāse*—even by a slight appreciation of the Hare Kṛṣṇa *mantra; sukhe*—without difficulty; *mukti haya*—one can get liberation.

TRANSLATION

"In this age of Kali, one cannot attain liberation without taking to the devotional service of the Lord. In this age, even if one does not chant the holy name of Kṛṣṇa perfectly, he still attains liberation very easily.

TEXT 31

শ্রেয়ঃস্তিং ভক্তিমুদস্য তে বিভো
ক্লিশ্যন্তি যে কেবলবোধলব্ধয়ে ।
তেষামসৌ ক্লেশল এব শিষ্যতে
নান্যদ্যথা স্থূলতুষাবঘাতিনাম্ ॥ ৩১ ॥

śreyaḥ-sṛtiṁ bhaktim udasya te vibho
kliśyanti ye kevala-bodha-labdhaye
teṣām asau kleśala eva śiṣyate
nānyad yathā sthūla-tuṣāvaghātinām

SYNONYMS

śreyaḥ-sṛtim—the auspicious path of liberation; *bhaktim*—devotional service; *udasya*—giving up; *te*—of You; *vibho*—O my Lord; *kliśyanti*—accept increased difficulties; *ye*—all those persons who; *kevala*—only; *bodha-labdhaye*—for obtaining knowledge; *teṣām*—for them; *asau*—that; *kleśalaḥ*—trouble; *eva*—only; *śiṣyate*—remains; *na*—not; *anyat*—anything else; *yathā*—as much as; *sthūla*—bulky; *tuṣa*—husks of rice; *avaghātinām*—of those beating.

ı RANSLATION

" 'My dear Lord, devotional service unto You is the only auspicious path. If one gives it up simply for speculative knowledge or the understanding that these living beings are spirit soul and the material world is false, he undergoes a great deal of trouble. He only gains troublesome and inauspicious activities. His actions are like beating a husk that is already devoid of rice. One's labor becomes fruitless.'

PURPORT

This is a quotation from *Śrīmad-Bhāgavatam* (10.14.4).

TEXT 32

যেঽন্যেঽরবিন্দাক্ষ বিমুক্তমানিন-
স্ত্বয্যস্তভাবাদবিশুদ্ধবুদ্ধয়ঃ ।

আরুহ্য কৃচ্ছ্রেণ পরং পদং ততঃ
পতন্ত্যধোঽনাদৃতযুষ্মদঙ্ঘ্রয়ঃ ॥ ৩২ ॥

ye 'nye 'ravindākṣa vimukta-māninas
tvayy asta-bhāvād aviśuddha-buddhayaḥ
āruhya kṛcchreṇa paraṁ padaṁ tataḥ
patanty adho 'nādṛta-yuṣmad-aṅghrayaḥ

SYNONYMS

ye—all those who; *anye*—others (nondevotees); *aravinda-akṣa*—O lotus-eyed one; *vimukta-māninaḥ*—who consider themselves liberated; *tvayi*—unto You; *asta-bhāvāt*—without devotion; *aviśuddha-buddhayaḥ*—whose intelligence is not purified; *āruhya*—having ascended; *kṛcchreṇa*—by severe austerities and penances; *param padam*—to the supreme position; *tataḥ*—from there; *patanti*—fall; *adhaḥ*—down; *anādṛta*—without respecting; *yuṣmat*—Your; *aṅghrayaḥ*—lotus feet.

TRANSLATION

" 'O lotus-eyed one, those who think they are liberated in this life but who are devoid of devotional service to You are of impure intelligence. Although they accept severe austerities and penances and rise to the spiritual position, to impersonal Brahman realization, they fall down again because they neglect to worship Your lotus feet.'

PURPORT

This is a verse from *Śrīmad-Bhāgavatam* (10.2.32).

TEXT 33

'ব্রহ্ম'-শব্দে কহে 'ষড়ৈশ্বর্যপূর্ণ ভগবান্' ।
তাঁরে 'নির্বিশেষ' স্থাপি, 'পূর্ণতা' হয় হান ॥ ৩৩ ॥

'brahma'-śabde kahe 'ṣaḍ-aiśvarya-pūrṇa bhagavān'
tāṅre 'nirviśeṣa' sthāpi, 'pūrṇatā' haya hāna

SYNONYMS

brahma-śabde—by the word *brahma; kahe*—is meant; *ṣaṭ-aiśvarya-pūrṇa bhagavān*—the Supreme Personality of Godhead, full in all six opulences; *tāṅre*—Him; *nirviśeṣa sthāpi*—if we make impersonal; *pūrṇatā haya hāna*—His completeness becomes damaged.

TRANSLATION

"The word Brahman means 'the greatest.' This means that the Supreme Personality of Godhead is full in all six opulences. However, if we take the one-sided impersonalist view, His fullness is diminished.

PURPORT

The Supreme Personality of Godhead is originally the Supreme Person. The Lord says in *Bhagavad-gītā* (9.4):

mayā tatam idaṁ sarvaṁ
jagad avyakta-mūrtinā
mat-sthāni sarva-bhūtāni
na cāhaṁ teṣv avasthitaḥ

"By Me, in My unmanifested form, this entire universe is pervaded. All beings are in Me, but I am not in them."

The potency of Kṛṣṇa that is spread everywhere is impersonal. The sunlight is the impersonal expansion of the sun globe and the sun-god. If we simply take one side of the Supreme Personality of Godhead—His impersonal effulgence—that one side does not fully explain the Absolute Truth. Impersonal appreciation of the Absolute Truth is one-sided and incomplete. One should also accept the other side, the personal side—Bhagavān. *Brahmeti paramātmeti bhagavān iti śabdyate.* One should not be satisfied simply by understanding the Brahman feature of the Personality of Godhead. One must also know the Lord's personal feature. That is complete understanding of the Absolute Truth.

TEXT 34

শ্রুতি-পুরাণ কহে—কৃষ্ণের চিচ্ছক্তি-বিলাস ।
তাহা নাহি মানি, পণ্ডিত করে উপহাস ॥ ৩৪ ॥

śruti-purāṇa kahe——kṛṣṇera cic-chakti-vilāsa
tāhā nāhi māni, paṇḍita kare upahāsa

SYNONYMS

śruti-purāṇa kahe—the Vedic literatures and the *Purāṇas* confirm; *kṛṣṇera*—of Lord Kṛṣṇa; *cit-śakti-vilāsa*—activities of spiritual potencies; *tāhā nāhi māni*—not accepting that; *paṇḍita kare upahāsa*—so-called scholars play jokes without perfect understanding.

TRANSLATION

"Vedic literatures, the Upaniṣads, the Brahma-sūtra and the Purāṇas all describe the activities of the spiritual potency of the Lord. If one cannot accept the personal activities of the Lord, he jokes foolishly and gives an impersonal description.

PURPORT

In the Vedic literatures, including the *Purāṇas,* there are full descriptions of the spiritual potency of Kṛṣṇa. All the pastimes of the Lord are eternal, blissful and full of knowledge, just as the form of Kṛṣṇa Himself is eternal, blissful and full of knowledge (*sac-cid-ānanda-vigraha*). Unintelligent people with a poor fund of knowledge compare their temporary bodies to the spiritual body of Kṛṣṇa, and by such foolishness they try to understand Kṛṣṇa as one of them. *Avajānanti māṁ mūḍhā mānuṣīṁ tanum āśritam. Bhagavad-gītā* (9.11) points out that foolish people think of Kṛṣṇa as one of them. Not understanding His spiritual potency, they simply decry the personal form of the Absolute Truth, foolishly thinking of themselves as *jñānīs* cognizant of the complete truth. They cannot understand that just as the material energy of the Lord has a variety of activities, the spiritual energy has variety also. They consider activities in devotional service the same as activities in material consciousness. Under such a wrong impression, they sometimes dare joke about the spiritual activities of the Lord and His devotional service.

TEXT 35

চিদানন্দ কৃষ্ণবিগ্রহ 'মায়িক' করি' মানি ।
এই বড় 'পাপ',— সত্য চৈতন্যের বাণী ॥ ৩৫ ॥

cid-ānanda kṛṣṇa-vigraha 'māyika' kari' māni
ei baḍa 'pāpa',——satya caitanyera vāṇī

SYNONYMS

cit-ānanda kṛṣṇa-vigraha—the transcendental form of Kṛṣṇa, which is completely spiritual; *māyika kari' māni*—accept as made of the external energy, *māyā; ei baḍa pāpa*—this is a great act of sin; *satya*—true; *caitanyera vāṇī*—the words of Śrī Caitanya Mahāprabhu.

TRANSLATION

"The Māyāvādīs do not recognize the personal form of the Lord as spiritual and full of bliss. This is a great sin. Śrī Caitanya Mahāprabhu's statements are actually factual.

PURPORT

Śrī Caitanya Mahāprabhu's movement especially aims at defeating the Māyāvāda conclusion about the Absolute Truth. Since the members of the Māyāvāda school cannot understand the spiritual form of the Lord, they incorrectly think the Lord's form is also made of material energy. They think that He is covered by a material body just like other living beings. Due to this offensive understanding, they cannot recognize that Śrī Kṛṣṇa's personal form is transcendental, not material. Their conclusion is a great offense at the lotus feet of the Lord. As explained by Śrī Caitanya Mahāprabhu, Śrī Kṛṣṇa has His eternal, blissful form that is full of knowledge, and all Vaiṣṇava *ācāryas* accept this. That is the proper understanding of the Absolute Truth.

TEXT 36

নাতঃ পরং পরম যদ্ভবতঃ স্বরূপ-
মানন্দমাত্রমবিকল্পমবিদ্ধবর্চঃ ।
পশ্যামি বিশ্বসৃজমেকমবিশ্বমাত্মন্
ভূতেন্দ্রিয়াত্মকমদস্ত উপাশ্রিতোঽস্মি ॥ ৩৬ ॥

nātaḥ paraṁ parama yad bhavataḥ svarūpam
ānanda-mātram avikalpam aviddha-varcaḥ
paśyāmi viśva-sṛjam ekam aviśvam ātman
bhūtendriyātmakam adas ta upāśrito 'smi

SYNONYMS

na—not; *ataḥ*—than this; *param*—more supreme; *parama*—O supreme one; *yat*—which; *bhavataḥ*—of Your Lordship; *sva-rūpam*—the personal form; *ānanda*—of transcendental bliss; *mātram*—only; *avikalpam*—where there is no creation; *aviddha*—without contamination; *varcaḥ*—having an effulgence; *paśyāmi*—I see; *viśva-sṛjam ekam*—who alone has created this universe; *aviśvam*—not belonging to the destructible material world; *ātman*—O Supreme Soul; *bhūta-indriya-ātmakam*—the original cause of the senses and the living beings; *adaḥ*—transcendental; *te*—unto You; *upāśritaḥ asmi*—I take full shelter.

TRANSLATION

" 'O supreme one, the transcendental form I am now seeing is full of transcendental bliss. It is not contaminated by the external energy. It is full of effulgence. My Lord, there is no better understanding of You than this. You are the Supreme Soul and the creator of this material world, but You are not connected with this material world. You are completely different from created

form and variety. I sincerely take shelter of that form of Yours which I am now seeing. This form is the original source of all living beings and their senses.'

PURPORT

This is a quotation from *Śrīmad-Bhāgavatam* (3.9.3). This verse was spoken by Lord Brahmā, who perfectly realized the Supreme Personality of Godhead after meditating upon the Lord within the water of the Garbhodhaka Ocean. Brahmā realized that the form of the Lord is completely spiritual. This is certainly a better understanding of the Absolute Truth than impersonal understanding.

TEXT 37

দৃষ্টং শ্রুতং ভূত-ভবদ্ভবিষ্যৎ স্থাস্নুশ্চরিষ্ণুর্মহদল্পকং বা।
বিনাচ্যুতাদ্বস্তু তরাং ন বাচ্যং স এব সর্বং পরমাত্মভূতঃ ॥৩৭॥

dṛṣṭaṁ śrutaṁ bhūta-bhavad-bhaviṣyat
sthāsnuś cariṣṇur mahad alpakaṁ vā
vinācyutād vastu-tarāṁ na vācyaṁ
sa eva sarvaṁ paramātma-bhūtaḥ

SYNONYMS

dṛṣṭam—experienced by direct perception; *śrutam*—experienced by hearing; *bhūta*—past; *bhavat*—present; *bhaviṣyat*—which will be in the future; *sthāsnuḥ*—immovable; *cariṣṇuḥ*—movable; *mahat*—the greatest; *alpakam*—the smallest; *vā*—or; *vinā*—except; *acyutāt*—the infallible Personality of Godhead; *vastu-tarām*—anything else; *na vācyam*—not to be spoken; *saḥ*—that Supreme Personality of Godhead; *eva*—certainly; *sarvam*—everything; *paramātma-bhūtaḥ*—the origin of all causes.

TRANSLATION

" 'Lord Śrī Kṛṣṇa, the Supreme Personality of Godhead, is the cause of all causes. He is past, present and future, and He is the movable and immovable. He is the greatest and the smallest, and He is visible and directly experienced. He is celebrated in Vedic literature. Everything is Kṛṣṇa, and without Him there is no existence. He is the root of all understanding, and He is that which is understood by all words.'

PURPORT

This verse from *Śrīmad-Bhāgavatam* (10.46.43) was spoken by Uddhava when he came to pacify all the inhabitants of Vṛndāvana during Kṛṣṇa's absence.

TEXT 38

তদ্বা ইদং ভুবনমঙ্গল মঙ্গলায়
ধ্যানে স্ম নো দরশিতং ত উপাসকানাম্ ।
তস্মৈ নমো ভগবতেঽনুবিধেম তুভ্যং
যোঽনাদৃতো নরকভাগ্ভিরসৎপ্রসঙ্গৈঃ ॥ ৩৮ ॥

tad vā idaṁ bhuvana-maṅgala maṅgalāya
dhyāne sma no daraśitaṁ ta upāsakānām
tasmai namo bhagavate 'nuvidhema tubhyaṁ
yo 'nādṛto naraka-bhāgbhir asat-prasaṅgaiḥ

SYNONYMS

tat—that; *vā*—or; *idam*—this; *bhuvana-maṅgala*—O most auspicious of the entire world; *maṅgalāya*—for the benefit; *dhyāne*—in meditation; *sma*—certainly; *naḥ*—of us; *daraśitam*—manifested; *te*—by You; *upāsakānām*—of devotees engaged in devotional service; *tasmai*—unto Him; *namaḥ*—all obeisances; *bhagavate*—the Supreme Personality of Godhead; *anuvidhema*—we offer obeisances, following in the footsteps of the *ācāryas; tubhyam*—unto You; *yaḥ*—who is; *anādṛtaḥ*—not much appreciated; *naraka-bhāgbhiḥ*—by persons who are destined to go to a hellish condition of life; *asat-prasaṅgaiḥ*—who discuss the Supreme Personality of Godhead illogically.

TRANSLATION

" 'O most auspicious one! For our benefit You are worshiped by us. You manifest Your transcendental form, which You show to us in our meditation. We offer our respectful obeisances unto You, the Supreme Person, and we worship You whom impersonalists do not accept due to their poor fund of knowledge. Thus they are liable to descend into a hellish condition.'

PURPORT

This is a quotation from *Śrīmad-Bhāgavatam* (3.9.4).

TEXT 39

অবজানন্তি মাং মূঢ়া মানুষীং তনুমাশ্রিতম্ ।
পরং ভাবমজানন্তো মম ভূতমহেশ্বরম্ ॥ ৩৯ ॥

avajānanti māṁ mūḍhā
mānuṣīṁ tanum āśritam

paraṁ bhāvam ajānanto
mama bhūta-maheśvaram

SYNONYMS

avajānanti—decry; *mām*—Me; *mūḍhāḥ*—rascals; *mānuṣīm*—just like a human being; *tanum*—a body; *āśritam*—accepted; *param*—supreme; *bhāvam*—position; *ajānantaḥ*—without knowing; *mama*—My; *bhūta-maheśvaram*—exalted position as the Supreme Person, creator of the material world.

TRANSLATION

" 'Fools disrespect Me because I appear like a human being. They do not know My supreme position as the cause of all causes, the creator of the material energy.'

PURPORT

This is a quotation from *Bhagavad-gītā* (9.11).

TEXT 40

তানহং দ্বিষতঃ ক্রূরান্ সংসারেষু নরাধমান্ ।
ক্ষিপাম্যজস্রমশুভানাসুরীষ্বেব যোনিষু ॥ ৪০ ॥

tān ahaṁ dviṣataḥ krūrān
saṁsāreṣu narādhamān
kṣipāmy ajasram aśubhān
āsurīṣv eva yoniṣu

SYNONYMS

tān—all of them; *aham*—I; *dviṣataḥ*—those who are envious; *krūrān*—always willing to do harm; *saṁsāreṣu*—in this material world; *nara-adhamān*—the lowest of men; *kṣipāmi*—throw; *ajasram*—again and again; *aśubhān*—engaged in inauspicious acts; *āsurīṣu*—demoniac; *eva*—certainly; *yoniṣu*—in families.

TRANSLATION

" 'Those who are envious of My form, who are cruel and mischievous and lowest among men, are perpetually cast by Me into hellish existence in various demoniac species of life.'

PURPORT

This is also a quotation from *Bhagavad-gītā* (16.19).

TEXT 41

সূত্রের পরিণাম-বাদ, তাহা না মানিয়া।
'বিবর্তবাদ' স্থাপে, 'ব্যাস ভ্রান্ত' বলিয়া ॥ ৪১ ॥

sūtrera pariṇāma-vāda, tāhā nā māniyā
'vivarta-vāda' sthāpe, 'vyāsa bhrānta' baliyā

SYNONYMS

sūtrera—of the codes of the *Vedānta-sūtra; pariṇāma-vāda*—the transformation of energy; *tāhā nā māniyā*—not accepting this fact; *vivarta-vāda*—the theory of illusion; *sthāpe*—establishes; *vyāsa bhrānta baliyā*—accusing Vyāsadeva to be mistaken.

TRANSLATION

"Not accepting the transformation of energy, Śrīpād Śaṅkarācārya has tried to establish the theory of illusion under the plea that Vyāsadeva has made a mistake.

PURPORT

For a further explanation of this verse, one may refer to Chapter Seven (verses 121-126).

TEXT 42

এই ত' কল্পিত অর্থ মনে নাহি ভায়।
শাস্ত্র ছাড়ি' কুকল্পনা পাষণ্ডে বুঝায় ॥ ৪২ ॥

ei ta' kalpita artha mane nāhi bhāya
śāstra chāḍi' kukalpanā pāṣaṇḍe bujhāya

SYNONYMS

ei ta'—this; *kalpita*—imaginary; *artha*—meaning; *mane*—to the mind; *nāhi*—does not; *bhāya*—appeal; *śāstra*—the authoritative scriptures; *chāḍi'*—giving up; *ku-kalpanā*—mischievous imagination; *pāṣaṇḍe*—to the atheistic class of men; *bujhāya*—teaches.

TRANSLATION

"Śrīpād Śaṅkarācārya has given his interpretation and imaginary meaning. It does not actually appeal to the mind of any sane man. He has done this to convince the atheists and bring them under his control.

PURPORT

Śrīpād Śaṅkarācārya's propaganda opposed the atheistic philosophy of Buddha. Lord Buddha's intention was to stop atheists from committing the sin of killing animals. Atheists cannot understand God; therefore Lord Buddha appeared and spread the philosophy of nonviolence to keep the atheists from killing animals. Unless one is free from the sin of animal killing, he cannot understand religion or God. Although Lord Buddha was an incarnation of Kṛṣṇa, he did not speak about God, for the people were unable to understand. He simply wanted to stop animal killing. Śrīpād Śaṅkarācārya wanted to establish the predominance of one's spiritual identity; therefore he wanted to convert the atheists through an imaginary interpretation of Vedic literatures. These are the secrets of the *ācāryas*. Sometimes they conceal the real purpose of the *Vedas* and explain the *Vedas* in a different way. Sometimes they enunciate a different theory just to bring the atheists under their control. Thus it is said that Śaṅkara's philosophy is for *pāṣaṇḍas,* atheists.

TEXT 43

পরমার্থ-বিচার গেল, করি মাত্র 'বাদ'।
কাহাঁ মুক্তি পাব, কাহাঁ কৃষ্ণের প্রসাদ ॥ ৪৩ ॥

paramārtha-vicāra gela, kari mātra 'vāda'
kāhāṅ mukti pāba, kāhāṅ kṛṣṇera prasāda

SYNONYMS

parama-artha-vicāra—discussion on spiritual matters; *gela*—has gone; *kari*—we do; *mātra vāda*—only argument and word jugglery; *kāhāṅ*—where; *mukti*—liberation; *pāba*—we shall get; *kāhāṅ*—where; *kṛṣṇera prasāda*—the mercy of the Supreme Personality of Godhead, Kṛṣṇa.

TRANSLATION

"The atheists, headed by the Māyāvādī philosophers, do not care for liberation or Kṛṣṇa's mercy. They simply continue to put forward false arguments and counter-theories to atheistic philosophy, not considering or engaging in spiritual matters.

TEXT 44

ব্যাসসূত্রের অর্থ আচার্য করিয়াছে আচ্ছাদন।
এই হয় সত্য শ্রীকৃষ্ণচৈতন্য-বচন ॥ ৪৪ ॥

vyāsa-sūtrera artha ācārya kariyāche ācchādana
ei haya satya śrī-kṛṣṇa-caitanya-vacana

SYNONYMS

vyāsa-sūtrera—of the codes of the Vedānta known as *Vyāsa-sūtra; artha*—the meanings; *ācārya*—Śaṅkarācārya; *kariyāche ācchādana*—has purposely covered; *ei*—this; *haya*—is; *sayta*—the truth; *śrī-kṛṣṇa-caitanya-vacana*—the words and explanation given by Lord Śrī Caitanya Mahāprabhu.

TRANSLATION

"The conclusion is that the import of the Vedānta-sūtra is covered by the imaginary explanation of Śaṅkarācārya. Whatever Śrī Kṛṣṇa Caitanya Mahāprabhu has said is perfectly true.

TEXT 45

চৈতন্য-গোসাঞি যেই কহে, সেই মত সার ।
আর যত মত, সেই সব ছারখার ॥" ৪৫ ॥

caitanya-gosāñi yei kahe, sei mata sāra
āra yata mata, sei saba chārakhāra"

SYNONYMS

caitanya-gosāñi—Śrī Caitanya Mahāprabhu; *yei kahe*—whatever He has said; *sei mata sāra*—that explanation is actually the essence of Vedic knowledge; *āra yata mata*—any other opinion not in collaboration with Śrī Caitanya Mahāprabhu's statement; *sei*—these; *saba chārakhāra*—all distortions.

TRANSLATION

"Whatever meaning Śrī Caitanya Mahāprabhu gives is perfect. Any other interpretation is only a distortion."

TEXT 46

এত কহি' সেই করে কৃষ্ণসংকীর্তন ।
শুনি' প্রকাশানন্দ কিছু কহেন বচন ॥ ৪৬ ॥

eta kahi' sei kare kṛṣṇa-saṅkīrtana
śuni' prakāśānanda kichu kahena vacana

SYNONYMS

eta kahi'—speaking so much; *sei*—the disciple of Prakāśānanda Sarasvatī; *kare*—performed; *kṛṣṇa-saṅkīrtana*—the chanting of the holy name of Kṛṣṇa; *śuni'*—hearing; *prakāśānanda*—the *guru,* Prakāśānanda Sarasvatī; *kichu*—something; *kahena*—says; *vacana*—words.

TRANSLATION

After saying this, the disciple of Prakāśānanda Sarasvatī began to chant the holy name of Kṛṣṇa. Hearing this, Prakāśānanda Sarasvatī made the following statement.

TEXT 47

আচার্যের আগ্রহ—'অদ্বৈতবাদ' স্থাপিতে ।
তাতে সূত্রার্থ ব্যাখ্যা করে অন্য রীতে ॥ ৪৭ ॥

ācāryera āgraha——'advaita-vāda' sthāpite
tāte sūtrārtha vyākhyā kare anya rīte

SYNONYMS

ācāryera—of Śaṅkarācārya; *āgraha*—the eagerness; *advaita-vāda*—monism; *sthāpite*—to establish; *tāte*—for that reason; *sūtra-artha*—the meaning of the *Brahma-sūtra,* or Vedānta philosophy; *vyākhyā*—explanation; *kare*—does; *anya rīte*—in a different way.

TRANSLATION

Prakāśānanda Sarasvatī said, "Śaṅkarācārya was very eager to establish the philosophy of monism. Therefore he explained Vedānta-sūtra, or Vedānta philosophy, in a different way to support monistic philosophy.

TEXT 48

'ভগবত্তা' মানিলে 'অদ্বৈত' না যায় স্থাপন ।
অতএব সব শাস্ত্র করয়ে খণ্ডন ॥ ৪৮ ॥

'bhagavattā' mānile 'advaita' nā yāya sthāpana
ataeva saba śāstra karaye khaṇḍana

SYNONYMS

bhagavattā—the Personality of Godhead; *mānile*—if one accepts; *advaita*—monism or nondualism; *nā*—not; *yāya*—is possible; *sthāpana*—establishing;

ataeva—therefore; *saba*—all; *śāstra*—revealed scriptures; *karaye*—does; *khaṇḍana*—refutation.

TRANSLATION

"If one accepts the Personality of Godhead, the philosophy that maintains that God and the living entity are one cannot be established. Therefore Śaṅkarācārya argued against and refuted all kinds of revealed scriptures.

TEXT 49

যেই গ্রন্থকর্তা চাহে স্ব-মত স্থাপিতে ।
শাস্ত্রের সহজ অর্থ নহে তাঁহা হৈতে ॥ ৪৯ ॥

yei grantha-kartā cāhe sva-mata sthāpite
śāstrera sahaja artha nahe tāṅhā haite

SYNONYMS

yei—anyone who; *grantha-kartā*—author; *cāhe*—wants; *sva-mata sthāpite*—to establish his own opinion; *śāstrera*—of the revealed scriptures; *sahaja*—the direct; *artha*—meaning; *nahe*—is not; *tāṅhā haite*—from such an author.

TRANSLATION

"Anyone who wants to establish his own opinion or philosophy certainly cannot explain any scripture according to the principle of direct interpretation.

TEXT 50

'মীমাংসক' কহে,—'ঈশ্বর হয় কর্মের অঙ্গ' ।
'সাংখ্য' কহে,—'জগতের প্রকৃতি কারণ-প্রসঙ্গ' ॥ ৫০

'mīmāṁsaka' kahe,——'īśvara haya karmera aṅga'
'sāṅkhya' kahe,——'jagatera prakṛti kāraṇa-prasaṅga'

SYNONYMS

mīmāṁsaka—the Mīmāṁsaka philosophers; *kahe*—say; *īśvara*—the Supreme Lord; *haya*—is; *karmera aṅga*—subject to fruitive activities; *sāṅkhya kahe*—the atheistic Sāṅkhya philosophers say; *jagatera*—of the cosmic manifestation; *prakṛti*—nature; *kāraṇa*—the cause; *prasaṅga*—thesis.

TRANSLATION

"The Mīmāṁsaka philosophers conclude that if there is a God, He is subjected to our fruitive activities. Similarly, the Sāṅkhya philosophers who analyze the cosmic manifestation say that the cause of the cosmos is material nature.

TEXT 51

'ন্যায়' কহে,—'পরমাণু হৈতে বিশ্ব হয়'।
'মায়াবাদী' নির্বিশেষ-ব্রহ্মে 'হেতু' কয় ॥ ৫১ ॥

'nyāya' kahe,——'paramāṇu haite viśva haya'
'māyāvādī' nirviśeṣa-brahme 'hetu' kaya

SYNONYMS

nyāya kahe—the philosophers following logic say; *paramāṇu*—the atom; *haite*—from; *viśva haya*—the cosmic manifestation has come; *māyāvādī*—the Māyāvādī philosophers, impersonalists; *nirviśeṣa-brahme*—in the impersonal Brahman effulgence; *hetu*—the cause; *kaya*—say.

TRANSLATION

"The followers of nyāya, the philosophy of logic, maintain that the atom is the cause of the cosmic manifestation, and the Māyāvādī philosophers maintain that the impersonal Brahman effulgence is the cause of the cosmic manifestation.

TEXT 52

'পাতঞ্জল' কহে,—'ঈশ্বর হয় স্বরূপ-জ্ঞান'।
বেদমতে কহে তাঁরে 'স্বয়ংভগবান্' ॥ ৫২ ॥

'pātañjala' kahe,——'īśvara haya svarūpa-jñāna'
veda-mate kahe tāṅre 'svayaṁ-bhagavān'

SYNONYMS

pātañjala kahe—the Pātañjala philosophers say; *īśvara haya*—the Supreme Lord is; *svarūpa-jñāna*—self-realization; *veda-mate*—in the Vedic version; *kahe*—they say; *tāṅre*—to Him; *svayam-bhagavān*—the Supreme Personality of Godhead.

TRANSLATION

"The Pātañjala philosophers say that when one is self-realized, he understands the Lord. Similarly, according to the Vedas and Vedic principles, the original cause is the Supreme Personality of Godhead.

TEXT 53

ছয়ের ছয় মত ব্যাস কৈলা আবর্তন ।
সেই সব সূত্র লঞা 'বেদান্ত'-বর্ণন ॥ ৫৩ ॥

chayera chaya mata vyāsa kailā āvartana
sei saba sūtra lañā 'vedānta'-varṇana

SYNONYMS

chayera—of the six philosophers; *chaya mata*—six different theses; *vyāsa*—Vyāsadeva; *kailā āvartana*—analyzed fully; *sei*—that; *saba*—all; *sūtra*—the codes; *lañā*—taking; *vedānta-varṇana*—explaining the Vedānta philosophy.

TRANSLATION

"After studying the six philosophical theses, Vyāsadeva completely summarized them all in the codes of Vedānta philosophy.

TEXT 54

'বেদান্ত'-মতে,—ব্রহ্ম 'সাকার' নিরূপণ ।
'নির্গুণ' ব্যতিরেকে তিঁহো হয় ত' 'সগুণ' ॥ ৫৪ ॥

'vedānta'-mate,——brahma 'sākāra' nirūpaṇa
'nirguṇa' vyatireke tiṅho haya ta' 'saguṇa'

SYNONYMS

vedānta-mate—according to Vedānta philosophy; *brahma*—the Absolute Truth; *sa-ākāra nirūpaṇa*—established as the Supreme Personality of Godhead, a person; *nirguṇa*—without material qualifications; *vyatireke*—by indirect explanations; *tiṅho*—the Supreme Personality of Godhead; *haya*—is; *ta'*—indeed; *saguṇa*—fully qualified with spiritual attributes.

TRANSLATION

"According to Vedānta philosophy, the Absolute Truth is a person. When the word nirguṇa [without qualities] is used, it is to be understood that the Lord has attributes that are totally spiritual.

TEXT 55

পরম কারণ ঈশ্বর কেহ নাহি মানে ।
স্ব-স্ব-মত স্থাপে পরমতের খণ্ডনে ॥ ৫৫ ॥

parama kāraṇa īśvara keha nāhi māne
sva-sva-mata sthāpe para-matera khaṇḍane

SYNONYMS

parama kāraṇa—the supreme cause, the cause of all causes; *īśvara*—the Supreme Lord; *keha nāhi māne*—none of the above-mentioned philosophers accept; *sva-sva-mata*—their own personal opinions; *sthāpe*—they establish; *para-matera khaṇḍane*—busy in refuting the opinions of others.

TRANSLATION

"Of the philosophers mentioned, none really cares for the Supreme Personality of Godhead, the cause of all causes. They are always busy refuting the philosophical theories of others and establishing their own.

TEXT 56

তাতে ছয় দর্শন হৈতে 'তত্ত্ব' নাহি জানি ।
'মহাজন' যেই কহে, সেই 'সত্য' মানি ॥ ৫৬ ॥

tāte chaya darśana haite 'tattva' nāhi jāni
'mahājana' yei kahe, sei 'satya' māni

SYNONYMS

tāte—therefore; *chaya darśana haite*—from the six philosophical principles; *tattva nāhi jāni*—we cannot understand the actual truth; *mahājana*—the great authorities; *yei kahe*—whatever they say; *sei*—that; *satya māni*—we can accept as truth.

TRANSLATION

"By studying the six philosophical theories, one cannot reach the Absolute Truth. It is therefore our duty to follow the path of the mahājanas, the authorities. Whatever they say should be accepted as the supreme truth.

PURPORT

In his *Amṛta-pravāha-bhāṣya,* Śrīla Bhaktivinoda Ṭhākura gives the following summary of the six philosophical processes. Prakāśānanda admitted that Śrīpād Śaṅkarācārya, being very eager to establish his philosophy of monism, took shelter of the Vedānta philosophy and tried to explain it in his own way. The fact is, however, that if one accepts the existence of God, he certainly cannot establish the theory of monism. For this reason Śaṅkarācārya refuted all kinds of Vedic literature that establishes the supremacy of the Personality of Godhead. In various ways, Śaṅkarācārya has tried to refute Vedic literature. Throughout the world, ninety-nine percent of the philosophers following in the footsteps of Śaṅkarācārya refuse to accept the Supreme Personality of Godhead. Instead they try to establish their own opinions. It is typical of mundane philosophers to want to establish their own opinions and refute those of others. Therefore: (1) The Mīmāṁsaka philosophers, following the principles of Jaimini, stress fruitive activity and say that if there is a God, He must be under the laws of fruitive activity. In other words, if one performs his duties very nicely in the material world, God is obliged to give one the desired result. According to these philosophers, there is no need to become a devotee of God. If one strictly follows moral principles, one will be recognized by the Lord, who will give the desired reward. Such philosophers do not accept the Vedic principle of *bhakti-yoga*. Instead, they give stress to following one's prescribed duty. (2) Atheistic Sāṅkhya philosophers like Kapila analyze the material elements very scrutinizingly and thereby come to the conclusion that material nature is the cause of everything. They do not accept the Supreme Personality of Godhead as the cause of all causes. (3) Nyāya philosophers like Gautama and Kaṇāda have accepted a combination of atoms as the original cause of the creation. (4) Māyāvādī philosophers say that everything is an illusion. Headed by philosophers like Aṣṭāvakra, they stress the impersonal Brahman effulgence as the cause of everything. (5) Philosophers following the precepts of Patañjali practice *rāja-yoga*. They imagine a form of the Absolute Truth within many forms. That is their process of self-realization.

All five of these philosophies completely reject the predominance of the Supreme Personality of Godhead and strive to establish their own philosophical theories. However, Śrīla Vyāsadeva wrote the *Vedānta-sūtra* and, taking the essence of all Vedic literature, established the supremacy of the Supreme Personality of Godhead. All five of the philosophers mentioned above understand that impersonal Brahman is without material qualities, and they believe that when the Personality of Godhead appears, He is contaminated and covered by the material qualities. The technical term used is *saguṇa*. They say, "*saguṇa* Brahman" and "*nirguṇa* Brahman." *Nirguṇa* Brahman means impersonal, and *saguṇa* Brahman means "accepting material contamination." More or less, this kind of philosophical speculation is called Māyāvāda philosophy. The fact is, however, that the Absolute Truth has nothing to do with material qualities because He is transcendental. He is always complete with full spiritual qualities. The five philosophers mentioned above do not accept Lord Viṣṇu as the Supreme Personality of Godhead, but they are very busy refuting the philosophy of other schools. There are six kinds of philosophical processes in India. Because Vyāsadeva is the Vedic authority, he is known as Vedavyāsa. His philosophical explanation of the *Vedānta-sūtra* is accepted by the devotees. As Kṛṣṇa confirms in *Bhagavad-gītā* (15.15):

sarvasya cāhaṁ hṛdi sanniviṣṭo
mattaḥ smṛtir jñānam apohanaṁ ca
vedaiś ca sarvair aham eva vedyo
vedānta-kṛd veda-vid eva cāham

"I am seated in everyone's heart, and from Me come remembrance, knowledge and forgetfulness. By all the *Vedas,* I am to be known; indeed, I am the compiler of Vedānta, and I am the knower of the *Vedas.*"

The ultimate goal of studying all Vedic literature is the acceptance of Kṛṣṇa as the Supreme Personality of Godhead. This Kṛṣṇa consciousness movement is propagating the philosophical conclusion of Śrīla Vyāsadeva and following other great *ācāryas* like Rāmānujācārya, Madhvācārya, Viṣṇusvāmī, Nimbārka and Śrī Caitanya Mahāprabhu Himself.

TEXT 57

তর্কোঽপ্রতিষ্ঠঃ শ্রুতয়ো বিভিন্না
নাসাবৃষির্যস্য মতং ন ভিন্নম্ ।
ধর্মস্য তত্ত্বং নিহিতং গুহায়াং
মহাজনো যেন গতঃ স পন্থাঃ ॥ ৫৭ ॥

tarko 'pratiṣṭhaḥ śrutayo vibhinnā
nāsāv ṛṣir yasya mataṁ na bhinnam
dharmasya tattvaṁ nihitaṁ guhāyāṁ
mahājano yena gataḥ sa panthāḥ

SYNONYMS

tarkaḥ—dry argument; *apratiṣṭhaḥ*—not fixed; *śrutayaḥ*—*Vedas; vibhinnāḥ*—possessing different departments; *na*—not; *asau*—that; *ṛṣiḥ*—great sage; *yasya*—whose; *matam*—opinion; *na*—not; *bhinnam*—separate; *dharmasya*—of religious principles; *tattvam*—truth; *nihitam*—placed; *guhāyām*—in the heart of a realized person; *mahā-janaḥ*—self-realized predecessors; *yena*—by which way; *gataḥ*—acted; *saḥ*—that; *panthāḥ*—the pure, unadulterated path.

TRANSLATION

" 'Dry arguments are inconclusive. A great personality whose opinion does not differ from others is not considered a great sage. Simply by studying the Vedas, which are variegated, one cannot come to the right path by which religious principles are understood. The solid truth of religious principles is hidden in the heart of an unadulterated self-realized person. Consequently, as the śāstras confirm, one should accept whatever progressive path the mahājanas advocate.'

PURPORT

This is a verse spoken by Yudhiṣṭhira Mahārāja in the *Mahābhārata, Vana-parva* (313.117).

TEXT 58

শ্রীকৃষ্ণচৈতন্য-বাণী—অমৃতের ধার।
তিঁহো যে কহয়ে বস্তু, সেই 'তত্ত্ব'—সার॥" ৫৮॥

śrī-kṛṣṇa-caitanya-vāṇī——amṛtera dhāra
tiṅho ye kahaye vastu, sei 'tattva'——sāra"

SYNONYMS

śrī-kṛṣṇa-caitanya-vāṇī—the message of Lord Śrī Caitanya Mahāprabhu; *amṛtera dhāra*—a continuous shower of nectar; *tiṅho*—the Lord; *ye kahaye vastu*—whatever He says to be the ultimate truth, the *summum bonum; sei tattva sāra*—that is the essence of all spiritual knowledge.

TRANSLATION

"The words of Śrī Caitanya Mahāprabhu are a shower of nectar. Whatever He concludes to be the ultimate truth is indeed the summum bonum of all spiritual knowledge."

TEXT 59

এ সব বৃত্তান্ত শুনি' মহারাষ্ট্রীয় ব্রাহ্মণ।
প্রভুরে কহিতে সুখে করিলা গমন॥ ৫৯॥

e saba vṛttānta śuni' mahārāṣṭrīya brāhmaṇa
prabhure kahite sukhe karilā gamana

SYNONYMS

e saba vṛttānta—all these descriptions; *śuni'*—hearing; *mahārāṣṭrīya brāhmaṇa*—the Mahārāṣṭrian *brāhmaṇa; prabhure*—Lord Śrī Caitanya Mahāprabhu; *kahite*—to inform; *sukhe*—very happily; *karilā gamana*—went.

TRANSLATION

After hearing all these statements, the Mahārāṣṭrian brāhmaṇa very jubilantly went to inform Lord Śrī Caitanya Mahāprabhu.

TEXT 60

হেনকালে মহাপ্রভু পঞ্চনদে স্নান করি' ।
দেখিতে চলিয়াছেন 'বিন্দুমাধব হরি' ॥ ৬০ ॥

hena-kāle mahāprabhu pañca-nade snāna kari'
dekhite caliyāchena 'bindu-mādhava hari'

SYNONYMS

hena-kāle—at this time; *mahāprabhu*—Śrī Caitanya Mahāprabhu; *pañca-nade snāna kari'*—taking His bath in the Ganges, called the Pañca-nada; *dekhite caliyāchena*—was going to see; *bindu-mādhava hari*—the Deity known as Lord Bindu Mādhava.

TRANSLATION

When the Mahārāṣṭrian brāhmaṇa went to see Caitanya Mahāprabhu, the Lord was going to the temple of Bindu Mādhava after bathing in the waters of Pañca-nada.

TEXT 61

পথে সেই বিপ্র সব বৃত্তান্ত কহিল ।
শুনি' মহাপ্রভু সুখে ঈষৎ হাসিল ॥ ৬১ ॥

pathe sei vipra saba vṛttānta kahila
śuni' mahāprabhu sukhe īṣat hāsila

SYNONYMS

pathe—on the way; *sei vipra*—that *brāhmaṇa; saba vṛttānta kahila*—explained the whole incident; *śuni'*—hearing; *mahāprabhu*—Śrī Caitanya Mahāprabhu; *sukhe*—in happiness; *īṣat*—mildly; *hāsila*—smiled.

TRANSLATION

While the Lord was on His way, the Mahārāṣṭrian brāhmaṇa informed Him about the incident that took place in the camp of Prakāśānanda Sarasvatī. Hearing this, Śrī Caitanya Mahāprabhu smiled happily.

TEXT 62

মাধব-সৌন্দর্য দেখি' আবিষ্ট হইলা ।
অঙ্গনেতে আসি' প্রেমে নাচিতে লাগিলা ॥ ৬২ ॥

mādhava-saundarya dekhi' āviṣṭa ha-ilā
aṅganete āsi' preme nācite lāgilā

SYNONYMS

mādhava-saundarya dekhi'—after seeing the beauty of Lord Bindu Mādhava; *āviṣṭa ha-ilā*—became ecstatic in love; *aṅganete āsi'*—coming to the courtyard; *preme*—in great love; *nācite lāgilā*—began to dance.

TRANSLATION

Upon reaching the temple of Bindu Mādhava, Śrī Caitanya Mahāprabhu, seeing the beauty of Lord Bindu Mādhava, became overwhelmed in ecstatic love. He then began to dance in the courtyard of the temple.

TEXT 63

শেখর, পরমানন্দ, তপন, সনাতন ।
চারিজন মিলি' করে নাম-সংকীর্তন ॥ ৬৩ ॥

śekhara, paramānanda, tapana, sanātana
cāri-jana mili' kare nāma-saṅkīrtana

SYNONYMS

śekhara—Candraśekhara; *paramānanda*—Paramānanda Purī; *tapana*—Tapana Miśra; *sanātana*—Sanātana Gosvāmī; *cāri-jana mili'*—all four of them; *kare*—perform; *nāma-saṅkīrtana*—chanting of the Hare Kṛṣṇa *mantra.*

TRANSLATION

There were four people accompanying Śrī Caitanya Mahāprabhu, and these were Candraśekhara, Paramānanda Purī, Tapana Miśra and Sanātana Gosvāmī. They were all chanting the Hare Kṛṣṇa mahā-mantra in the following way.

TEXT 64

“হরয়ে নমঃ কৃষ্ণ যাদবায় নমঃ ।
গোপাল গোবিন্দ রাম শ্রীমধুসূদন ॥” ৬৪ ॥

"haraye namaḥ kṛṣṇa yādavāya namaḥ
gopāla govinda rāma śrī-madhusūdana"

SYNONYMS

haraye—unto the Supreme Personality of Godhead; *namaḥ*—obeisances; *kṛṣṇa*—Lord Kṛṣṇa; *yādavāya*—to the descendant of the Yadu family; *namaḥ*—obeisances; *gopāla*—Gopāla; *govinda*—Govinda; *rāma*—Rāma; *śrī-madhusūdana*—Śrī Madhusūdana.

TRANSLATION

They chanted, "Haraye namaḥ kṛṣṇa yādavāya namaḥ/ gopāla govinda rāma śrī-madhusūdana."

PURPORT

This is another way of chanting the Hare Kṛṣṇa *mahā-mantra.* The meaning is: "I offer my respectful obeisances unto the Supreme Personality of Godhead, Kṛṣṇa. He is the descendant of the Yadu family. Let me offer my respectful obeisances unto Gopāla, Govinda, Rāma and Śrī Madhusūdana."

TEXT 65

চৌদিকেতে লক্ষ লোক বলে 'হরি' 'হরি'।
উঠিল মঙ্গলধ্বনি স্বর্গ-মর্ত্য ভরি' ॥ ৬৫ ॥

caudikete lakṣa loka bale 'hari' 'hari'
uṭhila maṅgala-dhvani svarga-martya bhari'

SYNONYMS

cau-dikete—all around; *lakṣa*—hundreds of thousands; *loka*—people; *bale*—chant; *hari hari*—O Supreme Personality of Godhead, Hari; *uṭhila*—there arose; *maṅgala-dhvani*—an auspicious sound; *svarga-martya bhari'*—overwhelming all the universe.

TRANSLATION

In all directions, hundreds and thousands of people began to chant, "Hari! Hari!" Thus there arose a tumultuous and auspicious sound filling the entire universe.

TEXT 66

নিকটে হরিধ্বনি শুনি' পরকাশানন্দ।
দেখিতে কৌতুকে আইলা লঞা শিষ্যবৃন্দ ॥ ৬৬ ॥

nikaṭe hari-dhvani śuni' parakāśānanda
dekhite kautuke āilā lañā śiṣya-vṛnda

SYNONYMS

nikaṭe—nearby; *hari-dhvani śuni'*—after hearing the chanting of the Hare Kṛṣṇa *mahā-mantra; parakāśānanda*—Prakāśānanda Sarasvatī; *dekhite*—to see; *kautuke*—in great eagerness; *āilā*—came; *lañā*—taking; *śiṣya-vṛnda*—all the disciples.

TRANSLATION

When Prakāśānanda Sarasvatī, who was staying nearby, heard this tumultuous chanting of the Hare Kṛṣṇa mahā-mantra, he and his disciples immediately came to see the Lord.

TEXT 67

দেখিয়া প্রভুর নৃত্য, প্রেম, দেহের মাধুরী ।
শিষ্যগণ-সঙ্গে সেই বলে 'হরি' 'হরি' ॥ ৬৭ ॥

dekhiyā prabhura nṛtya, prema, dehera mādhurī
śiṣya-gaṇa-saṅge sei bale 'hari' 'hari'

SYNONYMS

dekhiyā—seeing; *prabhura nṛtya*—the dancing of Śrī Caitanya Mahāprabhu; *prema*—ecstatic love; *dehera mādhurī*—the transcendental beauty of His body; *śiṣya-gaṇa-saṅge*—with his disciples; *sei*—Prakāśānanda Sarasvatī; *bale*—chants; *hari hari*—Lord Hari's name.

TRANSLATION

When Prakāśānanda Sarasvatī saw the Lord, he and his disciples also joined the chanting with Śrī Caitanya Mahāprabhu. Prakāśānanda Sarasvatī was charmed by the Lord's dancing and ecstatic love and by the transcendental beauty of His body.

TEXT 68

কম্প, স্বরভঙ্গ, স্বেদ, বৈবর্ণ্য, স্তম্ভ ।
অশ্রুধারায় ভিজে লোক, পুলক-কদম্ব ॥ ৬৮ ॥

kampa, svara-bhaṅga, sveda, vaivarṇya, stambha
aśru-dhārāya bhije loka, pulaka-kadamba

SYNONYMS

kampa—trembling; *svara-bhaṅga*—faltering voice; *sveda*—perspiration; *vaivarṇya*—fading of bodily color; *stambha*—becoming stunned; *aśru-dhārāya*—with showers of tears from the eyes; *bhije*—wet; *loka*—all the people; *pulaka-kadamba*—eruptions on the body like *kadamba* flowers.

TRANSLATION

Ecstatic spiritual transformations began to take place in the Lord's body. His body trembled, and His voice faltered. He perspired, turned pale and wept a constant flow of tears, which wet all the people standing there. The eruptions on the Lord's body appeared like kadamba flowers.

TEXT 69

হর্ষ, দৈন্য, চাপল্যাদি 'সঞ্চারী' বিকার ।
দেখি' কাশীবাসী লোকের হৈল চমৎকার ॥ ৬৯ ॥

harṣa, dainya, cāpalyādi 'sañcārī' vikāra
dekhi' kāśī-vāsī lokera haila camatkāra

SYNONYMS

harṣa—jubilation; *dainya*—humility; *cāpalya-ādi*—talking in ecstasy and so on; *sañcārī vikāra*—the transient transformations; *dekhi'*—seeing; *kāśī-vāsī*—the inhabitants of Benares; *lokera*—of all the people; *haila camatkāra*—there was astonishment.

TRANSLATION

All the people were astonished to see the Lord's jubilation and humility and to hear Him talk in ecstasy. Indeed, all the residents of Benares [Kāśī] saw the bodily transformations and were astonished.

TEXT 70

লোকসংঘট্ট দেখি' প্রভুর 'বাহ্য' যবে হৈল ।
সন্ন্যাসীর গণ দেখি' নৃত্য সম্বরিল ॥ ৭০ ॥

loka-saṅghaṭṭa dekhi' prabhura 'bāhya' yabe haila
sannyāsīra gaṇa dekhi' nṛtya saṁvarila

SYNONYMS

loka-saṅghaṭṭa dekhi'—by seeing the great crowd of people; *prabhura*—of Lord Caitanya; *bāhya*—external consciousness; *yabe haila*—when there was; *sannyāsīra gaṇa*—the groups of Māyāvādī *sannyāsīs,* headed by Prakāśānanda Sarasvatī; *dekhi'*—seeing; *nṛtya saṁvarila*—suspended His dancing.

TRANSLATION

When Śrī Caitanya Mahāprabhu regained His external consciousness, He saw that many Māyāvādī sannyāsīs and other people were gathered there. He therefore suspended His dancing for the time being.

TEXT 71

প্রকাশানন্দের প্রভু বন্দিলা চরণ ।
প্রকাশানন্দ আসি' তাঁর ধরিল চরণ ॥ ৭১ ॥

prakāśānandera prabhu vandilā caraṇa
prakāśānanda āsi' tāṅra dharila caraṇa

SYNONYMS

prakāśānandera—of Prakāśānanda Sarasvatī; *prabhu*—Śrī Caitanya Mahāprabhu; *vandilā*—prayed; *caraṇa*—at the feet; *prakāśānanda*—Prakāśānanda Sarasvatī; *āsi'*—coming; *tāṅra*—His; *dharila caraṇa*—immediately caught the lotus feet.

TRANSLATION

After stopping the kīrtana, Śrī Caitanya Mahāprabhu, who is a great example of humility, offered prayers unto the feet of Prakāśānanda Sarasvatī. At this, Prakāśānanda Sarasvatī immediately came forward and clasped the Lord's lotus feet.

TEXT 72

প্রভু কহে,—'তুমি জগদ্‌গুরু পূজ্যতম ।
আমি তোমার না হই 'শিষ্যের শিষ্য' সম ॥ ৭২ ॥

prabhu kahe,—'tumi jagad-guru pūjyatama
āmi tomāra nā ha-i 'śiṣyera śiṣya' sama

SYNONYMS

prabhu kahe—Śrī Caitanya Mahāprabhu continued to speak; *tumi*—you; *jagat-guru*—the spiritual master of the whole world; *pūjya-tama*—the most worshipable; *āmi*—I; *tomāra*—your; *nā ha-i*—am not; *śiṣyera śiṣya sama*—equal to the disciple of the disciple.

TRANSLATION

When Prakāśānanda Sarasvatī caught hold of the Lord's lotus feet, the Lord said, "My dear sir, you are the spiritual master of the whole world; therefore you are most worshipable. As far as I am concerned, I am not even on the level of the disciple of your disciple."

PURPORT

Māyāvādī *sannyāsīs* generally call themselves *jagad-guru,* the spiritual master of the whole world. Many consider themselves worshipable by everyone, although they do not even go outside India or their own district. Out of His great magnanimity and humility, Śrī Caitanya Mahāprabhu presented Himself as a subordinate disciple of Prakāśānanda Sarasvatī.

TEXT 73

শ্রেষ্ঠ হঞা কেনে কর হীনের বন্দন।
আমার সর্বনাশ হয়, তুমি ব্রহ্ম-সম ॥ ৭৩ ॥

śreṣṭha hañā kene kara hīnera vandana
āmāra sarva-nāśa haya, tumi brahma-sama

SYNONYMS

śreṣṭha hañā—being a more honorable person; *kene*—why; *kara*—you do; *hīnera*—of an inferior person; *vandana*—worship; *āmāra sarva-nāśa haya*—I become minimized in My strength; *tumi brahma-sama*—you are equal with the impersonal Brahman.

TRANSLATION

Śrī Caitanya Mahāprabhu continued, "You are a great, spiritually advanced personality, and therefore you cannot worship a person like Me. I am far inferior. If you do so, My spiritual power will be diminished, for you are as good as the impersonal Brahman.

TEXT 74

যদ্যপি তোমারে সব ব্রহ্ম-সম ভাসে।
লোকশিক্ষা লাগি' ঐছে করিতে না আইসে ॥' ৭৪ ॥

yadyapi tomāre saba brahma-sama bhāse
loka-śikṣā lāgi' aiche karite nā āise'

SYNONYMS

yadyapi—although; *tomāre*—for you; *saba*—everyone; *brahma-sama*—equal to the impersonal Brahman; *bhāse*—appears; *loka-śikṣā lāgi'*—for the enlightenment of people in general; *aiche*—in such a way; *karite nā āise*—you should not present yourself.

TRANSLATION

"My dear sir, for you everyone is on the level of impersonal Brahman, but for the enlightenment of people in general you should not behave in that way."

TEXT 75

তেঁহো কহে, 'তোমার পূর্বে নিন্দা-অপরাধ যে করিল।
তোমার চরণ-স্পর্শে, সব ক্ষয় গেল ॥ ৭৫ ॥

teṅho kahe, 'tomāra pūrve nindā-aparādha ye karila
tomāra caraṇa-sparśe, saba kṣaya gela

SYNONYMS

teṅho kahe—he replied; *tomāra*—of You; *pūrve*—formerly; *nindā-aparādha*—offenses and blasphemy; *ye karila*—whatever I have done; *tomāra caraṇa-sparśe*—by touching Your lotus feet; *saba kṣaya gela*—the effects of all those offenses have been destroyed.

TRANSLATION

Prakāśānanda Sarasvatī replied, "Formerly I have committed many offenses against You by blaspheming You, but now the effects of my offenses are counteracted by my touching Your lotus feet.

TEXT 76

জীবন্মুক্তা অপি পুনর্যান্তি সংসারবাসনাম্ ।
যদ্যচিন্ত্যমহাশক্তৌ ভগবত্যপরাধিনঃ ॥ ৭৬ ॥

jīvan-muktā api punar
yānti saṁsāra-vāsanām
yady acintya-mahā-śaktau
bhagavaty aparādhinaḥ

SYNONYMS

jīvat-muktāḥ—persons liberated during this life; *api*—also; *punaḥ*—again; *yānti*—go; *saṁsāra-vāsanām*—to desire material enjoyment; *yadi*—if; *acintya-mahā-śaktau*—to the possessor of inconceivable spiritual potency; *bhagavati*—the Supreme Personality of Godhead; *aparādhinaḥ*—offenders.

TRANSLATION

" 'If a person considered liberated in this life commits offenses against the reservoir of inconceivable potencies, the Supreme Personality of Godhead, he will again fall down and desire the material atmosphere for material enjoyment.'

TEXT 77

স বৈ ভগবতঃ শ্রীমৎপাদস্পর্শহতাশুভঃ ।
ভেজে সর্পবপুর্হিত্বা রূপং বিদ্যাধরার্চিতম্ ॥" ৭৭ ॥

sa vai bhagavataḥ śrīmat-
pāda-sparśa-hatāśubhaḥ
bheje sarpa-vapur hitvā
rūpaṁ vidyādharārcitam

SYNONYMS

saḥ—he (the serpent); *vai*—indeed; *bhagavataḥ*—of the Supreme Personality of Godhead, Kṛṣṇa; *śrīmat-pāda-sparśa*—by the touch of the lotus feet; *hata-aśubhaḥ*—relieved from all reactions of sinful life; *bheje*—achieved; *sarpa-vapuḥ*—the body of a snake; *hitvā*—giving up; *rūpam*—beauty; *vidyādhara-arcitam*—suitable for a person of Vidyādhara-loka.

TRANSLATION

" 'Being touched by the lotus feet of Śrī Kṛṣṇa, that serpent was immediately freed from the reactions of his sinful life. Thus the serpent gave up his body and assumed the body of a beautiful Vidyādhara demigod.' "

PURPORT

This is a quotation from *Śrīmad-Bhāgavatam* (10.34.9). The inhabitants of Vṛndāvana, under the leadership of Nanda Mahārāja, once wanted to go to the bank of the Sarasvatī on a pilgrimage. Nanda Mahārāja was fasting, and he lay down near the forest. At that time a serpent, who was formerly cursed by Āṅgirasa Ṛṣi, appeared. This serpent had formerly been named Sudarśana, and he had belonged to the Gandharvaloka planet. However, because he joked with the *ṛṣi,* he was condemned to take on the body of a big snake. When this serpent attacked Nanda Mahārāja, Nanda Mahārāja began to call, "Kṛṣṇa! Help!" Kṛṣṇa immediately appeared and began to kick the serpent with His lotus feet. Due to being touched by the Lord's lotus feet, the serpent was immediately freed from the reactions of his sinful life. Being freed, he again assumed his original form of Sudarśana, the Gandharva.

TEXT 78

প্রভু কহে,—'বিষ্ণু' 'বিষ্ণু', আমি ক্ষুদ্র জীব হীন।
জীবে 'বিষ্ণু' মানি—এই অপরাধ-চিহ্ন ॥ ৭৮ ॥

prabhu kahe,——'viṣṇu' 'viṣṇu', āmi kṣudra jīva hīna
jīve 'viṣṇu' māni——ei aparādha-cihna

SYNONYMS

prabhu kahe—Lord Śrī Caitanya Mahāprabhu said; *viṣṇu viṣṇu*—the holy name of Viṣṇu; *āmi*—I; *kṣudra*—infinitesimal; *jīva*—a living entity; *hīna*—bereft of all good qualities; *jīve*—such a low-grade living entity; *viṣṇu māni*—accepting as Lord Viṣṇu or the Personality of Godhead; *ei aparādha-cihna*—this is a great offense.

TRANSLATION

When Prakāśānanda Sarasvatī supported himself by quoting the verse from Śrīmad-Bhāgavatam, Śrī Caitanya Mahāprabhu immediately protested by uttering the holy name of Lord Viṣṇu. The Lord then presented Himself as a most fallen living entity, and He said, "If someone accepts a fallen conditioned soul as Viṣṇu, Bhagavān, or an incarnation, he commits a great offense."

PURPORT

Although Śrī Caitanya Mahāprabhu was Viṣṇu, the Supreme Personality of Godhead, He nonetheless, to teach us a lesson, denied belonging to the Viṣṇu category. Unfortunately, there are many so-called Viṣṇu incarnations in this age of Kali. People do not know that posing oneself as an incarnation is most offensive. People should not accept an ordinary man as an incarnation of God, for this also is a very great offense.

TEXT 79

জীবে 'বিষ্ণু' বুদ্ধি দূরে—যেই ব্রহ্ম-রুদ্র-সম ।
নারায়ণে মানে তারে 'পাষণ্ডীতে' গণন ॥ ৭৯ ॥

jīve 'viṣṇu' buddhi dūre——yei brahma-rudra-sama
nārāyaṇe māne tāre 'pāṣaṇḍīte' gaṇana

SYNONYMS

jīve—an ordinary living being; *viṣṇu*—as Lord Viṣṇu; *buddhi*—acceptance; *dūre*—let alone; *yei*—anyone who; *brahma-rudra-sama*—equal to personalities like Lord Brahmā and Lord Śiva; *nārāyaṇe*—Lord Nārāyaṇa, Viṣṇu; *māne*—accepts; *tāre*—such a person; *pāṣaṇḍīte gaṇana*—is grouped among the *pāṣaṇḍīs,* atheistic offenders.

TRANSLATION

Śrī Caitanya Mahāprabhu continued, "To say nothing of ordinary living entities, even Lord Brahmā and Lord Śiva cannot be considered on the level of Viṣṇu or Nārāyaṇa. If one considers them as such, he is immediately considered an offender and atheist.

TEXT 80

যস্তু নারায়ণং দেবং ব্রহ্মরুদ্রাদিদৈবতৈঃ ।
সমত্বেনৈব বীক্ষেত স পাষণ্ডী ভবেদ্ধ্রুবম্ ॥" ৮০ ॥

yas tu nārāyaṇaṁ devaṁ
brahma-rudrādi-daivataiḥ
samatvenaiva vīkṣeta
sa pāṣaṇḍī bhaved dhruvam"

SYNONYMS

yaḥ—any person who; *tu*—however; *nārāyaṇam*—the Supreme Personality of Godhead, the master of such demigods as Brahmā and Śiva; *devam*—the Lord; *brahma*—Lord Brahmā; *rudra*—Lord Śiva; *ādi*—and others; *daivataiḥ*—with such demigods; *samatvena*—on an equal level; *eva*—certainly; *vīkṣeta*—observes; *saḥ*—such a person; *pāṣaṇḍī*—*pāṣaṇḍī; bhavet*—must be; *dhruvam*—certainly.

TRANSLATION

" 'A person who considers demigods like Brahmā and Śiva to be on an equal level with Nārāyaṇa is to be considered an offender, a pāṣaṇḍī.' "

TEXT 81

প্রকাশানন্দ কহে,—"তুমি সাক্ষাৎ ভগবান্ ।
তবু যদি কর তাঁর 'দাস'-অভিমান ॥ ৮১ ॥

prakāśānanda kahe,——"tumi sākṣāt bhagavān
tabu yadi kara tāṅra 'dāsa'-abhimāna

SYNONYMS

prakāśānanda kahe—Prakāśānanda Sarasvatī replied; *tumi*—You; *sākṣāt*—directly; *bhagavān*—the Supreme Personality of Godhead, Kṛṣṇa; *tabu*—yet; *yadi*—if; *kara*—You pose; *tāṅra dāsa-abhimāna*—considering Yourself His servant.

TRANSLATION

Prakāśānanda replied, "You are the Supreme Personality of Godhead, Kṛṣṇa Himself. Nonetheless, You are considering Yourself His eternal servant.

TEXT 82

তবু পূজ্য হও, তুমি বড় আমা হৈতে ।
সর্বনাশ হয় মোর তোমার নিন্দাতে ॥ ৮২ ॥

tabu pūjya hao, tumi baḍa āmā haite
sarva-nāśa haya mora tomāra nindāte

SYNONYMS

tabu—still; *pūjya hao*—You are worshipable; *tumi baḍa*—You are much greater; *āmā haite*—than me; *sarva-nāśa haya*—everything becomes lost; *mora*—my; *tomāra nindāte*—by blaspheming You.

TRANSLATION

"My dear Lord, You are the Supreme Lord, and although You consider Yourself the Lord's servant, You are nonetheless worshipable. You are much greater than I am; therefore all my spiritual achievements have been lost because I have blasphemed You.

TEXT 83

মুক্তানামপি সিদ্ধানাং নারায়ণপরায়ণঃ ।
সুদুর্লভঃ প্রশান্তাত্মা কোটিষ্বপি মহামুনে ॥ ৮৩ ॥

muktānām api siddhānāṁ
nārāyaṇa-parāyaṇaḥ
sudurlabhaḥ praśāntātmā
koṭiṣv api mahā-mune

SYNONYMS

muktānām—of persons liberated or freed from the bondage of ignorance; *api*—even; *siddhānām*—of persons who have achieved perfection; *nārāyaṇa*—of the Supreme Personality of Godhead; *parāyaṇaḥ*—the devotee; *su-durlabhaḥ*—very rare; *praśānta-ātmā*—completely satisfied, desireless; *koṭiṣu*—among many millions; *api*—certainly; *mahā-mune*—O great sage.

TRANSLATION

" 'O great sage, out of many millions of materially liberated people who are free from ignorance, and out of many millions of siddhas who have nearly attained perfection, there is hardly one pure devotee of Nārāyaṇa. Only such a devotee is actually completely satisfied and peaceful.'

PURPORT

This verse is quoted from *Śrīmad-Bhāgavatam* (6.14.5).

TEXT 84

আয়ুঃ শ্রিয়ং যশো ধর্মং লোকানাশিষ এব চ ।
হন্তি শ্রেয়াংসি সর্বাণি পুংসো মহদতিক্রমঃ ॥ ৮৪ ॥

āyuḥ śriyaṁ yaśo dharmaṁ
lokān āśiṣa eva ca
hanti śreyāṁsi sarvāṇi
puṁso mahad-atikramaḥ

SYNONYMS

āyuḥ—duration of life; *śriyam*—opulence; *yaśaḥ*—reputation; *dharmam*—religion; *lokān*—possessions; *āśiṣaḥ*—benedictions; *eva*—certainly; *ca*—and; *hanti*—destroys; *śreyāṁsi*—good fortune; *sarvāṇi*—all; *puṁsaḥ*—of a person; *mahat*—of great souls; *atikramaḥ*—violation.

TRANSLATION

" 'When a person mistreats great souls, his life span, opulence, reputation, religion, possessions and good fortune are all destroyed.'

PURPORT

This is a statement made by Śukadeva Gosvāmī, who was relating *Śrīmad-Bhāgavatam* (10.4.46) to Mahārāja Parīkṣit.

TEXT 85

নৈষাং মতিস্তাবদুরুক্রমাঙ্ঘ্রিং
স্পৃশত্যনর্থাপগমো যদর্থঃ।
মহীয়সাং পাদরজোঽভিষেকং
নিষ্কিঞ্চনানাং ন বৃণীত যাবৎ ॥ ৮৫ ॥

naiṣāṁ matis tāvad urukramāṅghriṁ
spṛśaty anarthāpagamo yad-arthaḥ
mahīyasāṁ pāda-rajo-'bhiṣekaṁ
niṣkiñcanānāṁ na vṛṇīta yāvat

SYNONYMS

na—not; *eṣām*—of those who are attached to household life; *matiḥ*—the interest; *tāvat*—that long; *urukrama-aṅghrim*—the lotus feet of the Supreme Personality of Godhead, who is credited with uncommon activities; *spṛśati*—touches; *anartha*—of unwanted things; *apagamaḥ*—vanquishing; *yat*—of which; *arthaḥ*—results; *mahīyasām*—of the great personalities, devotees; *pāda-rajaḥ*—of the dust of the lotus feet; *abhiṣekam*—sprinkling on the head; *niṣkiñcanānām*—who are completely detached from material possessions; *na vṛṇīta*—does not do; *yāvat*—as long as.

TRANSLATION

" 'Unless human society accepts the dust of the lotus feet of great mahātmās—devotees who have nothing to do with material possessions—mankind cannot turn its attention to the lotus feet of Kṛṣṇa. Those lotus feet vanquish all the unwanted miserable conditions of material life.'

PURPORT

This verse appears in the *Śrīmad-Bhāgavatam* (7.5.32).

TEXT 86

এবে তোমার পাদাব্জে উপজিবে ভক্তি ।
তথি লাগি' করি তোমার চরণে প্রণতি ॥"৮৬ ॥

ebe tomāra pādābje upajibe bhakti
tathi lāgi' kari tomāra caraṇe praṇati"

SYNONYMS

ebe—now; *tomāra*—Your; *pāda-abje*—to the lotus feet; *upajibe*—will grow; *bhakti*—devotional service; *tathi lāgi'*—for that reason; *kari*—I do; *tomāra caraṇe praṇati*—humble obeisances at Your lotus feet.

TRANSLATION

"Henceforward I shall certainly develop devotional service unto Your lotus feet. For this reason I have come to You and have fallen down at Your lotus feet."

TEXT 87

এত বলি' প্রভুরে লঞা তথায় বসিল ।
প্রভুরে প্রকাশানন্দ পুছিতে লাগিল ॥ ৮৭ ॥

eta bali' prabhure lañā tathāya vasila
prabhure prakāśānanda puchite lāgila

SYNONYMS

eta bali'—saying this; *prabhure*—Śrī Caitanya Mahāprabhu; *lañā*—taking; *tathāya vasila*—sat down there; *prabhure*—unto Śrī Caitanya Mahāprabhu; *prakāśānanda*—Prakāśānanda Sarasvatī; *puchite lāgila*—began to inquire.

TRANSLATION

After saying this, Prakāśānanda Sarasvatī sat down with Śrī Caitanya Mahāprabhu and began to question the Lord as follows.

TEXT 88

মায়াবাদে করিলা যত দোষের আখ্যান ।
সবে এই জানি' আচার্যের কল্পিত ব্যাখ্যান ॥ ৮৮ ॥

māyāvāde karilā yata doṣera ākhyāna
sabe ei jāni' ācāryera kalpita vyākhyāna

SYNONYMS

māyāvāde—in the philosophy of Māyāvāda, impersonalism; *karilā*—You have done; *yata*—all; *doṣera ākhyāna*—description of the faults; *sabe*—all; *ei*—these; *jāni'*—knowing; *ācāryera*—of Śaṅkarācārya; *kalpita vyākhyāna*—imaginary explanations.

TRANSLATION

Prakāśānanda Sarasvatī said, "We can understand the faults You have pointed out in the Māyāvāda philosophy. All the explanations given by Śaṅkarācārya are imaginary.

TEXT 89

সূত্রের করিলা তুমি মুখ্যার্থ-বিবরণ ।
তাহা শুনি' সবার হৈল চমৎকার মন ॥ ৮৯ ॥

sūtrera karilā tumi mukhyārtha-vivaraṇa
tāhā śuni' sabāra haila camatkāra mana

SYNONYMS

sūtrera—of the *Brahma-sūtra; karilā*—have done; *tumi*—You; *mukhya-artha-vivaraṇa*—description of the direct meaning; *tāhā śuni'*—hearing that; *sabāra*—of everyone; *haila*—became; *camatkāra*—astonished; *mana*—the mind.

TRANSLATION

"My dear Lord, whatever direct meaning You have given when explaining the Brahma-sūtra is certainly very wonderful to all of us.

TEXT 90

তুমি ত' ঈশ্বর, তোমার আছে সর্বশক্তি ।
সংক্ষেপরূপে কহ তুমি শুনিতে হয় মতি ॥ ৯০ ॥

tumi ta' īśvara, tomāra āche sarva-śakti
saṅkṣepa-rūpe kaha tumi śunite haya mati

SYNONYMS

tumi ta'—indeed You are; *īśvara*—the Supreme Lord; *tomāra*—of You; *āche*—there are; *sarva-śakti*—all potencies; *saṅkṣepa-rūpe*—briefly; *kaha*—please explain; *tumi*—You; *śunite haya mati*—I wish to hear.

TRANSLATION

"You are the Supreme Personality of Godhead, and therefore You have inconceivable energies. I wish to hear from You briefly about the Brahma-sūtra."

PURPORT

Prakāśānanda Sarasvatī said that he had already understood Śrī Caitanya Mahāprabhu's explanation of the direct import of *Brahma-sūtra.* Nonetheless, he was requesting the Lord to briefly give the purpose and purport of the *Brahma-sūtra,* the *Vedānta-sūtra.*

TEXT 91

প্রভু কহে,—"আমি 'জীব', অতি তুচ্ছ-জ্ঞান !
ব্যাসসূত্রের গম্ভীর অর্থ, ব্যাস—ভগবান্ ॥ ৯১ ॥

prabhu kahe,—"āmi 'jīva', ati tuccha-jñāna!
vyāsa-sūtrera gambhīra artha, vyāsa—bhagavān

SYNONYMS

prabhu kahe—Lord Śrī Caitanya Mahāprabhu replied; *āmi jīva*—I am an insignificant living being; *ati tuccha-jñāna*—My knowledge is very meager; *vyāsa-sūtrera*—of the *Vedānta-sūtra,* written by Vyāsadeva; *gambhīra artha*—very grave meaning; *vyāsa*—Vyāsadeva; *bhagavān*—the Supreme Personality of Godhead.

TRANSLATION

Śrī Caitanya Mahāprabhu replied, "I am an ordinary living being, and therefore my knowledge is very insignificant. However, the meaning of the

Brahma-sūtra is very grave because its author, Vyāsadeva, is the Supreme Personality of Godhead Himself.

PURPORT

An ordinary living being cannot actually understand the purpose of the *Vedānta-sūtra.* One can understand the purpose if he hears it from the authority, Vyāsadeva himself. For this reason, Vyāsadeva gave a commentary on the *Brahma-sūtra* in the form of *Śrīmad-Bhāgavatam.* He had been instructed to do this by his spiritual master, Nārada. Of course, Śaṅkarācārya distorted the purpose of the *Brahma-sūtra* because he had a motive to serve. He wanted to establish Vedic knowledge in place of the atheistic knowledge spread by Lord Buddha. All these necessities are there according to time and circumstances. Neither Lord Buddha nor Śaṅkarācārya is to be blamed. The time required such an explanation for the understanding of various types of atheists. The conclusion is that one cannot understand the purpose of the *Vedānta-sūtra* without going through the *Śrīmad-Bhāgavatam* and rendering devotional service. Caitanya Mahāprabhu therefore further explains the matter in the following verses.

TEXT 92

তাঁর সূত্রের অর্থ কোন জীব নাহি জানে।
অতএব আপনে সূত্রার্থ করিয়াছে ব্যাখ্যানে ॥ ৯২ ॥

tāṅra sūtrera artha kona jīva nāhi jāne
ataeva āpane sūtrārtha kariyāche vyākhyāne

SYNONYMS

tāṅra sūtrera artha—the meaning of Vyāsadeva's *Vedānta-sūtra; kona*—any; *jīva*—living being; *nāhi jāne*—does not know; *ataeva*—therefore; *āpane*—personally; *sūtra-artha*—the meanings of the *sūtras; kariyāche vyākhyāne*—has described.

TRANSLATION

"The purpose of the Vedānta-sūtra is very difficult for an ordinary person to understand, but Vyāsadeva, out of his causeless mercy, has personally explained the meaning.

TEXT 93

যেই সূত্রকর্তা, সে যদি করয়ে ব্যাখ্যান।
তবে সূত্রের মূল অর্থ লোকের হয় জ্ঞান ॥ ৯৩ ॥

yei sūtra-kartā, se yadi karaye vyākhyāna
tabe sūtrera mūla artha lokera haya jñāna

SYNONYMS

yei sūtra-kartā—the person who has made the *Vedānta-sūtra; se*—that person; *yadi*—if; *karaye vyākhyāna*—explains the meaning; *tabe*—then; *sūtrera*—of the codes of *Vedānta-sūtra; mūla*—the original; *artha*—meaning; *lokera*—of the people in general; *haya jñāna*—comes within knowledge.

TRANSLATION

"If the Vedānta-sūtra is explained by Vyāsadeva himself, who has written it, its original meaning can be understood by the people in general.

TEXT 94

প্রণবের যেই অর্থ, গায়ত্রীতে সেই হয়।
সেই অর্থ চতুঃশ্লোকীতে বিবরিয়া কয় ॥ ৯৪ ॥

praṇavera yei artha, gāyatrīte sei haya
sei artha catuḥ-ślokīte vivariyā kaya

SYNONYMS

praṇavera—of the sound vibration, *oṁkāra; yei*—whatever; *artha*—meaning; *gāyatrīte*—in the Gāyatrī *mantra; sei*—that; *haya*—there is; *sei artha*—that same meaning; *catuḥ-ślokīte*—in *Śrīmad-Bhāgavatam* summarized in four *ślokas; vivariyā*—describing elaborately; *kaya*—has said.

TRANSLATION

"The meaning of the sound vibration oṁkāra is present in the Gāyatrī mantra. The same is elaborately explained in the four ślokas of Śrīmad-Bhāgavatam known as catuḥ-ślokī.

TEXT 95

ব্রহ্মারে ঈশ্বর চতুঃশ্লোকী যে কহিলা।
ব্রহ্মা নারদে সেই উপদেশ কৈলা ॥ ৯৫ ॥

brahmāre īśvara catuḥ-ślokī ye kahilā
brahmā nārade sei upadeśa kailā

SYNONYMS

brahmāre—to Lord Brahmā; *īśvara*—the Supreme Personality of Godhead; *catuḥ-ślokī*—the four famous verses known as *catuḥ-ślokī; ye kahilā*—whatever was explained; *brahmā*—Lord Brahmā; *nārade*—to Nārada Muni; *sei*—that; *upadeśa kailā*—instructed.

TRANSLATION

"Whatever was spoken by the Supreme Personality of Godhead to Lord Brahmā in the four verses of Śrīmad-Bhāgavatam, was also explained to Nārada by Lord Brahmā.

TEXT 96

নারদ সেই অর্থ ব্যাসেরে কহিলা ।
শুনি' বেদব্যাস মনে বিচার করিলা ॥ ৯৬ ॥

nārada sei artha vyāsere kahilā
śuni' veda-vyāsa mane vicāra karilā

SYNONYMS

nārada—the great sage Nārada; *sei artha*—the same purpose; *vyāsere kahilā*—explained to Vyāsadeva; *śuni'*—hearing; *veda-vyāsa*—Vyāsadeva; *mane*—within the mind; *vicāra karilā*—considered very carefully.

TRANSLATION

"Whatever Lord Brahmā told Nārada Muni was again explained by Nārada Muni to Vyāsadeva. Vyāsadeva later considered these instructions in his mind.

TEXT 97

"এই অর্থ—আমার সূত্রের ব্যাখ্যানুরূপ ।
'ভাগবত' করিব সূত্রের ভাষ্যস্বরূপ ॥"৯৭ ॥

"ei artha——āmāra sūtrera vyākhyānurūpa
'bhāgavata' kariba sūtrera bhāṣya-svarūpa"

SYNONYMS

ei artha—this explanation; *āmāra*—my; *sūtrera*—of *Brahma-sūtra; vyākhyā-anurūpa*—a suitable explanation; *bhāgavata*—*Śrīmad-Bhāgavata Purāṇa; kariba*—I shall make; *sūtrera*—of the *Brahma-sūtra; bhāṣya-svarūpa*—as the original commentary.

TRANSLATION

"Śrīla Vyāsadeva considered that whatever he had received from Nārada Muni as an explanation of oṁkāra he would elaborately explain in his book Śrīmad-Bhāgavatam as a commentary on Brahma-sūtra.

PURPORT

The sound vibration *oṁkāra* is the root of Vedic knowledge. This *oṁkāra* is known as *mahā-vākya,* or the supreme sound. Whatever meaning is in the supreme sound *oṁkāra* is further understood in the Gāyatrī *mantra.* Again, this same meaning is explained in *Śrīmad-Bhāgavatam* in the four *ślokas* known as *catuḥ-ślokī,* which begin with the words *ahaṁ evāsam evāgre.* The Lord says, "Only I existed before the creation." From this verse, four *ślokas* have been composed, and these are known as the *catuḥ-ślokī.* In this way the Supreme Personality of Godhead informed Lord Brahmā about the purpose of the *catuḥ-ślokī.* Again, Lord Brahmā explained this to Nārada Muni, and Nārada Muni explained it to Śrīla Vyāsadeva. This is the *paramparā* system, the disciplic succession. The import of Vedic knowledge, the original word *praṇava,* has been explained in *Śrīmad-Bhāgavatam.* The conclusion is that the *Brahma-sūtra* is explained in the *Śrīmad-Bhāgavatam.*

TEXT 98

চারিবেদ-উপনিষদে যত কিছু হয়।
তার অর্থ লঞা ব্যাস করিলা সঞ্চয় ॥ ৯৮ ॥

cāri-veda-upaniṣade yata kichu haya
tāra artha lañā vyāsa karilā sañcaya

SYNONYMS

cāri-veda—the four divisions of the *Vedas* (*Sāma, Yajur, Ṛg* and *Atharva*); *upaniṣade*—and in 108 *Upaniṣads; yata*—whatever; *kichu haya*—is there; *tāra artha*—the meanings of those Vedic literatures; *lañā*—taking together; *vyāsa*—Vyāsadeva; *karilā sañcaya*—collected.

TRANSLATION

"Vyāsadeva collected whatever Vedic conclusions were in the four Vedas and 108 Upaniṣads and placed them in the codes of the Vedānta-sūtra.

TEXT 99

যেই সূত্রে যেই ঋক্—বিষয়-বচন।
ভাগবতে সেই ঋক্ শ্লোকে নিবন্ধন ॥ ৯৯ ॥

yei sūtre yei ṛk——viṣaya-vacana
bhāgavate sei ṛk śloke nibandhana

SYNONYMS

yei sūtre—in the codes of *Vedānta-sūtra; yei*—whatever; *ṛk*—Vedic *mantra; viṣaya-vacana*—subject matter to be explained; *bhāgavate*—in *Śrīmad-Bhāgavatam; sei ṛk*—that same Vedic *mantra; śloke*—in eighteen thousand verses; *nibandhana*—compiling.

TRANSLATION

"In Vedānta-sūtra, the purpose of all Vedic knowledge is explained, and in Śrīmad-Bhāgavatam the same purpose has been explained in eighteen thousand verses.

TEXT 100

অতএব ব্রহ্মসূত্রের ভাষ্য—শ্রীভাগবত।
ভাগবত-শ্লোক, উপনিষৎ কহে 'এক'মত ॥ ১০০ ॥

ataeva brahma-sūtrera bhāṣya——śrī-bhāgavata
bhāgavata-śloka, upaniṣat kahe 'eka' mata

SYNONYMS

ataeva—therefore; *brahma-sūtrera bhāṣya*—the commentary on the *Brahma-sūtra* codes; *śrī-bhāgavata*—*Śrīmad-Bhāgavatam; bhāgavata-śloka*—the verses in *Śrīmad-Bhāgavatam; upaniṣat*—the explanations in the *Upaniṣads; kahe*—state; *eka mata*—the same version.

TRANSLATION

"That which is explained in the verses of Śrīmad-Bhāgavatam and in the Upaniṣads serves the same purpose.

TEXT 101

আত্মাবাস্যমিদং বিশ্বং যৎ কিঞ্চিজ্জগত্যাং জগৎ।
তেন ত্যক্তেন ভুঞ্জীথা মা গৃধঃ কস্যস্বিদ্ধনম্ ॥ ১০১ ॥

ātmāvāsyam idaṁ viśvaṁ
yat kiñcij jagatyāṁ jagat
tena tyaktena bhuñjīthā
mā gṛdhaḥ kasyasvid dhanam

SYNONYMS

ātma-āvāsyam—the expansion of the energy of the Supreme Soul, the Personality of Godhead; *idam*—this; *viśvam*—universe; *yat*—whatever; *kiñcit*—something; *jagatyām*—within the universe; *jagat*—all that is animate or inanimate; *tena*—by Him; *tyaktena*—by things allotted to every person; *bhuñjīthā*—you should accept for your maintenance; *mā*—never; *gṛdhaḥ*—encroach; *kasyasvit*—someone else's; *dhanam*—property.

TRANSLATION

" 'Everything animate or inanimate that is within the universe is controlled and owned by the Lord. One should therefore accept only those things for himself that are set aside as his quota, and one should not accept other things, knowing well to whom they belong.'

PURPORT

This is a quotation from *Śrīmad-Bhāgavatam* (8.1.10). Communists and socialists are trying to propagate the philosophy that everything belongs to the mass of people or to the state. Such an idea is not perfect. When this idea is expanded, we can see that everything belongs to God. That will be the perfection of the communistic idea. The purpose of *Śrīmad-Bhāgavatam* is here very nicely explained. Every one of us must be satisfied with those things the Supreme Personality of Godhead has allotted us. We should not encroach upon the possessions of others. This simple idea can be expanded in our daily lives. Everyone should have a piece of land given by the government, and everyone should possess a few cows. Both of these should be utilized for one's daily bread. Above that, if something is manufactured in a factory, it should be considered the property of the Supreme Personality of Godhead because the ingredients belong to the Supreme Lord. Actually, there is no need to manufacture such things artificially, but if it is done, one should consider that the goods produced belong to the Supreme Lord. Spiritual communism recognizes the supreme proprietorship of the Supreme Lord. As explained in *Bhagavad-gītā* (5.29):

bhoktāraṁ yajña-tapasāṁ
sarva-loka-maheśvaram
suhṛdaṁ sarva-bhūtānāṁ
jñātvā māṁ śāntim ṛcchati

"The sages, knowing Me as the ultimate purpose of all sacrifices and austerities, the Supreme Lord of all planets and demigods and the benefactor and well-wisher of all living entities, attain peace from the pangs of material miseries."

It is further explained in *Śrīmad-Bhāgavatam* that no one should claim anything as his property. Whatever property one claims to be his actually belongs to Kṛṣṇa.

One should be satisfied with whatever has been allotted by the Supreme Lord and should not encroach upon the property of others. This will lead to peace in the whole world.

TEXT 102

ভাগবতের সম্বন্ধ, অভিধেয়, প্রয়োজন ।
চতুঃশ্লোকীতে প্রকট তার করিয়াছে লক্ষণ ॥১০২॥

bhāgavatera sambandha, abhidheya, prayojana
catuḥ-ślokīte prakaṭa tāra kariyāche lakṣaṇa

SYNONYMS

bhāgavatera—of *Śrīmad-Bhāgavatam; sambandha*—a personal relationship with God; *abhidheya*—activities in that relationship; *prayojana*—the ultimate goal of life; *catuḥ-ślokīte*—in the four famous verses of *Śrīmad-Bhāgavatam; prakaṭa*—manifesting; *tāra*—of them; *kariyāche*—has done; *lakṣaṇa*—the symptoms.

TRANSLATION

"The essence of Śrīmad-Bhāgavatam—our relationship with the Supreme Lord, our activities in that connection and the goal of life—is manifest in the four verses of Śrīmad-Bhāgavatam known as the catuḥ-ślokī. Everything is explained in those verses.

TEXT 103

"আমি—'সম্বন্ধ'-তত্ত্ব, আমার জ্ঞান-বিজ্ঞান ।
আমা পাইতে সাধন-ভক্তি 'অভিধেয়'-নাম ॥ ১০৩ ॥

"āmi——'sambandha'-tattva, āmāra jñāna-vijñāna
āmā pāite sādhana-bhakti 'abhidheya'-nāma

SYNONYMS

āmi—I; *sambandha-tattva*—the center of all relationships; *āmāra*—of Me; *jñāna*—knowledge; *vijñāna*—practical application of that knowledge; *āmā pāite*—to obtain Me; *sādhana-bhakti*—the practice of devotional service; *abhidheya-nāma*—is called activities in that relationship.

TRANSLATION

"Lord Kṛṣṇa says, 'I am the center of all relationships. Knowledge of Me and the practical application of that knowledge is actual knowledge. Approaching Me for devotional service is called abhidheya.

PURPORT

Spiritual knowledge means fully understanding the Absolute Truth in three features—impersonal Brahman, localized Paramātmā and the all-powerful Supreme Personality of Godhead. Ultimately when one takes shelter at the lotus feet of the Supreme Personality of Godhead and engages in the Lord's service, the resultant knowledge is called *vijñāna,* special knowledge, or the practical application of spiritual knowledge. One should be engaged in the Lord's devotional service to achieve the aim of life, called *prayojana.* The practice of devotional service to attain that goal of life is called *abhidheya.*

TEXT 104

সাধনের ফল—'প্রেম' মূল-প্রয়োজন।
সেই প্রেমে পায় জীব আমার 'সেবন' ॥ ১০৪ ॥

sādhanera phala——'prema' mūla-prayojana
sei preme pāya jīva āmāra 'sevana'

SYNONYMS

sādhanera phala—the result of devotional service; *prema*—love of Godhead; *mūla-prayojana*—the chief goal; *sei preme*—by that love of Godhead; *pāya*—gets; *jīva*—the living entity; *āmāra*—My; *sevana*—service.

TRANSLATION

" 'By rendering devotional service, one gradually rises to the platform of love of Godhead. That is the chief goal of life. On the platform of love of Godhead, one is eternally engaged in the service of the Lord.

TEXT 105

জ্ঞানং পরমগুহ্যং মে যদ্বিজ্ঞান-সমন্বিতম্।
স-রহস্যং তদঙ্গঞ্চ গৃহাণ গদিতং ময়া॥ ১০৫ ॥

jñānaṁ parama-guhyaṁ me
yad vijñāna-samanvitam
sa-rahasyaṁ tad-aṅgaṁ ca
gṛhāṇa gaditaṁ mayā

SYNONYMS

jñānam—knowledge; *parama*—extremely; *guhyam*—confidential; *me*—of Me; *yat*—which; *vijñāna*—realization; *samanvitam*—fully endowed with; *sa-*

rahasyam—with mystery; *tat*—of that; *aṅgam*—supplementary parts; *ca*—and; *gṛhāṇa*—just try to take up; *gaditam*—explained; *mayā*—by Me.

TRANSLATION

" 'Please hear attentively what I shall speak to you, for transcendental knowledge about Me is not only scientific but full of mysteries.

PURPORT

This is a quotation from *Śrīmad-Bhāgavatam* (2.9.31).

TEXT 106

এই 'তিন' তত্ত্ব আমি কহিনু তোমারে ।
'জীব' তুমি এই তিন নারিবে জানিবারে ॥ ১০৬ ॥

ei 'tina' tattva āmi kahinu tomāre
'jīva' tumi ei tina nāribe jānibāre

SYNONYMS

ei tina tattva—all three of these features of the Absolute Truth; *āmi*—I; *kahinu*—shall speak; *tomāre*—unto you; *jīva*—a living being; *tumi*—you; *ei tina*—these three; *nāribe*—will not be able; *jānibāre*—to understand.

TRANSLATION

" 'O Brahmā, I shall explain all these truths to you. You are a living being, and without My explanation you will not be able to understand your relationship with Me, devotional activity and life's ultimate goal.

TEXT 107

যৈছে আমার 'স্বরূপ', যৈছে আমার 'স্থিতি' ।
যৈছে আমার গুণ, কর্ম, ষড়ৈশ্বর্য-শক্তি ॥ ১০৭ ॥

yaiche āmāra 'svarūpa', yaiche āmāra 'sthiti'
yaiche āmāra guṇa, karma, ṣaḍ-aiśvarya-śakti

SYNONYMS

yaiche—as far as; *āmāra*—My; *svarūpa*—original form; *yaiche*—as far as; *āmāra*—My; *sthiti*—situation; *yaiche*—as far as; *āmāra*—My; *guṇa*—attributes; *karma*—activities; *ṣaṭ-aiśvarya-śakti*—six kinds of opulence.

TRANSLATION

" 'I shall explain to you My actual form and situation, My attributes, activities and six opulences.'

TEXT 108

আমার কৃপায় এই সব স্ফুরুক তোমারে।"
এত বলি' তিন তত্ত্ব কহিলা তাঁহারে ॥ ১০৮ ॥

āmāra kṛpāya ei saba sphuruka tomāre"
eta bali' tina tattva kahilā tāṅhāre

SYNONYMS

āmāra—My; *kṛpāya*—by mercy; *ei saba*—all these; *sphuruka tomāre*—let them be awakened in you; *eta bali'*—saying this; *tina tattva*—the three truths; *kahilā tāṅhāre*—explained to him.

TRANSLATION

"Lord Kṛṣṇa assured Lord Brahmā, 'By My mercy all these things will be awakened in you.' Saying this, the Lord began to explain the three truths [tattvas] to Lord Brahmā.

TEXT 109

যাবানহং যথা-ভাবো যদ্রূপগুণকর্মকঃ ।
তথৈব তত্ত্ববিজ্ঞানমস্তু তে মদনুগ্রহাৎ ॥ ১০৯ ॥

yāvān ahaṁ yathā-bhāvo
yad-rūpa-guṇa-karmakaḥ
tathaiva tattva-vijñānam
astu te mad-anugrahāt

SYNONYMS

yāvān—as I am in My eternal form; *aham*—I; *yathā*—in whichever manner; *bhāvaḥ*—transcendental existence; *yat*—whatever; *rūpa*—various forms and colors; *guṇa*—qualities; *karmakaḥ*—activities; *tathā eva*—exactly so; *tattva-vijñānam*—factual realization; *astu*—let there be; *te*—your; *mat*—My; *anugrahāt*—by causeless mercy.

TRANSLATION

" 'By My causeless mercy, be enlightened in truth about My personality, manifestations, qualities and pastimes.

PURPORT

This is a quotation from *Śrīmad-Bhāgavatam* (2.9.32). For an explanation see *Ādi-līlā,* Chapter One, texts 51-52.

TEXT 110

স্বষ্টির পূর্বে ষড়ৈশ্বর্যপূর্ণ আমি ত' হইয়ে।
'প্রপঞ্চ', 'প্রকৃতি', 'পুরুষ' আমাতেই লয়ে ॥১১০॥

sṛṣṭira pūrve ṣaḍ-aiśvarya-pūrṇa āmi ta' ha-iye
'prapañca', 'prakṛti', 'puruṣa' āmātei laye

SYNONYMS

sṛṣṭira pūrve—before the creation of this cosmic manifestation; *ṣaṭ-aiśvarya-pūrṇa*—full of six opulences; *āmi*—I; *ta' ha-iye*—indeed existed; *prapañca*—the total material energy; *prakṛti*—material nature; *puruṣa*—the living entities; *āmātei laye*—were all existing in Me.

TRANSLATION

" 'Before the creation of the cosmic manifestation,' the Lord said, 'I existed, and the total material energy, material nature and the living entities all existed in Me.

TEXT 111

স্বষ্টি করি' তার মধ্যে আমি প্রবেশিয়ে।
প্রপঞ্চ যে দেখ সব, সেহ আমি হইয়ে ॥ ১১১ ॥

sṛṣṭi kari' tāra madhye āmi praveśiye
prapañca ye dekha saba, seha āmi ha-iye

SYNONYMS

sṛṣṭi kari'—after creating; *tāra madhye*—within the creation; *āmi praveśiye*—I enter as Lord Viṣṇu; *prapañca*—the cosmic manifestation; *ye*—whatever; *dekha*—you see; *saba*—all; *seha*—that; *āmi ha-iye*—I am.

TRANSLATION

" 'After creating the cosmic manifestation, I entered into it. Whatever you see in the cosmic manifestation is but an expansion of My energy.

TEXT 112

প্রলয়ে অবশিষ্ট আমি 'পূর্ণ' হইয়ে ।
প্রাকৃত প্রপঞ্চ পায় আমাতেই লয়ে ॥ ১১২ ॥

pralaye avaśiṣṭa āmi 'pūrṇa' ha-iye
prākṛta prapañca pāya āmātei laye

SYNONYMS

pralaye—at the time of annihilation; *avaśiṣṭa*—what remains; *āmi*—I; *pūrṇa*—full; *ha-iye*—am; *prākṛta prapañca*—the material cosmic manifestation; *pāya*—obtains; *āmātei*—in Me; *laye*—dissolution.

TRANSLATION

" 'When the whole universe dissolves, I remain full in Myself, and everything that is manifested is again preserved in Me.

TEXT 113

অহমেবাসমেবাগ্রে নান্যদ্যৎ সদসৎপরম্ ।
পশ্চাদহং যদেতচ্চ যোঽবশিষ্যেত সোঽস্ম্যহম্ ॥ ১১৩ ॥

aham evāsam evāgre
nānyad yat sad-asat-param
paścād ahaṁ yad etac ca
yo 'vaśiṣyeta so 'smy aham

SYNONYMS

aham—I, the Personality of Godhead; *eva*—certainly; *āsam*—existed; *eva*—only; *agre*—before the creation; *na*—never; *anyat*—anything else; *yat*—which; *sat*—the effect; *asat*—the cause; *param*—the supreme; *paścāt*—after; *aham*—I, the Personality of Godhead; *yat*—which; *etat*—this creation; *ca*—also; *yaḥ*—who; *avaśiṣyeta*—remains; *saḥ*—that; *asmi*—am; *aham*—I, the Personality of Godhead.

TRANSLATION

" 'Prior to the cosmic manifestation, only I exist, and no phenomena exist, either gross, subtle or primordial. After creation, only I exist in everything, and after annihilation, only I remain eternally.

PURPORT

This is a quotation from *Śrīmad-Bhāgavatam* (2.9.33). It is the first verse of the *catuḥ-ślokī*. For an explanation see *Ādi-līlā,* Chapter One, text 53.

TEXT 114

"অহমেব"-শ্লোকে 'অহম্'– তিনবার ।
পূর্ণৈশ্বর্য শ্রীবিগ্রহ-স্থিতির নির্ধার ॥ ১১৪ ॥

"aham eva"-śloke 'aham'——tina-bāra
pūrṇaiśvarya śrī-vigraha-sthitira nirdhāra

SYNONYMS

aham eva—I only; *śloke*—in this verse; *aham*—the word *aham; tina-bāra*—three times; *pūrṇa-aiśvarya*—full of all opulences; *śrī-vigraha*—of the transcendental form of the Lord; *sthitira*—of the existence; *nirdhāra*—confirmation.

TRANSLATION

" 'In the verse beginning "aham eva," the word "aham" is expressed three times. In the beginning there are the words "aham eva." In the second line there are the words "paścād aham." At the end are the words "so 'smy aham." This "aham" indicates the Supreme Person. By the repetition of "aham," the transcendental personality who is complete with six opulences is confirmed.

TEXT 115

যে 'বিগ্রহ' নাহি মানে, 'নিরাকার' মানে ।
তারে তিরস্করিবারে করিলা নির্ধারণে ॥ ১১৫ ॥

ye 'vigraha' nāhi māne, 'nirākāra' māne
tāre tiraskaribāre karilā nirdhāraṇe

SYNONYMS

ye—one who; *vigraha*—that Personality of Godhead; *nāhi māne*—does not accept; *nirākāra māne*—considers impersonal; *tāre*—him; *tiraskaribāre*—just to chastise; *karilā*—has done; *nirdhāraṇe*—ascertainment.

TRANSLATION

" 'Impersonalists do not accept the personal feature of the Supreme Personality of Godhead. The Personality of Godhead is stressed in this verse in order to impress upon them the necessity of accepting Him. Therefore the word "aham" is mentioned three times. To stress something important, one repeats it three times.

TEXT 116

এই সব শব্দে হয়—'জ্ঞান'-'বিজ্ঞান'-বিবেক ।
মায়া-কার্য, মায়া হৈতে আমি—ব্যতিরেক ॥ ১১৬ ॥

ei saba śabde haya——'jñāna'-'vijñāna'-viveka
māyā-kārya, māyā haite āmi——vyatireka

SYNONYMS

ei saba—all these; *śabde*—in the words; *haya*—there is; *jñāna*—of real spiritual knowledge; *vijñāna*—of the practical application of the knowledge; *viveka*—consideration; *māyā-kārya*—the activities of the external energy; *māyā haite*—from the activities of the material energy; *āmi*—I; *vyatireka*—distinct.

TRANSLATION

" 'Actual spiritual knowledge and its practical application are considered in all these sound vibrations. Although the external energy comes from Me, I am different from it.

TEXT 117

যৈছে সূর্যের স্থানে ভাসয়ে 'আভাস' ।
সূর্য বিনা স্বতন্ত্র তার না হয় প্রকাশ ॥ ১১৭ ॥

yaiche sūryera sthāne bhāsaye 'ābhāsa'
sūrya vinā svatantra tāra nā haya prakāśa

SYNONYMS

yaiche—just as; *sūryera*—of the sun; *sthāne*—in place; *bhāsaye*—appears; *ābhāsa*—the illumination; *sūrya vinā*—without the sun; *svatantra*—independently; *tāra*—of that; *nā haya*—is not; *prakāśa*—manifestation.

TRANSLATION

" 'Sometimes a reflection of the sun is experienced in place of the sun, but its illumination is never possible independent of the sun.

TEXT 118

মায়াতীত হৈলে হয় আমার 'অনুভব'।
এই 'সম্বন্ধ'-তত্ত্ব কহিলুঁ, শুন আর সব ॥ ১১৮ ॥

māyātīta haile haya āmāra 'anubhava'
ei 'sambandha'-tattva kahiluṅ, śuna āra saba

SYNONYMS

māyā-atīta haile—when one becomes transcendentally situated above this external energy; *haya*—there is; *āmāra anubhava*—perception of Me; *ei sambandha-tattva kahiluṅ*—this has been explained as the principle of a relationship with Me; *śuna*—please hear; *āra saba*—all the rest.

TRANSLATION

" 'When one is transcendentally situated, he can perceive Me. This perception is the basis of one's relationship with the Supreme Lord. Now let Me further explain this subject matter.

PURPORT

Real spiritual knowledge has to be received from revealed scriptures. After this knowledge is attained, one can begin to perceive his actual spiritual life. Any knowledge achieved by speculation is imperfect. One must receive knowledge from the *paramparā* system and from the *guru,* otherwise one will be bewildered, and will ultimately become an impersonalist. When one very scrutinizingly deliberates, he can realize the personal feature of the Absolute Truth. The Supreme Personality of Godhead is always transcendental to this material creation. *Nārāyaṇaḥ paro 'vyaktāt:* Nārāyaṇa, the Supreme Personality of Godhead, is always transcendental. He is not a creation of this material world. Without realizing spiritual knowledge, one cannot understand that the transcendental form of the Lord is always beyond the creative energy. The example of the sun and sunshine is given. The sunshine is not the sun, but still the sunshine is not separate from the sun. The philosophy of *acintya-bhedābheda-tattva* (simultaneously one and different) cannot be understood by one who is fully under the influence of the external energy. Consequently a person under the influence of the material energy cannot understand the nature and form of the Personality of the Absolute Truth.

TEXT 119

ঋতেঽর্থং যৎ প্রতীয়েত ন প্রতীয়েত চাত্মনি।
তদ্বিদ্যাদাত্মনো মায়াং যথাভাসো যথা তমঃ ॥ ১১৯ ॥

ṛte 'rthaṁ yat pratīyeta
na pratīyeta cātmani
tad vidyād ātmano māyāṁ
yathābhāso yathā tamaḥ

SYNONYMS

ṛte—without; *artham*—value; *yat*—that which; *pratīyeta*—appears to be; *na*—not; *pratīyeta*—appears to be; *ca*—certainly; *ātmani*—in relation to Me; *tat*—that; *vidyāt*—you must know; *ātmanaḥ*—My; *māyām*—illusory energy; *yathā*—just as; *ābhāsaḥ*—the reflection; *yathā*—just as; *tamaḥ*—the darkness.

TRANSLATION

" 'What appears to be truth without Me, is certainly My illusory energy, for nothing can exist without Me. It is like a reflection of a real light in the shadows, for in the light there are neither shadows nor reflections.

PURPORT

This is a quotation from *Śrīmad-Bhāgavatam* (2.9.34). It is the second verse of the *catuḥ-ślokī*. For an explanation of this verse, see *Ādi-līlā,* Chapter One, text 54.

TEXT 120

'অভিধেয়' সাধনভক্তির শুনহ বিচার ।
সর্ব-জন-দেশ-কাল-দশাতে ব্যাপ্তি যার ॥ ১২০ ॥

'abhidheya' sādhana-bhaktira śunaha vicāra
sarva-jana-deśa-kāla-daśāte vyāpti yāra

SYNONYMS

abhidheya—the means to obtain an end; *sādhana-bhaktira*—of the process of executing devotional service; *śunaha vicāra*—please hear the procedure; *sarva*—all; *jana*—people; *deśa*—countries; *kāla*—times; *daśāte*—and in circumstances; *vyāpti yāra*—which is all-pervasive.

TRANSLATION

" 'Now please hear from Me about the process of devotional service, which is applicable in any country, for any person, at all times and in all circumstances.

PURPORT

The cult of *bhāgavata-dharma* can be spread in all circumstances, among all people and in all countries. Many envious people accuse this Kṛṣṇa consciousness movement of spoiling the rigidity of so-called Hinduism. That is not actually the fact. Śrī Caitanya Mahāprabhu confirms that devotional service to the Lord—the cult of *bhāgavata-dharma,* which is now being spread as the Hare Kṛṣṇa movement—can be spread in every country, for every person, in any condition of life, and in all circumstances. *Bhāgavata-dharma* does not restrict pure devotees to the Hindu community. A pure devotee is above a *brāhmaṇa;* therefore it is not incompatible to offer the sacred thread to devotees in Europe, America, Australia, Japan, Canada, and so on. Sometimes these pure devotees, who have been accepted by Śrī Caitanya Mahāprabhu, are not allowed to enter certain temples in India. Some high-caste *brāhmaṇas* and *gosvāmīs* refuse to take *prasāda* in the temples of the International Society for Krishna Consciousness. Actually this is against the instruction of Śrī Caitanya Mahāprabhu. Devotees can come from any country, and they can belong to any creed or race. On the strength of this verse, those who are actually devotees and followers of Śrī Caitanya Mahāprabhu must accept devotees from all parts of the world as pure Vaiṣṇavas. They should be accepted not artificially but factually. One should see how they are advanced in Kṛṣṇa consciousness and how they are conducting Deity worship, *saṅkīrtana* and Ratha-yātrā. Considering all these points, an envious person should refrain from malicious atrocities.

TEXT 121

'ধর্মাদি' বিষয়ে যৈছে এ 'চারি' বিচার ।
সাধন-ভক্তি—এই চারি বিচারের পার ॥ ১২১ ॥

'dharmādi' viṣaye yaiche e 'cāri' vicāra
sādhana-bhakti——ei cāri vicārera pāra

SYNONYMS

dharma-ādi—of religious activities and so on; *viṣaye*—in the subject matter; *yaiche*—just as; *e cāri vicāra*—there is a consideration of four principles, namely the person, country, time and atmosphere; *sādhana-bhakti*—of devotional service; *ei*—these; *cāri*—four; *vicārera*—to the considerations; *pāra*—transcendental.

TRANSLATION

" 'As far as religious principles are concerned, there is a consideration of the person, the country, the time and the circumstance. In devotional service,

however, there are no such considerations. Devotional service is transcendental to all considerations.

PURPORT

When we are on the material platform, there are different types of religions—Hinduism, Christianity, Mohammedanism, Buddhism, and so on. These are instituted for a particular time, a particular country or a particular person. Consequently there are differences. Christian principles are different from Hindu principles, and Hindu principles are different from Mohammedan and Buddhist principles. These may be considered on the material platform, but when we come to the platform of transcendental devotional service, there are no such considerations. The transcendental service of the Lord (*sādhana-bhakti*) is above these principles. The world is anxious for religious unity, and that common platform can be achieved in transcendental devotional service. This is the verdict of Śrī Caitanya Mahāprabhu. When one becomes a Vaiṣṇava, he becomes transcendental to all these limited considerations. This is also confirmed in *Bhagavad-gītā* (14.26):

māṁ ca yo 'vyabhicāreṇa
bhakti-yogena sevate
sa guṇān samatītyaitān
brahma-bhūyāya kalpate

"One who engages in full devotional service, who does not fall down in any circumstance, at once transcends the modes of material nature and thus comes to the level of Brahman."

The devotional activities of the Kṛṣṇa consciousness movement are completely transcendental to material considerations. As far as different faiths are concerned, religions may be of different types, but on the spiritual platform, everyone has an equal right to execute devotional service. That is the platform of oneness and the basis for a classless society. In his *Amṛta-pravāha-bhāṣya,* Śrīla Bhaktivinoda Ṭhākura confirms that one has to learn from a bona fide spiritual master about religious principles, economic development, sense gratification and ultimately liberation. These are the four divisions of regulated life, but they are subjected to the material platform. On the spiritual platform, the four principles are *jñāna, vijñāna, tad-aṅga* and *tad-rahasya.* Rules, regulations and restrictions are on the material platform, but on the spiritual platform one has to be equipped with transcendental knowledge, which is above the principles of religious rituals. Mundane religious activity is known as *smārta-viddhi,* but transcendental devotional service is called *gosvāmi-viddhi.* Unfortunately many so-called *gosvāmīs* are on the platform of *smārta-viddhi,* yet they try to pass as *gosvāmi-viddhi,* and thus the people are cheated. *Gosvāmi-viddhi* is strictly explained in Sanātana Gosvāmī's *Hari-bhakti-vilāsa,* wherein it is stated:

yathā kāñcanatāṁ yāti
kāṁsyaṁ rasa-vidhānataḥ
tathā dīṣkā-vidhānena
dvijatvaṁ jāyate nṛṇām

The conclusion is that devotional service is open for everyone, regardless of caste, creed, time and country. This Kṛṣṇa consciousness movement is functioning according to this principle.

TEXT 122

সর্ব-দেশ-কাল-দশায় জনের কর্তব্য।
গুরু-পাশে সেই ভক্তি প্রষ্টব্য, শ্রোতব্য ॥ ১২২ ॥

sarva-deśa-kāla-daśāya janera kartavya
guru-pāśe sei bhakti praṣṭavya, śrotavya

SYNONYMS

sarva—all; *deśa*—countries; *kāla*—times; *daśāya*—and in circumstances; *janera*—of every man; *kartavya*—the duty; *guru-pāśe*—in the care of a spiritual master; *sei*—that; *bhakti*—devotional service; *praṣṭavya*—to be inquired; *śrotavya*—and to be heard.

TRANSLATION

" 'It is therefore the duty of every man—in every country, in every circumstance and at all times—to approach the bona fide spiritual master, question him about devotional service and listen to him explain the process.

TEXT 123

এতাবদেব জিজ্ঞাস্যং তত্ত্বজিজ্ঞাসুনাত্মনঃ।
অন্বয়-ব্যতিরেকাভ্যাং যৎ স্যাৎ সর্বত্র সর্বদা ॥ ১২৩ ॥

etāvad eva jijñāsyaṁ
tattva-jijñāsunātmanaḥ
anvaya-vyatirekābhyāṁ
yat syāt sarvatra sarvadā

SYNONYMS

etāvat—up to this; *eva*—certainly; *jijñāsyam*—to be inquired about; *tattva*—of the Absolute Truth; *jijñāsunā*—by the student; *ātmanaḥ*—of the self; *anvaya*—

directly; *vyatirekābhyām*—and indirectly; *yat*—whatever; *syāt*—it may be; *sarvatra*—everywhere; *sarvadā*—always.

TRANSLATION

" 'A person interested in transcendental knowledge must therefore always directly and indirectly inquire about it to know about the all-pervading truth.

PURPORT

This is a quotation from *Śrīmad-Bhāgavatam* (2.9.36). It is the fourth verse of the *catuḥ-ślokī*. For an explanation see *Ādi-līlā*, Chapter One, text 56.

TEXT 124

আমাতে যে 'প্রীতি', সেই 'প্রেম'—'প্রয়োজন' ।
কার্যদ্বারে কহি তার 'স্বরূপ'-লক্ষণ ॥ ১২৪ ॥

āmāte ye 'prīti', sei 'prema'——'prayojana'
kārya-dvāre kahi tāra 'svarūpa'-lakṣaṇa

SYNONYMS

āmāte—unto Me; *ye*—whatever; *prīti*—affection; *sei*—that; *prema*—love of Godhead; *prayojana*—the ultimate goal of life; *kārya-dvāre*—by practical example; *kahi*—let Me inform; *tāra*—its; *svarūpa-lakṣaṇa*—natural characteristics.

TRANSLATION

" 'Supreme affection for Me is called love of Godhead, and that is the ultimate goal of life. Let Me explain by practical example the natural characteristics of such love.

TEXT 125

পঞ্চভুত যৈছে ভুতের ভিতরে-বাহিরে ।
ভক্তগণে স্ফুরি আমি বাহিরে-অন্তরে ॥ ১২৫ ॥

pañca-bhūta yaiche bhūtera bhitare-bāhire
bhakta-gaṇe sphuri āmi bāhire-antare

SYNONYMS

pañca-bhūta—the five material elements; *yaiche*—just as; *bhūtera*—of the living entities; *bhitare*—inside; *bāhire*—and outside; *bhakta-gaṇe*—unto the devotees; *sphuri*—becoming manifest; *āmi*—I; *bāhire-antare*—externally and internally.

TRANSLATION

" 'The five material elements are existing inside and outside of every living entity. Similarly, I, the Supreme Personality of Godhead, am manifest within the heart of the devotee as well as outside his body.

PURPORT

The pure devotee knows that he is a servant of Kṛṣṇa eternally. He knows that everything can be used in the service of the Lord.

TEXT 126

যথা মহান্তি ভূতানি ভূতেষূচ্চাবচেষ্বনু ।
প্রবিষ্টান্যপ্রবিষ্টানি তথা তেষু ন তেষ্বহম্ ॥ ১২৬ ॥

yathā mahānti bhūtāni
bhūteṣūccāvaceṣv anu
praviṣṭāny apraviṣṭāni
tathā teṣu na teṣv aham

SYNONYMS

yathā—as; *mahānti*—the universal; *bhūtāni*—elements; *bhūteṣu*—in the living entities; *ucca-avaceṣu*—both gigantic and minute; *anu*—after; *praviṣṭāni*—situated internally; *apraviṣṭāni*—situated externally; *tathā*—so; *teṣu*—in them; *na*—not; *teṣu*—in them; *aham*—I.

TRANSLATION

" 'As the material elements enter the bodies of all living beings and yet remain outside them all, I exist within all material creations and yet am not within them.

PURPORT

This is a quotation from *Śrīmad-Bhāgavatam* (2.9.35). It is also the third verse of the *catuḥ-ślokī.* For an explanation see *Ādi-līlā,* Chapter One, text 55.

TEXT 127

ভক্ত আমা প্রেমে বান্ধিয়াছে হৃদয়-ভিতরে ।
যাহাঁ নেত্র পড়ে তাহাঁ দেখয়ে আমারে ॥ ১২৭ ॥

bhakta āmā preme bāndhiyāche hṛdaya-bhitare
yāhāṅ netra paḍe tāhāṅ dekhaye āmāre

SYNONYMS

bhakta—a devotee; *āmā*—Me; *preme*—by love; *bāndiyāche*—has bound; *hṛdaya-bhitare*—within his heart; *yāhāṅ*—wherever; *netra*—the eyes; *paḍe*—fall; *tāhāṅ*—there; *dekhaye*—he sees; *āmāre*—Me.

TRANSLATION

" 'A highly elevated devotee can bind Me, the Supreme Personality of Godhead, in his heart by love. Wherever he looks, he sees Me and nothing else.

TEXT 128

বিস্থজতি হৃদয়ং ন যস্য সাক্ষা-
দ্ধরিরবশাভিহিতোহপ্যঘৌঘনাশঃ ।
প্রণয়রসনয়া ধৃতাঙ্ঘ্রিপদ্মঃ
স ভবতি ভাগবতপ্রধান উক্তঃ ॥ ১২৮ ॥

visṛjati hṛdayaṁ na yasya sākṣād
dharir avaśābhihito 'py aghaugha-nāśaḥ
praṇaya-rasanayā dhṛtāṅghri-padmaḥ
sa bhavati bhāgavata-pradhāna uktaḥ

SYNONYMS

visṛjati—gives up; *hṛdayam*—the heart; *na*—not; *yasya*—whose; *sākṣāt*—directly; *hariḥ*—the Supreme Personality of Godhead; *avaśa-abhihitaḥ*—who is automatically glorified; *api*—although; *aghaugha-nāśaḥ*—who annihilates all kinds of inauspicious offenses for a devotee; *praṇaya-rasanayā*—with the rope of love; *dhṛta-aṅghri-padmaḥ*—whose lotus feet are bound; *saḥ*—such a devotee; *bhavati*—is; *bhāgavata-pradhānaḥ*—the most elevated devotee; *uktaḥ*—is said.

TRANSLATION

" 'Hari, the Supreme Personality of Godhead, who destroys everything inauspicious for His devotees, does not leave the hearts of His devotees even if they remember Him and chant about Him inattentively. This is because the rope of love always binds the Lord within the devotees' hearts. Such devotees should be accepted as most elevated.

PURPORT

This is a quotation from *Śrīmad-Bhāgavatam* (11.2.55).

TEXT 129

সর্বভূতেষু যঃ পশ্যেদ্ভগবদ্ভাবমাত্মনঃ।
ভূতানি ভগবত্যাত্মন্যেষ ভাগবতোত্তমঃ ॥ ১২৯ ॥

sarva-bhūteṣu yaḥ paśyed
bhagavad-bhāvam ātmanaḥ
bhūtāni bhagavaty ātmany
eṣa bhāgavatottamaḥ

SYNONYMS

sarva-bhūteṣu—in all objects (in matter, spirit, or combinations of matter and spirit); *yaḥ*—anyone who; *paśyet*—sees; *bhagavat-bhāvam*—the capacity to be engaged in the service of the Lord; *ātmanaḥ*—of the Supreme Spirit Soul, or the transcendence beyond the material conception of life; *bhūtāni*—all beings; *bhagavati*—in the Supreme Personality of Godhead; *ātmani*—the basic principle of all existence; *eṣaḥ*—this; *bhāgavata-uttamaḥ*—a person advanced in devotional service.

TRANSLATION

" 'A person advanced in devotional service sees within everything the soul of souls, the Supreme Personality of Godhead, Śrī Kṛṣṇa. Consequently he always sees the form of the Supreme Personality of Godhead as the cause of all causes and understands that all things are situated in Him.

PURPORT

This is a quotation from *Śrīmad-Bhāgavatam* (11.2.45).

TEXT 130

গায়ন্ত উচ্চৈরমুমেব সংহতাঃ
বিচিক্যুরুন্মত্তকবদ্বনাদ্বনম্।
পপ্রচ্ছুরাকাশবদন্তরং বহি-
র্ভূতেষু সন্তং পুরুষং বনস্পতীন্ ॥ ১৩০ ॥

gāyanta uccair amum eva saṁhatāḥ
vicikyur unmattakavad vanād vanam
papracchur ākāśavad antaraṁ bahir
bhūteṣu santaṁ puruṣaṁ vanaspatīn

SYNONYMS

gāyantaḥ—continuously singing; *uccaiḥ*—very loudly; *amum*—that one (Lord Śrī Kṛṣṇa); *eva*—certainly; *saṁhatāḥ*—being assembled together; *vicikyuḥ*—searched; *unmattaka-vat*—like those who have become mad; *vanāt*—from one forest; *vanam*—to another forest; *papracchuḥ*—asked about; *ākāśa-vat*—like the sky; *antaram*—within; *bahiḥ*—outside; *bhūteṣu*—in all living entities; *santam*—existing; *puruṣam*—the Supreme Person; *vanaspatīn*—all the trees and plants.

TRANSLATION

" 'All the gopīs assembled to chant the transcendental qualities of Kṛṣṇa very loudly, and they began to wander from one forest to another like madwomen. They began to inquire about the Lord, who is situated in all living entities internally and externally. Indeed, they even asked all the plants and vegetables about Him, the Supreme Person.' "

PURPORT

This is a quotation from *Śrīmad-Bhāgavatam* (10.30.4). The *gopīs* almost went mad due to Kṛṣṇa's suddenly leaving the *rāsa* dance. Because the *gopīs* were fully absorbed in thoughts of Kṛṣṇa, they were imitating His different postures and pastimes. They became very saddened because of His absence, and this incident is explained by Śukadeva Gosvāmī to Mahārāja Parīkṣit.

TEXT 131

অতএব ভাগবতে এই 'তিন' কয় ।
সম্বন্ধ-অভিধেয়-প্রয়োজন-ময় ॥ ১৩১ ॥

ataeva bhāgavate ei 'tina' kaya
sambandha-abhidheya-prayojana-maya

SYNONYMS

ataeva—therefore; *bhāgavate*—in *Śrīmad-Bhāgavatam; ei tina*—these three principles; *kaya*—are explained; *sambandha-abhidheya-prayojana-maya*—first one's relationship, then activities in devotional service, and then achieving the highest goal of life, love of Godhead.

TRANSLATION

Śrī Caitanya Mahāprabhu continued, "One's relationship with the Lord, activities and devotional service, and the attainment of the highest goal of life, love of Godhead, are the subject matters of Śrīmad-Bhāgavatam.

TEXT 132

বদন্তি তত্তত্ত্ববিদস্তত্ত্বং যজ্‌জ্ঞানমদ্বয়ম্ ।
ব্রহ্মেতি পরমাত্মেতি ভগবানিতি শব্দ্যতে ॥ ১৩২ ॥

vadanti tat tattva-vidas
tattvaṁ yaj jñānam advayam
brahmeti paramātmeti
bhagavān iti śabdyate

SYNONYMS

vadanti—they say; *tat*—that; *tattva-vidaḥ*—those who know the Absolute Truth; *tattvam*—the ultimate goal; *yat*—which; *jñānam advayam*—identical knowledge; *brahma iti*—as the impersonal Brahman; *paramātmā iti*—as the Supersoul; *bhagavān iti*—as the Supreme Personality of Godhead; *śabdyate*—it is described.

TRANSLATION

" 'The Absolute Truth is known by the self-realized souls as a unified identity known by different names—impersonal Brahman, localized Paramātmā, and Bhagavān, the Supreme Personality of Godhead.'

PURPORT

This is a quotation from *Śrīmad-Bhāgavatam* (1.2.11).

TEXT 133

ভগবানেক আসেদমগ্র আত্মাত্মনাং বিভুঃ ।
আত্মেচ্ছানুগতাবাত্মা অনানামত্যুপলক্ষণঃ ॥ ১৩৩ ॥

bhagavān eka āsedam
agra ātmātmanāṁ vibhuḥ
ātmecchānugatāv ātmā
anānāmaty-upalakṣaṇaḥ

SYNONYMS

bhagavān—the Supreme Personality of Godhead; *ekaḥ*—only; *āsa*—was; *idam*—this universe; *agre*—before (before the creation of this cosmic manifestation); *ātmā*—the living force; *ātmanām*—of all the living entities; *vibhuḥ*—the Supreme Lord; *ātma*—of the Supreme; *icchā*—the will; *anugatau*—according to;

ātmā—the Supersoul; *anānāmati-upalakṣaṇaḥ*—who is not realized by persons having many angles of vision.

TRANSLATION

" 'Before the cosmic manifestation was created, the creative propensity was merged in His person. At that time all potencies and manifestations were preserved in the personality of the Supreme Lord. The Lord is the cause of all causes, and He is the all-pervading, self-sufficient person. Before the creation, He existed with His spiritual potency in the spiritual world, wherein various Vaikuṇṭha planets are manifest.'

PURPORT

This is a quotation from *Śrīmad-Bhāgavatam* (3.5.23).

TEXT 134

এতে চাংশকলাঃ পুংসঃ কৃষ্ণস্তু ভগবান্ স্বয়ম্ ।
ইন্দ্রারি-ব্যাকুলং লোকং মৃড়য়ন্তি যুগে যুগে ॥ ১৩৪ ॥

ete cāṁśa-kalāḥ puṁsaḥ
kṛṣṇas tu bhagavān svayam
indrāri-vyākulaṁ lokaṁ
mṛḍayanti yuge yuge

SYNONYMS

ete—these; *ca*—and; *aṁśa*—plenary portions; *kalāḥ*—parts of plenary portions; *puṁsaḥ*—of the *puruṣa-avatāras; kṛṣṇaḥ*—Lord Kṛṣṇa; *tu*—but; *bhagavān*—the Supreme Personality of Godhead; *svayam*—Himself; *indra-ari*—the enemies of Lord Indra; *vyākulam*—full of; *lokam*—the world; *mṛḍayanti*—make happy; *yuge yuge*—at the right time in each age.

TRANSLATION

" 'All these incarnations of Godhead are either plenary portions or parts of the plenary portions of the puruṣa-avatāras. But Kṛṣṇa is the Supreme Personality of Godhead Himself. In every age He protects the world through His different features when the world is disturbed by the enemies of Indra.'

PURPORT

This is a quotation from *Śrīmad-Bhāgavatam* (1.3.28). For an explanation, see *Ādi-līlā,* Chapter Two, text 67.

TEXT 135

এইত' 'সম্বন্ধ', শুন 'অভিধেয়' ভক্তি ।
ভাগবতে প্রতি-শ্লোকে ব্যাপে যার স্থিতি ॥ ১৩৫ ॥

eita' 'sambandha', śuna 'abhidheya' bhakti
bhāgavate prati-śloke vyāpe yāra sthiti

SYNONYMS

eita'—this; *sambandha*—relationship; *śuna*—please hear; *abhidheya*—the function; *bhakti*—known as devotional service; *bhāgavate*—in *Śrīmad-Bhāgavatam; prati-śloke*—in each and every verse; *vyāpe*—pervades; *yāra*—of which; *sthiti*—the situation.

TRANSLATION

"This is one's eternal relationship with the Supreme Personality of Godhead. Now please hear about the execution of devotional service. This principle pervades practically all the verses of Śrīmad-Bhāgavatam.

TEXT 136

ভক্ত্যাহমেকয়া গ্রাহ্যঃ শ্রদ্ধয়াত্মা প্রিয়ঃ সতাম্ ।
ভক্তিঃ পুনাতি মন্নিষ্ঠা শ্বপাকানপি সম্ভবাৎ ॥ ১৩৬ ॥

bhaktyāham ekayā grāhyaḥ
śraddhayātmā priyaḥ satām
bhaktiḥ punāti man-niṣṭhā
śva-pākān api sambhavāt

SYNONYMS

bhaktyā—by devotional service; *aham*—I, the Supreme Personality of Godhead; *ekayā*—unflinching; *grāhyaḥ*—obtainable; *śraddhayā*—by faith; *ātmā*—the most dear; *priyaḥ*—to be served; *satām*—by the devotees; *bhaktiḥ*—the devotional service; *punāti*—purifies; *mat-niṣṭhā*—fixed only on Me; *śva-pākān*—the lowest grade of human beings, who are accustomed to eating dogs; *api*—certainly; *sambhavāt*—from all faults due to birth and so on.

TRANSLATION

" 'Being very dear to the devotees and sādhus, I am attained through unflinching faith and devotional service. This bhakti-yoga system, which

gradually increases attachment for Me, purifies even a human being born among dog-eaters. That is to say, everyone can be elevated to the spiritual platform by the process of bhakti-yoga.'

PURPORT

This verse is from *Śrīmad-Bhāgavatam* (11.14.21).

TEXT 137

ন সাধয়তি মাং যোগো ন সাংখ্যং ধর্ম উদ্ধব ।
ন স্বাধ্যায়স্তপস্ত্যাগো যথা ভক্তির্মমোর্জিতা ॥ ১৩৭ ॥

na sādhayati māṁ yogo
na sāṅkhyaṁ dharma uddhava
na svādhyāyas tapas tyāgo
yathā bhaktir mamorjitā

SYNONYMS

na—never; *sādhayati*—causes to remain satisfied; *mām*—Me; *yogaḥ*—the process of control; *na*—nor; *sāṅkhyam*—the process of gaining philosophical knowledge about the Absolute Truth; *dharmaḥ*—such an occupation; *uddhava*—My dear Uddhava; *na*—nor; *svādhyāyaḥ*—study of the *Vedas; tapaḥ*—austerities; *tyāgaḥ*—renunciation, acceptance of *sannyāsa,* or charity; *yathā*—as much as; *bhaktiḥ*—devotional service; *mama*—unto Me; *ūrjitā*—developed.

TRANSLATION

" 'The Supreme Personality of Godhead, Kṛṣṇa, said: "My dear Uddhava, neither through aṣṭāṅga-yoga [the mystic yoga system to control the senses], nor through impersonalism or an analytical study of the Absolute Truth, nor through study of the Vedas, nor through practice of austerities, nor through charity, nor through acceptance of sannyāsa, can one satisfy Me as much as one can by developing unalloyed devotional service unto Me." '

PURPORT

This is a quotation from *Śrīmad-Bhāgavatam* (11.14.20). For an explanation see *Ādi-līlā,* Chapter Seventeen, text 76.

TEXT 138

ভয়ং দ্বিতীয়াভিনিবেশতঃ স্যা-
দীশাদপেতস্য বিপর্যয়োঽস্মৃতিঃ ।

তন্মায়য়াতো বুধ আভজেত্তং
ভক্ত্যৈকয়েশং গুরুদেবতাত্মা ॥ ১৩৮ ॥

bhayaṁ dvitīyābhiniveśataḥ syād
īśād apetasya viparyayo 'smṛtiḥ
tan-māyayāto budha ābhajet taṁ
bhaktyaikayeśaṁ guru-devatātmā

SYNONYMS

bhayam—fear; *dvitīya-abhiniveśataḥ*—from the misconception of being a product of material energy; *syāt*—arises; *īśāt*—from the Supreme Personality of Godhead, Kṛṣṇa; *apetasya*—of one who has withdrawn (the conditioned soul); *viparyayaḥ*—reversal of position; *asmṛtiḥ*—no conception of his relationship with the Supreme Lord; *tat-māyayā*—because of the illusory energy of the Supreme Lord; *ataḥ*—therefore; *budhaḥ*—one who is wise; *ābhajet*—must worship; *tam*—Him; *bhaktyā*—by devotional service; *ekayā*—undiverted to *karma* and *jñāna; īśam*—the Supreme Personality of Godhead; *guru*—as the spiritual master; *devatā*—worshipable Lord; *ātmā*—Supersoul.

TRANSLATION

" 'When the living entity is attracted by the material energy, which is separate from Kṛṣṇa, he is overpowered by fear. Because he is separated from the Supreme Personality of Godhead by the material energy, his conception of life is reversed. In other words, instead of being the eternal servant of Kṛṣṇa, he becomes Kṛṣṇa's competitor. This is called viparyayo 'smṛtiḥ. To nullify this mistake, one who is actually learned and advanced worships the Supreme Personality of Godhead as his spiritual master, worshipful Deity and source of life. He thus worships the Lord by the process of unalloyed devotional service.'

PURPORT

This is a quotation from *Śrīmad-Bhāgavatam* (11.2.37).

TEXT 139

এবে শুন, প্রেম, যেই—মূল 'প্রয়োজন' ।
পুলকাশ্রু-নৃত্য-গীত– যাহার লক্ষণ ॥ ১৩৯ ॥

ebe śuna, prema, yei——mūla 'prayojana'
pulakāśru-nṛtya-gīta——yāhāra lakṣaṇa

SYNONYMS

ebe śuna—now hear; *prema*—love of Godhead; *yei*—which; *mūla prayojana*—the chief objective; *pulaka-aśru-nṛtya-gīta*—trembling of the body, tears in the eyes, dancing and chanting; *yāhāra lakṣaṇa*—the symptoms of which.

TRANSLATION

"Now hear from Me what actual love of Godhead is. It is the prime object of life and is symptomized by bodily trembling, tears in the eyes, chanting and dancing.

TEXT 140

স্মরন্তঃ স্মারয়শ্চ মিথোঽঘৌঘহরং হরিম্ ।
ভক্ত্যা সংজাতয়া ভক্ত্যা বিভ্রত্যুৎপুলকাং তনুম্ ॥ ১৪০ ॥

smarantaḥ smārayaś ca
mitho 'ghaugha-haraṁ harim
bhaktyā sañjātayā bhaktyā
bibhraty utpulakāṁ tanum

SYNONYMS

smarantaḥ—remembering; *smārayaḥ ca*—and reminding; *mithaḥ*—one another; *aghaugha-haram*—who takes away everything inauspicious from the devotee; *harim*—the Supreme Personality of Godhead; *bhaktyā*—by devotion; *sañjātayā*—awakened; *bhaktyā*—by devotion; *bibhrati*—possess; *utpulakām*—agitated by ecstasy; *tanum*—body.

TRANSLATION

" 'Pure devotees develop a spiritual body and symptoms of ecstatic love simply by remembering and reminding others of the Supreme Personality of Godhead, Hari, who takes away everything inauspicious from the devotee. This position is attained by rendering devotional service according to the regulative principles and then rising to the platform of spontaneous love.'

PURPORT

This is a quotation from *Śrīmad-Bhāgavatam* (11.3.31).

TEXT 141

এবংব্রতঃ স্বপ্রিয়নামকীর্ত্যা
জাতানুরাগো দ্রুতচিত্ত উচ্চৈঃ ।

হসত্যথো রোদিতি রৌতি গায়-
ত্যুন্মাদবন্নৃত্যতি লোকবাহ্যঃ ॥ ১৪১ ॥

evaṁ-vrataḥ sva-priya-nāma-kīrtyā
jātānurāgo druta-citta uccaiḥ
hastay atho roditi rauti gāyaty
unmādavan nṛtyati loka-bāhyaḥ

SYNONYMS

evam-vrataḥ—when one thus engages in a vow to chant and dance; *sva*—own; *priya*—very dear; *nāma*—holy name; *kīrtyā*—by chanting; *jāta*—in this way develops; *anurāgaḥ*—attachment; *druta-cittaḥ*—very eagerly; *uccaiḥ*—loudly; *hasati*—laughs; *atho*—also; *roditi*—cries; *rauti*—becomes agitated; *gāyati*—chants; *unmāda-vat*—like a madman; *nṛtyati*—dances; *loka-bāhyaḥ*—without caring for outsiders.

TRANSLATION

" 'When a person is actually advanced and takes pleasure in chanting the holy name of the Lord, who is very dear to him, he is agitated and loudly chants the holy name. He also laughs, cries, becomes agitated and chants like a madman, not caring for outsiders.'

PURPORT

This is a quotation from *Śrīmad-Bhāgavatam* (11.2.40).

TEXT 142

অতএব ভাগবত—সূত্রের 'অর্থ'-রূপ ।
নিজ-কৃত সূত্রের নিজ-'ভাষ্য'-স্বরূপ ॥ ১৪২ ॥

ataeva bhāgavata——sūtrera 'artha'-rūpa
nija-kṛta sūtrera nija-'bhāṣya'-svarūpa

SYNONYMS

ataeva—therefore; *bhāgavata*—*Śrīmad-Bhāgavatam; sūtrera*—of the *Brahma-sūtra; artha*—of the meaning; *rūpa*—the form; *nija-kṛta*—made by himself; *sūtrera*—of the *Vedānta-sūtra; nija-bhāṣya*—of his own commentary; *svarūpa*—the original form.

TRANSLATION

"Śrīmad-Bhāgavatam gives the actual meaning of the Vedānta-sūtra. The author of the Vedānta-sūtra is Vyāsadeva, and he himself has explained those codes in the form of Śrīmad-Bhāgavatam.

TEXTS 143-144

অর্থোঽয়ং ব্রহ্মসূত্রাণাং ভারতার্থবিনির্ণয়ঃ ।
গায়ত্রীভাষ্যরূপোঽসৌ বেদার্থপরিবৃংহিতঃ ॥ ১৪৩ ॥
পুরাণানাং সামরূপঃ সাক্ষাদ্ভগবতোদিতঃ ।
দ্বাদশস্কন্ধযুক্তোঽয়ং শতবিচ্ছেদ-সংযুতঃ ।
গ্রন্থোঽষ্টাদশসাহস্রঃ শ্রীমদ্ভাগবতাভিধঃ ॥ ১৪৪ ॥

artho 'yaṁ brahma-sūtrāṇāṁ
bhāratārtha-vinirṇayaḥ
gāyatrī-bhāṣya-rūpo 'sau
vedārtha-paribṛṁhitaḥ

purāṇānāṁ sāma-rūpaḥ
sākṣād-bhagavatoditaḥ
dvādaśa-skandha-yukto 'yaṁ
śata-viccheda-saṁyutaḥ
grantho 'ṣṭādaśa-sāhasraḥ
śrīmad-bhāgavatābhidhaḥ

SYNONYMS

arthaḥ ayam—this is the meaning; *brahma-sūtrāṇām*—of the codes of *Vedānta-sūtra; bhārata-artha-vinirṇayaḥ*—the ascertainment of the *Mahābhārata; gāyatrī-bhāṣya-rūpaḥ*—the purport of Brahma-gāyatrī, the mother of the Vedic literatures; *asau*—that; *veda-artha-paribṛṁhitaḥ*—expanded by the meanings of all the *Vedas; purāṇānām*—of the *Purāṇas; sāma-rūpaḥ*—the best (like the *Sāma* among the *Vedas*); *sākṣāt*—directly; *bhagavatā uditaḥ*—spoken by Vyāsadeva, an incarnation of the Supreme Personality of Godhead; *dvādaśa-skandha-yuktaḥ*—having twelve cantos; *ayam*—this; *śata-viccheda-saṁyutaḥ*—having 355 chapters; *granthaḥ*—this great literature; *aṣṭādaśa-sāhasraḥ*—having 18,000 verses; *śrīmad-bhāgavata-abhidhaḥ*—named *Śrīmad-Bhāgavatam.*

TRANSLATION

" 'The meaning of the Vedānta-sūtra is present in Śrīmad-Bhāgavatam. The full purport of the Mahābhārata is also there. The commentary of the Brahma-

gāyatrī is also there and fully expanded with all Vedic knowledge. Śrīmad-Bhāgavatam is the supreme Purāṇa, and it was compiled by the Supreme Personality of Godhead in His incarnation as Vyāsadeva. There are twelve cantos, 335 chapters and eighteen thousand verses.'

PURPORT

This is a quotation from the *Garuda Purāṇa.*

TEXT 145

সর্ব-বেদেতিহাসানাং সারং সারং সমুদ্ধৃতম্ ॥ ১৪৫ ॥

sarva-vedetihāsānāṁ
sāraṁ sāraṁ samuddhṛtam

SYNONYMS

sarva-veda—of all Vedic literature; *itihāsānām*—of historical literature; *sāram sāram*—the essence of the essence; *samuddhṛtam*—is collected (in *Śrīmad-Bhāgavatam*).

TRANSLATION

" 'The essence of all Vedic literature and all histories has been collected in this Śrīmad-Bhāgavatam.'

PURPORT

Śrīmad-Bhāgavatam was collected by the incarnation of God, Vyāsadeva, and it was later taught to his son, Śukadeva Gosvāmī. This is a quotation from *Śrīmad-Bhāgavatam* (1.3.42).

TEXT 146

সর্ববেদান্তসারং হি শ্রীমদ্ভাগবতমিষ্যতে ।
তদ্রসামৃততৃপ্তস্য নান্যত্র স্যাদ্রতিঃ ক্বচিৎ ॥ ১৪৬ ॥

sarva-vedānta-sāraṁ hi
śrīmad-bhāgavatam iṣyate
tad-rasāmṛta-tṛptasya
nānyatra syād ratiḥ kvacit

SYNONYMS

sarva-vedānta-sāram—the best part of all the Vedānta; *hi*—certainly; *śrīmad-bhāgavatam*—the great literature about Bhagavān; *iṣyate*—is accepted; *tat-rasa-*

amṛta—by the transcendental mellow derived from that great literature; *tṛptasya*—of one who is satisfied; *na*—never; *anyatra*—anywhere else; *syāt*—is; *ratiḥ*—attraction; *kvacit*—at any time.

TRANSLATION

" 'Śrīmad-Bhāgavatam is accepted as the essence of all Vedic literature and Vedānta philosophy. Whoever tastes the transcendental mellow of Śrīmad-Bhāgavatam is never attracted to any other literature.'

PURPORT

This is a quotation from *Śrīmad-Bhāgavatam* (12.13.15).

TEXT 147

গায়ত্রীর অর্থে এই গ্রন্থ-আরম্ভন ।
"সত্যং পরং"— **সম্বন্ধ,** "ধীমহি"— **সাধন-প্রয়োজন** ॥১৪৭

gāyatrīra arthe ei grantha-ārambhana
"satyaṁ paraṁ"——sambandha, "dhīmahi"——sādhana-prayojana

SYNONYMS

gāyatrīra arthe—with the meaning of Brahma-gāyatrī; *ei*—this; *grantha*—of the great literature; *ārambhana*—the beginning; *satyam param*—the supreme Absolute Truth; *sambandha*—shows a relationship; *dhīmahi*—we meditate (the end of the Gāyatrī *mantra*); *sādhana-prayojana*—the execution of service and the achievement of the ultimate goal.

TRANSLATION

"In the beginning of Śrīmad-Bhāgavatam there is an explanation of the Brahma-gāyatrī mantra. 'The Absolute Truth [satyaṁ param]' indicates the relationship, and 'we meditate [dhīmahi] on Him' indicates the execution of devotional service and the ultimate goal of life.

TEXT 148

জন্মাদ্যস্য যতোঽন্বয়াদিতরতশ্চার্থেষ্বভিজ্ঞঃ স্বরাট্
তেনে ব্রহ্ম হৃদা য আদিকবয়ে মুহ্যন্তি যৎ সূরয়ঃ ।
তেজোবারিমৃদাং যথা বিনিময়ো যত্র ত্রিসর্গোঽমৃষা
ধাম্না স্বেন সদা নিরস্তকুহকং সত্যং পরং ধীমহি॥ ১৪৮ ॥

janmādy asya yato 'nvayād itarataś cārtheṣv abhijñaḥ svarāṭ
tene brahma hṛdā ya ādi-kavaye muhyanti yat sūrayaḥ

tejo-vāri-mṛdāṁ yathā vinimayo yatra tri-sargo 'mṛṣā
dhāmnā svena sadā nirasta-kuhakaṁ satyaṁ paraṁ dhīmahi

SYNONYMS

janma-ādi—creation, maintenance and dissolution; *asya*—of this (the universe); *yataḥ*—from whom; *anvayāt*—directly from the spiritual connection; *itarataḥ*—indirectly from the lack of material contact; *ca*—also; *artheṣu*—in all affairs; *abhijñaḥ*—perfectly cognizant; *sva-rāṭ*—independent; *tene*—imparted; *brahma*—the Absolute Truth; *hṛdā*—through the heart; *yaḥ*—who; *ādi-kavaye*—unto Lord Brahmā; *muhyanti*—are bewildered; *yat*—in whom; *sūrayaḥ*—great personalities like Lord Brahmā and other demigods or great *brāhmaṇas; tejaḥ-vāri-mṛdām*—of fire, water and earth; *yathā*—as; *vinimayaḥ*—the exchange; *yatra*—in whom; *tri-sargaḥ*—the material creation of three modes; *amṛṣā*—factual; *dhāmnā*—with the abode; *svena*—His own personal; *sadā*—always; *nirasta-kuhakam*—devoid of all illusion; *satyam*—the truth; *param*—absolute; *dhīmahi*—let us meditate upon.

TRANSLATION

" 'I offer my obeisances unto Lord Śrī Kṛṣṇa, son of Vasudeva, who is the supreme all-pervading Personality of Godhead. I meditate upon Him, the transcendent reality, who is the primeval cause of all causes, from whom all manifested universes arise, in whom they dwell and by whom they are destroyed. I meditate upon that eternally effulgent Lord who is directly and indirectly conscious of all manifestations and yet is beyond them. It is He only who first imparted Vedic knowledge unto the heart of Brahmā, the first created being. Through Him this world, like a mirage, appears real even to great sages and demigods. Because of Him, the material universes, created by the three modes of nature, appear to be factual, although they are unreal. I meditate therefore upon Him, the Absolute Truth, who is eternally existent in His transcendental abode, and who is forever free of illusion.

PURPORT

This is the opening invocation of *Śrīmad-Bhāgavatam* (1.1.1).

TEXT 149

ধর্মঃ প্রোজ্ঝিতকৈতবোঽত্র পরমো নির্মৎসরাণাং সতাং
বেদ্যং বাস্তবমত্র বস্তু শিবদং তাপত্রয়োন্মূলনম্ ।
শ্রীমদ্ভাগবতে মহামুনিকৃতে কিংবাপরৈরীশ্বরঃ
সদ্যো হৃদ্যবরুধ্যতেঽত্র কৃতিভিঃ শুশ্রূষুভিস্তৎক্ষণাৎ ॥ ১৪৯ ॥

dharmaḥ projjhita-kaitavo 'tra paramo nirmatsarāṇāṁ satāṁ
vedyaṁ vāstavam atra vastu śivadaṁ tāpa-trayonmūlanam
śrīmad-bhāgavate mahāmuni-kṛte kiṁ vā parair īśvaraḥ
sadyo hṛdy avarudhyate 'tra kṛtibhiḥ śuśrūṣubhis tat-kṣaṇāt

SYNONYMS

dharmaḥ—religiosity; *projjhita*—completely rejected; *kaitavaḥ*—in which there is fruitive intention; *atra*—herein; *paramaḥ*—the highest; *nirmatsarāṇām*—of the one hundred percent pure in heart; *satām*—devotees; *vedyam*—to be understood; *vāstavam*—factual; *atra*—herein; *vastu*—substance; *śiva-dam*—giving well-being; *tāpa-traya*—of the threefold miseries; *unmūlanam*—causing uprooting; *śrīmat*—beautiful; *bhāgavate*—in the *Bhāgavata Purāṇa; mahā-muni*—by the great sage (Vyāsadeva); *kṛte*—compiled; *kim*—what; *vā*—indeed; *paraiḥ*—with others; *īśvaraḥ*—the Supreme Lord; *sadyaḥ*—at once; *hṛdi*—within the heart; *avarudhyate*—becomes confined; *atra*—herein; *kṛtibhiḥ*—by pious men; *śuśrūṣubhiḥ*—desiring to hear; *tat-kṣaṇāt*—without delay.

TRANSLATION

" 'Completely rejecting all religious activities which are materially motivated, this Bhāgavata Purāṇa propounds the highest truth, which is understandable by those devotees who are pure in heart. The highest truth is reality distinguished from illusion for the welfare of all. Such truth uproots the threefold miseries. This beautiful Bhāgavatam, compiled by the great sage Śrī Vyāsadeva, is sufficient in itself for God realization. As soon as one attentively and submissively hears the message of Bhāgavatam, he becomes attached to the Supreme Lord.'

PURPORT

This is a quotation from *Śrīmad-Bhāgavatam* (1.1.2). See also *Ādi-līlā,* Chapter One, text 91.

TEXT 150

'কৃষ্ণভক্তিরসস্বরূপ' শ্রীভাগবত।
তাতে বেদশাস্ত্র হৈতে পরম মহত্ত্ব ॥ ১৫০ ॥

'kṛṣṇa-bhakti-rasa-svarūpa' śrī-bhāgavata
tāte veda-śāstra haite parama mahattva

SYNONYMS

kṛṣṇa-bhakti—of devotional service to Kṛṣṇa; *rasa*—of the transcendental mellow; *svarūpa*—the very form; *śrī-bhāgavata*—*Śrīmad-Bhāgavatam; tāte*—

therefore; *veda-śāstra*—the Vedic literature; *haite*—than; *parama mahattva*—has greater utility and value.

TRANSLATION

"Śrīmad-Bhāgavatam gives direct information of the mellow derived from service to Kṛṣṇa. Therefore Śrīmad-Bhāgavatam is above all other Vedic literatures.

TEXT 151

নিগমকল্পতরোর্গলিতং ফলং
শুকমুখাদমৃতদ্রবসংযুতম্ ।
পিবত ভাগবতং রসমালয়ং
মুহুরহো রসিকা ভুবি ভাবুকাঃ ॥ ১৫১ ॥

nigama-kalpa-taror galitaṁ phalaṁ
śuka-mukhād amṛta-drava-saṁyutam
pibata bhāgavataṁ rasam ālayaṁ
muhur aho rasikā bhuvi bhāvukāḥ

SYNONYMS

nigama-kalpa-taroḥ—of the Vedic literature which is like a desire tree; *galitam*—completely ripened; *phalam*—fruit (which has come down without being distorted); *śuka-mukhāt*—from the mouth of Śukadeva Gosvāmī; *amṛta*—which is like nectar; *drava-saṁyutam*—mixed with juice; *pibata*—just drink; *bhāgavatam*—*Śrīmad-Bhāgavatam; rasam ālayam*—the reservoir of all mellows; *muhuḥ*—constantly; *aho*—O; *rasikāḥ*—intelligent and humorous devotees; *bhuvi*—in this world; *bhāvukāḥ*—thoughtful.

TRANSLATION

" 'The Śrīmad-Bhāgavatam is the essence of all Vedic literatures, and it is considered the ripened fruit of the wish-fulfilling tree of Vedic knowledge. It has been sweetened by emanating from the mouth of Śukadeva Gosvāmī. You who are thoughtful and who relish mellows should always try to taste this ripened fruit. O thoughtful devotees, as long as you are not absorbed in transcendental bliss, you should continue tasting this Śrīmad-Bhāgavatam, and when you are fully absorbed in bliss, you should go on tasting its mellows forever.'

PURPORT

This is a quotation from *Śrīmad-Bhāgavatam* (1.1.3).

TEXT 152

বয়ন্তু ন বিতৃপ্যাম উত্তমঃশ্লোকবিক্রমে।
যচ্ছৃণ্বতাং রসজ্ঞানাং স্বাদু স্বাদু পদে পদে ॥ ১·২ ॥

vayaṁ tu na vitṛpyāma
uttamaḥśloka-vikrame
yac chṛṇvatāṁ rasa-jñānāṁ
svādu svādu pade pade

SYNONYMS

vayam tu—we of course; *na*—never; *vitṛpyāmaḥ*—are satisfied; *uttamaḥ-śloka-vikrame*—in the activities and pastimes of the Supreme Personality of Godhead; *yat*—which; *śṛṇvatām*—of those hearing; *rasa-jñānām*—who know the taste of mellows; *svādu svādu*—more palatable; *pade pade*—in every step.

TRANSLATION

" 'We never tire of hearing the transcendental pastimes of the Personality of Godhead, who is glorified by hymns and prayers. Those who enjoy association with Him relish hearing His pastimes at every moment.' "

PURPORT

This is a quotation from *Śrīmad-Bhāgavatam* (1.1.19).

TEXT 153

অতএব ভাগবত করহ বিচার।
ইহা হৈতে পাবে সূত্র-শ্রুতির অর্থ-সার ॥ ১৫৩ ॥

ataeva bhāgavata karaha vicāra
ihā haite pābe sūtra-śrutira artha-sāra

SYNONYMS

ataeva—therefore; *bhāgavata*—*Śrīmad-Bhāgavatam; karaha vicāra*—try to understand scrutinizingly; *ihā haite*—from this; *pābe*—you will get; *sūtra-śrutira*—of the Vedic philosophy, the *Brahma-sūtra; artha-sāra*—the actual meaning.

TRANSLATION

Śrī Caitanya Mahāprabhu advised Prakāśānanda Sarasvatī, "Study Śrīmad-Bhāgavatam very scrutinizingly. Then you will understand the actual meaning of Brahma-sūtra."

TEXT 154

নিরন্তর কর কৃষ্ণনাম-সংকীর্তন।
হেলায় মুক্তি পাবে, পাবে প্রেমধন ॥ ১৫৪ ॥

nirantara kara kṛṣṇa-nāma-saṅkīrtana
helāya mukti pābe, pābe prema-dhana

SYNONYMS

nirantara kara—constantly perform; *kṛṣṇa-nāma-saṅkīrtana*—the chanting of the holy name of Kṛṣṇa; *helāya*—very easily; *mukti pābe*—you will get liberation; *pābe prema-dhana*—you will achieve the highest goal, ecstatic love of Kṛṣṇa.

TRANSLATION

Śrī Caitanya Mahāprabhu continued, "Always discuss Śrīmad-Bhāgavatam and constantly chant the holy name of Lord Kṛṣṇa. In this way you will be able to attain liberation very easily, and you will be elevated to the enjoyment of love of Godhead.

PURPORT

Śrīla Bhaktisiddhānta Sarasvatī Ṭhākura states that without studying *Śrīmad-Bhāgavatam,* one cannot understand the purport of *Brahma-sūtra* (*Vedānta-sūtra*) or the *Upaniṣads.* If one tries to understand Vedānta philosophy and the *Upaniṣads* without studying *Śrīmad-Bhāgavatam,* he will be bewildered and, construing a different meaning, will gradually become an atheist or an impersonalist.

TEXT 155

ব্রহ্মভূতঃ প্রসন্নাত্মা ন শোচতি ন কাঙ্ক্ষতি।
সমঃ সর্বেষু ভূতেষু মদ্ভক্তিং লভতে পরাম্ ॥ ১৫৫ ॥

brahma-bhūtaḥ prasannātmā
na śocati na kāṅkṣati
samaḥ sarveṣu bhūteṣu
mad-bhaktiṁ labhate parām

SYNONYMS

brahma-bhūtaḥ—freed from material conceptions of life but attached to an impersonal situation; *prasanna-ātmā*—fully joyful; *na śocati*—he does not lament; *na kāṅkṣati*—he does not hanker; *samaḥ*—equally disposed; *sarveṣu*—all; *bhūteṣu*—to the living entities; *mat-bhaktim*—My devotional service; *labhate*—achieves; *parām*—transcendental.

TRANSLATION

" 'One who is thus transcendentally situated at once realizes the Supreme Brahman and becomes fully joyful. He never laments nor desires to have anything; he is equally disposed to every living entity. In that state he attains pure devotional service unto Me.'

TEXT 156

"মুক্তা অপি লীলয়া বিগ্রহং কৃত্বা ভগবন্তং ভজন্তে ॥"১৫৬ ॥

"muktā api līlayā vigrahaṁ
kṛtvā bhagavantaṁ bhajante"

SYNONYMS

muktāḥ—liberated; *api*—although; *līlayā*—by pastimes; *vigraham*—the form of the Lord; *kṛtvā*—having installed; *bhagavantam*—the Supreme Personality of Godhead; *bhajante*—worship.

TRANSLATION

" 'Even a liberated soul merged in the impersonal Brahman effulgence is attracted to the pastimes of Kṛṣṇa. He thus installs a Deity and renders the Lord service.'

PURPORT

This is a quotation from Śaṅkarācārya's commentary on the *Nṛsiṁha-tāpanī.*

TEXT 157

পরিনিষ্ঠিতোঽপি নৈর্গুণ্যে উত্তমঃশ্লোকলীলয়া ।
গৃহীতচেতা রাজর্ষে আখ্যানং যদধীতবান্ ॥ ১৫৭ ॥

pariniṣṭhito 'pi nairguṇye
uttamaḥśloka-līlayā
gṛhīta-cetā rājarṣe
ākhyānaṁ yad adhītavān

SYNONYMS

pariniṣṭhitaḥ—situated; *api*—although; *nairguṇye*—in the transcendental position, freed from the material modes of nature; *uttamaḥ-śloka-līlayā*—by the pastimes of the Supreme Personality of Godhead, Uttamaḥśloka; *gṛhīta-cetā*—the mind became fully taken over; *rājarṣe*—O great King; *ākhyānam*—the narration; *yat*—which; *adhītavān*—studied.

TRANSLATION

" 'Śukadeva Gosvāmī addressed Parīkṣit Mahārāja, "My dear King, although I was fully situated in the transcendental position, I was nonetheless attracted to the pastimes of Lord Kṛṣṇa. Therefore I studied Śrīmad-Bhāgavatam from my father." '

PURPORT

This is a quotation from *Śrīmad-Bhāgavatam* (2.1.9).

TEXT 158

তস্যারবিন্দনয়নস্য পদারবিন্দ-
কিঞ্জল্কমিশ্রতুলসীমকরন্দবায়ুঃ ।
অন্তর্গতঃ স্ববিবরেণ চকার তেষাং
সংক্ষোভমক্ষরজুষামপি চিত্ততন্বোঃ ॥ ১৫৮ ॥

tasyāravinda-nayanasya padāravinda-
kiñjalka-miśra-tulasī-makaranda-vāyuḥ
antargataḥ svavivareṇa cakāra teṣāṁ
saṅkṣobham akṣara-juṣām api citta-tanvoḥ

SYNONYMS

tasya—of Him; *aravinda-nayanasya*—of the Supreme Personality of Godhead, whose eyes are like the petals of a lotus flower; *pada-aravinda*—of the lotus feet; *kiñjalka*—with saffron; *miśra*—mixed; *tulasī*—of *tulasī* leaves; *makaranda*—with the aroma; *vāyuḥ*—the air; *antargataḥ*—entered; *sva-vivareṇa*—through the nostrils; *cakāra*—created; *teṣām*—of them; *saṅkṣobham*—strong agitation; *akṣara-juṣām*—of the impersonally self-realized (Kumāras); *api*—also; *citta-tanvoḥ*—of the mind and the body.

TRANSLATION

" 'When the breeze carrying the aroma of tulasī leaves and saffron from the lotus feet of the lotus-eyed Personality of Godhead entered through the nostrils into the hearts of those sages [the Kumāras], they experienced a change in both body and mind, even though they were attached to impersonal Brahman understanding.'

PURPORT

This is a quotation from *Śrīmad-Bhāgavatam* (3.15.43).

TEXT 159

আত্মারামাশ্চ মুনয়ো নির্গ্রন্থা অপ্যুরুক্রমে ।
কুর্বন্ত্যহৈতুকীং ভক্তিমিত্থম্ভূতগুণো হরিঃ ॥ ১৫৯ ॥

ātmārāmāś ca munayo
nirgranthā apy urukrame
kurvanty ahaitukīṁ bhaktim
ittham-bhūta-guṇo hariḥ

SYNONYMS

ātma-ārāmāḥ—persons who take pleasure in being transcendentally situated in the service of the Lord; *ca*—also; *munayaḥ*—great saintly persons who have completely rejected material aspirations, fruitive activities, and so forth; *nirgranthāḥ*—without interest in any material desire; *api*—certainly; *urukrame*—unto the Supreme Personality of Godhead, Kṛṣṇa, whose activities are wonderful; *kurvanti*—do; *ahaitukīm*—causeless, or without material desires; *bhaktim*—devotional service; *ittham-bhūta*—so wonderful as to attract the attention of the self-satisfied; *guṇaḥ*—who has transcendental qualities; *hariḥ*—the Supreme Personality of Godhead.

TRANSLATION

" 'Those who are self-satisfied and unattracted by external material desires are also attracted to the loving service of Śrī Kṛṣṇa, whose qualities are transcendental and whose activities are wonderful. Hari, the Personality of Godhead, is called Kṛṣṇa because He has such transcendentally attractive features.' "

PURPORT

This is a quotation from *Śrīmad-Bhāgavatam* (1.7.10).

TEXT 160

হেনকালে সেই মহারাষ্ট্রীয় ব্রাহ্মণ ।
সভাতে কহিল সেই শ্লোক-বিবরণ ॥ ১৬০ ॥

hena-kāle sei mahārāṣṭrīya brāhmaṇa
sabhāte kahila sei śloka-vivaraṇa

SYNONYMS

hena-kāle—at this time; *sei*—that; *mahārāṣṭrīya brāhmaṇa*—the *brāhmaṇa* of Mahārāṣṭra province; *sabhāte*—in the meeting; *kahila*—declared; *sei*—that;

śloka-vivaraṇa—the description of the *ātmārāma-śloka* explained by Śrī Caitanya Mahāprabhu.

TRANSLATION

At this time the brāhmaṇa from the province of Mahārāṣṭra mentioned Lord Caitanya's explanation of the ātmārāma verse.

TEXT 161

এই শ্লোকের অর্থ প্রভু 'একষষ্টি' প্রকার ।
করিয়াছেন, যাহা শুনি' লোকে চমৎকার ॥ ১৬১ ॥

ei ślokera artha prabhu 'ekaṣaṣṭi' prakāra
kariyāchena, yāhā śuni' loke camatkāra

SYNONYMS

ei ślokera artha—the meanings of this verse; *prabhu*—Śrī Caitanya Mahāprabhu; *eka-ṣaṣṭi prakāra*—sixty-one varieties; *kariyāchena*—has done; *yāhā śuni'*—hearing which; *loke camatkāra*—everyone is astonished.

TRANSLATION

The Mahārāṣṭrian brāhmaṇa stated that Śrī Caitanya Mahāprabhu had already explained that verse in sixty-one ways. Everyone was astonished to hear this.

TEXT 162

তবে সব লোক শুনিতে আগ্রহ করিল ।
'একষষ্টি' অর্থ প্রভু বিবরি' কহিল ॥ ১৬২ ॥

tabe saba loka śunite āgraha karila
'ekaṣaṣṭi' artha prabhu vivari' kahila

SYNONYMS

tabe—then; *saba loka*—all the people gathered there; *śunite*—to hear; *āgraha karila*—expressed their eagerness; *eka-ṣaṣṭi artha*—sixty-one different meanings of the verse; *prabhu*—Śrī Caitanya Mahāprabhu; *vivari'*—elaborately; *kahila*—explained.

TRANSLATION

When all the people gathered there expressed the desire to hear again the sixty-one different meanings of the ātmārāma-śloka, Śrī Caitanya Mahāprabhu again explained them.

TEXT 163

শুনিয়া লোকের বড় চমৎকার হৈল ।
চৈতন্যগোসাঞি—'শ্রীকৃষ্ণ', নির্ধারিল ॥ ১৬৩ ॥

śuniyā lokera baḍa camatkāra haila
caitanya-gosāñi——'śrī-kṛṣṇa', nirdhārila

SYNONYMS

śuniyā—hearing; *lokera*—of all the people; *baḍa*—very great; *camatkāra*—wonder; *haila*—there was; *caitanya-gosāñi*—Śrī Caitanya Mahāprabhu; *śrī-kṛṣṇa*—personally Lord Kṛṣṇa; *nirdhārila*—they concluded.

TRANSLATION

When everyone heard Śrī Caitanya Mahāprabhu's explanation of the ātmārāma-śloka, everyone was astonished and struck with wonder. They concluded that Śrī Caitanya Mahāprabhu was none other than Lord Kṛṣṇa Himself.

TEXT 164

এত কহি' উঠিয়া চলিলা গৌরহরি ।
নমস্কার করে লোক হরিধ্বনি করি ॥ ১৬৪ ॥

eta kahi' uṭhiyā calilā gaurahari
namaskāra kare loka hari-dhvani kari

SYNONYMS

eta kahi'—after speaking that; *uṭhiyā*—standing; *calilā*—began to walk; *gaurahari*—Śrī Gaurasundara, Śrī Caitanya Mahāprabhu; *namaskāra kare loka*—all the people offered their obeisances; *hari-dhvani kari*—loudly chanting the Hare Kṛṣṇa *mahā-mantra.*

TRANSLATION

After giving those explanations again, Śrī Caitanya Mahāprabhu arose and took His leave. All the people there offered their obeisances unto Him and chanted the mahā-mantra.

TEXT 165

সব কাশীবাসী করে নামসংকীর্তন ।
প্রেমে হাসে, কাঁদে, গায়, করয়ে নর্তন ॥ ১৬৫ ॥

saba kāśī-vāsī kare nāma-saṅkīrtana
preme hāse, kāṅde, gāya, karaye nartana

SYNONYMS

saba kāśī-vāsī—all the inhabitants of Kāśī (Vārāṇasī); *kare*—performed; *nāma-saṅkīrtana*—chanting of the Hare Kṛṣṇa *mantra; preme*—in ecstatic love of Godhead; *hāse*—they laughed; *kāṅde*—they cried; *gāya*—chanted; *karaye nartana*—and danced.

TRANSLATION

All the inhabitants of Kāśī [Vārāṇasī] began chanting the Hare Kṛṣṇa mahā-mantra in ecstatic love. Sometimes they laughed, sometimes they cried, sometimes they chanted, and sometimes they danced.

TEXT 166

সন্ন্যাসী পণ্ডিত করে ভাগবত বিচার ।
বারাণসীপুর প্রভু করিলা নিস্তার ॥ ১৬৬ ॥

sannyāsī paṇḍita kare bhāgavata vicāra
vārāṇasī-pura prabhu karilā nistāra

SYNONYMS

sannyāsī—the Māyāvādī *sannyāsīs; paṇḍita*—the learned scholars; *kare*—do; *bhāgavata vicāra*—discussion on *Śrīmad-Bhāgavatam; vārāṇasī-pura*—the city known as Vārāṇasī; *prabhu*—Lord Śrī Caitanya Mahāprabhu; *karilā nistāra*—delivered.

TRANSLATION

After this, all the Māyāvādī sannyāsīs and learned scholars at Vārāṇasī began discussing Śrīmad-Bhāgavatam. In this way Śrī Caitanya Mahāprabhu delivered them.

TEXT 167

নিজ-লোক লঞা প্রভু আইলা বাসাঘর ।
বারাণসী হৈল দ্বিতীয় নদীয়া-নগর ॥ ১৬৭ ॥

nija-loka lañā prabhu āilā vāsāghara
vārāṇasī haila dvitīya nadīyā-nagara

SYNONYMS

nija-loka lañā—with His personal associates; *prabhu*—Śrī Caitanya Mahāprabhu; *āilā vāsa-aghara*—came to His residential place; *vārāṇasī*—the city of Vārāṇasī; *haila*—became; *dvitīya*—second; *nadīyā-nagara*—Navadvīpa (Nadia).

TRANSLATION

Śrī Caitanya Mahāprabhu then returned to His residence with His personal associates. Thus He turned the whole city of Vārāṇasī into another Navadvīpa [Nadīyā-nagara].

PURPORT

Both Navadvīpa and Vārāṇasī were celebrated for their highly educational activities. At the present time these cities are still inhabited by great, learned scholars, but Vārāṇasī is especially a center for Māyāvādī *sannyāsīs* who are learned scholars. However, unlike Navadvīpa, there are hardly any devotees in Vārāṇasī. Consequently a discussion of *Śrīmad-Bhāgavatam* was very rare in Vārāṇasī. In Navadvīpa, such a discussion was quite ordinary. After Śrī Caitanya Mahāprabhu visited Vārānaṣī and turned Prakāśānanda Sarasvatī and his disciples into Vaiṣṇavas, Vārāṇasī became like Navadvīpa because so many devotees began discussing *Śrīmad-Bhāgavatam.* Even at the present moment one can hear many discussions on *Śrīmad-Bhāgavatam* taking place on the banks of the Ganges. Many scholars and *sannyāsīs* gather there to hear *Śrīmad-Bhāgavatam* and perform *saṅkīrtana.*

TEXT 168

নিজগণ লঞা প্রভু কহে হাস্য করি'।
কাশীতে আমি আইলাঙ বেচিতে ভাবকালি ॥১৬৮॥

nija-gaṇa lañā prabhu kahe hāsya kari'
kāśīte āmi āilāṅa vecite bhāvakāli

SYNONYMS

nija-gaṇa lañā—with His personal associates; *prabhu kahe*—Śrī Caitanya Mahāprabhu said; *hāsya kari'*—laughingly; *kāśīte*—in Kāśī; *āmi āilāṅa*—I came; *vecite*—to sell; *bhāvakāli*—emotional ecstatic love.

TRANSLATION

Among His own associates, Śrī Caitanya Mahāprabhu laughingly said, "I came here to sell My emotional ecstatic love.

TEXT 169

কাশীতে গ্রাহক নাহি, বস্তু না বিকায়।
পুনরপি দেশে বহি' লওয়া নাহি যায়॥ ১৬৯॥

kāśīte grāhaka nāhi, vastu nā vikāya
punarapi deśe vahi' laoyā nāhi yāya

SYNONYMS

kāśīte—in Kāśī (Benares); *grāhaka nāhi*—there was no customer; *vastu nā vikāya*—it was not selling; *punarapi*—again; *deśe*—to My own country; *vahi'*—carrying (it); *laoyā*—to take; *nāhi yāya*—was not possible.

TRANSLATION

"Although I came to Vārāṇasī to sell My goods, there were no customers, and it appeared necessary for Me to carry them back to My own country.

TEXT 170

আমি বোঝা বহিমু, তোমা-সবার দুঃখ হৈল।
তোমা-সবার ইচ্ছায় বিনামূল্যে বিলাইল॥ ১৭০॥

āmi bojhā vahimu, tomā-sabāra duḥkha haila
tomā-sabāra icchāya vinā-mūlye bilāila

SYNONYMS

āmi—I; *bojhā*—burden; *vahimu*—shall carry; *tomā-sabāra duḥkha haila*—all of you became very unhappy; *tomā-sabāra icchāya*—only by your will; *vinā-mūlye bilāila*—I distributed without a price.

TRANSLATION

"All of you were feeling unhappy that no one was purchasing My goods and that I would have to carry them away. Therefore, by your will only, I have distributed them without charging."

PURPORT

When we began distributing the message of Śrī Caitanya Mahāprabhu in the Western countries, a similar thing happened. In the beginning we were very disappointed for at least one year because no one came forth to help this movement, but by the grace of Śrī Caitanya Mahāprabhu, some young boys joined this movement in 1966. Of course we distributed Śrī Caitanya Mahāprabhu's message of the Hare Kṛṣṇa *mahā-mantra* without bargaining or selling. As a result, this movement has spread all over the world, with the assistance of European and American boys and girls. We therefore pray for all the blessings of Śrī Caitanya Mahāprabhu upon all the devotees in the Western world who are spreading this movement.

TEXT 171

সবে কহে,— লোক তারিতে তোমার অবতার ।
'পূর্ব' 'দক্ষিণ' 'পশ্চিম' করিলা নিস্তার ॥ ১৭১ ॥

sabe kahe,——loka tārite tomāra avatāra
'pūrva' 'dakṣiṇa' 'paścima' karilā nistāra

SYNONYMS

sabe kahe—everyone says; *loka tārite*—to deliver the fallen souls; *tomāra avatāra*—Your incarnation; *pūrva*—east; *dakṣiṇa*—south; *paścima*—west; *karilā nistāra*—You have delivered.

TRANSLATION

All the Lord's devotees then said, "You have incarnated to deliver fallen souls. You have delivered them in the east and in the south, and now you are delivering them in the west.

TEXT 172

'এক' বারাণসী ছিল তোমাতে বিমুখ ।
তাহা নিস্তারিয়া কৈলা আমা-সবার সুখ ॥ ১৭২ ॥

'eka' vārāṇasī chila tomāte vimukha
tāhā nistāriyā kailā āmā-sabāra sukha

SYNONYMS

eka—one; *vārāṇasī*—the city of Vārāṇasī; *chila*—remained; *tomāte vimukha*—against Your missionary activities; *tāhā*—that; *nistāriyā*—delivering; *kailā*—have done; *āmā-sabāra*—of all of us; *sukha*—awakening of happiness.

TRANSLATION

"Only Vārāṇasī was left because the people there were against Your missionary activities. Now You have delivered them, and we are all very happy."

TEXT 173

বারাণসী-গ্রামে যদি কোলাহল হৈল ।
শুনি' গ্রামী দেশী লোক আসিতে লাগিল ॥ ১৭৩ ॥

vārāṇasī-grāme yadi kolāhala haila
śuni' grāmī deśī loka āsite lāgila

SYNONYMS

vārāṇasī-grāme—in the city of Vārāṇasī; *yadi*—when; *kolāhala haila*—there was broadcasting of this news; *śuni'*—hearing; *grāmī*—from the villages; *deśī*—from the towns; *loka āsite lāgila*—people began to pour in.

TRANSLATION

After the news of these events was broadcast, everyone from the surrounding neighborhoods began to pour in to see Śrī Caitanya Mahāprabhu.

TEXT 174

লক্ষ কোটি লোক আইসে, নাহিক গণন ।
সঙ্কীর্ণস্থানে প্রভুর না পায় দরশন ॥ ১৭৪ ॥

lakṣa koṭi loka āise, nāhika gaṇana
saṅkīrṇa-sthāne prabhura nā pāya daraśana

SYNONYMS

lakṣa koṭi—hundreds and thousands; *loka*—people; *āise*—come; *nāhika gaṇana*—there was no counting; *saṅkīrṇa-sthāne*—in a small place; *prabhura*—of Śrī Caitanya Mahāprabhu; *nā pāya daraśana*—could not get an audience.

TRANSLATION

Hundreds and thousands of people came to see Śrī Caitanya Mahāprabhu. There was no counting the number. Because the Lord's residence was very small, not everyone could see Him.

TEXT 175

প্রভু যবে স্নানে যান বিশ্বেশ্বর-দরশনে ।
দুইদিকে লোক করে প্রভু-বিলোকনে ॥ ১৭৫ ॥

prabhu yabe snāne yāna viśveśvara-daraśane
dui-dike loka kare prabhu-vilokane

SYNONYMS

prabhu—Śrī Caitanya Mahāprabhu; *yabe*—when; *snāne yāna*—goes to bathe; *viśveśvara-daraśane*—or to see the Deity of Lord Viśveśvara; *dui-dike*—on two sides; *loka*—all the people; *kare*—do; *prabhu-vilokane*—seeing of Śrī Caitanya Mahāprabhu.

TRANSLATION

When Śrī Caitanya Mahāprabhu went to take His bath in the Ganges and to see the temple of Viśveśvara, people would line up on both sides to see the Lord.

TEXT 176

বাহু তুলি' প্রভু কহে—বল 'কৃষ্ণ' 'হরি'।
দণ্ডবৎ করে লোকে হরিধ্বনি করি' ॥ ১৭৬ ॥

bāhu tuli' prabhu kahe——bala 'kṛṣṇa' 'hari'
daṇḍavat kare loke hari-dhvani kari'

SYNONYMS

bāhu tuli'—raising His two arms; *prabhu kahe*—Śrī Caitanya Mahāprabhu says; *bala*—please say; *kṛṣṇa hari*—Kṛṣṇa, Hari; *daṇḍavat kare*—offer their respects; *loke*—the people; *hari-dhvani kari'*—loudly chanting the name of Hari.

TRANSLATION

When Śrī Caitanya Mahāprabhu passed by the people, He would raise His arms and say, "Please chant Kṛṣṇa! Please chant Hari!" All the people received Him by chanting Hare Kṛṣṇa, and they offered their respects to Him by this chanting.

TEXT 177

এইমত দিন পঞ্চ লোক নিস্তারিয়া।
আর দিন চলিলা প্রভু উদ্বিগ্ন হঞা ॥ ১৭৭ ॥

ei-mata dina pañca loka nistāriyā
āra dina calilā prabhu udvigna hañā

SYNONYMS

ei-mata—in this way; *dina pañca*—five days; *loka*—the people; *nistāriyā*—delivering; *āra dina*—on the next day; *calilā*—departed; *prabhu*—Śrī Caitanya Mahāprabhu; *udvigna hañā*—being very eager.

TRANSLATION

In this way, for five days, Śrī Caitanya Mahāprabhu delivered the people of Vārāṇasī. Finally, on the next day, He became very eager to leave.

TEXT 178

রাত্রে উঠি' প্রভু যদি করিলা গমন ।
পাছে লাগ্ লইলা তবে ভক্ত পঞ্চ জন ॥ ১৭৮ ॥

rātre uṭhi' prabhu yadi karilā gamana
pāche lāg la-ilā tabe bhakta pañca jana

SYNONYMS

rātre uṭhi'—rising at night; *prabhu*—Śrī Caitanya Mahāprabhu; *yadi*—when; *karilā gamana*—departed; *pāche*—behind Him; *lāg la-ilā*—began to follow; *tabe*—then; *bhakta pañca jana*—five devotees.

TRANSLATION

After rising very early on the sixth day, Śrī Caitanya Mahāprabhu started to leave, and five devotees began to follow Him.

TEXT 179

তপন মিশ্র, রঘুনাথ, মহারাষ্ট্রীয় ব্রাহ্মণ ।
চন্দ্রশেখর, কীর্তনীয়া-পরমানন্দ,—পঞ্চ জন ॥ ১৭৯ ॥

tapana miśra, raghunātha, mahārāṣṭrīya brāhmaṇa
candraśekhara, kīrtanīyā-paramānanda,——pañca jana

SYNONYMS

tapana miśra—Tapana Miśra; *raghunātha*—Raghunātha; *mahārāṣṭrīya brāhmaṇa*—the Mahārāṣṭrian *brāhmaṇa; candraśekhara*—Candraśekhara; *kīrtanīyā-paramānanda*—Paramānanda, who used to perform *kīrtana; pañca jana*—these five persons.

TRANSLATION

These five devotees were Tapana Miśra, Raghunātha, the Mahārāṣṭrian brāhmaṇa, Candraśekhara and Paramānanda Kīrtanīyā.

TEXT 180

সবে চাহে প্রভু-সঙ্গে নীলাচল যাইতে।
সবারে বিদায় দিলা প্রভু যত্ন-সহিতে ॥ ১৮০ ॥

sabe cāhe prabhu-saṅge nīlācala yāite
sabāre vidāya dilā prabhu yatna-sahite

SYNONYMS

sabe cāhe—every one of them wanted; *prabhu-saṅge*—with Śrī Caitanya Mahāprabhu; *nīlācala yāite*—to go to Jagannātha Purī; *sabāre*—to all of them; *vidāya dilā*—bade farewell; *prabhu*—Śrī Caitanya Mahāprabhu; *yatna-sahite*—with great attention.

TRANSLATION

These five wanted to accompany Śrī Caitanya Mahāprabhu to Jagannātha Purī, but the Lord attentively bade them farewell.

TEXT 181

"যাঁর ইচ্ছা, পাছে আইস আমারে দেখিতে।
এবে আমি একা যামু ঝারিখণ্ড-পথে" ॥ ১৮১ ॥

"yāṅra icchā, pāche āisa āmāre dekhite
ebe āmi ekā yāmu jhārikhaṇḍa-pathe"

SYNONYMS

yāṅra—of one who; *icchā*—there is a desire; *pāche*—later; *āisa*—you may come; *āmāre dekhite*—to see Me; *ebe*—but at this time; *āmi*—I; *ekā*—alone; *yāmu*—shall go; *jhārikhaṇḍa-pathe*—through the forest known as Jhārikhaṇḍa.

TRANSLATION

Śrī Caitanya Mahāprabhu said, "If you want to see Me, you may come later, but for the time being I shall go alone through the Jhārikhaṇḍa forest."

TEXT 182

সনাতনে কহিলা,— তুমি যাহ' বৃন্দাবন।
তোমার দুই ভাই তথা করিয়াছে গমন ॥ ১৮২ ॥

sanātane kahilā,—— tumi yāha' vṛndāvana
tomāra dui bhāi tathā kariyāche gamana

SYNONYMS

sanātane kahilā—he advised Sanātana Gosvāmī; *tumi*—you; *yāha' vṛndāvana*—go to Vṛndāvana; *tomāra*—your; *dui bhāi*—two brothers; *tathā*—there; *kariyāche gamana*—have already gone.

TRANSLATION

Śrī Caitanya Mahāprabhu advised Sanātana Gosvāmī to proceed toward Vṛndāvana, and He informed him that his two brothers had already gone there.

TEXT 183

কাঁথা-করঙ্গিয়া মোর কাঙ্গাল ভক্তগণ ।
বৃন্দাবনে আইলে তাঁদের করিহ পালন ॥ ১৮৩ ॥

kāṅthā-karaṅgiyā mora kāṅgāla bhakta-gaṇa
vṛndāvane āile tāṅdera kariha pālana

SYNONYMS

kāṅthā—torn quilt; *karaṅgiyā*—a small waterpot; *mora*—My; *kāṅgāla*—poor; *bhakta-gaṇa*—devotees; *vṛndāvane āile*—when they come to Vṛndāvana; *tāṅdera*—of all of them; *kariha pālana*—take care.

TRANSLATION

Śrī Caitanya Mahāprabhu told Sanātana Gosvāmī, "All My devotees who go to Vṛndāvana are generally very poor. They each have nothing with them but a torn quilt and a small waterpot. Therefore, Sanātana, you should give them shelter and maintain them."

PURPORT

Following in the footsteps of Śrī Caitanya Mahāprabhu, we have constructed temples both in Vṛndāvana and Māyāpur, Navadvīpa, just to give shelter to the foreign devotees coming from Europe and America. Since the Hare Kṛṣṇa movement started, many Europeans and Americans have been visiting Vṛndāvana, but they have not been properly received by any *āśrama* or temple there. It is the purpose of the International Society for Krishna Consciousness to give them shelter and train them in devotional service. There are also many tourists eager to come to India to understand India's spiritual life, and the devotees in our temples both in Vṛndāvana and in Navadvīpa should make arrangements to accommodate them as far as possible.

TEXT 184

এত বলি' চলিলা প্রভু সবা আলিঙ্গিয়া ।
সবেই পড়িলা তথা মূর্চ্ছিত হঞা ॥ ১৮৪ ॥

eta bali' calilā prabhu sabā āliṅgiyā
sabei paḍilā tathā mūrcchita hañā

SYNONYMS

eta bali'—saying this; *calilā*—began to proceed; *prabhu*—Śrī Caitanya Mahāprabhu; *sabā*—all of them; *āliṅgiyā*—embracing; *sabei*—all of them; *paḍilā*—fell down; *tathā*—there; *mūrcchita hañā*—fainting.

TRANSLATION

After saying this, Śrī Caitanya Mahāprabhu embraced them all and began to proceed on His way, and they all fainted and fell down.

TEXT 185

কতক্ষণে উঠি' সবে দুঃখে ঘরে আইলা ।
সনাতন-গোসাঞি বৃন্দাবনেরে চলিলা ॥ ১৮৫ ॥

kata-kṣaṇe uṭhi' sabe duḥkhe ghare āilā
sanātana-gosāñi vṛndāvanere calilā

SYNONYMS

kata-kṣaṇe—after some time; *uṭhi'*—rising; *sabe*—all of them; *duḥkhe*—in great unhappiness; *ghare āilā*—returned to their homes; *sanātana-gosāñi*—Sanātana Gosvāmī; *vṛndāvanere calilā*—proceeded toward Vṛndāvana.

TRANSLATION

After some time, all the devotees got up and returned to their homes very much grief-stricken. Sanātana Gosvāmī proceeded toward Vṛndāvana alone.

TEXT 186

এথা রূপ-গোসাঞি যবে মথুরা আইলা ।
ধ্রুবঘাটে তাঁরে সুবুদ্ধিরায় মিলিলা ॥ ১৮৬ ॥

ethā rūpa-gosāñi yabe mathurā āilā
dhruva-ghāṭe tāṅre subuddhi-rāya mililā

SYNONYMS

ethā—there; *rūpa-gosāñi*—Rūpa Gosāñi; *yabe*—when; *mathurā āilā*—came to Mathurā; *dhruva-ghāṭe*—at the bank of the Yamunā known as Dhruva-ghāṭa; *tāṅre*—him; *subuddhi-rāya*—a devotee of Lord Caitanya named Subuddhi Rāya; *mililā*—met.

TRANSLATION

When Rūpa Gosvāmī reached Mathurā, he met Subuddhi Rāya on the banks of the Yamunā at a place called Dhruva-ghāṭa.

TEXT 187

পূর্বে যবে সুবুদ্ধি-রায় ছিলা গৌড়ে 'অধিকারী'।
হুসেন-খাঁ 'সৈয়দ' করে তাহার চাকরী ॥ ১৮৭ ॥

pūrve yabe subuddhi-rāya chilā gauḍe 'adhikārī'
husena-khāṅ 'saiyada' kare tāhāra cākarī

SYNONYMS

pūrve—formerly; *yabe*—when; *subuddhi-rāya*—Subuddhi Rāya; *chilā*—resided; *gauḍe*—in Bengal; *adhikārī*—a very respectable man; *husena-khāṅ*—Nawab Hussain Khān; *saiyada*—named Saiyada; *kare*—performed; *tāhāra cākarī*—service of Subuddhi Rāya.

TRANSLATION

Formerly Subuddhi Rāya had been a big landholder in Gauḍa-deśa [Bengal]. Saiyada Hussain Khān was then a servant of Subuddhi Rāya.

TEXT 188

দীঘি খোদাইতে তারে 'মুন্‌সীফ' কৈলা।
ছিদ্র পাঞা রায় তারে চাবুক মারিলা ॥ ১৮৮ ॥

dīghi khodāite tāre 'munsīpha' kailā
chidra pāñā rāya tāre cābuka mārilā

SYNONYMS

dīghi khodāite—to dig a big lake; *tāre*—Hussain Khān; *munsīpha kailā*—appointed as the supervisor; *chidra pāñā*—finding some fault; *rāya*—Subuddhi Rāya; *tāre*—him; *cābuka mārilā*—whipped.

TRANSLATION

Subuddhi Rāya put Hussain Khān in charge of digging a big lake, but, once, finding fault with him, he struck him with a whip.

TEXT 189

পাছে যবে হুসেন-খাঁ গৌড়ে 'রাজা' হইল।
সুবুদ্ধি-রায়েরে তিঁহো বহু বাড়াইল ॥ ১৮৯ ॥

pāche yabe husena-khāṅ gauḍe 'rājā' ha-ila
subuddhi-rāyere tiṅho bahu bāḍāila

SYNONYMS

pāche—later; *yabe*—when; *husena-khāṅ*—Hussain Khān; *gauḍe*—in Bengal; *rājā ha-ila*—was appointed Nawab, or governor, by the central Mohammedan government; *subuddhi-rāyere*—unto Subuddhi Rāya; *tiṅho*—he; *bahu bāḍāila*—increased the opulences.

TRANSLATION

Later Hussain Khān somehow or other was appointed Nawab by the central Mohammedan government. As a matter of obligation, he increased the opulences of Subuddhi Rāya.

TEXT 190

তার স্ত্রী তার অঙ্গে দেখে মারণের চিহ্নে।
সুবুদ্ধি-রায়েরে মারিতে কহে রাজা-স্থানে ॥ ১৯০ ॥

tāra strī tāra aṅge dekhe māraṇera cihne
subuddhi-rāyere mārite kahe rājā-sthāne

SYNONYMS

tāra strī—his wife; *tāra aṅge*—on his body; *dekhe*—sees; *māraṇera cihne*—the mark of the whip; *subuddhi-rāyere*—Subuddhi Rāya; *mārite*—to kill; *kahe*—says; *rājā-sthāne*—in the presence of the King.

TRANSLATION

Later, when the wife of Nawab Saiyada Hussain Khān saw the whip marks on his body, she requested him to kill Subuddhi Rāya.

TEXT 191

রাজা কহে,—আমার পোষ্টা রায় হয় 'পিতা'।
তাহারে মারিমু আমি,—ভাল নহে কথা ॥ ১৯১ ॥

rājā kahe,——āmāra poṣṭā rāya haya 'pitā'
tāhāre mārimu āmi,——bhāla nahe kathā

SYNONYMS

rājā kahe—the King said; *āmāra*—my; *poṣṭā*—maintainer; *rāya*—Subuddhi Rāya; *haya*—is; *pitā*—just like my father; *tāhāre mārimu*—shall kill him; *āmi*—I; *bhāla nahe kathā*—this is not a good proposal.

TRANSLATION

Hussain Khān replied, "Subuddhi Rāya has maintained me very carefully. He was just like a father to me," he said. "Now you are asking me to kill him. This is not a very good proposal."

TEXT 192

স্ত্রী কহে,—জাতি লহ', যদি প্রাণে না মারিবে।
রাজা কহে,—জাতি নিলে ইঁহো নাহি জীবে ॥ ১৯২

strī kahe,——jāti laha', yadi prāṇe nā māribe
rājā kahe,——jāti nile iṅho nāhi jībe

SYNONYMS

strī kahe—the wife replied; *jāti laha'*—then take his caste; *yadi*—if; *prāṇe nā māribe*—you will not kill him; *rājā kahe*—the King replied; *jāti nile*—if I take his caste; *iṅho nāhi jībe*—he will not live (he will commit suicide).

TRANSLATION

As a last alternative, the wife suggested that the Nawab take away Subuddhi Rāya's caste and turn him into a Mohammedan, but Hussain Khān replied that if he did this, Subuddhi Rāya would not live.

TEXT 193

স্ত্রী মরিতে চাহে, রাজা সঙ্কটে পড়িল।
করোঁয়ার পানি তার মুখে দেওয়াইল ॥ ১৯৩ ॥

strī marite cāhe, rājā saṅkaṭe paḍila
karoṅyāra pāni tāra mukhe deoyāila

SYNONYMS

strī—the wife; *marite cāhe*—wants to kill Subuddhi Rāya; *rājā*—the King; *saṅkaṭe paḍila*—became very perplexed; *karoṅyāra pāni*—water from a pitcher especially used by Mohammedans; *tāra mukhe*—on his head; *deoyāila*—forced to be sprinkled.

TRANSLATION

This became a perplexing problem for him because his wife kept requesting him to kill Subuddhi Rāya. Finally the Nawab sprinkled a little water on Subuddhi Rāya's head from a pitcher that had been used by a Mohammedan.

PURPORT

More than five hundred years ago in India, the Hindus were so rigid and strict that if a Mohammedan would sprinkle a little water from his pitcher upon a Hindu, the Hindu would be immediately ostracized. Recently, in 1947, during the partisan days, there was a big riot between Hindus and Muslims, especially in Bengal. The Hindus were forcibly made to eat cow's flesh, and consequently they began crying, thinking that they had become Mohammedans. Actually the Mohammedans in India did not come from the country of the Mohammedans, but Hindus instituted the custom that somehow or other if one contacted a Mohammedan, he became a Mohammedan. Rūpa and Sanātana Gosvāmī were born in a high *brāhmaṇa* family, but because they accepted employment under a Mohammedan government, they were considered Mohammedans. Subuddhi Rāya was sprinkled with water from the pitcher of a Mohammedan, and consequently he was condemned to have become a Mohammedan. Later, Aurangzeb, the Mohammedan emperor, introduced a tax especially meant for Hindus. Being oppressed in the Hindu community, many low-caste Hindus preferred to become Mohammedans. In this way the Mohammedan population increased. Later the British government made it a policy to divide the Hindus and the Muslims, and thus they maintained ill feelings between them. The result was that India was divided into Pakistan and Hindustan.

From early histories it appears that the entire earth was under one culture, Vedic culture, but gradually, due to religious and cultural divisions, the rule fragmented into many subdivisions. Now the earth is divided into many countries, religions and political parties. Despite these political and religious divisions, we advocate that everyone should unite again under one culture—Kṛṣṇa consciousness. People should accept one God, Kṛṣṇa; one scripture, *Bhagavad-gītā;* and one activity, devotional service to the Lord. Thus people may live happily upon this earth and combine to produce sufficient food. In such a society, there would be no question of scarcity, famine, or cultural or religious degradation. So-called caste systems and national divisions are artificial. According to our Vaiṣṇava philosophy, these are all external bodily designations. The Kṛṣṇa consciousness movement is not based upon bodily designations. It is a transcendental movement on the platform of spiritual understanding. If the people of the world understood that the basic principle of life is spiritual identification, they would understand that the business of the spirit soul is to serve the Supreme Spirit, Kṛṣṇa. As Lord Kṛṣṇa says in *Bhagavad-gītā* (15.7), *mamaivāṁśo jīva-loke jīva-bhūtaḥ sanātanaḥ*: "The living entities in this conditioned world are My eternal, fragmental parts." All living entities in different life forms are sons of Kṛṣṇa. Therefore they are all meant to serve Kṛṣṇa, the original supreme father. If this philosophy is accepted, the failure of the United Nations to unite all nations will be sufficiently compensated all over the world by a great Kṛṣṇa consciousness movement. Recently we had talks with Christian leaders in Australia, including the Bishop of Australia, and everyone there was pleased with our philosophy of oneness in religious consciousness.

TEXT 194

তবে সুবুদ্ধি-রায় সেই 'ছদ্ম' পাঞা ।
বারাণসী আইলা, সব বিষয় ছাড়িয়া ॥ ১৯৪ ॥

tabe subuddhi-rāya sei 'chadma' pāñā
vārāṇasī āilā, saba viṣaya chāḍiyā

SYNONYMS

tabe—upon this; *subuddhi-rāya*—Subuddhi Rāya; *sei*—that; *chadma*—plea; *pāñā*—getting an opportunity; *vārāṇasī āilā*—came to Vārāṇasī; *saba*—all; *viṣaya chāḍiyā*—giving up the implications of material activities.

TRANSLATION

Taking the Nawab's sprinkling water upon him as an opportunity, Subuddhi Rāya left his family and business affairs and went to Vārāṇasī.

PURPORT

It appears that Subuddhi Rāya was a big landholder and a responsible, respectable gentleman. He could not, however, avoid the social misconception that one becomes a Mohammedan when water is sprinkled on one's face from a Mohammedan's pitcher. Actually he was planning to give up his material life and leave his family. Hindu culture recommends four divisions—*brahmacarya, gṛhastha, vānaprastha* and *sannyāsa.* Subuddhi Rāya was thinking of taking *sannyāsa,* and by the grace of Kṛṣṇa, he received this opportunity. He therefore left his family and went to Vārāṇasī. The system of *varṇāśrama-dharma* is very scientific. If one is directed by the *varṇāśrama* institution, he will naturally think of retiring from family life at the end of his life. Therefore *sannyāsa* is compulsory at the age of fifty.

TEXT 195

প্রায়শ্চিত্ত পুছিলা তিঁহো পণ্ডিতের গণে ।
তাঁরা কহে,—তপ্ত-ঘৃত খাঞা ছাড়' প্রাণে ॥ ১৯৫ ॥

prāyaścitta puchilā tiṅho paṇḍitera gaṇe
tāṅrā kahe,——tapta-ghṛta khāñā chāḍa' prāṇe

SYNONYMS

prāyaścitta—atonement; *puchilā*—inquired; *tiṅho*—he; *paṇḍitera gaṇe*—among the learned scholars or *brāhmaṇa-paṇḍitas* in Vārāṇasī; *tāṅrā kahe*—they advised; *tapta-ghṛta*—hot clarified butter; *khāñā*—drinking; *chāḍa'*—give up; *prāṇe*—your life.

TRANSLATION

When Subuddhi Rāya consulted the learned brāhmaṇas at Vārāṇasī, asking them how his conversion to Mohammedanism could be counteracted, they advised him to drink hot ghee and give up his life.

TEXT 196

কেহ কহে,—এই নহে, 'অল্প' দোষ হয় ।
শুনিয়া রহিলা রায় করিয়া সংশয় ॥ ১৯৬ ॥

keha kahe,——ei nahe, 'alpa' doṣa haya
śuniyā rahilā rāya kariyā saṁśaya

SYNONYMS

keha kahe—some of the learned *brāhmaṇas* said; *ei*—this; *nahe*—not; *alpa*—insignificant; *doṣa*—fault; *haya*—is; *śuniyā*—hearing; *rahilā*—remained; *rāya*—Subuddhi Rāya; *kariyā*—making; *saṁśaya*—doubt.

TRANSLATION

When Subuddhi Rāya consulted some other brāhmaṇas, they told him that he had not committed a grievous fault and that consequently he should not drink hot ghee and give up his life. As a result, Subuddhi Rāya was doubtful about what to do.

PURPORT

This is another instance of Hindu custom. One *brāhmaṇa* would give advice condoning a particular fault, and another would give advice to the contrary. Typically, lawyers and physicians differ, giving one kind of instruction and then another. Due to the *brāhmaṇas'* different opinions, Subuddhi Rāya became further perplexed. He did not know what to do or what not to do.

TEXT 197

তবে যদি মহাপ্রভু বারাণসী আইলা।
তাঁরে মিলি' রায় আপন-বৃত্তান্ত কহিলা ॥ ১৯৭ ॥

tabe yadi mahāprabhu vārāṇasī āilā
tāṅre mili' rāya āpana-vṛttānta kahilā

SYNONYMS

tabe—at this moment; *yadi*—when; *mahāprabhu*—Śrī Caitanya Mahāprabhu; *vārāṇasī āilā*—came to Vārāṇasī; *tāṅre mili'*—meeting Him; *rāya*—Subuddhi Rāya; *āpana-vṛttānta kahilā*—explained his personal situation.

TRANSLATION

In his state of perplexity, Subuddhi Rāya met Śrī Caitanya Mahāprabhu when the Lord was at Vārāṇasī. Subuddhi Rāya explained his position and asked Śrī Caitanya Mahāprabhu what he should do.

TEXT 198

প্রভু কহে,— ইহাঁ হৈতে যাহ' বৃন্দাবন।
নিরন্তর কর কৃষ্ণনামসংকীর্তন ॥ ১৯৮ ॥

prabhu kahe,— ihāṅ haite yāha' vṛndāvana
nirantara kara kṛṣṇa-nāma-saṅkīrtana

SYNONYMS

prabhu kahe—the Lord advised; *ihāṅ haite*—from this place; *yāha' vṛndāvana*—go to Vṛndāvana; *nirantara*—incessantly; *kara*—perform; *kṛṣṇa-nāma-saṅkīrtana*—chanting of the holy name of Kṛṣṇa.

TRANSLATION

The Lord advised him, "Go to Vṛndāvana and chant the Hare Kṛṣṇa mantra constantly."

PURPORT

This is a solution to all sinful activities. In this age of Kali everyone is perplexed by so many inconveniences—social, political and religious—and naturally no one is happy. Due to the contamination of this age, everyone has a very short life. There are many fools and rascals who advise people to adopt this way of life or that way of life, but real liberation from life's perplexities means preparation for the next life. *Tathā dehāntara-prāptir dhīras tatra na muhyati.* One should be situated in his spiritual identity and return home, back to Godhead. The simplest method for this is recommended herein by Śrī Caitanya Mahāprabhu. We should constantly chant the holy names of the Lord, the Hare Kṛṣṇa *mahā-mantra.* Following in the footsteps of Śrī Caitanya Mahāprabhu, this Kṛṣṇa consciousness movement is recommending this process all over the world. We are saying, "Chant the Hare Kṛṣṇa *mahā-mantra,* be freed from all the complexities of life and realize Kṛṣṇa, the Supreme Personality of Godhead. Engage in His devotional service and perfect your life so that you can return home, back to Godhead."

TEXT 199

এক 'নামাভাসে' তোমার পাপ-দোষ যাবে ।
আর 'নাম' লইতে কৃষ্ণচরণ পাইবে ॥ ১৯৯ ॥

eka 'nāmābhāse' tomāra pāpa-doṣa yābe
āra 'nāma' la-ite kṛṣṇa-caraṇa pāibe

SYNONYMS

eka—one; *nāma-ābhāse*—by a reflection of the pure chanting of the Hare Kṛṣṇa *mahā-mantra; tomāra*—your; *pāpa-doṣa yābe*—all the sinful reactions will go away; *āra*—then again; *nāma la-ite*—after chanting purely the name of the Lord; *kṛṣṇa-caraṇa pāibe*—you will get shelter at the lotus feet of Kṛṣṇa.

TRANSLATION

Śrī Caitanya Mahāprabhu further advised Subuddhi Rāya: "Begin chanting the Hare Kṛṣṇa mantra, and when your chanting is almost pure, all your sinful

reactions will go away. After you chant perfectly, you will get shelter at the lotus feet of Kṛṣṇa.

PURPORT

The ten kinds of offenses should be considered. In the beginning, when one is initiated into the chanting of the Hare Kṛṣṇa *mahā-mantra,* there are naturally many offenses. However, the devotee should be very careful to avoid these offenses and chant purely. This does not mean that the Hare Kṛṣṇa *mahā-mantra* is sometimes pure and sometimes impure. Rather, the chanter is impure due to material contamination. He has to purify himself so that the holy names will be perfectly effective. Chanting the holy name of the Lord inoffensively will help one get immediate shelter at Kṛṣṇa's lotus feet. This means that by chanting purely, one will immediately be situated on the transcendental platform. We should note, however, that according to Śrī Caitanya Mahāprabhu's instructions, one should not wait to purify himself before chanting the Hare Kṛṣṇa *mantra.* Whatever our condition may be, we should begin chanting immediately. By the power of the Hare Kṛṣṇa *mantra,* we will gradually be relieved from all material contamination and will get shelter at the lotus feet of Kṛṣṇa, the ultimate goal of life.

TEXT 200

আর কৃষ্ণনাম লৈতে কৃষ্ণস্থানে স্থিতি ।
মহাপাতকের হয় এই প্রায়শ্চিত্তি ॥ ২০০ ॥

āra kṛṣṇa-nāma laite kṛṣṇa-sthāne sthiti-
mahā-pātakera haya ei prāyaścitti

SYNONYMS

āra—further; *kṛṣṇa-nāma*—the Hare Kṛṣṇa *mahā-mantra; laite*—continuously chanting; *kṛṣṇa-sthāne sthiti*—being situated in company with Lord Kṛṣṇa; *mahā-pātakera*—of all kinds of sinful activity; *haya*—is; *ei*—this; *prāyaścitti*—atonement.

TRANSLATION

"When you are situated at the lotus feet of Kṛṣṇa, no sinful reaction can touch you. This is the best solution to all sinful activity."

TEXT 201

পাঞা আজ্ঞা রায় বৃন্দাবনেরে চলিলা ।
প্রয়াগ, অযোধ্যা দিয়া নৈমিষারণ্যে আইলা ॥ ২০১॥

pāñā ājñā rāya vṛndāvanere calilā
prayāga, ayodhyā diyā naimiṣāraṇye āilā

SYNONYMS

pāñā ājñā—getting this order; *rāya*—Subuddhi Rāya; *vṛndāvanere calilā*—went toward Vṛndāvana; *prayāga*—Allahabad; *ayodhyā*—Ayodhyā (the kingdom of Lord Rāmacandra); *diyā*—through; *naimiṣāraṇye āilā*—came to Naimiṣāraṇya, (a place near Lucknow).

TRANSLATION

Thus receiving the order from Śrī Caitanya Mahāprabhu to go to Vṛndāvana, Subuddhi Rāya left Vārāṇasī and went through Prayāga, Ayodhyā and Naimiṣāraṇya toward Vṛndāvana.

TEXT 202

কতক দিবস রায় নৈমিষারণ্যে রহিলা।
প্রভু বৃন্দাবন হৈতে প্রয়াগ যাইলা ॥ ২০২ ॥

kataka divasa rāya naimiṣāraṇye rahilā
prabhu vṛndāvana haite prayāga yāilā

SYNONYMS

kataka divasa—a few days; *rāya*—Subuddhi Rāya; *naimiṣāraṇye rahilā*—stayed at Naimiṣāraṇya; *prabhu*—Śrī Caitanya Mahāprabhu; *vṛndāvana haite*—from Vṛndāvana; *prayāga*—to Allahabad; *yāilā*—went.

TRANSLATION

Subuddhi Rāya stayed for some time at Naimiṣāraṇya. During that time, Śrī Caitanya Mahāprabhu went to Prayāga after visiting Vṛndāvana.

TEXT 203

মথুরা আসিয়া রায় প্রভুবার্তা পাইল।
প্রভুর লাগ না পাঞা মনে বড় দুঃখ হৈল ॥ ২০৩ ॥

mathurā āsiyā rāya prabhu-vārtā pāila
prabhura lāga nā pāñā mane baḍa duḥkha haila

SYNONYMS

mathurā āsiyā—when he came to Mathurā; *rāya*—Subuddhi Rāya; *prabhu-vārtā pāila*—got information of the Lord's itinerary; *prabhura*—of Lord

Caitanya Mahāprabhu; *lāga*—contact; *nā pāñā*—not getting; *mane*—in the mind; *baḍa*—very great; *duḥkha*—unhappiness; *haila*—there was.

TRANSLATION

After reaching Mathurā, Subuddhi Rāya received information of the Lord's itinerary. He became very unhappy because he was not able to contact the Lord.

TEXT 204

শুষ্ককাষ্ঠ আনি' রায় বেচে মথুরাতে ।
পাঁচ ছয় পৈসা হয় এক এক বোঝাতে ॥ ২০৪ ॥

śuṣka-kāṣṭha āni' rāya vece mathurāte
pāṅca chaya paisā haya eka eka bojhāte

SYNONYMS

śuṣka-kāṣṭha āni'—collecting dry wood from the forest; *rāya*—Subuddhi Rāya; *vece*—sells; *mathurāte*—at Mathurā; *pāṅca chaya*—five or six; *paisā*—paise; *haya*—are; *eka eka bojhāte*—in exchange for each load of dry wood.

TRANSLATION

Subuddhi Rāya would collect dry wood in the forest and take it to the city of Mathurā to sell. For each load he would receive five or six paise.

TEXT 205

আপনে রহে এক পৈসার চানা চাবাইয়া ।
আর পৈসা বাণিয়া-স্থানে রাখেন ধরিয়া ॥ ২০৫ ॥

āpane rahe eka paisāra cānā cābāiyā
āra paisā bāṇiyā-sthāne rākhena dhariyā

SYNONYMS

āpane—personally; *rahe*—lives; *eka paisāra*—of one paisa's worth; *cānā*—fried chick-peas; *cābāiyā*—chewing; *āra*—the balance; *paisā*—four or five paise; *bāṇiyā-sthāne*—in the custody of a merchant; *rākhena*—keeps; *dhariyā*—depositing.

TRANSLATION

Earning his livelihood by selling dry wood, Subuddhi Rāya would live on only one paise's worth of fried chick-peas, and he would deposit whatever other paises he had with some merchant.

PURPORT

In those days there was no banking system like the one now found in Western countries. If one had excess money, he would deposit it with some merchant, usually a grocer. That was the banking system. Subuddhi Rāya would deposit his extra money with a mercantile man and spend it when necessary. When one is in the renounced order, saving money is not recommended. However, if one saves money for the service of the Lord or a Vaiṣṇava, that is accepted. These are the dealings of Subuddhi Rāya, who is one of the confidential devotees of Śrī Caitanya Mahāprabhu. Śrīla Rūpa Gosvāmī also followed this principle by spending fifty percent of his money in order to serve Kṛṣṇa through *brāhmaṇas* and Vaiṣṇavas. He gave twenty-five percent of his money to relatives, and twenty-five percent he deposited in the custody of a merchant. These are the approved methods recommended in *Caitanya-caritāmṛta.* Whether in the renounced order or in the *gṛhastha* order, a Vaiṣṇava should follow these principles set forth by the previous *ācāryas.*

TEXT 206

দুঃখী বৈষ্ণব দেখি' তাঁরে করান ভোজন ।
গৌড়ীয়া আইলে দধি, ভাত, তৈল-মর্দন ॥ ২০৬ ॥

duḥkhī vaiṣṇava dekhi' tāṅre karāna bhojana
gauḍīyā āile dadhi, bhāta, taila-mardana

SYNONYMS

duḥkhī vaiṣṇava—a poverty-stricken Vaiṣṇava; *dekhi'*—seeing; *tāṅre*—to him; *karāna bhojana*—gives food for eating; *gauḍīyā āile*—when a Bengali Vaiṣṇava came to Mathurā; *dadhi*—yogurt; *bhāta*—cooked rice; *taila-mardana*—massaging mustard oil on the body.

TRANSLATION

Subuddhi Rāya used to spend his savings to supply yogurt to Bengali Vaiṣṇavas who came to Mathurā. He also gave them cooked rice and oil massages. When he saw a poverty-stricken Vaiṣṇava, he would use his money to feed him.

PURPORT

There is a special reference for the maintenance of Bengali Vaiṣṇavas. A Gauḍīya Vaiṣṇava is a Bengali Vaiṣṇava. Most of the devotees of Lord Caitanya at that time were Gauḍīyas and Oriyās, inhabitants of Bengal and Orissa. There are still many hundreds and thousands of disciples in Bengal and Orissa. Bengalis are habituated to eating cooked rice as their staple food. When they went to

Mathurā in the North, they found that the people generally ate chapatis or *roṭi* made of wheat. The Bengalis could not digest this food because they were used to cooked rice. Therefore as soon as Subuddhi Rāya saw a Bengali Vaiṣṇava arriving in Mathurā, he would try to supply him with cooked rice. Bengalis are also accustomed to taking a massage with mustard oil. In any case, Subuddhi Rāya wanted to serve the Vaiṣṇavas according to their needs. Therefore he would supply yogurt to ease the digestion of food eaten in Mathurā, particularly the wheat-made chapatis and *roṭi*.

TEXT 207

রূপ-গোসাঞি, আইলে তাঁরে বহু প্রীতি কৈলা ।
আপন-সঙ্গে লঞা 'দ্বাদশ বন' দেখাইলা ॥ ২০৭ ॥

rūpa-gosāñi, āile tāṅre bahu prīti kailā
āpana-saṅge lañā 'dvādaśa vana' dekhāilā

SYNONYMS

rūpa-gosāñi—Rūpa Gosāñi; *āile*—when he came to Mathurā; *tāṅre*—unto him; *bahu*—much; *prīti*—love; *kailā*—showed; *āpana-saṅge lañā*—taking Rūpa Gosvāmī personally with him; *dvādaśa vana*—the twelve forests of Vṛndāvana; *dekhāilā*—showed.

TRANSLATION

When Rūpa Gosvāmī arrived at Mathurā, Subuddhi Rāya, out of love and affection for him, wanted to serve him in so many ways. He personally took Rūpa Gosvāmī to see all the twelve forests of Vṛndāvana.

PURPORT

Śrīla Rūpa Gosvāmī had been a minister in the government of Hussain Shah, and Subuddhi Rāya was also known to Hussain Shah, because as a boy, he had been Subuddhi Rāya's servant. It appears that Subuddhi Rāya was elderly, yet while he was living in Mathurā he showed Rūpa Gosvāmī the twelve forests of Vṛndāvana.

TEXT 208

মাসমাত্র রূপ-গোসাঞি রহিলা বৃন্দাবনে ।
শীঘ্র চলি' আইলা সনাতনানুসন্ধানে ॥ ২০৮ ॥

māsa-mātra rūpa-gosāñi rahilā vṛndāvane
śīghra cali' āilā sanātanānusandhāne

SYNONYMS

māsa-mātra—only one month; *rūpa-gosāñi*—Rūpa Gosāñi; *rahilā*—remained; *vṛndāvane*—at Vṛndāvana; *śīghra*—very soon; *cali' āilā*—returned; *sanātana-anusandhāne*—to search for Sanātana Gosvāmī.

TRANSLATION

Rūpa Gosvāmī remained in Mathurā and Vṛndāvana for one month in the association of Subuddhi Rāya. After that, he left Vṛndāvana to search for his elder brother, Sanātana Gosvāmī.

TEXT 209

গঙ্গাতীর-পথে প্রভু প্রয়াগেরে আইলা ।
তাহা শুনি' দুইভাই সে পথে চলিলা ॥ ২০৯ ॥

gaṅgā-tīra-pathe prabhu prayāgere āilā
tāhā śuni' dui-bhāi se pathe calilā

SYNONYMS

gaṅgā-tīra-pathe—on the road on the bank of the Ganges; *prabhu*—Śrī Caitanya Mahāprabhu; *prayāgere āilā*—came to Prayāga; *tāhā śuni'*—hearing this news; *dui-bhāi*—the two brothers named Rūpa and Anupama; *se pathe calilā*—traveled on that path.

TRANSLATION

When Rūpa Gosvāmī heard that Śrī Caitanya Mahāprabhu had gone to Prayāga on the road along the banks of the Ganges, both Rūpa and his brother Anupama went that way to meet the Lord.

TEXT 210

এথা সনাতন গোসাঞি প্রয়াগে আসিয়া ।
মথুরা আইলা সরান রাজপথ দিয়া ॥ ২১০ ॥

ethā sanātana gosāñi prayāge āsiyā
mathurā āilā sarāna rāja-patha diyā

SYNONYMS

ethā—here (at the other end); *sanātana gosāñi*—Sanātana Gosāñi; *prayāge āsiyā*—coming to Prayāga; *mathurā āilā*—he reached Vṛndāvana; *sarāna*—directly; *rāja-patha diyā*—on the government road or public road.

TRANSLATION

After reaching Prayāga, Sanātana Gosvāmī, following the order of Śrī Caitanya Mahāprabhu, went to Vṛndāvana along the public road.

PURPORT

This is especially significant because when Sanātana Gosvāmī went from Bengal to Benares, due to the political situation he did not go along the public road. After meeting Śrī Caitanya Mahāprabhu at Benares, however, he was ordered to proceed to Vṛndāvana along the public road leading to Mathurā. In other words, he was advised not to fear for his political situation.

TEXT 211

মথুরাতে স্থবুদ্ধি-রায় তাহারে মিলিলা ।
রূপ-অনুপম-কথা সকলি কহিলা ॥ ২১১ ॥

mathurāte subuddhi-rāya tāhāre mililā
rūpa-anupama-kathā sakali kahilā

SYNONYMS

mathurāte—at Mathurā; *subuddhi-rāya*—Subuddhi Rāya; *tāhāre mililā*—met him; *rūpa-anupama-kathā*—news about his younger brothers, Rūpa Gosvāmī and Anupama; *sakali*—everything; *kahilā*—described.

TRANSLATION

When Sanātana Gosvāmī met Subuddhi Rāya at Mathurā, Subuddhi Rāya explained everything about his younger brothers Rūpa Gosvāmī and Anupama.

TEXT 212

গঙ্গাপথে দুইভাই রাজপথে সনাতন ।
অতএব তাঁহা সনে না হৈল মিলন ॥ ২১২ ॥

gaṅgā-pathe dui-bhāi rāja-pathe sanātana
ataeva tāṅhā sane nā haila milana

SYNONYMS

gaṅgā-pathe—on the road on the bank of the Ganges; *dui-bhāi*—the two brothers Rūpa and Anupama; *rāja-pathe*—on the public road; *sanātana*—Sanātana Gosvāmī; *ataeva*—because of this; *tāṅhā sane*—with him; *nā haila milana*—there was not a meeting.

TRANSLATION

Since Sanātana Gosvāmī went along the public road to Vṛndāvana and Rūpa Gosvāmī and Anupama went on the road along the Ganges banks, it was not possible for them to meet.

TEXT 213

সুবুদ্ধি-রায় বহু স্নেহ করে সনাতনে ।
ব্যবহার-স্নেহ সনাতন নাহি মানে ॥ ২১৩ ॥

subuddhi-rāya bahu sneha kare sanātane
vyavahāra-sneha sanātana nāhi māne

SYNONYMS

subuddhi-rāya—Subuddhi Rāya; *bahu*—much; *sneha*—affection; *kare*—does; *sanātane*—unto Sanātana Gosvāmī; *vyavahāra-sneha*—love and affection because of a previous relationship; *sanātana*—Sanātana Gosvāmī; *nāhi māne*—was hesitant to accept.

TRANSLATION

Subuddhi Rāya and Sanātana Gosvāmī knew one another before accepting the renounced order. Therefore Subuddhi Rāya showed much affection to Sanātana Gosvāmī, but Sanātana Gosvāmī hesitated to accept his sentiments and affections.

TEXT 214

মহা-বিরক্ত সনাতন ভ্রমেন বনে বনে ।
প্রতিবৃক্ষে, প্রতিকুঞ্জে রহে রাত্রি-দিনে ॥ ২১৪ ॥

mahā-virakta sanātana bhramena vane vane
prati-vṛkṣe, prati-kuñje rahe rātri-dine

SYNONYMS

mahā-virakta—highly elevated in the renounced order of life; *sanātana*—Sanātana Gosvāmī; *bhramena*—wanders; *vane vane*—from forest to forest; *prati-vṛkṣe*—under every tree; *prati-kuñje*—in every bush; *rahe rātri-dine*—remains day and night.

TRANSLATION

Being very advanced in the renounced order, Sanātana Gosvāmī used to wander from forest to forest, never taking shelter of any habitation built of stone. He used to live under trees or beneath bushes both day and night.

TEXT 215

মথুরামাহাত্ম্য-শাস্ত্র সংগ্রহ করিয়া ।
লুপ্ততীর্থ প্রকট কৈলা বনেতে ভ্রমিয়া ॥ ২১৫ ॥

mathurā-māhātmya-śāstra saṅgraha kariyā
lupta-tīrtha prakaṭa kailā vanete bhramiyā

SYNONYMS

mathurā-māhātmya—giving a description of the greatness of Mathurā; *śāstra*—books; *saṅgraha kariyā*—collecting; *lupta-tīrtha*—lost holy places; *prakaṭa*—discovering; *kailā*—he did; *vanete bhramiyā*—traveling within the forest.

TRANSLATION

Śrīla Sanātana Gosvāmī collected some books about archaeological excavations in Mathurā, and, wandering in the forest, he sought to renovate all those holy places.

TEXT 216

এইমত সনাতন বৃন্দাবনেতে রহিলা ।
রূপ-গোসাঞি দুইভাই কাশীতে আইলা ॥ ২১৬ ॥

ei-mata sanātana vṛndāvanete rahilā
rūpa-gosāñi dui-bhāi kāśīte āilā

SYNONYMS

ei-mata—in this way; *sanātana*—Sanātana Gosvāmī; *vṛndāvanete rahilā*—remained in Vṛndāvana; *rūpa-gosāñi*—Rūpa Gosāñi; *dui-bhāi*—the two brothers; *kāśīte āilā*—came to Vārāṇasī (Kāśī).

TRANSLATION

Sanātana Gosvāmī remained in Vṛndāvana, and Rūpa Gosvāmī and Anupama returned to Vārāṇasī.

TEXT 217

মহারাষ্ট্রীয় দ্বিজ, শেখর, মিশ্র-তপন ।
তিনজন সহ রূপ করিলা মিলন ॥ ২১৭ ॥

mahārāṣṭrīya dvija, śekhara, miśra-tapana
tina-jana saha rūpa karilā milana

SYNONYMS

mahārāṣṭrīya dvija—the *brāhmaṇa* of Mahārāṣṭra province; *śekhara*—Candraśekhara; *miśra-tapana*—Tapana Miśra; *tina-jana*—these three persons; *saha*—with; *rūpa*—Rūpa Gosvāmī; *karilā milana*—met.

TRANSLATION

When Rūpa Gosvāmī arrived at Vārāṇasī, he met the Mahārāṣṭrian brāhmaṇa, Candraśekhara and Tapana Miśra.

TEXT 218

শেখরের ঘরে বাসা, মিশ্র-ঘরে ভিক্ষা।
মিশ্রমুখে শুনে সনাতনে প্রভুর 'শিক্ষা' ॥ ২১৮ ॥

śekharera ghare vāsā, miśra-ghare bhikṣā
miśra-mukhe śune sanātane prabhura 'śikṣā'

SYNONYMS

śekharera ghare vāsa—residence in the house of Candraśekhara; *miśra-ghare bhikṣā*—*prasāda* at the house of Tapana Miśra; *miśra-mukhe*—from the mouth of Tapana Miśra; *śune*—hears; *sanātane*—unto Sanātana; *prabhura śikṣā*—instructions of Śrī Caitanya Mahāprabhu.

TRANSLATION

While Rūpa Gosvāmī was staying at Vārāṇasī, he resided at the house of Candraśekhara and took prasāda at the house of Tapana Miśra. In this way he heard of Śrī Caitanya Mahāprabhu's instructions to Sanātana Gosvāmī in Vārāṇasī.

TEXT 219

কাশীতে প্রভুর চরিত্র শুনি' তিনের মুখে।
সন্ন্যাসীরে কৃপা শুনি' পাইলা বড় সুখে ॥ ২১৯ ॥

kāśīte prabhura caritra śuni' tinera mukhe
sannyāsīre kṛpā śuni' pāilā baḍa sukhe

SYNONYMS

kāśīte—at Vārāṇasī (Kāśī); *prabhura*—of Śrī Caitanya Mahāprabhu; *caritra*—the activity; *śuni'*—hearing; *tinera mukhe*—from the mouths of the three persons; *sannyāsīre kṛpā*—the mercy shown to the Māyāvādī *sannyāsīs; śuni'*—hearing about; *pāilā*—he got; *baḍa sukhe*—very great pleasure.

TRANSLATION

While staying at Vārāṇasī, Rūpa Gosvāmī heard of all Śrī Caitanya Mahāprabhu's activities. When he heard of His deliverance of the Māyāvādī sannyāsīs, he became very happy.

TEXT 220

মহাপ্রভুর উপর লোকের প্রণতি দেখিয়া ।
সুখী হৈলা লোকমুখে কীর্তন শুনিয়া ॥ ২২০ ॥

mahāprabhura upara lokera praṇati dekhiyā
sukhī hailā loka-mukhe kīrtana śuniyā

SYNONYMS

mahāprabhura—Śrī Caitanya Mahāprabhu; *upara*—upon; *lokera*—of the people in general; *praṇati dekhiyā*—seeing the surrender; *sukhī hailā*—became very happy; *loka-mukhe*—from the general public; *kīrtana śuniyā*—hearing the description.

TRANSLATION

When Rūpa Gosvāmī saw that all the people of Vārāṇasī respected Śrī Caitanya Mahāprabhu, he became very happy. He even heard stories from the general populace.

TEXT 221

দিন দশ রহি' রূপ গৌড়ে যাত্রা কৈল ।
সনাতন-রূপের এই চরিত্র কহিল ॥ ২২১ ॥

dina daśa rahi' rūpa gauḍe yātrā kaila
sanātana-rūpera ei caritra kahila

SYNONYMS

dina daśa—about ten days; *rahi'*—remaining; *rūpa*—Rūpa Gosvāmī; *gauḍe yātrā kaila*—went back to Bengal; *sanātana-rūpera*—of Śrī Sanātana Gosvāmī and Rūpa Gosvāmī; *ei*—thus; *caritra*—character; *kahila*—I have described.

TRANSLATION

After staying in Vārāṇasī for about ten days, Rūpa Gosvāmī returned to Bengal. In this way I have described the activities of Rūpa and Sanātana.

TEXT 222

এথা মহাপ্রভু যদি নীলাদ্রি চলিলা।
নির্জন বনপথে যাইতে মহা সুখ পাইলা ॥ ২২২ ॥

ethā mahāprabhu yadi nīlādri calilā
nirjana vana-pathe yāite mahā sukha pāilā

SYNONYMS

ethā—on the other side; *mahāprabhu*—Śrī Caitanya Mahāprabhu; *yadi*—when; *nīlādri calilā*—went back to Jagannātha Purī; *nirjana vana-pathe*—on a solitary forest path; *yāite*—traveling; *mahā sukha pāilā*—got very great pleasure.

TRANSLATION

When Śrī Caitanya Mahāprabhu returned to Jagannātha Purī, He passed through the solitary forest, and He received great pleasure in doing so.

TEXT 223

সুখে চলি' আইসে প্রভু বলভদ্র-সঙ্গে।
পূর্ব্ববৎ মৃগাদি-সঙ্গে কৈলা নানারঙ্গে ॥ ২২৩ ॥

sukhe cali' āise prabhu balabhadra-saṅge
pūrvavat mṛgādi-saṅge kailā nānā-raṅge

SYNONYMS

sukhe—in a very pleasing atmosphere; *cali' āise*—comes back; *prabhu*—Śrī Caitanya Mahāprabhu; *balabhadra-saṅge*—with the servant of Balabhadra Bhaṭṭācārya; *pūrva-vat*—as previously; *mṛga-ādi-saṅge*—with the forest animals; *kailā*—performed; *nānā-raṅge*—various pleasing activities.

TRANSLATION

Śrī Caitanya Mahāprabhu happily returned to Jagannātha Purī in the company of His servant, Balabhadra Bhaṭṭācārya. As previously, the Lord performed many pleasing pastimes with the forest animals.

TEXT 224

আঠারনালাতে আসি' ভট্টাচার্য ব্রাহ্মণে।
পাঠাঞা বোলাইলা নিজ-ভক্তগণে ॥ ২২৪ ॥

āṭhāranālāte āsi' bhaṭṭācārya brāhmaṇe
pāṭhāñā bolāilā nija-bhakta-gaṇe

SYNONYMS

āṭhāranālāte—to a place near Jagannātha Purī named Āṭhāranālā; *āsi'*—coming; *bhaṭṭācārya brāhmaṇe*—the *brāhmaṇa* known as Balabhadra Bhaṭṭācārya; *pāṭhāñā*—sending; *bolāilā*—called for; *nija-bhakta-gaṇe*—His own personal associates.

TRANSLATION

When Śrī Caitanya Mahāprabhu arrived at a place known as Āṭhāranālā near Jagannātha Purī, He sent Balabhadra Bhaṭṭācārya to call for His devotees.

TEXT 225

শুনিয়া ভক্তের গণ যেন পুনরপি জীলা ।
দেহে প্রাণ আইলে, যেন ইন্দ্রিয় উঠিলা ॥ ২২৫ ॥

śuniyā bhaktera gaṇa yena punarapi jīlā
dehe prāṇa āile, yena indriya uṭhilā

SYNONYMS

śuniyā—hearing; *bhaktera gaṇa*—the hordes of devotees at Jagannātha Purī; *yena*—as if; *punarapi*—again; *jīlā*—became alive; *dehe*—in the body; *prāṇa āile*—consciousness returned; *yena*—as if; *indriya*—senses; *uṭhilā*—became agitated.

TRANSLATION

Hearing news of the Lord's arrival from Balabhadra Bhaṭṭācārya, hordes of devotees became so happy that they seemed to be getting their lives back. It was as though their consciousness had returned to their bodies. Their senses also became agitated.

TEXT 226

আনন্দে বিহ্বল ভক্তগণ ধাঞা আইলা ।
নরেন্দ্রে আসিয়া সবে প্রভুরে মিলিলা ॥ ২২৬ ॥

ānande vihvala bhakta-gaṇa dhāñā āilā
narendre āsiyā sabe prabhure mililā

SYNONYMS

ānande—in great pleasure; *vihvala*—overwhelmed; *bhakta-gaṇa*—all the devotees; *dhāñā āilā*—very hastily came; *narendre āsiyā*—coming to the shore of Narendra Lake; *sabe*—all of them; *prabhure*—Śrī Caitanya Mahāprabhu; *mililā*—met.

TRANSLATION

Being overwhelmed with great pleasure, all the devotees hastily went to see the Lord. They met Him on the banks of Narendra-sarovara, the celebrated lake.

TEXT 227

পুরী-ভারতীর প্রভু বন্দিলেন চরণ ।
দোঁহে মহাপ্রভুরে কৈলা প্রেম-আলিঙ্গন ॥ ২২৭ ॥

purī-bhāratīra prabhu vandilena caraṇa
doṅhe mahāprabhure kailā prema-āliṅgana

SYNONYMS

purī—Paramānanda Purī; *bhāratīra*—and of Brahmānanda Bhāratī; *prabhu*—Lord Śrī Caitanya Mahāprabhu; *vandilena caraṇa*—worshiped the feet; *doṅhe*—both the elderly *sannyāsīs; mahāprabhure*—Śrī Caitanya Mahāprabhu; *kailā*—did; *prema-āliṅgana*—embracing in love.

TRANSLATION

When Paramānanda Purī and Brahmānanda Bhāratī met Śrī Caitanya Mahāprabhu, the Lord offered them His respectful obeisances due to their being Godbrothers of His spiritual master. They both then embraced Śrī Caitanya Mahāprabhu in love and affection.

TEXT 228

দামোদর-স্বরূপ, পণ্ডিত-গদাধর ।
জগদানন্দ, কাশীশ্বর, গোবিন্দ, বক্রেশ্বর ॥ ২২৮ ॥

dāmodara-svarūpa, paṇḍita-gadādhara
jagadānanda, kāśīśvara, govinda, vakreśvara

SYNONYMS

dāmodara-svarūpa—Svarūpa Dāmodara; *paṇḍita-gadādhara*—Gadādhara, the learned scholar; *jagadānanda*—Jagadānanda; *kāśīśvara*—Kāśīśvara; *govinda*—Govinda; *vakreśvara*—Vakreśvara.

TRANSLATION

Devotees like Svarūpa Dāmodara, Gadādhara Paṇḍita, Jagadānanda, Kāśīśvara, Govinda and Vakreśvara all came to meet the Lord.

TEXT 229

কাশী-মিশ্র, প্রদ্যুম্ন-মিশ্র, পণ্ডিত-দামোদর ।
হরিদাস-ঠাকুর, আর পণ্ডিত-শঙ্কর ॥ ২২৯ ॥

kāśī-miśra, pradyumna-miśra, paṇḍita-dāmodara
haridāsa-ṭhākura, āra paṇḍita-śaṅkara

SYNONYMS

kāśī-miśra—Kāśī Miśra; *pradyumna-miśra*—Pradyumna Miśra; *paṇḍita-dāmodara*—Dāmodara Paṇḍita; *haridāsa-ṭhākura*—Haridāsa Ṭhākura; *āra*—and; *paṇḍita-śaṅkara*—Śaṅkara Paṇḍita.

TRANSLATION

Kāśī Miśra, Pradyumna Miśra, Dāmodara Paṇḍita, Haridāsa Ṭhākura and Śaṅkara Paṇḍita also came there to meet the Lord.

TEXT 230

আর সব ভক্ত প্রভুর চরণে পড়িলা ।
সবা আলিঙ্গিয়া প্রভু প্রেমাবিষ্ট হৈলা ॥ ২৩০ ॥

āra saba bhakta prabhura caraṇe paḍilā
sabā āliṅgiyā prabhu premāviṣṭa hailā

SYNONYMS

āra saba bhakta—all the other devotees; *prabhura*—of Lord Śrī Caitanya Mahāprabhu; *caraṇe paḍilā*—fell down at the lotus feet; *sabā āliṅgiyā*—embracing all of them; *prabhu*—Śrī Caitanya Mahāprabhu; *prema-āviṣṭa*—overwhelmed in ecstatic love and emotion; *hailā*—became.

TRANSLATION

All the other devotees also came and fell down at the Lord's lotus feet. In return, Śrī Caitanya Mahāprabhu embraced them all with great ecstatic love.

TEXT 231

আনন্দ-সমুদ্রে ভাসে সব ভক্তগণে ।
সবা লঞা চলে প্রভু জগন্নাথ-দরশনে ॥ ২৩১ ॥

ānanda-samudre bhāse saba bhakta-gaṇe
sabā lañā cale prabhu jagannātha-daraśane

SYNONYMS

ānanda-samudre—in the ocean of transcendental bliss; *bhāse*—float; *saba bhakta-gaṇe*—all the devotees; *sabā lañā*—taking all of them; *cale*—goes; *prabhu*—Śrī Caitanya Mahāprabhu; *jagannātha-daraśane*—to see the Jagannātha Deity in the temple.

TRANSLATION

Thus they all merged in the ocean of transcendental bliss. Then the Lord and all His devotees proceeded toward the temple of Jagannātha to see the Deity.

TEXT 232

জগন্নাথ দেখি' প্রভু প্রেমাবিষ্ট হৈলা ।
ভক্ত-সঙ্গে বহুক্ষণ নৃত্য-গীত কৈলা ॥ ২৩২ ॥

jagannātha dekhi' prabhu premāviṣṭa hailā
bhakta-saṅge bahu-kṣaṇa nṛtya-gīta kailā

SYNONYMS

jagannātha dekhi'—seeing Lord Jagannātha; *prabhu*—Śrī Caitanya Mahāprabhu; *prema-āviṣṭa hailā*—became overwhelmed with love and affection; *bhakta-saṅge*--in the society of the devotees; *bahu-kṣaṇa*—for a long time; *nṛtya-gīta kailā*—chanted and danced.

TRANSLATION

As soon as Śrī Caitanya Mahāprabhu saw Lord Jagannātha in the temple, He was immediately overwhelmed with love and affection. He chanted and danced with His devotees for a long time.

TEXT 233

জগন্নাথ-সেবক আনি' মালা-প্রসাদ দিলা ।
তুলসী পড়িছা আসি' চরণ বন্দিলা ॥ ২৩৩ ॥

jagannātha-sevaka āni' mālā-prasāda dilā
tulasī paḍichā āsi' caraṇa vandilā

SYNONYMS

jagannātha-sevaka—the priests who were servitors of Lord Jagannātha; *āni'*—bringing; *mālā-prasāda dilā*—distributed flower garlands and *prasāda; tulasī paḍichā*—the temple servant known as Tulasī; *āsi'*—coming; *caraṇa vandilā*—worshiped the lotus feet of the Lord.

TRANSLATION

The priests immediately brought them flower garlands and prasāda. The temple's watchman, who was named Tulasī, also came and offered his obeisances to Śrī Caitanya Mahāprabhu.

TEXT 234

'মহাপ্রভু আইলা'—গ্রামে কোলাহল হৈল ।
সার্বভৌম, রামানন্দ, বাণীনাথ মিলিল ॥ ২৩৪ ॥

'mahāprabhu āilā'——grāme kolāhala haila
sārvabhauma, rāmānanda, vāṇīnātha milila

SYNONYMS

mahāprabhu āilā—Śrī Caitanya Mahāprabhu has arrived; *grāme*—in the town; *kolāhala haila*—there was spreading of the news; *sārvabhauma*—Sārvabhauma; *rāmānanda*—Rāmānanda; *vāṇīnātha*—Vāṇīnātha; *milila*—came and met Him.

TRANSLATION

When the news spread that Śrī Caitanya Mahāprabhu had arrived at Jagannātha Purī, devotees like Sārvabhauma Bhaṭṭācārya, Rāmānanda Rāya and Vāṇīnātha Rāya all came to meet Him.

TEXT 235

সবা সঙ্গে লঞা প্রভু মিশ্র-বাসা আইলা ।
সার্বভৌম, পণ্ডিত-গোসাঞি নিমন্ত্রণ কৈলা ॥ ২৩৫ ॥

sabā saṅge lañā prabhu miśra-vāsā āilā
sārvabhauma, paṇḍita-gosāñi nimantraṇa kailā

SYNONYMS

sabā saṅge lañā—taking all of them; *prabhu*—Śrī Caitanya Mahāprabhu; *miśra-vāsā āilā*—came to Kāśī Miśra's house; *sārvabhauma*—Sārvabhauma Bhaṭṭācārya; *paṇḍita-gosāñi*—Gadādhara Paṇḍita; *nimantraṇa kailā*—invited the Lord to take *prasāda.*

TRANSLATION

The Lord and all His devotees then went to the residence of Kāśī Miśra. Sārvabhauma Bhaṭṭācārya and Paṇḍita Gosāñi also invited the Lord to dine at their homes.

TEXT 236

প্রভু কহে,—"মহাপ্রসাদ আন' এই স্থানে ।
সবা-সঙ্গে ইহাঁ আজি করিমু ভোজনে ॥" ২৩৬ ॥

prabhu kahe,——"mahā-prasāda āna' ei sthāne
sabā-saṅge ihāṅ āji karimu bhojane"

SYNONYMS

prabhu kahe—Śrī Caitanya Mahāprabhu said; *mahā-prasāda āna'*—bring *mahā-prasāda; ei sthāne*—to this place; *sabā-saṅge*—with all; *ihāṅ*—here; *āji*—today; *karimu bhojane*—I shall dine.

TRANSLATION

Accepting their invitation, the Lord asked them to bring all the prasāda there so that He could eat it with His devotees.

TEXT 237

তবে দুঁহে জগন্নাথপ্রসাদ আনিল ।
সবা-সঙ্গে মহাপ্রভু ভোজন করিল ॥ ২৩৭ ॥

tabe duṅhe jagannātha-prasāda ānila
sabā-saṅge mahāprabhu bhojana karila

SYNONYMS

tabe—then; *duṅhe*—both Sārvabhauma and Paṇḍita Gosāñi; *jagannātha-prasāda ānila*—brought the *mahā-prasāda* of Jagannātha; *sabā-saṅge*—with all of them; *mahāprabhu*—Śrī Caitanya Mahāprabhu; *bhojana karila*—dined.

TRANSLATION

Upon receiving Śrī Caitanya Mahāprabhu's order, both Sārvabhauma Bhaṭṭācārya and Paṇḍita Gosāñi brought sufficient prasāda from the temple of Jagannātha. The Lord then dined with everyone at His own place.

TEXT 238

এই ত' কহিলুঁ,—প্রভু দেখি' বৃন্দাবন।
পুনঃ করিলেন যৈছে নীলাদ্রি গমন ॥ ২৩৮ ॥

ei ta' kahiluṅ,——prabhu dekhi' vṛndāvana
punaḥ karilena yaiche nīlādri gamana

SYNONYMS

ei ta' kahiluṅ—thus I have described; *prabhu*—Śrī Caitanya Mahāprabhu; *dekhi' vṛndāvana*—after visiting Vṛndāvana; *punaḥ*—again; *karilena*—did; *yaiche*—as; *nīlādri gamana*—coming back to Jagannātha Purī.

TRANSLATION

Thus I have described how Śrī Caitanya Mahāprabhu returned to Jagannātha Purī from Vṛndāvana.

TEXT 239

ইহা যেই শ্রদ্ধা করি' করয়ে শ্রবণ।
অচিরাৎ পায় সেই চৈতন্য-চরণ ॥ ২৩৯ ॥

ihā yei śraddhā kari' karaye śravaṇa
acirāt pāya sei caitanya-caraṇa

SYNONYMS

ihā—this; *yei*—anyone who; *śraddhā kari'*—with faith and love; *karaye śravaṇa*—hears; *acirāt*—very soon; *pāya*—gets; *sei*—he; *caitanya-caraṇa*—the lotus feet of Śrī Caitanya Mahāprabhu.

TRANSLATION

Whoever hears Śrī Caitanya Mahāprabhu's pastimes with faith and love very soon attains shelter at the Lord's lotus feet.

TEXT 240

মধ্যলীলার করিলুঁ এই দিগ্‌দরশন ।
ছয় বৎসর কৈলা যৈছে গমনাগমন ॥ ২৪০ ॥

madhya-līlāra kariluṅ ei dig-daraśana
chaya vatsara kailā yaiche gamanāgamana

SYNONYMS

madhya-līlāra—of this division, known as *Madhya-līlā; kariluṅ*—I have done; *ei dik-daraśana*—this summary inspection; *chaya vatsara*—continuously for six years; *kailā*—performed; *yaiche*—just as; *gamana-āgamana*—going and coming back.

TRANSLATION

I have thus given a summary of the Madhya-līlā, which is a special description of Śrī Caitanya Mahāprabhu's travels to and from Jagannātha Purī. Indeed, the Lord traveled to and fro continuously for six years.

TEXT 241

শেষ অষ্টাদশ বৎসর নীলাচলে বাস ।
ভক্তগণ-সঙ্গে করে কীর্তন-বিলাস ॥ ২৪১ ॥

śeṣa aṣṭādaśa vatsara nīlācale vāsa
bhakta-gaṇa-saṅge kare kīrtana-vilāsa

SYNONYMS

śeṣa aṣṭādaśa vatsara—the remaining eighteen years; *nīlācale vāsa*—residence at Jagannātha Purī; *bhakta-gaṇa-saṅge*—with devotees; *kare*—performs; *kīrtana-vilāsa*—the pastimes of chanting the Hare Kṛṣṇa *mantra.*

TRANSLATION

After taking sannyāsa at the age of twenty-four, Śrī Caitanya Mahāprabhu lived another twenty-four years. For six of these years, He traveled extensively throughout India, sometimes going to Jagannātha Purī and sometimes leaving. After traveling for six years, the Lord fixed His residence at Jagannātha Purī and stayed there for the eighteen remaining years of His life. During these eighteen years He mainly chanted Hare Kṛṣṇa with His devotees.

TEXT 242

মধ্যলীলার ক্রম এবে করি অনুবাদ।
অনুবাদ কৈলে হয় কথার আস্বাদ ॥ ২৪২ ॥

madhya-līlāra krama ebe kari anuvāda
anuvāda kaile haya kathāra āsvāda

SYNONYMS

madhya-līlāra krama—a chronological list of the pastimes described in the *Madhya-līlā* of *Caitanya-caritāmṛta; ebe*—now; *kari*—I may do; *anuvāda*—assessment; *anuvāda kaile*—by assessing in that way; *haya*—there is; *kathāra āsvāda*—tasting of all the topics.

TRANSLATION

I shall now chronologically reassess the chapters of Madhya-līlā so that one can relish the transcendental features of these topics.

TEXT 243

প্রথম পরিচ্ছেদে—শেষলীলার সূত্রগণ।
তথি-মধ্যে কোন ভাগের বিস্তার বর্ণন ॥ ২৪৩ ॥

prathama paricchede——śeṣa-līlāra sūtra-gaṇa
tathi-madhye kona bhāgera vistāra varṇana

SYNONYMS

prathama paricchede—in the First Chapter; *śeṣa-līlāra sūtra-gaṇa*—the codes of the *Antya-līlā,* Śrī Caitanya Mahāprabhu's pastimes at the end; *tathi-madhye*—within that; *kona bhāgera*—of some portion of the book; *vistāra varṇana*—a vivid description.

TRANSLATION

In the First Chapter I have given a synopsis of the last pastimes [Antya-līlā]. Within this chapter is a vivid description of some of the pastimes of the Lord that took place toward the end of His life.

TEXT 244

দ্বিতীয় পরিচ্ছেদে—প্রভুর প্রলাপ-বর্ণন।
তথি-মধ্যে নানা-ভাবের দিগ্‌দরশন ॥ ২৪৪ ॥

dvitīya paricchede——prabhura pralāpa-varṇana
tathi-madhye nānā-bhāvera dig-daraśana

SYNONYMS

dvitīya paricchede—in the Second Chapter; *prabhura*—of Śrī Caitanya Mahāprabhu; *pralāpa-varṇana*—a description of His behaving like a crazy man; *tathi-madhye*—within that; *nānā-bhāvera*—of different emotional ecstasies; *dik-daraśana*—indication.

TRANSLATION

In the Second Chapter I have described Śrī Caitanya Mahāprabhu's talking like a crazy man. Within this chapter it is indicated how Śrī Caitanya Mahāprabhu manifested His different emotional moods.

TEXT 245

তৃতীয় পরিচ্ছেদে—প্রভুর কহিলুঁ সন্ন্যাস ।
আচার্যের ঘরে যৈছে করিলা বিলাস ॥ ২৪৫ ॥

tṛtīya paricchede——prabhura kahiluṅ sannyāsa
ācāryera ghare yaiche karilā vilāsa

SYNONYMS

tṛtīya paricchede—in the Third Chapter; *prabhura*—of Śrī Caitanya Mahāprabhu; *kahiluṅ*—I have described; *sannyāsa*—acceptance of the renounced order of life; *ācāryera ghare*—at the house of Advaita Ācārya; *yaiche*—how; *karilā vilāsa*—enjoyed His pastimes.

TRANSLATION

In the Third Chapter I have described the Lord's acceptance of the renounced order and how He enjoyed His pastimes in the house of Advaita Ācārya.

TEXT 246

চতুর্থে—মাধব পুরীর চরিত্র-আস্বাদন ।
গোপাল স্থাপন, ক্ষীর-চুরির বর্ণন ॥ ২৪৬ ॥

caturthe——mādhava purīra caritra-āsvādana
gopāla sthāpana, kṣīra-curira varṇana

SYNONYMS

caturthe—in the Fourth Chapter; *mādhava purīra*—of Mādhavendra Purī; *caritra-āsvādana*—relishing the characteristics; *gopāla sthāpana*—the installation of Gopāla; *kṣīra-curira varṇana*—a description of Gopīnātha's stealing condensed milk at Remuṇā.

TRANSLATION

In the Fourth Chapter I have described Mādhavendra Purī's installation of the Gopāla Deity as well as Gopīnātha's stealing a pot of condensed milk at Remuṇā.

TEXT 247

পঞ্চমে —সাক্ষিগোপাল-চরিত্র-বর্ণন ।
নিত্যানন্দ কহে, প্রভু করেন আস্বাদন ॥ ২৪৭ ॥

pañcame——śakṣi-gopāla-caritra-varṇana
nityānanda kahe, prabhu karena āsvādana

SYNONYMS

pañcame—in the Fifth Chapter; *sākṣi-gopāla*—Sākṣi-gopāla; *caritra-varṇana*—a description of the characteristics; *nityānanda kahe*—Lord Nityānanda described this; *prabhu*—Lord Caitanya Mahāprabhu; *karena āsvādana*—tasted it.

TRANSLATION

In the Fifth Chapter I have narrated the story of Sākṣi-gopāla. Lord Nityānanda Prabhu narrated this while Śrī Caitanya Mahāprabhu listened.

TEXT 248

ষষ্ঠে— সার্বভৌমের করিলা উদ্ধার ।
সপ্তমে—তীর্থযাত্রা, বাসুদেব নিস্তার ॥ ২৪৮ ॥

ṣaṣṭhe——sārvabhaumera karilā uddhāra
saptame——tīrtha-yātrā, vāsudeva nistāra

SYNONYMS

ṣaṣṭhe—in the Sixth Chapter; *sārvabhaumera*—Sārvabhauma Bhaṭṭācārya; *karilā uddhāra*—the Lord delivered; *saptame*—in the Seventh Chapter; *tīrtha-yātrā*—going to different holy places; *vāsudeva nistāra*—delivering Vāsudeva.

TRANSLATION

In the Sixth Chapter I have told how Sārvabhauma Bhaṭṭācārya was delivered, and in the Seventh Chapter I have described the Lord's tour of different holy places and His deliverance of Vāsudeva.

TEXT 249

অষ্টমে –রামানন্দ-সংবাদ বিস্তার ।
আপনে শুনিলা 'সর্ব-সিদ্ধান্তের সার' ॥ ২৪৯ ॥

aṣṭame——rāmānanda-saṁvāda vistāra
āpane śunilā 'sarva-siddhāntera sāra'

SYNONYMS

aṣṭame—in the Eighth Chapter; *rāmānanda-saṁvāda vistāra*—an elaborate discussion with Śrī Rāmānanda Rāya; *āpane*—personally; *śunilā*—listened; *sarva*—all; *siddhāntera*—of conclusions; *sāra*—the essence.

TRANSLATION

In the Eighth Chapter I have recorded the Lord's elaborate discussion with Rāmānanda Rāya. The Lord personally listened as Rāmānanda gave the conclusive essence of all Vedic literatures.

TEXT 250

নবমে—কহিলুঁ দক্ষিণ-তীর্থ-ভ্রমণ ।
দশমে—কহিলুঁ সর্ব বৈষ্ণব-মিলন ॥ ২৫০ ॥

navame——kahiluṅ dakṣiṇa-tīrtha-bhramaṇa
daśame——kahiluṅ sarva-vaiṣṇava-milana

SYNONYMS

navame—in the Ninth Chapter; *kahiluṅ*—I have described; *dakṣiṇa-tīrtha-bhramaṇa*—going on pilgrimage in South India; *daśame*—in the Tenth Chapter; *kahiluṅ*—I have described; *sarva-vaiṣṇava-milana*—meeting of all kinds of devotees.

TRANSLATION

In the Ninth Chapter I have described the Lord's tour of South India and the different places of pilgrimage. In the Tenth Chapter I have described the meeting of all the devotees of the Lord.

TEXT 251

একাদশে—শ্রীমন্দিরে 'বেড়া-সংকীর্তন'।
দ্বাদশে –গুণ্ডিচা-মন্দির-মার্জন-ক্ষালন ॥ ২৫১ ॥

ekādaśe——śrī-mandire 'beḍā-saṅkīrtana'
dvādaśe——guṇḍicā-mandira-mārjana-kṣālana

SYNONYMS

ekādaśe—in the Eleventh Chapter; *śrī-mandire*—in the Jagannātha temple; *beḍā-saṅkīrtana*—chanting of the Hare Kṛṣṇa *mantra* all around; *dvādaśe*—in the Twelfth Chapter; *guṇḍicā-mandira*—of the temple known as Guṇḍicā; *mārjana-kṣālana*—cleansing and washing.

TRANSLATION

In the Eleventh Chapter I have described the great chanting of the Hare Kṛṣṇa mahā-mantra that surrounded the Lord. In the Twelfth Chapter I have given a narration of the cleansing and washing of the Guṇḍicā temple.

TEXT 252

ত্রয়োদশে—রথ-আগে প্রভুর নর্তন।
চতুর্দশে—'হেরাপঞ্চমী'-যাত্রা-দরশন ॥ ২৫২ ॥

trayodaśe——ratha-āge prabhura nartana
caturdaśe——'herā-pañcamī'-yātrā-daraśana

SYNONYMS

trayodaśe—in the Thirteenth Chapter; *ratha-āge*—in front of the Jagannātha Ratha; *prabhura nartana*—Lord Caitanya Mahāprabhu's dancing; *caturdaśe*—in the Fourteenth Chapter; *herā-pañcamī*—Herā-pañcamī, which takes place on the fifth day of Ratha-yātrā; *yātrā*—festival; *daraśana*—visiting.

TRANSLATION

In the Thirteenth Chapter I have described Śrī Caitanya Mahāprabhu's dancing before the chariot of Jagannātha. In the Fourteenth Chapter, there is an account of the Herā-pañcamī function.

TEXT 253

তার মধ্যে ব্রজদেবীর ভাবের শ্রবণ।
স্বরূপ কহিলা, প্রভু কৈলা আস্বাদন ॥ ২৫৩ ॥

tāra madhye vraja-devīra bhāvera śravaṇa
svarūpa kahilā, prabhu kailā āsvādana

SYNONYMS

tāra madhye—in that; *vraja-devīra*—of the *gopīs; bhāvera*—of ecstatic emotion; *śravaṇa*—hearing; *svarūpa kahilā*—Svarūpa Dāmodara Gosvāmī described; *prabhu*—Śrī Caitanya Mahāprabhu; *kailā āsvādana*—personally tasted.

TRANSLATION

Also in the Fourteenth Chapter the emotional ecstasy of the gopīs was described by Svarūpa Dāmodara and tasted by Śrī Caitanya Mahāprabhu.

TEXT 254

পঞ্চদশে—ভক্তের গুণ শ্রীমুখে কহিল ।
সার্বভৌম-ঘরে ভিক্ষা, অমোঘ তারিল ॥ ২৫৪ ॥

pañcadaśe——bhaktera guṇa śrī-mukhe kahila
sārvabhauma-ghare bhikṣā, amogha tārila

SYNONYMS

pañcadaśe—in the Fifteenth Chapter; *bhaktera*—of the devotees; *guṇa*—qualities; *śrī-mukhe kahila*—Caitanya Mahāprabhu personally described; *sārvabhauma-ghare*—at the house of Sārvabhauma; *bhikṣā*—accepting lunch; *amogha tārila*—He delivered Amogha.

TRANSLATION

In the Fifteenth Chapter Śrī Caitanya Mahāprabhu highly praised the qualities of His devotees and accepted lunch at the house of Sārvabhauma Bhaṭṭācārya. At that time, He delivered Amogha.

TEXT 255

ষোড়শে—বৃন্দাবনযাত্রা গৌড়দেশ-পথে ।
পুনঃ নীলাচলে আইলা, নাটশালা হৈতে ॥ ২৫৫ ॥

ṣoḍaśe——vṛndāvana-yātrā gauḍa-deśa-pathe
punaḥ nīlācale āilā, nāṭaśālā haite

SYNONYMS

ṣoḍaśe—in the Sixteenth Chapter; *vṛndāvana-yātrā*—departure for visiting Vṛndāvana; *gauḍa-deśa-pathe*—on the way through the province of Bengal;

punaḥ—again; *nīlācale āilā*—came back to Jagannātha Purī; *nāṭaśālā haite*—from Kānāi Nāṭaśālā.

TRANSLATION

In the Sixteenth Chapter Śrī Caitanya Mahāprabhu departed for Vṛndāvana and journeyed through Bengal. He later returned to Jagannātha Purī from Kānāi Nāṭaśālā.

TEXT 256

সপ্তদশে—বনপথে মথুরা-গমন ।
অষ্টাদশে—বৃন্দাবন-বিহার-বর্ণন ॥ ২৫৬ ॥

saptadaśe——vanapathe mathurā-gamana
aṣṭādaśe——vṛndāvana-vihāra-varṇana

SYNONYMS

saptadaśe—in the Seventeenth Chapter; *vana-pathe*—through the forest path; *mathurā-gamana*—Lord Caitanya Mahāprabhu's going to Mathurā; *aṣṭādaśe*—in the Eighteenth Chapter; *vṛndāvana-vihāra-varṇana*—description of His touring the forest of Vṛndāvana.

TRANSLATION

In the Seventeenth Chapter I have described the Lord's journey through the great forest of Jhārikhaṇḍa and His arrival at Mathurā. In the Eighteenth Chapter there is a description of His tour of the forest of Vṛndāvana.

TEXT 257

ঊনবিংশে—মথুরা হৈতে প্রয়াগ-গমন ।
তার মধ্যে শ্রীরূপেরে শক্তি-সঞ্চারণ ॥ ২৫৭ ॥

ūnaviṁśe——mathurā haite prayāga-gamana
tāra madhye śrī-rūpere śakti-sañcāraṇa

SYNONYMS

ūnaviṁśe—in the Nineteenth Chapter; *mathurā haite*—from Mathurā; *prayāga-gamana*—going to Prayāga; *tāra madhye*—within that; *śrī-rūpere*—Śrī Rūpa Gosvāmī; *śakti-sañcāraṇa*—empowering to spread devotional service.

TRANSLATION

In the Nineteenth Chapter, the Lord returned to Prayāga from Mathurā and empowered Śrī Rūpa Gosvāmī to spread devotional service.

TEXT 258

বিংশতি পরিচ্ছেদে—সনাতনের মিলন ।
তার মধ্যে ভগবানের স্বরূপ-বর্ণন ॥ ২৫৮ ॥

viṁśati paricchede——sanātanera milana
tāra madhye bhagavānera svarūpa-varṇana

SYNONYMS

viṁśati paricchede—in the Twentieth Chapter; *sanātanera milana*—meeting with Sanātana Gosvāmī; *tāra madhye*—within that; *bhagavānera*—of the Supreme Personality of Godhead; *svarūpa-varṇana*—description of personal features.

TRANSLATION

In the Twentieth Chapter the Lord's meeting with Sanātana is described. The Lord described the personal features of the Supreme Personality of Godhead in depth.

TEXT 259

একবিংশে – কৃষ্ণৈশ্বর্য-মাধুর্য বর্ণন ।
দ্বাবিংশে—দ্বিবিধ সাধনভক্তির বিবরণ ॥ ২৫৯ ॥

ekaviṁśe——kṛṣṇaiśvarya-mādhurya varṇana
dvāviṁśe——dvividha sādhana-bhaktira vivaraṇa

SYNONYMS

eka-viṁśe—in the Twenty-first Chapter; *kṛṣṇa-aiśvarya*—of the opulence of Kṛṣṇa; *mādhurya*—of the pleasing beauty; *varṇana*—description; *dvā-viṁśe*—in the Twenty-second Chapter; *dvi-vidha*—twofold; *sādhana-bhaktira*—of the discharge of devotional service; *vivaraṇa*—description.

TRANSLATION

In the Twenty-first Chapter there is a description of Kṛṣṇa's beauty and opulence, and in the Twenty-second Chapter there is a description of the twofold discharge of devotional service.

TEXT 260

ত্রয়োবিংশে—প্রেমভক্তিরসের কথন ।
চতুর্বিংশে—'আত্মারামাঃ'-শ্লোকার্থ বর্ণন ॥ ২৬০ ॥

trayoviṁśe——prema-bhakti-rasera kathana
caturviṁśe——'ātmārāmāḥ'-ślokārtha varṇana

SYNONYMS

trayaḥ-viṁśe—in the Twenty-third Chapter; *prema-bhakti*—of ecstatic love of Godhead; *rasera*—of the mellow; *kathana*—narration; *catuḥ-viṁśe*—in the Twenty-fourth Chapter; *ātmārāmāḥ*—known as *ātmārāma; śloka-artha*—the meaning of the verse; *varṇana*—description.

TRANSLATION

In the Twenty-third Chapter there is a description of the mellows of transcendental loving service, and in the Twenty-fourth Chapter the Lord analyzes the ātmārāma verse.

TEXT 261

পঞ্চবিংশে— কাশীবাসীরে বৈষ্ণবকরণ ।
কাশী হৈতে পুনঃ নীলাচলে আগমন ॥ ২৬১ ॥

pañcaviṁśe——kāśī-vāsīre vaiṣṇava-karaṇa
kāśī haite punaḥ nīlācale āgamana

SYNONYMS

pañca-viṁśe—in the Twenty-fifth Chapter; *kāśī-vāsīre*—the residents of Vārāṇasī (Kāśī); *vaiṣṇava-karaṇa*—making Vaiṣṇavas; *kāśī haite*—from Kāśī; *punaḥ*—again; *nīlācale āgamana*—coming back to Jagannātha Purī (Nīlācala).

TRANSLATION

In the Twenty-fifth Chapter there is a description of how the residents of Vārāṇasī were converted to Vaiṣṇavism. The Lord also returned to Nīlācala [Jagannātha Purī] from Vārāṇasī.

TEXT 262

পঞ্চবিংশতি পরিচ্ছেদে এই কৈলুঁ অনুবাদ ।
যাহার শ্রবণে হয় গ্রন্থার্থ-আস্বাদ ॥ ২৬২ ॥

pañcaviṁśati paricchede ei kailuṅ anuvāda
yāhāra śravaṇe haya granthārtha-āsvāda

SYNONYMS

pañca-viṁśati paricchede—in the Twenty-fifth Chapter; *ei*—this; *kailuṅ anuvāda*—I have made repetition; *yāhāra śravaṇe*—hearing which; *haya*—there is; *grantha-artha-āsvāda*—understanding of the whole contents of the book.

TRANSLATION

I have thus summarized these pastimes in the Twenty-fifth Chapter. Hearing this, one can understand the whole purport of this scripture.

TEXT 263

সংক্ষেপে কহিলুঁ এই মধ্যলীলার সার ।
কোটিগ্রন্থে বর্ণন না যায় ইহার বিস্তার ॥ ২৬৩ ॥

saṅkṣepe kahiluṅ ei madhya-līlāra sāra
koṭi-granthe varṇana nā yāya ihāra vistāra

SYNONYMS

saṅkṣepe—in brief; *kahiluṅ*—I have described; *ei*—this; *madhya-līlāra sāra*—essence of *Madhya-līlā; koṭi-granthe*—in millions of books; *varṇana*—description; *nā yāya*—is not possible; *ihāra vistāra*—elaborately.

TRANSLATION

I have now summarized the entire subject matter of the Madhya-līlā. These pastimes cannot be described elaborately even in millions of books.

TEXT 264

জীব নিস্তারিতে প্রভু ভ্রমিলা দেশে-দেশে ।
আপনে আস্বাদি' ভক্তি করিলা প্রকাশে ॥ ২৬৪ ॥

jīva nistārite prabhu bhramilā deśe-deśe
āpane āsvādi' bhakti karilā prakāśe

SYNONYMS

jīva nistārite—to deliver all the fallen souls; *prabhu*—Śrī Caitanya Mahāprabhu; *bhramilā*—traveled; *deśe-deśe*—in various countries; *āpane*—personally; *āsvādi'*—tasting; *bhakti*—devotional service; *karilā*—did; *prakāśe*—broadcasting.

TRANSLATION

To deliver all fallen souls, the Lord traveled from country to country. He personally tasted the transcendental pleasure of devotional service, and He simultaneously spread the cult of devotion everywhere.

PURPORT

Śrī Caitanya Mahāprabhu personally traveled to different regions of India to spread the *bhakti* cult throughout the country. He also personally relished transcendental activities. By His personal behavior He has given an example for devotees to follow. That is, one should broadcast the cult of devotional service. He specifically instructed His devotees to enjoin all Indians to broadcast this message throughout the world because at that time the Lord could not personally travel to other parts of the world. In this regard, He has left two instructions:

bhārata-bhūmite haila manuṣya-janma yāra
janma sārthaka kari' kara para-upakāra

"All Indians should seriously take up the cult of Śrī Caitanya Mahāprabhu and should perfect their lives by adopting the process of devotional service. After perfecting their lives, they should broadcast this message all over the world for the welfare of all human beings [*para-upakāra*]." (Cc. *Ādi* 9.41) A Vaiṣṇava is especially interested in *para-upakāra,* doing good to others. Prahlāda Mahārāja was also interested in this. He did not want to be delivered alone; rather, he wanted to deliver all fallen souls, who are bereft of knowledge of *bhakti* and who misuse their intelligence for the temporary benefit of the material body. Śrī Caitanya Mahāprabhu also wanted His mission spread all over the world.

pṛthivīte āche yata nagarādi grāma
sarvatra pracāra haibe mora nāma

"In every town and village, the chanting of My name will be heard."

Following in His footsteps, we are trying to broadcast His message throughout the world. By His mercy, people are taking this movement very seriously. Indeed, our books are extensively distributed in the Western countries, especially in America and Europe. Even the ecclesiastical orders in these countries are appreciating the value of this Kṛṣṇa consciousness movement and are ready to unite for the highest benefit of human society. The followers of Śrī Caitanya Mahāprabhu may therefore take this movement seriously and broadcast it throughout the world, from village to village and from town to town, just as Śrī Caitanya Mahāprabhu Himself did.

TEXT 265

কৃষ্ণতত্ত্ব, ভক্তিতত্ত্ব, প্রেমতত্ত্ব সার ।
ভাবতত্ত্ব, রসতত্ত্ব, লীলাতত্ত্ব আর ॥ ২৬৫ ॥

kṛṣṇa-tattva, bhakti-tattva, prema-tattva sāra
bhāva-tattva, rasa-tattva, līlā-tattva āra

SYNONYMS

kṛṣṇa-tattva—the truth of Kṛṣṇa; *bhakti-tattva*—the truth of devotional service; *prema-tattva*—the truth of ecstatic love of Godhead; *sāra*—the essence; *bhāva-tattva*—the emotional truth; *rasa-tattva*—the truth of transcendental mellow; *līlā-tattva*—the truth of pastimes of the Lord; *āra*—also.

TRANSLATION

Kṛṣṇa consciousness means understanding the truth of Kṛṣṇa, the truth of devotional service, the truth of love of Godhead, the truth of emotional ecstasy, the truth of transcendental mellow and the truth of the pastimes of the Lord.

TEXT 266

শ্রীভাগবত-তত্ত্বরস করিলা প্রচারে ।
কৃষ্ণতুল্য ভাগবত, জানাইলা সংসারে ॥ ২৬৬ ॥

śrī-bhāgavata-tattva-rasa karilā pracāre
kṛṣṇa-tulya bhāgavata, jānāilā saṁsāre

SYNONYMS

śrī-bhāgavata-tattva-rasa—the truth and transcendental taste of *Śrīmad-Bhāgavatam; karilā pracāre*—Caitanya Mahāprabhu preached elaborately; *kṛṣṇa-tulya*—identical with Kṛṣṇa; *bhāgavata*—*Śrīmad-Bhāgavatam; jānāilā saṁsāre*—has preached within this world.

TRANSLATION

Śrī Caitanya Mahāprabhu has personally preached the transcendental truths and mellows of Śrīmad-Bhāgavatam. Śrīmad-Bhāgavatam and the Supreme Personality of Godhead are identical, for Śrīmad-Bhāgavatam is the sound incarnation of Śrī Kṛṣṇa.

TEXT 267

ভক্ত লাগি' বিস্তারিলা আপন-বদনে ।
কাহাঁ ভক্ত-মুখে কহাই শুনিলা আপনে ॥ ২৬৭ ॥

bhakta lāgi' vistārilā āpana-vadane
kāhāṅ bhakta-mukhe kahāi śunilā āpane

SYNONYMS

bhakta lāgi'—especially for the purpose of His devotees; *vistārilā*—expansively described; *āpana-vadane*—personally, with His own mouth; *kāhāṅ*—sometimes; *bhakta-mukhe*—through the mouth of His devotees; *kahāi*—making describe; *śunilā āpane*—listened Himself.

TRANSLATION

Śrī Caitanya Mahāprabhu broadcast the purpose of Śrīmad-Bhāgavatam. He sometimes spoke for the benefit of His devotees and sometimes empowered one of His devotees to speak while He listened.

PURPORT

Śrī Caitanya Mahāprabhu, as an ideal teacher, or *ācārya,* explained *Śrīmad-Bhāgavatam* very elaborately Himself. He sometimes also empowered His devotees to speak while He listened. This is the way an *ācārya* should train His disciples. Not only should he describe the *bhāgavata* cult personally, but he should also train his disciples to speak on this sublime subject.

TEXT 268

শ্রীচৈতন্য-সম আর কৃপালু বদান্য ।
ভক্তবৎসল না দেখি ত্রিজগতে অন্য ॥ ২৬৮ ॥

śrī-caitanya-sama āra kṛpālu vadānya
bhakta-vatsala nā dekhi trijagate anya

SYNONYMS

śrī-caitanya-sama—equal to Śrī Caitanya Mahāprabhu; *āra*—anyone else; *kṛpālu*—merciful; *vadānya*—magnanimous; *bhakta-vatsala*—very kind to the devotees; *nā dekhi*—I do not see; *tri-jagate*—in these three worlds; *anya*—anyone else.

TRANSLATION

All sane men within these three worlds certainly accept the conclusion that no one is more merciful and magnanimous than Śrī Caitanya Mahāprabhu and that no one is as kind to His devotees.

TEXT 269

শ্রদ্ধা করি' এই লীলা শুন, ভক্তগণ ।
ইহার প্রসাদে পাইবা চৈতন্য-চরণ ॥ ২৬৯ ॥

śraddhā kari' ei līlā śuna, bhakta-gaṇa
ihāra prasāde pāibā caitanya-caraṇa

SYNONYMS

śraddhā kari'—having faith and love; *ei līlā*—these pastimes of Śrī Caitanya Mahāprabhu; *śuna*—hear; *bhakta-gaṇa*—O devotees; *ihāra prasāde*—by the grace of this transcendental hearing; *pāibā*—you will get; *caitanya-caraṇa*—the lotus feet of Śrī Caitanya Mahāprabhu.

TRANSLATION

All devotees should hear about Śrī Caitanya Mahāprabhu's pastimes with faith and love. By the grace of the Lord, one can thus attain shelter at His lotus feet.

TEXT 270

ইহার প্রসাদে পাইবা কৃষ্ণতত্ত্বসার ।
সর্বশাস্ত্র-সিদ্ধান্তের ইহাঁ পাইবা পার ॥ ২৭০ ॥

ihāra prasāde pāibā kṛṣṇa-tattva-sāra
sarva-śāstra-siddhāntera ihāṅ pāibā pāra

SYNONYMS

ihāra prasāde—by hearing these teachings of Śrī Caitanya Mahāprabhu; *pāibā*—you will get; *kṛṣṇa-tattva-sāra*—the essence of the truth of Kṛṣṇa; *sarva-śāstra*—of all revealed scriptures; *siddhāntera*—of conclusions; *ihāṅ*—here; *pāibā*—you will get; *pāra*—the ultimate limit.

TRANSLATION

By understanding the pastimes of Śrī Caitanya Mahāprabhu, one can understand the truth about Kṛṣṇa. By understanding Kṛṣṇa, one can understand the limit of all knowledge described in various revealed scriptures.

PURPORT

As stated in *Bhagavad-gītā* (7.3):

manuṣyāṇāṁ sahasreṣu
kaścid yatati siddhaye
yatatām api siddhānāṁ
kaścin māṁ vetti tattvataḥ

"Out of many thousands among men, one may endeavor for perfection, and of those who have achieved perfection, hardly one knows Me in truth."

It is very difficult to understand Kṛṣṇa, but if one tries to understand *Śrīmad-Bhāgavatam* through Caitanya Mahāprabhu's *bhakti* cult, one will undoubtedly understand Kṛṣṇa very easily. If somehow or other one understands Kṛṣṇa, his life will be successful. Again, as stated in *Bhagavad-gītā* (4.9):

janma karma ca me divyam
evaṁ yo vetti tattvataḥ
tyaktvā dehaṁ punar janma
naiti mām eti so 'rjuna

"One who knows the transcendental nature of My appearance and activities does not, upon leaving the body, take his birth again in this material world, but attains My eternal abode, O Arjuna."

TEXT 271

কৃষ্ণলীলা অমৃত-সার, তার শত শত ধার,
দশদিকে বহে যাহা হৈতে ।
সে চৈতন্যলীলা হয়, সরোবর অক্ষয়,
মনো-হংস চরাহ' তাহাতে ॥ ২৭১ ॥

kṛṣṇa-līlā amṛta-sāra, tāra śata śata dhāra,
daśa-dike vahe yāhā haite
se caitanya-līlā haya, sarovara akṣaya,
mano-haṁsa carāha' tāhāte

SYNONYMS

kṛṣṇa-līlā amṛta-sāra—the pastimes of Lord Kṛṣṇa are the essence of all eternal bliss; *tāra śata śata dhāra*—the flow of that eternal bliss is running in hundreds of branches; *daśa-dike*—in all the ten directions; *vahe*—flows; *yāhā haite*—from which; *se*—those; *caitanya-līlā*—pastimes of Śrī Caitanya Mahāprabhu; *haya*—are; *sarovara akṣaya*—a transcendental eternal lake; *manaḥ-haṁsa*—my mind, which is like a swan; *carāha'*—please wander; *tāhāte*—in that lake.

TRANSLATION

The pastimes of Lord Kṛṣṇa are the essence of all nectar. They flow in hundreds of rivulets and in all directions. The pastimes of Śrī Caitanya Mahāprabhu are an eternal reservoir, and one is advised to let his mind swim like a swan on this transcendental lake.

PURPORT

The essence of spiritual knowledge is found in the pastimes of Śrī Caitanya Mahāprabhu, which are identical with the pastimes of Lord Kṛṣṇa. This is the essence of knowledge. If knowledge does not include the understanding of Śrī Caitanya Mahāprabhu and Kṛṣṇa, it is simply superfluous. By Śrī Caitanya Mahāprabhu's grace, the nectar of Lord Śrī Kṛṣṇa's pastimes is flowing in different directions in hundreds and thousands of rivers. One should not think that the pastimes of Śrī Caitanya Mahāprabhu are different from Kṛṣṇa's pastimes. It is said: *śrī-kṛṣṇa-caitanya, rādhā-kṛṣṇa nahe anya.* Lord Caitanya Mahāprabhu is a combination of Rādhā-Kṛṣṇa, and without understanding His pastimes, one cannot understand Rādhā and Kṛṣṇa. Śrīla Narottama dāsa Ṭhākura therefore sings: *rūpa-raghunātha-pade haibe ākuti/ kabe hāma bujhaba se yugala pirīti.* "When shall I become very eager to study the books left by the six Gosvāmīs? Then I shall be able to understand the conjugal pastimes of Rādhā and Kṛṣṇa." Caitanya Mahāprabhu directly empowered Śrīla Rūpa Gosvāmī and Śrīla Sanātana Gosvāmī. Following in their footsteps, the other six Gosvāmīs understood Śrī Caitanya Mahāprabhu and His mission. One should understand Śrī Kṛṣṇa Caitanya and Lord Śrī Kṛṣṇa from the Gosvāmīs in the *paramparā* system. This Kṛṣṇa consciousness movement is following as strictly as possible in the footsteps of the Gosvāmīs. Narottama dāsa Ṭhākura says, *ei chaya gosāñi yāṅra, mui tāṅra dāsa:* "I am the servant of the six Gosvāmīs." The philosophy of Kṛṣṇa consciousness is to become the servant of the servant of the servant of the Lord. Whoever wants to understand the difficult subject matter of *kṛṣṇa-kathā* should accept the disciplic succession. If one is somehow or other able to understand Kṛṣṇa, his life will be successful. *Tyaktvā dehaṁ punar janma naiti mām eti so 'rjuna.* A perfect devotee is able to understand Kṛṣṇa through the disciplic succession, and his entrance into the kingdom of God is thereby certainly opened. When one understands Kṛṣṇa, there is no difficulty in transferring oneself to the spiritual kingdom.

TEXT 272

ভক্তগণ, শুন মোর দৈন্য-বচন।
তোমা-সবার পদধূলি, অঙ্গে বিভূষণ করি',
কিছু মুঞি করোঁ নিবেদন ॥ ২৭২ ॥ ধ্রু ॥

bhakta-gaṇa, śuna mora dainya-vacana
tomā-sabāra pada-dhūli, aṅge vibhūṣaṇa kari',
kichu muñi karoṅ nivedana

SYNONYMS

bhakta-gaṇa—O devotees; *śuna*—please hear; *mora*—my; *dainya-vacana*—humble submission; *tomā-sabāra*—of all of you; *pada-dhūli*—the dust of the feet; *aṅge*—on my body; *vibhūṣaṇa kari'*—taking as ornaments; *kichu*—something; *muñi*—I; *karoṅ nivedana*—wish to submit.

TRANSLATION

With all humility, I submit myself to the lotus feet of all of you devotees, taking the dust from your feet as my bodily ornaments. Now, my dear devotees, please hear one thing more from me.

TEXT 273

কৃষ্ণভক্তিসিদ্ধান্তগণ, যাতে প্রফুল্ল পদ্মবন,
তার মধু করি' আস্বাদন।
প্রেমরস-কুমুদবনে, প্রফুল্লিত রাত্রি-দিনে,
তাতে চরাও মনোভৃঙ্গগণ ॥ ২৭৩ ॥

kṛṣṇa-bhakti-siddhānta-gaṇa, yāte praphulla padma-vana,
tāra madhu kari' āsvādana
prema-rasa-kumuda-vane, praphullita rātri-dine,
tāte carāo mano-bhṛṅga-gaṇa

SYNONYMS

kṛṣṇa-bhakti-siddhānta-gaṇa—the conclusive understanding of devotional service to Kṛṣṇa; *yāte*—by which; *praphulla*—enlivened; *padma-vana*—the forest of lotus flowers; *tāra madhu*—the honey collected from those lotus flowers; *kari' āsvādana*—relishing; *prema-rasa*—of transcendental love of Kṛṣṇa; *kumuda-vane*—in the forest of *kumuda* flowers (a type of lotus); *praphullita*—being jubilant; *rātri-dine*—day and night; *tāte*—in that forest of lotus flowers; *carāo*—make wander; *manaḥ-bhṛṅga-gaṇa*—the bumblebees of your minds.

TRANSLATION

Devotional service to Kṛṣṇa is exactly like a pleasing, jubilant forest of lotus flowers wherein there is ample honey. I request everyone to taste this honey. If all the mental speculators bring the bees of their minds into this forest of lotus flowers and jubilantly enjoy ecstatic love of Kṛṣṇa day and night, their mental speculation will be completely transcendentally satisfied.

TEXT 274

নানা-ভাবের ভক্তজন, হংস-চক্রবাকগণ,
যাতে সবে' করেন বিহার ।
কৃষ্ণকেলি সুমৃণাল, যাহা পাই সর্বকাল,
ভক্ত-হংস করয়ে আহার ॥ ২৭৪ ॥

nānā-bhāvera bhakta-jana, haṁsa-cakravāka-gaṇa,
yāte sabe' karena vihāra
kṛṣṇa-keli sumṛṇāla, yāhā pāi sarva-kāla,
bhakta-haṁsa karaye āhāra

SYNONYMS

nānā-bhāvera bhakta-jana—devotees relishing relationships with Kṛṣṇa in different ecstasies; *haṁsa-cakravāka-gaṇa*—compared to swans and *cakravāka* birds; *yāte*—in that place; *sabe'*—all; *karena vihāra*—enjoy life; *kṛṣṇa-keli*—the pastimes of Kṛṣṇa; *su-mṛṇāla*—sweet buds; *yāhā pāi*—which one can get; *sarva-kāla*—eternally; *bhakta-haṁsa*—the devotees, who are just like swans; *karaye*—do; *āhāra*—eating.

TRANSLATION

The devotees who have a relationship with Kṛṣṇa are like the swans and cakravāka birds that play in the forest of lotus flowers. The buds of those lotus flowers are the pastimes of Kṛṣṇa, and they are edibles for the swanlike devotees. Lord Śrī Kṛṣṇa is always engaged in His transcendental pastimes; therefore the devotees, following in the footsteps of Śrī Caitanya Mahāprabhu, can always eat those lotus buds, for they are the pastimes of the Lord.

TEXT 275

সেই সরোবরে গিয়া, হংস-চক্রবাক হঞা,
সদা তাহাঁ করহ বিলাস ।

খণ্ডিবে সকল দুঃখ, পাইবা পরম সুখ,
অনায়াসে হবে প্রেমোল্লাস ॥ ২৭৫ ॥

sei sarovare giyā, haṁsa-cakravāka hañā,
sadā tāhāṅ karaha vilāsa
khaṇḍibe sakala duḥkha, pāibā parama sukha,
anāyāse habe premollāsa

SYNONYMS

sei sarovare giyā—going to that lake where the clusters of lotus flowers exist; *haṁsa-cakravāka hañā*—becoming swans or *cakravāka* birds; *sadā*—always; *tāhāṅ*—there; *karaha vilāsa*—enjoy life; *khaṇḍibe*—will be diminished; *sakala duḥkha*—all material anxieties and miseries; *pāibā*—you will get; *parama sukha*—the highest happiness; *anāyāse*—very easily; *habe*—there will be; *prema-ullāsa*—jubilation in love of God.

TRANSLATION

All the devotees of Śrī Caitanya Mahāprabhu should go to that lake and, remaining always under the shelter of the lotus feet of Śrī Caitanya Mahāprabhu, become swans and cakravāka birds in those celestial waters. They should go on rendering service to Lord Śrī Kṛṣṇa and enjoy life perpetually. In this way all miseries will be diminished, the devotees will attain great happiness, and there will be jubilant love of God.

TEXT 276

এই অমৃত অনুক্ষণ, সাধু মহান্ত-মেঘগণ,
বিশ্বোদ্যানে করে বরিষণ ।
তাতে ফলে অমৃত-ফল, ভক্ত খায় নিরন্তর,
তার শেষে জীয়ে জগজন ॥ ২৭৬ ॥

ei amṛta anukṣaṇa, sādhu mahānta-megha-gaṇa,
viśvodyāne kare variṣaṇa
tāte phale amṛta-phala, bhakta khāya nirantara,
tāra śeṣe jīye jaga-jana

SYNONYMS

ei amṛta—this nectar; *anukṣaṇa*—continuously; *sādhu mahānta-megha-gaṇa*—pure devotees and saintly persons, who are compared to clouds; *viśva-udyāne*—in the garden of the universe; *kare variṣaṇa*—rain down these nectarean pastimes of Śrī Caitanya Mahāprabhu and Lord Śrī Kṛṣṇa; *tāte*—because of that; *phale*—grows; *amṛta-phala*—the fruit of nectar; *bhakta khāya nirantara*—and the devotees eat such fruit continuously; *tāra śeṣe*—after their eating; *jīye jaga-jana*—the living entities all over the world live peacefully.

TRANSLATION

The devotees who have taken shelter of the lotus feet of Śrī Caitanya Mahāprabhu take the responsibility for distributing nectarean devotional service all over the world. They are like clouds pouring water on the ground that nourishes the fruit of love of Godhead in this world. The devotees eat that fruit to their hearts' content, and whatever remnants they leave are eaten by the general populace. Thus they live happily.

TEXT 277

চৈতন্যলীলা—অমৃতপূর, কৃষ্ণলীলা—সুকর্পূর,
দুহে মিলি' হয় সুমাধুর্য।
সাধু-গুরু-প্রসাদে, তাহা যেই আস্বাদে,
সেই জানে মাধুর্য-প্রাচুর্য ॥ ২৭৭ ॥

caitanya-līlā——amṛta-pūra, kṛṣṇa-līlā——sukarpūra,
duhe mili' haya sumādhurya
sādhu-guru-prasāde, tāhā yei āsvāde,
sei jāne mādhurya-prācurya

SYNONYMS

caitanya-līlā amṛta-pūra—the pastimes of Lord Śrī Caitanya Mahāprabhu are full of nectar; *kṛṣṇa-līlā su-karpūra*—the pastimes of Lord Kṛṣṇa are exactly like camphor; *duhe mili'*—the two meeting; *haya*—become; *su-mādhurya*—very, very palatable; *sādhu-guru-prasāde*—by the mercy of saintly persons and devotees in the transcendental position; *tāhā*—that; *yei*—anyone who; *āsvāde*—relishes this palatable nectar; *sei jāne*—he can understand; *mādhurya-prācurya*—the extensive quantity of sweetness in devotional service.

TRANSLATION

The pastimes of Śrī Caitanya Mahāprabhu are full of nectar, and the pastimes of Lord Kṛṣṇa are like camphor. When one mixes these, they taste very sweet. By the mercy of the pure devotees, whoever tastes them can understand the depths of that sweetness.

TEXT 278

যে লীলা-অমৃত বিনে, খায় যদি অন্নপানে,
তবে ভক্তের দুর্বল জীবন ।
যার একবিন্দু-পানে, উৎফুল্লিত তনুমনে,
হাসে, গায়, করয়ে নর্তন ॥ ২৭৮ ॥

ye līlā-amṛta vine, khāya yadi anna-pāne,
tabe bhaktera durbala jīvana
yāra eka-bindu-pāne, utphullita tanu-mane,
hāse, gāya, karaye nartana

SYNONYMS

ye—he who; *līlā*—of the pastimes of Lord Kṛṣṇa and Caitanya Mahāprabhu; *amṛta vine*—without nectar; *khāya yadi anna-pāne*—if one eats only ordinary food grains; *tabe*—then; *bhaktera*—of the devotees; *durbala jīvana*—life becomes weakened; *yāra*—of which; *eka-bindu-pāne*—if one drinks one drop; *utphullita tanu-mane*—the body and mind become jubilant; *hāse*—laughs; *gāya*—chants; *karaye nartana*—dances.

TRANSLATION

Men become strong and stout by eating sufficient grains, but the devotee who simply eats ordinary grains but does not taste the transcendental pastimes of Lord Caitanya Mahāprabhu and Kṛṣṇa gradually becomes weak and falls down from the transcendental position. However, if one drinks but a drop of the nectar of Kṛṣṇa's pastimes, his body and mind begin to bloom, and he begins to laugh, sing and dance.

PURPORT

All the devotees connected with this Kṛṣṇa consciousness movement must read all the books that have been translated (*Caitanya-caritāmṛta, Śrīmad-Bhāgavatam, Bhagavad-gītā* and others); otherwise, after some time, they will simply eat, sleep and fall down from their position. Thus they will miss the opportunity to attain an eternal, blissful life of transcendental pleasure.

TEXT 279

এ অমৃত কর পান, যার সম নাহি আন,
চিত্তে করি' সুদৃঢ় বিশ্বাস ।

না পড়' কুতর্ক-গর্তে, অমেধ্য কর্কশ আবর্তে,
যাতে পড়িলে হয় সর্বনাশ ॥ ২৭৯ ॥

e amṛta kara pāna, yāra sama nāhi āna,
citte kari' sudṛḍha viśvāsa
nā paḍa' kutarka-garte, amedhya karkaśa āvarte,
yāte paḍile haya sarva-nāśa

SYNONYMS

e amṛta kara pāna—all of you must drink this nectar; *yāra sama nāhi āna*—there is no comparison to this nectar; *citte*—within the mind; *kari' sudṛḍha viśvāsa*—having firm faith in this conclusion; *nā paḍa' kutarka garte*—do not fall down into the pit of false arguments; *amedhya karkaśa āvarte*—in the untouchable, harsh whirlpool; *yāte*—in which; *paḍile*—if one falls down; *haya sarva-nāśa*—the purpose of life will be spoiled.

TRANSLATION

The readers should relish this wonderful nectar because nothing compares to it. Keeping their faith firmly fixed within their minds, they should be careful not to fall into the pit of false arguments or the whirlpools of unfortunate situations. If one falls into such positions, he is finished.

TEXT 280

শ্রীচৈতন্য, নিত্যানন্দ, অদ্বৈতাদি ভক্তবৃন্দ,
আর যত শ্রোতা ভক্তগণ ।
তোমা-সবার শ্রীচরণ, করি শিরে বিভূষণ,
যাহা হৈতে অভীষ্ট-পূরণ ॥ ২৮০ ॥

śrī-caitanya, nityānanda, advaitādi bhakta-vṛnda,
āra yata śrotā bhakta-gaṇa
tomā-sabāra śrī-caraṇa, kari śire vibhūṣaṇa,
yāhā haite abhīṣṭa-pūraṇa

SYNONYMS

śrī-caitanya nityānanda—Śrī Caitanya Mahāprabhu and Lord Nityānanda; *advaita-ādi bhakta-vṛnda*—as well as the devotees like Advaita Ācārya; *āra*—and; *yata śrotā bhakta-gaṇa*—all the devotees who listen; *tomā-sabāra śrī-caraṇa*—the lotus feet of all of you; *kari śire vibhūṣaṇa*—I keep on my head as a helmet; *yāhā haite*—from which; *abhīṣṭa-pūraṇa*—all my purposes will be served.

TRANSLATION

In conclusion, I submit to Śrī Caitanya Mahāprabhu, Nityānanda Prabhu, Advaita Prabhu, and all the other devotees and readers that I accept your lotus feet as the helmet on my head. In this way, all my purposes will be served.

TEXT 281

শ্রীরূপ-সনাতন- রঘুনাথ-জীব-চরণ,
শিরে ধরি,—যার করেঁা আশ ।
কৃষ্ণলীলামৃতান্বিত, চৈতন্যচরিতামৃত,
কহে কিছু দীন কৃষ্ণদাস ॥ ২৮১ ॥

śrī-rūpa-sanātana- raghunātha-jīva-caraṇa,
śire dhari,——yāra karoṅ āśa
kṛṣṇa-līlāmṛtānvita, caitanya-caritāmṛta,
kahe kichu dīna kṛṣṇadāsa

SYNONYMS

śrī-rūpa-sanātana—of Śrīla Rūpa Gosvāmī and of Sanātana Gosvāmī; *raghunātha-jīva*—of Raghunātha dāsa Gosvāmī, Raghunātha Bhaṭṭa Gosvāmī and Śrīla Jīva Gosvāmī; *caraṇa*—the lotus feet; *śire dhari*—taking on my head; *yāra*—of which; *karoṅ āśa*—I always desire; *kṛṣṇa-līlā-amṛta-anvita*—mixed with the nectar of *kṛṣṇa-līlā; caitanya-caritāmṛta*—the pastimes of Lord Śrī Caitanya Mahāprabhu; *kahe*—is trying to speak; *kichu*—something; *dīna*—most humble; *kṛṣṇadāsa*—Kṛṣṇadāsa Kavirāja Gosvāmī.

TRANSLATION

Taking the feet of Śrīla Rūpa Gosvāmī, Śrī Sanātana Gosvāmī, Raghunātha dāsa Gosvāmī, Raghunātha Bhaṭṭa Gosvāmī and Jīva Gosvāmī on my head, I always desire their mercy. Thus I, Kṛṣṇadāsa, humbly try to describe the nectar of the pastimes of Śrī Caitanya Mahāprabhu, which are mixed with the pastimes of Lord Kṛṣṇa.

TEXT 282

শ্রীমন্মদনগোপাল-গোবিন্দদেব-তুষ্টয়ে ।
চৈতন্যার্পিতমস্ত্বেতচ্চৈতন্যচরিতামৃতম্ ॥ ২৮২ ॥

śrīman-madana-gopāla-
govindadeva-tuṣṭaye

caitanyārpitam astv etac
caitanya-caritāmṛtam

SYNONYMS

śrīman-madana-gopāla—of the Deity named Śrīman Madana-gopāla; *govinda-deva*—of the Deity named Govindadeva; *tuṣṭaye*—for the satisfaction; *caitanya-arpitam*—offered unto Śrī Caitanya Mahāprabhu; *astu*—let it be; *etat*—this; *caitanya-caritāmṛtam*—the book known as *Caitanya-caritāmṛta.*

TRANSLATION

For the satisfaction of Śrī Madana-gopāla and Govindadeva, we pray that this book, Caitanya-caritāmṛta, may be offered to Śrī Kṛṣṇa Caitanya Mahāprabhu.

TEXT 283

তদিদমতিরহস্যং গৌরলীলামৃতং যৎ
খল-সমুদয়-কোলৈর্নাদৃতং তৈরলভ্যম্ ।
ক্ষতিরিয়মিহ কা মে স্বাদিতং যৎ সমন্তাৎ
সহৃদয়-সুমনোভির্মোদমেষাং তনোতি ॥ ২৮৩ ॥

tad idam ati-rahasyaṁ gaura-līlāmṛtaṁ yat
khala-samudaya-kolair nādṛtaṁ tair alabhyam
kṣatir iyam iha kā me svāditaṁ yat samantāt
sahṛdaya-sumanobhir modam eṣāṁ tanoti

SYNONYMS

tat—that (*Caitanya-caritāmṛta*); *idam*—this; *ati-rahasyam*—full of spiritual mysteries; *gaura-līlā-amṛtam*—the nectar of the pastimes of Śrī Caitanya Mahāprabhu; *yat*—which; *khala-samudaya*—envious rascals; *kolaiḥ*—by pigs; *na*—never; *ādṛtam*—praised; *taiḥ*—by them; *alabhyam*—not obtainable; *kṣatiḥ iyam iha kā*—what is the loss in this connection; *me*—of me; *svāditam*—tasted; *yat*—which; *samantāt*—completely; *sahṛdaya-sumanobhiḥ*—by those who are friendly and whose minds are very clean; *modam*—enjoyment; *eṣām*—of them; *tanoti*—expands.

TRANSLATION

The Caitanya-caritāmṛta pastimes of Lord Śrī Caitanya Mahāprabhu constitute a very secret literature. It is the life and soul of all devotees. Those who are not fit to relish this literature, who are envious like hogs and pigs, will certainly not adore it. However, this will not harm my attempt. These pastimes of

Lord Śrī Caitanya Mahāprabhu will certainly please all saintly people who have clear hearts. They will certainly enjoy it. We wish that this will enhance their enjoyment more and more.

Thus end the Bhaktivedanta purports to the Śrī Caitanya-caritāmṛta, Madhya-līlā, *Twenty-fifth Chapter, describing how the inhabitants of Vārāṇasī were converted to Vaiṣṇavism.*

Note:

The author of *Śrī Caitanya-caritāmṛta,* Kṛṣṇadāsa Kavirāja Gosvāmī, has condemned all his enemies by comparing them to envious hogs and pigs. This Kṛṣṇa consciousness movement, which is spreading throughout the world, is being appreciated by sincere people, although they have never previously heard of Śrī Caitanya Mahāprabhu and Kṛṣṇa's pastimes. Now even the higher, priestly circles are appreciating this movement. They have concluded that this movement is very nice and that they have something to learn from it. Nonetheless, in India there are some people who say that they belong to this cult but who are actually very envious of the *ācārya.* They have tried to suppress our activities in many ways, but as far as we are concerned, we follow in the footsteps of Kṛṣṇadāsa Kavirāja Gosvāmī and take them as envious pigs and hogs. We simply wish to present the pastimes of Lord Kṛṣṇa and Śrī Caitanya Mahāprabhu to the best of our ability so that those who are really honest can cleanse their hearts. We hope that they enjoy this literature and bestow their blessings upon us. It appears that even such a great personality as Kṛṣṇadāsa Kavirāja Gosvāmī met with some envious obstacles; what, then, to speak of us, who are only insignificant creatures in this universe. We are simply trying to execute the orders of our spiritual master to the best of our ability.

END OF THE MADHYA-LĪLĀ

References

The statements of *Śrī Caitanya-caritāmṛta* are all confirmed by standard Vedic authorities. The following authentic scriptures are quoted in this book on the pages listed. Numerals in bold type refer the reader to *Śrī Caitanya-caritāmṛta's* translations. Numerals in regular type are references to its purports.

Agni Purāṇa, 30

Amṛta-pravāha-bhāṣya (Bhaktivinoda Ṭhākura), **1,** 81, 326, 363

Anubhāṣya (Bhaktisiddhānta Sarasvatī Ṭhākura), 300

Bhagavad-gītā, 53, 63, 66, **129,** 137, 141, 153, **157, 168, 176, 186, 188,** 195, 223, 230, 263, 272-273, 275, 288, 313, 314,**318,** 328, 351, 363, 404, 442

Bhakti-rasāmṛta-sindhu (Rūpa Gosvāmī), 4, 5, 12, 14, 18, 20, 21, 26, 27-28, 30, 31, 32, 35, 44, 46, 49, 50-51, 65, **151, 189,** 273

Brahma-saṁhitā, 73, 244

Caitanya-candrodaya-nāṭaka (Kavi Karṇapūra), **289-291**

Caitanya-caritāmṛta (Kṛṣṇadāsa Kavirāja), 300

Garuḍa Purāṇa, **378**

Hari-bhakti-sudhodaya, 14, **99, 149, 205**

Hari-bhakti-vilāsa (Sanātana Gosvāmī), 64, 273, 274-275, 276, 279-281, **284,** 363

Hari-vaṁśa, **72**

Kṛṣṇa-karṇāmṛta (Bilvamaṅgala Ṭhākura), 19, 21

Kṛṣṇa-sandarbha (Jīva Gosvāmī), 76

Laghu-bhāgavatāmṛta (Rūpa Gosvāmī), 76

Mahābhārata, 75, **328**

Mahā Upaniṣad, **146**

Nārada-pañcarātra, 6, 64, 132-133

Nāradīya Purāṇa **175**

Nārāyaṇa-saṁhitā, 300

Nṛsiṁha-tāpanī Upaniṣad, **141, 160**

Padma Purāṇa, 26, 277

Pāṇini's *sūtras,* **94, 164, 250**

Sarva-saṁvādinī (Jīva Gosvāmī), 76

Skanda Purāṇa, **236, 240,** 272, 282-283

Śrīmad-Bhāgavatam, 10, 15, **24, 43,** 64, 70, 71, 143, **148, 156, 166, 172, 174, 178, 179, 183, 203, 262,** 269, 271, **321, 316, 361, 370, 375, 377**

Ṛg-saṁhitā, 73-74, 91

Tattva-sāgara, 276

Ujjvala-nīlamaṇi (Rūpa Gosvāmī), 36-37, 41, 56

Upadeśāmṛta (Rūpa Gosvāmī), 268

Viṣṇu Purāṇa, 75, **118,** 129, **255**

Viśva-prakāśa dictionary, **93, 116**

Glossary

A

Abhidheya—activities in one's personal relationship with God; devotional service.

Ācārya—a spiritual master who teaches by his own example.

Acintya-bhedābheda-tattva—Lord Caitanya's "simultaneously one and different" doctrine, which establishes the inconceivable simultaneous oneness and difference of the Lord and His expansions.

Adhirūḍha—an advanced symptom of *mahā-bhāva* found only in the *gopīs.*

Akāma—one who is desireless.

Anapekṣa—indifference to mundane people.

Anartha-nivṛtti—giving up unwanted things.

Anubhāva—bodily symptoms manifested by a devotee in ecstatic love for Kṛṣṇa.

Anurāga—subattachment in ecstatic love of God.

Arcanā—worship of the Deity in the temple.

Āsana—a sitting place.

Asuras—demons; people who are averse to the supremacy of the Supreme Lord, Viṣṇu.

Ātma-nivedana—the devotional process of surrendering everything to the Lord.

Ātmārāmas—transcendentalists.

Ayoga—See: *Viyoga.*

Ayukta—the ecstatic condition of not having yet met one's lover.

B

Bhāgavata-dharma—the science of God consciousness.

Bhakta—a devotee of Kṛṣṇa.

Bhakti—devotional service.

Bhakti-rasa—the mellow relished in the transcendental loving service of the Lord.

Bhakti-yoga—the method for developing pure devotional service.

Bhāva—ecstatic love of God.

Bhāva-bhakti—the platform of purified goodness when one's heart melts in devotional service; the first stage of love of Godhead.

Brahmacārī—a celibate student under the care of a spiritual master.

Brāhmaṇa—the intelligent class of men.

Brahmānanda—the bliss derived from merging into the existence of the Absolute.

Bhukti—material enjoyment.

Brahma-bhūta—the state of being freed from material contamination.

Brahma-muhūrta—the hour and a half just before sunrise.

Brahma-randhra—the hole at the top of the skull through which a *yogī* passes on quitting his body.

Brahma-upāsaka—a worshiper of the impersonal Brahman.

Brahmavādīs—those who are absorbed in the thought of impersonal Brahman.

C

Caṇḍālas—low-class men who eat dogs; untouchables.

Catuḥsana—the four Kumāras.
Catuḥ-ślokī—the four nutshell verses of the *Śrīmad-Bhāgavatam* (2.9.33-36).

D

Daṇḍavats—offering obeisances to a superior by falling flat on the ground like a rod.
Dāsya—the devotional process of serving the Lord.
Devī-dhāma—the material world, under the control of the goddess Devī, or Durgā.
Dharma—the capacity to render service, which is the essential quality of a living being.
Dīkṣā—spiritual initiation.
Dhṛti—perseverance or endurance.
Duḥsaṅga—bad association.

G

Gosvāmī—one who can control his senses and mind.
Gosvāmi-viddhi—transcendental devotional service.
Gṛhastha—one who lives in God conscious married life.
Guru—the bona fide spiritual master.

H

Hari—the Supreme Lord, who removed all inauspicious things from the heart.

J

Jagad-guru—the spiritual master of the whole world.
Jīva—the spirit soul or atomic living entity.
Jīvan-muktas—those liberated in this life.
Jñāna—knowledge.
Jñānī—one who is engaged in the cultivation of knowledge.

K

Kaitava—cheating religious processes.
Kāka—crow.
Kali-yuga—the age of quarrel and hypocrisy in which we are now living.
Kāma—lust.
Kaniṣṭha-adhikārīs—those in the lowest stage of devotional service.
Karma—any material action which will incur a subsequent reaction.
Keśa-avatāras—the false story of the incarnations of Kṛṣṇa and Balarāma from respective black and white hairs of Kṣīrodakaśāyī Viṣṇu.
Keśava—a name of Kṛṣṇa meaning one who has beautiful hair.
Kīrtana—the devotional process of chanting.
Krodha—anger.
Kṛṣṇa-kathā—topics spoken by or about Kṛṣṇa.

Kṛṣṇāliṅgita-vigraha—the spiritual master, who is always embraced by Kṛṣṇa.
Kṛṣṇa-prema-dhana—the treasure of love for Kṛṣṇa.
Kṣatriya—the administrative or protective class of men.
Kṣepaṇa—subordinate ecstatic symptoms including dancing and bodily contortions; a division of *anubhāva.*
Kṣetrajña—the living entity who is the knower of the body.

L

Lobha—greed.

M

Mada—intoxication.
Mādana—a category of highly advanced ecstasy in which the lovers meet together and there is kissing and many other symptoms.
Madana-mohana—Kṛṣṇa, the attractor of Cupid.
Mahā-bhāgavata—a first-class pure devotee of the Lord.
Mahābhāva—sublime ecstatic love of God.
Mahākāśa—(lit., the greatest sky of all) the space occupied by Goloka Vṛndāvana.
Mahā-mantra—the chanting for deliverance: Hare Kṛṣṇa, Hare Kṛṣṇa, Kṛṣṇa Kṛṣṇa, Hare Hare/ Hare Rāma, Hare Rāma, Rāma Rāma, Hare Hare.
Mahā-pūrṇa—the highest level of perfection.
Māna—the mood of the lover and the beloved experienced in one place or in different places; this mood obstructs their looking at one another and embracing one another, despite their attachment to one another.
Mātsarya—envy.
Mauṣala-līlā—the pastimes of the disappearance of Lord Kṛṣṇa and of the Yadu dynasty.
Māyā—the energy of Kṛṣṇa which deludes the living entity who desires to forget the Supreme Lord.
Māyayāpahṛta-jñānāḥ—persons whose knowledge has been stolen by illusion.
Moha—illusion.
Mohana—highly advanced ecstasy in which the lovers are separated; divided into *udghūrṇā* and *citra-jalpa.*
Mokṣa-kāma—one who desires liberation.
Mokṣākāṅkṣī—See: *Mokṣa-kāma.*
Mukti—liberation.
Mumukṣu—See: *Mokṣa-kāma.*
Muni—a sage or self-realized soul.

N

Nigarbha-yogī—a *yogī* who worships the Supersoul without form.
Nirgrantha-muni—a completely liberated saint.
Nirguṇa—(without qualities) means that the Lord has totally spiritual attributes.

Niyamāgraha—either following rules and regulations insufficiently (*niyama-agraha*) or fanatically without understanding the goal (*niyama-āgraha*).

O

Oṁkāra—the root of Vedic knowledge known as *mahā-vākya,* the supreme sound.

P

Pāda-sevana—the devotional process of serving the lotus feet of the Lord.
Paramahaṁsa—the topmost class of God realized devotees.
Paramparā—the disciplic succession through which spiritual knowledge is transmitted.
Para-upakāra—helping others.
Pāsaṇḍī—an atheist who thinks the demigods and Viṣṇu to be on the same level.
Prākṛta-sahajiyās—pseudo-devotees with a mundane concept of the pastimes of Kṛṣṇa.
Prakṛti—material nature.
Praṇaya—intimacy in ecstatic love of God.
Prāpta-brahma-laya—one who has already attained the Brahman position.
Prāpta-svarūpas—those merged in Brahman realization.
Pravāsa—the condition of separation of lovers who were previously intimately associated.
Prayojana—the ultimate goal of life, love of God.
Prema—the stage of pure love of Godhead.
Prema-vaicittya—an abundance of love that brings about grief from fear of separation; although the lover is present.
Puruṣa-avatāras—the three primary Viṣṇu expansions of Kṛṣṇa who are involved in the creation, maintenance and destruction of the material universe.
Pūrva-rāga—the ecstasy of lovers before their meeting.

R

Rāga—attachment in ecstatic love of God.
Rāja-yoga—Patañjalis' process of imagining a form of the Absolute Truth within many forms.
Rati—strong attraction in ecstatic love of God.
Rati-ābhāsa—a preliminary glimpse of attachment.
Rūḍha—advanced symptom of conjugal mellow found among the queens of Dvārakā; included in *mahābhāva.*

S

Sac-cid-ānanda-vigraha—the eternal form of the Supreme Lord which is full of bliss and knowledge.
Sādhaka—those who are nearing the perfection of Brahman realization.
Sādhana-bhakti—the development of devotional service through the regulative principles.
Sādhu—a holy man.
Sādhu-varya—the best of gentlemen.

Sagarbha-yogī—a *yogī* who worships the Supersoul in the Viṣṇu form.
Sakhya—the devotional process of making friendship with the Lord.
Śālagrāma-śilā—a Deity incarnation of Nārāyaṇa in the form of a stone.
Śama—control of the mind.
Sambandha—one's personal relationship with God.
Sambhoga—the ecstasy of the meeting and embracing of lovers.
Saṅkīrtana—the congregational chanting of the holy name of the Lord.
Sannyāsa—the renounced order of life.
Śānta-bhaktas—devotees in the neutral stage of devotional service.
Śārkarākṣa—those situated in the gross bodily conception of life.
Sarva-kāma—one who desires material perfection.
Sarva-kāma-deha—the body engaged for the satisfaction of all kinds of material desires.
Sarvārambha-parityāgī—one who is indifferent to both pious and impious activities.
Satyaṁ param—the Supreme Absolute Truth, Kṛṣṇa.
Sevā-aparādha—offenses in Deity worship.
Siddhi—perfection in *yoga*.
Śīta—subordinate ecstatic symptoms including singing, yawning, etc.; a division of *anubhāva*.
Smaraṇa—the devotional process of remembering the Lord.
Smārta-brāhmaṇa—a caste *brāhmaṇa* who believes that a person not born in a *brāhmaṇa* family can never be elevated to that platform.
Smārta-guru—a professional spiritual master.
Smārta-viddhi—mundane religious activity.
Smṛti—scriptures compiled by living entities under transcendental direction.
Sneha—affection in ecstatic love of God.
Śravaṇa—the devotional process of hearing.
Śṛṅgāra—conjugal love.
Sthāyi-bhāva—permanent ecstasies.
Śuddha-sattva-viśeṣātmā—the position of being situated on the transcendental platform of pure goodness.
Śūdra—the laborer class of men.
Sukṛti—auspicious activity.
Svarūpa-lakṣaṇa—the position when the soul is purified of all material contamination.

T

Tapasvīs—persons who undergo severe penances for elevation to higher planets.
Tattva—knowledge of the actual truth.
Tilaka—sacred clay used to mark Viṣṇu temples on twelve places of the body of a devotee.
Triveṇī—the confluence of three sacred rivers at Prayāga.
Tulasī—Kṛṣṇa's favorite plant.

U

Udbhāsvara—eternal ecstatic symptoms or bodily transformations which indicate ecstatic emotions in the mind.

Uttama-adhikārīs—the first-class devotees.

Uttamaśloka—a name for Kṛṣṇa indicating that choice prayers are offered to Him.

V

Vaiśya—the class of men involved in business and farming.

Vānaprastha—retired life, in which one travels to holy places in preparation for the renounced order of life.

Vandana—the devotional process of offering prayers to the Lord.

Varṇāśrama-dharma—the regulation of society by establishing different social and spiritual orders of life.

Vidyādharas—inhabitants of one of the heavenly planets.

Vijñāna—the practical realization of spiritual knowledge.

Vipralambha—ecstasy in separation.

Virakti—detachment.

Viṣayīs—those who are attached to sense gratification.

Viśuddha-sattva—the position of uncontaminated goodness.

Viyoga—the stage of separation when the mind is fully absorbed in thoughts of Kṛṣṇa.

Vyabhicārī—thirty-three varieties of transitory ecstasies.

Y

Yajñas—sacrifices.

Yoga—linking of the consciousness of the infinitesimal living entity with Kṛṣṇa.

Bengali Pronunciation Guide

BENGALI DIACRITICAL EQUIVALENTS AND PRONUNCIATION

Vowels

অ a   আ ā   ই i   ঈ ī   উ u   ঊ ū   ঋ ṛ

ৠ ṝ   এ e   ঐ ai   ও o   ঔ au

ং ṁ *(anusvāra)*   ঁ ṅ *(candra-bindu)*   ঃ ḥ *(visarga)*

Consonants

Gutterals:	ক ka	খ kha	গ ga	ঘ gha	ঙ ṅa
Palatals:	চ ca	ছ cha	জ ja	ঝ jha	ঞ ña
Cerebrals:	ট ṭa	ঠ ṭha	ড ḍa	ঢ ḍha	ণ ṇa
Dentals:	ত ta	থ tha	দ da	ধ dha	ন na
Labials:	প pa	ফ pha	ব ba	ভ bha	ম ma
Semivowels:	য ya	র ra	ল la	ব va	
Sibilants:	শ śa	ষ ṣa	স sa	হ ha	

Vowel Symbols

The vowels are written as follows after a consonant:

া ā   ি i   ী ī   ু u   ূ ū   ৃ ṛ   ৄ ṝ   ে e   ৈ ai   ো o   ৌ au

For example: কা kā   কি ki   কী kī   কু ku   কূ kū   কৃ kṛ

কৄ kṝ   কে ke   কৈ kai   কো ko   কৌ kau

The letter *a* is implied after a consonant with no vowel symbol.

The symbol *virāma* (৲) indicates that there is no final vowel. ক্ k

The letters above should be pronounced as follows:

a –like the *o* in hot; sometimes like the *o* in go; final *a* is usually silent.
ā –like the *a* in far.
i, ī –like the *ee* in meet.
u, ū –like the *u* in rule.
ṛ –like the *ri* in *ri*m.
ṝ –like the *ree* in *ree*d.
e –like the *ai* in pain; rarely like *e* in bet.
ai –like the *oi* in b*oi*l.
o –like the *o* in go.
au –like the *ow* in *ow*l.
ṁ –*(anusvāra)* like the *ng* in so*ng*.
ḥ –*(visarga)* a final *h* sound like in Ah.
ṅ –*(candra-bindu)* a nasal *n* sound like in the French word *bon*.
k –like the *k* in *k*ite.
kh –like the *kh* in Ec*kh*art.
g –like the *g* in *g*ot.
gh –like the *gh* in bi*g-h*ouse.
ṅ –like the *n* in ba*n*k.
c –like the *ch* in *ch*alk.
ch –like the *chh* in mu*ch-h*aste.
j –like the *j* in *j*oy.
jh –like the *geh* in colle*ge-h*all.
ñ –like the *n* in bu*n*ch.
ṭ –like the *t* in *t*alk.
ṭh –like the *th* in ho*t-h*ouse.
ḍ –like the *d* in *d*awn.
ḍh –like the *dh* in goo*d-h*ouse.
ṇ –like the *n* in g*n*aw.
t–as in *t*alk but with the tongue against the the teeth.
th–as in ho*t-h*ouse but with the tongue against the teeth.
d–as in *d*awn but with the tongue against the teeth.
dh–as in goo*d-h*ouse but with the tongue against the teeth.
n–as in *n*or but with the tongue against the teeth.
p –like the *p* in *p*ine.
ph –like the *ph* in *ph*ilosopher.
b –like the *b* in *b*ird.
bh –like the *bh* in ru*b-h*ard.
m –like the *m* in *m*other.
y –like the *j* in *j*aw. য
y –like the *y* in *y*ear. য়
r –like the *r* in *r*un.
l –like the *l* in *l*aw.
v –like the *b* in *b*ird or like the *w* in d*w*arf.
ś, ṣ –like the *sh* in *sh*op.
s –like the *s* in *s*un.
h–like the *h* in *h*ome.

This is a general guide to Bengali pronunciation. The Bengali transliterations in this book accurately show the original Bengali spelling of the text. One should note, however, that in Bengali, as in English, spelling is not always a true indication of how a word is pronounced. Tape recordings of His Divine Grace A. C. Bhaktivedanta Swami Prabhupāda chanting the original Bengali verses are available from the International Society for Krishna Consciousness, 3764 Watseka Ave., Los Angeles, California 90034.

Index of Bengali and Sanskrit Verses

This index constitutes a complete alphabetical listing of the first and third line of each four-line verse and both lines of each two-line verse in *Śrī Caitanya-caritāmṛta.* In the first column the transliteration is given, and in the second and third columns respectively the chapter-verse references and page number for each verse are to be found.

A

'abhidheya' sādhana-bhaktira śunaha vicāra	25.120	361
ācārya 'kalpanā' kare āgraha kariyā	25.26	309
ācārya-kalpita artha ye paṇḍita śune	25.27	309
ācāryera āgraha—'advaita-vāda' sthāpite	25.47	322
ācāryera ghare yaiche karilā vilāsa	25.245	429
acirād eva sarvārthaḥ	24.170	174
acirāt milaye tāṅre kṛṣṇa-prema-dhana	23.126	79
acirāt pāya sei caitanya-caraṇa	25.239	426
ādau śraddhā tataḥ sādhu-	23.14	9
adhikāri-bhede rati—pañca-parakāra	23.45	25
adhirūḍha-mahābhāva—dui ta' prakāra	23.58	37
adhyagān mahad-ākhyānaṁ	24.117	144
advaita-vīthī-pathikair upāsyāḥ	24.133	154
adveṣṭā sarva-bhūtānāṁ	23.106	65
advitīya-jñāna, yāṅhā vinā nāhi āna	24.73	118
āge 'tera' artha kariluṅ, āra 'chaya' ei	24.210	198
āge yata yata artha vyākhyāna kariba	24.105	137
ahaitukī bhakti kare nirgrantha hañā	24.167	172
aham evāsam evāgre	24.76	120
aham evāsam evāgre	25.113	351
"aham eva"-śloke 'aham'—tina-bāra	25.114	358
ahaṁ sarvasya prabhavo	24.189	185
ahaṁ vedmi śuko vetti	24.313	257
"aho dhanyo 'si devarṣe	24.278	239
aho mahātman bahu-doṣa-duṣṭo	24.125	149
aiche eka śaśaka dekhe āra kata-dūre	24.233	212
aiche kṛpālu kṛṣṇa, aiche tāṅra guṇa	24.63	113
aiśvarya-mādhurya-kāruṇye svarūpa-pūrṇatā	24.42	101
ajā-gala-stana-nyāya anya sādhana	24.93	128
ajāta-rati sādhaka-bhakta,—e cāri prakāra	24.291	247
akāmaḥ sarva-kāmo vā	24.90	127
akāmaḥ sarva-kāmo vā	24.197	190
akāma, mokṣa-kāma, sarva-kāma āra	24.89	126
akaraṇe doṣa, kaile bhaktira lambhana	24.342	286
akleśāṁ kamala-bhuvaḥ praviśya goṣṭhīṁ	24.120	146
alaukika rūpa, rasa, saurabhādi guṇa	24.43	102
alaukika śakti-guṇe kṛṣṇa-kṛpāya bāndhe	24.39	100
āliliṅga parighāyata-dorbhyāṁ	24.349	290
āmā-hena yebā keha 'vātula' haya	24.323	263
āmā pāite sādhana-bhakti 'abhidheya'-nāma	25.163	352
āmāra eka śiṣya āche, calaha dekhite"	24.268	233
āmāra kṛpāya ei saba sphuruka tomāre"	25.108	355
āmāra sarva-nāśa haya, tumi brahma-sama	25.72	335
āmāte ye 'prīti', sei 'prema'—'prayojana'	25.124	365
āmi bojhā vahimu, tomā-sabāra duḥkha haila	25.170	392
"āmi—'sambandha'-tattva, āmāra jñāna	25.103	352
āmi tomāra na ha-i 'śiṣyera śiṣya' sama	25.73	336
āmi tomāya bahu anna pāṭhāimu dine	24.262	230
aṁśena giriśādiṣu	23.78	50
ānanda-samudre bhāse saba bhakta-gaṇe	25.231	423
ānande vihvala bhakta-gaṇa dhāñā āilā	25.226	420
ananta guṇa śrī-rādhikāra, pañciśa—	23.86	54
ananta kṛṣṇera guṇa, cauṣaṭṭi—pradhāna	23.69	45
ananya-mamatā viṣṇau	23.8	5
anapekṣaḥ śucir dakṣa	23.109	67
anartha-nivṛtti haile bhaktye 'niṣṭhā' haya	23.11	7
aneka dainyādi kari' dharila caraṇa	25.14	303
aṅganete āsi' preme nācite lāgilā	25.62	331
aniketaḥ sthira-matir	23.112	69
anivedita-tyāga, viaṣṇava-nindādi-varjana	24.338	284
antar-bhakti-rasena pūrṇa-hṛdayo bāhye	24.348	289
antargataḥ svavivareṇa cakāra teṣāṁ	24.45	103
antargataḥ svaviveraṇa cakāra teṣāṁ	24.115	143
antargataḥ svavivareṇa cakāra teṣāṁ	25.158	386
antarvāṇibhir apy asya	23.40	23
antaryāmi-upāsaka 'ātmārāma' kaya	24.154	165
'anubhāva'—smita, nṛtya, gītādi udbhāsvara	23.51	29
anuvāda kaile haya kathāra āsvāda	25.242	428
anvaya-vyatirekābhyāṁ	25.123	364
āpāmaraṁ yo vitatāra gauraḥ	23.1	2
āpanāra bale kare sarva-vismāraṇa	24.38	100
āpana-saṅge lañā 'dvādaśa vana' dekhāilā	25.207	412
āpane āsvādi' bhakti karilā prakāśe	25.264	437

āpane karaha yadi hṛdaye praveśa	24.326	265
āpane rahe eka paisāra cānā cābāiyā	25.205	410
āpane śunilā 'sarva-siddhāntera sāra'	25.249	431
āpāyayati govinda-	24.215	202
'api'-śabda—avadhāraṇe, seha cāri bāra	24.304	253
api-śabde mukhya artha sāta vikhyāta	24.68	116
api sambhāvanā-praśna-	24.69	116
aprāptātīta-naṣṭārthā-	24.181	181
āra artha śuna, yāhā—arthera bhāṇḍāra	24.284	243
āra artha śuna, yaiche sādhura saṅgama	24.226	208
āra dina calilā prabhu udvigna hañā	25.177	395
āra dina madhyāhna kari' tāṅra ghare gelā	25.15	303
āra eka artha kahe parama samartha	24.148	162
āra eka artha śuna pramāṇe samartha	24.306	254
āra eka bheda śuna arthera prakāśa	24.294	249
āra eka-dāna āmi māgi tomā-ṭhāñi	24.246	217
āra kata-dūre eka dekhena śūkara	24.232	211
āra kṛṣṇa-nāma laite kṛṣṇa-sthāne sthiti	25.200	408
āra 'nāma' la-ite kṛṣṇa-caraṇa pāibe	25.199	407
āra paisā bāṇiyā-sthāne rākhena dhariyā	25.205	410
āra saba bhakta prabhura caraṇe paḍilā	25.230	422
āra tina artha śuna parama samartha	24.220	205
āra yata mata, sei saba chārākhāra"	25.45	321
ardha-māra jīva yadi dhaḍ-phaḍa kare	24.243	216
ardha-mārā kara kene, nā lao parāṇa?"	24.241	215
ardha mārile kibā haya, tāhā kaha more"	24.248	218
ārta, arthārthī,—dui sakāma-bhitare gaṇi	24.95	130
artha śuni' sanātana vismita hañā	24.314	258
artho 'yaṁ brahma-sūtrāṇāṁ	25.143	376
ārto jijñāsur arthārthī	24.94	129
āruhya kṛcchreṇa paraṁ padaṁ tataḥ	24.131	152
āruhya kṛcchreṇa paraṁ padaṁ tataḥ	24.141	159
āruhya kṛcchreṇa paraṁ padaṁ tataḥ	25.32	312
āruhya ye druma-bhujān rucira-prabālān	24.176	178
ārurukṣor muner yogaṁ	24.159	168
āśā-bandhaḥ samutkaṇṭhā	23.18	11
āsakti haite citte janme kṛṣṇe	23.12	7
āsaktis tad-guṇākhyāne	23.19	11
asamānordhva-rūpa-śrī	23.83	52
asatsaṅga-tyāga, śrī-bhāgavata-śravaṇa	24.339	284
āścarya śuniyā mora utkaṇṭhita mana	24.6	84
asmin sukha-ghana-mūrtau param-	24.128	151
"asmin vane vṛkṣāḥ phalanti" yaiche	24.300	251
aspandanaṁ gatimatāṁ pulakas tarūṇāṁ	24.207	196
aśru-dhārāya bhije loka, pulaka-kadamba	25.68	333
aṣṭādaśe—vṛndāvana-vihāra-varṇana	25.256	434
aṣṭame—rāmānanda-saṁvāda vistāra	25.249	431
āste-vyaste dhāñā āse, patha nāhi pāya	24.270	234
aśvattha-vṛkṣāś ca baṭa-vṛkṣāś ca	24.299	251
ataeva āpane sūtrārtha kariyāche vyākhyāne	25.92	346
ataeva bhāgavata karaha vicāra	25.153	383
ataeva bhāgavata—sūtrera 'artha'-rūpa	25.142	375
ataeva bhāgavate ei 'tina' kaya	25.131	369
ataeva brahma-sūtrera bhāṣya—śrī-	25.100	350
ataeva hari bhaje buddhimān jana	24.93	128
ataeva saba śāstra karaye khaṇḍana	25.48	322
ataeva tāṅhā sane nā haila milana	25.212	414
'āṭānna' bāra ātmārāma nāma la-iye	24.295	249
āṭānna ca-kārera saba lopa haya	24.298	250
ātatatvāca ca mātṛtvād ātmā hi paramo	24.78	121
atha pañca-guṇā ye syur	23.78	50
āṭhāranālāte āsi' bhaṭṭācārya brāhmaṇe	25.224	420
athāsaktis tato bhāvas	23.15	9
atha vṛndāvaneśvaryāḥ	23.87	54
athocyante guṇāḥ pañca	23.80	51
"ātmā deha-mano-brahma-svabhāva	24.12	86
ātma-madhye goṣṭhī kare chāḍi' adhyayana	25.22	307
"ātmārāmā api"—'api' 'garhā'-artha	24.225	208
'ātmārāmā api' bhaje,—gauṇa artha	24.224	207
'ātmārāmā eva' hañā śrī-kṛṣṇa bhajaye	24.202	193
ātmārāma-gaṇākarṣīty	23.81	51
ātmārāma-gaṇera āge kariba gaṇana	24.13	87
ātmārāma jīva yata sthāvara-jaṅgame	24.200	192
"ātmārāmāś ca api" kare kṛṣṇe ahaitukī	24.146	161
'ātmārāmāś ca ātmārāmāś ca' āṭānna	24.296	249
"ātmārāmāś ca ātmārāmāś ca" kari'	24.149	162
"ātmārāmāś ca munayaś ca" kṛṣṇere	24.152	164
'ātmārāmāś ca munayaś ca' kṛṣṇere	24.221	206
'ātmārāmāś ca munayaś ca nirgranthāś	24.303	252
ātmārāmāś ca munayo	24.5	83
'ātmārāmāś ca' samuccaye kahiye ca-kāra	24.301	251
ātmārāmatayā me vṛthā	24.128	151
ātmārāmeti padyārkasy-	24.1	81
'ātmā'-śabde brahma, deha, mana, yatna,	24.11	86
'ātmā'-śabde 'buddhi' kahe buddhi-viśeṣa	24.156	184
'ātma'-śabde 'deha' kahe,—cāri artha tāra	24.211	199

'ātmā-śabde 'dhṛti' kahe,—dhairye yei 24.174 177
'ātma'-śabde kahe kṛṣṇa bṛhattva-svarūpa 24.77 120
'ātmā'-śabde kahe 'kṣetrajña jīva'-lakṣaṇa 24.307 254
'ātmā'-śabde kahe—sarva-vidha bhagavān 24.285 244
'ātmā'-śabde 'mana' kaha—mane yei rame 24.165 171

'ātmā'-śabde 'svabhāva' kahe, tāte yei rame 24.200 192
'ātmā'-śabde 'yatna' kahe—yatna kariyā 24.168 173
ātmāvāsyam idaṁ viśvaṁ 25.101 351
ātmecchānugatāv ātma 25.133 370
atulya-madhura-prema 23.82 52
autkaṇṭhya-bāṣpa-kalayā muhur ardyamānas 24.157 166

avajānanti māṁ mūḍhā 25.39 317
avatārāvalī-bījaṁ 23.81 51
avicintya-mahā-śaktiḥ 23.80 51
avidyā-karma-saṁjñānyā 24.308 255
ayaṁ netā suramyāṅgaḥ 23.70 45
āyuḥ śriyaṁ yaśo dharmaṁ 25.84 342

B

bahunā kiṁ guṇās tasyāḥ 23.91 55
bāhu tuli' prabhu kahe—bala 'kṛṣṇa' 'hari' 25.176 395
bāṇa-viddha bhagna-pāda kare dhaḍ-phaḍi 24.231 211
'baṭo, bhikṣām aṭa, gāṁ cānaya' yaiche 24.223 207
batriśe chābbiśe mili' aṣṭa-pañcāśa 24.294 249

bhagavān eka āsedam 25.133 370
'bhāgavata' kariba sūtrera bhāṣya-svarūpa" 25.97 348
bhāgavata-siddhānta gūḍha sakali kahilā 23.115 71
bhāgavata-śloka, upaniṣat kahe 'eka' mata 25.100 350
bhāgavate prati-śloke vyāpe yāra sthiti 25.135 372

bhāgavatera sambandha, abhidheya, 25.102 352
bhāgavatera svarūpa kene nā kara vicāraṇa? 24.317 260
bhāgavate sei ṛk śloke nibandhana 25.99 350
'bhagavattā' mānile 'advaita' nā yāya 25.48 322
bhakta āmā preme bāndhiyāche hṛdaya- 25.127 366

bhakta-deha pāile haya guṇera smaraṇa 24.111 140
bhakta-duḥkha dekhi' prabhu manete cintila 25.13 302
bhakta-duḥkha khaṇḍāite tāre kṛpā kaila 25.5 298
bhakta-gaṇa-saṅge kare kīrtana-vilāsa 25.241 427
bhakta-gaṇa, śuna mora dainya-vacana 25.272 444

bhakta-gaṇe sphuri āmi bāhire-antare 25.125 365
bhaktāḥ śravan-netra-jalāḥ samagram 23.23 14
bhakta lāgi' vistārilā āpana-vadane 25.267 440
bhaktānāṁ hṛdi rājantī 23.97 58

bhakta-saṅge bahu-kṣaṇa nṛtya-gīta kailā 25.232 423
bhakta-vatsala nā dekhi trijagate anya 25.268 440
bhakta-vātsalya, ātma-paryanta vadānyatā 24.42 101
bhakti-bale 'prāpta-svarūpa' divya-deha pāya 24.134 154
bhaktiḥ punāti man-niṣṭhā 25.136 372

bhakti-nirdhūta-doṣāṇāṁ 23.95 58
bhakti-prabhāva,—sei kāma chāḍāñā 24.198 191
bhaktira svabhāva,—brahma haite kare 24.110 139
bhaktir ity ucyate bhīṣma- 23.8 5
'bhakti'-śabdera artha haya daśa-vidhākāra 24.30 96
'bhakti'-śabdera ei saba arthera mahimā 24.33 97

bhakti sādhana kare yei 'prāpta-brahma-laya' 24.109 139
bhakti-smṛti-śāstra kari' kariha pracāra 23.104 62
bhakti vinā kevala jñāne 'mukti' nāhi haya 24.109 139
bhakti vinā mukti nahe, bhāgavate kaya 25.30 310
bhakti vinu kona sādhana dite nāre phala 24.92 128

bhakti vinu mukti nāhi, bhaktye mukti haya 24.139 157
bhaktyā bhāgavataṁ grāhyaṁ 24.313 257
bhaktyāham ekayā grāhyaḥ 25.136 372
bhaktyā sañjātayā bhaktyā 25.140 373
'bhaktye jīvan-mukta' guṇākṛṣṭa hañā kṛṣṇa 24.130 152

'bhaktye jīvan-mukta', 'jñāne jīvan-mukta' 24.129 151
bhaktye mukti pāileha avaśya kṛṣṇere 24.143 160
bhartur mithaḥ suyaśasaḥ kathanānurāga- 24.88 125
bhāvaḥ sa eva sāndrātmā 23.7 5
bhāva-rūpā, mahābhāva-lakṣaṇa-rūpā āra 24.31 96

bhāva-tattva, rasa-tattva, līlā-tattva āra 25.265 439
bhayaṁ dvitīyābhiniveśataḥ syād 24.137 156
bhayaṁ dvitīyābhiniveśataḥ syād 25.138 374
bheje sarpa-vapur hitvā 25.77 337
bhikṣām aṭann ari-pure 23.27 16

'bhramara-gītā'ra daśa śloka tāhāte 23.60 38
bhramite bhramite yadi sādhu-saṅga pāya 24.310 256
bhukti-mukti-siddhi-sukha chāḍaya yāra 24.39 100
bhukti, siddhi, indriyārtha tāre nāhi 23.24 15
bhukti, siddhi, mukti—mukhya ei tina 24.27 94

bhūtāni bhagavaty ātmany 25.129 368
bīja, ikṣu, rasa, guḍa tabe khaṇḍa-sāra 23.43 24
'brahma-ātmā'-śabde yadi kṛṣṇere kahaya 24.82 123
brahma-bhūtaḥ prasannātmā 24.132 153

brahma-bhūtaḥ prasannātmā 25.155 384
brahmādi kīṭa-paryanta—tāṅra śaktite 24.307 254
brahmā nārade sei upadeśa kailā 25.95 348

brahma, paramātmā, bhagavattā, 24.80 122
brahmāre īśvara catuḥ-ślokī ye kahilā 25.95 348
'brahma'-śabde kahe 'ṣaḍ-aiśvarya-pūrṇa 25.33 312
'brahma' śabdera artha—tattva sarva- 24.71 117
brahmeti paramātmeti 24.74 118
brahmeti paramātmeti 24.81 122

brahmeti paramātmeti 25.132 370
bṛhattvād bṛṁhaṇatvāc ca 24.72 117
brūhi yogeśvare kṛṣṇe 24.320 261
buddhimān-arthe—yadi 'vicāra-jña' haya 24.91 127
buddhi, svabhāva,—ei sāta artha-prāpti 24.11 86
buddhye rame ātmārāma—dui ta' prakāra 24.187 184

C

'ca' 'api', dui śabda tāte 'avyaya' haya 24.65 114
'ca'—avadhāraṇe, ihā 'api'—samuccaye 24.185 184
'ca' evārthe—'munayaḥ eva' kṛṣṇere bhajaya 24.225 208
caitanya-caritāmṛta kahe kṛṣṇadāsa 23.127 80
caitanya-caritāmṛta kahe kṛṣṇadāsa 24.355 293

caitanya-gosāñi—'śrī-kṛṣṇa', nirdhārila 25.163 389
caitanya-gosāñi yei kahe, sei mata sāra 25.45 321
caitanya-līlā—amṛta-pūra, 25.277 447
caitanyārpitam astv etac 25.282 451
candraśekhara, kīrtanīyā-paramānanda, 25.179 396

cānvācaye samāhāre 24.67 115
caraṇa-cālane kāṅpāila tribhuvana 24.20 90
cāri-jana mili' kare nāma-saṅkīrtana 25.63 331
cāri puruṣārtha chāḍāya, guṇe hare 24.64 114
cāri-śabda-saṅge evera karibe uccāra 24.304 253

cāri-veda-upaniṣade yata kichu haya 25.98 349
cāri-vidha tāpa tāra kare saṁharaṇa 24.60 111
cāru-saubhāgya-rekhāḍhyā 23.88 55
ca-śabda api-arthe, 'api'—avadhāraṇe 24.171 175
ca-śabde 'anvācaye' artha kahe āra 24.223 207

ca-śabde 'api'ra artha ihāṅo kahaya 24.162 169
ca-śabde 'eva', 'api'-śabda samuccaye 24.202 193
ca-śabde kari yadi 'itaretara' artha 24.148 162
ca-śabde 'samuccaye', āra artha kaya 24.221 206
caskambha yaḥ sva-raṁhasāskhalatā 24.21 91

catuḥ-ṣaṣṭir udāhṛtāḥ 23.85 53
catuḥ-ślokīte prakaṭa tāra kariyāche 25.102 352
catur-bhujaṁ kañja-rathāṅga-śaṅkha- 24.156 166
caturdaśe—'herā-pañcami'-yātrā-daraśana 25.252 432

caturthe—mādhava purīra caritra-āsvādana 25.246 429
catur-vidhā bhajante māṁ 24.94 129
caturviṁśe—'ātmārāmāḥ'-ślokārtha 25.260 436
caudikete lakṣa loka bale 'hari' 'hari' 25.65 332
chaya vatsara kailā yaiche gamanāgamana 25.240 427

chayera chaya mata vyāsa kailā āvartana 25.53 325
chidra pāñā rāya tāre cābuka mārilā 25.188 400
cid-ānanda kṛṣṇa-vigraha 'māyika' kari' 25.35 314
cirād adattaṁ nija-gupta-vittaṁ 23.1 2
cīrāṇi kiṁ pathi na santi diśanti bhikṣāṁ 23.114 70
citra-jalpera daśa aṅga—prajalpādi-nāma 23.60 38

D

dadāmi buddhi-yogaṁ taṁ 24.173 176
dadāmi buddhi-yogaṁ taṁ 24.192 187
dadhi yena khaṇḍa-marica-karpūra-milane 23.49 28
daivī hy eṣā guṇamayī 24.138 157
dakṣiṇo vinayī hrīmān 23.74 47
dāmodāra-svarūpa, paṇḍita-gadādhara 25.228 421

daṇḍavat kare loke hari-dhvani kari' 25.176 395
daṇḍavat-sthāne pipīlikāre dekhiyā 24.271 235
danta-dhāvana, snāna, sandhyādi vandana 24.332 278
daśame—kahiluṅ sarva-vaiṣṇava-milana 25.250 431
dāsya-bhaktera rati haya 'rāga'-daśā-anta 24.32 97

dāsya-rati 'rāga' paryanta krameta bāḍaya 23.54 33
dāsya-sakhyādi-bhāve puruṣādi gaṇa 24.57 110
dattābhayaṁ ca bhuja-daṇḍa-yugaṁ vilokya 24.50 106
dehārāmī dehe bhaje 'dehopādhi brahma' 24.212 200
dehārāmī karma-niṣṭha—yājñikādi jana 24.214 201

dehārāmī, sarva-kāma—saba ātmārāma 24.218 204
dehe ātma-jñāne ācchādita sei 'jñāna' 24.201 192
dehe prāṇa āile, yena indriya uṭhilā 25.225 420
dekhi' kāśī-vāsī lokera haila camatkāra 25.69 333
dekhite caliyāchena 'bindu-mādhava hari' 25.60 330

dekhite kautuke āilā lañā śiṣya-vṛnda 25.66 332
dekhiyā prabhura nṛtya, prema, dehera 25.67 333
dekhiyā vyādhera mane haila camatkāra 24.264 231
dekhiyā vyādhera prema parvata-mahāmuni 24.277 238
deśa-kāla-supātrajñaḥ 23.72 46

devī kṛṣṇamayī proktā 23.68 44
dhairyavanta eva hañā karaya bhajane 24.174 177
dhana-sañcayī—nirgrantha, āra ye nirdhana 24.17 89
dhanuka bhāṅgi' vyādha tāṅra caraṇe 24.258 227

dhanur-bāṇa haste,—yena yama daṇḍa-dhara 24.235 213
dhanyasyāyaṁ navaḥ premā 23.40 23
dhanyeyam adya dharaṇī tṛṇa-vīrudhas tvat 24.206 195
'dharmādi' viṣaye yaiche e 'cāri' vicāra 25.121 362
dharmaḥ projjhita-kaitavo 'tra paramo 24.100 133

dharmaḥ projjhita-kaitavo 'tra paramo 25.149 381
dharmasya tattvaṁ nihitaṁ guhāyāṁ 25.57 328
dhṛtiḥ syāt pūrṇatā jñāna 24.181 181
dhṛtimanta hañā bhaje pakṣi-mūrkha-caye 24.185 184
dhruva-ghāṭe tāṅre subuddhi-rāya mililā 25.186 400

dīghi khodāite tāre 'munsīpha' kailā 25.188 400
dīkṣā, prātaḥ-smṛti-kṛtya, śauca, 24.331 274
dina daśa rahi' rūpa gauḍe yātrā kaila 25.221 418
dina-kṛtya, pakṣa-kṛtya, ekādaśy-ādi 24.340 285
dine tata laya, yata khāya dui jane 24.267 233

divya deha diyā karāya kṛṣṇera bhajana 24.110 139
doṅhe mahāprabhure kailā prema-āliṅgana 25.227 421
dṛṣṭaṁ śrutaṁ bhūta-bhavad-bhaviṣyat 25.37 316
duḥkhābhāve uttama-prāptye mahā-pūrṇa 24.180 181
duḥkha pāñā prabhu-pade kailā nivedana 25.12 302
duḥkhī vaiṣṇava dekhi' tāṅre karāna 25.206 411

'duḥsaṅga' kahiye—'kaitava', 'ātma-vañcanā' 24.99 133
dui-dike loka kare prabhu-vilokane 25.175 394
dui mārge ātmārāmera batriśa vibheda 24.292 248
dui-vidha bhakta haya cāri cāri prakāra 24.287 245
dūra haite vyādha pāila gurura daraśane 24.269 234
durūhādbhuta-vīrye 'smin 24.195 189

dvādaśa-skandha-yukto 'yaṁ 25.144 377
dvādaśe—guṇḍicā-mandira-mārjana 25.251 432
dvāviṁśe—dvividha sādhana-bhaktira 25.259 435
dvijopasṛṣṭaḥ kuhakas takṣako vā 23.21 13
dvitīya paricchede—prabhura pralāpa- 25.244 429
dvividha 'vibhāva',—ālambana, uddīpana 23.50 29

E

e amṛta kara pāna, 25.279 449
ebe āmi ekā yāmu jhārikhaṇḍa-pathe" 25.181 397
ebe kari ślokera mūlārtha prakāśa 24.106 138
ebe ślokārtha kari, yathā ye lāgaya 24.70 116
ebe śuna bhakti-phala 'prema'-prayojana 23.3 3

ebe śuna, prema, yei—mūla 'prayojana' 25.139 374
ebe tomāra pādābje upajibe bhakti 25.86 343
e dui,—bhāvera 'svarūpa', 'taṭastha' lakṣaṇa 23.6 4
eho kṛṣṇa-guṇākṛṣṭa mahā-muni hañā 24.167 172

ei amṛta anukṣaṇa, 25.276 44
ei āra tina artha gaṇanāte pāila 24.283 242
"ei artha—āmāra sūtrera vyākhyānurūpa 25.97 348
ei baḍa 'pāpa',—satya caitanyera vāṇī 25.35 314
ei cāri artha saha ha-ila 'teiśa' artha 24.220 205

ei cāri sukṛti haya mahā-bhāgyavān 24.96 131
ei chaya ātmārāma kṛṣṇere bhajaya 24.145 161
ei chaya yogī sādhu-saṅgādi-hetu pāñā 24.161 169
ei-dṛṣṭe bhāgavatera artha jānaya" 24.323 263
ei dui artha mili' 'chābbiśa' artha haila 24.283 242

ei haya satya śrī-kṛṣṇa-caitanya-vacana 25.44 321
ei jīva—sanakādi saba muni-jana 24.203 193
ei-mata dāsye dāsa, sakhye sakhā-gaṇa 23.93 57
ei-mata dina pañca loka nistāriyā 25.177 395
ei mata kahiluṅ eka ślokera vyākhyāna 24.322 262

ei mata mahāprabhu dui māsa paryanta 25.3 297
ei-mata sanātana vṛndāvanete rahilā 25.216 416
ei nava prīty-aṅkura yāṅra citte haya 23.20 12
ei-pañca-madhye eka 'svalpa' yadi haya 24.194 188
ei pañca sthāyī bhāva haya pañca 'rasa' 23.46 26

ei pāpa yāya mora, kemana upāye? 24.254 224
ei rasa anubhave yaiche bhakta-gaṇa 23.94 57
ei rasa-āsvāda nāhi abhaktera gaṇe 23.99 59
ei saba śabde haya—'jñāna'-'vijñāna'-viveka 25.110 359
ei saba śānta yabe bhaje bhagavān 24.164 170

ei sabe viddhā-tyāga, aviddhā-karaṇa 24.342 286
eita' 'sambandha', śuna 'abhidheya' bhakti 25.135 372
ei 'sambandha'-tattva kahiluṅ, śuna āra 25.118 360
ei saṅkṣepe sūtra kahiluṅ dig-daraśana 24.345 287
ei sāta artha prathame kariluṅ vyākhyāne 24.153 164

ei sāte rame yei, sei ātmārāma-gaṇa 24.13 87
ei ślokera artha prabhu 'ekaṣaṣṭi' prakāra 25.161 388
ei śloke śrīdhāra-svāmī kariyāchena 24.101 134
ei svabhāva-guṇe, yāte mādhuryera sāra 24.40 100
ei ta' ekādaśa padera artha-nirṇaya 24.70 116

ei ta' kahiluṅ,—prabhu dekhi' vṛndāvana 25.238 426
ei ta' kahiluṅ sanātane prabhura prasāda 24.351 291
ei ta' kahiluṅ ślokera 'ṣaṣṭi' saṅkhyaka 24.306 254
ei ta' kahiluṅ tomāya vyādhera ākhyāna 24.282 242

ei ta' kahilu prabhura sanātane prasāda 24.346 288
ei ta' kalpita artha mane nāhi bhāya 25.42 319
ei tera artha kahiluṅ parama samartha 24.163 170
ei tina bhede haya chaya prakāra 24.158 167

ei 'tina' tattva āmi kahinu tomāre 25.106 354
ei tomāra vara haite habe mora bala" 23.123 78
ei 'ūnaṣaṣṭi' prakāra artha kariluṅ 24.302 252
ei ūniśa artha karilu, āge śuna āra 24.211 199
ei yāṅhā nāhi, tāhā bhakti—'ahaitukī' 24.29 95

eka 'ātmārāma'-śabda avaśeṣa rahe 24.150 163
eka ātmārāma-śabde āṭānna artha kaya 24.298 250
eka 'ātmārāma'-śabde chaya-jana kahe 24.150 163
eka bhakta-vyādhera kathā śuna sāvadhāne 24.229 210
eka bhukti kahe, bhoga—ananta-prakāra 24.28 95

ekādaśa-skandhe tāṅra bhakti-vivaraṇa 24.119 145
ekādaśa pada ei śloke sunirmala 24.10 85
ekādaśe—śrī-mandire 'beḍā-saṅkīrtana' 25.251 432
ekādaśī, janmāṣṭamī, vāmana-dvādaśī 24.341 285
eka-dina anna āne daśa-biśa jane 24.267 233

eka-dina nārada kahe,—"śunaha, parvate 24.268 233
eka dina śrī-nārada dekhi' nārāyaṇa 24.230 210
eka eka guṇa śuni' juḍāya bhakta-kāṇa 23.69 45
eka eka tina bhede chaya vibheda 24.155 165
eka eka vastra pari' bāhira hao dui-jana 24.259 228

eka 'nāmābhāse' tomāra pāpa-doṣa yābe 25.199 407
eka—'sādhana', 'prema-bhakti'—nava 24.307 96
'eka-ṣaṣṭi' artha ebe sphurila tomā-saṅge 24.312 257
'ekaṣaṣṭi' artha prabhu vivari' kahila 25.162 388
eka śloke āṭhāra artha kairācha vyākhyāne 24.4 83

eka 'svayaṁ bhagavān', āra 'bhagavān' 24.285 244
'eka' vārāṇasī chila tomāte vimukha 25.172 393
ekaviṁśe—kṛṣṇaiśvarya-mādhurya varṇana 25.259 435
e saba vṛttānta śuni' mahārāṣṭrīya 25.59 329
eta anna nā pāṭhāo, kichu kārya nāi 24.280 241

eta bali' calilā prabhu sabā āliṅgiyā 25.184 399
eta bali' dui-jana ha-ilā antardhāna 24.281 241
eta bali' prabhure lañā tathāya vasila 25.87 343
eta bali' tina tattva kahilā tāṅhāre 25.108 355
eta cinti' nimantrila sannyāsīra gaṇe 25.11 301

eta kahi' sei kare kṛṣṇa-saṅkīrtana 25.46 321
eta kahi' uṭhiyā calilā gaurahari 25.164 389
etāvad eva jijñāsyaṁ 25.123 364
ete cāṁśa-kalāḥ puṁsaḥ 25.134 371

ete 'linas tava yaśo 'khila-loka-tīrthaṁ 24.177 179
ete na hy adbhutā vyādha 24.273 236
ethā mahāprabhu yadi nīlādri calilā 25.222 419
ethā rūpa-gosāñi yabe mathurā āilā 25.186 400

ethā sanātana gosāñi prayāge āsiyā 25.210 413
e tine saba chāḍāya, kare kṛṣṇe 'bhāva' 24.104 136
evaṁ guṇāś catur-bhedāś 23.85 53
evaṁ harau bhagavati pratilabdha-bhāvo 24.157 166
evaṁ-vrataḥ sva-priya-nāma-kīrtyā 23.41 23
evaṁ-vrataḥ sva-priya-nāma-kīrtyā 25.141 374

G

gā gopakair anuvanaṁ nayator udāra 24.207 196
gaṅgā-pathe dui-bhāi rāja-pathe 25.212 414
gaṅgā-tīra-pathe prabhu prayāgere āilā 25.209 413
gauḍendrasya sabhā-vibhūṣaṇa-maṇis 24.348 289
gauḍiyā āile dadhi, bhāta, taila-mardana 25.206 411

gāyanta uccair amum eva saṁhatāḥ 25.130 368
gāyatrī-bhāṣya-rūpo 'sau 25.143 376
gāyatrīra arthe ei grantha-ārambhana 25.147 379
ghare gela vyādha, guruke kari' namaskāra 24.264 231
"ghare giyā brāhmaṇe deha' yata āche dhana 24.259 228

gokula-prema-vasatir 23.90 55
gopāla govinda rāma śrī-madhusūdana" 25.64 331
gopāla sthāpana, kṣīra-curira varṇana 25.246 429
gopīcandana-mālya-dhṛti, tulasī-āharaṇa 24.333 278
"gosāñi, prayāṇa-patha chāḍi' kene 24.238 214

grāme dhvani haila,—vyādha 'vaiṣṇava' ha-ila 24.266 232
grāmera loka saba anna ānite lāgila 24.266 232
grantha bāḍe, punarukti haya ta' kathana 25.17 304
grantho dhane 'tha sandarbhe 24.18 89
grantho 'ṣṭādaśa-sāhasraḥ 25.144 377

gṛhīta-cetā rājarṣe 24.47 104
gṛhīta-cetā rājarṣe 25.157 385
guṇākṛṣṭa hañā kare kṛṣṇera bhajana 24.119 145
guṇākṛṣṭa hañā kare nirmala bhajana 24.111 140
guṇākṛṣṭa hañā kare nirmala bhajana 24.114 142

'guṇa' śabdera artha—kṛṣṇera guṇa ananta 24.41 101
guru-lakṣaṇa, śiṣya-lakṣaṇa, doṅhāra 24.330 267
guru-pāśe sei bhakti praṣṭavya, śrotavya 25.122 364
guru-sevā, ūrdhva-puṇḍra-cakrādi-dhāraṇa 24.332 278
guru-tulya strī-gaṇera vātsalye ākarṣaṇa 24.57 110
gurv-arpita-guru-snehā 23.91 55

H

hanti śreyāṁsi sarvāṇi 25.84 342
harau ratiṁ vahann eṣa 23.27 16
"haraye namaḥ kṛṣṇa yādavāya namaḥ 25.64 331

harer guṇākṣipta-matir 24.117 144
harer nāma-ślokera yei karilā vyākhyāna 25.29 310
hari-bhaktau pravṛttā ye 24.273 236
hari-bhaktye hiṁśa-śūnya haya sādhu-varya 24.272 235
haridāsa-ṭhākura, āra paṇḍita-śaṅkara 25.229 422

'hariḥ'-śabde nānārtha, dui mukhyatama 24.59 111
harim upāsata te yata-cittā 24.178 179
hariṇā cāśv adeyeti 24.172 175
'hari'-śabdera ei mukhya kahiluṅ lakṣaṇa 64.64 114
hari-vaṁśe kahiyāche goloke nitya-sthiti 23.116 72

harṣa, dainya, cāpalyādi 'sañcāri' vikāra 25.69 333
harṣāmarṣa-bhayodvegair 23.108 66
hasaty atho roditi rauti gāyaty 23.41 23
hasaty atho roditi rauti gāyaty 25.141 374

helāya mukti pābe, pābe prema-dhana 25.154 384
hena-kāle mahāprabhu pañca-nade snāna 25.60 330
hena-kāle nindā śuni' śekhara, tapana 25.12 302
hena-kāle sei mahārāṣṭrīya brāhmaṇa 25.160 287

hena-kāle vipra āsi' karila nimantraṇa 25.14 303
'hetu'-śabde kahe—bhukti-ādi vāñchāntare 24.27 94
hīnārthādhika-sādhake tvayi tathāpy 23.29 17
hṛṣīkeśe hṛṣīkāṇi 24.184 183
husena-khāṅ 'saiyada' kare tāhāra cākarī 25.187 400

I

ihā dekhi' sannyāsi-gaṇa habe iṅhāra 25.9 299
ihā haite pābe sūtra-śrutira artha-sāra 25.153 383
ihāra prasāde pāibā caitanya-caraṇa 25.269 441
ihāra prasāde pāibā kṛṣṇa-tattva-sāra 25.270 441

ihāra śravaṇe bhakta jānena saba anta 24.353 292
ihā yaiche krame nirmala, krame bāḍe svāda 23.44 25
ihā yei śraddhā kari' karaye śravaṇa 25.239 426

indra āsi' karila yabe śrī-kṛṣṇere stuti 23.116 72
indrāri-vyākulaṁ lokaṁ 25.134 371
īśvara tumi,—ye karāha, sei siddha haya" 24.327 266

itaretara 'ca' diyā samāsa kariye 24.295 249
iti matvā bhajante māṁ 24.189 185
'ittham-bhūta-guṇaḥ'-śabdera śunaha 24.35 98

'ittham-bhūta'-śabdera artha— 24.36 98
'itthaṁ'-śabdera bhinna artha, 'guṇa' 24.35 98
ity ādayo 'nubhāvāḥ syur 23.19 11
ity asādhāraṇaṁ proktaṁ 23.84 53

J

jagadānanda, kāśīśvara, govinda, 25.228 421
jagannātha dekhi' prabhu premāviṣṭa 25.232 423
jagannātha-sevaka āni' mālā-prasāda dilā 25.233 424
jagat-tamo jahārāvyāt 24.1 81
jahau yuvaiva malavad 23.25 15

jala āni' bhaktye doṅhāra pāda prakṣālila 24.275 237
janmādy asya yato 'nvayād itarataś cārtheṣv 25.148 380
janma haite śuka-sanakādi 'brahmamaya' 24.113 142
japa, stuti, parikramā, daṇḍavat vandana 24.337 283
jāta-ajāta-rati-bhede sādhaka dui bheda 24.288 245

jāta-rati sādhaka-bhakta—cāri-vidha jana 24.290 247
jayādvaita-candra jaya gaura-bhakta-vṛnda 23.2 2
jayādvaita-candra jaya gaura-bhakta-vṛnda 24.2 82
jayādvaita-candra jaya gaura-bhakta-vṛnda 25.2 296
jaya jaya gauracandra jaya nityānanda 23.2 2

jaya jaya śrī-caitanya jaya nityānanda 24.2 82
jijñāsu, jñānī,—dui mokṣa-kāma māni 24.95 130
jīvanī-bhūta-govinda 23.96 58
jīva nistārite prabhu bhramilā deśe-deśe 25.264 437
'jīvan-mukta' aneka, sei dui bheda jāni 24.129 151

jīvan-muktā api punar 25.76 337
'jīva' tumi ei tina nāribe jānibāre 25.106 354
jīve duḥkha ditecha, tomāra ha-ibe aiche 24.249 218
jīvera duḥkha dekhi' nārada vyākula-anantare 24.233 212
jīvera svabhāva—kṛṣṇa-'dāsa'-abhimāna 24.201 192

jīveṣv ete vasanto 'pi 23.77 49
jīve 'viṣṇu' buddhi dūre—yei brahma-rudra- 25.79 339
jīve 'viṣṇu' māni—ei aparādha-cihna 25.78 338
jñāna-mārge—nirviśeṣa-brahma prakāśe 24.83 123

jñāna-mārge upāsaka—duita' prakāra 24.107 138
jñānaṁ parama-guhyaṁ me 25.105 353
jñāna, yoga, bhakti,—tinera pṛthak lakṣaṇa 24.79 121
jñāninām cātma-bhūtānāṁ 24.86 124

K

kācaṁ vicinvann api divya-ratnaṁ 24.219 204
kadāhaṁ yamunā-tīre 23.37 21
kadarthanā diyā māra'—e pāpa 'apāra' 24.250 220
kadarthiyā tumi yata mārilā jīvere 24.251 221
kāhāṅ bhakta-mukhe kahāi śunilā āpane 25.267 440
kāhāṅ mukti pāba, kāhāṅ kṛṣṇera prasāda 25.43 320

kalau naṣṭa-dṛśām eṣa 24.321 262
kālena vṛndāvana-keli-vārtā 24.350 290
kāli haite tumi yei mṛgādi māribā 24.247 218
kali-kāle nāmābhāse sukhe mukti haya 25.30 310
kali-kāle sannyāse 'saṁsāra' nāhi jini 25.28 309

kāmādi 'duḥsaṅga' chāḍi' śuddha-bhakti 24.97 131
kampa-pulakāśru haila kṛṣṇa-nāma gāñā 24.276 238
kampa, svara-bhaṅga, sveda, vaivarṇya, 25.68 333
kāntā-gaṇera rati pāya 'mahābhāva'-sīmā 24.34 98
kāṅthā-karaṅgiyā mora kāṅgāla bhakta-gaṇa 25.183 398

kariyāchena, yāhā śuni' loke camatkāra 25.161 388
karmaṇy asminn anāśvāse 24.215 202
kāro mana kona guṇe kare ākarṣaṇa 24.43 102
karoṅyāra pāni tāra mukhe deoyāila 25.193 403
kartavyākartavya saba 'smārta' vyavahāra 24.344 287

kārya-dvāre kahi tāra 'svarūpa'-lakṣaṇa 25.124 365
kāśī haite punaḥ nīlācale āgamana 25.261 436
kāśī-miśra, pradyumna-miśra, paṇḍita 25.229 422
kāśīte āmi āilāṅa vecite bhāvakāli 25.168 391
kāśīte grāhaka nāhi, vastu nā vikāya 25.169 392

kāśīte prabhura caritra śuni' tinera mukhe 25.219 417
kā stry aṅga te kala-padāmṛta-veṇu-gīta 24.56 109
kasyānubhāvo 'sya na deva vidmahe 24.54 108
kata-dūre dekhe vyādha vṛkṣe oṅta hañā 24.234 212
kataka divasa rāya naimiṣāraṇye rahilā 25.202 409

kata-kṣaṇe uṭhi' sabe duḥkhe ghare āilā 25.185 399
kecit svadehāntar hṛdyāvakāśe 24.156 166
keha kahe,—ei nahe, 'alpa' doṣa haya 25.196 405
kemane tarimu muñi pāmara adhama? 24.253 223
keśāvatāra, āra yata viruddha vyākhyāna 23.117 74

kevala brahmopāsaka, mokṣākāṅkṣī āra 24.107 138
kevala brahmopāsaka tina bheda haya 24.108 138
khaṇḍibe sakala duḥkha, 25.275 446
kibā pralāpilāṅa, kichu nāhika smaraṇe 24.8 85
kiṁvā 'dhṛti'-śabde nija-pūrṇatādi-jñāna 24.180 181

kirāta-hūnāndhra-pulinda-pukkaśā 24.179 180
kirāta-hūnāndhra-pulinda-pukkaśā 24.209 198
kīrtyamānaṁ yaśo yasya 24.98 132
kona bhāgye kona jīvera 'śraddhā' yadi haya 23.9 6

kona prakāre pāroṅ yadi ekatra karite 25.9 229
koṭi-granthe varṇana nā yāya ihāra vistāra 25.263 437
"kramaḥ śaktau paripāṭyāṁ kramaś cālana 24.24 92
'krama'-śabde kahe ei pāda-vikṣepaṇa 24.19 90

kṛpā kari' kaha yadi, juḍāya śravaṇa' 24.6 84
kṛpāmṛtenābhiṣiṣeca devas 24.350 290
kṛṣṇa-bahirmukha-doṣe māyā haite bhaya 24.136 155
kṛṣṇa-bhajana karāya, 'mumukṣā' chāḍāya 24.124 148
kṛṣṇa bhaje kṛṣṇa-guṇe ākṛṣṭa hañā 24.161 169

kṛṣṇa-bhakta—duḥkha-hīna, vāñchāntara 24.182 182
kṛṣṇa-bhakta-gaṇa kare rasa āsvādane 23.99 59
kṛṣṇa-bhakti rasa-rūpe pāya pariṇāme 23.47 27
'kṛṣṇa-bhakti-rasa-svarūpa' śrī-bhāgavata 25.150 381
kṛṣṇa-bhakti-rasera ei 'sthāyi-bhāva'-nāma 23.4 3

kṛṣṇa-bhakti-siddhānta-gaṇa, 25.273 444
kṛṣṇādibhir vibhāvādyair 23.98 58
kṛṣṇa-guṇākṛṣṭa hañā bhaje kṛṣṇa 24.134 154
kṛṣṇa guṇākṛṣṭa hañā karena bhajana 24.116 144
kṛṣṇa-guṇākṛṣṭa hañā kṛṣṇere 24.113 142

kṛṣṇa-guṇākṛṣṭa hañā tāṅhāre bhajaya 24.205 194
kṛṣṇa-guṇākhyāne haya sarvadā āsakti 23.34 20
kṛṣṇa-guṇāsvādera ei hetu jāniba 24.105 137
kṛṣṇa-keli sumṛṇāla, 25.274 445
kṛṣṇa-kṛpādi-hetu haite sabāra udaya 24.205 194

'kṛṣṇa kṛpā karibena'—dṛḍha kari' jāne 23.28 17
kṛṣṇa-kṛpāya kṛṣṇa bhaje chāḍi' saba 24.218 204
kṛṣṇa-kṛpāya sādhu-kṛpāya doṅhāra 24.175 177
kṛṣṇa-kṛpāya sādhu-saṅge rati-buddhi 24.188 185
kṛṣṇa, kṛṣṇa-bhakti vinu anya kāmanā 24.99 133

kṛṣṇa-kṣetra-yātrā, kṛṣṇa-mūrti 24.335 281
kṛṣṇa-līlāmṛtānvita, 25.281 450
kṛṣṇa-līlā amṛta-sāra, 25.271 442
kṛṣṇa-līlā-sthāne kare sarvadā vasati 23.36 21
kṛṣṇa-manane muni kṛṣṇe sarvadā bhajaya 24.224 207

kṛṣṇa-pade bhakti karāya guṇe ākarṣiyā 24.198 191
'kṛṣṇa-prema', 'bhakti-rasa', bhaktira 24.353 292
kṛṣṇa-prema-sevā-pūrṇānanda-pravīṇa 24.182 182
"kṛṣṇa-premera' cihna ebe śuna sanātana 23.38 22
kṛṣṇa-priyāvalī-mukhyā 23.91 55

'kṛṣṇārāmāś ca' eva—haya kṛṣṇa-manana 24.228 209
kṛṣṇa-sambandha vinā kāla vyartha nāhi 23.22 13
kṛṣṇa sei sei tomā karābe sphuraṇa 24.328 266
kṛṣṇa-sukha-nimitta bhajane tātparya 24.25 93

kṛṣṇa-tattva, bhakti-tattva, prema-tattva 25.265 439
kṛṣṇa-tulya bhāgavata, jānāilā saṁsāre 25.266 439
kṛṣṇa-tulya bhāgavata—vibhu, sarvāśraya 24.318 260
kṛṣṇera darśane, kāro kṛṣṇera kṛpāya 24.127 151

kṛṣṇera svarūpa-gaṇera sakala haya 'jñāna'	24.352	291
kṛṣṇe rati gāḍha haile 'prema'-abhidhāna	23.4	3
kṛṣṇe 'ratira' cihna ei kailuṅ vivaraṇa	23.38	22
kṛṣṇe svadhāmopagate	24.321	262
kṛṣṇonmukha bhakti haite māyā-mukta haya	24.136	155
kṛtvā bhagavantaṁ bhajante"	24.112	141
kṛtvā bhagavatnaṁ bhajante"	24.144	160
kṛtvā bhagavantaṁ bhajante"	25.156	385
kruddha hañā vyādha tāṅre gāli dite cāya	24.237	214
kṣāntir avyartha-kālatvaṁ	23.18	11
kṣatir iyam iha kā me svāditaṁ yat samantāt	25.283	451
"kṣetrajña ātmā puruṣaḥ	24.309	255
kṣipāmy ajasram aśubhān	25.40	318
kurari vilapasi tvaṁ vīta-nidrā na śeṣe	23.65	42
'kurvanti'-pada ei parasmaipada haya	24.25	93
kurvanty ahaitukīṁ bhaktim	24.5	83
kurvanty ahaitukīṁ bhaktim	25.159	387
kuśāsana āni' doṅhāre bhaktye vasāila	24.274	237

L

lajjā-śīlā sumaryādā	23.89	55
lakṣa koṭi loka āise, nāhika gaṇana	25.174	394
līlā premṇā priyādhikyaṁ	23.84	53
loka-saṅghaṭṭa dekhi' prabhura 'bāhya'	25.70	334
loka-śikṣā lāgi' aiche karite nā āise'	25.74	336
lokera saṅghaṭṭa āise prabhure dekhite	25.19	305
lupta-tīrtha prakaṭa kailā vanete bhramiyā	25.215	416

M

'mādane'—cambanādi haya ananta vibheda	23.59	37
mādhava-saundarya dekhi' āviṣṭa ha-ilā	25.62	331
madhu-gandhi mṛdu-smitam etad aho	23.35	20
madhuraṁ madhuraṁ vapur asya vibhor	23.35	20
madhura-nāma sṛṅgāra-rasa—sabāte prābalya	23.53	33
madhureyaṁ nava-vayāś	23.87	54
mādhurya-śaktye goloka, aiśvarye paravyoma	24.22	91
madhya-līlāra kariluṅ ei dig-daraśana	25.240	427
madhya-līlāra krama ebe kari anuvāda	25.242	428
'mahājana' yei kahe, sei 'satya' māni	25.56	326
mahā-pātakera haya ei prāyaścitti	25.200	408
'mahāprabhu āila'—grāme kolāhala haila	25.234	424
mahāprabhura upara lokera praṇati dekhiyā	25.220	418
mahārāṣṭrīya dvija, śekhara, miśra-tapana	25.217	416
mahā-virakta sanātana bhramena vane vane	25.214	415
mahiṣī-gaṇera 'rūḍha', 'adhirūḍha' gopikā	23.57	36
mahiṣī-haraṇa ādi, saba—māyāmaya	23.118	74
mahīyasāṁ pāda-rajo-'bhiṣekaṁ	25.85	342
mām eva ye prapadyante	24.138	157
mane eka saṁśaya haya, tāhā khaṇḍāite	24.239	214
mantra-adhikārī, mantra-siddhy-ādi-śodhana	24.331	274
māsa-kṛtya, janmāṣṭamyādi-vidhi-vicārāṇa	24.340	285
māsa-mātra rūpa-gosāñi rahilā vṛndāvane	25.208	412
mathurā āilā sarāna rāja-patha diyā	25.210	413
mathurā āsiyā rāya prabhu-vārtā pāila	25.203	409
mathurā-māhātmya-śāstra saṅgraha kariyā	25.215	416
mathurāte subuddhi-rāya tāhāre mililā	25.211	414
mathurāya lupta-tīrthera kariha uddhāra	23.103	61
mat-sevayā pratītaṁ te	24.183	182
mauṣala-līlā, āra kṛṣṇa-antardhāna	23.117	74
māyā-kārya, māyā haite āmi—vyatireka	25.116	359
māyā-śaktye brahmāṇḍādi-paripāṭī	24.23	92
māyātīta haile haya āmāra 'anubhava'	25.118	360
māyāvāde karilā yata doṣera ākhyāna	25.88	344
'māyāvādī' nirviśeṣa-brahme 'hetu' kaya	25.51	324
mayy arpita-mano-buddhir	23.107	66
'mīmāṁsaka' kahe,—'īśvara haya karmera	25.50	323
miśra-mukhe śune sanātane prabhura 'śikṣā'	25.218	417
mo-haite kaiche haya smṛti-paracāra	24.325	264
mokṣākāṅkṣī jñānī haya tina-prakāra	24.121	146
mora mana chuṅite nāre ihāra eka-bindu	23.121	77
mṛga-chāla cāha yadi, āisa mora ghare	24.245	217
mṛga māribāre āche bāṇa yuḍiyā	24.234	212
mukhe 'haya' 'haya' kare, hṛdaya nā māne	25.27	309
"muktā api līlayā vigrahaṁ	24.112	141
"muktā api līlayā vigrahaṁ	24.144	160
"muktā api līlayā vigrahaṁ	25.156	385
muktānām api siddhānāṁ	25.83	341
'mukti' lāgi' bhaktye kare kṛṣṇera bhajana	24.122	147
muktir hitvānyathā-rūpaṁ	24.135	155
mumukṣā chāḍiyā guṇe bhaje tāṅra pā'ya	24.127	151
mumukṣā chāḍiyā kailā kṛṣṇera bhajana	24.126	150
mumkṣavo ghora-rūpān	24.123	148
'mumukṣu' jagate aneka saṁsārī jana	24.122	147
mumukṣu, jīvan-mukta, prāpta-svarūpa āra	24.121	146

"munayaḥ santaḥ" iti kṛṣṇa-manane āsakti 24.146 161
'munayaś ca' bhakti kare,—ei artha tāra 24.301 251
"munayo 'pi" kṛṣṇa bhaje guṇākṛṣṭa hañā 24.168 173
'muni'-ādi śabdera artha śuna, sanātana 24.14 87
muñi—nīca-jāti, kichu nā jānoṅ ācāra 24.325 264

'muni', 'nirgrantha', 'ca' 'api',—cāri śabdera 24.293 248
'muni', 'nirgrantha'-śabdera pūrvavat 24.162 169
'muni'-śabde manana-śīla, āra kahe maunī 24.15 88
'muni'-śabde—pakṣī, bhṛṅga; 'nirgranthe' 24.175 177
'muñi ye śikhāluṅ tore sphuruka sakala' 23.123 78
mūrkha, nīca, mleccha ādi śāstra-rikta-gaṇa 24.17 89

N

na bhajanty avajānanti 24.142 159
nadī-tīre eka-khāni kuṭīra kariyā 24.260 228
nadyo 'drayaḥ khaga-mṛgāḥ sadayāvalokair 24.206 195
naiṣāṁ matis tāvad urukramāṅghriṁ 25.85 342
nāma-gāne sadā ruci, laya kṛṣṇa-nāma 23.32 19

nāma-mahimā, nāmāparādha dūre varjana 24.336 282
namaskāra kare loka hari-dhvani kari 25.164 389
nānā-bhāvera bhakta-jana, 25.274 445
nānā kāme bhaje, tabu pāya bhakti-siddhi 24.196 189
nānā śāstre paṇḍita āise śāstra vicārite 25.19 305

nā paḍa' kutarka-garte, 25.279 449
na premā śravaṇādi-bhaktir api vā yogo 23.29 17
nārada kahe,—'aiche raha, tumi bhāgyavān' 24.281 241
nārada kahe,—'āmi anna diba prati-dine' 24.257 226
nārada kahe,—"ardha mārile jīva pāya vyathā 24.249 218

nārada kahe,—'dhanuka bhāṅga, tabe se 24.256 226
nārada kahe,—'eka-vastu māgi tomāra sthāne' 24.244 216
nārada kahe,—"ihā āmi kichu nāhi cāhi 24.246 217
nārada kahe,—"patha bhuli' āilāṅa puchite 24.239 214
nārada kahe,—'vaiṣṇava, tomāra anna 24.279 240

nārada kahe,—"vyādha, ei nā haya āścarya 24.272 235
nārada kahe,—'yadi dhara āmāra vacana 24.255 225
nārada kahe,—"yadi jīve māra' tumi bāṇa 24.241 215
nārada-prabhāve mukhe gāli nāhi āya 24.237 214
nārada-saṅge vyādhera mana parasanna ha-ila 24.252 222

nārada sei artha vyāsere kahilā 25.96 348
nārade dekhi' mṛga saba palāñā gela 24.236 213
nāradera saṅge śaunakādi muni-gaṇa 24.126 150
nāradera upadeśe sakala karila 24.265 232

nāradere kahe,—tumi hao sparśa-maṇi 24.277 238
nārāyaṇa-kalāḥ śāntā 24.123 148
nārāyaṇe māne tāre 'pāṣaṇḍīte' gaṇana 25.79 339
narendre āsiyā sabe prabhure mililā 25.226 420
nārīgaṇa-manohārī 23.75 48

na sādhayati māṁ yogo 25.137 373
na svādhyāyas tapas tyāgo 25.137 373
nātaḥ paraṁ parama yad bhavataḥ svarūpam 25.36 315
navame—kahiluṅ dakṣiṇa-tīrtha-bhramaṇa 25.250 431
nava-yogīśvara janma haite 'sādhaka' jñānī 24.118 145

nāyakānāṁ śiroratnaṁ 23.67 43
nāyaka, nāyikā,—dui rasera 'ālambana' 23.92 56
nāyikāra śiromaṇi—rādhā-ṭhākurāṇī 23.66 43
nāyaṁ sukhāpo bhagavān 24.86 124
necchanti sevayā pūrṇāḥ 24.183 182

"nīca-jāti, nīca-sevī, muñi—supāmara 23.120 76
nīco 'py utpulako lebhe 24.278 239
nigama-kalpa-taror galitaṁ phalaṁ 25.151 382
nija-gaṇa lañā prabhu kahe hāsya kari' 25.168 391
nija-granthe karṇapūra vistāra kariyā 24.347 288

nija-guṇe tabe hare dehendriya-mana 24.63 113
nija-kāma lāgiha tabe kṛṣṇere bhajaya 24.91 127
nija-kṛta sūtrera nija-'bhāṣya'-svarūpa 25.142 375
nija-loka lañā prabhu āilā vāsāghara 25.167 390
nikaṭe hari-dhvani śuni' parakāśānanda 25.66 332

nirantara kara kṛṣṇa-nāma-saṅkīrtana 25.154 384
nirantara kara kṛṣṇa-nāma-saṅkīrtana 25.198 406
nirantara kṛṣṇa-nāma kariha kīrtana 24.261 229
"nirgranthā api"ra ei 'api'—sambhāvane 24.153 164
'nirgranthā eva' hañā, 'api'—nirdhāraṇe 24.302 252

'nirgrantha hañā'—ei duṅhāra 'viśeṣaṇa' 24.226 208
"nirgranthāḥ"—avidyā-hina, keha—vidhi- 24.147 162
'nirgranthāḥ' hañā ihāṅ 'api'—nirdhāraṇe 24.222 206
'nirgrantha'—mūrkha, nīca, sthāvara-paśu- 24.203 193
'nirgrantha'-śabde kahe, avidyā-granthi-hīna 24.16 88

nirgrantha-śabde kahe tabe 'vyādha', 22.227 209
'nirgrantha' sthāvarādira śuna vivaraṇa 24.204 194
'nirguṇa' vyatireke tiṅho haya ta' 'saguṇa' 25.54 325
nirjana vana-pathe yāite mahā sukha pāilā 25.222 419

nirmamo nirahaṅkāraḥ 23.106 65
nir niścaye niṣ kramārthe 24.18 89
nirodho 'syānu śayanam 24.135 155

nirveda-harṣādi—tetriśa 'vyabhicārī' 23.52 32
nistāra karaha more, paḍoṅ tomāra pāye" 24.254 224
niṣṭhā haite śravaṇādye 'ruci' upajaya 23.11 7
nityānanda kahe, prabhu karena āsvādana 25.247 430
nivedana kare dante tṛṇa-guccha lañā 23.119 76
'nyāya' kahe,—'paramāṇu haite viśva haya' 25.51 324

P

pāche lāg la-ilā tabe bhakta pañca jana 25.178 396
pāche yabe husena-khāṅ gauḍe 'rājā' ha-ila 25.189 401
pakṣī, mṛga, vṛkṣa, latā, cetanācetana 24.58 110
pāñā ājñā rāya vṛndāvanere calilā 25.201 409
pañca ātmārāma chaya ca-kāre lupta haya 24.149 162

pañca-bhūta yaiche bhūtera bhitare-bāhire 25.125 365
pāṅca chaya paisā haya eka eka bojhāte 25.204 410
pañcadaśe—bhaktera guṇa śrī-mukhe kahila 25.254 433
pañca-kāla pūjā ārati, kṛṣṇera bhojana- 24.334 279
pañcama-puruṣārtha—ei 'kṛṣṇa-prema'- 23.101 60

pañcame—sākṣi-gopāla-caritra-varṇana 25.247 430
pañca, ṣoḍaśa, pañcāśat upacāre arcana 24.334 279
pañca-tattvākhyāne tāhā kariyāchi vistāra 25.16 303
pañca-vidha rasa—śānta, dāsya, sakhya, 23.53 33
pañcaviṁśati paricchede ei kailuṅ anuvāda 25.262 436

pañcaviṁśe—kāśī-vāsīre vaiṣṇava-karaṇa 25.26 436
'paṇḍita' muni-gaṇa, nirgrantha 'mūrkha' āra 24.187 184
paṅgu nācāite yadi haya tomāra mana 23.122 77
papracchur ākāśavad antaraṁ bahir 25.130 368
parama kāraṇa īśvara keha nāhi māne 25.55 326

'paramānanda kīrtanīyā'—śekharera saṅgī 25.4 297
paramārtha-vicāra gela, kari mātra 'vāda' 25.43 320
paraṁ bhāvam ajānanto 25.39 318
pariniṣṭhito 'pi nairguṇye 24.47 104
pariniṣṭhito 'pi nairguṇye 25.157 385

paripūrṇatayā bhānti 23.77 49
pāriṣada, sādhana-siddha, sādhaka-gaṇa āra 24.287 245
paścād ahaṁ yad etac ca 24.76 120
paścad ahaṁ yad etac ca 25.113 357
paśyāmi viśva-sṛjam ekam aviśvam ātman 25.36 315

'pātañjala' kahe,—īśvara haya svarūpa-jñāna' 25.52 324
patha chāḍi' nārada tāra nikaṭe calila 24.236 213
pāṭhāñā bolāilā nija-bhakta-gaṇe 25.224 420
pathera pipīlikā iti-uti dhare pāya 24.270 234

pathe sei vipra saba vṛttānta kahila 25.61 330
pathe ye śūkara-mṛga, jāni tomāra haya" 24.240 215
pibata bhāgavataṁ rasam ālayam 25.151 382
pitāra śikṣāte āmi kari aiche kāma 24.242 216
pitṛ-mātṛ-sneha ādi 'anurāga'-anta 24.34 98

"prabhu ājñā dilā 'vaiṣṇava-smṛti' karibāre 24.324 264
prabhu kahe,—āmi 'jīva', ati tuccha-jñāna! 25.91 345
prabhu kahe,—"āmi vātula, āmāra vacane 24.7 84
prabhu kahe,—'ihāṅ haite yāha' vṛndāvana 25.198 406
prabhu kahe,—"kene kara āmāra stavana 24.317 260

prabhure kīrtana śunāya, ati baḍa raṅgī 25.4 297
prabhure prakāśānanda puchite lagila 25.87 343
prabhure praṇata haila sannyāsīra gaṇa 25.22 307
prabhu vṛndāvana haite prayāga yāilā 25.202 409
prabhu yabe snāne yāna viśveśvara 25.175 394

prakāśānanda āsi' tāṅra dharila caraṇa 25.71 334
prakāśānanda kahe,—"tumi sākṣāt 25.81 340
prakāśānandera prabhu vandilā caraṇa 25.71 334
prakāśānandera śiṣya eka tāṅhāra 25.23 307
prākṛta kṣobhe tāṅra kṣobha nāhi 23.20 12

prākṛta prapañca pāya āmātei laye 25.112 357
pralaye avaśiṣṭa āmi 'pūrṇa' ha-iye 25.112 357
praṇata-bhāra-viṭapā madhu-dhārāḥ 24.208 197
praṇavera yei artha, gāyatrīte sei haya 25.94 347
praṇaya-rasanayā dhṛtāṅghri-padmaḥ 25.128 367

'prapañca', 'prakṛti', 'puruṣa' āmātei 25.110 356
prapañca ye dekha saba, seha āmi ha-iye 25.111 356
'pra'-śabde—mokṣa-vāñchā kaitava 24.101 134
praśnottare bhāgavate kariyāche nirdhāra 24.319 261
prathama paricchede—śeṣa-līlāra 25.243 428

prabhu kahe,—"mahā-prasāda āna' ei sthāne 25.236 425
prabhu kahe,—'tumi jagad-guru pūjyatama 25.73 336
prabhu kahe,—'viṣṇu' 'viṣṇu', āmi kṣudra jīva 25.78 338
prabhu kahe,—"ye karite karibā tumi mana 24.328 266
prabhura lāga nā pāñā mane baḍa duḥkha 25.203 409

"prabhura svabhāva,—yebā dekhe 25.8 299
prabhura upadeśāmṛta śune yei jana 23.126 79
prabhure kahite sukhe karilā gamana 25.59 329
prathamei māribā, ardha-mārā nā karibā" 24.247 218

pratāpī kīrtimān rakta- 23.75 48
prati-śloke prati-akṣare nānā artha kaya 24.318 260
prati-vṛkṣe, prati-kuñje rahe rātri-dine 25.214 415

prauḍhānandaś camatkāra-	23.98	58
pravāsākhya, āra prema-vaicittya-ākhyāna	23.63	40
praviṣṭāny apraviṣṭāni	29.126	366
prayāga, ayodhyā diyā naimiṣāraṇye	25.201	409
prāyaścitta puchilā tiṅho paṇḍitera	25.195	405
prāyo amī muni-gaṇā bhavadīya-mukhyā	24.177	179
prāyo batāmba munayo vihagā vane 'smin	24.176	178
premādika sthāyi-bhāva sāmagrī-milane	23.47	27
premā krame bāḍi' haya—sneha, māna,	23.42	24
premāntaraṅga-bhūtāni	23.96	58
prema-rasa-kumuda-vane,	25.273	444
'prema-vaicittya' śrī-daśame mahiṣī-gaṇe	23.64	42
preme hāse, kāṅde, gāya, karaye nartana	25.165	390
preme matta kari' ākarṣaye kṛṣṇa-guṇa	24.58	110
premera lakṣaṇa ebe śuna, sanātana	23.6	4
pṛthak nānā artha pade kare jhalamala	24.20	85
pṛthak pṛthak artha pāche kariba milana	24.14	87
pṛthak pṛthak ca-kāre ihā 'api'ra artha	24.145	161
pulakāśru-nṛtya-gīta——yāhāra lakṣaṇa	25.139	374
punaḥ karilena yaiche nīlādri gamana	25.238	426
punaḥ nīlācale āilā, nāṭaśālā haite	25.255	433
punaḥ sanātana kahe yuḍi' dui kare	24.324	264
punarapi deśe vahi' laoyā nāhi yāya	25.169	392
punarapi kahe kichu vinaya kariyā	24.3	82
purāṇānāṁ sāma-rūpaḥ	25.144	377
puraścaraṇa-vidhi, kṛṣṇa-prasāda-bhojana	24.338	284
purī-bhāratīra prabhu vandilena caraṇa	25.227	421
pūrṇaiśvarya śrī-vigraha-sthitira	25.114	358
'pūrva' 'dakṣiṇa' 'paścima' karilā	25.171	393
pūrvavat mṛgādi-saṅge kailā	25.223	419
pūrve prayāge āmi rasera vicāre	23.102	61
'pūrve śuniyāchoṅ, tumi sārvabhauma-sthāne	24.4	83
pūrve yabe subuddhi-rāya chilā gauḍe	25.187	400

R

rādhikādye 'pūrva-rāga' prasiddha	23.64	42
rāga, anurāga, bhāva, mahābhāva haya	23.42	24
rāga-bhakti-viddhi-bhakti haya dui-rūpa	24.84	123
rāga-bhaktye vraje svayaṁ-bhagavāne	24.85	124
rāga-mārge aiche bhakte ṣoḍaśa vibheda	24.292	248
rājā kahe,——āmāra poṣṭā rāya haya	25.191	402
rājā kahe,——jāti nile iṅho nāhi jībe	25.192	402
'rāmaś ca kṛṣṇaś ca' yathā viharaye	24.222	206
rāmaś ca rāmaś ca rāmaś ca rāmā	24.151	
'rasālākhya' rasa haya apūrvāsvādane	23.49	28
'rati'-lakṣaṇā, 'prema'-lakṣaṇā, ityādi	24.31	96
rati-premādira taiche bāḍaye āsvāda	23.44	25
ratir ānanda-rūpaiva	23.97	58
rātre uṭhi' prabhu yadi karilā gamana	25.178	396
rodana-bindu-maranda-syandi-	23.33	19
ṛte 'rthaṁ yat pratīyeta	25.119	361
rucibhiś citta-māsṛṇya-	23.5	4
ruci haite bhaktye haya 'āsakti' pracura	23.12	7
ruciras tejasā yukto	23.70	45
ruddhā guhāḥ kim ajito 'vati nopasannān	23.114	70
'rūḍha', 'adhirūḍha' bhāva——kevala	23.57	36
'rūḍhi-vṛttye' nirviśeṣa antaryāmī	24.82	123
rūpa-anupama-kathā sakali kahilā	25.211	414
rūpa-gosāñi, āile tāṅre bahu prīti	25.207	412
rūpa-gosāñi dui-bhāi kāśīte āilā	25.216	416
rūpa-guṇa-śravaṇe rukmiṇy-ādira	24.51	106
rūpaṁ dṛśāṁ dṛśimatām akhilārtha	24.52	107

S

sabā āliṅgiyā prabhu premāviṣṭa hailā	25.230	422
saba chāḍi' śuddha-bhakti kare kṛṣṇa-pāya	24.188	185
saba kāśī-vāsī kare nāma-saṅkīrtana	25.165	390
sabā lañā cale prabhu jagannātha-daraśane	25.231	423
saba mili' 'rasa' haya camatkārakārī	23.52	32
saba phala deya bhakti svatantra prabala	24.92	128
sabāre vidāya dilā prabhu yatna-sahite	25.180	397
sabā-saṅge ihāṅ āji karimu bhojane"	25.236	425
sabā saṅge lañā prabhu miśra-vāsā āilā	25.235	425
sabā-saṅge mahāprabhu bhojana karila	25.237	425
saba tyaji' tabe tiṅho kṛṣṇere bhajaya	24.310	256
sabe cāhe prabhu-saṅge nīlācala yāite	25.180	397
sabe dui-janāra yogya bhakṣya-mātra cāi"	24.280	241
sabe ei jāni' ācāryera kalpita vyākhyāna	25.88	344
sabei paḍilā tathā mūrcchita hañā	25.184	399
sabe kahe,—loka tārite tomāra avatāra	25.171	393
sabhā-madhye kahe prabhura kariyā	25.23	307
sabhāte kahila sei śloka-vivaraṇa	25.160	387
sac-cid-ānanda-sāndrāṅgaḥ	23.79	51
sac-cid-rūpa-guṇa sarva pūrṇānanda	24.41	101
sadā svarūpa-samprāptaḥ	23.79	51
sad-dharmasyāvabodhāya	24.170	174

sādhaka, brahmamaya, āra prāpta-brahma-	24.108	138
sādhakānām ayaṁ premṇaḥ	23.15	9
sādhana-bhakti—ei cāri vicārera pāra	25.121	362
sādhana-bhaktye haya 'sarvānartha-nivartana'	23.10	6
sādhana-siddha—dāsa, sakhā, guru, kāntā-	24.290	247
sādhanaughair anāsaṅgair	24.172	175
sādhanera phala—'prema' mūla-prayojana	25.104	353
sādhu-guru-prasāde,	25.277	447
sādhu-lakṣaṇa, sādhu-saṅga, sādhu-sevana	24.339	284
sādhu-saṅga haite haya 'śravaṇa-kīrtana'	23.10	6
sādhu-saṅga-kṛpā kimvā kṛṣṇera kṛpāya	24.97	131
sādhu-saṅga, kṛṣṇa-kṛpā, bhaktira svabhāva	24.104	136
sādhu-saṅge seha bhaje śrī-kṛṣṇa-caraṇe	24.165	171
sādhu-saṅge seha kare śrī-kṛṣṇa-bhajana	24.227	209
sādhu-saṅge tapa chāḍi' śrī-kṛṣṇa bhajaya	24.216	203
sadyaḥ kṣiṇoty anvaham edhatī satī	24.217	203
sa eva dhairyam āpnoti	24.184	183
sagarbha, nigarbha,—ei haya dui bheda	24.155	165
sahaje āmāra kichu artha nāhi bhāse	24.9	85
sakāma-bhakta 'ajña' jāni' dayālu bhagavān	24.102	135
sakāraṇa likhi ādau guru-āśrayaṇa	24.329	267
sakhā-gaṇera rati haya 'anurāga' paryanta	24.33	97
'sakhā' 'guru', 'kāntā gaṇa'—cāri-	24.289	246
sakhya-vātsalya-rati pāya 'anurāga'-sīmā	23.55	34
sakhya-vātsalye yogādira aneka vibheda	23.56	35
"sākṣāt īśvara tumi vrajendra-nandana	24.315	259
śakti, kampa, paripāṭī, yukti, śaktye	24.20	90
samaḥ sarveṣu bhūteṣu	24.132	153
samaḥ sarveṣu bhūteṣu	25.155	384
samaḥ śatrau ca mitre ca	23.111	68
sāmānya-buddhi-yukta yata jīva avaśeṣa	24.186	184
'sāmānya' sad-ācāra, āra 'vaiṣṇava'-ācāra	24.344	287
samatvenaiva vīkṣeta	25.80	340
sambandha-abhidheya-prayojana-maya	25.131	369
'sambhoga'-'vipralambha'-bhede dvividha	23.62	39
sambhoge 'mādana', virahe 'mohana' nāma	23.58	37
sambhogera ananta aṅga, nāhi anta tāra	23.62	39
samudrā iva pañcāśad	23.76	48
samutkaṇṭhā haya sadā lālasā-pradhāna	23.30	18
samyaṅ masṛṇita-svānto	23.7	5
sanakādira mana harila saurabhādi guṇe	24.44	102
sanakādyera kṛṣṇa-kṛpāya saurabhe hare	24.114	142
sanātana-gosāñi vṛndāvanere calilā	25.185	399
sanātanaṁ susaṁskṛtya	25.1	295
sanātana-rūpera ei caritra kahila	25.221	418
sanātane kahilā,—"tumi yāha' vṛndāvana	25.182	398
sanātane prabhura prasāda rākhiyāche likhiyā	24.347	288
saṅgīta-prasarābhijñā	23.88	55
śaṅkha-jala-gandha-puṣpa-dhūpādi-lakṣaṇa	24.337	283
'sāṅkhya' kahe,—'jagatera prakṛti kāraṇa-	25.50	323
saṅkīrṇa-sthāne prabhura nā pāya daraśana	25.174	394
saṅkṣepa-rūpe kaha tumi śunite haya mati	25.90	345
saṅkṣepe kahiluṅ ei madhya-līlāra sāra	25.263	437
saṅkṣepe kahiluṅ ei 'prayojana'-vivaraṇa	23.101	60
saṅkṣepe kahiluṅ—'prema'-prayojana-	23.125	79
sannyāsī paṇḍita kare bhāgavata vicāra	25.166	390
sannyāsīra gaṇa dekhi' nṛtya saṁvarila	25.70	334
sannyāsīra gaṇa prabhure yadi upekṣila	25.5	298
sannyāsīra mana phirāite mana ha-ila	25.13	302
sannyāsīre kṛpā pūrve likhiyāchoṅ vistāriyā	25.6	298
sannyāsīre kṛpā śuni' pāilā baḍa sukhe	25.219	417
śānta-ādi rasera 'yoga', 'viyoga'—dui bheda	23.56	35
'śānta' bhakta kari' tabe kahi tāṅra nāma	24.164	170
śānta-bhaktera rati bāḍe 'prema'-paryanta	24.32	97
śānta, dāsya, sakhya, vātsalya, madhura āra	23.45	25
śānta-rase śānti-rati 'prema' paryanta haya	23.54	33
santuṣṭaḥ satataṁ yogī	23.107	65
saptadaśe—vanapathe mathurā-gamana	25.256	434
saptame—tīrtha-yātrā, vāsudeva nistāra	25.248	430
sa rahasyaṁ tad-aṅgaṁ ca	25.105	353
sāraṁ sāraṁ samuddhṛtam	25.145	378
sarasi sārasa-haṁsa-vihaṅgāś	24.178	179
śarkarā, sitā-michari, śuddha-michari āra	22.43	24
"sarūpāṇām eka-śeṣa eka-vibhaktau"	24.151	163
sarūpāṇām eka-śeṣa eka-vibhaktau,	24.297	250
sarva amaṅgala hare, prema diyā hare mana	24.59	111
sārvabhauma-ghare bhikṣā, amogha tārila	25.254	433
sārvabhauma, paṇḍita-gosāñi nimantraṇa	25.235	425
sārvabhauma, rāmānanda, vāṇīnātha milila	25.234	424
sārvabhauma vātula tāhā satya kari' māne	24.7	84
sarva-bhūteṣu yaḥ paśyed	25.129	368
sarvādbhuta-camatkāra-	23.82	52
sarva-deśa-kāla-daśāya janera kartavya	25.122	364
sarva-jana-deśa-kāla-daśāte vyāpti yāra	25.120	361
sarva-kāla duḥkha pāba, ihā nā karile"	25.10	301
sarvākarṣaka, sarvāhlādaka, mahā-rasāyana	24.38	100

sarva-lakṣmīmayī sarva-	23.68	44
sarva-loka hāse, gāya, karaye nartana	25.21	306
sarva-nāśa haya mora tomāra nindāte	25.82	340
sarvārambha-parityāgī	23.109	67
sarva-samuccaye āra eka artha haya	24.303	252
sarva-saṅkalpa-sannyāsī	24.160	168
sarva-śāstra khaṇḍi' prabhu 'bhakti' kare sāra	25.20	305
sarva-śāstra-siddhāntera ihāṅ pāibā pāra	25.270	441
sarvathaiva durūho 'yam	23.100	60
sarvatra pramāṇa dibe purāṇa-vacana	24.343	286
sarva-vedānta-sāraṁ hi	25.146	378
sarva-vedetihāsānāṁ	25.145	378
sarva-vyāpaka, sarva-sākṣī, parama-svarūpa	24.77	120
'sarvottama' āpanāke 'hīna' kari māne	23.26	16
ṣaṣṭhe—sārvabhaumera karilā uddhāra	25.248	430
śāstra chāḍi' kukalpanā pāṣaṇḍe bujhāya	25.42	319
śāstra-yukti nāhi ihāṅ siddhānta-vicāra	24.40	100
śāstrera sahaja artha nahe tāṅhā haite	25.49	323
satāṁ prasaṅgān mama vīrya-saṁvido	23.16	10
śaṭhena kenāpi vayaṁ haṭhena	24.133	154
ṣāṭi artha kahiluṅ, saba—kṛṣṇera bhajane	24.311	256
sat-saṅga, kṛṣṇa-sevā, bhāgavata, nāma	24.193	188
sat-saṅgamākhyena sukhāvahena	24.125	149
sat-saṅgān mukta-duḥsaṅgo	24.98	131
sat-saṅge 'karma' tyaji' karaya bhajana	24.214	201
sat-saṅge seha kare kṛṣṇera bhajana	24.212	200
satyaṁ diśaty arthitam arthito nṛṇāṁ	24.103	135
satyaṁ diśaty arthitam arthito nṛṇāṁ	24.199	191
"satyaṁ paraṁ"—sambandha, "dhīmahi"	25.147	379
sa vai bhagavataḥ śrīmat-	25.77	337
sayuktika vākye mana phirāya sabāra	25.20	305
se caitanya-līlā haya,	25.271	442
se divasa haite grāme kolāhala haila	25.18	304
sei advaya-tattva kṛṣṇa—svayaṁ-bhagavān	24.75	119
sei anna labe, yata khāo dui-jane"	24.262	230
sei artha catuḥ-ślokīte vivariyā kaya	25.94	347
sei artha haya ei saba udāharaṇe	24.311	256
sei ātmārāma yogīra dui bheda haya	24.154	165
sei 'bhāva' gāḍha haila dhare 'prema'-nāma	23.13	8
sei brahma-śabde kahe svayaṁ-bhagavān	24.73	118
sei buddhi dena tāṅre, yāte kṛṣṇa pāya	24.191	187
sei dui śreṣṭha,—rādhā, vrajendra-nandana	23.92	56
sei jala strī-puruṣe piyā śire la-ila	24.275	237
sei kṛṣṇa-prāpti-hetu trividha 'sādhana'	24.79	121
sei premā—'prayojana' sarvānanda-dhāma	23.13	8
sei preme pāya jīva āmāra 'sevana'	25.104	353
sei saba sūtra lañā 'vedānta'-varṇana	25.53	325
sei sabera sādhu-saṅge guṇa sphurāya	24.124	148
sei sarovare giyā,	25.275	446
sei satya sukhadārtha parama pramāṇa	25.29	310
sei upāsaka haya trividha prakāra	24.89	126
śekhara, paramānanda, tapana, sanātana	25.63	331
śekharera ghare vāsā, miśra-ghare bhikṣā	25.218	417
śeṣa aṣṭādaśa vatsara nīlācale vāsa	25.241	427
śeṣe saba lopa kari' rākhi eka-bāra	24.296	249
sevya—bhagavān, sarva-mantra-vicāraṇa	24.330	267
siddhānta śikhāilā,—yei brahmāra agocara	23.120	76
siddhi—aṣṭādaśa, mukti—pañca-vidhākāra	24.28	95
śīghra cali' āilā sanātanānusandhāne	25.208	412
śikhāilā tāṅre bhakti-siddhāntera anta	25.3	297
śiṣya-gaṇa-saṅge sei bale 'hari' 'hari'	25.67	333
śītoṣṇa-sukha-duḥkheṣu	23.111	68
śloka-vyākhyā lāgi' ei kariluṅ ābhāsa	24.106	138
smarantaḥ smārayaś ca	25.140	373
ṣoḍaśe—vṛndāvana-yātrā gauḍa-deśa-pathe	25.255	433
śraddadhānā mat-paramā	23.113	69
śraddhā kari' ei līlā śuna, bhakta-gaṇa	25.269	441
śravaṇādyera phala 'premā' karaye prakāśa	24.62	113
śreṣṭha hañā kene kara hīnera vandana	25.72	335
śreyaḥ-sṛtiṁ bhaktim udasya te vibho	24.140	158
śreyaḥ-sṛtiṁ bhaktim udasya te vibho	25.31	311
śrī-aṅga-rūpe hare gopīkāra mana	24.49	105
śrī-bhāgavata-raktānāṁ	23.95	58
śrī-bhāgavata-tattva-rasa karilā pracāre	25.266	439
śrī-caitanya, nityānanda,	25.280	449
śrī caitanya-nityānanda-advaita-caraṇa	24.354	292
śrī-caitanya-sama āra kṛpālu vadānya	25.268	440
śrī-kṛṣṇa-caitanya haya 'sākṣāt nārāyaṇa'	25.24	308
śrī-kṛṣṇa-caitanya-vākya dṛḍha satya māni	25.28	309
śrī-kṛṣṇa-caitanya-vāṇī—amṛtera dhāra	25.58	329
śrīmad-bhāgavate mahāmuni-kṛte kiṁ	24.100	133
śrīmad-bhāgavate mahāmuni-kṛte kiṁ	25.149	381
śrīman-madana-gopāla-	25.282	450
śrī-mūrti-lakṣaṇa, āra śālagrāma-lakṣaṇa	24.335	281
śrī-mūrti-viṣṇu-mandira karaṇa-lakṣaṇa	24.343	286
śrī-rāma-navamī, āra nṛsiṁha-caturdaśī	24.341	285
śrī-rūpa-raghunātha-pade yāra āśa	23.127	80
śrī-rūpa-raghunātha-pade yāra āśa	24.355	293

śrī-rūpa-sanātana- 25.281 450
sṛṣṭi kari' tāra madhye āmi praveśiye 25.111 356
sṛṣṭira pūrve ṣaḍ-aiśvarya-pūrṇa āmi 25.110 356
śruti-purāṇa kahe—kṛṣṇera cic-chakti- 25.34 313
śrutvā guṇān bhuvana-sundara śṛṇvatāṁ 24.52 107

stambhādi—'sāttvika' anubhāvera bhitara 23.51 29
sthānābhilāṣī tapasi sthito 'haṁ 24.219 204
sthāyi-bhāva 'rasa' haya ei cāri mili' 23.48 28
sthiro dāntaḥ kṣamā-śīlo 23.73 47
sthūle 'dui' artha, sūkṣme 'batriśa' prakāra 24.284 243

strī kahe,—jāti laha', yadi prāṇe nā māribe 25.192 402
strī marite cāhe, rājā saṅkaṭe paḍila 25.193 403
stuti kare mahāprabhura caraṇe dhariyā 24.314 258
subalādyera 'bhāva' paryanta premera 23.55 34
śubhāśubha-parityāgī 23.110 68
subuddhi janera haya kṛṣṇa-premodaya 24.194 188

subuddhi-rāya bahu sneha kare sanātane 25.213 415
subuddhi-rāyere mārite kahe rājā-sthāne 25.190 401
subuddhi-rāyere tiṅho bahu bāḍāila 25.189 401
śuddha-sattva-viśeṣātmā 23.5 4
sudurlabhaḥ praśāntātmā 25.83 341

śukadevera mana harila līlā-śravaṇe 24.46 103
sukhāni goṣpadāyante 24.37 99
sukhe cali' āise prabhu balabhadra-saṅge 25.223 419
sukhī bhakta-suhṛt prema- 23.74 47
sukhī haila loka-mukhe kīrtana śuniyā 25.220 418

śuni' duḥkhe mahārāṣṭrīya vipra karaye 25.7 298
śuni' grāmī deśī loka āsite lāgila 25.173 394
śuni' mahāprabhu sukhe īṣat hāsila 25.61 330
śuni' prakāśānanda kichu kahena vacana 25.46 321
śuni' veda-vyāsa mane vicāra karilā 25.96 348

śuniyā bhaktera gaṇa yena punarapi jīlā 25.225 420
śuniyā lokera baḍa camatkāra haila 25.163 389
śuniyā paṇḍita-lokera juḍāya mana-kāṇa 25.25 308
śuniyā rahilā rāya kariyā saṁśaya 25.196 405
sūrya vinā svatantra tāra nā haya prakāśa 25.117 359
śuṣka-jñāne jīvan-mukta aparādhe adho 24.130 152

śuṣka-kāṣṭha āni' rāya vece mathurāte 25.204 410
śuṣka-vairāgya-jñāna saba niṣedhila 23.105 63
sustha hañā mṛgādi tine dhāñā palāila 24.263 231
sūtra kari' diśā yadi karaha upadeśa 24.326 265
sūtra-upaniṣadera mukhyārtha chāḍiyā 25.26 309
sūtrera karilā tumi mukhyārtha-vivaraṇa 25.89 344
sūtrera pariṇāma-vāda, tāhā nā māniyā 25.41 319

suvilāsā mahābhāva- 23.90 55
sva-caraṇa diyā kare icchāra pidhāna 24.102 135
svāṁ kāṣṭhām adhunopete 24.320 261
"svaritañitaḥ kartrabhiprāye kriyā-phale" 24.26 94
svarūpa aiśvarya kari' nāhi yāṅra sama 24.71 117

'svarūpa' anubhavi' tāṅre 'īśvara' kari' māne 25.8 299
svarūpa kahilā, prabhu kailā āsvādana 25.253 433
svasukha-nibhṛta-cetās tad-vyudastānya- 24.48 104
sva-sva-mata sthāpe para-matera khaṇḍane 25.55 326
'svayaṁ-bhagavattve', bhagavattve—prakāśa 24.84 123

svayaṁ vidhatte bhajatām anicchatām 24.103 135
svayaṁ vidhatte bhajatām anicchatām 24.199 191
śyāma-varṇa rakta-netra mahā-bhayaṅkara 24.235 213

T

tabe dui ṛṣi āilā sei vyādha-sthāne 24.269 234
tabe duṅhe jagannātha-prasāda ānila 25.237 425
tabe kare bhakti-bādhaka karma, avidyā 24.62 113
tabe mahāprabhu tāṅra nimantraṇa mānilā 25.15 303
tabe mahāprabhu tāṅra śire dhari' kare 23.124 78

tabe saba loka śunite āgraha karila 25.162 388
tabe sanātana prabhura caraṇe dhariyā 23.119 76
tabe sanātana prabhura caraṇe dhariyā 24.3 82
tabe sanātana saba siddhānta puchilā 23.115 71
tabe sei jīva 'sādhu-saṅga' ye karaya 23.9 6

tabe sei mṛgādi tine nārada sustha kaila 24.263 231
tabe sei vipra āila mahāprabhura sthāne 25.11 301
tabe sei vyādha doṅhāre aṅgane ānila 24.274 237
tabe se karite pāri tomāra mocana' 24.255 225
tabe subuddhi-rāya sei 'chadma' pāñā 25.194 404

tabe sūtrera mūla artha lokera haya jñāna 25.93 347
tabe ta' ānanda mora bāḍaye antare" 24.243 216
tabe tāra diśā sphure mo-nīcera hṛdaya 24.327 266
tabe yadi mahāprabhu vārāṇasī āilā 25.197 406
tabe ye ca-kāra, sei 'samuccaya' kaya 24.152 164

tabu pūjya hao, tumi baḍa āmā haite 25.82 340
tabu yadi kara tāṅra 'dāsa'-abhimāna 25.81 340
tad idam ati-rahasyaṁ gaura-līlāmṛtaṁ yat 25.283 451
tad-rasāmṛta-tṛptasya 25.146 378
tad vā idaṁ bhuvana-maṅgala maṅgalāya 25.38 317

tad vidyād ātmano māyāṁ 25.119 361
tāhā nāhi māni, paṇḍita kare upahāsa 25.34 313
tāhā nistāriyā kailā āmā-sabāra sukha 25.172 393

tāhāṅ yaiche kailā prabhu sannyāsīra	25.16	303
tāhāṅ ye nā likhiluṅ, tāhā kariye	25.17	304
tāhāre mārimu āmi, bhāla nahe kathā	25.191	402
tāhā śuni' dui-bhāi se pathe calilā	25.209	413
tāhā śuni' sabāra haila camatkāra mana	25.89	344
taiche saba ātmārāma kṛṣṇe bhakti karaya	24.300	251
taiche viddha bhagna-pāda kare dhaḍ-phaḍa	24.232	211
taj-joṣaṇād āśv apavarga-vartmani	23.16	10
tal labhyate duḥkhavad anyataḥ sukhaṁ	24.169	174
taṁ mopayātaṁ pratiyantu viprā	23.21	13
taṁ sanātanam upāgatam akṣṇor	24.349	290
tān ahaṁ dviṣataḥ krūrān	25.40	318
tāṅhāte eteka cihna sarva-śāstre kaya	23.17	11
tan-māyayāto budha ābhajet taṁ	24.137	156
tan-māyayāto budha ābhajet taṁ	25.138	374
tāṅrā kahe,—tapta-ghṛta khāñā chāḍa'	25.195	405
tāṅra sūtrera artha kona jīva nāhi jāne	25.92	346
tāṅra vākya, kriyā, mudrā vijñeha nā	23.39	22
tāṅra vākya śuni' mane bhaya upajila	24.25	222
tāṅre mili' rāya āpana-vṛttānta kahilā	25.197	406
tāṅre 'nirviśeṣa' sthāpi, 'pūrṇatā' haya	25.33	312
tāṅte rame yei, sei saba—'ātmārāma'	24.286	244
tapana miśra, raghunātha, mahārāṣṭrīya	25.199	396
'tapasvī' prabhṛti yata dehārāmī haya	24.216	203
tapasvī, vratī, yati, āra ṛṣi, muni	24.15	88
tāra āge eka-piṇḍi tulasī ropiyā	24.260	228
tāra artha lañā vyāsa karilā sañcaya	25.98	349
tāra madhye bhagavānera svarūpa-varṇana	25.258	435
tāra madhye śrī-rūpere śakti-sañcāraṇa	25.257	434
tāra madhye vraja-devīra bhāvera śravaṇa	25.253	433
tāra strī tāra aṅge dekhe māraṇera cihne	25.190	401
tārā taiche tomā māribe janma-janmāntare'	24.251	221
tāre tiraskaribāre karilā nirdhāraṇe	25.115	358
tāre uṭhāñā nārada upadeśa kaila	24.258	227
tarko 'pratiṣṭhaḥ śrutayo vibhinnā	25.57	328
tasmai namas te sarvātman	24.72	117
tasmai namo bhagavate 'nuvidhema tubhyaṁ	25.38	317
tasyaiva hetoḥ prayateta kovido	24.169	173
tasyāravinda-nayanasya padāravinda-	24.45	103
tasyāravinda-nayanasya padāravinda-	24.115	143
tasyāravinda-nayanasya padāravinda-	25.158	386
tata udagād ananta tava dhāma śiraḥ	24.166	171
tata udagād ananta tava dhāma śiraḥ	24.213	200
tāte chaya darśana haite 'tattva' nāhi jāni	25.56	326
tāte phale amṛta-phala,	25.276	446
tāte sūtrārtha vyākhyā kare anya rīte	25.47	322
tāte veda-śāstra haite parama mahattva	25.150	381
tathaiva tattva-vijñānam	25.109	355
tathā mad-viṣayā bhaktir	24.61	112
tathāpi ca-kārera kahe mukhya artha sāta	24.66	115
tathāpi ei sūtrera śuna dig-daraśana	24.329	267
tathā yukta-padārtheṣu	24.69	116
tathi lāgi' kari tomāra caraṇe praṇati'	25.86	343
tathi-madhye kona bhāgera vistāra varṇana	25.243	428
tathi-madhye nānā-bhāvera dig-daraśana	25.244	429
tat kiṁ karomi viralaṁ muralī-vilāsi	23.31	18
tato 'nartha-nivṛttiḥ syāt	23.14	9
tat pādāmbuja-sarvasvair	23.100	60
tat-tat-kāmādi chāḍi' haya śuddha-	24.96	131
tava madhura-svara-kaṇṭhī	23.33	19
tejo-vāri-mṛdāṁ yathā vinimayo yatra	25.148	380
tena tyaktena bhuñjīthā	25.101	351
teṅho kahe, 'tomāra pūrve nindā-aparādha	25.75	336
teṣām asau kleśala eva śiṣyate	24.140	158
teṣām asau kleśala eva śiṣyate	25.31	311
teṣāṁ satata-yuktānāṁ	24.173	176
teṣāṁ satata-yuktānāṁ	24.192	187
te vai vidanty atitaranti ca deva-māyāṁ	24.190	186
tina-jana saha rūpa karilā milana	25.217	416
tina-kāle satya tiṅho—śāstra-pramāṇa	24.75	119
tina sādhane bhagavān tina svarūpe bhāse	24.80	122
tiṅho ye kahaye vastu, sei 'tattva'—sāra"	25.58	329
tīvreṇa bhakti-yogena	24.90	127
tīvreṇa bhakti-yogena	24.197	190
tomā dekhi' mora lakṣya mṛga	24.238	214
tomāra bhāi rūpe kailuṅ śakti-sañcāre	23.102	61
tomāra bhakti-vaśe uṭhe arthera taraṅge	24.312	257
tomāra caraṇa-sparśe, saba kṣaya gela	25.75	336
tomāra dui bhāi tathā kariyāche gamana	25.182	398
tomāra niśvāse sarva-veda-pravartana	24.315	259
tomāra saṅga-bale yadi kichu haya mane	24.8	85
tomā-sabāra icchāya vinā-mūlye bilāila	25.170	392
tomā-sabāra pada-dhūli, aṅge vibhūṣaṇa	25.272	444
tomā-sabāra saṅga-bale ye kichu prakāśe	24.9	85
tomā-sabāra śrī-caraṇa,	25.280	449
tomā vinā anya jānite nāhika samartha"	24.316	259
trailokya-saubhagam idaṁ ca nirīkṣya	24.56	109
trayodaśe—ratha-āge prabhura nartana	25.252	432

trayoviṁśe—prema-bhakti-rasera kathana	25.260	436
trijagan-mānasākarṣi-	23.83	52
triveṇī-snāne prayāga karilā gamana	24.230	210
tṛtīya paricchede—prabhura kahiluṅ sannyāsa	25.245	429
tulasī paḍichā āsi' caraṇa vandilā	25.133	424
tulasī-parikramā kara, tulasī-sevana	24.261	229
tulya-nindā-stutir maunī	23.113	68
tumiha kariha bhakti-śāstrera pracāra	23.103	61
tumi ta' īśvara, tomāra āche sarva-śakti	25.90	345
tumi—vaktā bhāgavatera, tumi jāna artha	24.316	259
tumi ke kahilā, ei siddhāntāmṛta-sindhu	23.121	77
tvac-chaiśavaṁ tri bhuvanādbhutam ity avehi	23.31	18
tvat-sākṣāt-karaṇāhlāda-	24.37	99

U

udāra mahatī yāṅra sarvottamā buddhi	24.196	189
udaram upāsate ya ṛṣi-vartmasu kūrpa-	24.166	171
udaram upāsate ya ṛṣi-vartmasu kūrpa-	24.213	200
udbāṣpaḥ puṇḍarīkākṣa	23.37	21
uddeśe kahiye ihāṅ saṅkṣepa kariyā	25.6	298
'udghūrṇā', 'citra-jalpa'—'mohane' dui	23.59	37
udghūrṇā, vivaśa-ceṣṭā—divyonmāda-nāma	23.61	38
uktārthānām aprayogaḥ	24.151	163
uktārthānām aprayoga iti	24.297	250
ūnaviṁśati artha ha-ila mili' ei dui	24.210	198
ūnaviṁśe—mathurā haite prayāga-gamana	25.257	434
upadeśa lañā kare kṛṣṇa-saṅkīrtana	25.21	306
upaniṣadera karena mukhyāratha vyākhyāna	25.25	308
ūrdhva bāhu nṛtya kare vastra uḍāñā	24.276	238
urukrama'-śabde kahe, baḍa yāṅra krama	24.19	90
'urukrama'-śabdera ei artha nirūpaṇa	24.13	92
urukrame ahaitukī kāhāṅ kona artha	24.163	170
"urukrame eva bhaktim eva ahaitukīm	24.305	253
uṭhila maṅgala-dhvani svarga-martya bhari'	25.65	332
uttuṅgaṁ yadu-pura-saṅgamāya raṅgaṁ	24.120	146

V

vadanti tat tattva-vidas	24.74	118
vadanti tat tattva-vidas	24.81	122
vadanti tat tattva-vidas	25.132	370
vadānyo dhārmikaḥ śūraḥ	23.73	47
vāgbhiḥ stuvanto manasā smarantas	23.23	14
vaiṣṇava-lakṣaṇa, sevāparādha-	24.336	282
vaiṣṇavī-kṛtya sannyāsi-	25.1	295
vaṁśī-gīte hare kṛṣṇa lakṣmy-ādira mana	24.53	108
vaṁśī-svarādi—'uddīpana, kṛṣṇādi—	23.50	29
vana-latās tarava ātmani viṣṇuṁ	24.208	197
vana-patha dekhe mṛga āche bhūme paḍi'	24.231	211
vara deha' mora māthe dhariyā caraṇa	23.122	77
vara dilā—'ei saba sphuruka tomāre'	23.124	78
vārāṇasī āilā, saba viṣaya chāḍiyā	25.194	404
vārāṇasī-grāme yadi kolāhala haila	25.173	394
vārāṇasī haila dvitīya nadīyā-nagara	25.167	390
vārāṇasī-pura prabhu karilā nistāra	25.166	390
vārāṇasī-vāsa āmāra haya sarva-kāle	25.10	301
varīyān īśvaraś ceti	23.76	48
vastra-pīṭha-gṛha-saṁskāra, kṛṣṇa-	24.333	278
vastre sthāna jhāḍi' paḍe daṇḍavat hañā	24.271	235
vātsalye mātā pitā āśrayālambana	23.93	57
vātulera pralāpa kari' ke kare pramāṇa?	24.322	262
vāvadūkaḥ supāṇḍityo	23.71	46
vayam iva sakhi kaccid gāḍha-nirviddha-cetā	23.65	42
vayaṁ tu na vitṛpyāma	25.152	383
veda-mate kahe tāṅre 'svayaṁ-bhagavān'	25.52	324
'vedānta'-mate,—brahma 'sākāra' nirūpaṇa	25.54	325
vibhāva, anubhāva, sāttvika, vyabhicārī	23.48	28
vibhu-rūpe vyāpe, śaktye dhāraṇa-poṣaṇa	24.22	91
vicāra kariyā yabe bhaje kṛṣṇa-pāya	24.191	187
vidagdhaś caturo dakṣaḥ	23.72	46
'vidhi-bhakta', 'rāga-bhakta',—dui-vidha	24.286	244
vidhi-bhaktye nitya-siddha pāriṣada—'dāsa'	24.289	246
vidhi-bhaktye pārṣada-dehe vaikuṇṭhete	24.87	125
vidhi-mārge bhakte ṣoḍaśa bheda pracāra	24.291	247
vidhi-niṣedha-veda-śāstra-jñānādi-vihīna	24.16	88
vidhi-rāga-mārge cāri cāri—aṣṭa bheda	24.288	245
vidhi-rāga-mārge 'sādhana bhakti'-ra vidhāna	24.352	291
vidhi-śiva-nārada-mukhe kṛṣṇa-guṇa śuni'	24.188	145
vīkṣyālakāvṛta-mukhaṁ tava kuṇḍala-śrī-	24.50	106
viṁśati paricchede—sanātanera milana	25.258	435
vinācyutād vastu-tarāṁ na vācyaṁ	25.37	316
vinītā karuṇā-pūrṇā	23.89	55
'vipralambha' catur-vidha—pūrva-rāga,	23.63	40
virahe kṛṣṇa-sphūrti, āpanāke 'kṛṣṇa'-	23.61	38
viṣṇor nu vīrya-gaṇanāṁ katamo 'rhatīha	24.21	91
viṣṇu-śaktiḥ parā proktā	24.308	254
viṣṇu-śaktiḥ parā proktā	24.308	254
visṛjati hṛdayaṁ na yasya sākṣād	25.128	367
vistāri' kahana nā yāya prabhura prasāda	23.125	79

'vivarta-vāda' sthāpe, 'vyāsa bhrānta' 25.41 319
vividhādbhuta-bhāṣā-vit 23.71 46
vrajendra-nandana kṛṣṇa—nāyaka-śiromaṇi 23.66 43
vraje vāsa,—ei pañca sādhana pradhāna 24.193 188
vṛkṣāś ca āmra-vṛkṣāś ca vṛkṣāḥ 24.299 251

vṛndāvane āila tāṅdera kariha pālana 25.183 398
vṛndāvane kṛṣṇa-sevā, vaiṣṇava-ācāra 23.104 62
vyādha hañā haya pūjya bhāgavatottama 24.228 209
vyādha kahe,—"bālya haite ei āmāra karma 24.253 223
vyādha kahe,—'dhanuka bhāṅgile 24.257 226

vyādya kahe,—"kibā dāna māgilā āmāre 24.248 218
vyādha kahe,—"mṛgādi laha, yei tomāra 24.244 216
vyādha kahe,—"śuna, gosāñi, 'mṛgāri' 24.242 216
vyādha kahe, "yāre pāṭhāo, sei diyā yāya 24.279 240
vyādha kahe,—'yei kaha, sei ta' kariba' 24.256 226

vyādha kahe,—"yei kaha, sei ta' niścaya" 24.240 215
vyādha tumi, jīva māra—'alpa' aparādha 24.250 220
vyākhyā śikhāila yaiche susiddhānta 23.118 74
vyāsa-kṛpāya śukadevera līlādi-smaraṇa 24.116 144
vyāsa-śuka-sanakādira prasiddha bhajana 24.204 194

vyāsa-sūtrera artha ācārya kariyāche 25.44 321
'vyāsa-sūtrera' artha karena ati-manorama 25.24 308
vyāsa-sūtrera gambhīra artha, vyāsa— 25.91 345
vyatanuta kṛpayā yas tattva-dīpaṁ purāṇaṁ 24.48 104
vyavahāra-sneha sanātana nāhi māne 25.213 415

Y

yabe tumi likhibā, kṛṣṇa karābe sphuraṇa 24.345 287
yac ca vrajanty animiṣām ṛṣabhānuvṛttyā 24.88 125
yac chṛṇvatāṁ rasa-jñānāṁ 25.152 383
yadā hi nendriyārtheṣu 24.160 168
yad-vāñchayā śrīr lalanācarat tapo 24.54 108

yady acintya-mahā-śaktau 25.76 337
yady adbhuta-krama-parāyaṇa-śīla- 24.190 186
yadyapi tomāre saba brahma-sama bhāse 25.74 336
ya eṣāṁ puruṣaṁ sākṣād 24.142 159
yāhā haite haya sat-saṅga-mahimāra 24.229 210

yāhā haite vaśa haya śrī-kṛṣṇa kautukī 24.29 95
yāhāṅ netra paḍe tāhāṅ dekhaya āmāre 25.127 366
yāhāṅ tāhāṅ prabhura nindā kare sanyāsīra 25.7 298
yāhāṅ yei lāge, tāhā kariye samartha 24.293 248
yāhāṅ yei yukta, sei arthera adhīna 24.147 162
yāhāra śravaṇe cittera khaṇḍe avasāda 24.346 288

yāhāra śravaṇe cittera khaṇḍe avasāda 24.351 291
yāhāra śravaṇe haya bhakti-rasa-jñāna 13.3 3
yāhāra śravaṇe haya granthārtha-āsvāda 25.262 436
yaiche āmāra guṇa, karma ṣaḍ-aiśvarya-śakti 15.107 354
yaiche āmāra 'svarūpa', yaiche āmāra 25.107 354

yaiche rasa haya, śuna tāhāra lakṣaṇa 23.94 57
yaiche sūryera sthāne bhāsaye 'ābhāsa' 25.117 359
yaiche taiche yohi kohi karaye smaraṇa 24.60 111
yāṅhāra hṛdaye ei bhāvāṅkura haya 23.17 11
yāṅhāra śravaṇe loke lāge camatkāra 24.319 261

yāṅra āge brahmānanda tṛṇa-prāya haya 24.36 98
yāṅra citte kṛṣṇa-premā karaye udaya 13.39 22
"yāṅra icchā, pāche āisa āmāre dekhite 25.181 397
yāṅra prāṇa-dhana, sei pāya ei dhana 24.354 292
yāra eka-bindu-pāne, 25.278 448

yasmān nodvijate loko 23.108 66
yas tu nārāyaṇaṁ devaṁ 25.80 340
yā śunile haya sādhu-saṅga-prabhāva-jñāna 24.282 242
yathā-sthāne nārada gelā, vyādha ghare āila 24.265 232
yathāgniḥ susamṛddhārciḥ 24.61 112

yathā mahānti bhūtāni 25.126 366
yatnāgraha vinā bhakti nā janmāya preme 24.171 175
yatnāntare tathā pāde- 24.67 115
yat-pāda-sevābhirucis tapasvinām 24.217 203
yatra nityatayā sarve 23.67 43

yatra svalpo 'pi sambandhaḥ 24.195 189
yāvān ahaṁ yathā-bhāvo 25.109 355
ye divasa prabhu sannyāsīre kṛpā kaila 25.18 304
yei artha lagāiye, sei artha haya 24.65 114
yei cāha tāhā diba mṛga-vyāghrāmbare" 25.245 217

yei grantha-kartā cāhe sva-mata sthāpite 25.49 323
yei guṇera 'vaśa' haya kṛṣṇa bhagavān 23.86 54
yei sūtra-kartā, se yadi karaye vyākhyāna 25.93 347
yei sūtre yei ṛk—viṣaya-vacana 25.99 350
ye līlā-amṛta vine, 25.278 448

ye 'nye ca pāpā yad-upāśrayāśrayāḥ 24.179 180
ye 'nye ca pāpā yad-upāśrayāśrayāḥ 24.209 198
ye 'nye 'ravindākṣa vimukta-māninas 24.131 152
ye 'nye 'ravindākṣa vimukta-māninas 24.141 158
ye 'nye 'ravindākṣa vimukta-māninas 25.32 312

ye-rase bhakta 'sukhī', kṛṣṇa haya 'vaśa' 23.46 26
ye tu dharmāmṛtam idaṁ 23.113 69
ye 'vigraha' nāhi māne, 'nirākāra' māne 25.115 358

yo dustyajān dāra-sutān 23.25 15
yoga-mārge—antaryāmi-svarūpete bhāse 24.83 123
yogārūḍhasya tasyaiva 24.159 168
'yogārurukṣu', 'yogārūḍha' 'prāpta- 24.158 167
yogya-bhāve jagate yata yuvatīra gaṇa 24.55 109
yo na hṛṣyati na dveṣṭi 23.110 68
yukta-vairāgya-sthiti saba śikhāila 23.105 63

General Index

Numerals in bold type indicate references to *Śrī Caitanya-caritāmṛta's* verses. Numerals in regular type are references to its purports.

A

Abhidheya
explanation of, **352**
Absolute Truth
according to Vedānta philosophy, **325**
as unified identity, **370**
can't be reached by philosophical theories, **326**
eternally exists in transcendental abode, **380**
impersonal appreciation of as one-sided and incomplete, 313
is complete with full spiritual qualities, 327
Kṛṣṇa not fully satisfied by study of, **373**
three features of, **119, 122, 123,** 353
Vaiṣṇava *ācāryas* have proper understanding of, 315
word *brahma* indicates, **117-118**
See also: Kṛṣṇa, Supreme Lord
Ācārya
describes and accepts the Lord, 53
duties of, 64
secrets of, 320
should be considered incarnation of Kṛṣṇa's potency, 300
Vaiṣṇava accepts form of Kṛṣṇa, 315
See also: Spiritual master
Acintya-bhedābheda-tattva
one fully under external energy can't understand 360
Activities
boastful as aspect of transcendental madness, **39**
educational in Navadvīpa and Vārāṇasī, 391
fruitive stressed by Mīmāṁsaka philosophy, 327
in relation to God explained in *catuḥ-ślokī,* **352**
Activities
of Caitanya as evidence of His Supreme Lordship, 300
of Kṛṣṇa as wonderful, **387**
of Kṛṣṇa make awakening possible, 31
of one in love of God can't be understood by learned man, **22-23**
of pure devotees, **14**
of spiritual potency described in scriptures, **314**
symptoms of transcendental emotion as visible in, **11**
See also: Karma
Adhirūḍha
as ecstatic symptom in conjugal mellow, **36-**37
Advaita Ācārya
as member of Pañca-tattva, **304**
Affection
as manifestation of love of God, **24**
for Lord's residences as symptom of ecstatic emotion, **12**
friendship increases to, 34
increased to position of *sthāyi-bhāva,* **3**
of Rādhā for elderly people, **56**
Agni Purāṇa
quoted on *vibhāva,* 30
Ahaitukī
word always applicable to Lord, **170**
Ahaṁ tvāṁ sarva-pāpebhyo
quoted, 112
Ālambana
as division of *vibhāva,* 30
Amānya-matsaro dakṣo nirmamo
verses quoted, 270
Amara-koṣa dictionary
quoted on meaning of word *kṣetrajña,* **255**
Amṛta-pravāha-bhāṣya
cited on learning from spiritual master, 363

Amṛta-pravāha-bhāṣya
six philosophical processes summarized in, 326
summary of Chapter Twenty-four in, 81
summary of Chapter Twenty-three in, **1**
Ananyāś cintayanto māṁ
verses quoted, 230
Anāsaktasya viṣayān
verses quoted, 65
Andhā yathāndhair upanīyamānāḥ
quoted, 219
Anger
based on love as counter-love, 34
one is dear to Kṛṣṇa if he is free from, **67**
Āṅgīrasa Ṛṣi
cursed Sudarśana, 338
Animal killing
Buddha stopped, 320
punishment for, **219-221**
Antavat tu phalaṁ teṣāṁ
verses quoted, 272
Anubhāṣya
quoted on empowered spiritual master, 300
Anubhāva
activates hearing and chanting, 28
symptoms of, 31
symptoms of ecstatic emotion as, **12**
Anubhāvas tu citta-stha-
verse quoted, 31
Anupama
as younger brother of Sanātana, **414**
returned to Vārāṇasī, **416**
Anurāga
attraction of devotees in friendship increases up to, **97**
Anxiety
expressed by Parīkṣit, 14
one is dear to Kṛṣṇa if he is free from, **67**
Anyābhilāṣitā-śūnyaṁ jñāna-
verses quoted, 273-274
Āpani ācari-bhakti karila pracāra
quoted, 133
Api
seven chief meanings of word, **116**
Ārādhyo bhagavān vrajeśa-tanayas
verse quoted, 274
Āruṇa Ṛṣi
path of, **172**
Association
absence of Supreme Lord's, 35
Kṛṣṇa's pastimes relished by those in His, **383**
Association of devotees
as necessary for hearing spiritual message, **10**
brings great happiness, **125**
results in discharging devotional service, 8
value of, **136-**137
Aṣṭāṅga-yoga
does not satisfy Kṛṣṇa as much as *bhakti,* **373**
Aṣṭāvakra
as Māyāvādī philosopher, 327
Asuras
describe Kṛṣṇa as incarnation of black crow, 75
Āṭhāranālā
Caitanya arrived at, **420**
Athāsyāḥ keśava-rater
verses quoted, 27-28
Atheists
Māyāvādīs as, 53
Śaṅkarācārya's theory meant to control and convince, **319**
Athocyante guṇāḥ pañca
verses quoted, 51
Athocyante trayas triṁśad-
verses quoted, 32
Ātmā
another meaning of, **175**
meaning of, **192, 199, 244**
seven meanings of, **86-87**
word indicates Kṛṣṇa, **120**
Ātmārāmas
all serve and worship Kṛṣṇa, **164, 251**
defined, **87**
six kinds of, **161**
six meanings of, **199**
two types of, **185**
Ātmārāma-śloka
compared to sun, **82**
different meanings of explained, **388-389**
eleven words in listed, **86**
more meanings of, **205**
quoted, **83-84**

Atonement
compared to elephant's bathing, 224
Attachment
arises from taste, **7**
as manifestation of love of God, **24**
false symptoms of praised by fools, 26
friendship increases to, 34
Kṛṣṇa as everyone's object of, **48**
to chanting and describing Lord's qualities in *bhāva* stage, **20**
to description of Lord as symptom of ecstatic emotion, **12**
to devotional service, 8, **10**
to Supreme Lord as result of hearing *Bhāgavatam,* **381**
Austerities
don't satisfy Kṛṣṇa as much as *bhakti,* **373**
Kṛṣṇa as ultimate purpose of, 351
Avajānanti māṁ mūḍhā mānuṣīṁ tanum āśritam
quoted, **314**
Avatārāvalī-bījaṁ
verses quoted, 51
Aviruddhān viruddhāṁś ca
verse quoted, 27
Ayoga
two divisions of, 36
Ayoga-yogavetāsya
quoted, 35

B

Balabhadra Bhaṭṭācārya
as servant of Caitanya, **419**
Baladeva Vidyābhūṣaṇa
supports Rūpa's refutation of theory of hair incarnation, 76
Balarāma
as incarnation of a white hair, **74**-76
glorified by Kṛṣṇa, **179**
Balitvāt kṛṣṇa-mantrāṇāṁ
quoted, 276
Beauty
even animals and trees stunned by Kṛṣṇa's, **110**
gopīs attracted to Kṛṣṇa's, **105-106**
of Kṛṣṇa as beyond compare, **52**
Beauty
of Kṛṣṇa's body, **45**
of Rādhārāṇī, **56**
Bengalis
cooked rice as staple food of, 411
Bhagavad-gītā
cited on *asuras'* forgetfulness of Kṛṣṇa, 75
explained by *asuras,* 75
foolish rascals described in, 220
quoted on activities carried out by modes of nature, 220
quoted on appearance of Kṛṣṇa, 263, 442
quoted on becoming dear to Kṛṣṇa, 66
quoted on *brahma-bhūta* platform, 141
quoted on Brahman realization, **153**
quoted on demigod worship, 272-273
quoted on devotee transcending modes of material nature, 363
quoted on difficulty of overcoming divine energy, **157**
quoted on disciplic succession, 288
quoted on eligibility of lowborn to approach Kṛṣṇa, 195
quoted on envy of Kṛṣṇa's form, **318**
quoted on foolishness of thinking Kṛṣṇa ordinary, 314
quoted on four kinds of men who come to devotional service, **129**
quoted on full engagement in devotional service, 273
quoted on full surrender to Kṛṣṇa, 223
quoted on impersonal potency of Kṛṣṇa, 313
quoted on knowledge from Kṛṣṇa in the heart, 328
quoted on Kṛṣṇa as source of everything, **186**
quoted on Kṛṣṇa as ultimate goal of sacrifice, 351
quoted on Kṛṣṇa giving intelligence to devotee, **188**
quoted on Kṛṣṇa providing for His devotee, 230
quoted on Kṛṣṇa's direction in heart, **176**
quoted on living beings as parts of Kṛṣṇa, 404

Bhagavad-gītā
quoted on practice of *yoga* system, **168**
quoted on qualities of *brāhmaṇas,* 269
quoted on rareness of knowing Kṛṣṇa, 442
quoted on renunciation, 63
quoted on transmigration, 137
quoted on understanding Kṛṣṇa, 53
quoted on women's ability to approach supreme destination, 275

Bhagavān
as personal side of Absolute Truth, 313
See also: Kṛṣṇa

Bhāgavata Purāṇa
propounds highest truth, **381**
See also: Śrīmad-Bhāgavatam

Bhakti
Caitanya's liberal demonstration of cult of, 65
characteristics of, **6**
cult must be spread all over world, 66
Sanātana instructed to preach cult of, **62**
ten meanings of word, **96**
See also: Devotional service, *Prema-bhakti*

Bhakti-rasāmṛta-sindhu
dhṛti defined in, **182**
one must understand Kṛṣṇa from statements in, 53
quoted on advanced devotee reaching highest platform of wonder and bliss, **59**
quoted on *anubhāva,* 31
quoted on *ayoga,* 35
quoted on chanting and dancing in ecstasy, 21
quoted on connection and separation, 35
quoted on devotional service in pure goodness, 4
quoted on five processes which awaken love of God, **189**
quoted on five qualities found in demigods, 50-51
quoted on Kṛṣṇa's bodily beauty, 46
quoted on Kṛṣṇa's mercy, 18
quoted on Kṛṣṇa's qualities, 44

Bhakti-rasāmṛta-sindhu
quoted on love of God as composed of mellows, 27-28
quoted on one situated in love of God, **23**
quoted on *prema,* 5
quoted on proper renunciation, 65
quoted on pure devotees, 14
quoted on pure devotional service, 273
quoted on Rādhikā, 20
quoted on *rati,* 26
quoted on seed of ecstatic emotion for Kṛṣṇa, 12
quoted on *sthāyi-bhāva,* 27
quoted on Supreme Lord's qualities manifested in living beings, 49
quoted on transitory elements, 32
quoted on *udbhāsvara,* 31
quoted on understanding transcendental mellows, **60**
quoted on uselessness of impersonal cultivation, **151**
quoted on *vibhāva,* 30

Bhaktisiddhānta Sarasvatī
cited on Narottama dāsa Ṭhākura as *brāhmaṇa* by qualification, 269
cited on neutrality increasing to love of God, 34
cited on qualities of bona fide disciple, 271
cited on studying *Bhāgavatam,* 384
dry renunciation forbidden by, 64
gave sacred thread to bona fide Vaiṣṇavas, 270
gives sixteen divisions of *mantras,* 275
quoted on empowered spiritual master, 300

Bhaktivinoda Ṭhākura
cited on learning from spiritual master, 363
cited on two classes of transcendentalists, 140
cited on Vaiṣṇavas as touchstones, 239
summarizes growth of love of God, 8

Bhakti-yoga
increases attachment for Kṛṣṇa, **372-373**

Bhakti-yoga
See also: Bhakti, Devotional service
Bhārata-bhūmite haila manuṣya
verses quoted, 438
Bharata Mahārāja
activities of, **16**
gave up family, friends and kingdom, **15**
Bhāva
characteristics of, **20**
symptoms of, **4**
Bhāva-bhakti
as stage of devotional life, 8-9
Bhāvārtha-dīpikā
quoted on Hari as Supersoul of everything, **121**
Bhīṣma
defines *bhakti,* **6**
Bhoktāraṁ yajña-tapasāṁ
verses quoted, 351
Bhukti
is of unlimited variety, **95**
Bilvamaṅgala Ṭhākura
quoted on his attraction to Kṛṣṇa, **154**
Bindu Mādhava
Caitanya went to see, **330**
Body, material
four divisions of, **199**
Body, spiritual
acquired by devotee, **140-**141
developed by devotional service, **375**
Brahmā
as living being, **354**
Kṛṣṇa as Lord of, 75
Kṛṣṇa imparted Vedic knowledge unto, **380**
questioned by Indra on Goloka Vṛndāvana, 73
realized Kṛṣṇa's spiritual form, 316
Sanātana taught conclusions unknown to, **77**
Yogendras entered association of, **146**
Brahma-bhūta
attaining platform of, 140-141
Brahmacārī
may take only one bath a day, 277
Brahma-gāyatrī
Bhāgavatam contains commentary of, **377-378, 379**
Brahmaloka
those advancing in spiritual knowledge reside in, 73
Brahman
as cause of cosmos, **324**
as devoid of material qualities, 327
as feature of Absolute Truth, 353
impersonalist view diminishes fullness of, **313**
Kumāras were attached to, **386**
one in bodily concept worships his own body as, **200**
one who is transcendentally situated realizes Supreme, **385**
philosophical speculation leads to realization of, **123**
said by Māyāvādīs to be cause of everything, 327
said to be located in abdomen by *yogīs,* **172**
those devoid of devotional service fall down from realization of, **312**
three categories of those who wish to merge into, **147**
three types of people who worship, **139**
Brāhmaṇa
duty of public to present gift to, 233
never supposed to be engaged for anyone's service, 265
pure devotee is above, 362
Śṛṅgi curses Parīkṣit, 13
Brahmānanda
like straw compared to transcendental bliss, **99**
Brahmānanda Bhāratī
met Caitanya at Purī, **421**
Brahma-saṁhitā
quoted on Goloka Vṛndāvana, 73
quoted on incarnations of the Lord, 244
Brahma-sūtra
can't be understood without studying *Bhāgavatam,* 384
describes activities of Kṛṣṇa's spiritual potency, **314**
Prakāśānanda should study *Bhāgavatam* to understand, **384**
See also: Vedānta-sūtra

Brahmeti paramātmeti bhagavān iti śabdyate
quoted, 313
Bṛhad-gautamīya-tantra
quoted on Rādhārāṇī, 44
Buddha
stopped animal killing, 320

C

Ca
meaning of word, **206, 207, 208**
word can be explained in seven ways, **115**
Caitanya-candrodaya-nāṭaka
quoted on mercy of Caitanya on Sanātana, **289-291**
Caitanya Mahāprabhu
as combination of Rādhā-Kṛṣṇa, 443
as eastern horizon where *ātmārāma* verse rises, 82
as Kṛṣṇa Himself, **259**
as member of Pañca-tattva, **304**
has complexion of golden *campaka* flower, **290**
personally preached truths of *Bhāgavatam,* **439**
politely changed people's minds, **306**
presented Himself as a fallen living entity, **339**
words of are firm and convincing, **310**
Caitanya-caritāmṛta
as very secret literature, **451-452**
deliverance of Vārāṇasī *sannyāsīs* described in, **299**
quoted on *saṅkīrtana,* 300
Caṇḍālas
Bharata offers respects to, **27**
Candraśekhara
met Rūpa at Vārāṇasī, **417**
Paramānanda Kīrtanīyā as friend of, **297**
unhappy upon hearing blasphemy of Caitanya, **302**
wanted to accompany Lord to Purī, **396-397**
Catuḥ-ślokī
first verse of quoted, **358**
fourth verse of quoted, **365**
Oṁkāra and Gāyatrī mantra explained in, **347**
second verse of quoted, **361**
third verse of quoted, **366**
Chanting
activated by *vibhāva,* etc., 28
awakening taste for, **7**
in Kali-yuga Kṛṣṇa worshiped by, 300
interest in as result of association with devotees, 8
of advanced devotee, **24**
of *mahā-mantra* after Caitanya's explanation of *ātmārāma-śloka,* **389-390**
of Paramānanda Kīrtanīyā as humorous, **297**
one who is advanced takes pleasure in, **376**
taste for as symptom of ecstatic emotion, **12**
though imperfect still gives liberation, **311**
Charity
doesn't satisfy Kṛṣṇa as much as *bhakti,* **373**
trees give alms in, **70**
Cintāmaṇi-prakara-sadmasu
as *mantra* quoted while bathing Deities, 280
Citra-jalpa
as division of *mohana* stage, **38**
Citraka
as shelter in servitorship mellow, **57**
Cleanliness
of Kṛṣṇa, **47**
one is dear to Kṛṣṇa if he practices, **67**
Conjugal love
as mellow of sweetness, **33**
as transcendental mellow, **25**
object and shelter of mellow of, **57**
special activities of found only in Kṛṣṇa, **52**
two departments of, **39**
two ecstatic symptoms in, **36-**37

D

Dāmodara Paṇḍita
met Caitanya at Purī, **422**
Dampatayor bhāva ekatra
verse quoted on *māna,* 41
Darśanāliṅganādīnām
verse quoted, 40
Daśāśvamedha-ghāṭa
Caitanya instructed Rūpa at, **61**
Death
Parīkṣit prepares for imminent, 13
Dehino 'smin yathā dehe
verses quoted, 137
Deity
installed by Māyāvādī *sannyāsīs,* **141-**142
liberated soul installs, **385**
Sanātana instructed to install, 62
Deity worship
offenses in, **282-**283
rules for, **279-**281
Demigods
asuras as enemies of, 76
devotees don't worship, **148**
five qualities not present in, **51**
five qualities partially present in, **50**
Kṛṣṇa as Supreme Lord of, 351
material world seems real to, **380**
no need to worship, 272
not on level with Nārāyaṇa, **340**
Detachment
as symptom of ecstatic emotion for Kṛṣṇa, **12**
found in persons who have developed *bhāva,* 15
Devakī
Kṛṣṇa born from, 76
Devotees
as nonviolent, **236**
can bind Supreme Lord by love, **367**
can spread chanting of *mahā-mantra* only when empowered by Kṛṣṇa, 300
in stage of *ayoga* think of attaining Kṛṣṇa's association, 35
Kṛṣṇa as well-wisher of, **48**
Devotees
mental concoction not meant for, 300
of Caitanya can deliver whole world, 225
of Kṛṣṇa awaken symptoms of ecstatic love, 31
possess unequalled love for Kṛṣṇa, **52**
Rādhā as most famous of submissive, **56**
satisfied by hearing Kṛṣṇa's qualities, **45**
seed of love expands in heart of advanced, **59**
shouldn't flatter materialists, **70**
situated in endurance and patience, **183**
Supreme Lord manifest within heart of, **366**
thirty-two kinds of regular and spontaneous, 243-**249**
three categories of, **126**
very few in Vārāṇasī, 391
Devotional service
ācārya accepts essence of, 64
according to regulative principles, **375**
advanced devotees understand varieties of, **59-60**
all other methods of self-realization useless without, **128-**129
as means and end, **353**
as only auspicious path, **158-159**
Bhāgavatam learned only through, **258**
Caitanya personally tasted pleasure of, **438**
causes one to forget material happiness, **100**
compared to forest of lotus flowers, **445**
developing interest in, 8
difficult to attain for two reasons, **176**
even birds and illiterates can engage in, **184**
five processes for elevation to, **188-189**
four kinds of pious men render, **129-131**
in Dvāpara-yuga according to *pāñcarātrika* principles, 300
in love of God becomes composed of transcendental mellows, **27**

Devotional service
- in pure goodness, **4**
- is applicable everywhere, in all circumstances, **361**
- is causeless and unmotivated, **95**
- is transcendental to all considerations of time or place, **362-363**
- leads to love of God, **3**
- one cannot understand *Vedānta-sūtra* without, 346
- one is dear to Kṛṣṇa if he determinedly engages in, **66**
- one is very dear to Kṛṣṇa if he is fixed in, **69**
- one who is transcendentally situated attains pure, **385**
- Sanātana inquired about conclusive statements concerning, **71**
- Sanātana instructed to establish in Vṛndāvana, **62**
- satisfies Kṛṣṇa more than any other process, **373**
- sincere endeavor necessary in, **175**
- spiritual master should be questioned about, **364**
- taste for hearing and chanting awakens from firm faith in, **7**
- two kinds of, **124-126**
- *See also: Bhakti-yoga*

Dharma
- devotional service as, 71

Dhṛti
- word defined, **181-182**

Dhruva-ghāṭa
- Rūpa met Subuddhi Rāya at, **400**

Dhrūva Mahārāja
- came to Kṛṣṇa in need of money, 130
- while searching for glass found valuable jewel, **205**

Dīpārcir eva hi dasāntaram
- verses quoted, 244

Disciple
- qualifications of, 270-271

Dreams
- meetings of lovers in, 40

Durgā
- *See:* Kālī

Durlabhe sad-gurūṇāṁ ca
- verses quoted, 276

Duty
- of everyone to follow *mahājanas,* **326**
- of everyone to hear from bona fide spiritual master, **364**

Dvāpara-yuga
- *pāñcarātrika* principles practiced in, 300

Dvāparīyair janair viṣṇuḥ
- verses quoted, 300

Dvārakā
- advanced ecstasy found among queens of, **36**-37
- *prema-vaicittya* feelings prominent in queens of, **42**
- queens in attracted to Kṛṣṇa by hearing about Him, **107**-108

E

Ecstasies
- highly advanced found among *gopīs,* **36**-37
- particular (*vibhāva*), **29**
- permanent, 27-**28**
- subordinate (*anubhāva*), **30**

Ecstatic symptoms
- as *anubhāvas,* 31
- ecstasy of continuous existence of, 34
- in conjugal mellow, **36**-37
- manifest in *bhakti-yoga,* **157**
- mixed with permanent ecstasy, **29**
- of advanced devotee while chanting, **24, 376**
- of Caitanya at Bindu Mādhava temple, **331**
- of inhabitants of Vārāṇasī, **390**
- of pure devotees developed by preaching, **375**

Ei chaya gosāñi yāṅra, mui
- quoted, 443

Ekādaśī
- should be observed, **286**

Eko bahūnāṁ yo vidadhāti kāmān
- quoted, 50, 227

Elements
thirty-three transitory, 32-33
Energies
of Caitanya as inconceivable, **345**
Energy, external
acintya-bhedābheda-tattva not understood by one fully under, 360
causes illusion of truth without Kṛṣṇa, **361**
existed in Kṛṣṇa before cosmic manifestation, **356**
has variety of activities, 314
Kṛṣṇa as creator of, **318**
Kṛṣṇa is different from, **359**
Kṛṣṇa's form not contaminated by, **315**
universes created and maintained by, **92**-93
Energy, internal
has variety of activities, 314
Enjoyment
materialists interested in material, **15**
of mellows in *sthāyi-bhāva,* **3**
Envy
asuras describe Kṛṣṇa as black crow due to, 75
by spreading *bhakti* cult one gives up, 66
Evaṁ paramparā-prāptam imaṁ
quoted, 288
Existence
of Kṛṣṇa as eternal, **358**
without Kṛṣṇa there is no, **316**

F

Faith
as beginning of devotional service, **6, 10**
Fame
equiposition in infamy and, **69**
Fasting
awakens symptoms of ecstatic love, 31
Fear
living entities overpowered by, **156**
one is dear to Kṛṣṇa if he is free from, **67**
Flute of Kṛṣṇa
birds and swans enchanted by, **178, 180**
Flute of Kṛṣṇa
goddess of fortune attracted by, **108**
women captivated by, **110**
Food
devotee doesn't have to endeavor to get, 70-71
Form of Kṛṣṇa
is eternal, blissful and full of knowledge, 314
Māyāvādīs do not recognize, **314**
those envious of cast into demoniac species, **318**
Fortune
faith developed by good, **6**
interest in Kṛṣṇa consciousness developed by good, 8
of one who mistreats great souls destroyed, **342**
Friendship
as transcendental mellow, **25**
divisions of connection and separation in, **35**
increases to subordinate spontaneous love, **34**
object and shelter in mellow of, **57**
varieties of *yoga* and *viyoga* in, 36

G

Gadādhara Paṇḍita
as one of Pañca-tattva, **304**
met Caitanya at Purī, **422**
Gajendra
came to Kṛṣṇa in distress, 130
Gaṇapati
See: Gaṇeśa
Gaṇeśa
one who worships, 273
Ganges
Caitanya bathed in, **395**
discussions of *Bhāgavatam* take place on banks of, 391
taste of devotional service like water of, **203**

Garbhodaka Ocean
Brahmā meditated upon the Lord in, 316
Garuda Purāṇa
quoted on *Bhāgavatam,* **378**
Gatiḥ śama-damāṭyānāṁ
verses quoted, 72-73
Gaurakṛṣṇa
Supreme Lord known as, **2**
Gaurāṅgera bhakta-gaṇe jane jane
quoted, 225
Gautama
as Nyāya philosopher, 327
Gavām eva tu goloko
verses quoted, 73
Gāyatrī *mantra*
meaning of *oṁkāra* present in, **347**
to be chanted three times daily, 277
Goddess of fortune
attracted to Kṛṣṇa, **108-109**
Goddesses of fortune
Rādhārāṇī as central figure for, **44**
Gokula
Rādhā as reservoir of loving affairs in, **56**
Goloka-nāmni nija-dhāmni tale
verses quoted, 73
Goloka Vṛndāvana
Hari-vaṁśa describes, **72**
maintained by conjugal potency of Kṛṣṇa, **92,** 93
Goodness
bhāva-bhakti as platform of purified, 9
devotional service in pure, **4**
Gopīs
advanced ecstasies found among, **36-**37
as very dear to Kṛṣṇa, **53**
attracted by beauty of Kṛṣṇa, **105-106**
can attain *mahābhāva,* **98**
inquired about the Lord from plants. **369**
Rādhā as chief of, **56**
three kinds of separation celebrated in, **42**
Gosvāmīs, six
glorification of, 62
understood Caitanya and His mission, 443
Govardhana Hill
raised by Kṛṣṇa, **72,** 73
Govinda
met Caitanya at Purī, **422**
Gṛhastha
should bathe twice a day, 277
should live outside the temple, 233
shouldn't live at home until he dies, 228
Guṇa
meaning of word, **101**

H

Habits
freedom from unwanted, **10**
Happiness
attained in course of time, **174**
derived from attraction to one mellow, **26**
equiposition in distress and, **69**
in devotional service as life of advanced devotees, **59**
of Kṛṣṇa, **48**
of Kṛṣṇa derived from Rādhā's bodily aroma, **56**
one is dear to Kṛṣṇa if he is equal in distress and, **66**
Hare Kṛṣṇa
one who relishes holy name can chant constantly, **32**
Hare Kṛṣṇa movement
See: Kṛṣṇa consciousness movement
Hari
as Supersoul of everything, **121**
as Supreme Lord destroys inauspiciousness for devotees, **367**
is called Kṛṣṇa, **83-84, 387**
Hari
two foremost meanings of word, **111-114**
Hari-bhakti-sudhodaya
quoted on association of devotees, **149**
quoted on Dhruva Mahārāja, **205**
quoted on pure devotees, 14
quoted on transcendental bliss, **99**

Hari-bhakti-vilāsa
cited on becoming *brāhmaṇa* by initiation, 64
enunciates behavior of a Vaiṣṇava, 62
Gosvāmi-viddhi explained in, 363
quoted on purity of *mahā-mantra,* 275
quoted on spiritual initiation, 276
quoted on thinking Viṣṇu and demigods to be equal, 273
quoted on women as eligible for spiritual life, 274-275
rules for Deity worship in, 279-281, **284**
specifically meant for India, 64
Haridāsa Ṭhākura
met Caitanya at Purī, **422**
Hari-vaṁśa
description of Vṛndāvana in, **72**
quoted on Goloka Vṛndāvana, 72
Hearing
activated by *vibhāva,* etc., 28
awakening taste for, **7**
Bhāgavatam submissively, **381**
interest in as result of association with devotees, 8
Kṛṣṇa's qualities satisfies devotees, **45**
pure devotees attached to, **132-**133
Heart
fructification of seed of love in, **12**
highest truth understood by devotees pure in, **381**
melting of, 9
melts in *rati* stage, 26
peculiar conditions of in *vyabhicārī,* 33
seed of love grows in, **7, 59**
seed of transcendental emotion in, **11**
softened in *bhāva* stage, **4, 5**
Heavenly planets
obit of sun as entrance to, 73
Hetu
meaning of word, **94**
Hindus
conflict between Mohammedans and, 403-404
Holy name
can only be distributed by empowered person, 300-301
distributed by Gaurakṛṣṇa, **2**
having great relish for, **32**
Holy name
Prakāśānanda advised to chant, **384**
taste for chanting as symptom of ecstatic emotion, **12**
Honor
equiposition in dishonor and, **69**
Hṛṣīkeṇa hṛṣīkeśa sevanaṁ bhaktir
verse quoted, 133, 141
Humility
Caitanya exemplified, **335**
of Kṛṣṇa, **48**
of Rādhārāṇī, **56**

I

Illusion
Absolute Truth free from, **380**
Māyāvādīs say everything is, 327
reality distinguished from, **381**
Śaṅkarācārya tried to establish theory of, **319**
Impersonalism
does not satisfy Kṛṣṇa as much as *bhakti,* **373**
Impersonalists
do not accept Kṛṣṇa due to poor fund of knowledge, **317**
Incarnations
as plenary portions of *puruṣa-avatāra,* **371**
demigods and living entities not source of all, **51**
Lord has innumerable, 244
most offensive to pose oneself as one of, 339
offense of accepting a conditioned soul as one of, **339**
of Kṛṣṇa and Balarāma from Viṣṇu's hairs, **74-**76
India
Caitanya traveled in different regions of, 438
followed principle of *smārta-vidhi,* 64
Hindu-Mohammedan conflict in, 403-404
ISKCON temples in, 398-399
so-called *brāhmaṇas* in, 265

India
so-called *gurus* in, 268-269
Indra
gave information on Goloka Vṛndāvana, **72**-73
Initiation, spiritual
anyone can be elevated to position of *brāhmaṇa* by, 64
follows association with devotees, 8, **10**
process of, **226, 227**
Intelligence
given by Lord to devotees, **187**
of Kṛṣṇa, **46**
of those devoid of devotional service impure, **312**
one is dear to Kṛṣṇa if he dedicates his, **66**
one who considers everyone as God has no, 50
International Society for Krishna Consciousness
See: Kṛṣṇa consciousness movement
Ittham-bhūta
meaning of word, **99-101**

J

Jagadānanda
met Caitanya at Purī, **422**
Jagannātha Deity
Caitanya went to see, **423**
Jagannātha Purī
Caitanya returned to, **419-426**
Caitanya stayed at for last eighteen years of His life, **427**
Jaimini
Mīmāṁsaka philosophers follow principles of, 327
Janma karma ca me divyam
quoted, 263, 442
Janmāṣṭamī
should be observed, **285-286**
Judeo-Christian scriptures
"Thou shalt not kill" as injunction in, 221

K

Kālī, Goddess
one who worships, 273
Kali-kālera dharma kṛṣṇa-nāma-saṅkīrtana
verses quoted, 300
Kāliya
touched by Kṛṣṇa's lotus feet, **108-109**
Kali-yuga
animals sacrificed in, 221
Bhāgavatam has risen like sun in, **262**
everyone perplexed in, 407
renounced order cannot deliver one in, **310**
Kāmais tais tair hṛta-jñānāḥ
verses quoted, 272
Kaṇāda
as Nyāya philosopher, 327
Kaniṣṭha-adhikārīs
can't turn others into Vaiṣṇavas, 239
Kapila
as Sāṅkhya philosopher, 327
Kāśī
See: Vārāṇasī
Kāśī Miśra
met Caitanya at Purī, **422**
Kāśīśvara
met Caitanya at Purī, **422**
Kintu bāla-camatkāra-
verses quoted, 26
Kirāta-hūṇāndhra-pulinda-pulkaśā
verse quoted, 64
Knowledge
one interested in must always inquire about, **365**
practical application of spiritual, **359**
speculative like beating empty husk, **311**
spiritual explained, **352**
spiritual has to be received from revealed scriptures, 360
Supreme Lord as concentrated form of eternity, bliss and, **51**
Kṣepaṇa
as symptom of *anubhāva,* 31

Kṛṣṇa
absorption in thoughts of as inward cleanliness, 68
all good qualities situated in, **44**
always under Rādhā's control, **56**
as compiler of Vedānta and knower of *Vedas,* 328
as example of particular ecstasies, **29**
as incarnation of a black hair, **74**-76
as lotus-eyed, **43**
as maintainer of everyone, 227
as more exalted than living beings and demigods, **53**
as most sublime abode of bliss, **100**
as object in transcendental mellows, **57**
as *uttama-śloka,* **15**
as very funny, **95**
attained by faith and devotional service, **372-373**
Bhāgavatam as sound incarnation of, **439**
Bhāgavatam is as great as, **260**
Caitanya as, **259**
characteristics and activities of, **380**
comes under control of devotee, **26**
controlled by qualities of Rādhārāṇī, **54**
everything can be used in service of, 366
everything is, **316**
existed before creation of cosmic manifestation, **356**
explains His form, situation, attributes, activities and opulences, **355**
explains to Uddhava what pleases Him most, **373**
Hari is called, **83-84**
in separation one thinks oneself to be, **39**
living entity becomes competitor of, **374**
nothing can exist without, **361**
qualities and paraphernalia of awaken symptoms of ecstatic love, 31
raised Govardhana Hill, **72,** 73

Kṛṣṇa
says "I am the center of all relationships", **352**
sixty-four transcendental qualities of, **45-54**
spiritual master empowered by direct potency of, 300
sweetness of early age of, **19**

Kṛṣṇa consciousness movement
accused by envious of spoiling so-called Hinduism, 362
Caitanya desired worldwide preaching of, 301
continues tradition of six Gosvāmīs, 63
devotional service is open for everyone in, 363
gaining ground due to logical presentation, 306
high caste *brāhmaṇas* and *gosvāmīs* envious of, 362
impeded by Māyāvādī philosophers, 53
one is very very dear to Kṛṣṇa if he follows principle of, **69**
stories opposed to conclusions of, **74**-76

Kṛṣṇa-karṇāmṛta
quoted on Kṛṣṇa's qualities, 19
quoted on Kṛṣṇa's sweetness, 21

Kṛṣṇa-prema-dhana
as beyond platform of liberation, **61**

Kṛṣṇa-sandarbha
discussion of hair incarnation in, 76

Kṛṣṇaś ca kṛṣṇa-bhaktāś ca
verses quoted, 30

Kṛṣṇena saṅgamo yas tu
quoted, 35

Kṣīrodakaśāyī Viṣṇu
Kṛṣṇa and Balarāma as incarnations of hairs of, **74-**76

Kumāras
attracted by aroma of *tulasī,* **102-103, 142-143**
devotional service of as celebrated, **194**

Kurvanti
purport of word, **93-**94

L

Laghu-bhāgavatāmṛta
contains information on hair incarnation, 76

Lakṣmī
Nārāyaṇa as Lord of, **51**

Lamentation
one is dear to Kṛṣṇa if he is free from, **110**

Law of nature
a life for a life according to, 220

Liberation
as situation in one's original form, **155**
atheist do not care for, **320**
by devotional service, **152**
cannot be attained without devotional service, **157, 311**
desire for given up by association of devotees, **148, 150-151**
from material contamination as *anartha-nivṛtti,* 8
kṛṣṇa-prema-dhana as beyond platform of, **61**
Prakāśānanda can attain, **384**
readily granted by Kṛṣṇa, 176

Living entities
all have some intelligence, **184-185**
as marginal potency, **254-255,** 257
attracted by material energy become fearful, **374**
Brahmā as one of, **354**
Caitanya presented Himself as one of, **339**
equal disposition to, **385**
existed in Kṛṣṇa before cosmic manifestation, **356**
five qualities not present in, **51**
kinds of, **194**
Kṛṣṇa as more exalted than, **53**
Kṛṣṇa as well-wisher of, 351
Kṛṣṇa's form as source of, **316**
material elements are within and without the, **366**
Supreme Lord astonishes all, **52**

Living entities
Supreme Lord's qualities exhibited in, **49-**50

Lokānām asau pūjyo yathā hariḥ
quoted, 268

Lotus feet of Caitanya
offenses counteracted by touching, **337**
Prakāśānanda Sarasvatī caught hold of, **335**
Sanātana desires to keep on his head, **78**

Lotus feet of Kṛṣṇa
attained by offenseless chanting, **407-408**
free one from material miseries, **181**
free one from all sinful reactions, **338**
Kāliya touched by dust of, **108-109**
Kṛṣṇa forcibly gives one shelter of, **136**
Kumāras attracted to, **102-103**
Māyāvāda conclusion an offense against, 315
mellows understand by one dedicated to, **60**
neglect of causes fall down from Brahman realization, **312**
three ways to attain, **121**
vanquish all miserable conditions of material life, **343**

Love of God
as life's ultimate goal, **8, 79, 365, 375**
as result of devotional service, **3**
attraction of devotees in neutrality increases up to, **97**
development of compared to sugar, **25**
five processes which awaken, **188-189**
gradual development of, **10**
Kṛṣṇa's qualities and paraphernalia awaken symptoms of ecstatic, 31
learned man can't understand person situated in, **22**
manifestations of, **24**
mellows gradually increase to, **34**
Prakāśānanda can be elevated to enjoyment of, **384**
symptoms of fructifying seed of, **12**
See also: Prema-bhakti

M

Mādana
as division of highly advanced ecstasy, **37-38**
Madana-mohana
Sanātana established temple of, 62
Madhvācārya
Kṛṣṇa consciousness movement follows, 328
Madness
aspects of transcendental, **39**
Madhyama-adhikārīs
can turn others into Vaiṣṇavas, 239
Magnanimity
of Caitanya, 335
Mahā-bhāgavata
spiritual master on platform of, 300
Mahā-bhāgavata-śreṣṭho
verses quoted, 268
Mahābhārata
Bhāgavatam contains full purport of, **377-378**
Kṛṣṇa's pastimes mentioned in, 75
quoted on *keśa-avatāra,* 75
quoted on *mahājanas,* **328**
Mahābhāva
gopīs can attain, **98**
includes *rūḍha* and *adhirūḍha,* 37
Mahājanas
one should accept path of, **328**
Mahā-kula-prasūto 'pi
verses quoted, 268
Mahā-mantra
as solution to all sinful activities, 407-**408**
chanted after Caitanya's explanation of *ātmārāma-śloka,* **389-390**
chanted humorously, **297**
frees one from all contamination, 223
message of distributed without bargaining or selling, 392-393
no question of *śodhana* for, 276
offenses in chanting, 408
one can bathe by chanting, 277
one who relishes holy name can chant constantly, **32**
Mahārāja Parīkṣit
See: Parīkṣit Mahārāja
Mahārāṣṭrian *brāhmaṇa*
invitation of to Vārāṇasī *sannyāsīs* and Caitanya, **301, 303**
mentioned Caitanya's explanation of *ātmārāma* verse, **388**
met Rūpa at Vārāṇasī, **417**
unhappy hearing blasphemy of Caitanya, **299**
wanted to accompany Caitanya to Purī, **396-397**
Mahā Upaniṣad
quoted on nine Yogendras, **146**
Mahā-Viṣṇu
living entities merge in, **155**
Mamaivāṁśo jīva-loke jīva-bhūtaḥ
quoted, 49, 404
Māṁ ca yo 'vyabhicāreṇa
verses quoted, 273, 363
Māṁ hi pārtha vyapāśritya
verses quoted, 195, 275
Māna
as division of *vipralambha,* **40-**41
as transcendental quality, **25**
Mantras
different kinds of for different devotees, **274**
Manuṣya-lokād ūrdhvaṁ tu
verses quoted, 72-73
Manuṣyāṇāṁ sahasreṣu kaścid
verses quoted, 442
Material energy
See: Energy, external
Mathurā
Rūpa met Subuddhi Rāya at, **400**
Sanātana instructed to excavate in, **103**
Mauṣala-līlā
related for bewilderment of *asuras,* 75
Māyāpur
ISKCON temple in, 398-399
Mayā tatam idaṁ sarvaṁ
verses quoted, 313
Māyāvādīs
say Brahman effulgence is cause of everything, **324,** 327
consider everyone as God, 50

Māyāvādīs
discussed *Bhāgavatam*, **390**
don't understand Kṛṣṇa's qualities, 52-53
Māyāvādī *sannyāsīs*
blasphemed Caitanya, **299**
call themselves *jagad-guru*, 335
gave up studies of Vedānta, **307**
Mellows
devotional service in love of God becomes composed of transcendental, **27**
enjoyed in *sthāyi-bhāva*, **3**
five transcendental, **25-26, 33**
hero and heroine as basis of transcendental, **56**
nondevotees can't understand exchange of Kṛṣṇa and devotees in different, **59, 60**
object and shelter in transcendental, **57**
Rūpa empowered to understand, **61**
yoga and *viyoga* always exist in five, 36
Mental speculation
forbidden by Caitanya, **63**
Mercy
of Caitanya can't be described expansively, **79**
of Kṛṣṇa awoke knowledge in Brahmā, **355**
of Kṛṣṇa not cared for by atheists, **320**
Rādhā always full of, **56**
value of Kṛṣṇa's, **136-**137
Mīmāṁsaka philosophers
conclusion of, **324**
stress fruitive activity, 327
Mind
as a sense, 49
Kumāras experienced change in, **386**
of everyone in three worlds attracted by Kṛṣṇa's flute, **52**
of pure devotee always remembers Lord, **14**
of women attracted by Kṛṣṇa, **48**
one is dear to Kṛṣṇa if he dedicates his, **66**
Miseries
highest truth uproots threefold, **381**
Miseries
Kṛṣṇa's lotus feet vanquish all kinds of, **343**
sages who know Kṛṣṇa attain peace from, 351
Modes of nature
material universes created by, **380**
Mohammedans
conflict between Hindus and, 403-404
Mohana
as division of highly advanced ecstasy, **37-38**
Monism
cannot be established if one accepts existence of God, 326-327
Śaṅkarācārya eager to establish, **322-323**
Motives
three kinds of, **94**
Mṛgāri
story of Nārada and, **210-242**
Muni
meanings of, **88, 177**
Mukti
word has five varieties, **95**
Muktiṁ dadāti karhicit
quoted, **176**
Mystic powers
materialists interested in, **15**
Vaiṣṇava possesses, **18**
Supreme Lord as possessor of all, **51**
Mystic *yoga*
See: Yoga

N

Na cātra śātravā doṣā
verses quoted, 275-276
Naimiṣāraṇya
Subuddhi Rāya stayed for some time at, **409**
Nānā-śāstra-vicāraṇaika-nipuṇau
verse quoted, 62, 270
Nanda Mahārāja
as father of Kṛṣṇa, **43,** 56, 57

Nanda Mahārāja
as shelter in mellow of paternal affection, **57**
saved from serpent by Kṛṣṇa, 338
Vṛndāvana as kingdom of, 73
Nārada Muni
as spiritual master of Vyāsadeva, 222, 346
called a touchstone by Parvata Muni, **238**-239
defines *bhakti,* **6**
story of hunter Mṛgāri and, **210-242**
Nārada-pañcarātra
cited on becoming *brāhmaṇa* by initiation, 64
quoted on *bhakti,* 6
quoted on pure devotional service, 132-133
Nāradīya Puraṇa
quoted on attaining desired goal of life, **175**
Nārāyaṇa
as the Lord of Lakṣmī, **51**
Brahmā and Śiva not on level of, **339**
by regulative devotional service one becomes an associate of, **125**
Caitanya as, **308**
five qualities exist in, **51**
four qualities not found in, **52-53**
is always transcendental, 360
Kṛṣṇa as more exalted than, **53**
pure devotees always engaged in service of, 73
Nārāyaṇaḥ paro 'vyaktāt
quoted, 360
Nārāyaṇa-saṁhitā
quoted on empowered spiritual master, 300
Narendra-sarovara
devotees met Caitanya on banks of, **421**
Narottama dāsa Ṭhākura
as *brāhmaṇa* by qualification, 269
as servant of Gosvāmīs, 443
quoted on understanding pastimes of Kṛṣṇa, 443
Nature, material
existed in Kṛṣṇa before cosmic manifestation, **356**
Navadvīpa
ISKCON temple in, 398-399
Vārāṇasī turned into another, **391**
Na vinā vipralambhena
quoted, 39
Neutrality
as permanent ecstasy, **27**
as transcendental mellow, **45**
increases to appreciation of love of God, **34**
yoga and *viyoga* in, 36
Nigrantha
meanings of, **88-89, 162, 177**
Nīlakaṇṭha
quoted on *brāhmaṇas* by quality, 269
Nimbārka
Kṛṣṇa consciousness movement follows, 328
Nirguṇa
explained, **325**
Nityānanda Prabhu
as member of Pañca-tattva, **304**
Nondevotees
can't understand exchange of Kṛṣṇa and devotees in different mellows, **59, 60**
Nṛsiṁha-caturdaśī
should be observed, **285, 286**
Nṛsiṁha-tāpanī
quoted on impersonalists' attraction to pastimes of Kṛṣṇa, **141, 160**
Nyāya philosophy
says cause of cosmos is the atom, **324,** 327

O

Offenses
cause desire for material enjoyment, **337**
in chanting *mahā-mantra,* 408
in Deity worship, **282**-283
of considering a conditioned soul to be an incarnation, **339**

Offenses
of Prakāśānanda Sarasvatī counteracted, **337**
Oṁkāra
Gāyatrī *mantra* contains meaning of, **347**
Omniscience
of Supreme Lord, **51**
Oṁ viṣṇor nu vīryāṇi kaṁ
verses quoted, 91
Opulence
Bharata Mahārāja gave up, **15**
of Kṛṣṇa as beyond compare, **52**
of one who mistreats great souls destroyed, **342**
Vaikuṇṭha maintained by the Lord's, **92,** 93

P

Padma Purāṇa
quoted on always remembering Viṣṇu, 277
quoted on Bharata Mahārāja, 26
quoted on characteristics of *guru,* 268
Pain
mitigation of material, 63
one is dear to Kṛṣṇa if he is free from, **67**
Pañca-nada
Caitanya bathed in, **330**
Pañca-tattva
members of listed, **304**
Paṇḍita Gosāñi
invited Caitanya to dinner, **425**
Pāṇini's *sūtras*
quoted, **94, 164, 250**
Paramānanda Kīrtanīyā
chanted to Caitanya in humorous way, **297**
wanted to accompany Lord to Purī, **396-397**
met Caitanya at Purī, **421**
Paramātmā
localized as one aspect of Absolute Truth, 353
Paramparā
knowledge must be received from, 360
Parental affection
See: Paternal love
Parental love
as transcendental mellow, **25**
divisions of connection and separation in, **35**
Parīkṣit Mahārāja
advised by Śukadeva on independence of devotee, 70
cursed by *brāhmaṇa* boy, 13
Parvata Muni
called Nārada a touchstone, **238**-239
visits Mṛgāri with Nārada, **234-242**
Pastimes of Caitanya
are full of nectar, **447**
identical with pastimes of Kṛṣṇa, 443
in *Caitanya-caritāmṛta* as very secret literature, **451-452**
truth about Kṛṣṇa understood by understanding, **441**
Pastimes of Kṛṣṇa
as eternal, blissful and full of knowledge, 314
compared to buds of lotus flowers, **445**
compared to camphor, **447**
devotees never tire of hearing, **383**
even impersonalists attracted to, **141**-142
evoke wonder, **52**
identical with pastimes of Caitanya, 443
liberated soul is attracted to, **385**
mentioned in *Mahābhārata,* 75
one is ecstatic emotion resides in place of, **21**
Śukadeva Gosvāmī attracted to, **104-105, 144**
Patañjali
followers of practice *rāja-yoga,* 327
says one must be self-realized to understand the Lord, **324**
Paternal love
increases to subordinate spontaneous love, **34**
object and shelter in mellow of, **57**
varieties of *yoga* and *viyoga* in, 36
Patraka
as shelter in servitorship mellow, **57**

Peace
how to attain world, 351-352
Pious activities
one is dear to Kṛṣṇa if he rejects, **67**
Planets
Kṛṣṇa as Supreme Lord of, 351
Vaikuṇṭha manifest in spiritual world, **371**
Pleasure
experienced by advanced devotee from chanting, **24**
love of God as reservoir of all, **8**
Possessions
of others should not be encroached upon, 351
Possessiveness
being rightly situated above, 65
in relation to the Lord, **5-6**
Potency
Rādhārāṇī as primeval internal, **44**
Power
inconceivable supreme not present in demigods, etc., **51**
of Kṛṣṇa's body, **45**
Pradyumna Miśra
met Caitanya at Purī, **422**
Prahlāda Mahārāja
defines *bhakti,* **6**
interested in doing good to others, 438
Prajalpa
as division of mad emotional talks, **38**
Prakāśānanda Sarasvatī
became Vaiṣṇava, 391
charmed by Caitanya's dancing and beauty, **333**
instructions to, **383-384**
requested Caitanya to explain *Vedānta-sūtra,* **345**
Prakṛteḥ kriyamāṇāni guṇaiḥ
verses quoted, 220
Praṇava
explained in *Bhāgavatam,* 349
Prāpañcikatayā buddhyā
verses quoted, 65
Pravāsa
as division of *vipralambha,* **40-**41
Prayāga
Caitanya went to, **409**
Prayāga
Daśāśvamedha-ghāṭa located in, **61**
Prayers
of Caitanya to Prakāśānanda Sarasvatī, **335-336**
offered by pure devotees, **14**
offered to Kṛṣṇa for His favor, **15**
Supreme Lord glorified by, **383**
Prema
characteristics of, **5**
Prema-bhakti
nine varieties of, **96-98**
See also: Love of God
Prema-vaicittya
as division of *vipralambha,* **40-**41
Priyasya sannikarṣe 'pi
verse quoted, 41
Pṛthivīte āche yata nagarādi grāma
verses quoted, 438
Pure devotees
are not restricted to Hindu community, 362
attached to hearing about Kṛṣṇa, **132-**133
consider themselves in lowest stage of life, **16**
dedicate their whole lives to Lord's service, **14**
know they are eternal servants of Kṛṣṇa, 366
never attracted to material opulence, **136-**137
promoted to Vaikuṇṭha, 73
spiritual body of, **375**
understand highest truth, **381**
Purification
of soul in *svarūpa-lakṣaṇa,* 4-5
of Vaiṣṇava by following rules of spiritual master, 64
Pūrva-rāga
as division of *vipralambha,* **40-**41
Pūrva-saṅga-tayor yūnor
verse quoted, 41

Q

Qualities
five not present in demigods, **51**

Qualities
five partially present in demigods, **50-51**
four not found in Nārāyaṇa, **52-53**
Kṛṣṇa has all transcendental good, **44**
Kṛṣṇa's sixty-four transcendental, **45-54**
Kṛṣṇa's unlimited, **101-102**
of Kṛṣṇa as transcendental, **387**
of Kṛṣṇa attract even animals and trees, **111**
of Kṛṣṇa make awakening possible, 31
of Rādhārāṇī, **54-55**
of Supreme Lord compared to depth of an ocean, **49**
Rukmiṇī attracted to Kṛṣṇa by hearing about His, **107**-108

R

Rādhā-kuṇḍa
Sanātana instructed to re-establish, 62
Rādhārāṇī
as shelter of mellow of conjugal love, **57**
as topmost heroine in all dealings, **43**
characteristics of, **44**
constantly pours forth tears, **19**
three kinds of separation celebrated in, **42**
verses spoken by as example of *prajalpa,* **38**
Vṛndāvana as kingdom of, 73
Rādhikā
See: Rādhārāṇī
Rāga
attraction of devotees in servitorship increases up to, **97**
Rāja-yoga
followers of Patañjali practice, 327
Raghunātha
wanted to accompany Caitanya to Purī, **396-397**
Raktaka
as shelter in servitorship mellow, **57**
Rāma-navamī
should be observed, **285, 286**
Rāmānanda Rāya
met Caitanya at Purī, **424**
Rāmānujācārya
Kṛṣṇa consciousness movement follows, 328
Raṅga-kṣetra
achieved by Yogendras, **146**
Ratha-yātrā
conducted by Western Vaiṣṇavas, 362
Rati
as seed of love of God, **25, 59**
Rati-ābhāsa
expert devotee defines symptoms of attachment as, 26
Ratir yā saṅgamāt pūrvaṁ
verse quoted, 41
Regulative principles
devotional service executed according to, **96, 375**
executed under orders of spiritual master, **10**
followed in *sādhana-bhakti,* 8
following of as freedom from contamination, **7**
purification by, **193**
should not be followed without effect, 64-65
synopsis of Vaiṣṇava, **267-287**
Religion
different types of on material platform, 363
of one who mistreats great souls destroyed, **342**
one who kills animals cannot understand, 320
real principle of, 306
rejection of materially motivated, **381**
Renunciation
Caitanya instructs Sanātana about proper, **63**
incomplete, 65
process of at stage of *vānaprastha,* 228
Reputation
of one who mistreats great souls destroyed, **342**
Ṛg-saṁhitā
quoted on Vṛndāvana, 73-74
Ṛg Veda mantra
quoted on Vāmana, 91

Rohiṇī
Balarāma born from, 76
Rūḍha
as ecstatic symptom in conjugal mellow, **36**-37
Rūḍhoktebhyo 'nubhāvebhyaḥ
verse quoted, 37
Rukmiṇī
attracted to Kṛṣṇa by hearing about Him, **107**-108
Rūpa Gosvāmī
as younger brother of Sanātana, **414**
empowered to understand mellows, **102**
established temple of Govindajī, 62
how he divided his money, 411
refutes argument about hair incarnation, 76
returned to Vārāṇasī, **416**
showed forests of Vṛndāvana by Subuddhi Rāya, **412**
Rūpa-raghunātha-pade haibe
quoted, 443

S

Sa cāpi keśau harir uccakarta
verses quoted, 75
Sacrifice
Kṛṣṇa as ultimate purpose of, 351
Sadā svarūpa-samprāptaḥ
verses quoted, 51
Sādhana-bhakti
as devotional service according to regulative principles, **10**
as stage of devotional life, 8
Saiyada Hussain Khān
as servant of Subuddhi Rāya, **400**
Śālagrāma-śilā
should be worshiped with *tulasī,* 282
Śamādibhir eva brāhmaṇādi
verses quoted, 269
Sambhoga
four categories of, 40
Śamīka
as father of Śṛṅgi, 13
Śamo damas tapaḥ śaucaṁ
verses quoted, 269
Sanātana Gosvāmī
accepts position as lower than straw, **76**
as author of *Hari-bhakti-vilāsa,* 363
blessed with specific mercy by Caitanya, **288-291**
Caitanya explained confidential meanings of *Bhāgavatam* to, **71**
compared to deep lake covered with moss, **289**
directed by Caitanya to write book on Vaiṣṇava behavior, **267-287**
instructed by Caitanya for two months, **297**
remained in Vṛndāvana, **416**
Rūpa and Anupama as younger brothers of, **414**
served in Mohammedan government, 264-265
Sañcārayanti bhāvasya
verses quoted, 32
Saṅgābhāvo harer dhīrair
verse quoted, 35
Śaṅkarācārya
imaginary interpretations of, **309,** 344
quoted on liberated soul becoming attracted to Kṛṣṇa's pastimes, **385**
tried to establish theory of illusion, **319**
tried to refute Vedic literature, 326-327
Śaṅkara Paṇḍita
met Caitanya at Purī, **422**
Sāṅkhya philosophy
by analysis concludes that material nature is supreme cause, **324,** 327
Saṅkīrtana
in Western countries, 306, 362
sannyāsīs gather to perform, 391
Sannyāsa
acceptance of does not satisfy Kṛṣṇa as much as *bhakti,* **373**
compulsory at age fifty, 405
vānaprastha as stage preliminary to, 228
Sannyāsīs
asuras in dress of, 75
Bhāgavatam discussed by Māyāvādī, **390**
should bathe three times a day, 277

Sārvabhauma Bhaṭṭācārya
Caitanya explained *ātmārāma* verse at home of, **82**
called madman by Caitanya, **84**
met Caitanya at Purī, **424**
Sarva-dharmān parityajya
verses quoted, 223
Sarva-saṁvādinī
discussion of hair incarnation in, 76
Sarvasya cāhaṁ hṛdi sanniviṣṭo
verse quoted, 328
Sarvopādhi-vinirmuktaṁ tat-paratvena
verses quoted, 132-133, 141
Śāstras
confirm that one should accept the path of *mahājanas,* **328**
Sāttvika
activates hearing and chanting, 28
Sa vai puṁsāṁ paro dharmo
verse quoted, 71
Scripture
devotional service is enjoined in every, 306
principle of direct interpretation of, **323**
real spiritual knowledge has to be received from, 360
Śaṅkarācārya argued against, **323**
Sense gratification
materialists interested in, **15**
some engage in devotional service for, **127**
Senses
Kṛṣṇa's form as original source of, **316**
living entities struggle with, 49
of Kṛṣṇa are controlled, **47**
Separation
as department of conjugal love, **39**
devotees think of attaining Kṛṣṇa's association in, 35
feelings of in Rādhārāṇī, *gopīs* and Dvārakā queens, **42**
See also: Viyoga
Servitorship
as permanent ecstasy, **27**
as transcendental mellow, **25**
increases to spontaneous love of God, **34**
Servitorship
object and shelter in mellow of, **57**
yoga and *viyoga* in, 36
Siddhaloka
space travel on, 211
Siddhi
word has eighteen varieties, **95**
Sin
chanting Hare Kṛṣṇa as solution to all, 407-**408**
four kinds of, 112
of animal killing stopped by Buddha, **319**
Śīta
as symptom of *anubhāva,* 31
Śiva
five qualities not present in, **51**
five qualities partially present in, **50**
Kṛṣṇa as more exalted than, **53**
one who worships, 273
quoted on *Bhāgavatam,* **258**
resides above Devī-dhāma, 73
Śivaloka
inhabitants of, 73
Skanda Purāṇa
offenses in Deity worship mentioned in, 282-283
quoted on demigod worship, 272
quoted on Nārada Muni, **240**
quoted on nonviolence of devotees, **236**
Smartavyaḥ satataṁ viṣṇur
verses quoted, 277
Sneha
as transcendental quality, **25**
Socialists
philosophy of, 351
Spiritual master
can initiate *brāhmaṇas,* 64
characteristics of bona fide, 268
duty of everyone to approach a bona fide, **364**
empowered by direct potency of Kṛṣṇa, 300
offers everything to the Lord, 279
orders of must be strictly followed, 229, 232

Spiritual master
taking shelter of, **267**
worshiped to become free from fear, **374**
Śrama eva hi kevalam
quoted, 137
Śrīdāma
as shelter in friendship mellow, **57**
Śrīdhara Svāmī
cited, **135**
quoted on brahminical qualifications, 269
Śrī-kṛṣṇa-caitanya, rādhā-kṛṣṇa nahe anya
quoted, 443
Śrīmad-Bhāgavatam
advanced devotees attached to understanding meaning of, **59**
as commentary on *Brahma-sūtra,* 346
as essence of all Vedic literature, **378-379**
as essence of Vedic literature, **382**
as sound incarnation of Kṛṣṇa, **439**
as sufficient for God realization, **381**
as the spotless *Purāṇa,* **258**
ātmārāma verse in quoted, **83-84**
Caitanya explained confidential meanings of, **71**
Caitanya personally preached truths of, **439-440**
cited on qualities of *brāhmaṇas,* 269
described in *Guruḍa Purāṇa,* **377**
devotional service compared to fire in, **112**
eighteen thousand verses in, **350**
explained by *asuras,* 75
form of given in questions and answers, **261**
gives actual meaning of *Vedānta-sūtra,* **377-378**
gives information on mellow of service, **382**
invocation of quoted, **380**
is as great as Kṛṣṇa, **260**
learned only through devotional service, **258**
one must be madman like Caitanya to understand, **263**
Śrīmad-Bhāgavatam
Parīkṣit's desire for imminent death stated in, 13
quoted on Absolute Truth as unified identity, **370**
quoted on anyone becoming *brāhmaṇa* by initiation, 64
quoted on apparent truth, **361**
quoted on approaching a spiritual master, 271
quoted on attainment of happiness and distress, **174**
quoted on attainment of yogic perfection, **172**
quoted on bees chanting glories of Balarāma, **179**
quoted on *Bhāgavatam* rising like sun in age of Kali, **262**
quoted on *bhakti-yoga,* **372-373**
quoted on Bharata Mahārāja, 15
quoted on birds listening to Kṛṣṇa's flute, **178**
quoted on Brahman realization as temporary, **312**
quoted on characteristics of Kṛṣṇa, **316**
quoted on conditioned soul as competitor of Kṛṣṇa, **156**
quoted on demigod worship, **148**
quoted on development of spiritual body, **375**
quoted on devotees' dependence upon Lord, 70
quoted on devotees' lack of material desires, **183**
quoted on devotional service as only auspicious path, **158-159, 311**
quoted on *dharma* for all humanity, 71
quoted on ecstatic symptoms, **167**
quoted on ecstatic symptoms of advanced devotee, **24**
quoted on enlightenment by Kṛṣṇa's mercy, **356**
quoted on existence of Kṛṣṇa, **358**
quoted on falling from Brahman realization, **153**
quoted on fear of living entity, **374**

Śrīmad-Bhāgavatam
quoted on glories of Vṛndāvana, **196-197**
quoted on good fortune of Kāliya, **108-109**
quoted on *gopīs* absorbed in thoughts of Kṛṣṇa, **369**
quoted on *gopīs'* attraction to Kṛṣṇa, **106**
quoted on Hari bound by rope of love, **367**
quoted on hearing in association of devotees, 10
quoted on hearing pastimes of Kṛṣṇa, **383**
quoted on highest truth, **381**
quoted on how advanced devotee sees Kṛṣṇa everywhere, **368**
quoted on how Kṛṣṇa pervades material creations, **366**
quoted on how Kṛṣṇa's lotus feet vanquish misery, **343**
quoted on impersonalists poor fund of knowledge, **317**
quoted on Kṛṣṇa as Supreme Lord, **371**
quoted on Kṛṣṇa's fulfilling material desires of devotees, **136, 191**
quoted on Kṛṣṇa's lotus feet, **338**
quoted on Kṛṣṇa's spiritual form, **315-316**
quoted on Kumāras, **386**
quoted on Kumāras attraction to aroma of *tulasī,* **103**
quoted on Lord's existence before during and after creation, **120**
quoted on lowborn creatures purified by Viṣṇu, **180-181, 186-187**
quoted on meaning of liberation, **155**
quoted on mystery of transcendental knowledge, **354**
quoted on necessity of inquiry into knowledge, **365**
quoted on qualifications of spiritual master, 270
quoted on rarity of pure devotees, **341**
quoted on ritualistic ceremonies at Naimiṣāraṇya, **202**

Śrīmad-Bhāgavatam
quoted on self-satisfied becoming attracted to Kṛṣṇa, **387**
quoted on sleepless lamentation, **43**
quoted on spiritual communism, **351**
quoted on spiritual planets, **371**
quoted on spontaneous devotional service, **125, 126**
quoted on Śukadeva becoming attracted to Kṛṣṇa's pastimes, **386**
quoted on Śukadeva Gosvāmī, **104-105**
quoted on Śukadeva's study of *Bhāgavatam,* **144**
quoted on taste of devotional service, **203**
quoted on tasting mellow of *Bhāgavatam,* **379, 383**
quoted on the glories of *Bhāgavatam,* **134**
quoted on three categories of devotees, **127**
quoted on three features of Absolute, **119**
quoted on three kinds of men who worship Kṛṣṇa, **190**
quoted on Vāmana, **91**
quoted on worship of Lord in heart, **166**
rejects materially motivated religions, **134**
Rukmiṇī's letter to Kṛṣṇa in quoted, **107**
studied and described by Śukadeva Gosvāmī, **104-105**
subject matters of, **369**
Śukadeva studied from father, **386**
Vyāsadeva explained *oṁkāra* in, **349**

Śrīnivāsa Ācārya
quoted on six Gosvāmīs, 62

Śrīvāsa Ṭhākura
as one of Pañca-tattva, **304**

Śṛṅgi
cursed Parīkṣit, 13

Sthāyi-bhāva
love of God in devotional service as, **3**

Subala
as shelter in friendship mellow, **57**
greatness of love of, **34**

Subuddhi Rāya
earned livelihood by selling dry wood, **410**
history of, **400-413**
instruction of Caitanya to, **406-408**
showed Rūpa the forests of Vṛndāvana, **412**
Sudāma
as shelter in friendship mellow, **57**
Śūdras
accepting service for livelihood as business of, 265
can approach supreme destination, 195, 275
Śukadeva Gosvāmī
advises Parīkṣit on independence of devotee, 70
attracted to pastimes of Kṛṣṇa, **104-105, 144, 386**
Bhāgavatam increases in sweetness when spoken by, **382**
Bhāgavatam taught to, 378
came to Kṛṣṇa in search of knowledge, 130
devotional service of as celebrated, **194**
explained incident of *gopīs* to Parīkṣit, 369
Sun
ātmārāma verse compared to, **82**
situated above sky, 73
Supersoul
mystic *yoga* leads to realization of, **123**
six types of worshipers of, **165**-166
Śuṣka-vairāgya-jñāna saba
quoted, 65
Supreme Lord
activities of spiritual potency of described in Vedic literatures, **314**
as creator of planetary systems, 73
as protector of surrendered souls, **70**
astonishes all living entities, **52**
attracted by Rādhārāṇī, **44**
Caitanya as, **299**-300, **308**
glorified by hymns and prayers, **383**
has inconceivable energies, **345**
hearing *Bhāgavatam* attaches one to, **381**
Supreme Lord
indicated by repetition of *"aham"*, **358**
is always transcendental, 360
is bound by love, **367**
is manifest within the heart of the devotee, **366**
known as Gaurakṛṣṇa, **2**
Kṛṣṇa glorified as, **49**
living entities have qualities of, 50
one should depend solely on, 67
one who sees Caitanya's character accepts Him as, **299**
relationship with explained in *catuḥ-ślokī*, **352**
supreme proprietorship of, 351
Surrendered soul
Kṛṣṇa as protector of, **48**
Parīkṣit asks to be accepted as, **13**
receives protection from Supreme Lord, **70**
Svarūpa Dāmodara
met Caitanya at Purī, **422**
Sweetness
conjugal love as mellow of, **33**
of Kṛṣṇa's body, face and smile, **20**
of Kṛṣṇa's early age, **19**
of Rādhārāṇī, **56**
Śyāmānanda Gosvāmī
as *brāhmaṇa* by qualification, 269

T

Tāntrikeṣu ca mantreṣu
verses quoted, 274-275
Tapana Miśra
met Rūpa at Vārāṇasī, **417**
unhappy hearing blasphemy of Caitanya, **302**
wanted to accompany Caitanya to Purī, **396-397**
Tasmād gurum prapadyeta
verse quoted, 271
Taste
arises from firm faith, 8
awakens for hearing and chanting, **7**
develops from becoming fixed in devotional service, **10**

Taste
for chanting as symptom of ecstatic emotion, **12**
heart softened by, **4**-5
of love of God increases, **25**
of permanent ecstasy mixed with other ecstatic symptoms, **28-29**
Taṭastha-lakṣaṇa
as marginal symptom of *bhāva,* 5
Tathā dehāntara-prāpti dhīras tatra
quoted, 407
Tatra jñeyā vibhāvās tu
verse quoted, 30
Tatra soma-gatiś caiva
verses quoted, 72-73
Tattva-sāgara
quoted on spiritual initiation, 276
Tā vāṁ vāstūnyuśmasi gamadhyai
verse quoted, 74
Tayor eko balabhadro babhūva
verses quoted, 75
Time
happiness and distress attained in course of, **174**
incarnations presented Vedic knowledge according to, 346
must be utilized for Kṛṣṇa, **14**
should not be wasted, **12,** 14
Tolerance
of all obstacles on path of Kṛṣṇa consciousness, 14
Transcendentalists
two classes of, 140-141
Transmigration
Gītā quoted on, 137
Truth
apparent is illusory energy without Kṛṣṇa, **361**
Tulasī
as Kṛṣṇa's favorite plant, 31
Kumāras attracted by aroma of, **102-103, 143, 386**
leaves of to be collected in morning, **278**
śālagrāma-śilā should be worshiped with, 282
value of worship of, 229-230
Tyaktvā dehaṁ punar janma naiti
quoted, 53, 263, 443

U

Udāra-dhīḥ
meaning of word, **127**
Udbhāsante svadhāmnīti
verse quoted, 31
Udbhāsvara
symptoms of, 32
Uddhava
defines *bhakti,* **6**
quoted on characteristics of Kṛṣṇa, **316**
Uddīpana
as division of *vibhāva,* 30
Uddīpanās tu te proktā
verses quoted, 30-31
Udghūrṇā
as division of *mohana* stage, **38**
as aspect of transcendental madness, **39**
Ujjahārātmanaḥ keśau sita-kṛṣṇau
quoted, 75
Ujjvala-nīlamaṇi
quoted on *adhirūḍha* ecstasies, 36-37
quoted on *pūrva-rāga,* 41
quoted on qualities of Rādhārāṇī, 56
quoted on *vipralambha,* 39
Umā
as wife of Śiva, 73
United Nations
failure of, 404
Universes
created by external potency, **92-**93
Urukrama
meanings of word, **90-93**
Upadeśāmṛta
quoted on what is a *gosvāmī,* 268
Upaniṣads
Caitanya explains direct meaning of, **308**
can't be understood without studying *Bhāgavatam,* 384
Śaṅkarācārya gives up direct meaning of, **309**

Upayurpari tatrāpi
verses quoted, 72-73
Utkaṇṭhitam viyogaś cety
quoted, 36

V

Vaikuṇṭha
by regulative devotional service one attains, **125**
five qualities exist in Nārāyaṇa in, **51**
maintained by opulences of the Lord, **92,** 93
Nārada can go to, 211
situated in spiritual world, 73
Vaikuṇṭha-lokas
See: Vaikuṇṭha
Vaiṣṇava
ācāryas accept form of Kṛṣṇa, 315
anyone can become, 66
doesn't stock food for next day, 241
duty of to travel and preach, 239
must be accepted from all parts of the world, 362
needs not be anxious for bodily maintenance, 240
possesses mystic power, **18**
Prakāśānanda became, 391
Sanātana instructed to enunciate behavior of, 62
Vaiśyas
can approach supreme destination, 195, 275
Vakreśvara
met Caitanya at Purī, **422**
Vāmana
caused three worlds to tremble, **90-91**
Vāmana-dvādaśī
should be observed, **286**
Vāṇīnātha Rāya
met Caitanya at Purī, **424**
Vānaprastha
process of renunciation at stage of, 228
should bathe twice a day, 277
Vārāṇasī
Caitanya came to sell ecstatic love in, **391-392**
Caitanya delivered people of, **396**
deliverance of *sannyāsīs* of described in *Ādi-līlā,* Chapter Seven, **298**
inhabitants of discussed conversion of Māyāvādīs, **305-306**
mahā-mantra chanted by inhabitants of, **390**
Rūpa and Anupama returned to, **416**
turned into another Navadvīpa, **391**
Varṇāśrama
without worship of Viṣṇu one falls down from, **159**
Varṇāśramācāravatā puruṣeṇa
verses quoted, 129
Varṇāśrama-dharma
as scientific system, 405
meant for human beings, 129-130
spiritual master above considerations of, 300
Vasudeva
Kṛṣṇa as son of, **380**
Vedas
Kṛṣṇa is to be known by, 328
one can't come to the right path by studying, **328**
study of doesn't fully satisfy Kṛṣṇa, **373**
Vedānta-sūtra
Absolute Truth as person according to, **325**
Bhāgavatam gives actual meaning of, **377-378**
Caitanya explains, **308**
Māyāvādī *sannyāsīs* gave up study of, **307**
Śaṅkarācārya covered import of, **321**
Vedic literature
celebrates Kṛṣṇa, **316**
descriptions of Kṛṣṇa's spiritual potency in, **314**
Śaṅkarācārya tried to refute, 326-327
Vibhāva
activates hearing and chanting, 28
divisions of, 30-31

Vibhāvair anubhāvaiś ca
verses quoted, 28
Vibhāvyate hi raty-ādir
verses quoted, 30
Vijñāna
as result of devotional service, 353
Vipralambha
defined, 40
four divisions of, **40**-41
Viṣṇu
as Supreme Lord, 339
Brahmā and Śiva not on level of, **339**
feelings of possessiveness in relation to, **6**
form of worshiped in heart, **166**
one should always remember, 277
Parīkṣit requests saints to chant names of, 13
three categories of potency of, **255**
Vāmana as incarnation of, 90
without worship of one falls down from *varṇāśrama-dharma,* **159**
Viṣṇu Purāṇa
quoted on Absolute Truth as *summum bonum,* **118**
quoted on *keśa-avatāra,* 75
quoted on three potencies of Viṣṇu, **255**
quoted on *varṇāśrama-dharma,* 129
Viṣṇusvāmī
Kṛṣṇa consciousness movement follows, 328
Viśva-prakāśa dictionary
ātmā defined in, **87**
ca defined in, **115**
nirgrantha defined in, **89**
quoted on meaning of *api,* **116**
quoted on meaning of *karma,* **93**
Viśveśvara
Caitanya visited temple of, **395**
Vivaśa-ceṣṭā
as aspect of transcendental madness, **39**
Vivasvān
one who worships, 273
Viyoga
as division of each mellow, **35**
See also: Separation
Vrajabhūmi
See: Vṛndāvana
Vṛndāvana
as holy place, **12**
attraction of men and women of to Kṛṣṇa, **110**
Caitanya ordered Sanātana to give shelter to devotees in, **398**
Caitanya sent Subuddhi Rāya to, **407**
glories of described, **196-197**
ISKCON temple in, 398-399
Sanātana and Rūpa empowered to carry out work in, **62, 291**
Sanātana remained in, **416**
spontaneous devotional service in, **124-125**
Subuddhi Rāya showed Rūpa forests of, **412**
Vyabhicārī
activates hearing and chanting, 28
as ecstatic emotions, 33
Vyaktaṁ maṣṛṇitevāntar-
verses quoted, 26
Vyāsadeva
as author of *Vedānta-sūtra,* **347, 377-378**
as compiler of *Bhāgavatam,* **381**
as spiritual master of author's disciplic succession, 222
as Supreme Lord, **346**
causeless mercy of, **346**
devotional service of as celebrated, **194**
made a mistake according to Śaṅkarācārya, **319**
Śukadeva Gosvāmī as son of, **105**
Śukadeva studied *Bhāgavatam* by grace of, **144**
summarized six philosophical theses in Vedānta codes, **325**

W

War
as result of animal killing, 221
Wealth
devotees shouldn't flatter those intoxicated by, **70**

Wealth
of Kṛṣṇa, **48**
Women
can approach supreme destination, 275
captivated by flute of Kṛṣṇa, **110**
Kṛṣṇa attracts minds of, **48**
World, material
appears real to sages and demigods, **380**
ātmārāma verse eradicates darkness of, **82**
Kṛṣṇa Supreme Soul of, **315**
spiritual master extinguishes fire of, 300
Supreme Lord is not a creation of, 360
under control of Devī, 73
World, spiritual
before creation Kṛṣṇa existed in, **371**
everything in is one, 211
Vaikuṇṭha-lokas situated in, 73
Worship
of Deity conducted by Western Vaiṣṇavas, 362
of Kṛṣṇa by everyone, **48**
Sanātana instructed to establish Vṛndāvana method of, 62

Y

Yadu dynasty
stories concerning destruction of, **74-**75
Yamunā
dancing in ecstasy on bank of, **37**
Yāre dekha, tāre kaha 'kṛṣṇa'-upadeśa
verses quoted, 239
Yaśodā
as shelter in mellow of paternal affection, **57**
Vṛndāvana as kingdom of, 73
Yas tu nārāyaṇaṁ devaṁ
verses quoted, 273
Yasya deve parā bhaktir yathā
quoted, 225, 258
Yathā kāñcanatāṁ yāti
verses quoted, 64, 276, 363
Ye 'py anya-devatā bhakta
verses quoted, 272
Yoga
as division of each mellow, **35**
Gītā quoted on practice of system of, **168-169**
leads to realization of Supersoul, **123**
three divisions of advancement in, **167**
three types of, 36
Yogendras
attracted to qualities of Kṛṣṇa, **145-146**
Yogīs
thirteen types of, 170
two types of *ātmārāmas,* **165-**166
Yogo 'pi kathitaḥ siddhis
quoted, 36
Youthfulness
of Kṛṣṇa's body, **45**
of Supreme Lord, **51**
Yudhiṣṭhira Mahārāja
quoted on *mahājanas,* **328**
Yuktāhāra-vihārasya
verse quoted, 63
Yūnor ayuktayor bhāvo
verses quoted, 39

The Author

His Divine Grace A. C. Bhaktivedanta Swami Prabhupāda appeared in this world in 1896 in Calcutta, India. He first met his spiritual master, Śrīla Bhaktisiddhānta Sarasvatī Gosvāmī, in Calcutta in 1922. Bhaktisiddhānta Sarasvatī, a prominent devotional scholar and the founder of sixty-four Gauḍīya Maṭhas (Vedic Institutes), liked this educated young man and convinced him to dedicate his life to teaching Vedic knowledge. Śrīla Prabhupāda became his student, and eleven years later (1933) at Allahabad he became his formally initiated disciple.

At their first meeting, in 1922, Śrīla Bhaktisiddhānta Sarasvatī Ṭhākura requested Śrīla Prabhupāda to broadcast Vedic knowledge through the English language. In the years that followed, Śrīla Prabhupāda wrote a commentary on the *Bhagavad-gītā,* assisted the Gauḍīya Maṭha in its work and, in 1944, without assistance, started an English fortnightly magazine, edited it, typed the manuscripts and checked the galley proofs. He even distributed the individual copies freely and struggled to maintain the publication. Once begun, the magazine never stopped; it is now being continued by his disciples in the West.

Recognizing Śrīla Prabhupāda's philosophical learning and devotion, the Gauḍīya Vaiṣṇava Society honored him in 1947 with the title "Bhaktivedanta." In 1950, at the age of fifty-four, Śrīla Prabhupāda retired from married life, and four years later he adopted the *vānaprastha* (retired) order to devote more time to his studies and writing. Śrīla Prabhupāda traveled to the holy city of Vṛndāvana, where he lived in very humble circumstances in the historic medieval temple of Rādhā-Dāmodara. There he engaged for several years in deep study and writing. He accepted the renounced order of life (*sannyāsa*) in 1959. At Rādhā-Dāmodara, Śrīla Prabhupāda began work on his life's masterpiece: a multivolume translation and commentary on the eighteen thousand verse *Śrīmad-Bhāgavatam* (*Bhāgavata Purāṇa*). He also wrote *Easy Journey to Other Planets.*

After publishing three volumes of *Bhāgavatam,* Śrīla Prabhupāda came to the United States, in 1965, to fulfill the mission of his spiritual master. Since that time, His Divine Grace has written over forty volumes of authoritative translations, commentaries and summary studies of the philosophical and religious classics of India.

In 1965, when he first arrived by freighter in New York City, Śrīla Prabhupāda was practically penniless. It was after almost a year of great difficulty that he established the International Society for Krishna Consciousness in July of 1966. Under his careful guidance, the Society has grown within a decade to a worldwide confederation of almost one hundred *āśramas,* schools, temples, institutes and farm communities.

In 1968, Śrīla Prabhupāda created New Vṛndāvana, an experimental Vedic community in the hills of West Virginia. Inspired by the success of New Vṛndāvana, now a thriving farm community of more than one thousand acres, his students have since founded several similar communities in the United States and abroad.

In 1972, His Divine Grace introduced the Vedic system of primary and secondary education in the West by founding the *Gurukula* school in Dallas, Texas. The school began with 3 children in 1972, and by the beginning of 1975 the enrollment had grown to 150.

Śrīla Prabhupāda has also inspired the construction of a large international center at Śrīdhāma Māyāpur in West Bengal, India, which is also the site for a planned Institute of Vedic Studies. A similar project is the magnificent Kṛṣṇa-Balarāma Temple and International Guest House in Vṛndāvana, India. These are centers where Westerners can live to gain firsthand experience of Vedic culture.

Śrīla Prabhupāda's most significant contribution, however, is his books. Highly respected by the academic community for their authoritativeness, depth and clarity, they are used as standard textbooks in numerous college courses. His writings have been translated into eleven languages. The Bhaktivedanta Book Trust, established in 1972 exclusively to publish the works of His Divine Grace, has thus become the world's largest publisher of books in the field of Indian religion and philosophy. Its latest project is the publishing of Śrīla Prabhupāda's most recent work: a seventeen-volume translation and commentary—completed by Śrīla Prabhupāda in only eighteen months—on the Bengali religious classic *Śrī Caitanya-caritāmṛta.*

In the past ten years, in spite of his advanced age, Śrīla Prabhupāda has circled the globe twelve times on lecture tours that have taken him to six continents. In spite of such a vigorous schedule, Śrīla Prabhupāda continues to write prolifically. His writings constitute a veritable library of Vedic philosophy, religion, literature and culture.